民法典物权编概要

（中英文对照版）

Civil Code of China Real Rights

史国政 著

WUHAN UNIVERSITY PRESS
武汉大学出版社

图书在版编目(CIP)数据

民法典物权编概要：汉英对照/史国政著. -- 武汉：武汉大学出版社,2024.11(2025.2 重印). -- ISBN 978-7-307-24482-5

Ⅰ.D923

中国国家版本馆 CIP 数据核字第 2024W65X75 号

责任编辑:张　欣　　　责任校对:汪欣怡　　　版式设计:马　佳

出版发行:**武汉大学出版社**　　(430072　武昌　珞珈山)

(电子邮箱:cbs22@whu.edu.cn 网址:www.wdp.com.cn)

印刷:湖北云景数字印刷有限公司

开本:787×1092　1/16　印张:29.25　字数:637 千字　插页:2

版次:2024 年 11 月第 1 版　　2025 年 2 月第 2 次印刷

ISBN 978-7-307-24482-5　　定价:98.00 元

序

以中华人民共和国成立七十多年以来的积淀，中国的《民法典》经过全民热烈讨论、理论界的激烈争论应运而生。改革开放导引了中国社会主义市场经济制度的确立和发展，并促使民商事法律如雨后春笋般蓬勃发展，而在这众多日臻完善的法律制度中，物权法(制度)作为一个独具特色且与人们生活息息相关的制度显得更加重要。

编纂一部真正属于中国人民的民法典，是新中国几代法律人的夙愿。党和国家曾于1954年、1962年、1979年和2001年先后四次启动民法制定工作。经过长期的编纂工作，2020年5月28日，十三届全国人大三次会议表决通过了《中华人民共和国民法典》(以下简称《民法典》)，《民法典》对原有的、制定于不同时期的《民法通则》《物权法》《合同法》《担保法》《婚姻法》《收养法》《继承法》《侵权责任法》和人格权方面的民事法律规范进行全面系统的编订纂修，形成了一部具有中国特色、体现时代特点、反映人民意愿的法典，这是一部适应新时代中国特色社会主义发展要求，符合中国国情和实际，体例科学、结构严谨、规范合理、内容完整并协调一致的法典。

新中国成立70多年特别是改革开放40多年来，中国共产党团结带领中国人民不懈奋斗，成功开辟了中国特色社会主义道路，取得了举世瞩目的发展成就，中国特色社会主义制度展现出强大生命力和显著优越性。中国民事法律制度正是伴随着新时期改革开放和社会主义现代化建设的历史进程而形成并不断发展完善的，是中国特色社会主义法律制度的重要组成部分。《民法典》的出台不仅充分彰显了中国特色社会主义法律制度的成果和制度自信，促进和保障中国特色社会主义事业不断发展，也为人类法治文明的发展进步贡献出中国智慧和中国方案。

民法是中国特色社会主义法律体系的重要组成部分，是民事领域的基础性、综合性法律，它规范各类民事主体的各种人身关系和财产关系，涉及社会和经济生活的方方面面，《民法典》是"社会生活的百科全书"。建立健全完备的法律规范体系，以良法保障善治，是全面依法治国的前提和基础。民法通过确立民事主体、民事权利、民事法律行为、民事责任等民事总则制度，确立物权、合同、人格权、婚姻家庭、继承、侵权责任等民事分则制度，来调整各类民事关系。民法与国家其他领域法律规范一起，支撑着国家制度和国家治理体系，是保证国家制度和国家治理体系正常有效运行的基础性法律规范。

《民法典》进一步确立：公有制为主体、多种所有制经济共同发展，按劳分配为主体、多种分配方式并存，社会主义市场经济体制等社会主义基本经济制度，是以法治为基础、在法治轨道上运行、受法治规则调整的经济制度，社会主义市场经济本质上是法治经济。《民法典》的制定进一步完善了中国民商事领域基本法律制度和行为规则，为各类民商事活动提供基本遵循，有利于充分调动民事主体的积极性和创造性、维护交易安全、维护市场秩序，有利于营造各种所有制主体依法平等使用资源要素、公开公平公正参与竞争、同等受到法律保护的市场环境，推动经济高质量发展。

《民法典》坚持以人民为中心，以保护民事权利为出发点和落脚点，切实回应人民的法治需求，更好地满足了人民日益增长的美好生活需要，健全和充实了民事权利种类，形成了更加完备的民事权利体系，进一步完善权利保护和救济规则，形成了规范有效的权利保护机制，更好地维护人民权益，保护民权，不断增加人民群众获得感、幸福感和安全感，促进人的全面发展。中国的《民法典》与资本主义制度下的民法典有着本质区别。

物权法（制度）是规范财产关系的民事基本法律，调整因物的归属和利用而产生的民事关系，包括明确国家、集体、私人和其他权利人的物权以及对物权的保护。物权法（制度）是民法的重要组成部分，是在中国特色社会主义法律体系中起支架作用、不可或缺的重要法律制度。

《民法典》规定的物权制度，明确国有财产和集体财产的范围、国家所有权和集体所有权的行使、加强对国有财产和集体财产的保护，有利于巩固和发展公有制经济；明确私有财产的范围、依法对私有财产给予平等保护，有利于鼓励、支持和引导非公有制经济的发展。

《民法典》规定的物权制度保护公民通过辛勤劳动积累的合法财产、保护依法享有的土地承包经营权等合法权益。孟子曰："民之为道也，有恒产者有恒心，无恒心者无恒心。"这凸显恒产在手对治国安邦的重要意义。物权法（制度）明确并保护私人所有权、业主的建筑物区分所有权、土地承包经营权、宅基地使用权、居住权等财产权益，以维护人民群众的切身利益，激发人们创造财富的活力，促进社会和谐。

从清末变法开始，中国就一直效法德、日，进行中国法制改革，但近百年来的历史实践表明，只有符合中国特色的社会主义法律制度才能真正解决中国的问题，这也是中国物权法（制度）源于西方却又符合中国国情的特色所在。就目前中国物权法（制度）的发展来看，其理论不仅有着不亚于大陆法系物权理论的深厚的法哲学根基，而且其制定、立法之精细，用语之严谨，逻辑之严密也不亚于大陆法系国家之物权立法。在中国经济快速发展并成为世界经济重要部分之同时，让世界各国特别是"一带一路"沿线国家准确、全面了解中国物权制度的发展极为必要。

有鉴于此，笔者作为一个浸淫民商事法律领域数十年的法律人，历经多年编著了这本《民法典物权编概要》，并由武汉大学出版社出版，旨在通过该书向世界各国全面介绍中国物权制度，让世界了解中国物权制度发展的渊源和当代中国灿烂的民事法律文化，促进中国法律制度的发展，服务法律实践，推动中国民商事法制的全面发展。

本着对读者负责的态度，编写期间邀请相关学者、编辑进行了全面校对和完善。当然笔者驽马铅刀、绵力薄材，尽管朝乾夕惕、废寝忘食，也难免有所疏漏，还请各位读者和相关同仁不吝赐教。今日本书得以付梓，理当言表却又难以言表的是谢意。对多方协力与襄助的各位，我会常怀感恩之心，永存感激之情！

　　谨以此书献给我的家人和我的祖国！

史国政

2024 年 10 月 8 日

于中国郑州

Preface

With more than seven decades' accumulation since the founding of the People's Republic of China and after much wide-ranging discussion and heated debate both outside and within the academia, the Civil Code of the People's Republic of China (Civil Code) came out as required. The reform and opening-up policy has been signposting the establishment and growth of the socialist market economy, fostering the development of civil and commercial laws and regulations, among which the real right law(system) sparkles noticeably by reason of its unique features and close bond with daily life.

Since the founding of the PRC, generations of Chinese jurists have yearned for a civil code that could be truly called Chinese people's own. The compilation of a unified civil code was launched four times by the Communist Party and the State, in 1954, 1962, 1979 and 2001, but a complete code never came to fruition. On May 28, 2020, after a long legislative marathon, the Civil Code of the People's Republic of China was adopted at the third session of the thirteenth National People's Congress. The Civil Code comprehensively and systematically incorporates and modifies the various private laws and regulations previously enacted in different periods including the General Principles of the Civil Law, the Real Right Law, the Contract Law, the Guaranty Law, the Marriage Law, the Adoption Law, the Inheritance Law, the Tort Liability Law and provisions related to personality rights, forming a civil code that boasts Chinese characteristics, embodies the nature of the times, and reflects the will of the people. Suited to the development requirements of the socialism with Chinese characteristics in the new era and national conditions and practices, the Code is scientifically structured, well-knit, reasonably stipulated, and embodies comprehensive content in great coherence.

In more than 70 years since the founding of the PRC, and particularly in more than 40 years since the launch of reform and opening up, the path of socialism with Chinese characteristics has been found out successfully through the constant efforts of the Chinese people united under the leadership of the Communist Party of China, and remarkable accomplishments have captured the attention of the world. The system of socialism with Chinese characteristics has demonstrated great vitality and immense strength. The Chinese civil legal system, which is an important component of the Chinese socialist legal system, has gradually taken shape and been developed and refined on a consistent basis along with the historical process of reform and opening up and socialist modernization in the new era. Compilation of the Civil Code not only fully demonstrates the progress made in developing the Chinese socialist legal system and the nation's confidence in this system while promoting and guaranteeing constant advancement of the Chinese socialist cause, but also contributes Chinese wisdom and Chinese solutions to global progress in building the rule of law.

As an important component of the socialist system of laws with Chinese characteristics and a fundamental and comprehensive legal department in the area of civil matters, the civil law regulates various types personal and proprietary relationships among the persons of the civil law, covers all aspects of our social and economic life, and thus is dubbed an "encyclopedia on social life". The establishment and improvement of a comprehensive legal system and the safeguard of good governance by good law is a prerequisite and basis for comprehensively advancing law-based governance. Through formulating general civil-law institutions such as civil-law persons, civil-law rights, civil juristic acts and civil liabilities and establishing specific systems on real right, contract, personality right, marriage and family, inheritance and tort liability, the civil law regulates all kinds of civil relationships. Together with laws in other areas, it supports the state system and national governance system. It is a basic law that ensures the effective functioning of these systems.

The Civil Code reinforces that the basic socialism economic system in which the public ownership is dominant and diverse forms of ownership develop side by side, the distribution system in which distribution according to work is dominant and diverse modes of distribution coexist and the socialist market economy system are based on rule of law, operating within the orbit and limits prescribed by law, and that the socialist market economy is essentially a rule of law economy. The enactment of the Civil Code further improves the fundamental legal systems and behavioral rules in China's civil and commercial areas, thereby setting benchmarks for various kinds of civil and commercial activities. It shall foster the full activation of the activeness and creativity of civil-law persons, insurance of transaction security, maintenance of the market orders, and contribute to creating a market environment in which entities of all ownerships legally and equally use resource factors, openly, fairly and equitably participate in competition, and receive equal protection from the law, thereby advancing the high-quality growth of the economy.

The Civil Code firmly adheres to centering itself around the people and taking the protection of civil rights as its starting point and finishing point. By constructively responding to the people's need for law-based governance, better satisfying the people's increasing desire for a good life as well as perfecting and enriching categories of civil rights, it has formulated a more complete civil rights systems to improve rules for rights' protection and remedies and a more regulated and effective rights protection mechanism to better defend people's rights and interests, thereby persistently enhancing people's sense of fulfillment, happiness and security as well as fostering the well-rounded personal development. This is what essentially distinguishes the Chinese Civil Code from its counterparts under capitalist systems.

The real right law (system) is a basic civil law governing proprietary relationships. It regulates the civil-law relations arising from the attribution and utilization of things, which includes the ascertaining of real rights attributed to the State, collectives, private entities or other right holders and the protection of such real rights. As a significant component of the civil law, the real right law (system) is an indispensable and important legal system that functions as a supporting pillar in the socialist system of laws with Chinese characteristics.

Through clearly defining the scope of properties owned by the State and collectives, the ways of exercising State and collective ownership, and the strengthened protection of state-owned or collectively owned properties, the real right law (system) in the Civil Code is conducive to enhancing and developing the public sector of the economy; by clarifying the scope of private properties and rendering equal protection thereto, it helps to encourage, support and guide the development of non-public sectors of the economy.

The real right law (system) of the Civil Code protects citizens' properties legally obtained by the sweat of their brow as well as other lawful interests and rights such as the right to contractual management of land. According to Mencius, "the way of the people is this: If they have a certain livelihood, they will have a fixed heart; if they have not a certain livelihood, they have not a fixed heart. "①This reflects the significance of possessing fixed assets for the state governance and national security. By clarifying and protecting private ownership, ownership of a building's units, rights to contractual management of land, rights to use house sites and rights of habitation, etc. , the real right law (system) seeks to safeguard people's vital interests and motivate them to create wealth, thereby promoting social harmony.

China has been borrowing from Germany and Japan when undertaking the reform of its legal system ever since it commenced reform movements in the late Qing Dynasty. Nonetheless, centuries' historical practice has shown that a socialist system of laws with Chinese characteristics is the only authentic solution to China's problems. This is why the real right law (system) owes its origin to the West but still is tailor-made for the conditions and reality of China. In view of the current state of the PRC real right law (system), not only is its jurisprudential basis as profound and solid as that of any other civil law country, but also the statute itself is by no means inferior to any of its counterparts in the civil law system with its fine legislative techniques, careful selection of terms and its undeniably strict logic. As the

---

① It is interpreted "If a person has certain property income, he will have a persistent moral sense and code of conduct; if a person has not any property income, he will not have a persistent moral sense and code of conduct. "

development of Chinese economy, China starts to play a significant role in the world economy. It is of great importance to make viable to the rest of the world especially the countries along the Belt and Road Initiative an accurate and comprehensive understanding of the development of the PRC real right law (system).

Taking note of this and being a lawyer who has been practicing in the field of civil and commercial law for decades, I write this book, *Civil Code of China Real Rights*, published by the Wuhan University Press with years' unremitting efforts. The book aims to present to the rest of the world a comprehersive introduction of the Chinese real right system, its origin together with a depiction of the brilliant legal culture in the contemporary China, thus promoting the development of Chinese legal system, doing a service to the legal practice, and facilitating the comprehensive development of the Chinese civil and commercial legal system.

Bearing in mind the responsibilities towards my readers, I have had the book revised and collated several times by various scholars and editors. Flaws and weaknesses, unfortunately, may still be inevitable to the best of my endeavor. Any advice or suggestion, therefore, will be appreciated whole-heartedly. To those who have rendered most valuable assistance to me in editing this volume for publication, my gratitude is beyond words. I am and always will be appreciated for your untiring and wise support.

This book is dedicated to my family and my country!

Guozheng, Shi
Oct. 8th, 2024
Zhengzhou, China

目　　录

Table of Contents

第一章　中国物权法(制度)概述

《中华人民共和国物权法》(以下简称《物权法》)经过中华人民共和国全国人大及其常委会八次审议,于2007年3月16日由全国人民代表大会表决通过,于2007年10月1日起生效实施,物权制度自此比较完整地建立。

2020年5月28日,十三届全国人大三次会议审议通过了《中华人民共和国民法典》(以下简称《民法典》),其第二编为"物权",于2021年1月1日生效实施,中国物权制度自此全面、完整地建立起来。

一、中国物权制度、物权法①的形成及发展历程

在中国长达两千多年的封建社会,各个朝代多采用诸法合一的立法体例,刑事法律、民商事法律、行政管理法律及诉讼法律等合在一起,构建成一个国家或者一个朝代的法典,如唐朝时期的《贞观律》,明朝时期的《大明律》,以维护皇权、官僚、地主的利益为其明显特点。1911年前中国没有独立的民法典,也没有独立的物权法。

《大清民律草案》是清政府于1911年完成的中国历史上第一部专门民法典草案,但未正式颁布与施行。它分为总则、债、物权、亲属、继承五编。其中前三编由日本法学家松冈义正等仿照德日民法典的体例和内容草拟而成,吸收了大量的欧美及日本的民法理论、制度和原则;后两编则由修订法律馆和礼学馆起草,带有浓厚的中国封建制度和封建礼教色彩。

《中华民国民法典》是中国历史上第一部民法典,1929—1931年由中华民国政府颁布。该法典在中国施行近20年,《中华民国民法典》共1225条,分为五编,依次为总则、债、物权、亲属、继承,该法典建立了完善的中国物权制度。1949年中国共产党发布文告,终止了中华民国的全部法律的实施,废止了包括《中华民国民法典》在内的中华民国的《六法全书》。

中华人民共和国的物权制度在1949年10月之后逐步建立起来,全民所有制是在中国共产党领导的人民民主革命取得胜利之后建立起来的。通过没收地主、富农的土地和生产资料等财产分给其他贫困农民,建立了农村的土地私有制度,之后又在互助组、初

---

① 物权法,本书有广义与狭义之分。广义的物权法,指的是所有的与物权制度有关的法律规范的总称,其渊源为法律、行政法规、司法解释等,譬如《民法典·物权编》《农村土地承包法》《不动产登记暂行条例》等;狭义的物权法仅指《民法典·物权编》。

级社的基础上，建立了合作社所有制，20 世纪 50 年代通过合作社改制为人民公社的形式，建立了农村的农民集体所有权制度。通过对城市的工厂实行私有制，资本家享有工厂的私有财产权，而后在 1956 年的社会主义改造中，采取和平赎买的政策，通过国家资本主义形式，成立了公私合营的所有权制度。因此，中华人民共和国成立初期，所有权的形式包括国家所有权、合作社所有权、个体劳动者所有权、资本家所有权，以及公民生活资料所有权。这个时期的物权体系的主要形式就是所有权。

1966—1976 年的"无产阶级文化大革命"运动，酿成十年内乱，法律制度几乎被废止，人权受到侵害的现象时有发生，物权立法被搁置。

1978 年 12 月十一届三中全会之后，经过拨乱反正，受到摧残的物权制度得到恢复，但主要的物权仍然是所有权。那时候的教科书也仅仅研究所有权，并不研究他物权。所有权的形式包括国家所有权、劳动群众集体所有权、个体劳动者生产资料所有权和公民生活资料所有权。

在中国改革开放的大潮中，中国的物权制度逐步建立起来，中国人创造了更多形式的物权种类，特别是在他物权中，出现了土地承包经营权、宅基地使用权、国有土地使用权、全民所有制企业经营权等用益物权，以及抵押权、质权和留置权等担保物权。民间存在典权、居住权、让与担保、所有权保留等物权的形式。

自 1949 年中华人民共和国成立至《中华人民共和国民法通则》（以下简称《民法通则》）公布实施，中国大陆在宪法以及其他法规中，对物权制度有所规定，但都是原则性的规定，内容不统一、不完整、不系统。

1986 年制定的《民法通则》距今已有近 40 年，限于当时的经济社会发展程度和立法技术，其中许多制度已经过时，如"联营"；而许多勃兴于成熟市场经济条件下的内容又没能被规定在《民法通则》中，如环境权、公司股东权。《民法通则》在我国民事立法史上具有里程碑意义，发挥了重要作用。《民法通则》既规定了民法的一些基本制度和一般性规则，也规定了合同、所有权及其他财产权、知识产权、民事责任、涉外民事关系法律适用等具体内容，被称为一部"小民法典"。但是《民法通则》只是关于民法适用的一些笼统的概括性的规定，《民法通则》确立的制度是在民事法律实践中被普遍适用的，但具体到调整每一个特定的民事法律关系时，还需要依据民法的其他部门法才能胜任。所以虽然中国之《民法通则》已经有物权、知识产权、侵权责任等方面的规定，但依然还是要制定《物权法》《知识产权法》《侵权责任法》等民法法律。

《民法总则》于 2017 年 3 月 15 日第十二届全国人民代表大会第五次会议通过，自 2017 年 10 月 1 日起实施。《民法总则》实施，暂不废止《民法通则》，然而《民法总则》与《民法通则》的规定是不一致的，根据新法优于旧法的原则，适用《民法总则》的规定。《民法总则》为民法典各编之冠，总汇民法典共同适用之原理、原则，其主要内容就是规定民事活动必须遵循的一些基本原则和一般性规则。《民法总则》生效后，基本上《民法通则》就不再适用。

1987 年 1 月 1 日起实施的《民法通则》在第五章第一节规定了"财产所有权以及与财

产所有权有关的财产权"。这一部分规定实际上就是物权法，从第 71 条至第 83 条，共计 13 个条文：规定了所有权的概念及其取得制度；规定了国家所有权、集体所有权和公民的个人所有权；规定了继承权、共有权等关于所有权制度的内容；规定了国有土地使用权、土地承包经营权、采矿权等用益物权；规定了相邻关系即相邻权。尽管《民法通则》的这一部分的条文较少，但是涉及了物权法的核心制度内容，因此，构成了中国大陆物权法的基本架构。其缺点是过于简单，缺乏详细的物权规则及具体制度。

1995 年 10 月 1 日起施行的《担保法》对担保物权制度作出完整规定：规定了抵押权、质权和留置权。

1993 年，中共中央决定建立社会主义市场经济体制，全国人大常委会启动民法典的立法进程，决定尽快起草《物权法》，并且采用制定单行法的方法，分别制定民法典的各个部分，最后编纂为完整的民法典。因此，《合同法》和《物权法》的起草工作开始启动。1999 年《合同法》制定并公布实施之后，《物权法》的起草工作进入了实质性阶段。

2007 年 3 月 16 日，第十届全国人民代表大会第五次会议参加表决的近 3000 名人大代表以 2799 票赞成、52 票反对、37 票弃权的表决结果，通过了《物权法》，其自 2007 年 10 月 1 日起施行。

2020 年 5 月 28 日，十三届全国人大三次会议审议通过了《民法典》，这是我国首部以法典命名的法律，在中国法治史上具有划时代的意义。《民法典》的编纂始于对以《德国民法典》为典范的潘德克顿法学体系的继受，最终形成了"总则编 + 六分编"的体系结构。《民法典》共 7 编、1260 条，各编依次为总则、物权、合同、人格权、婚姻家庭、继承、侵权责任，以及附则。物权编排在总则后的第一编，足以证明物权制度的重要地位。《民法典·物权编》在保持《物权法》的基本制度与基本规则不变的情况下，以问题为导向，作出了必要的修改，即以《物权法》为基础，按照中共中央提出的完善产权保护制度，健全归属清晰、权责明确、保护严格、流转顺畅的现代产权制度的要求，结合现实需要，进一步完善了物权法律制度。对其中存在的不当之处予以纠正，对其中某些制度与规则的不足之处予以完善，对部分阙如的制度予以增补。

《民法典·物权编》共 5 个分编、20 章、258 条。

二、中国物权法(制度)的属性及中国特色

(一)物权法(制度)是社会主义市场经济的基本法

《中华人民共和国宪法》明确规定中国实行社会主义市场经济。而衡量一个国家或地区的经济体制是不是市场经济，关键要看市场是否在资源的配置中发挥基础性作用，其中一个重要的标志就是规范市场经济的民商法体系是否建立和健全。中国千余年来商品经济、市场经济始终没有得到充分发育，其根本原因在于中国封建制度之下，私有财产无法得到法律的全方位的支持和保护。社会主义市场经济体制的构建首先要求产权清晰、权责明确，这样交易关系才有可能顺利进行。物权法律制度不仅是确认和保护所有

制关系的法律，而且是规范市场经济的基本法律规则。《法国民法典》确认了法国作为资本主义市场经济国家的财产制度，系法国的基本法，物权法（制度）则是中国特色社会主义市场经济的基本法。

（二）物权法（制度）是维护中国社会主义基本经济制度的重要法律

《民法典》第207条规定："国家、集体、私人的物权和其他权利人的物权受法律平等保护，任何组织或者个人不得侵犯。"这就是对平等保护原则的具体规定。其一，《民法典·物权编》强化对国有财产的保护，明确了行使国家所有权的主体。国有财产由国务院代表国家行使所有权，但法律另有规定的，依照规定。其二，《民法典·物权编》明确界定了国有财产尤其是国家专有财产的范围。其三，《民法典·物权编》对国家机关、国有企事业单位管理和使用国家财产的权限作出了规定。在国有财产受到侵犯后，《民法典》赋予国有财产的管理机关和企事业单位可以请求不法行为人停止侵害、排除妨碍、消除危险、返还原物、恢复原状、赔偿损失的权利，从而保护国家所有权。

《民法典·物权编》强化了对私人所有权的保护。物权法规定的私人所有权，就是指公民个人依法对其所有的动产或者不动产享有的权利，以及私人投资到各类企业中所依法享有的出资人的权益。私人所有权是私人所有制在法律上的反映。《民法典·物权编》从三种所有制形态的分类出发，分别确定国家、集体和私人所有权。《民法典·物权编》扩大了对私人所有权的保护范围，强化对非公经济的保护，鼓励非公经济的发展。

（三）物权法（制度）是保护最广大人民群众利益的基本法律

《中华人民共和国宪法》将"依法治国，建设社会主义法治国家"确立为一项基本治国方略。而衡量一个国家是否属于法治国家的重要标志，就是要看是否有一套完善的法律制度，以充分保护公民的人身和财产权利。

民法典物权制度始终以维护最广大人民群众根本利益为目的，关注民生，保护老百姓即最基层民众的切身利益。民法典物权制度中详细规定有关保护农民财产权的制度，切实维护了广大农民的利益。

民法典物权制度切实维护了广大城市居民的财产权益。《民法典》第359条规定："住宅建设用地使用权期限届满的，自动续期。续期费用的缴纳或者减免，依照法律、行政法规的规定办理。"民法典物权制度还确认了对物权的保护制度和方法，确立了物权的各项规则。可以说，民法典物权制度通过对各类财产权的保护，奠定了中国法治社会的基础。

物权法是固有法，因此，任何一部民法典的物权法都应当有自己的特色。中国物权法（制度）也具有自己鲜明的民族和社会特点，极具中国特色。

中国物权法（制度）规定了具有独创性的物权，体现了强烈的中国特色。中国物权法（制度）的鲜明中国特色，更主要地体现在它所规定的那些独具特色的物权类型上。

在《民法典·物权编》规定的物权体系中，规定了所有权、业主的建筑物区分所有权、共有权、相邻权(相邻关系)、土地承包经营权、建设用地使用权、宅基地使用权、居住权、地役权、特许物权、抵押权、质权、留置权等共 13 种基本物权，其中的土地承包经营权、建设用地使用权、宅基地使用权和特许物权，都是中国独具特色的物权形态。所有权是任何民事立法都要规定的物权，但是《民法典》规定的所有权也有自己的特点。

物权法还创造了很多具有中国特色的一般规则和具体规则，这也体现了中国物权法的鲜明中国特色。物权法规定了诸多的具有中国特色的创新制度如：(1)鼓励创造财富原则；(2)不动产物权的统一登记制度；(3)确立了完善的动产交付形式；(4)确立物权保护请求权；(5)不动产征收补偿制度；(6)相邻关系；(7)地役权；(8)浮动抵押制度；等等。

三、物权法(制度)的功能作用及重要社会意义

(一)确认和保护物权——定分止争

物权法(制度)首要的功能作用在于确定财产的归属，从而平息冲突与纷争。而物权法(制度)的这一功能是通过确认物权类型并对其加以保护来实现的。由于人类可控制的资源具有稀缺性，而人类的欲望是无穷的，若不能划定个人控制财产的界限，则人类对财产的争夺不会休止，社会生活亦不能维持，于是就有将一定的财产归属于特定主体，使该主体能对归属于他的财产进行排他性支配的必要，物权制度遂应运而生。财产权之确立，可以停止人们掠夺性的经营消费活动，并减少财产权之纠纷，从而有助于人们安定地从事生产活动，增加社会之总生产量。在中国社会主义市场经济条件下，民法典物权制度的这一功能表现为以下几点：

第一，确认以公有制为主体的多种经济形式并保护多种所有制经济，充分发挥公有制的优越性。

《民法典》第 206 条规定，国家坚持和完善公有制为主体、多种所有制经济共同发展，按劳分配为主体、多种分配方式并存，社会主义市场经济体制等社会主义基本经济制度。中国是以公有制为主体的多种经济形式并存的社会主义国家。公有制作为一种所有制关系，必须经过物权法(制度)的调整使之成为一种财产法律关系，从而明确权利归属，确定权利义务的内容，才能使其优越性得到充分体现。多年来，以公有制为主体的多种所有制并存已得到长足的发展，国家、企业、公民的财富得以积累。但是物权制度不完善，造成公有财产中所有者虚位、产权界限不清等一系列问题，公有制的优越性难以发挥，生产力受到极大束缚，并导致了国有资产的严重流失。这均与社会生活中缺乏规范财产归属关系的基本民事法律规则有关。在中国，国家与国有企业的财产关系长期以来没有理顺，存在政企不分的现象，企业缺乏应有的活力。通过物权法(制度)确认企业作为独立自主、自负盈亏的法人所应有的财产权利，就能够使企业对其资产进行有效的经营管理，实现国有资产的保值和增值，防止国有资产的流失。物权法(制度)

通过解决集体所有权的主体、内容及权利的行使问题，通过对集体所有权的合理规范，使集体所有制经济的优越性能够得到充分发挥。此外，物权法（制度）还确认一系列保护物权的规则、制度，从而能够保护国家财产和集体财产不受侵犯。

第二，民法典物权制度确认国家、集体以及个人所有权，对各类财产权实行平等保护，平等保护原则是物权法的基本原则之一。

民法典物权制度不仅强调对公有财产的保护，而且也将对个人财产所有权的保护置于相当重要的地位，对各类财产实行一体确认、平等保护。① 由于受到旧的意识形态的影响，国家所有权历来被置于优先保护的地位，而个人所有权却受到较大的限制。这一状况直接妨碍了社会经济的发展，也影响了广大人民群众创造财富积极性的发挥。当前，某些个人资金的外流以及某些过度的挥霍浪费与个人财产权没有得到充分的保护就存在一定的关系。因此，民法典物权制度对公有财产和个人财产实行平等保护，有助于人们将一定的资金投入生产领域，满足社会投资的需要，促进市场经济的发展。

第三，民法典物权制度通过对物权的确认和保护，鼓励、刺激国民努力创造财富，从而促进社会财富的增长，促进国民经济的健康发展。

法律本身虽不能直接创造财产，但是可以通过确认和保护财产来鼓励财富的创造。法律的这一功能，主要就是通过物权法来发挥的。孟子认为有恒产才能有恒心。一个国家缺乏完备的物权法（制度），就不能形成一整套对财产予以确认和保护的完整规则，则人们对财产权利的实现和利益的享有都将是不确定的，就不会形成所谓的恒产，也很难使人们产生投资的信心、置产的愿望和创业的动力。物权法对各类物权的确认和保护将会造成一种激励机制，调动人民创造、积累和爱护财产的积极性，促进社会经济的发展。

(二)《民法典》的物权制度和规则支持、保障与促进市场交易的顺利进行

物权法（制度）不仅是确认和保护所有制关系的法律，而且也是规范市场经济的基本法律规则。物权法的制度和规则是中国市场经济得以发展、繁荣的不可或缺的要素，也是建立中国社会主义市场经济秩序的迫切需要。物权法（制度）对中国市场经济的重要作用是通过其所具有的支持、保障与促进交易顺利进行的功能来实现的，这主要表现在以下几个方面：

1. 确认物权形态，为交易的进行提供基础条件、前提

市场经济的核心概念是交换。在表面上，交换似乎是物与物或物与货币的交换，即物或货币从一个市场主体移转到另一个市场主体；但实质上，交换是物或货币上权利的交换，也就是说交换是物权在市场主体间的移转，而交换得以发生的基本前提是交易主体拥有物权。在具体的交换过程中，如果没有交易主体拥有物权的事实以及交易双方对彼此物权的尊重，交易是不可能发生的。物权法（制度）通过确认各种具体的物权形态，

---

① 《民法典》第 206 条第 3 款、第 207 条。

并予以切实的保障从而为交易的顺利进行奠定了基础。

2. 物权法(制度)确立物权变动的规则,规范交易主体取得物权的方式、方法,实现其交易目的

交换实际上就是基于交易主体的自由意思而发生的物权移转,或者说交易过程实际上就是物权变动过程。对一个正常的交易而言,它以某一交易主体享有某一物权为起点,至另一交易主体取得该物权而结束。在这一完整的交易过程中,不仅合同法或者债法要发挥作用,而且物权法也要发挥其功能。物权法(制度)对交易过程的规范主要是通过确立物权变动的规则来实现的。在交易过程中,交易主体双方必然要利用买卖、赠与等合同形式,但这些合同仅为发生债的关系的协议,并不发生物权变动(交易主体取得物权从而实现交易目的)的效果。欲发生物权变动的效果,尚需依物权法的规定践行一定的公示方法,如动产需交付、不动产需登记。

3. 物权法(制度)确立公示公信原则、善意取得制度,保护交易安全

法律上的安全分为静的安全与动的安全。静的安全又称所有的或享有的安全,是指法律对主体已经享有的既定利益加以保护,使其免受他人任意侵夺。动的安全又称交易安全,是指法律对主体取得利益的行为加以保护,使其合理期待能够得到法律上的实现。法律对交易安全的保护往往是通过对善意无过失的交易者的保护来实现的,其目的在于畅通财产流通、实现社会整体效益。一般认为,债权制度旨在确保动的安全,物权制度则在于实现静的安全。实际上,物权法(制度)亦有维护交易秩序、保护动的安全的功能。物权法(制度)的这一功能主要通过公示公信原则以及善意取得制度发挥出来。

作为物权法(制度)上的一种维护交易安全的重要法律措施,善意取得制度实际上是通过阻却原权利人物权的追及效力而使善意第三人取得动产所有权。由于此项制度的存在,第三人在交易的过程中不必费时费力地调查交易相对人财产的来源,或者担心其为无权处分人从而使自己取得的所有权为他人所追夺。

(三)增进财产的利用效益,实现物尽其用的目标

物权法(制度)是鼓励人民群众创造财富的法律。物权法律制度是构建社会主义和谐社会的重要保障,法律本身虽不能直接创造财产,但是可以通过确认和保护财产来鼓励财富的创造。法律的这一功能,主要就是通过物权法(制度)来实现的。现代物权法以效益作为重要的目标。根据经济分析法学派的观点,所有的法律规范、法律制度和法律活动归根结底都是以有效地利用资源、最大限度地增加社会财富为目的,也就是通过法律手段促进资源的优化配置,实现帕累托最优效益。尽管将效益的目标扩张于所有的法律部门的观点,其合理性值得商榷,但其作为物权法(制度)立法中应确立的基本价值却依然十分必要。作为一种解决因资源的有限性与需求的无限性而引发的紧张关系的法律手段,物权法(制度)的功能不仅仅在于界定财产归属、明晰产权从而达到定分止争、实现社会秩序的效果,更在于使有限的自然资源的效益得到充分发挥,从而更好地满足人类的需求。无论是从物权法自身的演变来看,还是从制度构建来看,物权法(制

度)都以充分发挥资源的经济社会效益作为其追求的目标。

物权法(制度)从"归属到利用"或从"所有到利用"的历史演变过程体现了物尽其用的基本价值。

自物权制度产生以来,人类社会就形成了两种各具特色的物权体系,即以"所有"为中心的罗马法物权体系和以"利用"为中心的日耳曼法物权体系。罗马法物权体系由于受个人主义思想的影响,强调所有而非利用;而日耳曼法物权体系受团体主义的影响,强调利用而非所有。罗马法以所有为中心的物权体系由于适应了早期资本主义经济发展的需要,因而为大多数资本主义国家所接受。在这种物权体系下,物权法注重保护所有权本体的完整性,强调对所有人享有的各项权能进行全面保护。此时,物由所有人进行现实的支配并由其自己利用,从而导致权利主体对物的所有关系和利用关系趋于一致。然而,所有权仅意味着权利主体对财产的支配、控制状态获得了法律的确认和保障,这一确认本身并不意味着一定能实现物尽其用、促进社会财富的增长。首先,强调仅能由所有人对物加以利用就排斥了他人对物的利用,当所有人不能或不愿利用时,他人亦无法利用。其次,欲使资源最大限度地发挥其效用,就必须由最能有效利用资源的人来利用资源,才能达到物尽其用、地尽其利的效果。在判断财产权制度是否有效率或者效率高低的标准中,一个重要的标准就是财产权具有可转让性。因为如果财产权具有可转让性,就意味着资源能够流向最能有效利用该资源的主体,从而实现资源的优化配置。在财产只能由所有人利用的情形下,由于所有人不一定就是财产的最佳利用人,从而并不一定能做到物尽其用。由此产生了所有权权能分离的必要性,即所有人在保留所有权的前提下,将所有权的部分权能分离给他人。

此时,所有权获得了一种观念的存在,变成了对物的抽象的支配,但所有人却通过权能的分离使自身的利益获得了最大的实现,而非所有人则可以利用所有人的财产组织生产经营,物的效益由此得到充分发挥。《中华人民共和国物权法》详尽规定从"归属到利用"或从"所有到利用"的转变中各种制度、规则。物权法除具有界定财产归属、明晰产权的功能外,其重心已表现为最大限度地发挥资源的效用以获得最佳的经济社会效益。物权法(制度)是鼓励人民群众创造财富的法律。

物权法(制度)在中国现实的社会生活中,具有如下重要意义:

第一,《民法典·物权编》全面肯定和完善建立了中国的物权制度和物权体系,规定权利人依法享有物权。特别是规定对所有权平等保护:不仅保护国家所有权、集体所有权,而且特别强调了保护私人所有权——这是一个重大的突破,具有极为重要的意义。应当看到的是,物权就是财产权,是人权的组成部分。人权以生存权、发展权和尊严权为核心,但是必须有财产权作为重要保障。尊重个人的物权,就是尊重人权的基础,就是尊重人权。因此,没有对物权的保护,人权是不完善的,规定物权,就是要保障人权。

第二,《民法典》是中华人民共和国成立70多年来特别是改革开放40多年成果的记录和体现,是将改革开放取得的成果转化为法律的形式固定下来,保证其继往开来。例如，宅基地使用权、土地承包经营权、建设用地使用权、居住权等，都是在改革开放中创造出来的他物权，业主的建筑物区分所有权是改革开放创造出来的所有权形式，《民法典·物权编》对此都加以肯定，使之成为现实的物权制度。《民法典·物权编》确认这些物权制度，就是肯定改革开放的成果，使其变为法律，可以继往开来，世代延续下去，使人民得到的这些物权，能够得到法律的保障。

第三，《物权法》的通过，标志着《民法典》的起草工作完成了关键的核心部分。完成了《物权法》，就完成了《民法典》制定过程中的核心部分，从此《民法典》的制定工作进入快车道。《物权法》的制定、通过标志着中国社会主义市场经济法制体系完成了最为重要的部分。因为构建社会主义市场经济法制体系的标志就是《民法典》制定完成。那么，《民法典》等民事法律的通过，标志着社会主义市场经济法制体系已经建立。

(四)《民法典》物权制度的基本结构和主要内容

《民法典》"第一编 总则 第五章　民事权利"第114～第117条，规定了"物权""物"的概念与内容，同时明确"物权法定"的基本原则。将"物权"作为民事主体的最基本的民事权利。

《民法典·物权编》严格遵循潘得克顿民法体系的传统，共有5个分编、20章、256条。

第一分编为"总则"，规定的是物权的一般性问题，包括三章："一般规定"，"物权的设立、变更、转让和消灭"，以及"物权的保护"。从条文上说，是从第205条至第239条，共35个条文。

第二分编为"所有权"，对所有权的形式和规则作出全面的规定。该编为六章，分别为"一般规定""国家所有权和集体所有权、私人所有权""业主的建筑物区分所有权""相邻关系""共有"，以及"所有权的取得的特别规定"。本编从第240条至第322条，共83个条文。

第三分编为"用益物权"，共六章，包括"一般规定""土地承包经营权""建设用地使用权""宅基地使用权""居住权""地役权"，"居住权"是法律第一次规定。本编共六章，从第323条至第385条，共63个条文。

第四分编为"担保物权"，除了担保物权的一般规定外，还规定了三种担保物权，即抵押权、质权和留置权。本编共四章，从第386条至第457条，共72个条文。

第五分编为"占有"，对占有的一般规则和保护作出了规定。这一分编内容较少，只有一章，从第458条至第462条，共5个条文。

从《民法典·物权编》规定的内容上分析，中国的物权体系分为两部分，一部分是自物权，就是所有权；另一部分是他物权，包括用益物权和担保物权。自物权调整的是物的归属法律关系问题，他物权调整的是物的利用法律关系问题。

任何一部物权法都必须具备自己的特色。中国民法典物权制度施行于中国大陆法域，必须适合施行法域的具体情况。民法典物权制度的施行将新中国成立以来实践的物权制度固定下来，在中国共产党的执政中发挥了卓有成效的作用，具有鲜明的中国特色。

在各国民法典中，物权制度从来都是具有民族性和固有性特征的民事权利制度。言下之意，一个民族的物权法应当具有自己的特点，是一个民族确认财产归属和利用关系的权利制度体系。物权法的基本内容是规定一个国家的基本所有制，以及在所有制的基础上建立的各项物权制度。由于特定的国家具有自己不同的发展历史和观念，物权法的发展具有更为浓厚的自己国家和民族的特色，体现与自己国家和民族发展相一致的物权制度，因而使物权法所规定的制度千差万别，各有自己的特点，而与他国不同。在现代世界上，各国的物权制度由于相互借鉴，在很多制度上采用了相同的或者相似的内容，但是与债权法和知识产权法等相比较，物权法（制度）还是具有鲜明的民族性和固有性。

在民法典中最需要有共同性而非民族性和固有性的法律是合同法。因为合同法是规范交易规则的法律，凡是进行国际交易，都必须采取相同的规则，才能保证交易的顺利进行，维护交易各方的权益。如果合同法规定与别国不同，就难以取得交易上的优势。

而物权的流转则是本国自己的事情：只要本国人民认可，适合于本国人民的需要和本国国情，就可以确认这样的制度，保持物权法（制度）的民族性和固有性。中国《民法典》没有移植和照搬他国的物权和物权规则，但是立法者在制定《民法典》的过程中，缜密学习与引入了外国的物权制度、物权规则，因此中国民法典物权制度具有鲜明的中国特色与社会主义特色，具有民族性、独创性。本书以简约手笔向世界各国介绍中国物权制度，让世界人民了解中国，了解中国灿烂的法律文化。

Chapter 1　Synopsis: Chinese Real Right Law (System)

After eight reviews by the National People's Congress and its standing committee, the Real Right Law of the People's Republic of China (Real Right Law) was adopted on March 16th, 2007, and came into effect as of October 1st, 2007. Thenceforth a relatively comprehensive real right system was established in China.

On May 28, 2020, the Civil Code of the People's Republic of China (Civil Code) was adopted at the third session of the thirteenth National People's Congress, of which the Book Two regulates real rights. The Civil Code entering into force on January 1st, 2021; thence forward a comprehensive and complete Chinese real right system was formulated.

1. Chinese Real Right System and the Establishment and Development of Real Right Law[1]

In feudal China, which marked a period of over 2000 years in Chinese history, a legislation pattern of "all laws in one" was adopted by monarchs of various dynasties: criminal laws, civil laws, business laws, administrative laws and procedural laws were combined into one uniform law code of an empire or a dynasty, such as the Code of Zhenguan in the Tang Dynasty and the Great Ming Code of the Ming Dynasty. These codes served to maintain the imperial power and guard the interests of the bureaucrat and landlord classes. There were neither separate civil code nor any real right statute in China until 1911.

The Draft Civil Code of Qing Dynasty compiled by Qing Government in 1911 is the first separate draft civil code in Chinese history. However, it was never officially promulgated or implemented. It consists of five parts: general provisions, real rights, claims, relatives and inheritance. The first three parts were drafted by Japanese jurists led by Matsuoka Yoshimasa following the structure and contents of the Japanese and German Civil Codes and incorporating

---

[1]　Real right law, is interpreted in this book, either in a broad sense as the entire Chinese real right institution, whose source of law encompasses statutes, administrative regulations, judicial interpretations etc. , or in a narrow sense as the book on real rights of the Civil Code of the PRC. the Law on land contract in Rural Areas , the Interim Regulations on Real Estate Registration etc. , all fall into the former's source of law.

an abundance of theories, systems and principles excerpted from the European and Japanese civil law. The rest two parts were compiled by codifiers from Bureau for Compilation of Law and the Bureau of Rites Science, which retained conspicuous features of Chinese feudal ethics.

The first civil code in a strict sense should be the Civil Code of the Republic of China, which was promulgated by the government of the Republic of China in from 1929 to 1931 and was in effect nationwide for over two decades. This code was composed of five parts with 1, 225 articles: general provisions, law of property, law of obligations, family law and law of succession, establishing a relatively sophisticated property law system. The code ceased to be valid with an edict issued by the Communist Party of China, which annulled the whole body of laws enacted by the Republic of China government, including the Complete Literatures on Six Laws into which the civil code was incorporated.

The real right system of PRC is established step by step since October 1949. As the Communist Party successfully led China to the victory of the new democratic revolution, properties of Kuomintang government and bureaucratic capitalists were confiscated and nationalized, which laid a solid foundation for the system of ownership by the whole people. The confiscated lands and other means of production of the landlords and rich farmers were then allotted to the poor farmers. That was how the system of the private land ownership was set up, which later developed into the system of ownership of cooperative on the basis of the mutual-aid teams and the elementary agricultural producers' cooperatives. In 1950s, the cooperative system was replaced by people's commune, which indicated the system of collective ownership of farmers was established in the country. By way of privatization in urban factories, capitalists obtained the ownership upon private properties; in the socialist transformation of 1956, national capitalism form was adopted through redeeming the capitalists' enterprises. These two changes paved the way for the building of joint state-private ownership system. Therefore, during the initial stage when the New China had just been founded, various forms of ownership coexisted in the country, including ownership of the State, cooperative, individual worker and capitalist, State ownership, the co-operative ownership, the ownership by individual workers, the ownership by capitalists and the ownership of means of subsistence by citizens. Among all, ownership took up the bulk of the property rights system.

During the "Proletarian Cultural Revolution" that took place in China from 1966 to 1976, and led to the ten years of turmoil, the Chinese legal system existed almost in name only. human rights were violated massively and rampantly, and the legislation of the real right law almost came to a complete standstill.

After the Third Plenary Session of the 11th Central Committee of the Chinese Communist Party in December of 1978 and the succeeding restoration of order, the setbacks in the work was gradually removed to improve the real right system, but the ownership remained the major form of property rights. Textbooks of that period largely studied the complete and full ownership (*jus in re propia*), letting pass the rights over the property of another (*jus in re aliena*). Ownership of the State, the collective ownership by the working people, ownership of means of production by individual worker and the ownership of means of subsistence by citizens, all fell into the categories of ownership.

With the adoption of the reform and opening up policy, the Chinese real right law system gradually came into being. A variety of new types of real rights, especially those other than ownership have been created, including rights to usufruct such as the right to contractual management of land, the right to the use of house sites, the right to use of state-owned land, the right to management of state-owned enterprises as well as certain security interests in property rights such as right to mortgage, pledge, and lien. Other forms of real rights like vadium mortuum, right of habitation, alienation guarantee and ownership retention coexisted in private practices.

During the period between the founding of RPC in 1949 and the implementation of the General Principles of the Civil Law of the PRC (General Principles of the Civil Law), the Constitution and other laws and regulations in Chinese mainland did regulate on the real right system but only in a general sense, with the content being incompatible, incomplete and unsystematic.

It has been four decades since the General Principles of the Civil Law was promulgated in 1986. Confined to the social and economic condition as well as legislative techniques at that given time, the statute contains many legal regimes such as the "economic association" that could no longer catch up with the social advance as time went on. On the other hand, it hasn't included certain systems that have well developed the nation's market economy, such as "the environmental right", "shareholder's right", etc. Undeniably, the statute has played an important role during the nation's history of civil legislation. Its significance is monumental, in that it has not only stipulated basic systems and general rules for the civil law, but also such specified rules as those on the contract, ownership and other property rights, intellectual property right, civil liability and application of law in foreign-related civil relations, etc. These earned it the name "small-scale civil code". However, it should also be noticed that the legal systems established therein only concern generalized and abstract rules on the application of the civil law. That these rules are universally applied in the civil law practice doesn't eliminate the need for other departments of civil law in regulating particular type of civil relationship. For this reason, it is still needed to legislate civil statutes such as the Real Right Law, Law on Intellectual Property Right, the Tort Liability Law, in addition to the existing relevant stipulations in the General Principles of the Civil Law.

On March 15, 2017, the General Rules of the Civil Law was adopted at the Fifth Session of the Twelfth National People's Congress of the People's Republic of China. It came into force on October 1, 2017. The implementation of this statute doesn't terminate the validity of the General Principles of the Civil Law deservedly. Pursuant to the principle "new laws precede over old laws", provisions in the new statute shall prevail in cases of contradictions with those in the older one. As the leading part of the civil code, the General Rules of the Civil Law encapsulates doctrines and principles that are universally applicable in the civil code, and it mainly encompasses certain fundamental principles and rules that must be observed in civil activities. Basically, the General Principles of the Civil Law no longer applies after the General Rules of the Civil Law goes into effect.

The General Principles of the Civil Law which came into effect on January 1st, 1987. In Chapter 5, Section 1 "property ownership and related property rights", it employs 13 articles (Articles 71 to 83) to stipulate the definition and acquisition of ownership such as the State ownership, the collective ownership and the private ownership, the right of inheritance and co-ownership, right to usufruct such as the right to land contractual management, right to use of state-owned land, right of mining, together with relationship of adjacency (or adjacent relationships). Presumably, the aforementioned section may be deemed as equivalent to the real right law, as it has encompassed the essentials of the latter statute though the clauses are small in number. The section forms the skeleton of the Chinese mainland's real right law system. Nonetheless, it lacks specific and concrete rules or systems regarding real right, which is not sophisticated enough.

Detailed and thorough stipulations regarding security interests have been found in the Guaranty Law of the People's Republic of China (Guaranty Law), which came into effect on October 1st, 1995. This law provides three forms of security interests in property rights: right to mortgage, pledge and lien.

In 1993, the Central Committee of the CPC decided to practice the socialist market economy. Against such a background, the Standing Committee of NPC commenced the legislation of civil code. According to the legislative schedule, parts of the civil code will be first separately enacted in form of single acts, and then compiled into one integral civil code. A draft of real right law was cried out for. Consequently, its draft began together with that of the contract law. The draft of the Real Right Law, however, didn't enter into a material stage until 1999 when the Contract Law of the People's Republic of China (Contract Law) was promulgated and implemented.

The draft underwent multiple reviews and was finally issued and opened up for public suggestion in 2005. It aroused the passion among the public and the legislature received more than ten thousand pieces of advice within months. Subsequently, the draft was amended and scrutinized several times before it was adopted by the NPC with an overwhelming vote.

On March 16th, 2007, the Real Right Law of the People's Republic of China was adopted at the fifth session of the tenth NPC with 2,799 affirmative, 52 dissenting and 37 waiver votes recorded by near 3,000 NPC representatives that attended the meeting. It came into effect on October 1, 2007.

On May 28, 2020, the third session of the thirteenth NPC adopted the Civil Code, which is the first Chinese law carrying the title "code" since the founding of the PRC and of epoch-making significance in the Chinese legal history. Compilation of this code began with the inheritance of the Pandekten system modeled after the German Civil Code, and ended up in a structure consisting of "book of general provisions and six books on specific provisions". The Civil Code is divided into 1260 provisions in seven books, i. e. , General Principles, Real Rights, Contracts, Personality Rights, Marriage and Family, Succession, Tort Liability, and Supplementary Provisions. That the book on Real Rights is positioned closely after the book on General Provisions sufficiently evidences the paramount significance of the real right system. While mainly keeping the basic systems and rules of the Real Right Law, Book Two Real Rights is problem-oriented and has made various necessary revisions. Grounded upon the Real Right Law, the book on Real Rights followed the requirement of the Central Committee of the CPC for improving the property rights system and perfecting the modern property rights system featuring clear ownership, defined rights and duties, strict protection and smooth circulation and at the same time tended to diverse practical needs to further refine the real right legal system. It has rectified existing irregularities, made up the deficiency in some institutions and provisions, and added up certain systems that were absent in the past.

The Book on Real Rights of the Civil Code is divided into five subsections, consisting of 20 chapters and 256 provisions.

2. Nature and Chinese Characteristic of Chinese Real Right Law (System)

2.1   Real Right Law (System) is a Basic Law of a Socialist Market Economy

As prescribed in the Constitution, the State of China practices socialist market economy. However, what is the key criterion when judging whether a country adopts market economy? What truly matters is whether market plays a fundamental function in the country's resource deployment, with the establishment and completion of a system of civil and commercial laws that regulate the market economy being one of the import symbols. For thousands of years, neither commodity economy nor market economy has been fully developed in China, of which one underlying reason is that private properties were not sufficiently protected by the law under a feudal system. In view of this, to clearly define the property rights, rights and responsibilities becomes the first requisite in establishing a socialist market economy system, so as to make it possible to achieve smoothly proceeded transactions. The real right law system serves not only to confirm and protect property rights, but also as one of basic laws to regulate the socialist market economy. Just as the French Civil Code substantiates a property system for France as a capitalist market economy and thus amounts to one of the nation's fundamental laws, real right law (system) also constitutes one of the fundamental laws of the socialist market economy with Chinese characteristics.

2.2 Real Right Law (System) Upholds China's Basic Socialist Economic System as an Important Law

Article 207 of the Civil Code stipulates that "The real rights of the State, collectives, private individuals, and the other right holders are equally protected by law and free from infringement by any organization or individual". This is a specific provision on the principle of equal protection. First, Book Two Real Rights strengthens the protection of state-owned property by manifesting the subject that exercises the ownership of the state, The State Council shall exercise ownership of state-owned property on behalf of the state; and where laws provide for otherwise, the provisions there shall prevail. Second, Book Two Real Rights clearly defines the scope of property owned by the state, especially those concerns exclusive property of state ownership. Third, Book Two Real Rights sets limits on the power exercised by government departments, state-owned enterprises and institutions in the administration and use over state-owned property. In cases where state-owned property right is infringed upon, according to the Civil Code, these entities may seek cessation of the infringements, removal of the nuisance, elimination of dangers, restitution of property, restoration of the original state or compensation for losses from the infringer, so as to protect such right.

Book Two Real Rights also reinforces protection over private property right, which is stipulated by the law including the right enjoyed by individuals over their movable property and immovable property, and the rights and interests enjoyed by private investors in enterprises. Private property right is a reflection of the private ownership system in law. Based on the three patterns of ownership, Book Two Real Rights marks separate boundaries on property rights owned by the state, the collectives and individuals. It extends the protection, inter alia, of the ownership of private property by strengthening the protection and encouraging the development of the non-public sectors of the economy.

2.3 Real Right Law (System) is a Fundamental Law that Seeks to Promote the Interests of the Overwhelming Majority of the People

The Constitution has established it as a basic strategy to govern the country by law and build a socialist country under the rule of law. One touchstone of whether a state is a nomocracy is the presence of a sophisticated legal system that aims to provide an adequate safeguard for the personal and property rights of citizens.

One theme runs through the entire real right law is to promote the interests of the overwhelming majority of the people. The law pays regards to the livelihood and other vital interests of the grassroots. It stipulates in detail certain legal institutions regarding the farmers' property rights to render service to the protection thereof.

The real right system in the Civil Code has been committed to guarding the interests of the overwhelming majority of the people, paying close attention to the people's wellbeing and defending the interests of the people at grass-roots level. It contains detailed provisions for the protection of farmers' property rights to safeguard the latter's interests.

The real right system in the Civil Code also takes the rights and interests of urban residents into consideration. Article 359 of the Civil Code provides that, "The right to use a lot of land for construction of residential buildings is automatically renewed upon expiration of the term. The payment, reduction, or exemption of the renewal fees shall be dealt with in accordance with the provisions of laws and administrative regulations". This, together with other institutions and methods for real right protection, lays a solid foundation for a society under the rule of law.

Property law is native law, which means it varies from different nations or cultural contexts by means of encompassing unique characteristics. As might be expected, the real right law (system) in China also has distinguishing national and social characteristics of its own, and thus embodies prominent Chinese characteristics.

These characteristics are well demonstrated through the originality and uniqueness in certain types of real right it has created.

In the system of real rights Book Two Real Rights provides thirteen categories of basic real rights including ownership, ownership of a building's units, co-ownership, adjacent right (or adjacent relationship), right to contractual management of land, right to use land for construction purposes, right to use a house site, right of habitation, easement, chartered real right, mortgage, pledge and lien. Among these real rights, the right to contractual management of land, the right to use land for construction purposes, the right to use a house site and chartered real rights are all unique types of real rights embodying Chinese characteristics. Whilst ownership is one type of real right that is indispensable to any civil legislations, the ownership system stipulated by the Civil Code boasts its own special features.

Among the various rules provided by real right law, there are ones that are especially innovative with Chinese characteristics. For example, (1) the principle of encouraging wealth creation, (2) a uniform registration system of immovable property, (3) a relatively comprehensive delivery system of movable property, (4) various claims for protection over real right, (5) the compensation system for expropriation, (6) adjacent relationship, (7) easement, (8) floating mortgage, etc.

3. Function and Social Significance of Real Right Law (System)

3.1 Confirmation and Protection of Real Right: Validation and Elimination of Conflicts and Disputes

The primary function of real right law (system) is to decide to whom a property right goes, so that conflicts or disputes may be settled. This purpose is achieved by first defining various categories of real right and then rendering accordant protection. Due to the scarcity of resources viable to the human beings on the one hand, and the insatiable desire in human nature on the other, the combat over possessions will never come to an end, unless a clear-cut boundary is set upon the scope of controllability by each person over a particular thing. That's why it becomes necessary for the sustainability of a social community, to distribute a certain property to a specific subject and let him or her exercise exclusive control thereupon. That is why the real right system was created. The establishment of property right puts a stop to the predatory activities in operation and consumption, preventing disputes arising from properties, and enabling people to engage in productive activities peacefully to increase social productivity. Against the background of a socialist market economy, this function of the Civil Code is reflected in the following aspects:

First, it achieves the superiority of the public ownership system by confirming that the public ownership is dominant and diverse forms of ownership should be protected side by side.

Article 206 of the Civil Code stipulates that "The State upholds and improves the fundamental socialist economic systems, such as the ownership system under which diverse forms of ownership co-develop with public ownership as the mainstay, the distribution system under which multiple forms of distribution co-exist with distribution according to work as the mainstay, as well as the system of socialist market economy." China is a socialist country upholding the basic economic system in which the public ownership is dominant and diverse forms of ownership develop side by side. Public ownership, as one category of ownership, can assume its advantage only if it is shaped through the regulation of the real right law (system) into a type of proprietary legal relationship where lawful holders of ownership are clearly defined and scope of rights and obligations ascertained. Over decades, the diverse forms of ownership have been continuously developing under the dominance of the public ownership, which brought about a noticeable increase in the wealth of enterprises, citizens and the nation as a whole. In spite of this, the imperfection in the real right system still caused a series of problems in public property system e. g. , owner phantom and ambiguity in definition which greatly restrained the productivity inflicted heavy loss on the state-owned property. As a result, the superiority of public ownership failed to materialize. All of these were attributable to the lack of fundamental laws and regulations regarding property ownership in social life. In China, the property relationship between the state and state-owned enterprises has long been in a tangle with no clear distinction between the functions of the government and enterprises, resulting in the lack of vigor in businesses. Taking these into consideration, the real right law (system) establishes the property rights due to enterprises that hold the status of legal persons with independent operation and full responsibility for profits and losses, so that effective management may be exercised, and the state-owned property can be preserved or increase free from drain. The law (system) also sets viable rules in relation to the subject, contents, and exercise of collective ownership thus enables the advantages of a collective ownership economy to sufficiently materialize. In addition, the real right law (system) has also established a system of regulations and institutions for protection of real rights, so that properties owned by the state and collective organizations may be safeguarded from infringement.

Second, the real right law (system) provides equal protection to different categories of property rights including state ownership, collective ownership and private ownership under the principle of equal protection which is one of its basic principles.

On the one hand, the real right system of the Civil Code lays much emphasis on the protection of public properties; on the other hand, it also attaches great importance to ownership of individuals. Properties in various kinds are systematically categorized for equal protection. ①
Under the influence of traditional ideology, ownership of the state has always been prioritized in terms of protection while private ownership has been suppressed in development. The immediate repercussion thereof is the hindered development of the social economy and waning the passion to make fortune in most people. Undeniably, the current affairs could be partially responsible for the private capital drain or extravagance and waste in the current stage. Consequently, equal protection for both public and private properties by the real right system of the Civil Code may encourage investment in production, satisfying the demands in social financing and promoting the development of the market economy.

Third, the real right system of the Civil Code seeks to increase social wealth and foster a healthy growth of the national economy by encouraging and stimulating wealth creation on the people with clear definition and effective protection of real rights.

The law itself can not directly create any wealth, but it may do that in an indirect way by first recognizing properties and then rendering accordant protection thereto. Such function is primarily achieved by the system of real right laws. According to Mencius, fixed property makes

①   See Paragraph 3, Article 206 and Article 207 of the Civil Code.

fixed heart. When a relatively sophisticated system of real right law is absent in a nation, there can be no clear expectation on one's property rights and interests, because there will not be a comprehensive body of rules for reference in recognizing and protecting property rights. Lacking the so-called "fixed property", it becomes also unlikely for people to have any confidence in making investments, or any willingness to acquire assets, or any incentive to launch new businesses. An incentive mechanism, in contrast, will be provided by real right law with its definition and safeguards for various kinds of properties, which will inspire the people to create, accumulate and protect their properties and stimulate social and economy development one stage further.

3.2 Real Right System of the Civil Code Ensures That Transactions Proceed Smoothly in the Market

With providing definition and protection to ownership, the real right law (system) also regulates the market economy as a basic law. The institutions and rules therein are indispensable to a growing and prosperous Chinese market economy, as they meet the compelling needs in imposing an order on building the socialist market economy. The aforementioned role real right law (system) plays in the Chinese market economy is fulfilled by ways of effecting transactions and ensuring their smooth proceedings, and mainly to be shown from the following aspects:

First, the Real Right Law defines the various categories of real rights and prerequisite for transactions.

The core concept of market economy is exchange. Superficially, exchange seems to mean the exchanges between goods or of goods and money, namely, the transfer of goods or money from one market subject to another. But essentially, the object of exchange is the rights invested upon the goods or money. In other words it is the transfer of real right between different market subjects, of which one precondition is the entitlement of subjects to such certain real right. Without the satisfaction of this prerequisite or the mutual respect to each other's real rights of the parties, a transaction is not likely to go smoothly. It is in this way that real right law (system) lays a solid foundation for the smoothy proceeding of transactions.

Second, the real right law (system) sets a system of rules regarding the change of real right, providing the means by which transactors may acquire these rights and fulfill the purpose of their transactions.

As a matter of fact, transaction is a transfer of real right between transactors out of their free will, in other words, the process in which real right changes. A typical transaction starts with one party holding a particular real right and ends up in the acquisition of the other party of the same real right. In this process, real right law (system) works with contract law or law of obligations mainly through its regulation on the change of real rights. As is often the case, parties in a transaction adopt contracts, e. g. , purchase and sale contract or donation contract to create obligations for each other. However, these contracts do not exert such effects as the change of real right, which fails the direct fulfilment of transaction purpose. To achieve transactors' acquisition of real right, certain publication procedures are to be gone through in accordance with the real right law. For example, delivery is required for movable property and the immovables, the proper registration is required for the immovable property.

Third, the real right law (system) protects the security of transaction with its principle of publication and credibility and rule of good faith acquisition (or bona fide acquisition).

In legal sense, security can be decoded in two ways: the static security and dynamic security. The former is also known as the security from ownership or possession, which means the legal protection of vested interests and resistance to encroachment. The latter, which is the so-called transaction security, on the other hand, refers to the legal protection over the acts conducted by a subject to acquire such interests, ensuring that his or her legitimate expectation will be satisfied. The law safeguards transaction security by rendering the party who is a faultless bona fide purchaser his due protection. The underlying purpose is to encourage property transfers and raise the social benefits. It is generally believed that the law of obligations aims to ensure dynamic security whilst the law of real right the static security. In fact, the real right law (system) also carries out a function in maintaining transaction order and providing dynamic security, which is fulfilled through the principle of publication and credibility and rule of good faith acquisition.

The rule of good faith acquisition, as an important legal measure for protecting transaction security, terminates the retroactive effect of the real right vested in the real right holder, thus makes the bona fide third party acquire the ownership with respect to the movable property. As a result, a third party in a transaction will no longer need to conduct time-and energy-consuming investigations into the source of property that the other party presents with, for the sole purpose of freeing himself from any concern arising from the unauthorized disposal the transaction might have involved, which otherwise could deprive him of the ownership he is about to acquire.

3. 3   Real Right Law (System) Seeks to Give Play to the Usefulness of Things and Encourage People to Create More Wealth

The real right system is a necessary safeguard for building a harmonious socialist society. The law itself can not directly create any wealth, but it may do that in an indirect way by first recognizing properties and then rendering accordant protection thereto. Such function is primarily achieved by the system of real right law (system). For modern systems of real right law, efficiency is a central theme. According to the school of economic analysis of law, all legal rules, institutions and activities may be concluded to one aim, that is, the efficient utilization of resources and the maximization of social wealth. In other words, to get into the pareto optimal state, the optimal state of resources allocation. Admittedly, such massive expansion of efficiency into every law department is questionable upon a second thought, the necessity of adopting efficiency as a basic value in the legislation of the real right law (system) is hard to deny. The real right law (system), as a legal instrument for compromising the finitude of resources and the infinitude of human needs, compromising the strained relations between the limited resources and infinite desires, does not only function in clearly defining the attribution of things and property rights to settle disputes and maintain the social order, but also in giving full play to the usefulness of the limited resources to meet the demands of the mankind. Viewed from the perspective of its own evolution and the development of system, the real right law (system) seeks to achieve the full potential of resources in terms of increasing the social and economic benefits.

The historical transition in focus of real right law (system) from attribution or ownership to utilization reflects the basic value of the principle "making the most use of things".

Ever since the system of real right came into being, two unique forms of it coexist in the human society: the Roman real right system that focuses on "ownership" and the Germanic real right system that focuses on "utilization". The former is the product of individualism, while the latter is collectivism. Adapting to the needs of economic development of early capitalism, the Roman real right system was gradually adopted by most capitalist countries. Under such real right system, much importance is attached to protecting the integrity of the ownership itself and the various contents of ownership enjoyed by the right holder. As a result, a thing is under the actual control and for the use of its owner. Hence, the ownership and utilization of the thing are compatible. Nonetheless, ownership only means that the disposal of and control over a thing by its right holder is legally recognized and protected, which does not necessarily help to make the most use of such thing to foster the increase of social wealth. First, when the owner is the only person that is entitled to the use of a thing, other individuals are excluded from such use, including the situation when the owner is unable or unwilling to make use of his property. Second, if the usefulness of resources is to be given full play, then they must be at the disposal of the person who is most likely to make it happen. Only in that way can the material and land resources be turned to best account. Following that, what matters greatly is that the transferability of property rights becomes a key criterion in judging whether and to what extent a property right system is efficient. This is because transferability means the possibility of a thing going to the person who can make the best use of it, thus optimizing the allocation of resources. In cases where the property is at the exclusive disposal of its owner, it may not be made the most use because the owner is not necessarily the best user. As a result, it becomes necessary to divide the contents of ownership, namely, to deliver part of its contents to another on the condition that the owner still retains the ownership.

Now the existence of ownership becomes one conceptual in nature, which means that the disposal of a thing becomes abstract but with the owner maximizing his own interest by sharing some contents of his ownership and other ones undertaking production and operation by using the thing. The usefulness of the thing is thus given full play. Real right law sets down a system of rules for the transfer of attribution or ownership to utilization. It focuses on making the best use of resources to achieve the maximal social and economic benefits, in addition to clearly define the attribution of things and property rights. In this sense, the real right law (system) is a law that encourages people to create wealth.

The significance of real right law (system) in the Chinese social life is to be viewed in the following aspects:

First, the real right system of the Civil Code has established and improved the Chinese real right system. It stipulates that a right holder enjoys real rights in accordance with the law. In particular, it reinforces the protection of private ownership along with the state ownership and collective ownership. Such equal protection over ownership is a major breakthrough with profound significance. It is to be noticed that real right is the same as the right of property, which is a component of human rights. The core of human rights is the right of subsistence, development and human dignity, with the right of property being its solid foundation. To respect an individual's real right, is to respect the foundation of his human right, and ultimately human right as a whole. In the light of this, human rights will not be complete absent proper protection of the real right. The purpose of establishing real right lies in securing human rights.

Second, the Civil Code reflects the great accomplishments achieved in more than 70 years since the founding of the PRC, particularly through the launch of reform and opening up in the past four decades. It sets down such fruit in the form of law to make sure that the policy will be carried on by next generations. For example, certain forms of jus in re aliena including the right to use a house site, the right to contractual management of land, the right to use land for construction purposes, the right of habitation and ownership of a building's units were all created in the process of reforming and opening up. The confirmation of these rights in Book Two Real Rights of the Civil Code demonstrates the achievements of the reform and opening up policy. By granting these forms of right a legal status, it is possible to keep the succession between generations and provide unimpeded access protection of real right for people.

Third, the adoption of the Real Right Law marks the completion of the core component in the draft work of the civil code. The legislation of the civil code thenceforth got in a fast lane.

The enactment and adoption also symbolize that the legal system of socialist market economy managed to build the mainstay, whilst the full establishment of such legal system shall be marked by the enactment of a civil code. Hence, adoption of civil legislations such as the Civil Code symbolizes that the a legal system for the socialist market economy has been established.

4. Real Right System of the Civil Code: Basic Structure and Major Contents

Articles 114 to 117 of the Chapter V Civil-law Rights in Book One General Part of the Civil Code have stipulated the concept and content of "real rights" and "thing" and defined the basic principle of numerus clausus. The real right is placed as one of the most fundamental civil-law rights.

The book on real rights of the Civil Code has strictly followed the traditional Pandekten system in civil law, consisting of five subsections divided into 20 chapters and 258 provisions.

The first subsection stipulates "General Rules". This part stipulates some general questions in real right and falls into three chapters, namely, "General Rules", "Creation, Alteration, Transfer and Extinction of Real Rights", and "Protection of Real Rights". The related articles are Articles 205 to 239, 35 provisions in total.

The second subsection concerns "Ownership". This part stipulates the categories and related rules of ownership. It falls into six chapters: "General Rules", "State Ownership, Collective Ownership and Private Ownership", "Ownership of a Building's Units", "Adjacent Relationships", "Co-ownership" and "Special Provisions on the Acquisition of Ownership". This part covers 83 provisions from Articles 240 to 322.

The third subsection regulates "Rights of Usufruct". This part falls into six chapters: "General Rules", "Right to Contractual Management of Land", "Right to Use Land for Construction Purposes", "Right to Use a House Site", "Right of Habitation" and "Easements". This is the first time that the right of habitation has been stipulated by law. This part covers 63 articles from Articles 323 to 385.

The fourth subsection governs "Security Interests". In addition to the general rules on security interests, it stipulates three categories of security interests in property, namely, mortgage, pledge and lien. This part falls into four chapters and covers 72 articles from Articles 386 to 457.

The fifth subsection deals with "Possession". This part provides for the general rules and protection of possession. It contains less contents than the other parts, having only one chapter with 5 articles from Articles 458 to 462.

In view of its contents, the book on real rights of the Civil Code can be divided into two parts: jus in re propria and jus in re aliena. ① The former refers to ownership and regulates on the attribution of properties. The latter mainly includes right to usufruct and security interests in property rights, which regulates on the utilization of properties.

Every real right law must have its own characteristics. The real right system of the Civil Code is to be implemented in Chinese mainland, thus must adapt to the reality and conditions thereof. By setting down the real right system established during the past seven decades since the founding of the PRC, the book on real rights in the Civil Code has played an extraordinary role with its unique Chinese characteristics under the leadership of the CPC.

Among the various civil codes of different nations, the real right system has always been a body of civil rights that is national and native. In other words, the real right system of a nation should have its own features as a right system that define the attribution and utilization of things It basically stipulates the fundamental ownership system of a state together with the various real right institutions established thereupon. Because the history and notions vary geographically among nations, the real right law systems, whose adaptation to the development of its country or nation bestows on it certain features that are different from that of any other countries. It is true that modern countries are borrowing from each other to improve its real right system, resulting in much identicalness or similarity in these systems. Still, the real right law (system) carries with conspicuous features when compared with universal laws such as the law of obligations and intellectual property law.

Admittedly, the department of law which calls for the most commonness instead of nationality or nativeness would be the contract law. It is a law that regulates the transaction. International transactions may proceed smoothly only on the condition that parties of both sides accept the same rules in defending their rights and interests. When the contract law of a country is too dissimilar from that of other nations, it may lose its competitive edge in transaction.

The transfer of real right is mainly a domestic affair and may be established as a system with nationality and nativeness, as long as such transfer system adapts to the needs of the nationals and the reality and conditions of the country, which is also accepted by the people. The legislators thoroughly studied and introduced real right systems and rules of foreign countries in drafting the Civil Code. It refused undiscriminating implantation or full plagiarism. That's why the real right system in the Civil Code is marked with distinctive Chinese or socialist characteristics and much nationality and originality. This book will briefly introduce to the world the real right system of the PRC and offer an insight into the country's splendid legal culture.

---

① *Jus in re aliena*, or right over property of another, means the right holder is entitled to exert limited dominance over a property of another according to the stipulations of law or a contract between it and another. One example is easements.

第二章 物 权 概 述

第一节 物权的概念、特征和效力

一、物权的概念和特征

"物权"一词，在法律上正式使用始于 1811 年制定的《奥地利民法典》，该法典第 307 条规定："物权是属于个人的财产上的权利，可以对抗任何人。"1896 年制定的《德国民法典》以"物权"作为其第三编的编名，系统地规定了所有权、地上权、用益权、地役权、抵押权、质权等物权。自此以后，大陆法系各国纷纷仿效德国民法典，在自己的民法典中规定符合本国国情的物权制度。中国的《民法通则》虽然没有使用"物权"一词，但其第五章第一节对"财产所有权与财产所有权有关的财产权"的规定，基本上构成了中国民法中的物权制度。迄今为止，物权在其他各国民法典中基本上没有一个明确定义。

《民法典·物权编》不仅明确规定"本编调整因物的归属和利用产生的民事关系"（第205 条），而且《民法典》明文规定"民事主体依法享有物权。物权是权利人依法对特定的物享有直接支配和排他的权利，包括所有权、用益物权和担保物权"（第 114 条）。

在理解物权的概念时，不能把物权仅仅视为对物的权利。物权，实质上反映的是人与人之间的关系。因为法律在确认和保护权利主体以自己的意志支配物，并取得该物的利益的同时，亦意味着对权利主体之外的人支配该物或取得该物利益的限制，从而形成权利义务关系。物权法律关系的内容，就是物权权利主体所享有的权利和义务主体所负有的义务。

物权是和债权相对应的一种民事权利，它们共同组成民法中最基本的财产权形式。在商品经济条件下，人和财产的结合表现为物权；当财产进入流通领域之后，在不同主体之间的交换则体现为债权。主体享有物权是交换前提，交换过程则表现为债权，交换的结果往往导致物权的让渡和转移。在商品交换中，所有权权能也可以依据交换原则与所有权发生分离。可见，民法关于物权和债权的规定构成了商品经济运行的基本规则。物权和债权作为社会经济生活中最基本的财产权，两者密切联系在一起，相辅相成地对商品经济发挥着积极的媒介作用。

物权作为一项独立的民事权利，和债权比较具有以下特征：

（一）物权的权利主体是特定的，而义务主体是不特定的——物权是绝对权，债权是相对权

物权是指特定的主体所享有的、排除一切不特定人的侵害的财产权利（《民法典》第114条）。作为绝对权和"对世权"，物权的权利主体是特定的，其他任何人都负有不得非法干涉和侵害权利人所享有的物权的义务。物权法律关系的主体就是物权法律关系的权利人和义务人，主体既可以是自然人，也可以是法人。权利主体是特定的，义务主体是不特定的。在中国，国家、集体和个人都可以作为权利主体。这就是说，一切不特定的人都是义务主体。而债权只是发生在债权人和债务人之间的关系，债权的主体是特定的。《民法典》第118条第2款规定："债权是因合同、侵权行为、无因管理、不当得利以及法律的其他规定，权利人请求特定义务人为或者不为一定行为的权利。"债权人的请求权只对特定的债务人发生效力。正是从这个意义上说，债权又被称为对人权。

（二）物权的标的或者客体是特定的物

物权关系是民事主体之间对物质资料的占有关系，所以，物权的标的是物而不是行为。物权的标的在范围上是十分广泛的，它们在法律上有一个共同的特点，即必须是特定物。如果物没有特定化，权利人对其就无从支配，而且在物权转移时，也无法登记和交付。此外，作为物权客体的物必须是独立物和有体物，而不可能是行为。否则，物权便很难确定，法律也难以对国家所有权、集体组织所有权等的客体作出规定。

大陆法系关于物主要有三种立法例：第一种是兼指有体物和无体物（权利），以《法国民法典》为代表；第二种是只承认有体物，不承认无体物，以《德国民法典》和《日本民法典》为代表；第三种是例外承认"自然力"是物，以《瑞士民法典》为代表。笔者认为，法律上的物，是指存在于人身之外可以满足人们的社会生活需要并且能够被人们所实际控制或支配的物质实体和自然力。随着社会的发展、科技的进步，"物"的外延应不断扩大，如脱离人体的器官及组织、死胎、尸体、人体医疗废物和胎盘等，只要不违背公共秩序与善良风俗，在特定情况下可以成为物权客体，再如空间、无线电频谱资源亦成为物权客体。

《民法典》规定了物的概念。该法第115条规定："本法所称物，包括不动产和动产。法律规定权利作为物权客体的，依照其规定。"在物的定义上加上了"法律规定权利作为物的客体的，依照其规定"。法律规定有的权利也可以作为物权法律规范的对象，包括权利质权和权利抵押权，如有人认为我国建设土地使用权就是这种类型。所以如果有特别法的规定的话，从其规定。该条规定是对传统物权法物权客体——物的定义的否定，拒绝以有体物定义物权客体。随着科技的进步，特别是空间和自然力纳入物权法的调整范围，《民法典》的物权客体包括物和法律规定的权利两大类，这对于重新构建统一物的概念提供了机遇和法律依据，即以物权客体为上位概念进行构建；但未能给物下一个明确的定义。将权利作为物权的客体不符合逻辑。

债权的标的因债权的种类不同而各不相同。一般来说，债权直接指向的是行为，而间接涉及物。在债权关系存续期间，债权人一般不直接占有债务人的财产，只有在债务人交付财产以后，债权人才能直接支配物，但交付以后往往导致债权的消灭和物权的产生。

（三）物权是一种支配权，是权利人对物的直接支配

所谓直接支配，一方面是指物权的权利人可以依据自己的意志直接依法占有、使用其物，或采取其他的支配方式，他人无义务实施积极的行为协助；另一方面是指物权人对物可以以自己的意志独立进行支配，无须得到他人的同意。在无须他人的意思和行为的情况下，物权人就能够依据自己的意志依法直接占有、使用其物，或者采取其他支配方式。

物权中的支配主要是对特定的动产和不动产的支配，也包括对物的价值的支配。当然，实物的支配与价值的支配是不能完全分开的。例如，恢复用益物权人对土地和房产的支配，也就保护了用益物权人对不动产的使用价值的支配。保护担保物权人对实物的支配，实际上也就保护了对交换价值的支配。物权人对物的支配范围，不仅受物本身性质和效用等的限制，而且要受到物权本身的内容限制。例如，所有权人对物的支配，只受法律限制，一般不受他人意志的限制，但当所有权人在其物上设定了他物权以后，则要受到他物权的限制。对于他物权人来说，因其是在他人之物上所设定的权利，所以其支配的范围不仅要受到法律的限制，而且要受到所有权的限制。他物权的类型不同，其权利内容也是不一样的。

物权人直接支配一定的标的物，必然享有一定的利益。物权所体现的利益一般可分为三种：第一，所有权人享有的利益，这是物的全部利益；第二，用益物权人所享有的利益，是物的使用价值或利用价值；第三，担保物权人所享有的利益，是依法获取物的交换价值，即债务人届期不清偿时，债权人可以依法变卖、拍卖担保物，就其价金满足债权。在市场经济条件下，由于信用制度的发达，获取物的交换价值利益也日益重要。

物权的支配性决定了物权所具有的优先性、追及性等特征。

（四）物权是排他的权利，具有对世性

物权的排他性主要是指物权具有对世效力，即对世性。它是指物权人的权利可以对抗一切不特定的义务人。除物权人以外，其他任何人都对物权人的权利负有不可侵害和妨害的义务。正由于物权是一种对世权、绝对权，因此属于侵权行为法所保障的对象。当发生侵害物权的情形时，权利人不仅可以行使物上请求权[1]，以排除他人的侵害并恢复物权应有的圆满支配状态，而且可以基于侵权行为提起诉讼。也正因为物权属于对世

---

[1]　物上请求权是指当物权的完整性受到或者可能受到损害时，为回复物权的圆满状态，物权人要求加害人作为或者不作为的请求权。

权，所以物权的设立、移转必须要公示，从而使他人知晓，是一种公开性的权利。

物权的排他性还表现在，内容相同的物权之间具有相互排斥的性质，即同一物上不容两个以上相同内容的物权并存，也即"一物一权"，如不能在同一物上设立两个所有权、两个经营权或两个使用权。数人共有一物是所有权的量的分割而非质的分割。数人共有一物，不是共有人对"该物"各自享有独立的所有权，而是平等地或按份额地共同享有一个所有权。此外，一物之上设立数个抵押权也仅是对抵押物交换价值的量的分割而非质的分割。

债权的特征与物权相反：债权人一般不是直接支配一定的物，而是请求债务人依照债的规定为一定行为或不为一定行为。债权也具有不可侵犯性，在第三人侵犯债权（如第三人阻止债务人履行债务）给债权人造成损失时，债权人也可以请求该第三人赔偿损失。但是债权不能像物权那样可以产生排他性效力。在同一物之上，可以设立多个债权，各个债权之间都具有平等的效力。至于某些债权也可能依法具有某些排他效力（如租赁权的排他性）的情况下，该债权已经具有了物权的性质。此时的权利主体相对于债务人是债权人和某种物权人，相对于第三人则是完全的物权人。

物权的支配性和对世性，是物权的基本属性，概括了物权关系的特点。物权作为支配权，强调的是一种主体与客体之间的关系。物权关系在性质上是民事主体对物质资料的占有关系，因此物权的客体只能是物而不是行为。如果认为行为是物权的客体，则物权很难确定。尤其是应看到物权的客体主要是有体物而且必须是特定物、独立物，这不仅是由物权的经济属性决定的，而且也是物权区别于知识产权等权利的一个重要标志。如果物不能特定化，虽然可以成为债权的标的，但不能作为物权的客体，正如法谚所称："所有权不得未确定。"如果物不能确定，则物权支配的对象亦不能确定，从而物权也难以存在。所以，民法理论认为物权客体的特定主义亦应为物权的一项规则。

物权是一种对世权，强调的是人与人之间的关系。对世权表述的是一种权利人和义务人之间的关系，这是一种人与人之间的关系：权利人享有支配特定的物并享受其利益的权利，而义务人负有不得侵害权利人的权利并不得妨碍权利人行使权利的义务。这种权利义务关系也构成了物权与债权关系的本质区别。物权的支配性、对世性的关系还表现在：支配权是对世权的基础和前提，正是因为物权人享有支配权，才有可能享有对世权。但支配并不一定能够对世。例如，实际占有他人的财产，并不一定能够对抗第三人。对世的特点也就表现了物权绝不仅仅是一种单纯的对物的权利，而是一种人与人之间的关系。物权的定义本身就是要强调支配和对世两个特点。至于优先权等，都是从前两个特点中产生出来的，并不能表现出物权的根本属性。

（五）物权是优先权

物权的优先权，基本含义是指权利效力的强弱，即同一标的物上有数个利益相互矛盾、相互冲突的权利并存时，具有较强效力的权利排斥或先于具有较弱效力的权利的实现。可以分为对内优先和对外优先。对外优先是指当物权与债权并存时，物权优先于债权。对内优先是指物权相互之间的效力，在多个物权并存的情况下，原则上先设定的物权优先于后设定的物权。《民法典》第 414 条规定："同一财产向两个以上债权人抵押的，拍卖、变卖抵押财产所得的价款依照下列规定清偿：（一）抵押权已登记的，按照登记的先后顺序清偿；顺序相同的，按照债权比例清偿；（二）抵押权已登记的先于未登记的受偿；（三）抵押权未登记的，按照债权比例清偿。其他可以登记的担保物权，清偿顺序参照适用前款规定。"这就是物权法中所谓"先来后到"的规则，也有人将其称为"时间在先，权利在先"规则。物权相互间的权利也扩大适用并产生另一项规则，即后成立的物权不得妨碍先成立的物权。但是，先物权的实现可能导致后物权的消灭或在某些情况下自然排除后物权，法律基于社会公共利益的考虑，规定某些发生在后的物权有优先于发生在先的某些物权的效力，如规定海商法上的留置权应优先于船舶抵押，此时应依据法律规定确定物权的效力。债权是平等性的权利。债权原则上不具有优先的效力，在同一物之上可以设立多个债权，各个债权在受清偿时，应当适用"债权人平等"的原则，其设立采取合同自由主义。债权特别是合同债权，主要由当事人自由确定。

（六）物权的追及性特征

物权都具有追及性。所谓追及的效力，是指物权的标的物不管辗转流通到什么人手中，所有人可以依法向物的占有人索取，请求其返还其物。任何人都负有不得妨碍权利人行使其权利的义务，无论任何人非法取得所有人的财产，都有义务返还。不仅所有权，而且担保物权的标的物，不论辗转到何人之手，也不影响这些权利的行使。而债权通常只具有相对性，只能在合同当事人之间发生效力。

应当指出的是，物权的追及效力并不是绝对的，因为在法律上确立善意取得制度之后，物权的追及权应当受到善意取得制度的限制。

（七）物权是公开的权利

物权是一种对世权，具有强烈的排他性，直接关系到第三人利益。因此，物权必须对外公开，使第三人知道，由此决定了物权设定、变动时必须公示。动产所有权以动产的占有为权利表征，动产质权、留置权亦以占有为权利表征；而不动产则以登记为权利表征。公示往往伴随物权的存在，一旦公示不存在，物权也将不存在。而债权只是在特定的当事人之间存在，并不具有公开性，设立债权亦不需要公示。因此当事人之间设立合同设立某项物权时，如未公示，可能仅产生债权而不产生物权。

（八）物权的设立采取法定主义

物权的设立采取法定主义，即物权的种类和基本内容由法律规定，不允许当事人自由创设物权种类或随意确定物权的内容。而债权的设立采取合同自由主义。债权特别是合同债权，主要由当事人自由确定。

(九)物权是无期限限制或长期的权利

物权为永久性或长期性的权利，尤其是所有权来说，法律上并无期限限制。只要所有人存在，则所有权将必然存在，如果所有物发生转让，尽管原所有人丧失了所有权，但新所有人取得了所有权。正是从这个意义上，通常认为所有权具有永恒性。根据《民法典》第196条之规定，"下列请求权不适用诉讼时效的规定：（一）请求停止侵害、排除妨碍、消除危险；（二）不动产物权和登记的动产物权的权利人请求返还财产……"物权人请求对物权的保护一般不适用诉讼时效的规定。

而债权都是有期限限制的权利，在法律上不存在无期限限制的债权。即使在一些合同之债中没有规定合同的存续期限，债权人享有的债权与债务人所应承担的债务，也应受到时效的限制。

上述特征中，前四个特征是物权的基本特征和主要特征。

二、物权的效力

按传统民法学的观念，物权的效力是指物权人基于其对物的支配权和排他性产生的特殊法律效力。物权的效力与物权的权能有关，但并非物权权能本身，而是物权权能进一步作用的结果。物权的效力，有的人认为包括物的追及力，即物权的标的物不管流入谁的手中，物权人都可以依法向物的不法占有人索取、请求返还原物，而债权原则上不具有追及的效力。债权的标的物在没有移转所有权之前，由债务人非法转让并由第三人占有时，债权人不得请求物的占有人返还财产，只能请求债务人履行债务和承担违约责任。但大多数人认为，物的追及力属于物上请求权的内容，无独立的必要。

(一)物权的排他效力

物权的排他效力，指在同一物之上不容许两种以上同一内容或同一性质的物权同时存在。由于物权具有排他效力，也决定了一物一权规定的产生。但也有学者认为物权本质中具有排他性，而不认为物权有排他效力。笔者认为，排他性既是物权的性质，也是物权的效力。因为，一方面，物权在性质区分于债权的原因之一，即是物权具有排他性，而债权不具有排他性；另一方面，物权的排他效力是客观存在的，因为在许多情况下，经当事人协商转让不动产的所有权或使用权，如未经登记，受让人不能取得所有权，受让人即使占有了不动产，也不能享有法律上的所有权。但如果依法办理了登记过户手续，即使没有实际占有该不动产，也可以使其权利具有排他的效力，从而使其权利转化为所有权。所以，排他效力的取得是物权是否取得的标志。由此可见，排他的效力具有一定的独立性。排他的占有与独占的支配是很难分开的。也就是说，当某人依法取得对某物的支配权利后，他人不得再享有相同内容的支配权利，因此排他效力的产生必须以主体能够对物进行事实上和法律上的支配为前提。但这种支配并不一定要有明显的、外在的表示，如不一定以实际控制某物作为排他性权利的标志，因为现代公示制度的发展已经极大地减少了外部占有的事实对权利归属的决定作用。只要符合法定的公示要求，物权人即使未实际占有和控制某物，也应享有对该物的所有权或其他物权。

排他效力具体来说表现在：

1. 所有权的排他性

同一物之上不得存在两个所有权，即一物不容二主。

2. 他物权上的排他性

同一物之上不得设定两个内容相互矛盾的用益物权。如在某块土地之上为某人设定建设用地使用权后，又设立宅基地使用权。

以下情形，数个物权可以同时存在于同一物上：（1）所有权与他物权；（2）以占有为内容的他物权与非以占有为内容的物权；（3）非以占有为内容的数个物权。

3. 对世效力

物权的效力可以对抗权利人之外的一切不特定的人。任何人"无权占有不动产或者动产的，权利人可以请求返还原物"（《民法典》第 235 条）。任何人"妨害物权或者可能妨害物权的，权利人可以请求排除妨害或者消除危险"（《民法典》第 236 条）。任何人"造成不动产或者动产毁损的，权利人可以依法请求修理、重作、更换或者恢复原状"（《民法典》第 237 条）。任何人"侵害物权，造成权利人损害的，权利人可以依法请求损害赔偿，也可以依法请求承担其他民事责任"（《民法典》第 238 条）。

4. 不可侵犯性

物权是一种不可侵犯的权利，系侵权行为的客体。

现代民事权利理论规定，权利是由法律明文规定、明文宣示的，由国家保障其实现的财产利益和人身利益，具有不可侵性。侵害权利将构成侵权行为。物权是侵权责任法所保护的最重要的、最基本的客体，从侵权法的滥觞和演进来看，侵权法主要围绕的就是物权，尤其是财产权的所有权的侵害而发展起来的。

（二）物权的优先效力

物权的优先效力包括两方面：

（1）当物权与债权并存时，物权优先于债权，即物权破除债权。例如，享有担保物权的人较之普通债权人具有优先受偿的权利。当然，中国法律和司法实践也赋予某些债的关系优先效力。例如，已出租的私有房屋由出租人出卖时，承租人享有优先于他人购买该房屋的权利，[①] 但这种优先效力不是基于物权产生的，所以不具有优先于物权的效力。例如，甲、乙、丙三人将其共有的房屋出租给丁，此后三人协商同意将该房屋出卖，在出卖给何人时发生了争议。甲、乙要将房屋出卖给戊，丙根据其物权主张优先购买权，丁则根据其债权主张优先购买权。这时，应该根据物权优先于债权的原则，裁定

---

① 《民法典》第 726 条规定，出租人出卖租赁房屋的，应当在出卖之前的合理期限内通知承租人，承租人享有以同等条件优先购买的权利。优先购买权是指出卖人在出卖标的物时，在同等条件下根据法律规定或者合同约定，赋予特定对象其他权利人购买标的物的权利。

房屋应出卖给丙。但也有少数例外，如不动产租赁中的"买卖不破除租赁"。

（2）在某些情况下，当事人可以在同一物之上设立多个物权，先设立的物权优先于后设立的物权，这就是物权相互间的优先效力（《民法典》第414条）。而债权不具有对内优先的效力。在同一物上可以设立多个债权，各个债权都具有平等的效力，债权人在依法受偿时都是平等的。

（三）追及效力

物权的追及效力，又称物权的"追及权"或物权的"追及效"，指物权成立之后，物权的标的物不论辗转入何人之手，物权人均可以依法向物的占有人索取，请求其返还原物（《民法典》第235条）。任何人都负有不得妨碍权利人行使权利的义务。不仅所有权，而且担保物权的标的物，不论辗转到任何人之手，都不影响该权利的存在。

物权的追及效力，是否为一项独立的效力，有否定和肯定两种意见。否定意见以中国台湾地区的郑玉波先生和日本的松坂佐一先生为代表。松坂佐一先生认为物权的追及效力只不过是物上请求权的一个侧面，无单独列为物权的效力的必要。郑玉波先生认为，物权的追及效力实质已为物权的优先效力所包含。持相反立场的学者是中国台湾地区的学者王泽鉴先生等，认为物权的追及效力与物上请求权、物权的优先效力有重叠之虞，因此认为其为一项独立的物权效力。梁慧星、王利明先生都赞成后说。王利明先生认为，一方面，物权具有追及的效力是相对于债权而言的，它是在与债权的比较中所确定的独有的效力。债权原则上不具有追及效力，债权的标的物在没有转移所有权之前，由债务人非法转让或第三人非法占有时，债权人不得请求物的占有人返还财产，只能请求债务人履行债务和承担违约责任。另一方面，物权的追及效力需要通过行使物上请求权得以实现，但物上请求权是由物权的追及效力所决定的，追及效力是物上请求权中返还原物请求权产生的基础，但并不是说它应当包括在返还原物请求权之中。还应看到，追及权只能由物权人享有，但物上请求权中的返还原物请求权，不仅仅由物权人享有并行使，占有人也可以行使。所以，不应将追及的效力概括在物上请求权之中。

《中华人民共和国刑法》第64条规定："犯罪分子违法所得的一切财物，应当予以追缴或者责令退赔；对被害人的合法财产，应当及时返还。"该立法例系物权之追及效力的有力例证。

应当指出，物权追及效力并不是绝对的，因为在法律上确立善意取得制度之后，物权的追及效力应当受到善意取得适用的限制。

（四）物上请求权

物上请求权是指物权人对物的支配因受到他人妨碍而出现缺陷时，为回复其对物的支配之圆满状态而产生的请求权。物上请求权基于物权的支配权受到妨碍而发生。法律赋予物权人以物上请求权的目的在于维护物权人对物的圆满支配状态。物上请求权也被称为物权请求权，或物权保全请求权、物上关系请求权。其中包括《民法典》第235~238条的排除妨害或停止侵害请求权；返还财产请求权；财产损害赔偿请求权。

物上请求权基于物权的支配权受到妨碍而发生，而且只能在有可能回复物的原有支配状态时才能行使。它虽然不是物权权能，却是保障物权人对物的支配权所必需的、不能与物权相分离的权利，因此物上请求权成为物权所特有的效力。债权是债权人请求债务人为一定行为或不为一定行为的权利，而并非对物的支配权。因此，在债权受到侵害时，要使债权人的损失得到补救和恢复，一般只宜采取损害赔偿的方式。

物上请求权的性质，在理论上有三种不同的见解：(1)认为物上请求权为独立的请求权；(2)认为物上请求权纯为债权，不承认物上请求权与债权请求权的差别；(3)认为物上请求权是依附物之支配权的附从权利。笔者认为第三种观点较为妥当。

物上请求权不是债权。物上请求权不同于债权请求权，其分别如下：(1)发生的根据不同。物上请求权发生的根据是物之支配权受到侵害，债的请求发生的根据是合同、无因管理①、不当得利②或侵权损害赔偿之债的义务履行。(2)两者的目的不同。从微观上讲，债权请求权的目的在于满足债权人获得物质资料、知识产品、劳动力、服务等利益的要求；而物上请求权的目的在于回复物权人对物的原有支配状态，满足物权人享受物的各种利益的要求。(3)后果不同。债权请求权的实现产生消灭债权关系的后果，而物上请求权的实现则产生回复物之支配权，使其能继续顺利行使的后果。

但是，物上请求权与物之支配权的关系上，物上请求权也不是独立于物之支配权的独立权利，而是附从于物之支配权的权利，表现在：(1)物上请求权的发生以物之支配权受侵害为前提条件，只有支配权存在才有产生物上请求权的可能性，支配权消灭产生物上请求权的可能性就随之而消灭。(2)物上请求服务于物之支配权。返还原物请求权服务于物的占有权能，排除妨碍请求权、恢复原状请求权则共同服务于物的使用、收益、处分权能。

鉴于物上请求权与物的支配权的上述关系，物上请求权只能在物的支配权遭受侵害与妨碍时发生，也只有在回复物的支配原状有可能时才能行使。如果物权标的物毁损灭失，回复物权人对原物的支配权无可能，则物权人不能行使物上请求权，只能依照损害赔偿之债的规定请求加害人赔偿经济损失。

物上请求权与损害赔偿请求权也是有重大区别的，主要有：(1)物上请求权为物权的效力，损害赔偿请求权为债权的效力。(2)损害赔偿请求权以致害行为具有违法性并造成实际损失为要件，而物上请求权则不以此为要件，只要行为人的行为对物权人正当行使物的支配权构成了妨碍，即使行为人的行为并不违法，也未给物权人造成实际损失，物权人也可提出物上请求。例如，物的所有人可以基于合理需要向物的合法使用人请求返还原物。

---

① 无因管理是指无法律上的义务，也无合同上的义务，为避免他人利益损失而为他人管理事务或者提供服务的事实行为。

② 不当得利是指没有法律上的依据，使他人受到损失而自己获得利益之法律事实。

第二节　物权的种类

物权在法理上通常作如下分类：

一、所有权与他物权

根据物权的权利主体是否为财产的所有人划分，所有权是所有人对自己的财产享有的全面支配的权利，包括对物的占有、使用、收益和处分的权利。它是物权中最完整、最充分的权利。他物权是非财产所有人根据法律的规定或所有人的意思对他人所有的财产享有的有限支配的物权。它是在所有权权能与所有权人发生分离的基础上产生的。

两者的区别在于：

1. 权利主体不同

所有权的权利主体是所有人，而他物权的权利主体是非所有人，即除所有人以外的其他民事主体，其他物权只能由非所有人享有而不能由所有人享有。尽管非所有人享有所有人的部分权能，但非所有人并不能取代所有人的地位而成为所有人。对于所有人来说，尽管在财产之上设定他物权而使其在一定程度上脱离了所有权的权能，但他仍然对其财产享有最终的处分权。所有人没有必要在自己的财产上享有他物权，而他物权只能由非所有人享有。他物权因一定的法律事实产生而由所有人享有时，就因所有权与他物权的混同而导致他物权的消灭。此时，所有权即恢复其完整状态。

2. 权利的内容不同

所有权是完全物权，而他物权只在一定程度上具有所有权的权能。没有法律的依据和所有人的授权，他物权人不能行使处分权。所以他物权又称"限制物权"。

3. 权利存在的期限不同

所有权的存在通常不受时间限制，也即不因法律事实的产生或终止而使所有权绝对地消灭，所以叫"无期物权"。他物权如果是通过合同取得的，则就只能在合同的有效期内存在，所以又叫"有期物权"。

二、用益物权和担保物权

根据物权设立的目的的不同对他物权所作的进一步划分。

用益物权，是指非所有人对他人所有之物享有的占有、使用和收益的权利，是以物的使用收益为目的而设立的物权，中国法律中用益物权包括土地承包经营权、建设用地使用权、宅基地使用权、居住权、地役权。

用益物权的基本内容，是对用益物权的标的物享有占有、使用和收益的权利，是通过直接支配他人之物而占有、使用和收益。这是所有权权能分离出来的权能，表现的是对财产的利用关系。

担保物权是以保证债务的履行、债权的实现为目的而设立的物权，如抵押权、质权、留置权。

两者的区别在于：

1. 对标的物的要求不同

用益物权以追求物的使用价值或者使用效能为内容，标的物必须有使用价值。而担保物权以追求物的价值和优先受偿为内容，标的物必须具有交换价值。

2. 是否具有从属性（独立性）

用益物权具有独立性，担保物权则具有从属性。用益物权根据法律的规定或与财产所有人的约定独立存在，不以用益物权人对财产所有人享有其他财产权利为前提。而担保物权的存在则以担保物权人对担保物的所有人或其关系人享有债权为前提，债权消灭担保物权也随之消灭。

3. 是否必须占有标的物

用益物权的行使以占有标的物为前提，因为用益物权人如不占有标的物就无法对标的物进行使用收益。而担保物权的行使除留置权、质权依其性质必须占有标的物外，其他担保物权均不以直接占有标的物为前提。

4. 是否具有代位性

担保物权具有代位性。而用益物则不具有这一性质。如担保物权的标的物因不能归责于担保物权人的原因灭失，担保物权人可以请求担保人以其他物替补，担保物权的标的物转化为价值形态（如货币）时，担保权就以变形物为客体，因而具有代位性。而用益物权的标的物灭失，无论其灭失的原因如何，均导致用益物权的消灭而不得请求所有人以其他物替补。

三、动产物权和不动产物权

动产物权和不动产物权是按物权的客体是动产或不动产所作的划分。

动产物权是以能够移动的财产为客体的物权。不动产物权是以土地房屋等不动产为客体的物权，如不动产所有权、土地使用权。《不动产登记暂行条例》第2条将不动产界定为土地、海域以及房屋、林木等定着物。中国的不动产物权包括不动产所有权、地上权、地役权、房屋典权、国有土地的使用权、不动产的抵押权等。动产物权包括动产所有权、留置权、动产的抵押权、动产质权等。现阶段以权利作为客体的物权形式，如权利上的抵押权等并不发达，但是中国之现行立法承认某些有价证券如国库券可以抵押，因此权利上的物权形式实际上是存在的。这些物权形式可以视为动产物权。

第三节　物权法（制度）的基本原则

物权法（制度）的基本原则，是物权法（制度）的主旨和根本准则，是指导、解释、执行和研究物权法的出发点。物权法的基本原则贯穿在整个物权法制度和规范之中，体现物权立法的基本理念和精神。物权法基本原则有民法学上的基本原则和物权立法上的基本原则之分。民法学上的基本原则通常有四个：物权法定、一物一权、公示公信和物权效力优先。物权立法上的基本原则，《民法典》规定了三个基本原则，即平等保护原则（第113条、第206条、第207条），物权法定原则（第116条），公示公信原则（第208条）。

一、平等保护原则

(一)平等保护原则的概念和意义

物权法上的平等保护原则，是指物权主体在法律地位上平等，依法享有相同的权利，遵守相同的规定；其物权受到侵害以后应当受到物权法的平等保护。《民法典》第206条第3款规定："国家实行社会主义市场经济，保障一切市场主体的平等法律地位和发展权利。"第207条规定："国家、集体、私人的物权和其他权利人的物权受法律平等保护，任何组织或者个人不得侵犯。"

平等保护是物权法（制度）的首要原则，也是中国物权法（制度）具有中国特色的鲜明体现。

平等保护原则是中国民法基本原则在物权制度中的具体体现。

(二)平等保护原则的内容

平等保护原则的内容主要包括：

1. 法律地位的平等

法律地位平等是指所有的市场主体在物权法中都具有平等的地位。这是《中华人民共和国宪法》所确认的法律面前人人平等原则的具体体现。

2. 适用规则的平等

除了法律有特别规定的情况外，任何物权主体在取得、设定和移转物权时，应当遵循共同的规则。

3. 保护的平等

保护的平等包括两个方面：一是在物权发生冲突时，针对各个主体都应当适用平等的规则解决其纠纷；二是在物权受到侵害之后，各个物权主体都应当受到平等保护。

二、物权法定原则

(一)物权法定原则的概念和内容

从历史上言之，关于物权的创设，有放任主义和法定主义之别。放任主义允许当事人依占有或登记，予其使用收益权以物权的效力，此为普鲁士普通法所采用。例如，租赁权本为债权关系，但依普鲁士普通法，以不动产为其标的时，则当事人得以自由意思，加以登记，使之变为物权。法定主义由法律明定物权之种类及内容等，不许当事人自由创设。物权法定主义最早起源于罗马法，以后逐渐为大陆法系各国和地区如法国、德国、日本、奥地利、荷兰民法及中国台湾地区加以继受。《日本民法典》第 175 条规定："物权除本法或其他法律有规定外，不得创设。"《民法典》第 116 条规定："物权的种类和内容，由法律规定。"

物权法定原则，是指物权的种类、内容都必须由法律明确规定，不得由法律之外的规范性文件确定，或当事人根据自己的意愿决定。

物权法定原则的内容包括：

1. 物权种类法定

它包括两方面要求：一是物权的具体的类型必须由法律明确确认，法律之外的规范性文件不得创设物权。当事人不得创设法律未明确规定的新的类型的物权。二是当事人也不允许当事人通过约定改变现行法律规定的物权类型。例如，法律规定以动产设立质押必须移转占有，当事人不得设立不移转占有的动产质权，否则与现行法律规定不符。

2. 物权内容法定

一方面，物权的内容必须由法律规定，当事人不得创设与法定物权内容不符合的物权。例如，（1）所有权权能必须由法律作出明确规定；（2）对所有权的限制必须由法律作出规定。对所有权的限制必须来自法律的规定，任何非所有人不得擅自对他人的所有权权能施加限制或妨碍他人行使所有权，否则构成对他人所有权的侵害。另一方面，内容法定强调当事人不得作出与物权法关于物权内容的强行性规定相背离的约定。例如，《民法典》第 399 条规定："下列财产不得抵押：（一）土地所有权……"该条规定明确土地所有权不能被抵押，当事人不得通过协议改变这一规定，协议内容不得违反这一规定。

物权法定原则与合同自由原则的区别体现了合同法与物权法（制度）的不同之处。

（二）物权法定原则存在的根据

对于物权法定原则存在的根据，学者的看法归纳起来，有如下原因：

（1）基于历史原因。物权法定原则虽源于罗马法，但正式确立始于资本主义民法。然而，资产阶级在制定民法并建立物权制度时，面临着如何清理封建时代的旧物权及防止封建制物权复活的问题。封建时代的所有权实行双重甚至多重所有，物权与对人的支配权不分，谁享有土地的权利，谁就享有对土地之上的臣民的支配权，物权是对人的支配权的基础。如果封建时代的物权不予以废除，物权不能作为真正的财产权存在，资本主义市场所要求的自由的所有权制度就不能建立，资本主义生产方式也从根本上难以存在和发展。

（2）与债权相比，物权是一种对物的排他的支配权，具有对抗第三人的效力，对第三人的利益影响更大。如果允许当事人自由创设物权，必然会损害第三人的利益。

（3）从有利于物权的公示，确保交易安全与迅速的作用来看，物权法定十分必要。

（4）物权直接反映社会所有制关系，对社会经济关系影响重大，不能允许当事人随意创设物权。

(三)物权法定原则的现实意义

(1)坚持物权法定原则,对各种类财产实行平等保护,有利于鼓励和刺激人们努力创造财富,促进社会财富的增长。

(2)坚持物权法定原则,通过物权法将一些权利确认为物权,也有利于充分发挥公有制的优越性和巨大的潜力。

(3)通过强调物权法定,有利于在物权法(制度)中建立一套完整的物权体系。

三、公示、公信原则

(一)公示原则

所谓公示,是指物权在设立、变动时,必须将物权设立、变动的事实通过一定的公示方法向社会公开,使第三人知道物权变动的情况,以避免第三人遭受损害并保护交易安全。

《民法典》第 208 条规定:"不动产物权的设立、变更、转让和消灭,应当依照法律规定登记。动产物权的设立和转让,应当依照法律规定交付。"

物权的变动之所以要公示也是由物权的性质本身所决定的。因为物权具有排他的、优先的效力。如果物权的变动不采用一定的公示方法,某人享有某种物权,第三人并不知道,而该人要向第三人主张优先权时,必然会使第三人遭受损害。

物权公示制度的建立极大地减少了产权变动中的纠纷,从而维护了交易的安全和秩序。公示制度是物权变动所特有的制度,而债权因不具有优先效力而不需要公示。如无公示制度,则物权亦不复存在。例如质权人一旦将质物返还给出质人,由出质人代为占有,或者因丧失对质物的占有而又不能请求返还,则质权亦将发生消灭。

物权的公示方法必须要由法律明确规定,而不能由当事人随意创设。关于公示方法,原则上应当采用不动产登记、动产交付的规则。登记的效力表现为在当事人达成设定、移转物权为目的的合同以后,一经登记便可以产生物权设定和移转的效力。物权的登记绝不是一个行政管理的过程,而在于将物上权利设立和变动的信息向社会公开,使第三人了解这些信息,这样不仅能够使权利的移转获得公信力,使已经形成的权利成为一种干净的权利,更重要的是使第三人能够通过登记了解权利的状况以及权利上是否存在负担等,为不动产交易的当事人提供一种风险的警示,从而决定是否与登记的权利人从事各种交易。完备的登记制度不仅是财产交易有序化的条件,而且也是物权制度赖以生存的基础,只有在一个完备的登记制度的基础上,绝大多数不动产物权才能得以设立和有秩序地移转。

就动产而言,应当以交付为公示方法。在物权的设定过程中,通过交付而移转占有也可以成为动产物权设定的一种公示方法。例如,质权的设定必以移转占有即交付为要件，只要动产已实际交付便可设立质权。至于交付行为本身是否为第三人知道并不重要。

此外，对于动产、不动产之外的其他权利，《民法典》也规定了相应的公示方法。例如，《民法典》第 445 条规定："以应收账款出质的，质权自办理出质登记时设立。"第 443 条规定："以基金份额、股权出质的，质权自办理出质登记时设立。"

《民法典》第 333 条规定："土地承包经营权自土地承包经营权合同生效时设立。"这是对于不动产物权登记公示的例外规定。

公示原则的功能在于：明确物权的归属，维护交易安全，提高物的利用效率。

（二）公信原则

所谓公信，是指对于通过法定公示方法所公示出来的物权状态，相对人有合理的理由相信其为真实的权利状态，并与登记权利人进行交易，法律应当对这种信赖利益予以保护。也就是说，一旦当事人变更物权时，依据法律的规定进行了公示，则即使依公示方法表现出来的物权事实上不存在或存在瑕疵，但对于信赖该物权的存在并已从事了物权交易的人，法律仍然承认该物权具有与真实的物权相同的法律效果，以保护交易安全。

例如，甲将乙的房屋登记在自己的名义下，并将该房屋转让给丙，丙因信赖甲所提出的产权证书等文件，而与甲订立了房屋买卖合同，则尽管甲不是真正的权利人，但法律上仍承认该项交易所导致的所有权移转之效果，以保护当事人的利益并维护交易安全。假如在此情况下确认该项交易无效，登记不具有公信力，则人们进行交易时，很难相信通过登记所表现出来的权利，这就不利于正常交易的进行。再如对动产的占有，根据许多国家的民法规定，可推定占有者享有权利。由此可见，公信原则实际上是赋予公示的内容具有公信力。公示如不能产生公信力，其作用必然大为减弱。可见公示与公信是密切联系在一起的。公信原则最早适用于动产物权，以后逐渐扩展到不动产物权。

公信原则表现为两方面的内容：

1. 登记记载的权利人在法律上推定其为真正的权利人

《民法典》第 216 条规定："不动产登记簿是物权归属和内容的根据。"这一条实际上就是确立了登记的权利推定效力。不动产登记簿是物权归属的依据。第一，凡是记载于登记簿的权利人，就在法律上推定其为的权利人。第二，如果当事人通过合同设定某种物权，但尚未进行登记，也没有完成公示的要求，人们便可以相信此种物权并没有产生。第三，如果某种物权虽然已经发生了变动，但没有通过公示予以表彰，人们也没有理由相信此种物权已经发生变动。这就是说，未经公示，不能对抗第三人。从法律效果上看，只要作为公示内容的物权现状没有变动，法律便视物权变动未曾发生。这种信赖态样，学说称之为消极信赖。凡是信赖登记所记载的权利而与权利人进行交易的人，在没有相反的证据证明其明知或应当知道不动产登记簿上记载的权利人并非真正的权利人时，都应当推定其具有善意。①

2. 凡是信赖登记所记载的权利而与权利人进行的交易，在法律上应当受到保护

登记记载的权利和内容，第三人会产生信赖，这种信赖应当受到保护，这就是公信力。严格地说，公信力实际上是在交易过程中因涉及第三人才可能发生的效力。这就是说，一方面，所谓公信力实际上保护的是第三人的信赖利益，在双方当事人之间如果发生产权争议，实际上只是涉及登记的推定效力问题，而不涉及公信力。另一方面，公信力维护的是交易过程中的交易安全。

《民法典》第216条规定其实也包括了对登记产生的信赖利益的保护，而最直接保护信赖利益的规则，是《民法典》第311条关于不动产或者动产善意取得的规定。

公信制度的设立能够促使人们从事登记行为，从而有利于建立一种真正的信用经济，并使权利的让渡能够顺利、有序地进行。公示和公信对于鼓励交易具有极为重要的作用：一方面，由于交易当事人不需要花费更多的时间和精力去调查了解标的物的权利状态，从而可以较为迅速地达成交易。另一方面，交易当事人不必要因为过多担心处分人非真正的权利人而犹豫不决。公信原则使交易当事人形成了一种对交易的合法性、对受让的标的物的不可追夺性的信赖与期待，从而为当事人快捷的交易形成了一种激励机制，为交易的安全确立了一种保障机制。

当然，公信制度的适用也有一些例外，如：善意取得制度不适用于恶意的第三人。

第四节　物权的变动

一、物权变动概述

物权变动，是指物权的设立、变更、转让和消灭。物权变动的实质，是人与人之间对于权利客体的支配关系和归属关系的变更。

物权的设立，是当事人依据法律规定的物权类型、物权设定的条件，通过法律行为和其他方式创设某项物权。设立物权的过程是物权从无到有的发生的过程，从权利人角度则称为物权的取得。物权取得包括原始取得和继受取得。物权的原始取得，又称物权的固有取得或权利的绝对发生，指非依他人既存的权利而取得物权。一般而言，基于事实行为取得的物权，多属于物权原始取得。物权的继受取得，又称物权的传来取得或物权的相对发生，指基于他人既存的权利而取得物权。一般而言，基于法律行为取得的物权，多属于继受取得。

物权的变更，有广义和狭义之分。广义的变更包括物权主体的变更、物权的内容的变更和物权客体的变更。狭义的变更则不包括物权主体的变更。因为物权主体的变更，同时引起原物权人物权的丧失和新物权人物权的取得，可分别归入物权的取得和

---

① 肖厚国：《物权变动研究》，中国社会科学院研究生院博士学位论文，第6页。

丧失之中。

物权的转让，是当事人基于法律规定或合同约定移转物权，从而使物权的主体发生变化。这是最典型的交易形式。

物权的消灭，是指当事人依据法律规定或合同的约定，通过实施一定的行为暂时地或永久地消灭物权。

物权变动的原因。物权变动是物权法上的一种民事法律效果。物权作为一种民事法律关系，也是因一定的法律事实产生、变更、终止的。能引起物权变动的民事法律事实有两类：

(1)民事法律行为(《民法典》称之为民事法律行为)。《物权法》第 25 条称之为法律行为。《民法总则》将其修改为民事法律行为，《民法典》第 133 条规定，民事法律行为是民事主体通过意思表示设立、变更、终止民事法律关系的行为。包括双方行为和单方行为。

(2)民事法律行为以外的法律事实。包括生产、天然孳息的收取、继承、时效、先占、添附、拾得遗失物、发现埋藏物、国有化、征收、没收、法院强制执行、标的物消费、标的物灭失、混同、存续期限届满(限于有期物权)、债务清偿(限于担保物权)等。

二、基于民事法律行为的物权变动

(一)基于民事法律行为的物权变动的规范模式

在引起物权变动的法律事实中，最重要的是民事法律行为。物权如何依法律行为而变动，是现代各国物权立法政策与立法技术上的重要问题。前述物权行为理论就是涉及基于法律行为的物权变动的问题。

1. 英美法系

英美法有关不动产权利变动系采取"契据交付主义"。如前所述，依美国法，有关不动产权利变动之情形，除让与(人)债权意思表示外，仅须作成契据，交付给受让人，即发生不动产权利变动之效力。受让人可以将契据拿去登记，但一般而言(各州规定不一致)，登记不是生效要件而是对抗要件。依英国法，不动产土地权利的变动须有两项要件始可发生，即"合同的要件"和"严格证书"。所谓严格证书，与美国法所指的"契据"(covenant)有同一含义。可见，美国法和英国法，不动产交易的过程同样被明确地区分为订立合同和交付契据两个阶段，可以形象地说，买卖合同类似债权契约，存在合同是否履行问题，购买人基于买卖合同的签订取得衡平地产权；契据交付类似物权契据，承载着出让人出让产权和受让人受让产权的意思表示，不存在履行与否问题，而是直接以产权变动为内容，发生权利移转的法律后果。

2. 大陆法系

至 20 世纪初，大陆民法就物权的变动就已形成了"三足鼎立"的规制格局，至今无新的模式。

(1)物权形式主义。以德国民法为典范。依此主义，物权变动依独立于债权契约而存在的物权合意及交付、登记而发生。买卖标的物的所有权移转，除须有买卖合同、登记或交付外，还须有当事人就标的物所有权的移转做成一个独立于买卖合同之外的合意。此合意是专门以物权的变动为内容的，学说上称为物权的合意(物权合同、物权契约)。例如，①甲和乙签订买卖合同(债权行为)；②甲和乙还要签订两个物权合同：一是甲愿意将房屋卖给乙，乙愿买，二是乙将价金交付给甲，甲愿意接收；③登记。②和③是物权行为，是独立存在的，因为物权行为是无因的。

(2)意思主义。以法国、日本为代表。意思主义也称债权意思主义，物权的变动依当事人的债权意思表示即发生效力。例如，甲和乙买卖合同生效时，乙即取得房屋所有权。登记是对抗要件，是不允许甲再将房屋卖给丙(登记产生对抗第三人的效力)。

(3)债权形式主义。债权形式主义，又称意思主义与登记或交付的结合，是指物权因法律行为而发生变动时，除有当事人之间的债权合意外，还必须履行交付或者登记才能生效。与法国物权变动的意思主义不同之处在于，其否认当事人的债权合意本身得直接引起物权变动，而强调交付和登记对物权变动的发生作用。但与德国之物权变动的物权形式主义的不同之处在于，虽然其将物权变动系于交付或者登记之外部形式(故为物权变动的形式主义之一种)，但其将当事人之间的债权合意作为物权变动的内在动力和原因，并不承认在债权合意之外，尚存在一个独立的物权合意(物权契约)。物权的变动在合意基础上依交付或者登记而发生，故不承认物权行为的存在。《瑞士民法典》常被认为是债权形式主义的典型。奥地利、瑞士、苏联、韩国均采用此主义，物权因法律行为发生变动时，除当事人间须有债权合意外，必须另外践行登记或交付的法定方式才能生效。例如，①甲和乙须签订买卖合同；②须登记。甲自登记取得所有权，买卖合意是直接引起物权的变动的原因。

(二)中国《民法典》对物权变动模式的选择：采取意思主义与登记或交付的结合即债权形式主义

1. 动产变动

《民法典》第224条规定："动产物权的设立和转让，自交付时发生效力，但是法律另有规定的除外。"根据此规定可以明确：

首先，基于买卖合同、赠与合同、互易合同而发生所有权转移的，以交付为所有权转移的时间。动产物权因民事法律行为而发生变动时，除有当事人之间的债权合意外，交付为动产物权变动的生效要件。但是，船舶、航空器和机动车等的物权的设立、变更、转让和消灭，未经登记，不得对抗善意第三人(《民法典》第225条)。

其次，所有权的移转不要求另有移转所有权的合意(物权的合意)，而是将所有权的移转直接作为债权合同的当然结果。

因此，中国法律对动产的变动采取意思主义与登记或交付的结合的模式。

2. 不动产变动

关于不动产的变动，在《物权法》生效前被规定在若干单行法律、法规中。如 1983 年颁布的《城市私有房屋管理条例》①第 6 条规定："城市私有房屋的所有人，须到房屋所在地房管机关办理所有权登记手续，经审查核实后，领取房屋所有权证；房屋所有权转移或房屋现状变更时，须到房屋所在地房管机关办理所有权转移或房屋现状变更登记手续。"1990 年颁布的《城镇国有土地使用权出让和转让暂行条例》（2020 年 11 月修订）第 25 条第 1 款规定："土地使用权和地上建筑物、其他附着物所有权转让，应当依照规定办理过户登记。"1994 年颁布实施的《城市房地产管理法》（2019 年修订）第 41 条规定："房地产转让，应当签订书面转让合同，合同中应当载明土地使用权取得的方式。"第 61 条第 3 款规定，房地产转让或者变更时，应当向县级以上地方人民政府房产管理部门申请房产变更登记，并凭变更后的房屋所有权证书向同级人民政府土地管理部门申请土地使用权变更登记。

《民法典》第 209 条第 1 款规定："不动产物权的设立、变更、转让和消灭，经依法登记，发生效力；未经登记，不发生效力，但是法律另有规定的除外。"第 215 条规定："当事人之间订立有关设立、变更、转让和消灭不动产物权的合同，除法律另有规定或者当事人另有约定外，自合同成立时生效；未办理物权登记的，不影响合同效力。"前述规定非常明确地表明，在中国不动产物权因民事法律行为而发生变动时，除有当事人之间的债权合意外，经依法登记，发生物权变动效力；采取的是意思主义与登记的结合的模式。

（三）基于民事法律行为的不动产物权变动模式——登记要件模式和登记对抗模式

1. 登记要件模式和登记对抗模式的含义

不动产物权变动是指不动产物权产生、变更、消灭的法定方式。由于不动产物权的外在公示方法是登记，所以就不动产的物权变动而言又主要可以分为两种模式，即登记要件模式和登记对抗模式。

登记要件模式，是指登记是不动产物权变动的生效要件，未经登记，不动产物权不发生变动。德国、瑞士民法采取了此种方式。中国《民法典》第 209 条的规定，明确了登记要件应当成为不动产物权变动的基本原则。

登记对抗模式，是指未经登记物权的变动在法律上也可以有效成立，在当事人之间产生效力，不能对抗善意第三人。法国、日本民法采取了此种形式。《民法典》第 209 条规定的"但是法律另有规定的除外"，其中就包括了登记对抗模式。例如，《民法典》第 335 条规定："土地承包经营权互换、转让的，当事人可以向登记机构申请登记；未经登记，不得对抗善意第三人。"登记对抗模式的特点有：（1）登记不是一种法定义务，但

---

① 该条例根据 2008 年 1 月 15 日《国务院关于废止部分行政法规的决定》已经废止。

可以作为约定义务。(2)移转物权如果需要交付,必须要实际交付。(3)未经登记发生物权的变动,受让人既可对抗转让人,也可对抗恶意第三人。(4)受让人享有的物权非经登记不得对抗善意的第三人。

2. 登记要件模式和登记对抗模式的区别

(1)登记是否为物权变动的生效要件。

(2)登记是否为强制性的要件。在登记要件主义模式下,登记是一种强制性的规范,实际上属于物权法定的一部分内容。如果没有登记将无法产生物权变动的效果,这样就强制要求当事人登记才能够发生物权设立、变更和消灭的后果。

(3)是否存在物权的冲突问题。登记对抗模式存在一个物上出现权利冲突的可能。

(4)是否需要以交付或登记为要件。在登记对抗的情况下,需要以交付为物权变动的要件。

(5)是否要考虑第三人的善意问题。在登记对抗的模式下,即使没有办理登记仍然可以发生物权变动,只不过这种物权不能对抗善意的第三人。因而登记对抗模式的适用要求考虑第三人主观上是否善意。

(6)从适用范围来说,由于《民法典》采取登记要件为一般原则、登记对抗为例外的做法,所以登记对抗模式只能适用于法律特别规定的情况。《民法典》第 209 条第 1 款规定:"不动产物权的设立、变更、转让和消灭,经依法登记,发生效力;未经登记,不发生效力,但是法律另有规定的除外。"

《民法典》第 209 条第 1 款规定的法律另有规定的情况主要包括:

第一,在《民法典》中明确规定可以采取登记对抗的情况。例如,第 335 条规定:"土地承包经营权互换、转让的,当事人可以向登记机构申请登记;未经登记,不得对抗善意第三人"。再如,第 374 条规定:"地役权自地役权合同生效时设立。当事人要求登记的,可以向登记机构申请地役权登记;未经登记,不得对抗善意第三人。"

第二,依法属于国家所有的自然资源。《民法典》第 209 条第 2 款规定:"依法属于国家所有的自然资源,所有权可以不登记。"

第三,非基于民事法律行为发生的物权变动,如继承、征收、合法建造房屋,虽不经登记也发生效力,但是未经登记不得处分该物权,如《民法典》第 229 条至第 231 条之规定。

三、非基于法律行为的物权变动

(一)非基于法律行为的物权变动的概念

《民法典·物权编》第 2 章第 3 节规定了非法律行为的物权变动模式。所谓非基于法律行为的物权变动,是指直接由法律规定的原因导致物权的设立、变更和消灭。其特点主要有:

(1)必须依据法律的规定。物权的公示方法是由物权法规定的,对不适用法定的公示方法的情况，也须由法律明确规定。非基于法律行为的物权变动通常是直接基于法律规定的原因而发生的，而不取决于当事人的意思。法律规定的原因通常包括：因继承、强制执行、公用征收、法院的判决、因公权力、因合法建造、拆除房屋等事实行为取得不动产物权等。只要发生法律规定的事实，就会发生物权的取得和变动。

(2) 须有特定的事实或事实行为的发生。

(3) 不以登记为物权变动的生效要件。

(4) 是物权变动的例外情况。

(二) 非基于法律行为的不动产物权变动

不动产非基于法律行为而发生变动的情形，主要有继承、强制执行、公用征收和法院判决等。一般而言，不动产物权变动非因法律行为而发生的，都不以登记为物权变动的生效要件。依据《民法典》第 232 条，处分该物权时，依照法律规定需要办理登记的，非经登记，不发生物权效力。

(1) 法院、仲裁机构的生效法律文书或者人民政府的征收决定等。《民法典》第 229 条规定："因人民法院、仲裁机构的法律文书或者人民政府的征收①决定等，导致物权设立、变更、转让或者消灭的，自法律文书或者征收决定等生效时发生效力。"

(2) 继承。《民法典》第 230 条规定："因继承取得物权的，自继承开始时发生效力。"

(3) 合法建造、拆除房屋等事实行为。《民法典》第 231 条规定："因合法建造、拆除房屋等事实行为设立或者消灭物权的，自事实行为成就时发生效力。"

(三) 非基于法律行为的动产物权变动

按照《民法典》的规定，动产物权非依法律行为而发生变动的，其原因除了法院、仲裁机构法律文书、征收、继承外，还包括因遗失物拾得、埋藏物或者隐藏物发现等事实行为引起的动产物权变动。

四、不动产登记

(一) 不动产登记的概念和特征

不动产登记是《民法典》确立的一项物权制度，是指经权利人或利害关系人申请或国家专职登记机构依职权，由登记机构将有关不动产物权设立、变更、消灭等事项记载于不动产登记簿的事实。笔者认为作为物权公示手段，不动产登记本质上为产生司法效果的事实行为而非登记机关的行政管理行为。其特点包括：

(1) 是登记机构将不动产物权的设立和变动的事实记载于登记簿。

---

① 征收是指征收主体(国家)基于公共利益需要，以行政权取得集体、个人财产所有权并给予适当补偿的行政行为。

（2）是对不动产物权的设立、变更、转让和消灭等事项进行的登记。

（3）仅限于不动产。

（4）性质上是一种公示方法。

有学者认为不动产物权登记是一种行政行为，它所体现的是国家行政权力对不动产物权关系的合理干预。干预的目的是明晰各种不动产物权，依法保护物权人的合法权益。

中国以土地为中心的登记制度源远流长，从一开始就与土地税赋息息相关。据学者考证，中国古代以土地交易为中心形成的登记制度，肇始于周朝中后期。唐代以后，中国在土地管理方面出现了立契、申牒或过割制度。土地买卖必须通过官府，进行书面申报和登记，才能发生效力。否则，不仅交易无效，而且还要受到严厉的制裁。

2015 年 3 月 1 日前在中国，对不动产物权登记享有职权的行政机关有土地管理机关、房产管理机关、矿产管理机关、水行政管理机关、渔政管理机关、林业管理机关等。2014 年 11 月 24 日，国务院公布《不动产登记暂行条例》，自 2015 年 3 月 1 日起施行，该条例于 2019 年 3 月 24 日修订。

制定出台《不动产登记暂行条例》或《不动产登记法》的目的是整合不动产登记职责、建立不动产统一登记制度，是完善社会主义市场经济体制、建设现代市场体系的必然要求，对于保护不动产权利人合法财产权、提高政府治理效率和水平，尤其是方便企业、方便群众，具有重要意义。根据《民法典》第 210 条的规定，不动产实行统一登记，并授权法律、行政法规对统一登记的范围、登记机构和登记办法作出规定。国务院制定出台该《不动产登记暂行条例》，通过立法规范登记行为、明确登记程序、界定查询权限，整合土地、房屋、林地、草原、海域等登记职责，实现不动产登记机构、登记簿册、登记依据和信息平台"四统一"。《不动产登记暂行条例》共 6 章 35 条，对不动产登记机构、登记簿、登记程序、登记信息共享与保护等作出规定。

《不动产登记暂行条例》第 5 条规定："下列不动产权利，依照本条例的规定办理登记：（一）集体土地所有权；（二）房屋等建筑物、构筑物所有权；（三）森林、林木所有权；（四）耕地、林地、草地等土地承包经营权；（五）建设用地使用权；（六）宅基地使用权；（七）海域使用权；（八）地役权；（九）抵押权；（十）法律规定需要登记的其他不动产权利。"

（二）物权登记的效力

对物权登记的效力，各国立法规定不尽一致。大陆法系国家主要有两种不同的观点：登记要件说和登记对抗说。

依照《民法典》第 209 条的规定，中国采取的是登记要件作为一般原则，以登记对抗作为例外。

不动产登记的效力包括：

1. 自记载于不动产登记簿之日起发生物权设立和变动的效力

《民法典》第 214 条规定："不动产物权的设立、变更、转让和消灭，依照法律规定应当登记的，自记载于不动产登记簿时发生效力。"

2. 权利推定效力

《民法典》第 216 条规定，不动产登记簿是物权归属和内容的根据。例如，登记簿登记记载的权利人在法律上推定其为真正的权利人，本书"公信原则"部分对此已做论述。

3. 善意保护的效力

不动产权属证书是权利人享有该不动产物权的证明。《民法典》第 217 条规定了登记与权属证明之间的关系："不动产权属证书记载的事项，应当与不动产登记簿一致；记载不一致的，除有证据证明不动产登记簿确有错误外，以不动产登记簿为准。"

要区分登记的效力和合同的效力。《民法典》第 215 条规定："当事人之间订立有关设立、变更、转让和消灭不动产物权的合同，除法律另有规定或者当事人另有约定外，自合同成立时生效；未办理物权登记的，不影响合同效力。"登记的效力和合同的效力相互区别又相互联系。登记的效力具有独立的法律后果。

将登记确定为权利移转的公示要件，也可以明确区分登记和行政审批的概念。

(三)登记机构及其审查义务

登记应当在登记机构办理。登记机构是指负责在登记机构所管辖的行政区划内依法接受申请人递交的申请材料办理所有权和其他物权变动登记的机构。

1995—2015 年，不动产物权变动登记的事务，主要由有关行政机关及其设立的事业单位负责，登记机构比较多。《民法典》第 210 条规定："不动产登记，由不动产所在地的登记机构办理。国家对不动产实行统一登记制度。统一登记的范围、登记机构和登记办法，由法律、行政法规规定。"

《不动产登记暂行条例》第 7 条规定："不动产登记由不动产所在地的县级人民政府不动产登记机构办理；直辖市、设区的市人民政府可以确定本级不动产登记机构统一办理所属各区的不动产登记。跨县级行政区域的不动产登记，由所跨县级行政区域的不动产登记机构分别办理。不能分别办理的，由所跨县级行政区域的不动产登记机构协商办理；协商不成的，由共同的上一级人民政府不动产登记主管部门指定办理。国务院确定的重点国有林区的森林、林木和林地，国务院批准项目用海、用岛，中央国家机关使用的国有土地等不动产登记，由国务院国土资源主管部门会同有关部门规定。"

同时《不动产登记暂行条例》第 8 条第 3 款规定："不动产登记簿应当记载以下事项：(一)不动产的坐落、界址、空间界限、面积、用途等自然状况；(二)不动产权利的主体、类型、内容、来源、期限、权利变化等权属状况；(三)涉及不动产权利限制、提示的事项；(四)其他相关事项。"

关于登记机构的在登记中的审查中承担何种义务，在制定《民法典》过程中曾有实质审查说和形式审查说之分。《民法典》最终采取了形式审查为主、实质审查为辅的审查制度。《民法典》第 212 条规定："登记机构应当履行下列职责：(一)查验申请人提供的权属证明和其他必要材料；(二)就有关登记事项询问申请人；(三)如实、及时登记有关事项；（四）法律、行政法规规定的其他职责。申请登记的不动产的有关情况需要进一步证明的，登记机构可以要求申请人补充材料，必要时可以实地查看。"

（四）登记查询

《民法典》第218条规定："权利人、利害关系人可以申请查询、复制不动产登记资料，登记机构应当提供。"

（五）更正登记和异议登记

更正登记，是指权利人、利害关系人认为不动产登记簿记载的事项有错误时，经其申请，经过权利人书面同意更正或者有证据证明登记确有错误的，登记机构对错误事项进行更正的登记。

《民法典》第220条第1款规定："权利人、利害关系人认为不动产登记簿记载的事项错误的，可以申请更正登记。不动产登记簿记载的权利人书面同意更正或者有证据证明登记确有错误的，登记机构应当予以更正。"

异议登记，是指利害关系人对不动产登记簿记载的物权归属等事项有异议的，可以通过异议登记以保护其权利。《民法典》第220条第2款规定："不动产登记簿记载的权利人不同意更正的，利害关系人可以申请异议登记。登记机构予以异议登记，申请人在异议登记之日起十五日内不提起诉讼的，异议登记失效。异议登记不当，造成权利人损害的，权利人可以向申请人请求损害赔偿。"

（六）预告登记

《民法典》第221条规定了预告登记。该条规定："当事人签订买卖房屋的协议或者签订其他不动产物权的协议，为保障将来实现物权，按照约定可以向登记机构申请预告登记。预告登记后，未经预告登记的权利人同意，处分该不动产的，不发生物权效力。预告登记后，债权消灭或者自能够进行不动产登记之日起九十日内未申请登记的，预告登记失效。"

预告登记，是指为了确保债权的实现、保障将来实现物权等目的，按照约定向登记机构申请办理的预先登记。

预告登记是与本登记相对应的概念。本登记就是指对于已经实际发生的物权变动进行的登记。通常所说的物权登记都是本登记。两者之间的区别主要在：登记权利的客体不同；登记的申请材料不同；登记的法律效力不同。预告登记的效果是限制登记权利人的处分行为，以保障债权请求权的实现。

预告登记的作用主要是：保障将来实现物权；保障债权请求权的效力；顺位保证；破产保护作用。

（七）登记的请求权

登记的请求权，是指登记权利人对登记义务人所享有的请求其履行登记义务或协助履行登记义务的权利。

在中国，立法长期以来一直将登记、审批等作为合同成立并生效的要件，导致实践中当事人在签订合同后为获取不正当利益而不愿意办理登记，致合同不能生效，法院也不能在合同无效后强制其办理登记、审批的手续。所以，将登记与合同的效力分开，使登记义务成为合同请求权内容，才能在一方故意不办理登记手续时，另一方可请求法院强制其办理登记手续，也可以请求追究不办理登记方的违约责任。

登记义务人原则上由法律与合同加以确定。如果法律和合同没有规定的，双方都应当负有办理登记的义务。《不动产登记暂行条例》第14条规定：因买卖、设定抵押权等申请不动产登记的，应当由当事人双方共同申请。但是尚未登记的不动产首次申请登记，继承、接受遗赠取得不动产权利等七种情况；可以由当事人单方申请。

五、动产交付与动产物权登记

(一)动产交付的概念和效力与动产物权登记

交付是指权利人将自己占有的物移转给其他人占有的行为。

《民法典》第224条规定："动产物权的设立和转让，自交付时发生效力，但法律另有规定的除外。"

可见，动产物权的设立和转让，除法律另有规定外，以交付为其公示方法。交付是法定义务，当事人要完成物权变动，必须要依法履行交付的义务。交付完成将发生物权的变动。

这里所称法律另有规定者，包括以民用航空器、船舶、机动车辆为客体的物权、动产抵押权和某些权利质权。除这些动产物权外，其他动产物权均以交付为其公示方法。按照法律规定，这些动产物权不以交付为其公示方法，而以登记为其公示方法。但这些动产物权登记的效力，立法上一般采取登记对抗主义，即登记并非这些动产物权变动的要件，只是不经登记其物权变动不能产生对抗善意第三人的效力。《民法典》第225条规定："船舶、航空器和机动车等的物权的设立、变更、转让和消灭，未经登记，不得对抗善意第三人。"以航空器、船舶、车辆抵押的，为运输工具的登记部门，中国《海商法》第9条规定："船舶所有权的取得、转让和消灭，应当向船舶登记机关登记；未经登记的，不得对抗第三人。"第13条规定："设定船舶抵押权，由抵押权人和抵押人共同向船舶登记机关办理抵押权登记；未经登记的，不得对抗第三人。"

一般动产物权登记，依据《国务院关于实施动产和权利担保统一登记的决定》国发〔2020〕18号，通知自2021年1月1日起，在全国范围内实施动产和权利担保统一登记。生产设备、原材料、半成品、产品等动产抵押登记的设立、变更、注销，登录人民银行征信中心动产融资统一登记公示系统办理。但机动车抵押、船舶抵押、航空器抵押、债券质押、基金份额质押、股权质押、知识产权中的财产权质押除外。以企业或者其他组织、自然人的设备和其他动产抵押的，工商行政管理部门、公证部门不再负责抵押登记。一般情况下，登记的动产抵押权优于未登记的动产抵押权。

单纯的交付只能表示物的占有的转移，不能表示物权的让与，因此交付作为动产物权让与的公示方法，须以交付人让与动产物权的意思为前提。交付人让与动产物权的意思，通常通过交付人单方的民事法律行为或交付人与受交付人双方的民事法律行为表现出来。

交付与登记不同，登记可以作为一切不动产物权变动形式的公示手段，而交付则不能作为一切动产物权变动形式的公示手段，只能作为以民事法律行为让与动产物权的公示手段。这里所说的让与，包括转让所有权、设定以占有为要素的他主物权。动产物权的其他变动形式都不以交付为其公示手段。例如，以原始取得方法取得动产所有权，或者不发生交付（如以收益、添附、先占、时效取得等方式取得动产物权），或者交付在其中不具有法律意义（如以继承方式取得动产所有权）。留置权是债权人先占有债务人的财产，在债务人到期不履行债务时才发生的，因此交付也不是取得留置权的公示。实际上，只有以民事法律行为让与动产所有权与设定质权时，交付才是动产物权变动的公示手段。其中具有普遍意义的又只有动产所有权的让与。

关于交付的效力，有生效要件主义与对抗要件主义两种不同的立法。采取生效要件主义的立法，以《德国民法典》为代表，把交付作为让与动产物权的要件，非经交付不发生动产物权让与的法律效果。采取对抗要件主义的立法，当事人让与动产物权的意思表示直接具有移转动产物权的法律效力，交付只是对抗第三人的要件。中国采取的是生效要件主义。

（二）交付方式

交付分为现实交付和观念交付两种情况：

1. 现实交付

现实交付是指动产物权的出让人将动产的占有实际地移转给受让人，由受让人直接占有该动产。这是通常的交付方式，包括：（1）在约定的时间和地点由转让人与受让人直接交接物品。此种交付以受让人点收后完成。（2）根据受让人的指示将物品托运或邮寄。此种交付自转让人办完托运或邮寄手续时完成。

2. 观念交付

观念交付是指在特殊情况下，法律允许当事人通过特别的约定，并不现实地交付动产，而采取一种变通的交付办法来代替实际交付。允许观念交付可以充分尊重当事人的意志，减少因实际交付所付出的交易费用，使交易更为便捷。

观念交付主要采取三种方式：

（1）简易交付。即根据当事人的协议，受让人将已经他主占有的财产（财产已实际被受让人占有）变为自主占有。《民法典》第 226 条规定："动产物权设立和转让前，权利人已经占有该动产的，物权自民事法律行为生效时发生效力。"

（2）占有改定。即动产物权的让与人与受让人之间特别约定，将转让人的自主占有改为他主占有。此种交付自占有改定的协议达成时或者协议约定的时间到来时完成。此处的特定契约并非订立单纯的无法律关系存在的间接占有契约，而是达成租赁、借用、保管、让与担保等特定法律关系的合意，否则，抽象的改定不能使受让人取得间接占有，故不能使其取得所有权。《民法典》第228条规定："动产物权转让时，当事人又约定由出让人继续占有该动产的，物权自该约定生效时发生效力。"

（3）指示交付（又称返还财产请求权的让与）。所有人在转让由第三人占有的财产时，可以用让与返还原物请求权的方式为交付。《民法典》第227条规定："动产物权设立和转让前，第三人占有该动产的，负有交付义务的人可以通过转让请求第三人返还原物的权利代替交付。"

（三）船舶、航空器和机动车等物权的变动——登记对抗主义

《民法典》第225条规定："船舶、航空器和机动车等的物权的设立、变更、转让和消灭，未经登记，不得对抗善意第三人。"船舶、航空器和机动车因价值超过一般动产，在法律上被视为一种准不动产，但是船舶、航空器和机动车等本身具有动产的属性，其物权变动并不是在登记时发生效力，依照《民法典》规定，其所有权转移一般在交付时发生效力，其抵押权在抵押合同生效时设立。但是，因这类动产的价值较大，法律对这类动产规定有登记制度，其物权的变动如果未在登记部门进行登记，就不产生社会公信力，即使已经发生物权变动效力也不能对抗善意第三人。所谓善意第三人，就是指不知道也不应当知道物权发生了变动的物权关系相对人。例如，甲将其汽车卖给乙并已经完成交付，但没有进行登记，这时该汽车所有权已经转移给乙，但如果甲又背着乙将汽车卖给不知情的丙并进行了登记，乙就不能以事先已经取得该汽车所有权而对抗丙，丙获得该汽车的所有权。

第五节　物权的民法保护

一、物权的民法保护概述

物权的民法保护，是指在物权受到侵害的情况下，为维护物权人的利益、保障权利人不受侵害的各种民法保护方法。

保护物权不仅是民法的任务，也是中国各个法律部门的共同任务。各个法律部门对物权都作出了规定，并设立了不同的法律责任。《民法典·物权编》第一分编专设一章（第三章）规定了物权的民法保护，主要是在物权的效力和物权的特殊规则方面，对权利人提供充分的保障。它主要有以下特征：

（1）在物权受到侵害情况下，可以通过多种途径获得救济：诉讼外和解、具有法律效力的调解（专门调解机构的调解或者法院调解、仲裁机关调解）、诉讼。

（2）设立了确认物权的请求权，专门用于解决因物权归属不明产生的争议。

（3）设立了专门保护物权的方式：物权请求权，包括返还原物、排除妨碍、消除危险、恢复原状请求权四种方式。

（4）对于物权的保护，不仅可以采用物权请求权，而且可以采用侵权请求权，加大了物权的保护力度。

（5）针对侵害物权的情况，不仅仅规定了民事责任，而且规定了违反行政管理规定的应当依法承担行政责任，构成犯罪的依法承担刑事责任。这就构成了一个保护物权的完整的责任体系。

物权的民法保护，包括确认物权确认请求权和物权（上）请求权。特别注意一点，因继承、强制执行、公用征收、法院的判决、因公权力、因合法建造、拆除房屋等事实行为取得不动产物权的，依据《最高人民法院关于适用〈中华人民共和国民法典〉物权编的解释（一）》（以下简称：《〈民法典〉物权编的解释（一）》）第 8 条，"依据民法典第 229 条至第 231 条规定享有物权，但尚未完成动产交付或者不动产登记的权利人，依据民法典第 235 条至第 238 条的规定，请求保护其物权的，应予支持"，物权人享有物权确认请求权和物权请求权。

二、确认物权的请求权

（一）概念

确认物权的请求权，是指利害关系人在物权归属和内容发生争议时，有权请求确认物权的归属，明确物权的内容。《民法典》第 234 条规定："因物权的归属、内容发生争议的，利害关系人可以请求确认权利。"

物权的确认并不是一项独立的请求权。因为，一方面，民法上的请求权是以实体权利的存在为前提的，如物权请求权就是以物权的存在为前提的。然而，物权的确认是因为物权这一实体权利本身的归属或内容存在争议而产生的。既然物权的归属和内容仍存在争议，那么就不能认为请求确认物权的人就当然享有物权。另一方面，确认物权的请求权只能通过公力救济的方式来实现，常常要通过登记主管机关或者人民法院来进行确认。另外，确认请求权不能直接针对特定的人行使，也是它与一般请求权不同的表现。

（二）物权的确认的特点

（1）是物权保护的前提。
（2）内容：确认物权归属和物权内容。
（3）确认物权的归属必须向有关物权登记机关或人民法院提出请求。
（4）确认物权必须由利害关系人提出请求。
确认物权原则上不适用诉讼时效。

（三）物权请求权

见前述"物权效力"中的物权请求权。

Chapter 2　Survey of Real Right

Section One　Definition, Characters and Effects of Real Right

1. Concept and Characters of Real Right

The term "real right" was first officially used in law by the Austrian Civil Code that was enacted in 1811. Article 307 of this code provides that, "Real right is a private property right that can be asserted against anyone. " In 1896, the German Civil Code was enacted. In the third part of this code, the term "Law of Property" was used as the title, being followed by stipulations of other real rights including ownership, superficies (or surface rights), usufructuary right, easement, mortgage, pledge, etc. Thenceforth, other civil law jurisdictions also began to model after the German Civil Code by establishing in their civil codes real right systems that were adapted to their own reality and conditions. Section 1, Chapter 5 of the General Principles of the Civil Law of PRC providing "Property Ownership and Related Property Rights" basically brings into the real right system of PRC, though the term "real right" is not specifically used. As of today, there is no clear definition about the real right in the civil codes of other nations.

Book Two Real Rights of the Civil Code stipulates that "This Book regulates the civil-law relations arising from the attribution and utilization of things" (Article 205). Added to that, the Civil Code specifies that "Persons of the civil law enjoy real rights in accordance with law. Real rights are the rights to directly and exclusively control a specific thing by the right holder in accordance with law, which consists of the ownership, right to usufruct, and security interests in the property" (Article 114).

To understand the concept of real right properly, one should bear in mind that such right is not only a right that is asserted against a thing. Rather, it reflects the relations between or among different parties. Whilst the law confirms that the right holder is entitled to dispose a thing at his free will for the purpose of acquiring the interests thereupon, it also has set limits on others in terms of disposing the same thing or enjoying the interests thereupon. This is how rights and obligations are created. The content of the legal relationship of real right is the rights enjoyed by the real right holder and the obligations undertaken by the obligor.

The real right and creditors' rights are two different sets of civil-law rights and together build up the most fundamental forms of proprietary right. In a commodity economy, combination of person and property forms the real right. As property gets into circulation, exchange between different parties forms the creditor's right. One prerequisite of such exchange is that transactors respectively hold their real rights, whilst the process of the exchange is reflected in creditors' rights. A transaction ends up in the assignment and transfer of real rights. When goods are exchanged, various contents of ownership can be separated from this right in accordance with the exchange principle. In light of this, in the area of civil law real right law and the law of obligations are the basic rules regulating the functioning of a commodity economy. As two forms of basic proprietary rights in social and economic life, real rights and creditor's rights interact with each other when exerting positive repercussions on the commodity economy.

Compared with creditors' rights, real rights have the following features as a separate category of civil-law right:

1. 1   A Real Right Holder is Specified, but its Obligor not—The Real Right is an Absolute Right, whilst the Creditor's Right a Relative Right

The real right refers to those proprietary rights enjoyed by a specified holder which exclude the encroachment of all other unspecified individuals (Article 114 of the Civil Code). The subject of the legal relationship of real right is the right holder and obligor of the legal relationship, and the subject can be either a natural person or a legal person. The subject of the right is specific, while the obligation subject is not. In China, the State, collectives and individuals can be a right holder. As an absolute right and a "right against the whole world", the real right is vested in a specific right holder, creating for others an obligation not to interfere with or infringe upon such right. That is to say, anyone other than the right holder is an obligor. Unlike the real right, the creditor's right is vested in a determinate holder effective between the obligee and its obligor. The right holder is specified. Para. 2, Article 118 of the Civil Code provides that "A right in personam is the right of an obligee to request a specific obligor to do or not to do a certain act, as arising from a contract, a tortious act, a negotiorum gestio, or unjust enrichment, or otherwise arising by operation of law". The obligee of a creditor's right may only assert claims against the determinate person. In this sense, the claim is a personal right (jura in personam).

1. 2   Object of Real Rights are Specific Things

As the real right concerns the possession of material goods by civil persons, objects of real rights are things rather than performance. Objects of real rights have a broad scope, but share one thing in common—they must be specified. Otherwise, the right holder will be unable to control the object and registration or delivery cannot be conducted when the real right is transferred. Added to that, object of a real right must be independent and tangible thing rather than performance. Otherwise, it will be difficult for the law to define real rights or objects of State ownership and collective ownership.

There are mainly three patterns of legislation on things adopted by continental jurisdictions. The first pattern is represented by the French Civil Code, which defines things as tangible or intangible objects (rights). The second is represented by the German Civil Code and the Japanese Civil Code, which only recognize tangible objects. The third pattern is similar to the second one but exceptionally recognizes "force of nature" as things. It is represented by the Swiss Civil Code. In my opinion, things in legal sense shall refer to substances and natural forces that can not only satisfy people's needs in social life but also be subjected to human beings' actual control or disposal. Denotation of "things" should be expanded as the science and technology advances. For example, organs and tissues separated from human body, dead fetus, corpses, medical wastes, placenta, etc. may all be taken as objects of real rights in special cases, so long as it does not violate public policy. Another example could be space or radio spectrum resources, which could also be taken as potential object of real rights.

The Civil Code defines the concept of property in its Article 115, which stipulates that "Property consists of immovable and movable property. Where the law provides that a right shall be treated as property over which a real right lies, such provisions shall be followed. " The second sentence following the first sentence that defines the concept property states that certain rights can also be object regulated by the real right law. These include pledge on a right and mortgage on a right. Some also argue that the right to use land for construction purposes in the Chinese law fall into this category as well. Where there exist provisions under specific laws, such rules shall prevail. Article 115 seems to have denied the traditional definition in real right law which defines things as object of real rights in that it does not use tangible things to conceptualize object of real rights. As science and technology advance, especially as space and natural forces get encompassed into the regulation scope of the real right law, object of real rights in the Civil Code has also been enriched and comes to include both things and rights. This presents both a challenge and a legal basis for reframing a unified concept of property—the concept could be restructured by adopting object of real rights as a hypernym. But a clear definition for property remains absent here. It is arguably illogical to treat rights as object of real rights.

Object of creditors' rights may differ according to specific types of claims. Generally speaking, a creditor's right usually directly targets the performance of an act and points to a thing. During the term of existence of an obligatory relationship, an obligee normally does not take direct possession of the property held by the obligor; he may do so only after the obligor has delivered such property to him. Upon delivery, the creditor's right generally terminates and certain real right(s) would be created.

1. 3　Real Right is a Dominating Right with which an Obligee May Achieve Direct Domination over Property

By direct domination, we mean that, on the one hand, a real right holder may lawfully possess, use or adopt other means to dispose of his property at his own will without imposing any obligation on any other person to actively provide any assistance; on the other hand, it also means that the right holder may freely exercise domination over the property, without having to acquire consent from another person. In other words, the right holder may freely and lawfully possess, use or by other means dispose of his property regardless of any intentions or acts of another party.

In the real right, domination mainly refers to the control over a specified movable or immoveable thing. It also alludes to the dominance over the property's value. Of course, a complete separation of these two is impossible. For example, where a right to usufruct holder restores his domination over a piece of land or a house, the value in use of realty is also resumed. Protecting a security interest holder's control over the secured property also in fact secures the corresponding exchange value. The extent to which a right holder may exert influence or control over a property largely depends not only on the property's nature and utility, but also on the contents of the real right itself. For instance, an owner may, in general cases, exercise whatever domination the law entitles him to have over a thing, free from any interference by others. However, once a jus in re aliena is established upon the same property, his ownership will be subject to restrictions of such newly created right. At the same time, the holder of the newly created real right also exerts limited control over the property subject to the stipulation of law and influence of the ownership, because the new right is established over a property belonging to another. The contents of a real right over a property belonging to another differ according to the type of jus in re aliena.

A real right holder obtains profit from the specific property he controls. Such interests basically take three forms: the first form refers to those interests vested in the owner, which constitutes the entire interests existing on the property; the second form lies in the interests enjoyed by usufruct right holder(s), namely, the value in use or utility value of the property; the third form manifests in the interests vested in security interest holder (s), i. e., the exchange value of the thing, meaning that the obligee may be given the priority in being paid with the money into which the secured property is converted or the proceeds obtained from auction or sale of the property in the case where the debtor defaults. In alignment with the increasingly sophisticated credit system in market economy, exchange value in property also becomes increasingly vital.

The dominative feature of the real right gives rise to its other characters such as the preferential effect and retroactive effect.

1.4 Real Right is an Exclusive Right that Can be Asserted against the Whole World

Exclusivity of the real right means that effects of this right overshadow the whole world. Any person other than the real right holder is legally bound to refrain from encroaching on or impairing such real right. Because the real right is exclusive and absolute, when it comes to the protection of the real right, the tort law applies. The obligee could either make claims on property rights[1] to restore his original status of full domination over the property through removal of impairment, or file a suit against the tortfeasor relying on the tort law. For the same reason, transfer and creation of a real right should be publicized. Hence, the real right is a publicized right.

The exclusive effect also manifests in the principle of "one property one right", meaning that real right with same contents are mutually exclusive and may not exist on one property at the same time. For example, one may not establish two ownerships or two rights of management or use on the same property. Where several subjects share the ownership on one property, what is divided and shared is the ownership in terms of its quantity instead of the quality or nature. Co-ownership does not mean that each co-owner respectively enjoys an independent ownership on the property. Instead, they share one ownership either equally or in proportion to the amount of their shares. Likewise, creation of several mortgages upon one property is also a mere division of the quantity instead of quality or nature of the exchange value of the mortgaged property.

In the setting of creditors' rights, however, blatantly different characters are to be observed. The obligee, though generally doesn't exercise direct dominance over the thing, may request the obligor for an act or inaction. Creditors' rights are also inviolable, because the obligee may request any third party who has infringed his right (e. g. such third party unlawfully prevent the obligor from performing his obligations) for recovery of damage. On the other hand, the creditors' rights are not exclusive as real right. More than one creditor's right can be set simultaneously regarding one property, with each having equal effects. As for some creditors' rights that have exclusivity to such extent as the law allows (e. g. , exclusivity in leasehold), which have already acquired some features of real right, the right holder is the

---

[1] Claim on property rights refers to that when the integrity of real right is impaired or might be impaired, the right holder enjoys the right to require the impairing people to take or stop certain action to recover the integrity of real right.

obligee or holder of certain real right compared with the obligor, but a complete real right holder for the third parties.

As two basic characteristics of real right, domination and absoluteness also well characterize the real right relation itself, which is a dominating right, underlines the relationship between a subject and object. Such relationship denotes the possession of the property taken by civil persons. Thus, the object of real right has to be a thing, and shall not be performance. Otherwise, real right will be not easily ascertainable. What we should pay particular attention to is that the objects of real right are tangible, and in most cases they must be specified and independent. This is determined by the economic nature of real right, which also distinguishes it from other rights such as intellectual property rights. As is put by a proverb, "the ownership shouldn't be uncertain". If property is unspecified, then it may only be the object of creditors right, not that of real right, because the uncertainty will deprive the right of the object over which it dominates, thus undermine the right itself. Consequently, specificity of object is deemed by the academia as an indispensable rule in real right law.

As a right against the whole world, the real right emphasizes the relationship between persons. It denotes such relations between obligee(s) and obligor(s), with the former being entitled to dispose and obtain profits from a specified thing, while the latter being obliged not to encroach on or impair the right. This is an interpersonal relationship, which constitutes one of the fundamental differences between creditor's right and real right. Another interaction between the feature of domination and absoluteness in real right lies in that the former is a foundation and prerequisite for the latter. It is possible to hold the right against the whole world only when there is the domination over a thing on the part of the obligee, though such domination doesn't necessarily lead to absoluteness, like in the case where the actual possession of anothers' property cannot be asserted against a third party. Absoluteness indicates that real right is not only the right over a thing, but also a relation between people. The above mentioned two features should be encompassed in the definition of real right. Other features such as priority deriving from the two features cannot manifest the nature of real right.

1.5   Real Right is a Preferential Right

The preferential effect of real right refers to the strength of the right's effects. Where several conflicting interests co-exist on one property, rights with stronger effects exclude or prevail over those with weaker effects. Such effect may be viewed from two aspects: the internal aspect and the external aspect. External preferential effect denotes the priority of real right over creditor's right, while internal preferential effect alludes to cases where several real rights coexist on one property, the right established earlier in time prevails over that created later. Article 414 of the Civil Code provides that, "Where a property is mortgaged to two or more creditors, the proceeds obtained from auction or sale of the mortgaged property shall be applied in accordance with the following provisions: (1) where the mortgages have all been registered, the order of payment is based on the priority in time of registration; (2) a registered mortgage has priority over an unregistered mortgage to be paid; and (3) where none of the mortgages are registered, payment shall be made on a pro rata basis against the claims. The preceding paragraph shall be applied mutatis mutandis with regard to the priority order of payment for other security interests that are registrable". This is the so-called rule of "first come, first served" or "first in time, first in right". When applied in a broader sense, such hierarchy of effects among real right evolve into another rule, that is, a real right established earlier in time is not to be impaired by the ones created later, which means its realization may eliminate or exclude these rights. At times, however, the law, taking into consideration of the public interests, may provide quite opposite rules such as the maritime law where maritime lien is given priority over a mortgage of a ship. Under this condition, such stipulation of law shall prevail. Unlike real rights, creditor's rights are equal without priority. Even though more than one creditor's right is established on the property, each right holder shall abide by the principle of equality upon liquidation.

1. 6   Retroactive Effect of Real Right

Every real right is with retroactivity. When, by whatever means and to whomever a thing is transferred, the owner may lawfully recover his property from the possessors. Anyone else is obliged not to interfere when the right holder exercises his right. Anyone who has illegally acquired the property is obliged to return it. This rule also applies in the field of security interests in property rights. In most cases, creditor's rights are only with privity and binding on the parties to the contract. Generally the creditor's rights only bear the nature of relativity, being valid only between the parties of the contract.

It should be pointed out that, the retroactive effect of real right is not absolute. It is subject to limitation set by the rule of good faith acquisition.

1. 7   Real Right is a Public Right

As a right against the whole world, real right is strongly exclusive, thus directly affects the interests of others. On account of this, real right should be publicized for the knowledge of the parties concerned. As such, publication of real right establishment and changes becomes necessary. Ownership of movable properties manifests in possession, as is the same with pledge and lien, while ownership of immovable properties is displayed through registration. Publication generally comes along with real right. Absent publication, real right will not exist. Creditor's rights, on the other hand, comes into being only between certain parties. It usually concerns no public, thus requires no publication. Therefore, if the parties enter into a contract to establish a real right, the contract will stand without publication, but the real right will not.

1. 8　Establishment of the Real Right Shall be Stipulated by law

The creation of real right is under the rule of the doctrine of numerus clausus, which requires the categories and contents of real right be stipulated by law, leaving little room for the discretion of the parties. Creditor's rights are established in accordance with the principle of freedom of contract. Particularly, a contractual obligation is to be ascertained by the parties themselves at their free will.

1. 9　Real Right is Permanent or Long Standing

The real right is permanent or long standing. In the case of ownership, it is subject to no time limitation. As long as the owner lives, so will his ownership be kept. When the property is transferred, the ownership therein goes to a new owner, though the original owner loses his right in the property. In this sense the ownership is viewed to be eternal. According to Article 196 of the Civil Code, "The limitation period does not apply to the following rights to claim: (1) a claim for cessation of the infringement, removal of the nuisance, or elimination of the danger; (2) a claim for return of property of a person who has a real right in an immovable or a registered movable property..." Hence, the limitation period does not apply to cases where a real right holder claims for protection of his real rights.

In contrast, creditor's rights are temporal rights. There is no such obligatory right under the law that is permanent and free from time limitation. It is true that in some situations where no terms regarding the validity period of the contract can be found. Under such circumstances, the obligee's right and the obligor's obligation are still subject to limitation period.

Among the above-mentioned features, the first four features are the most fundamental and principal characters of real right.

2.　Effects of Real Right

Under traditional notion of civil law, the effect of real right derives from the exclusive domination by the right holder over the property. It is closely related to the content of real right but is not equal to the content itself. Rather. In fact, it is the result of such content being in function. Some hold the view that retroactive effects constitute part of the effects of real right. This means, a right holder is entitled to exercise restitution of his property from an illegal possessor to whom the property by whatever means has been transferred, while a creditor's right holder usually is not boast. When a obligor illegally assigns the property to a third party and the third party manages to control the property before the creditor is able to acquire the ownership of the property, the original obligor has no right to require the possessor to return the property in dispute. He is only entitled to assert performance of the contract and liability for breach of contract against the obligor. Nonetheless, the majority of opinions deny the necessity of encompassing the retroactive effect into the content of a claim on right.

2.1　Exclusivity of Real Right

Due to the exclusive effect, two or more than two real rights with the same content or of the same nature may not coexist in one property, which further gives rise to the rule of "one property one right". According to some scholars, the real right does contain exclusivity, and no exclusive effect is necessary. As I see, exclusivity is not only part of the nature but also the effect of real right. For the reason is that, on the one hand, it is one of the major features that distinguished real right from creditor's right, and on the other hand its existence is a fact. This second point can be illustrated by such a scenario where two parties agree upon a transfer of the ownership or exercise the right of a property. Absent registration, the assignee may not acquire the ownership in accordance with the law even if he has actually possessed the property. However, once the registration procedures are gone through, the right holder enjoys his right to obtain such effect as exclusivity regardless of whether he is possessing the property. Therefore, the acquisition of exclusive effect symbolizes the acquisition of real right. Thus, the exclusive effect is relatively independent. It's difficult to tell apart the exclusive possession from a monopolistic domination. In other words, it is a precondition that the right holder has access to the factual and legal disposition of a thing for an exclusive effect arising along with his right, because others will be excluded from the right with the same content only when the property has been subject to the disposal of the right holder, which disposal, of course, does not necessarily have to be displayed out in an easily noticeable way such as an actual control. Such mitigation of the once decisive influence of outward possession on the attribution of the ownership in a thing is possible, thanks to the development of the modern publication system. As long as the requirements of publication are met, the right holder shall be entitled the ownership or other real rights in property even though he does not exercise actual possession or control over such property.

To be specific, exclusive effect is to be observed in the following aspects:

The first is exclusivity of ownership. More than one real right cannot coexist in one property. In other words, one property cannot be subject to two owners.

The second is exclusivity in jus in re aliena. On one property cannot stands two rights to usufruct whose contents conflict with each other. For instance, if the right to use land for construction purposes has been set up, the right to use a house site cannot be established simultaneously thereupon.

In the following cases, two or more real rights may co-exist on one property: (1) ownership (jus in re propria) and jus in re aliena; (2) jus in re aliena whose contents include possession and real right whose contents do not; and (3) real rights whose contents don't encompass possession.

The third is absoluteness. The effect of real right may be asserted against any person other than the right holder. Where an immovable or movable property is possessed by a person not entitled to do so, the right holder may request for restitution. (Article 235 of the Civil Code) Where there is a nuisance or a potential nuisance against a real right, the right holder may request for removal of the nuisance or elimination of the danger. (Article 236 of the Civil Code) Where an immovable or movable property is destructed or damaged, the right holder may request for the repair, redoing, replacement, or restoration to the original condition in accordance with law. (Article 237 of the Civil Code) Where a real right is infringed upon and damage is thus caused, the right holder may, in accordance with law, request the infringing person to pay damages or bear other civil liabilities. (Article 238 of the Civil Code)

The fourth is inviolability. The real right is inviolable and qualified object for tortious acts.

Under modern civil-law right theory, rights refer to proprietary and personal interests explicitly defined and declared by law and realized through safeguard of the State. They are inviolable. Any infringement upon rights would constitute a tortious act. The real right is one of the most important and fundamental objects protected by tort liability law. The origin and evolution of tort law also evidences that its development is mainly centered around real rights, especially the ownership, which is a proprietary right.

2. 2　Preferential Effect

Preferential effect consists of two parts:

First, in cases where real right and creditor's right coexist, the former has priority over the latter, namely, real right may challenge creditors right. For example, the holder of a security interest in property right enjoys the priority in having his debts paid compared with a common obligee. Of course, the Chinese law and judicial practice do, on certain occasions, grant some creditors' rights preferential effects. For instance, where a lessor intends to sell a leased house, the lessee has the priority to purchase the house under equal conditions (or the right of first refusal)①. Nonetheless, such priority does not arise from real right, thus may not challenge the

---

①　Article 726 of the Civil Code stipulates that a lessor intending to sell a leased house shall notify the lessee within a reasonable period of time prior to the sale, and the lessee shall have the priority right to purchase the house under equivalent conditions. The right of first refusal, according to the provisions of law or contracts, means the right of a particular person to purchase the subject matter in preference to a third party under equal conditions when the seller wants to sell the subject matter to the latter.

latter's preferential effect. For instance, A, B and C share the ownership of a house and have leased it to D. As the three co-owners negotiate with each other on to whom they will sell the leased house, dispute arises. While A and B prefer to sell the house to E, C contends that he has the priority to purchase as the co-owner. Meanwhile, D also insists on his right of first refusal based on his creditor's right. Under such circumstances, the house should be sold to C in accordance with the principle "real right precedes creditor's right". However, such principle also makes a few exceptions. As in the lease of the immovable property, the rule of "sale doesn't break hire (emptio non tollit locatum)" applies.

Second, in cases where parties are allowed to establish several real rights on one thing, the real right established earlier in time prevails, which indicates the preferential effect among real rights (Article 414 of the Civil Code). The internal priority in contrast does not manifest in the setting of creditors' rights. When more than one creditor's right co-exist in one thing, each of them are equally valid and each creditor is equally situated when being paid.

2.3 Retroactive Effect

Retroactive effect, also known as "the right of pursuit" or "retroactivity", means that when, by whatever means and to whomever a thing is transferred, the owner may lawfully recover his property from such possessor (Article 235 of the Civil Code). Everyone else is obliged not to interfere when the obligee is exercising his right. Anyone who has illegally acquired the thing is obliged to return it. This regulation applies also in the field of security interests in property rights.

As to whether the retroactive effect is with independence, opinions diverge considerably. Antagonists, represented mainly by Taiwan scholar Zheng Yubo and Japanese scholar, deny such independence. According to Mr. Saichi Matsusaka, the retroactive effect of real right is merely one facet of the claim on real right, which doesn't necessitate its being categorized as a part of the effect of real right. Mr. Zheng Yubo bases his argument on a different ground that the retroactive effect has been incorporated into the preferential effect. As their fellow contestant, Mr. Wang Zejian leads the affirmative opinion, which contends that the retroactive effect is self-contained as one type of the real right effect, or else, it may overlap with the claim on real right and the preferential effect. Such latter opinion is also accepted by Mr. Liang Huixing and Wang Liming. As Mr. Wang Liming sees, on the one hand, retroactivity of real right is a concept mentioned mainly in comparison with creditor's right, whose effect is primarily non-retroactive. When a obligor illegally assigns the property to a third party and the third party manages to control the property before the creditor is able to acquire the ownership of the property, the original obligee has no right to ask the possessor to return the thing in dispute. He is only entitled to assert performance of contract and liability for breach of contract against the obligor. On the other hand, the retroactive effect works by way of the claim on real right, which is actually determined by such effect. The basis of the claim for restitution of property, one subcategory of the claim, arises from the retroactivity, though it does not inherently encompass such effect. It is also to be observed that, while only the real right holder enjoys the retroactive effect of the property, the claim on real right may be exercised by a possessor as well. This explains why the retroactive effect should not be included in the claim on real right.

Another supporting rule indicating the retroactivity in real right is Article 64 of the Criminal Law of PRC, which provides, "All property illegally obtained by a criminal shall be recovered, or compensation shall be ordered. Contrabands and possessions of the criminal that were used in the crime shall be confiscated. "

It is worth pointing out that the retroactive effect is by no means absolute. It is subject to the limitation set by the rule of good faith acquisition.

2. 4   Claims on Real Rights

The claim on real right arises when the control of a real right holder over a thing is hindered and becomes defective due to act of another person and recovery of full control is demanded. In short, it results from the impaired control of a real right. The law grants the real right holder claims on real right for the purpose of enabling him to recover his complete control over his property. The claim on real right is also known as claim of property rights, claim for real right protection or claim on real right relationships. Such claims include claim for removal of nuisance or elimination of danger, claim for restitution of property, and claim for compensation of damages, which are stipulated in Articles 235 to 238 of the Civil Code.

A claim on real right arises because the domination over the thing is hindered. It is exercisable only when the restoration of the initial status is possible. Although not being a part of the contents of real right, it is still indispensable for the protection of the domination over a thing, thus shall not be separated from real right, but rather a unique power held by the latter. Unlike claim on real right, a creditor's right is the right for an obligee to ask the obligor to do or not do a certain act. It is not a dominating right over a thing, thus its restoration upon impairment from others may, in most cases, tan be achieved only by way of compensation for damage so as to reimburse or restore any loss the obligee might have incurred.

As to the nature of claim on real right, three opinions may be observed in the academia: the first opinion is that it is an independent type of claim, the second is that it is a creditor's right in nature and thus bears little dissimilarities from claim on creditors rights, and the third is that it is an accessory right attached to the dominating right over a thing. The author is for the third view.

Claim on real right is not equal to a creditor's right, neither is it the same as the claim on creditor's right. This is because first, the two rights arise under different circumstances. While a claim on real right is based on impaired status of a dominating right over a thing, while a claim on a creditor's right is founded on the performance of obligations arising from a contract, negotiorum gestio① (or agency without specific authorization), unjust enrichment②, or tort liability. Second, the two rights serve for different purposes. From the micro perspective, a claim on creditor's right is aimed to meet people's needs in such various kinds of interests of substances, intellectual products, labor force and service, while a claim on real rights targets to restore the right holder's domination over a thing, satisfying his needs in obtaining profits from such thing. Third, their legal effects are non-identical. A claim on creditors' rights terminates the obligatory relationship when exercised, but a claim on real rights recovers the domination over a thing when it is exercised, allowing for the continuous existence of the right.

Regarding the relationships between claim on real right and the dominating right over a thing, the former should not be deemed as independent of the latter, but rather, it is an accessory to the latter. First, claim on real right is created on the condition that a dominating right is in existence. Once the latter extinguishes, the former will not arise. Second, the claim on real right renders service to the dominating right. More specifically, the claim for restitution of property protects the possessory power in a thing, and the claims for removal of the nuisance and for restoration of original status contribute to the exercise of such powers for·obtain profits from and disposal of a thing.

In light of this, claim on real right may only arise when the dominating right in a thing is violated or impaired and be exercised, and then the restoration of the original status is possible. Absent any of the two prerequisites, a claim on real right cannot be exercised. The only remedy for economic damage leaves with the claim for compensation for loss.

Of course, the mentioned two claim rights are differentiated from each other to great extent. First, the claim on real right is one effect radiated from real right while the claim for compensation for damage is that from a creditor's right. Second, a claim for compensation for damage requires two conditions, namely, unlawfulness of the act and actual loss. Neither, nonetheless, is a precondition to a claim on real right. Because in the latter scenario, as long as one's acts have obstructed the right holder in dominating the thing, the real right holder is entitled to bring a claim on real right, even if nothing is unlawful with such acts and no actual loss has been resulted in. For example, an owner may require a legitimate user to return the property out of reasonable needs.

---

① *Negotiorum gestio* , means a person acts as manager or provides services in order to protect another person's interests when he is not legally or contractually obligated to do so.

② Unjust enrichment is a legal fact that a person has benefited from the property or labor of others without legal cause and has thereby caused loss to others.

Section Two   Categories of Real Rights

In jurisprudence, real rights may be categorized in the following ways.

1. Jus in re propria and Jus in re aliena (or Ownership and Right over the Property of Another)

Based on whether its holder is the owner of the property, real right may be divided into two kinds: The first one is ownership, which is an all-inclusive and complete right enjoyed by an owner in his property, including the rights to possess, utilize, obtain profits from and dispose of the property, and, the second category is jus in re aliena or right over the property of another, which denotes a limited right of domination over the property enjoyed by a non-owner in accordance to law or the owner's intention. The ownership is the most complete and full right among all real rights, while jus in re aliena arises from the separation of powers of ownership.

Distinction between the two types of real right mainly lies in the following aspects:

The first distinction lies in their different subjects. While the ownership is held by the owner, jus in re aliena is not held by a non-owner, namely, any civil persons other than the owner. Although such subjects may enjoy some powers derived from the ownership, they cannot take the place of the owner, who, in any case, still have the last right in the disposal of the property, though some power of ownership has been, to certain degree, separated from him due to the establishment of a jus in re aliena. Thus, it is unnecessary for the owner to hold a jus in re aliena in his property. Such right is to be held by a subject other than himself. If, upon the occurrence of certain legal facts. For example an ownership and right over the property of another being with respect to the same property have been vested in the same person (the owner), such rights will be extinguished because of being merged and held by the same person. As a result, the ownership is to resume its complete and full state.

The second distinction lies their various contents. Ownership is a complete real right, but the right over the property of another contains the power of an ownership only to certain extent. The right holder of the latter may not dispose of the thing absent a statutory basis or the authorization of the owner. In such sense, the right over the property of another is also termed as "qualified or limited right in property".

The third distinction lies in their different durations. In most cases, ownership is not subject to time limitation and will not be permanently extinguished upon the advent or expiration of certain legal facts. Thus, it is called "real right for an indefinite period of time". ① In

---

① Real right for an indefinite period of time is a real right which is permanent or without time limits, for example, ownership.

contrast, the right over the property of another may only be valid during the existence of a contract if it has been created by such contract. Therefore, it is also-called "real right for a definite period of time". ①

2. Rights to Usufruct and Security Interests in Property Rights

According to different purposes of creation, the right over the property of another may be further divided into the following subcategories.

The right to usufruct refers to the right enjoyed by a non-owner to possess, utilize and derive profit from another person's property. It is established for the purpose of using or obtaining profits from a property. In Chinese law, rights to usufruct include the right to contractual management of land, right to use land for construction purposes, right to use a house site, right of habitation and easement.

The basic contents of a right to usufruct include in the right to possess, utilize and obtain profit from the object. Such power of directly controlling and thereby possessing, utilizing and obtaining profit from a property owned by another person is a competence severed from the ownership and reflects the utilization relationship concerning a property.

Security interests are created to guarantee the performance of an obligation and the realization of the creditor's right. Mortgage, pledge, and lien are typical examples of security interests.

The right to usufruct and security interest are different in the following aspects:

First, the requirements for their objects are different. The right to usufruct aims to realize the use value or efficacy of a thing, which makes the use value a vital element of its object. In the case of the security interests in property right, on the other hand, the exchange value of the object is much emphasized, in that security interests in property right aims at getting the priority in having one's claim paid and focuses on the value of a thing.

The second difference lies in whether the right is incidental in nature (appurtenant nature). The right to usufruct is independent while the security interests in property right is incidental. The former come into existence through the provision of law or the agreement between the usufructuary and the owner of the property. That the usufructuary may assert other property rights against the owner is not a precondition to the creation of the right. This, however, is not the case with security interests in property right, whose holder must have a creditor's right towards the owner of the object or a related party for such interests to come into existence. When such creditor's right extinguishes, the security interests in property right is eliminated.

---

① Real right for a definite period of time is a real right whose period is specific.

The third difference lies in the necessity of possessing the object. While the possession of the object is a premise for exercising a right to usufruct, or the obtaining of profits may not be conducted, the security interests in property right does not require direct possession of the object, though some such as lien and pledge do require possession due to their nature.

Fourth, there is difference in whether their objects are subrogative. The object of security interests in property right is subrogative in nature, but not that of a right to usufruct. In cases where the object is destroyed or lost due to certain circumstances not attributable to the holder of such interests, a replacement may be required by the right holder. If the object is transformed into other valuables such as currency, the object of the security interests in property right may also change accordingly to such variations. As a result, the security interests in property right has an object subrogatory in nature. In the setting of the right to usufruct, when the object is destroyed or lost, the right extinguishes regardless of the cause of such destruction or loss. The former right holder has no right to demand for any replacement of the object.

3. Real Rights in Movable Properties and in Immovable Properties

Such classification is based on whether the object of a real right is movable property or not.

The object of a real right in movable properties is movable property, whilst that of a real right in immovable properties is immovable property such as a tract of land or a house. Typical real rights in immovable properties include ownership of immovable property, right to the use of land, etc. A concrete definition of the immovable property may be found in Article 2 of the Interim Regulations on Real Estate Registration of the PRC, which defines "real estate" as land, sea areas and fixtures such as buildings and woods. In China typical types of real rights in immovable property include ownership of immovable property, superficies, easement, pawning right of buildings, right to use the state-owned land, mortgage in immovable property etc. Typical real rights in movable properties include ownership of movable property, lien, mortgage in movable property, pledge in movable property, etc. At present, practice as to take a right as the object of real right, for example, a right to mortgage of a right, has not been well developed, though the legislation does recognize certain securities, such as treasury bounds, maybe mortgaged. In light of this, the real right in rights does exist. Such right may be deemed as real right in movable property.

Section Three　Basic Principles of Real Right Law (System)

Basic principles of the real right law(system) are the purport and fundamental rules of the real right law (system) that serve as the starting point when it comes to guide, interpret, implement and research on real right law. As a common thread uniting the whole system and rules of real right law, they demonstrate the essential notions and values behind such legislation. Denotation of basic principles is discussed in two different contexts, which are within the civil law jurisprudence and legislation. The former generally adopts four basic principles, namely, numerus clausus, one property one right, publication and presumption of accuracy and preferential effect. The Civil Code stipulates three basic principles on the legislative level, namely, the principle of equal protection (Articles 113, 206 and 207), the principle of numerus clausus (Article 116), and the principle of publication and presumption of accuracy (Article 208).

1. The Principle of Equal Protection

1. 1 Definition and Significance of the Principle of Equal Protection in Real Right Law

The principle of equal protection means that, various right holders have equal status under the law; they enjoy the same rights, abide by the same rules and are equally protected when their real rights are infringed. Para. 3, Article 206 of the Civil Code provides that "The State implements a socialist market economy and protects the equal legal status and development rights of all market participants." Article 207 of the Civil Code stipulates that "The real rights of the State, collectives, private individuals, and the other right holders are equally protected by law and free from infringement by any organization or individual."

As the first and foremost principle of real right law (system), equal protection also reflects a unique Chinese characteristic of the Chinese real right law (system).

This principle is also a concrete manifestation of the general principles of Chinese civil law in the area of Chinese real right law (system).

1. 2 Contents

The principle of equal protection mainly encompasses the following contents:

1. 2. 1 Equal legal status. All the mainstays in the market enjoy equal status under real right law. This echoes with the principle of equality before the law as is confirmed by the Constitution.

1. 2. 2 Equal application of rules. Unless otherwise provided by laws, any subject of real right must abide by the same rules when acquiring, creating or transferring a real right.

1. 2. 3 Equal protection. This means, first, each party in dispute will be applied the same rules in case of conflicts between or among any subjects of real rights; second, equal

protection of right holders is guaranteed should their real rights be infringed.

2. The Principle of Numerus Clausus

2. 1　Definition and Contents of the Principle of Numerus Clausus

Historically speaking, two diverged opinions regarding the creation of real right have been developed. The first one is the laissez-faire theory, which allows the real right effect of a use right or profit right created by parties based on their possession or registration. Such approach was adopted by the General Law of the Land of the Prussian States. Under this law, for instance, a leasehold, which is generally accepted now as a creditor's right, may acquire the status of real right provided that it is created on an immovable property and registered out of the free will of the parties. Under the principle of numerus clausus, on the other hand, the categories and contents of real right must be stipulated by law, leaving no room for the parties' discretion. This latter approach may be traced back to the Roman law, and has been gradually succeeded by such civil law jurisdictions as France, Germany, Japan, Austria, Holland, and China's Taiwan Province ever since. Article 175 of the Japanese Civil Code provides that "No real rights can be established other than those prescribed by laws including this Code." Likewise, Article 116 of the Civil Code stipulates that "The categories and content of the real right are provided by law".

Under the principle of numerus clausus, the categories and contents of real right must be specifically provided by law, allowing for neither regulation of other legal documents nor discretion of the parties.

The principle mainly encompasses the following aspects:

2. 1. 1　The categories of real right shall be prescribed by law. Two layers of meaning may be found thereunder. First, the specific categories of real right shall be defined by law, not any other normative documents. Also, parties cannot create real right that does not fall into the statutory categories. Second, any deviation from the given categories under the current law is also not allowed, ever if it is generated by agreement between parties. For example, the law requires the transfer of possession in creating a pledge on a movable property. As such, any parties may not waive such prerequisite of transferring possession. Otherwise, it constitutes a deviation from the law.

2. 1. 2　Contents of real right shall be prescribed by law. On the one hand, the contents of real right are stipulated by law. Parties shall not create real right whose contents are inconsistent with what is provided by law. For instance, the contents and limitation of ownership are to be ascertained by law. Non-owners may not, in any case, restrict or obstruct the exercise of such right. Any deviation therefrom constitutes an encroachment upon the

ownership. On the other hand, the principle of numerus clausus prohibits the parties from entering into any agreement that is incompatible with the mandatory rules set forth by real right law. For example, Article 399 of the Civil Code provides that "The following property may not be mortgaged: (1) land ownership..." This provision has explicitly forbidden mortgage in land ownership. The parties may not exclude this provision through agreement; neither may the content of their agreement otherwise violate this rule.

The distinction between the principle of numerus clausus and that of freedom of contract also demonstrates the difference between the contract law and the real right law (system).

2. 2 Rationale for the Principle of Numerus Clausus

Regarding the rationale behind the principle of numerus clausus, opinions in the academia are diverged but may be summed up into the following few points:

2. 2. 1 Historical reasons. Though originated in the Roman law, the principle of numerus clausus is formally established by capitalist civil law. When enacting the civil law and building the legal system of real right, the bourgeoisie was faced with the problem that how to clean up the old real right system built in the feudal era and eliminate the possibility of its revival. Under feudal system, tenure of property was held by dual or sometimes, even multiple subjects. The domination right over a thing and that over a person are indiscrete without a clear boundary. Those who owned the land acquired the domination right over the people living thereupon. The real right was the foundation of the domination right of people. For these reasons, a free ownership system called for by a capitalist market would never be built up and the capitalist ways of production could not come into being and prosper if the feudal real right system was not abolished.

2. 2. 2 Since a real right, unlike a creditor's right, is a dominating right over a thing that can be asserted against a third party, it exerts more influence upon the interests of others. If parties are allowed to create real rights freely, the interests of a third party may stand in great peril.

2. 2. 3 The principle is necessary for the publication of real right status and transaction security and efficiency.

2. 2. 4 As a reflection of the ownership system in society, the real right exerts considerable impact on the social economic relationships, thus shall not be subject to discretion of parties.

2. 3 Practical Significance

2. 3. 1 The principle of numerus clausus renders equal protection to diverse kinds of property, thereby encouraging the creation of wealth and fostering the increase of social

affluence.

2. 3. 2　By defining certain rights as real rights, the doctrine achieves the advantage and potential of the public ownership system.

2. 3. 3　Emphasis laid on the principle of numerus clausus also contributes to the establishment of a sophisticated real rights framework in the real right law (system).

3. The Principle of Publication and Presumption of Accuracy

3. 1　The Principle of Publication

Publication of real right means that, upon the creation or change of real right, certain means of publication should be taken to make such information available to the public so that any third party will be informed of the change of circumstances and avoid any possible damage that may arise, thus protecting the transaction security.

According to Article 208 of the Civil Code, "The real right of the movable property shall be created or transferred upon delivery in accordance with the provisions of law. The creation, alteration, alienation, or extinguishment of the real rights in immovable property shall be registered in accordance with law. The creation and alienation of real rights in movable property shall be subject to the delivery of the movable property in accordance with law. "

The necessity of publication comes from the nature of real right. Since the real right is exclusive and preferential, a third party may suffer damage when on the one hand, a right holder claims for priority while on the other hand, the right is not acknowledged by the third party.

The publication system safeguards the security and order in transaction by preventing potential disputes arising from the real right transaction. It is unique for the real right system because creditor's right system doesn't encompass priority in its effect. One may say that, the real right cannot stand without publication. For example, a pledge extinguishes when the pledgee returns the pledged property to the pledgor for the latter's possession on his behalf, or when the pledgee loses the possession to someone that he cannot require the return of the property.

The ways of publication are to be stipulated by law and not open to the agreement of the parties. In principle, the immovable property should be registered and movable property should be delivered. The effect of registration manifests in the fact that a real right is created or transferred upon registration after the parties have concluded a contract with the same purpose. Registration of real right is by no means a procedure of administrative nature, but rather, a process adopted to make it known to the public, especially a third party that the relevant information on the creation and alienation of real right. In this way, not only will the transfer of a real right acquire its credibility, but also the newly created right grows into a clean right. More importantly, a third party may be informed of the status and encumbrances, if any, on a right. With the knowledge of the potential risks, such party may then further decide whether to conduct transaction about the registered obligee. A sophisticated registration system is a precondition to the orderly proceeding of transactions, as well as a cornerstone of the real right system. Only when such a system is established, will the transfer and creation of most real rights be conducted in order.

As for the movable property, their publication requires delivery. While being created, a real right of movable property may be publicated in such a way as delivery through transfer of possession. For instance, the creation of a pledge requires delivery, namely the transfer of possession of the property. As long as the movable property has been actually delivered, a pledge will be established regardless of the knowledge thereof by a third party.

At the same time, the Civil Code also provides means of publication regarding other real rights. Take Article 445 of the Civil Code as an example, it stipulates that "A pledge on an account receivable is created upon registration". Article 445 of this code provides that "A pledge on fund shares or equity is created upon registration of the pledge. "

According to Article 333 of the Civil Code, "A right to contractual management of land① is created at the time when the contract on the right to contractual management of land enters into effect. " This provision is an exception to the rule on the registration of real rights in immovable property.

The function of the principle of publication lies in ascertaining the attribution of and improving the utilization efficiency in property. Meanwhile, it safeguards the transaction security.

3. 2   The Principle of Presumption of Accuracy

The principle of presumption of accuracy means, the contents of the registration published by statutory means are presumed to be real and correct, and the party concerned may reasonably be expected to rely on the credibility of such appearance and conduct transaction about the

---

① The right to contractual management of land means the right of the member of a village collective economic organization to enter into a contract with the latter and utilize or make benefits from the land, forests, mountains, grasslands, unreclaimed lands, tidal flats and water surface to engage in farming, forestry, fishing or other production or operation projects. China resorts to a socialist public ownership i. e. an ownership by the whole people and ownership by collective organizations of land. Land in the rural areas and suburban areas, except otherwise provided for by the State, shall be collectively owned by peasants including land for building houses, land and hills allowed to be retained by peasants. No organization or individual may appropriate, buy, sell or otherwise engage in the transfer of land by unlawful means. However, the right to use land may be transferred according to law. Land collectively owned by peasant shall be operated and managed by village collective economic organizations or villagers' committee and shall be contracted out to members of the collective economic organizations for use in crop farming, forestry, animal husbandry and fisheries production.

registered property. His reliance interests should be protected by law. In other words, as long as there is lawful publication upon the alteration of real right by the parties, any transaction conducted out of reliance on such publicized contents will be admitted by law because the parties relied on that fact that such a real right does exist. Even if it does not actually exist or is defective, the transaction security will be protected.

For example, A registered B's house under his own name and assigned the house to C. Since C has reasonably relied on such documents as A presented to prove his ownership, a sale and purchase contract regarding the house was finally concluded. Under such circumstance, the legal effect of the transaction, namely, the transfer of the ownership in the realty is still acknowledged by law, even though A is actually not a right holder. Because the transaction security needs to be safeguarded by protecting the interest of such third party. Otherwise, that is, if the transaction was invalidated, then the published contents will lose its credibility. Consequently, parties when carrying out a transaction, may not place trust on the published rights, which will result in much difficulties in making dealings with each other. As to the movable property, the laws of many civil law jurisdictions presume that a possessor lawfully has the rights that he exercises with respect to properties in his possession. Viewed in this, the principle of presumption of accuracy essentially endows the contents published with credibility. Otherwise, the effect of publication may be greatly reduced. In conclusion, the principle of publication and that of presumption of accuracy are inter-related. Initially, the principle of presumption of accuracy applies only to real right in movable property; gradually its application extends to the real right in immovable property.

The contents of the principle of presumption of accuracy are to be observed in two aspects:

First, the registered right holder is presumed to be the lawful right holder. Article 216 of the Civil Code provides that "The register of immovable property is the basis for determining the attribution and contents of the real rights in immovable property". This provision in fact has established the presumption effect of registration. The realty register is the basis for the attribution of the real right. First, the right holder recorded in the register is presumed to be the lawful right holder. Second, if the parties have contracted to create a real right but have not yet registered or adopted other means of publication, then reasonable conclusion may be drawn that such right has not been established. Third, when a real right has already been altered but not yet published, then people may lack reasonable ground to believe that such alteration has actually occurred. That is, the alteration of real right may not challenge a third party. In terms of the legal effects, a real right transaction may not be recognized by the law as long as the status of the register remain as it is. Such reliance, according to theories, is termed as negative reliance. Anyone who enters into transactions on basis of the rights registered are to be presumed to be in good faith, unless evidences prove that he knew or should have known the registered right holder was not the lawful holder. ①

Second, anyone who has transacted out of reliance with the registered right holder is protected under law.

The reliance of a third party on the rights and contents recorded in the register should be protected. This is the credibility. In a strict sense, credibility is possible only when a third party is involved in a transaction. That is to say, on the one hand, what the credibility principle intends to protect is the reliant interests of a third party. It will be the issue when there only involves a dispute between the transacting parties, only presumptive effect of registration is concerned. On the other hand, the principle of presumption of accuracy also safeguards the transaction security.

While Article 216 of the Civil Code does involve protection for reliant interests, the most direct protection, however, comes from Article 311 of the Civil Code, which stipulates the rules of good faith acquisition of immovable or movable property.

The principle of credibility encourages registration and contributes to the founding of a credit economy. Meanwhile, it promotes the smooth and orderly proceeding of transactions. Publication and credibility are important: on the one hand, they save transactors a significant amount of time otherwise they would be invested into investigating the legal status of an object, thus transactions are entered into soon. On the other hand, they free the parties from the concerning that the disposer could be unauthorized. The principle of credibility has created for the parties a mechanism that encourages fast transactions by protecting such reliance and expectation that the deal is legal and the object will not be pursued by others. A safeguard mechanism is thus founded for transaction security.

Admittedly, the principle of credibility also allows for exception. For instance, in cases where a third party is in bad faith, the rule on good-faith acquisition does not apply.

Section Four　Changes in Real Right

1. Changes in Real Right: An Overview

The change in real right refers to the creation, alteration, transfer and extinction of real rights. Quite essentially, it is the change of inter-personal relationships regarding the disposal and attribution of the object of the right.

The creation of real right is a process in which parties create certain real right(s) within the statutory categories in accordance with relevant requirements through juristic acts or by other

---

① Xiao Houguo, *Real Right Alternation*, PhD thesis of Graduate School of Chinese Academy of Social Science, 2000, p. 6.

means. Such process is where the real right comes into being out of nothing. Which is called the acquisition of real right from the obligee's point of view. It falls into two categories, namely, original acquisition and derivative acquisition. The former is also known as inherent acquisition or the absolute creation of real right, meaning the real right is independent of any existing right of another. Real right created by de facto acts mostly is of original acquisition. As for the latter, the derivative acquisition, or the relative creation of real right, refers to the obtainment of real right based on a right of another person. Generally speaking, real rights created by juristic acts are of derivative acquisition.

The alteration of real right may be decoded in two senses. In a wide sense, it encompasses the alteration of the subjects, contents and objects of real right. In a narrow sense, it excludes that of the subjects. This is because, when real right changes its subjects, there must be an extinction of such right on the transferor, coinciding with an acquisition on the transferee. In such sense, the alteration of subject may be respectively categorized as an acquisition and extinction of a real right. The transfer of real right is the most typical transaction mode.

It refers to the change in the subjects of real right based on either statutory provisions or on a contract between parties.

Regarding the extinction of real rights, it is the temporary or permanent elimination in effect of real right triggered by certain acts of the parties according to the statutory provisions or mutual consent.

With respect to the causes of changes in real right, there may be observed two sets of legal facts. These changes, as particular types of legal effects, derive from such civil relationship as the real right relations, which are created, altered or terminated by legal effects. These mentioned two sets of legal facts are the juristic acts and legal facts:

First, juristic acts (in the Civil Code termed as "civil juristic acts") can cause changes in real rights. Article 25 of the Real Right Law utilizes the term "juristic acts", but the General Rules of the Civil Law of the People's Republic of China ("General Rules of the Civil Law") revised it and termed it "civil juristic acts". Article 133 of the Civil Code provides that "A civil juristic act is an act through which a person of the civil law, by expression of intent, creates, alters, or terminates a civil juristic relationship." Civil juristic acts can be divided into bilateral acts and unilateral acts.

Second, juristic facts except juristic acts may also cause changes in real rights. Such juristic facts include production, acquisition of natural fruits, successions, prescription, appropriation, accession, finding of a lost thing, treasure trove (or buried things①), nationalization, requisition, confiscation, court enforcement, consumption, loss, mixture,

---

① Buried things, in a narrow sense, means things that are buried in land and the ownership of which is unclear. In a broad sense, subjects that are hidden in chattel or real property and the owner of which is unclear are all buried things.

expiration of duration (only in cases of real right with a definite period of time), liquidation of a debt (only in cases of security interests), etc.

2. Changes Caused by Civil Juristic Acts

2. 1 Various Regulatory Modes of Changes in Real Rights Caused by Civil Juristic Acts

Among all legal facts that may cause changes in real rights, civil juristic acts are the most important. Modern countries have put great weight in their legislative policies and techniques on giving clear guidance as to how should real right change according to juristic acts. It is on this matter that the aforementioned theory of juristic acts in real right gives a sharp focus.

2. 1. 1 The Common Law Approach

The common law system adopts the transaction mode of "deed delivery" in transfers of real right concerning the immovable rights. As explained before, under the US law, the immovable rights are transferred immediately upon delivery of deed, provided only that there is a manifestation of intention to transfer. The assignee may have the deed registered. Such registration, however, in most states, is only a requirement of perfection or antagonism, rather than that of validity. Under the British law, two prerequisites need to be satisfied for the immovable rights to be transacted, namely, that of a contract and that of a "strict certificate". The latter has the same implication as the "covenant" under the US law. It may thus be concluded that under both American and British laws the process of a real estate transaction is also clearly divided into two stages, namely, the stage of contract conclusion and the stage of deed delivery. To put it more vividly, the sales contract is similar to a covenant on obligations, from which possible issues may arise over contract enforcement, and the buyer acquires the estate in equity through such contact. The delivery of deed is similar to a real right deed, which carries the manifested intentions of the transferor and transferee to respectively assign and accept the real estate. No enforcement issue would arise from such delivery act. Instead, the direct contents of such delivery are the changes in estate, giving rise to the legal consequence of right assignment.

2. 1. 2 The Continental Law Approach

Ever since the dawn of the 20th century, the triangle of three transaction modes of real right has been in existence in the civil law system, with no advent of a new one as of today.

First, formalism of real right. The German Civil Code sets a fine example. In such mode, changes in real right require agreement, delivery and registration concerning the real right independent of the juristic acts of creditor's rights. In a sale and purchase contract, the transfer of ownership over the targeted matter necessitates a separate agreement thereof in addition to the sale and purchase contract and the registration or delivery. Since the contents of such agreement mainly concern changes in real right, it is termed agreement over real right (or contract of real right, agreement of real right) in theory. For example, after A and B concluded a sale contract regarding a house (juristic act of creditor's right), they should further conclude two contracts on real right, with one manifesting A's intention of selling and B's willingness of purchasing the house, and the other manifesting B's intention of paying the price and A's willingness of accepting such delivery. Subsequent to these, the transaction is to be registered. As may be seen, the conclusion of real right contracts and the registration are independent juristic acts of real right with abstract nature.

Second, consensualism. This approach is typically adopted by France and Japan. According to this transaction mode, which is also known as the consensualism of creditor's right, a change in real right occurs upon the manifestation of intentions of the parties concerned. For instance, the moment when the sale and purchase contract concerning a house between A and B comes into effect, the purchaser B acquires the ownership in the targeted matter, with registration only being a perfection requirement, i. e. , A cannot sell the house to a third party C. (B's right may be asserted against a third party).

Third, formalism of creditor's right. This theory requires delivery or registration in addition to an agreement of creditor's right between parties, for a change in real right arising from a juristic act. Such approach is also termed a combination of consensualism and registration or delivery. Unlike the French approach of consensualism, formalism of creditor's right denies that a change in real right can directly arise from an agreement on creditor's right (a claim). Instead, it lays much emphasis on the effect of delivery and registration upon changes in real right. It also differs from the German approach in that though it also makes such external formality as delivery or registration indispensable for changes in real right (thus is deemed as a subcategory of formalism) but it is the agreement concerning creditor's right that constitutes the primary impetus and cause of such change. An independent agreement over real right (contract of real right) is denied under the theory, because a change in real right arises from a delivery or registration based on an agreement over creditor's right. The Swiss Civil Code is considered as the best representative, followed by its counterparts in other countries including Austria, Soviet Union and South Korea. In these countries, a juristic act causes a change in real right, provided that there is an agreement concerning creditor's right between the parties and registration or delivery has been conducted in accordance with the statutory provisions. For instance, for a change in real right concerning an immovable property between A and B, the two should first conclude a sale and purchase contract and then have the transaction registered. The purchaser B doesn't acquire the ownership until registration, and the consensus regarding the sale and purchase serves as a direct cause of the change.

2. 2 The Chinese Approach: A Combination of Consensualism and Requirement for Registration or Delivery, i. e. Formalism of Creditor's Right

2. 2. 1 Changes Concerning Movable Property

Article 224 of the Civil Code stipulates that "The creation or alienation of a real right in movable property shall take effect upon delivery, unless otherwise provided by law". This provision makes two points clear:

First, in cases where ownership is transferred based on a purchase and sale contract, donation contract or barter contract, the transfer is valid upon the time of delivery. Where changes to real right in movables are caused by civil juristic acts, delivery is a requirement of validity for such change in real right, unless otherwise contracted by the parties. Nevertheless, the creation, alteration, alienation, or extinguishment of the real rights in vessels, aircrafts, motor vehicles, and the like, that have not been registered is not effective against a bona fide third person. (Article 225 of the Civil Code)

Second, the transfer of ownership is a direct result of the performance over a contract of creditor's right, not requiring a separate agreement over real right.

Therefore, Chinese legislation has adopted a transaction mode of consensualism combined with registration or delivery regarding changes in real right concerning the immovable property.

2. 2. 2 Changes Concerning Immovable Property

Stipulation regarding changes in real right concerning the immovable property can be found in various single acts or regulations. For example, Article 6 of the Private Houses in Urban Management Regulations①of 1983 prescribed that the owner of urban private house should implement the registration procedures of the ownership at the housing administration department at the place of the house, and get the ownership certificate of the house after examination and verification; in the event the ownership of the house is transferred or the conditions of the house has changed, an application for altering registration of ownership transfer or the conditions of the house shall be submitted to the housing administration department at the place of the house. Para. 1, Article 25 of the Interim Regulations Concerning the Assignment and Transfer of the Right to the Use of the State-owned Land in the Urban Areas (amended in November 2020), an administrative regulation promulgated in 1990, prescribes that "With respect to the transfer of the right to the use of the land and of the ownership of the above-ground buildings and other attached objects, registration for the transfer shall be undertaken in accordance with the relevant

---

① This regulation according to "the Decision of Repealing Part of the Administrative Rules and Regulations" by the state council on January 15, 2008 has been abolished.

provisions①", Article 41 of the Urban Real Estate Administration Law, a statute promulgated in 1994, which was revised in 2019, provides that "written contract must be signed in real estate transfer, and the contract shall carry the clause on the form of obtaining the right of land use." Para. 3 of Article 61 of the same statute stipulates that "When a real estate is transferred or changed, an application should be made with the real estate administration department of people's government above the county level for registration of the change and upon the modified title certificate, an application should be made with the land administration department of the people's government at same level for a change to the right of land use. After a verification made by the land administration department of the people's government at the same level, the people's government at the same level shall renew or modify the land use certificate."

Para. 1, Article 209 of the Civil Code provides that "The creation, alteration, alienation, or extinguishment of a real right in immovable property shall become effective upon registration in accordance with law, and shall not take effect without registration, unless otherwise provided by law". Article 215 further stipulates that "A contract concluded by the parties on the creation, alteration, alienation, or extinguishment of a real right becomes effective upon its formation, unless it is otherwise provided by law or agreed upon by the parties, and the validity of the contract is not affected by the fact that the real right is not registered". These provision make it quite explicit that in China changes to real rights in immovables caused by civil juristic acts become effective upon registration in addition to the parties' agreement. Regarding changes in real rights concerning immovables China adopts a transaction mode of consensualism combined with requirement for registration.

2.3　Transaction Mode of Real Right Concerning the Immovable Property Based on Juristic Act—Registration as a Requirement of Validity and as a Requirement of Perfection

2.3.1　Registration as a Requirement of Validity and as a Requirement of Perfection or Antagonism: Meanings and Definitions

The transaction mode of real right concerning the immovable property is the statutory means by which a real right over an immovable property is created, altered or extinguished. Because changes in real rights concerning the immovable property are published through registration, two transaction modes may derive therefrom, namely, that in which registration is a requirement of validity and that in which a requirement of perfection.

According to the former transaction mode, registration is a requirement of validity for changes in real right concerning the immovable property. Otherwise, no such change may

---

①　As prescribed previously, China resorts to a socialist public ownership, land in urban districts shall be owned by the State while the land use right can be transferred.

become effective. Such mode have been adopted by civil laws in jurisdictions such as Germany, Switzerland. Pursuant to Article 209 of the Civil Code, registration is a principal element of changes in real right.

Under the latter transaction mode, changes in real right may become legally valid even if without registration. Such validity binds the parties concerned and may not be asserted against a third party in good faith. Such approach has been the choice of the French and Japanese civil codes. According to Article 209 of the Civil Code, there is an exception for the principle it has established, namely, registration is a requirement of validity, by stating "unless it is otherwise provided by law". Thus registration may also be a requirement of perfection. For example, Article 335 of the Civil Code stipulates that, "Where the rights to contractual management of land are exchanged or transferred, the parties may apply to the registration authority for registration; without registration, such exchange or transfer may not be asserted against a bona fide third person". As can be seen, the latter transaction mode encompasses the following few characteristics. First, registration may be a contractual obligation, though it's not necessarily legal obligation. Second, if the transfer of a real right necessitates delivery, then the property has to be delivered. Third, change in real right is possible in the absence of registration, which effect may be asserted by the transferee against both the transferor and a third party in bad faith. Fourth, the real right enjoyed by the assignee is not to be held against a third party in good faith before registration.

2.3.2 Differences between Registration as a Requirement of Validity and as a Requirement of Perfection or Antagonism

First, whether registration is indispensable for a change in real right to become valid.

Second, whether registration is mandatory. Under the transaction mode where registration is a requirement of validity, registration is mandatory, and constitutes a part of the principle of numerus clausus. A change in real right cannot arise in the absence of registration, which makes it a mandatory requirement for the party to register so that the creation, alteration or extinguishment of a real right will be valid.

Third, whether conflicts arise among real rights is possible. The conflicts of rights in one property will possibly arise only under the transaction mode where registration is a requirement of challenge.

Fourth, whether delivery or registration is required. When registration is a requirement of perfection, the change in real right necessitate delivery.

Fifth, whether the good faith of a third party should be taken into consideration. A change in real right may be valid without registration under the transaction mode where registration is a requirement of perfection, but such change may not be asserted against a third party in good faith. Therefore, whether a third party is in good faith or not is one factor to be considered under such mode.

Sixth, the application scopes are different. The transaction mode of antagonism applies only when there are special statutory provisions, because the Civil Code has made it an exception to the principle that registration is a requirement of validity. According to Para. 1, Article 209 of the Civil Code, "The creation, alteration, alienation, or extinguishment of a real right in immovable property shall become effective upon registration in accordance with law, and shall not take effect without registration, unless otherwise provided by law".

Cases that may be deemed as "otherwise provided by law" mainly include the following scenarios.

First, cases explicitly defined by the Civil Code that the transaction mode of antagonism is applicable thereunder. Article 335 prescribes that "Where the rights to contractual management of land are exchanged or transferred, the parties may apply to the registration authority for registration; without registration, such exchange or transfer may not be asserted against a bona fide third person". Article 374 stipulates that, "An easement is created at the time the easement contract enters into effect. Where the parties request for registration, applications may be filed with the registration authority for the registration of the easement; without registration, such an easement may not be asserted against a bona fide third person".

Second, cases where natural resources owned by the State are involved. According to Para. 2, Article 209 of the Civil Code, "Ownership registration is not required for natural resources that are owned by the State in accordance with law".

Third, cases where a change in real right does not arise from a civil juristic act, for example, inheritance, requisition, lawful construction of houses can cause changes in real right absent registration. However, when such changed real right is disposed, registration is still required in accordance with law, or the successive change will be invalid (Articles 229 to 231 of the Civil Code).

3. Changes Not Arising from Juristic Acts

3. 1   Definition

Provisions on changes in real right not arising from juristic acts are mainly to be found in Section 3, Chapter 2 of the Civil Code's book on real rights. Under such transaction mode, the creation, alteration and extinction of real right are directly caused by statutory provisions. Its major features follow below.

3. 1. 1   This transaction mode is applicable only when there are statutory provisions. As the means of publication are provided for by law, so there should be situations where such means are inapplicable. Changes in real right not arising from juristic acts usually occur in

accordance with statutory provisions, regardless of the parties' will. Such statutory reasons generally include inheritance, court enforcement, requisition, judgments of the court, eminent domain, de facto acts such as lawful construction or demolition, etc. A change in real right takes place so long as the factual situation prescribed by the law occurs.

3. 1. 2   The transaction mode requires certain facts or conduct of de facto acts.

3. 1. 3 Registration is not a requirement of validity.

3. 1. 4   The transaction mode applies as an exception to the principle of real right changes.

3. 2   Changes to Real Right Concerning the Immovable Property Not Arising from Juristic Acts

Inheritance, court enforcement, requisition, judgments of court, etc. , are the most common cases where a change in real right concerning the immovable property arises without a juristic act. In most cases, changes to such nature do not necessitate registration when becoming effective. Nonetheless, according to 232 of the Civil Code, where disposition of such a real right in is required by law to be registered, the disposition of the real right, if not so registered, is not effective.

3. 2. 1   Effective legal documents of a court or arbitration institution or expropriation decision made by the people's government. Article 229 of the Civil Code stipulates that, "Where a real right is created, altered, alienated, or extinguished as a result of a legal document issued by the people's court or an arbitration institution, or based on an expropriation decision made by the people's government①, the creation, alteration, alienation, or extinguishment of the real right becomes effective at the time when the legal document or expropriation decision enters into effect".

3. 2. 2   Inheritance. Article 230 of the Civil Code provides that "Where a real right is acquired through succession, the real right as inherited becomes effective at the time when the succession opens".

3. 2. 3   De facto acts such as lawful construction and demolition of houses. Article 231 of the Civil Code provides that, "Where a real right is created or extinguished as a result of a de facto act such as lawful construction or demolition of a house, the creation or extinguishment of the real right becomes effective when the de facto act is accomplished".

3. 3   Changes to Real Right in the Movable property not Caused by Juristic Acts

As is provided by the Civil Code, where a change of real rights in movable property does

---

①   An administrative act conducted by the authority to expropriate properties owned by collectives or individuals for public interests with payment of compensation.

not arise from a juristic act, the causes may, apart from issuance of legal documents by a court or arbitration institution, requisition, inheritance, also include such de facto acts as finding of lost things, discovery of a thing buried underground or hidden, etc.

4. Registration of Immovable Property

4. 1   Concept and Characteristics

Realty registration is a real right institution established by the Civil Code whereby the realty registration authority, upon the application of real right holders or other interested parties or by its own authority, records such matters as the creation, alteration or extinguishment of a real right in the realty registry. The author opines that as a way of publicizing real rights, registration of immovable property in its nature is a de facto act instead of an administrative act on the part of the registration authority. It embodies the following characteristics:

4. 1. 1   It is the realty registration authority who is responsible for the recording of the creation and changes to real right in the realty register.

4. 1. 2   The matters registered include the creation, alteration, alienation and extinguishment of real right.

4. 1. 3   The rules apply only to the immovable property.

4. 1. 4   The registration is a means of publication in essence.

Some scholars hold the view that as an administrative act, the realty registration embodies the reasonable states intervention in real right relationships on the immovable property, for the purpose of clearly defining the attribution of property and protection of lawful rights and interests of the real right holder.

The registration system centered around land has a long history in China, and was closely related to land taxation from the very beginning. According to textual research, the ancient registration system centered around land originated in China in the middle or late Zhou Dynasty. From the Tang Dynasty onwards, institutions such as contract conclusion (in Chinese: 立契), administrative examination (in Chinese: 申牒) or settlement (in Chinese: 过割) began to appear in China's land administration regime. All land transactions must be examined by the authority, filed in written form and registered accordingly to be effective. Otherwise, not only was the transaction void but also the parties would be severely punished.

In China before March 1st, 2015, administrative organs for land, house, mining, waters, fishing and forestry, etc. are realty registration authorities that were duly empowered. On November 24, 2014, the Interim Regulations on Real Estate Registration was issued by the State Council. It came into effect on March 1st, 2015 and was amended on March 24, 2019.

The Interim Regulations on Real Estate Registration or Real Estate Registration Law is legislated to integrate real estate registration responsibilities and establish a unified registration system over immovable property. It echoes the demand in the socialist market economy and constructs a modern market system. Meanwhile, it plays a crucial role in protecting the lawful rights of the immovable property and promoting the efficiency and performance of governance. Particularly, it facilitates the people's application for registration. According to Article 210 of the Civil Code, the State implements a unified registration system with respect to immovable property, and the scope, authorities, and measures for the unified registration shall be specified by laws and administrative regulations. In light of this, the State Council promulgated the Interim Regulations on Real Estate Registration, so as to regulate via legislation on the registration activities, clarify the registration procedures, define the registration authorities and integrate registration responsibilities regarding land, house, forest, grassland and sea area, etc. In order to realize a unification of realty registration authorities, register, basis and information platform. The Interim Regulations on Real Estate Registration falls into 6 chapters with 35 provisions, stipulating on registration authority, register, procedure, and sharing and protection of registration information.

According to Article 5 of the Regulation, the following real rights shall be registered in accordance with the provisions of this Regulation: (1) Collective land ownership; (2) Ownership of constructions and structures, such as buildings; (3) Ownership of forests and woods; (4) Right to the contracted management of land such as farmland, forest land and grassland; (5) Right to use land for construction purposes;[1] (6) Right to use homestead land; (7) Right to use sea area; (8) Easement; (9) Mortgage right; and (10) Other real estate rights required to be registered according to the relevant laws.

4. 2　Effects of Registration

Regarding the effects of registration, legislations vary greatly. In civil law jurisdictions, two major approaches may be observed, namely, registration as a requirement of validity and that of perfection.

According to Article 209 of the Civil Code, Chinese law principally makes registration a requirement for validity, whilst adopting the antagonism mode as an exception.

---

[1]　China is to place a strict control on the use of land. The State shall compile general plans to set use of land including those of farm or construction used or unused. "Land for farm use" refers to land directly used for agricultural production, including cultivated land, wooded land, grassland, land for farmland water conservancy and water surfaces for breeding; "land for construction purposes" refers to land on which buildings and structures are put up, including land for urban and rural housing and public facilities, land for industrial and mining use, land for building communications and water conservancy facilities, land for tourism and land for building military installations. The term "land unused" refers to land other than that for agricultural and construction uses. Land should be used strictly in line with the purposes of land use defined in the general plan for the utilization of the land whether by units or individuals.

The effects of realty registration mainly encompass the following aspects:

4. 2. 1   Upon registration into the realty register, creations or other changes in real right come into effect. Article 214 of the Civil Code prescribes that "The creation, alteration, alienation, or extinguishment of a real right of the immovable property that is required by law to be registered becomes effective at the time when it is recorded in the register of immovable property".

4. 2. 2   The effect of presumption of accuracy. Article 216 of the Civil Code prescribes that the register of immovable property is the basis for determining the attribution and contents of the real rights in immovable property. For instance, the registered right holder is presumed to be the real holder, such has been discussed in the section of "principle of presumption of accuracy".

4. 2. 3   The effect in protection of parties in good faith. The real right ownership certificate is the proof of the holder's ownership of real right. Article 217 of the Civil Code stipulates the relationship between real right registration and certificate, stating that "The items recorded in the real right certificate for immovable property shall be consistent with what are recorded in the register of immovable property; in case of inconsistency between the two, what is recorded in the register of immovable property shall prevail, unless there is evidence establishing a clear error in the register of immovable property".

Distinction should be made between the effects of registration and that of a contract. Article 215 of the Civil Code provides that "A contract concluded by the parties on the creation, alteration, alienation, or extinguishment of a real right becomes effective upon its formation, unless it is otherwise provided by law or agreed upon by the parties, and the validity of the contract is not affected by the fact that the real right is not registered". The effects of registration and of contract distinguish from each other but are also correlated. Effects from registration also give rise to independent legal consequences.

Another benefit of making registration a requirement of publication in transfer is that it sets clear boundaries between registration and administrative approval.

4. 3   The Registration Organ and Its Duty of Examination

Registration shall be handled by the registration organ which is the institution that records in its jurisdiction after applicants submitting the required materials to prove the ownership and such statutory matters in the real estate register in accordance with the law.

From 1995 to 2015, relevant authorities and institutions which were set up by the authorities are in charge of matters regarding registration of real right. The number of agencies is multiple. Article 210 of the Civil Code provides that "The registration of immovable property shall be handled by the registration authority at the place where the immovable property is located. The State implements a unified registration system with respect to immovable property. The scope, authorities, and measures for the unified registration shall be specified by laws and administrative regulations".

Article 7 of the Interim Regulation on Real Estate Registration provides that, real estate shall be registered by the real estate registration authority of the county people's government at the place where the real estate is located; and the people's government of a municipality directly under the Central Government or a districted city may determine the real estate registration authority at the same level to uniformly register real estate in all districts under its jurisdiction. The real estate across administrative regions at the county level shall be registered respectively by the real estate registration authorities of administrative regions at the county level where the real estate is located. If separate registration could not be realized, the real estate registration authorities of relevant administrative regions where the real estate is located shall consult for the registration; if no agreement could be reached, the real estate shall be registered by the authority designated by the competent real estate registration authority of the people's government at the next higher level which administrates both the aforesaid two administrative regions. The registration of real property such as the forests, woods and forest land in key state-owned forest areas determined by the State Council, the sea area and island used for projects approved by the State Council, and the state-owned land used by central state authorities, shall be provided for by the competent department of land and resources of the State Council together with other relevant departments.

Meanwhile, Para. 3, Article 8 of the Interim Regulations on Real Estate Registration provides that "The real estate register shall record: (1) the natural conditions such as the location, boundary, space, acreage, and usage of the real estate; (2) the ownership conditions such as the owner, type, content, resource, term, and change of ownership of real estate rights; (3) the matters involving the limitation on and reminder of real estate rights; and (4) other relevant matters".

As for what kind of responsibility the registration organ shall undertake while performing its duty of examination, there once goes two opinions in the drafting of the Civil Code, namely, that for formal examination and that for substantive examination. The Civil Code finally adopts a mode that combined both two ways, with formal examination as principal way and substantive examination as a supplementary way. Article 212 of the Civil Code prescribes that "The registration authority shall perform the following responsibilities: (1) to examine the proof of real rights and other necessary materials provided by the applicant; (2) to inquire the relevant registration items of the applicant; (3) to register the relevant items truthfully and in a timely manner; and (4) to perform other responsibilities as provided by laws and administrative regulations. Where further proof is required for the relevant information of the immovable property to be registered, the registration authority may require the applicant to provide supplementary materials, and may conduct onsite inspection where necessary".

4.4   Consultation of Registration

Article 218 of the Civil Code prescribes that "A right holder or an interested person may apply for retrieving and making copies of the information of the registered immovable property, and the registration authority shall provide the information".

4.5   Correction Registration and Dissidence Registration

Correction registration is a process where the registration organ makes corrections to wrongly recorded items, when the right holder or the interested party believes that there are some wrong items recorded in the realty register and accordingly applies for correction, and the right holder recorded in the realty register agrees in written form to make corrections or there is evidence to prove that there are definitely errors in the registration.

Para. 1, Article 220 of the Civil Code provides that "A right holder or an interested person may apply for rectification of the registration if he believes that an item is incorrectly recorded in the register of immovable property. Where the right holder as recorded in the register of immovable property agrees in writing to make rectification, or where there is evidence establishing a clear error in the register, the registration authority shall rectify it".

Dissidence registration is method that an interested party may resort to for the protection of its own right when it dissents from the ownership or other matters recorded in the realty register. Para. 2, Article 220 of the Civil Code prescribes that "Where the right holder as recorded in the register of immovable property does not agree to make rectification, an interested person may apply for registration of a demurrer. Where the registration authority registers the demurrer but the applicant fails to file a lawsuit within 15 days from the date of such a registration, the registration of demurrer becomes ineffective. Where a demurrer is improperly registered and damage is thus caused to the right holder, the right holder may request the applicant to pay damages".

4.6   Registration of Priority Notice

The registration of priority notice is stipulated in Article 221 of the Civil Code, which provides that "Where the parties enter into an agreement for the sale of a house or on any other real right in immovable property, they may apply for registration of a priority notice to a registration authority in accordance with the agreement so as to ensure the realization of the real right in the future. Where, after the priority notice is registered, the immovable property is disposed of without the consent of the right holder as registered in the priority notice, the disposition is not effective in terms of the real right. Where, after the priority notice is registered, no application for registration of the real right of immovable property has been made within 90 days from the date on which the creditor's claim extinguishes or the immovable property is eligible for registration, the registration of the priority notice becomes ineffective".

The purpose of registration of priority notice is to guarantee the realization of creditor's right or potential real right. It should be applied to the registration organ in accordance with previous agreement between parties.

Registration of priority notice is a counterpart concept of principal registration. The latter is a registration procedure for real right that have already changed. In most cases, a real right registration is endowed with such nature. The differences between an registration of priority notice and a principal registration lies in their objects, materials for application and legal effects. The registration of priority notice aims to realize a creditor's right by restricting the disposal of the right holder in the realty register.

The major functions of the registration of priority notice is to ensure the realization of real right in the future, maintain the validity of a claim, guarantee the order of priority and render protection in cases of bankruptcy.

4.7 Claim for Registration

The claim for registration is a right asserted by a right holder of registration to require performance or assistance of the duty holder of registration to fulfill the obligation to register.

For a long period of time, the Chinese law has made registration or administrative approval a requirement for conclusion and validity of contract, which results in the dilemma that one party of a contract refuses to register for unlawful interests. As a result, the contract cannot come into effect, rendering the court's inability to impose performance of such obligation due to the invalidity of the contract. Viewed from this, a proper solution is to separate the validity of the contract from that of registration. When registration becomes a contractual obligation, the party will be able to request court enforcement or claim for liability for contractual breach when the other party intentionally refuses to register.

In principle, the right holder of registration is to be stipulated by law or contract. Absent such stipulations, both parties are the obligors of registration. According to Article 14 of the Interim Regulations on Real Estate Registration, the registration of real estate to be traded or mortgaged shall be jointly applied for by both parties. Under seven circumstances, including where the application for the registration of the unregistered real estate is filed for the first time, the real estate rights are obtained by inheritance or acceptance of bequests, etc., the real estate registration may be unilaterally applied for by a party.

5. Delivery of Movable Property and Registration of Real Rights in Movable Property

5.1　Definition and Effects of Delivery of Movable Property and Registration of Real Rights in Movable Property

Delivery is an action whereby a right holder transfers the property under his possession to another person.

Article 224 of the Civil Code prescribes that "The creation or alienation of a real right in movable property shall take effect upon delivery, unless otherwise provided by law".

Thus, unless otherwise prescribed by law, the creation or alienation of real right regarding movable property shall be publicized by delivery. As a statutory obligation, delivery is a prerequisite for a change in real right to be fulfilled. The change in real right occurs upon delivery.

Cases otherwise prescribed by law may include real rights whose objects are civil aircrafts, vessels and motor vehicles, mortgages in movable properties and pledges on rights. Except for these real rights in movable property, other real rights in movables are publicized through delivery. According to the law, these real rights in movable properties are not publicized by delivery, but through registration. However, concerning the effect of such registration the legislation usually adopts the mode whereby registration is a perfection requirement, which means that registration is not a requirement of validity and the absence of registration only results in the real right's ineffectiveness against a bona fide third party. Article 225 of the Civil Code stipulates that "The creation, alteration, alienation, or extinguishment of the real rights in vessels, aircrafts, motor vehicles, and the like, that have not been registered is not effective against a bona fide third person". Where aircrafts, vessels, or motor vehicles are mortgaged, the competent authority for real right registration shall be the registration organs of such means of transport. Article 9 of the Maritime Law prescribes that "The acquisition, transference or extinction of the ownership of a ship shall be registered at the ship registration organ; no acquisition, transference or extinction of the ship's ownership may act against a third party unless registered". Article 13 of the same statute stipulates that "the mortgage of a ship shall be established through registering the mortgage of the ship by both the mortgagee and the mortgagor at the ship registration organ. No right to mortgage may act against a third party unless registered".

Regarding registration of general real rights in movables, the Decision on the Implementation of Unified Registration of Security Over Chattel and Rights (Guo Fa [2020] No. 18) notified that from January 1, 2021, the unified registration of security over chattel and rights shall be implemented nationwide. All registration concerning the establishment, alteration and deregistration of mortgage in movable property such as production equipment, raw materials, semi-finished products, and products, etc. shall be made in an online system launched by the credit reference center of People's Bank of China, except mortgage over motor vehicles, ships and aircrafts, pledge over bonds, fund units and equity, and pledge over property rights in intellectual property. Where equipment or other movable property of enterprises, other organizations, or natural persons are mortgaged, administration for industry and commerce or notary public office authorities are no longer responsible for registering mortgages. In general cases, registered mortgages in movable property prevail unregistered ones.

Simple delivery can only denote a transfer of possession, but not the transfer of the real right. Therefore, delivery, as a means of publication for changes in the real right concerning movable properties, requires the intention of the transferor to transfer his real right. Such intention usually manifests through a unilateral civil juristic act on part of the transferor or a bilateral civil juristic act by the parties.

Unlike registration, delivery cannot be the means of publication for every form of change in real right concerning movable properties. It is a publication method only for transfer arising from juristic acts. In other words, we refer to transfer of ownership or creation of nonproprietary real rights that requires possession. As to other forms of changes in real right concerning movable properties, they are not publicated by delivery. For example, in cases where ownership of a movable property is obtained through original acquisition, the delivery may not occur at all (such as acquisition by profits, accession, appropriation, prescription, etc.), or have no legal significance (such as acquisition through inheritance). With regard to lien, it occurs only when a creditor has first occupied the property of the obligor and then the obligor fails to pay its due debts. Thus, delivery does not publicate the acquisition of the lien. In fact, it is a publication method for change in real right concerning movable property, only when a transfer of real right or creation of pledge arise from certain civil juristic acts, with the former scenario to be the most typical.

Two legislative models may be observed regarding effects of delivery, namely, which are where delivery is a requirement of validity and that of perfection. The former is well represented by the German Civil Code, which makes delivery a requirement for the validity of transfer of the real right concerning movable properties. Under the latter legislation model, the manifestation of intention of the parties can lead to directly legal effect of transfer the real right concerning movable property, with delivery only being a requirement of perfection against a third party. The former approach is adopted by China.

5. 2   Forms of Delivery

Delivery falls into two categories, i. e. , actual delivery and conceptual delivery.

5. 2. 1   Actual delivery. It refers to the physical transfer of possession regarding a movable property from the transferor to the transferee. The transferee will directly possess the movable property. Actual delivery is most typical, and it includes: (1) the transferor transfers the property to the transferee directly at the promissory time and place. Such delivery is accomplished after a compliance check and acceptance by the transferee; (2) the transferor consigns for shipment or mails the property in accordance with transferee's instructions. Such delivery is accomplished when the transferor finishes the procedures for the consignment or mailing.

5. 2. 2   Conceptual delivery. Under special circumstances, parties are allowed to adopt a flexible measure instead of actual delivery through agreement. Such approach shows sufficient respect to private autonomy, and reduces transaction cost incurred by actual delivery, facilitating the convenience in transaction.

There are three principal methods under conceptual delivery:

First, traditio brevi manu. It means that according to the agreement of the parties, the transferee may change the possession of a third party (the property has been practically occupied by the transferee) to possession of his own. Article 226 of the Civil Code prescribes that, "Where a right holder is already in possession of a movable property before a real right in the movable property is created or alienated, the real right in the movable property becomes effective at the time when the civil juristic act is effected".

Second, constructive transfers. This occurs when the proprietary possession of a transferor turns into nonproprietary through an agreement between such owner of movable property and the acquirer. Such delivery is accomplished when the agreement is concluded or is specified by the agreement itself. The agreement hereby referred to cannot be simply an agreement for indirect possession without any legal basis. Rather, it shall be an agreement regarding entering into certain legal relationship such as lease, gratuitous loan, custody and transfer guaranty etc. Otherwise, the transferee may not acquire the indirect possession and the ownership. Article 228 of the Civil Code stipulates that, "Where, upon alienation of a real right in movable property, the parties agree that the transferor continues to be in possession of the movable property, the real right in the movable property becomes effective at the time when such an agreement enters into effect".

Third, delivery by instructions (or assignment of claim for possession). When an owner transfers a property that is occupied by a third party, delivery may be replaced by the way of transferring the claim for restitution of property. Article 227 of the Civil Code stipulates that,

"Where a third person is in possession of a movable property before a real right in the movable property is created or alienated, the person obligated to deliver the movable property may transfer his right to restitution against the third person as substitute for delivery".

5.3 Change in Real Right Concerning Vessels, Aircrafts and Motor Vehicles, etc. : the Antagonism Mode

Article 225 of the Civil Code stipulates that "The creation, alteration, alienation, or extinguishment of the real rights in vessels, aircrafts, motor vehicles, and the like, that have not been registered is not effective against a bona fide third person". Because the value of vessels, aircrafts, and motor vehicles well exceeds that of general chattels, these movable properties are deemed as a type of quasi-immovable property. At the same, however, they also boast features of movable property. Alteration of real rights in these property takes effect not at the time of registration. According to the Civil Code, alienation of ownership usually becomes effective upon the time of delivery and mortgage is created at the time when the mortgage contract is concluded. Nonetheless, due to the high value of these chattels, the law stipulates a registration system for them to record changes to real rights of these property. Absent registration at the competent registration organ, the real right changes have no social credibility; even if such changes do become effective, the effectiveness cannot be claimed against a bona fide third party. The bona fide third party hereby refers to a person neither knew nor ought to have known the changes to real right. For instance, A sold his car to B and completed delivery accordingly but without registration. In such case, the ownership of the car has gone to B. However, if A secretly sold the same car to C, who had no knowledge of prior transaction, and completed registration accordingly, then B may not claim against C on the ground that he has obtained the ownership over the car earlier. The ownership of the car was attributed to C.

Section Five   Protection of Real Right in Civil Law

1. Protection of Real Right in Civil Law: An Overview

The protection of the real right in civil law refers to the various measures adopted under civil law so as to safeguard the interests of right holders of real rights against infringement, when any encroachment arises.

When it comes to the protection of real right, it requires the joint effort of various departments of law including the civil law. Therefore, different stipulations and rules of liabilities regarding the real right can be found within a variety of laws. In the first subsection of Book Two Real Rights of the Civil Code, a special chapter (Chapter Three) has been set forth to regulate the protection of real rights. Special rules and the effects of the real right are established thereunder. The major characters of Chapter 3 are to be viewed from the following perspectives:

1.1　When a real right is infringed upon, multiple approaches may be taken as remedy. For example, compromise out of lawsuits, mediation with binding effect (conducted by a special institution for mediation, a court or an arbitral institution) and litigation.

1.2　The claim for confirmation of real right has been set forth for the settlement of disputes arising from ambiguous attribution of real right.

1.3　Particularly, various means that one may exert to the protection of a real right are brought into being. This includes claims on property rights such as claim for restitution of property, removal of the nuisance, elimination of danger and restoration of original status.

1.4　Besides claims of real rights, claims of tort are also powerful instruments for the protection of real right.

1.5　A comprehensive system of liabilities safeguarding the real right has been founded, with civil liabilities, administrative liabilities and criminal liabilities respectively being clarified regarding the violation of real right in civil law, administrative regulations and the criminal law.

In civil law means of protection for the real right include claims for confirmation of real rights and claims of real rights. Particularly noteworthy is that according to Article 8 of the Interpretations (I) of the Supreme People's Court on the Application of Property Right Part of the Civil Code of the People's Republic of China 2020 (hereafter "Interpretations (I) on the Property Right Part of the Civil Code"), where real rights in immovable property are obtained through inheritance, court enforcement, requisition, judgments of the court, eminent domain, de facto acts such as lawful construction or demolition, etc., "Where a right holder enjoys certain real rights pursuant to Articles 229 to 231 of the Civil Code but has not completed the delivery of movable property or registration of immovable property, and claims for protection of real rights in accordance with Articles 235 to 238 of the Civil Code, such claim shall be sustained". The real right holder enjoys the claims for confirmation of real rights and claims of real rights.

2. Claim for Confirmation of Real Rights

2.1　Definition

Claim for confirmation of real right arises when the parties seek for confirmation regarding matters which are concerned dispute over the attribution or contents of a real right. Article 234 of the Civil Code provides that "Where a dispute arises over the attribution or contents of a real right, an interested person may request for confirmation of the right".

The claim for confirmation of real right is not an independent claim. Because on the one hand, while every claim under the civil law is based on a substantive right, like the case with claim of real right, which is based on the existence of a real right, the claim for confirmation on real right actually relies on a substantive right whose attribution or contents are disputed. Viewed in this, one may not take for granted that the party who has claimed for confirmation necessarily enjoys the real right. On the other hand, the claim for confirmation of real right has to be put up through public remedies for realization. The decision is usually made by a competent registration organ or a court. In addition, such claim for confirmation may not be asserted against a particular person, which marks another difference between it and other claims.

2.2 Features of the Claim for Confirmation of Real Rights

2.2.1 It is a precondition for real right protection.

2.2.2 The claim is aimed to confirm the attribution and contents of real right.

2.2.3 It is necessary to apply to the relevant real right registration organ or a people's court to confirm the attribution.

2.2.4 The application for confirmation can be put up Only by the party concerned.

Claim for confirmation of real right is not subject to prescription.

2.3 Claim of Property Rights

See related argument and explanation made in the former section on "Effects of Real Rights".

第三章　所　有　权

第一节　所有权概述

一、所有权的概念、特征和本质

(一)所有权的概念

所有权的概念，在民法学上通常在三种不同意义上使用：

一是指所有权法律制度，即有关所有权法律规范的总和。所有权法律制度，不仅是物权法的基本制度，也是整个民法的基本制度之一，同时还涉及宪法、行政法、刑法等许多法律部门中有关财产所有权关系的法律规定。

二是指所有权法律关系，即法律确认特定所有人与不特定的义务人基于物质资料的归属和支配而发生的权利义务关系。

作为民事法律关系，所有权法律关系包括三要素：主体、客体和内容(参见本书第二章第一节内容)。根据物权法定原则，物权的客体"物"也就是所有权的客体包括动产和不动产，以有体物为主。但是法律规定有的权利也可以作为物权的客体，所以如果有特别法的规定的话，从其规定。

三是指所有权(人)对其所有(权)物依法享有的权利，也即所有权法律关系内容的权利方面。

各国民法给所有权下定义都从第三种角度考虑。《法国民法典》第544条规定："所有权为对物完全按个人意愿使用及处分的权利，但法令所禁止的使用不在此限。"即只是抽象规定所有权的作用。《民法典》第240条规定："所有权人对自己的不动产或者动产，依法享有占有、使用、收益和处分的权利。"这条仅规定了所有权人的权利内容。

(二)所有权的特征

作为物权，所有权除具有物权的共性特征外，还具有区别于其他物权的特殊性。

1. 所有权是自物权

所有权是所有人对自己的财产享有物权。他物权都是对别人的财产享有的权利。

2. 所有权是绝对权、对世权

所有权的实现不需要他人的积极行为，只要他人不加干预，所有人自己便能实现其所有权。所有权关系的义务主体是所有权人以外的一切人，所负的义务是不得非法干涉所有权人行使其所有权。这是一种特定的不作为义务。债权的实现，必须依靠债务人履行债务的行为——主要是作为。

3. 所有权是独占权

所有人独占其所有物，独享其所有物的价值与使用价值。所有人使用其所有物，除在公法范围内可能向国家负担一定税费外，在私法范围内无须向任何人支付代价。他人处分所有人的财产，其所得价金，作为所有权的一般价值的表现形态，应归所有人所有，而不归处分人所有。与此相反，使用他人的财产，除法律另有规定或与所有人另有约定外，一般均需向所有人支付相应的对价。因此，对财产进行使用、收益时是否需要将所得价金给予他人或为他人保存，可作为区别所有权与他物权的一个标准。

4. 所有权是原始物权

所有权不是从其他财产权派生出来的，而是法律直接确认财产归属关系的结果。与所有权不同，其他物权则是由所有权派生出来的，是所有权的权能与所有权分离的结果。

5. 所有权是完全物权

从对物的支配方面来看，所有权是一种总括的、全面的、一般的支配权，全部囊括了占有、使用、收益、处分四项权能，而且所有人行使这些权能，除受法律的限制外，不受他人单方面的限制，有充分的自由。与所有权相比，他物权是受限制的，不完全或不充分的物权。他物权人一般只能就物的使用价值或交换价值的特定方面进行支配，只能享有占有、使用、处分四项权能中的一项、两项或三项权能。即使享有全部四项权能，与所有权相比，也是不充分的，须受到所有人的一定制约。

6. 所有权具有强烈的排他性

财产所有人对其财产享有的所有权，可以依法排斥他人的非法干涉，不允许其他任何人加以妨碍或者侵害。对所有权而言，必须严格实行一物一权主义，即在一物之上只能有一个所有权，不能形成双重所有权。而他物权则在实行一物一权方面并不十分严格。同一物之上可以成立数个物权(如一个所有权与一个他物权或者数个他物权)。当财产所有权受到不法占有或者侵害时，财产所有人有权请求返还原物、停止侵害、排除妨碍或者赔偿损失。

7. 具有回归力的权能(弹力性)

所有权人根据自己利益的需要在自己的所有物上设定他物权。他物权设定后，即构成对所有权的限制，所有权处于不圆满状态。但日后他物权消灭，所有权所受限制除去，所有权可以回复。他物权的权能是有限的与非恒定的，一旦丧失即引起他物权消灭，因此也就不具有弹力性与回归力。

(三)所有权与财产及产权的区别

财产是英美法所经常采用的概念,但大陆法学者也经常使用财产概念。财产和所有权在很多情况下是可以通用的,但严格地说,财产与所有权的概念是有区别的。第一,财产可以是有形物也可以为无形物,是有体物与无体物的总称。然而所有权必须以有体物为客体,一旦所有权的客体包括了无体物,则所有权与其他权利的区分将不复存在。第二,财产并不限于绝对权,可以包括各种权利与利益。也就是说,财产既可以指所有权、其他物权,知识产权,也可能是指债权。从这个意义上说,所有权只是财产的一种形态。

所有权与产权也是不同的。产权又称为财产权,是指以财产利益为内容直接体现某种物质利益的权利,是与非财产权相对应的概念。非财产权是指并非以财产利益为内容,而是以人身所体现的利益为内容的、与权利人的人身不可分的民事权利,主要是指人身权,包括人格权与身份权。财产权包含的内容较为广泛,凡是具有经济价值的权利都可以纳入财产权的范畴。可见,产权是一个上位概念,所有权是一个下位概念。所有权不过是产权的一种。所有权和其他物权制度构成民法中一项相对独立的制度,统称为物权法(制度)。而财产权并非一种单一权利,而是多项民事权利的集合,所以财产法是民法中多项制度如物权法、债权法、知识产权法等的集合。物权、债权、继承权等财产权虽都以经济利益为内容,但权利的性质和特点是根本不同的,权利的内容与保护方法也是完全不同的。可以说,它们相互间个性大于共性。

二、所有权的权能

所有权的权能,是所有人为利用所有物实现其对所有物的独占利益,在法律规定的范围内可以采取的各种措施与手段。所有权的不同权能表现为所有权的不同作用。每一种权能意味着所有人或所有人授权他人实施一类或一系列行为的可能性。例如,所有权的处分权能,意味着所有人有权将财产用于消费、清偿、赠与、交换、出租、加工等。其中除生活消费外,包括生产消费在内的其他各种处分行为,都可委托他人进行。随着社会经济的发展,物的利用方式不断增多,所有权权能所体现的作用也就随之而扩大。

根据《民法典》第240条的规定,占有、使用、收益和处分,构成了所有权的四项权能或内容。

(一)占有权

占有是主体对于物基于占有的意思进行控制的事实状态。占有是对物的一种事实上的控制。对物的控制也称为对物的管领,需要借助身体与物发生一种外部的接触。但是,占有人必须具有占有的意图,且事实上控制或管领了某物。占有尽管是主体对物事实上的控制状态,但并非在法律上没有意义;相反,占有常常形成一种法律关系。占有人因占有可能取得占有权甚至所有权。即使不能形成权利的占有,在法律上也可获得保护，故占有具有重要的法律意义。

根据占有人是否有权占有某物，可分为有权占有和无权占有。有权占有，是指基于法律或合同的规定而享有对某物进行占有的权利。此种对物可以进行占有的权利，在法律上又称为本权。本权主要包括依合同取得的合同债权（如因保管、租赁合同等而取得对物的占有）、物权（如所有权、用益物权）等。在有权占有的情况下，占有背后通常有本权。占有和本权的关系表现为当本权受到侵害时，保护占有则具有保护本权的作用。另外，本权可以强化占有，保护本权当然可以维护占有人对物的合法占有。总之，在有本权的情况下的占有，称为有权占有，亦称正权原占有。所谓无权占有，是指无本权的占有。如窃贼对赃物的占有，承租人在租赁期届满以后对租赁物的占有。

无权占有通常可以分为两类：善意占有与恶意占有。所谓善意占有，是指不法占有人在占有他人财产时，不知道或者不应当知道其占有是非法的。例如，不知道他人在市场上出售的财产是其无权处分的财产而以合理的价格购买了该财产并对该财产进行占有，占有人占有该财产主观上是善意的。如果占有人明知其无占有的权利或对其有无占有的权利有怀疑，则应为恶意占有。

区分善意占有和恶意占有在民法上的意义在于：

(1)当所有人的动产由占有人非法转让给第三人时，如果第三人占有该动产是出于善意，就可以依法取得所有权。

(2)如果占有人基于将财产据为己有的意思，善意、和平、公然、持续不间断地占有某项财产，经过法定的占有时效期间，则可依占有时效制度而取得对其占有财产的所有权。

(3)在不当得利的返还上，善意占有人一般只返还现存的利益，对于已经灭失的利益不负返还的责任。而恶意占有人在此情况下应负赔偿责任。

(4)在返还原物时，善意占有人可请求所有人返还为其保管、保存占有物所支付的必要的费用，并对已经在占有物上获得的孳息负返还义务。而恶意占有人在返还原物时，不仅无权请求所有人偿付其支付的费用，而且有义务返还其所获得的孳息。

(二)使用权

使用，是按照物的性质和用途对物加以利用，以满足生产生活需要。使用权就是这种利用财产的权利。

使用权在本质上是由物的使用价值决定的。实现物的使用价值以满足所有人的需要是所有人的意志和利益的体现。而所有人以外的其他人，负有不妨碍所有人实现其物的使用价值的义务。

使用权意味着所有人可以在法律规定的范围内，依自身的意志使用其物，同时可以取得所有物的孳息，包括天然孳息和法定孳息。

使用权是直接在所有物之上行使的权利，因而使用权的存在要以实际占有物为前提。当物与所有人分离以后，所有人的使用权也与所有权发生分离。因而使用权和占有权一样，也可以由非所有人享有。非所有人的使用权是从所有权中派生出来的一项权利，非所有人必须根据法律和合同的规定行使使用权。

（三）收益权

收益权是在物上获得经济利益的权利，即收取由原物产生出来的新增经济价值的权利。这里的新增经济价值，包括天然孳息和法定孳息。

任何所有权都要求在经济上得到实现。人们拥有某物，是为了从物上获得物的使用价值（使用）和换取物的价值（处分）。此外，权利人还要取得物所派生出来的价值（收益），特别是在市场经济社会。这正是商品生产者所追求的。

在现代市场经济条件下，收益权不仅是所有权中的一项独立的权能，而且是所有权最基本的一项权能。在现实经济生活中，物的收益与物的使用密切联系，物的收益常常表现为运用物质资料进行生产经营活动的结果。但是，生产经营的结果与生产经营的过程毕竟是两个不同的范畴，因此表现在法律上，收益权与使用权也就可能彼此分离而属于不同的主体。如股东出资后，其出资财产虽由公司占有与使用，然而股东却能凭借股权单独取得其出资财产的收益。企业租赁经营也是类似。现代市场经济是一种货币经济，财产所有人所看重的是经济价值，财产的占有、使用则并不重要，只要能使自己的财产增值，他们宁可让渡财产的占有权、使用权甚至处分权。在这种经济条件下，收益权能也就凸显，成为体现所有权的最基本的权能。

收益权也可以与所有权分离而属非所有人。在他主经营日益成为社会普遍现象的现代经济条件下，收益权与所有权分离的通常形式是：（1）所有人与经营人订立契约，在让与资产占有权、使用权、处分权的同时，让与部分收益权，保留部分收益权，从而与资产经营人按一定比例分享资产收益。（2）所有人让与占有权、使用权和部分收益权，保留处分权与部分收益权，如中国的土地使用权。（3）在一定期限内让与使用权和全部收益权而仅仅保留处分权。如国家为鼓励开发自然资源，将国有的荒山、滩涂划给集体或个人开发，在一定期限内国家不分利润，但永久性地全部让与收益权而保留所有权是不可能的。因为在这种情况下，所有权无法从经济上实现。

（四）处分权

是指依法对物进行处置，从而决定物的命运的权利。

处分包括事实上的处分和法律上的处分。事实上的处分是指对物进行消费，包括生产消费和生活消费。事实上的处分是对物的实物形态进行的处分，将导致物的形体变更或消灭。关于生产性消费，由于在生产过程凝聚的人类劳动能够转移到产品上，物的形态反而得以扩大。生活消费则常常引起物的形体与价值的同时消灭，如大米被做成米饭吃掉。事实上的处分与对物的使用不同，因为使用只引起物的磨损，并不引起物的形体的变更或消灭。当物使用到不能再使用的程度时，人们才会进而采用处分行为（如抛弃）。

法律上的处分，是指通过法律行为对物进行处置，即转让。它是对物的价值形态上的处分，意味着交换价值的转移。

事实上的处分和法律上的处分，分别引起所有权的绝对消灭和相对消灭。所以处分权决定着财产的归属，是财产所有权的核心。但处分权也可以基于法律的规定和所有权人的意志与所有权分离而属非所有权人，如留置、抵押、设质。

三、所有权的种类

所有权的种类就是指所有权的不同类型，是对所有制形式的反映。在中国，所有权的形式主要有国家所有权、集体组织所有权和私人所有权，是中国现阶段财产所有权的三种基本形式。尽管这几种所有权都体现了社会主义公有制的特点，但是又反映了不同所有制的性质和要求，在法律上也具有不同的特点。这些特点不仅表现在权利主体的区别上，而且也表现在客体的范围上（如土地只能为国家和集体组织所有，不能为个人所有）和权利的行使方式上（如国家所有权要借助与行政相关的职能活动来行使）。这些区别也是划分不同所有权形式的依据。另外，《民法典》还规定了社会团体法人、捐助法人所有权。

（一）国家所有权

1. 国家所有权概念和特征

在中国，社会主义国家不仅是国家政权的承担者，而且是国有财产的所有者。社会主义国家所有权作为社会主义条件下的一种所有权形式，是国家对国有财产的占有、使用、收益和处分的权利，国家所有权本质上是社会主义全民所有制在法律上的表现。

全民所有制是社会全体成员共同占有社会生产资料的一种所有制形式。由于现阶段不可能由社会全体成员直接占有社会生产资料，单个社会成员也不可能代表全体社会成员支配生产资料。因此，必须通过一个社会中心来实现对全民的生产资料进行支配。在国家依然存在的情况下，这个社会中心只能是国家。公有制的建立，使社会主义国家能够按照全体人民的共同利益，对全民所有制领域的经济活动进行统一领导和必要的管理。因此，社会主义全民所有制在法律上表现为国家所有权，有其客观的必然性。

（1）权利主体的特定性。国家所有权作为一种法律关系，权利主体是国家，义务主体则是除国家以外的任何不特定的组织和个人。这些组织和个人都负有不侵犯国有财产的义务。作为权利主体的国家，同时也是国家行政权的主体。但是，国家在行使其权利时，其作为两种不同性质的主体身份是可以分离的。国家作为所有权主体和行政权主体的分离，是促使政企职责分开、发展社会主义市场经济的必要条件。在中国现行体制下，国家所有权是通过国务院代表国家来行使的。国家在行使所有权时，可以将其所有权的权能转移给社会组织和个人享有或者行使，但任何组织和个人都不得成为国有财产的所有人。同样，国家的各个机构，无论其属于哪一个行政层次，都只是代表国家行使所有权的机关，其本身并不是所有人。如果认为从中央到地方的各级政府部门都是国有财产的所有人，则必然导致将统一的国家所有权分割为中央政府所有权、地方政府所有权和部门所有权，将从根本上改变中国全民所有制的性质。

（2）客体的广泛性。《民法典》第 242 条规定："法律规定专属于国家所有的不动产和动产，任何组织个人不能取得所有权。"根据中国宪法和民法之规定，城市的土地、矿藏、水流、森林、草原、荒地、渔场等自然资源属于国家专有，禁止侵占或以买卖及其他方式非法转让。《民法典》第 247～254 条具体规定了国家所有的财产，包括法律规定属于国家所有的野生动植物资源、无线电频谱资源、法律规定属于国家所有的文物等。相对于集体组织财产所有权和公民个人财产所有权而言，国家所有权的客体具有广泛性。也就是说，任何财产都可以成为国家所有权的客体，但不一定能够成为集体组织和私人所有权的客体。但国有财产的广泛性的特征并不意味着对集体组织的财产可以随意"拔高升级"，使之转化为国有财产，更不意味着对于集体组织和公民个人的财产，国家可以任意通过国有化而取得。

（3）取得方式的特殊性。由于国家本身是主权的享有者和政权的承担者，国家可以凭借其公共权力通过征收、国有化、没收等方式强制性地将公民个人或集体的财产收归国有；还可以依据行政权强制性地无偿地征收税金，从而取得国有财产；还可以通过其他特殊方式取得所有权，如获得无人认领的拾得物、漂流物、发现的所有权不明的埋藏物或者隐藏物，获得无人继承又无人受遗赠的财产。

（4）行使方式的特殊性。国家作为一个抽象的实体，难以直接行使所有权，必须通过法律法规授权的国家机关、企事业单位以及国家投资的企业，在法律规定的范围内行使。

2. 国家所有权的保护

对国家所有权实行保护是中国各个法律部门的重要任务。中国《宪法》明确规定："社会主义的公共财产神圣不可侵犯。"《民法典》第 258 条规定："国家所有的财产受法律保护，禁止任何单位或者个人侵占、哄抢、私分、截留、破坏。"这里，所谓侵占，是指非经国家的授权或者是国家机关的同意，而占有国有财产。例如，未经批准使用国有土地和自然资源，抢占国有房屋和其他财产，挪用公款，化公为私，或以权谋私，侵吞国家财产。所谓哄抢，是指故意以非法手段抢占国家财产，如趁国有企业关停并转之机而哄抢财物。所谓私分，是指未经批准而将国有财产分配给个人或组织所有。例如，巧立名目，滥发奖金和实物。所谓截留，指将应上交给国家的利税以各种手段不交或少交。所谓破坏，是指以非法手段直接损害国有财产，如滥挖矿床、滥伐林木、捕杀珍稀动物、盗掘古墓、毁损古迹。上列各种违法行为，都侵犯了国家财产所有权，应依法追究行为人的民事责任。对国有财产的保护，还应注重对动态利益的保护，要重视保护国有资产的利益，保障国家所有权在经济上的实现。

为了防止国有资产流失的特别规定。《民法典》第 259 条第 1 款规定："履行国有财产管理、监督职责的机构及其工作人员，应当依法加强对国有财产的管理、监督，促进国有财产保值增值，防止国有财产损失；滥用职权，玩忽职守，造成国有财产损失的，应当依法承担法律责任。"第 2 款规定："违反国有财产管理规定，在企业改制、合并分立、关联交易等过程中，低价转让、合谋私分、擅自担保或者以其他方式造成国有财产损失的，应当依法承担法律责任。"

(二)集体所有权

1. 集体所有权的概念和特征

中国《宪法》规定，中华人民共和国的经济制度的基础是生产资料的社会主义公有制，即全民所有制和劳动群众集体所有制。集体所有制经济是中国公有制经济的重要组成部分。在中国，集体所有权是指劳动群众集体组织以及集体组织全体成员对集体财产享有的占有、使用、收益和处分的权利，它是劳动群众集体所有制在法律上的表现。集体所有权的特征可以从以下三个方面来看：

(1)集体所有权的主体

集体所有权没有全国性的统一的主体。各个劳动群众集体组织都是独立的集体所有权的主体。集体组织大都是具有法人资格的主体，它们相互之间是平等的相互合作关系或者相互独立，主要是农村集体组织，也包括城镇集体企业和合作社集体组织。集体所有权的主体还包括集体的全体成员。《民法典》第 261 条规定："农民集体所有的不动产和动产，属于本集体成员集体所有。"在法律上，劳动群众集体所有的财产和集体组织成员的个人财产是分开的。集体组织的某个成员或某部分成员都不能成为集体所有权的主体。可见，集体的概念在民法上有特定的含义，集体既可能是指组织，也可能是指集体成员。但是，集体组织并不包括各种不具有法人资格的团体，如合伙组织、各种非法人团体。

(2)集体所有权的客体

依法归劳动群众集体所有的土地，是集体所有权的重要客体。在中国实行土地全民所有和集体所有两种形式。中国《宪法》第 10 条规定："城市的土地属于国家所有。农村和城市郊区的土地，除由法律规定属于国家所有的以外，属于集体所有；宅基地和自留地、自留山，也属于集体所有。"《民法典》对集体所有权的客体作了专门规定。第 260 条规定："集体所有的不动产和动产包括：(1)法律规定属于集体所有的土地和森林、山岭、草原、荒地、滩涂；(2)集体所有的建筑物、生产设施、农田水利设施；(3)集体所有的教育、科学、文化、卫生、体育等设施；(4)集体所有的其他不动产和动产。"集体所有权的客体虽然不包括专属于国家所有的自然资源等专属性的财产，但相对于个人所有的财产而言，集体所有的财产范围也是非常广泛的。

(3)集体所有权的内容

集体所有权的内容是指集体组织对它所有的财产享有占有、使用、收益和处分的权利。一般来说，集体所有权的各项权能都是由集体组织自己行使的，但是根据生产和经营活动的需要，某个集体组织也可以将其所有权的权能转移给个人行使。

2. 集体所有权的行使和保护

中国《宪法》第 17 条规定："集体经济组织在遵守有关法律的前提下，有独立进行经济活动的自主权。"集体经济组织是自负盈亏的生产经营组织，依照法律的规定，它有权因地制宜地从事生产经营活动，有权决定其生产经营方式，有权独立自主地参与各种民事流转活动，对其在生产经营活动中取得的收益，在照章纳税以后，有权就盈余部分独立进行支配。对于农村集体所有的宅基地、自留山、自留地，集体组织的管理机构有权进行统一规划，或根据实际情况合理调整。集体组织在行使其财产所有权时，必须遵守法律和国家计划，认真实行民主管理。在生产和分配活动中要兼顾国家、集体和个人三方面的利益。《民法典》对集体所有权的行使作了一些具体规定。

劳动群众集体所有的财产，是中国社会主义公共财产的重要组成部分，受国家法律的保护。中国《宪法》规定，社会主义公共财产神圣不可侵犯，其中包括劳动群众集体组织所有的财产。根据《宪法》规定的原则，中国《民法通则》（2009 年修正）第 74 条第 3 款明确规定："集体所有的财产受法律保护，禁止任何组织或者个人侵占、哄抢、私分、破坏或者非法查封、扣押、冻结、没收。"《民法典》第 265 条规定："集体所有的财产受法律保护，禁止任何组织或者个人侵占、哄抢、私分、破坏。农村集体经济组织、村民委员会或者其负责人作出的决定侵害集体成员合法权益的，受侵害的集体成员可以请求人民法院予以撤销。"任何单位和个人不得非法干预集体组织的内部事务，不得以任何借口平调、挪用、侵吞或私分集体所有制企业的资金、利润、厂房、设备、原材料产品等一切资产，不得无偿调动集体所有制企业的劳动力。对于侵犯集体所有制企业的合法权益的行为，企业有权予以抵制，或依法提起诉讼和提出请求。中国民法保护所有权的确认产权、返还原物、恢复原状、排除妨害、赔偿损失等方法，也是保护集体所有权的重要措施。除民事制裁外，必要时还应根据侵犯集体财产的不同程度和细节，另行追究不法行为人的行政责任或刑事责任。

（三）私人所有权

1. 私人所有权的概念和特征

私人所有权是公民个人依法对其所有的动产或者不动产享有的占有、使用、收益和处分的权利。私人所有权是公民个人所有制在法律上的表现。在任何社会条件下，所有权的存在必然导致个人所有权存在。如果消灭了财产的个人所有，使一切财产都成为公有财产，则所有权概念本身也就失去了存在的意义。在社会主义阶段，私人所有权具有其客观存在的必然性。马克思和恩格斯指出："共产主义并不剥夺任何人占有社会产品的权力，它只剥夺利用这种占有去奴役他人劳动的权力。"①把个人所有与社会主义对立起来是不正确的。在中国社会主义初级阶段，个人财产不仅不能消灭，而且必须在法定范围内稳定地发展，这样方能推动竞争和市场的发展，以繁荣国家的社会主义商

---

① 《马克思恩格斯选集》（第一卷），人民出版社 1972 年版，第 288 页。

品经济。

私人所有权具有以下特点：

(1)私人所有权的主体是自然人。

(2)私人所有权的客体范围是非常宽泛的。《民法典》确定的私人所有权的概念，较之于个人所有权，在客体上更为宽泛，不仅包括生活资料，也包括生产资料。《民法典》第 266 条规定："私人对其合法的收入、房屋、生活用品、生产工具、原材料等不动产和动产享有所有权"；该条对私人所有权的客体采取了具体列举和抽象概括相结合的方式。

(3)私人所有权取得的方式是多样的。既可以是合法的劳动，也可以通过投资以及继承、赠与。只要不是法律禁止的方式，都可以采用。

(4)私人所有权的内容广泛。

2. 私人所有权的行使和保护

《宪法》第 13 条规定："公民的合法的私有财产不受侵犯。国家依照法律规定保护公民的私有财产权和继承权。国家为了公共利益的需要，可以依照法律规定对公民的私有财产实行征收或者征用并给予补偿。"《民法典》第 267 条规定："私人的合法财产受法律保护，禁止任何组织或者个人侵占、哄抢、破坏。"私人依法对其所有的生产资料和生活资料享有完全的占有、使用、权益和处分的权利。私人在法律规定的范围内行使其生产资料所有权，从事正当的生产经营活动，或利用其生活资料满足个人的需要，都受法律的保护。任何单位和个人都不得以任何方式无偿平调私人的财产。对于各种非法摊派和收费，公民有权予以拒绝。私人在其所有权受到侵犯时，有权要求侵权行为人停止侵害、返还财产、排除妨害、恢复原状、赔偿损失，或依法向人民法院提起诉讼。

私人在行使所有权时，应当遵守法律和社会公德，遵循诚信原则，不得滥用所有权。

(四)社会团体法人、捐助法人财产所有权

1. 社会团体法人、捐助法人财产所有权的概念和特征

社会团体法人、捐助法人财产所有权，是指社会团体法人、捐助法人依法对其所有的不动产和动产所享有的权利。《民法典》第 270 条规定："社会团体法人、捐助法人依法所有的不动产和动产，受法律保护。"即社会团体法人、捐助法人对其依法所有的财产，享有直接的支配权，不受他人非法干涉。任何组织和个人都不得侵占、挪用、哄抢、破坏和任意调拨社会团体法人、捐助法人依法所有的财产。非经法律规定的权限和程序，不得征收、征用。社会团体所有权的法律特征有：

(1)不能按照所有制归属于任何一类所有权。它实际上是国家、集体和私人所有权以外的一类所有权。

(2)它是一种特殊的法人财产。

(3)其主体是社会团体包括社会团体法人、捐助法人。

2. 关于"社会团体法人、捐助法人"其他法律规范，参见《民法典》第 87 条至第 95 条内容。

第二节　业主的建筑物区分所有权

一、业主的建筑物区分所有权的概念和特征

《民法典》第 271 条规定，业主的建筑物区分所有权，是指业主对建筑物内的住宅、经营性用房等专有部分享有所有权，对专有部分以外的共有部分享有共有和共同管理的权利。

建筑物区分所有制度在德国法上称为"住宅所有权"，法国法中称为"住宅分层所有权"，瑞士法上称为"楼层所有权"，英美法中称为"公寓所有权"。日本称为"区分所有权"，中国大陆学者一般采纳了"建筑物区分所有"概念。中国《民法典》也采纳了这一观点。而建筑物区分所有又是由单独所有和共有构成的。《民法典》第 271 条规定："业主对建筑物内的住宅、经营性用房等专有部分享有所有权，对专有部分以外的共有部分享有共有和共同管理的权利。"在法律上建立区分所有制度，可以明确在区分所有情况下的产权和利益关系，解决各种产权纠纷，维护住户生活的安定，从经济上也可以通过促进房地产交易的繁荣而带动整个经济的发展。业主建筑物区分所有权有以下特征：

1. 集合性（复合性）

业主建筑物区分所有权是由建筑物区分所有人对专有部分的所有权、建筑物区分所有人对共有部分的共有权和共同管理权三种权利组成的，不同于普通物权，如所有权、抵押权等，这些权利具有单一性。

2. 专有部分所有权的主导性

在构成业主的建筑物区分所有权的三要素中，专有所有权具有主导性。表现在：(1)区分所有人取得专有所有权即取得了共有权和成员权；(2)专有所有权大小，决定区分所有权人共有权和管理权(如表决权)的大小；(3)在区分所有权成立登记上，只登记专有所有权，而共有权和成员权则不需要单独登记；(4)业主转让其建筑物专有部分所有权的，其对建筑物共有部分享有的共有和共同管理的权利视为一并转让。

3. 一体性

即构成建筑物区分所有权的三要素须结为一体，不可分离。权利人不能对建筑物区分所有权进行分割行使、转让、抵押、继承或抛弃。

4. 权利主体身份的多重性

这具体表现在：(1)业主是建筑物专有部分的所有权人，可以对其专有部分进行占有、使用、收益和处分，但这些权能又受到其他建筑物专有部分所有权人的制约，即权利人负有不危害其他人利益的义务。(2)业主是建筑物共有部分的共有权人，既可以对全体区分所有人在生活中必须使用的共有财产，如公共楼梯、公共走廊、大门等进行使

用，还可以对依据法律规定和区分所有人之间的共同约定，由其专有使用的共有财产，如地下停车场车位、与一楼连接的庭院等进行排他的、独占性的使用。(3)业主是建筑物区分所有权人组织的成员，享有相应的管理权。

5. 客体的复杂性

业主建筑物区分所有权的客体主要是建筑物，但不限于建筑物。在中国，由于商品房开发都是以小区为单位进行规划和建设的，所以业主的区分所有权的范围已经从建筑物拓展到整个小区，包括小区规划范围内的绿地、道路，小区中的其他公共场所和公共设施。

二、专有部分所有权

(一)专有部分所有权的概念和特征

专有所有权，又称"专有权"或"特别所有权"，是指业主对其建筑物专有部分享有占有、使用、收益和处分的权利。其特征可以概括如下：

(1)具有所有权的效力。其本质上属于所有权。

(2)客体具有特殊性。只能是建筑物经分割后形成的具有一定独立性和可公示性的专有部分。

(3)在权利行使上具有特殊性、限定性。业主与他人基于建筑物会形成共同生活关系，他在行使专有部分所有权时必须受到共同生活规则的制约。《民法典》第272条规定了两方面限制：一是业主行使权利不得危及建筑物的安全，二是业主行使权利不得损害其他业主的合法权益。《民法典》第279条规定："业主不得违反法律、法规以及管理规约，将住宅改变为经营性用房。业主将住宅改变为经营性用房的，除遵守法律、法规以及管理规约外，应当经有利害关系的业主一致同意。"

4. 在建筑物区分所有权中居于主导地位。

(二)专有所有权的客体

专有所有权的客体，是建筑物中的专有部分。专有部分，指在构造上能够明确区分，具有排他性且可独立作用的建筑物部分。一栋建筑物，若无构造与利用上的独立性的专有部分，仅能成立单独所有或共有，不得成立区分所有。因而，专有部分的存在，是建筑物区分所有权成立的基础。

构成专有部分，须具备以下条件：

1. 必须具有构造上的独立性

构造上的独立性又称为"物理上的独立性"，各个部分在建筑物的构造上可以被区分开，可与建筑物其他部分完全隔离，也只有这样才能客观地划分不同部分并为各个所有人独立支配。如一排房屋以墙壁间隔成户。在法律上要求构成上的独立性的原因在于，一方面，由于区分所有是要将建筑物分割为不同部分而为不同所有者单独所有，因此单独所有权的支配权效力所及的客体范围必须明确，要明确划分范围就必须以墙壁、楼地板、大门等作间隔和区分标志。另一方面，只有在客体范围十分明确的情况下，才能确定权利范围，同时准确地判断他人的行为是否构成对某一专有权的损害，如果各个权利的客体都不能区分开，也就很难判定某人的权利是否受到侵害。

2. 必须具有使用上的独立性

也就是说，建筑物被区分为各个部分以后，每一部分都可以被独立地使用或具有独立的经济效用，不需借助其他部分，如区分的部分可以用来住人，用作店铺、办公室、仓库、停车场等。假如区分为各个房间以后，该房间并无独立的出入门户，必须利用相邻的出入单位门户才能出入，则该房间并不具有使用上的独立性，从而不能成为区分所有的客体。

3. 通过登记予以公示并表现出法律上的独立性

构造上和使用上的独立性，乃是经济上的独立性，只有通过登记才能表现为法律上的独立。也就是说，通过登记使被分割的各个部分在法律上形成各个所有权的客体。如果被分割的各个部分登记为各个主体所有，则建筑物作为整体不能再作为一个独立物存在。应当指出的是，通过登记表现出来的法律上独立性，是以构造上和使用上的独立性为基础的，如果构造上或使用上的独立性不复存在，则法律上的独立性也难以存在。例如，原被区分所有的两部分同属于一人，间隔除去后，两部分合二为一，则各部分失去其构造上的独立性或使用上的独立性，应解释为一个所有权。

（三）专有部分范围的确定

《民法典》对专有部分范围、界限如何确定未作规定。在理论上，如何界定区分所有建筑物的专有部分，有五种不同的主张。

1. "中心"说，即"壁心"说

该学说认为区分所有建筑物的专有部分的范围达到墙壁、柱、地板、天花板等境界部分厚度的中心。这种观点对于界定权利的范围较为明确，但是对于建筑物的维护与管理则较为不妥。

2. "空间"说

此学说认为专有部分的范围仅限于墙壁、地板、天花板所围成的空间部分，而界线点上的分割部分如墙壁、地板、天花板等则为全体或者部分区分所有人所共有。该说恰好与"壁心"说相对立，此说实质是扩张区分所有中共有部分的范围，排斥区分所有人对墙壁、地板等进行任何专属性支配。

3. "最后粉刷表层"说

该说认为专有部分包含壁、柱等部分表层所粉刷的部分，亦即壁和其他境界的本体属共用部分，但境界壁最后粉刷的表层部分为专有部分。此说的好处是既可以兼顾区分所有人现实支配的需要，又不会危及建筑物整体的安全。不过其缺点仅在于交易上计算建筑物面积时，所计算的面积实际上包含到壁心的面积，从而与一般的交易习惯所不相符，不易被大众所接受。

4. 折中了壁心说和最后粉刷表层说

由该说形成的主张，称为"壁心和最后粉刷表层"说。该学说认为中央部分属于共有部分，表面层属于专有部分，并认为专有部分的范围应分内部关系与外部关系：在业主内部，专有部分的范围仅及于墙壁、地板等境界部分"表层粉刷的部分"；对于第三人的外部关系，如对专有部分的买卖、保险等，则专有部分之范围及于境界构造物之"中心线"。此说的实质是对"最后粉刷表层说"结合交易习惯而作出的修正，对各方利益的关照更为合理，似乎为最佳之说。

5. "双重性"说

该说主张墙壁具有双重属性，既具有专有财产的性质，又具有共有财产的性质。

在上述各种主张中，通说采用"壁心和最后粉刷表层说"。这是建筑物区分所有权理论中最为精致的理论，能够很好地确定区分所有建筑物的专有部分和共用部分的虚实界限。虚的权利界限，在于壁心，实的权利界限，在于最后粉刷表层。

三、共有权

(一)建筑物区分所有人对共有部分的共有权的概念和特征

共有权，也称"共用部分持分权"或"持分共有所有权部分"，是指建筑物区分所有人依照法律或管理规约的规定，对区分所有建筑物的共有部分所享有的占有、使用和收益的权利。其与一般共有权相比具有以下特征：

1. 从主体上看，身份具有复合性

既是共有权人，也是专有所有权人和区分所有人管理团体的一个成员。而一般的共有所有权人，其身份则是单一的，即只能是共有所有权人。

2. 从客体上看，范围较广泛

共有部分的范围主要包括六个方面：(1)建筑物的基本构造部分，如支柱、屋顶、外墙或地下室等；(2)建筑物的共有部分及附属物，如楼梯、消防设备、走廊、水塔、自来水管道，以及仅为部分区分所有人的共有的部分，如各层楼之间的楼板；(3)建筑物占有的地基的使用权；(4)住宅小区的绿地、道路、物业管理用房；(5)公共场所和公共设施、如小区大门建筑、艺术装饰物等地上或地下共有物和水电、照明、消防、安保等公用配套设施，以及除依法归属于国家或有关法人所有外，原则上应当归属于全体住宅小区的业主的共有物；(6)小区内的空地。

3. 从内容上看，权利义务较为广泛

主要包括：(1)全体区分所有人对建筑物整体所共同享有的权利、义务；(2)对建筑物某一部分共同享有的权利；(3)因一部分区分所有人在一部分共用部分上设定专用使用权而产生的权利、义务；(4)因对建筑物基地的利用而发生的区分所有人与土地所有人之间的权利、义务。

4. 从种类上看,可依不同标准分为不同的种类

如法定共有权和约定共有权,全体共有权和部分共有权,对建筑物的共有权和对附属建筑物的共有权,无负担的共有权和有负担的共有权等。而一般共有权则仅分为按份共有与共同共有两种。

5. 从权利变动上看,区分共有所有权的取得、丧失、变更决定于专有所有权的取得、丧失、变更

即前者系从属于后者而存在,后者处于主导地位。而一般共有权的取得、丧失、变更,则以各共有人独立的行为进行,没有主从关系。

6. 共有权,从标的物的分割上看,区分共有所有权的标的物不得请求分割

而一般共有权的标的物,共有权人可以请求其应有部分的量的分割。

(二)共有部分的范围

1. 法定共有

法定共有,是指依照法律规定由业主对于共有部分享有的共有权。其特点在于,当事人不得在购房合同中通过约定变更归属。《民法典》第 274 条规定:"建筑区划内的道路,属于业主共有,但是属于城镇公共道路的除外。建筑区划内的绿地,属于业主共有,但是属于城镇公共绿地或者明示属于个人的除外。建筑区划内的其他公共场所、公用设施和物业服务用房,属于业主共有。"第 275 条第 2 款规定:"占用业主共有的道路或者其他场地用于停放汽车的车位,属于业主共有。"第 281 条规定:"建筑物及其附属设施的维修资金,属于业主共有。"可见,法定共有主要有:(1)建筑区划内的道路;(2)建筑区划内的绿地;(3)建筑区划内的物业服务用房;(4)占用业主共有的道路或者其他场地用于停放汽车的车位;(5)建筑区划内的其他公共场所、公用设施;(6)建筑物及其附属设施的维修资金。

2. 约定共有

约定共有,是指法律允许当事人通过合同约定为共有而享有的共有权。

(1)车库、车位。《民法典》第 275 条第 1 款规定:"建筑区划内,规划用于停放汽车的车位、车库应当首先满足业主的需要。建筑区划内,规划用于停放汽车的车位、车库的归属,由当事人通过出售、附赠或者出租等方式约定。"《民法典》第 276 条规定:"建筑区划内,规划用于停放汽车的车位、车库应当首先满足业主的需要。"

(2)会所。《民法典》未规定。实务界有两种观点:一种观点认为,取决于商品房销售合同的具体约定,如果合同中没有提及会所,则会所的所有权属于开发商;另一种观点认为,如果没有约定,则会所属于业主共同所有。

四、管理权

(一)业主管理权的概念和特征

业主管理权,是指建筑物区分所有人基于一栋建筑物的构造、权利归属和使用上的

密切关系而形成的作为建筑物管理团体的一员而享有的权利和承担的义务。也可定义为，是指业主基于专有部分的所有权从而对业主的共同财产和共同事务的管理权。业主管理权具有以下特征：

(1)是专属于业主的权利，以专有部分的所有权为基础。

(2)是独立于专有所有权与共有权以外的权利。管理权是对全体业主对共有财产和共同事务所享有的权利和承担的义务。它不仅仅是单纯的财产关系，其中有很大部分是管理关系，具有人法性(管理制度)的因素存在。而专有所有权与共有所有权则为"物法性"因素。

(3)是基于业主之间的共同关系而产生的权利。

(4)是一种具有永续性的权利。由于区分所有人之间的共同关系是基于建筑物的专有部分与共有部分、专有所有权与共有所有权的相互粘连而产生的，因而只要建筑物存在，区分所有人间的团体关系即会存续，原则上不得解散。基于共同关系而产生的成员权与共同关系共始终，并具有永续性。

(5)是一项与专有所有权、共有权密不可分的权利。三者共同构成区分所有权的完整内容。

(6)是针对共有财产和公共事务的权利。管理权与专有所有权和共有所有权一样，是现代区分所有权不可或缺的基本要素。它主要表现的是各区分所有人如何在共同关系事务上决定其意思以及该意思如何得以执行，故本质上属于区分所有权的人法上的范畴，从而也就决定了其不得单独作为让与的客体。

(二)管理权的内容

《民法典》第278条规定："下列事项由业主共同决定：(1)制定和修改业主大会议事规则；(2)制定和修改管理规约；(3)选举业主委员会或者更换业主委员会成员；(4)选聘和解聘物业服务企业或者其他管理人；(5)使用建筑物及其附属设施的维修资金；(6)筹集建筑物及其附属设施的维修资金；(7)改建、重建建筑物及其附属设施；(8)改变共有部分的用途或者利用共有部分从事经营活动；(9)有关共有和共同管理权利的其他重大事项。业主共同决定事项，应当由专有部分面积占比三分之二以上的业主且人数占比三分之二以上的业主参与表决。决定前款第六项至第八项规定的事项，应当经参与表决专有部分面积四分之三以上的业主且参与表决人数四分之三以上的业主同意。决定前款其他事项，应当经参与表决专有部分面积过半数的业主且参与表决人数过半数的业主同意。"

(三)业主大会和业主委员会

《民法典》和国务院于2003年6月8日公布、2007年8月26日、2016年2月6日修订的《物业管理条例》对业主大会和业主委员会分别作了规定。

1. 业主大会

业主大会是物业管理区域内全体业主组成的、管理其共有财产和共同生活事务的自治组织。

《物业管理条例》第 10 条规定，同一个物业管理区域内的业主，应当在物业所在地的区、县人民政府房地产行政主管部门或者街道办事处、乡镇人民政府的指导下成立业主大会，并选举产生业主委员会。但是，只有一个业主的，或者业主人数较少且经全体业主一致同意，决定不成立业主大会的，由业主共同履行业主大会、业主委员会职责。

业主大会应当代表和维护物业管理区域内全体业主在物业管理活动中的合法权益，其职权是由法律、法规以及规约的规定来决定的。《民法典》第 278 条第 1 款规定了业主共同决定的事项，即为对业主大会职权的规定。有关业主大会的职权，除了法律规定之外，还可以通过管理规约来特别决定。

业主大会会议分为定期会议和临时会议。

2. 业主委员会

业主委员会是业主大会的执行机构，受业主大会委托来管理全体业主的共有财产或者共有生活事务。业主可以设立业主大会，选举业主委员会。业主委员会应当自选举产生之日起 30 日内，向物业所在地的区、县人民政府房地产行政主管部门和街道办事处、乡镇人民政府备案。业主委员会委员应当由热心公益事业、责任心强、具有一定组织能力的业主担任。业主委员会主任、副主任在业主委员会成员中推选产生。

业主委员会执行业主大会的决定事项，依照法律、法规履行职责。

3. 业主大会和业主委员会决定的效力及日常管理权

《民法典》第 280 条规定："业主大会或者业主委员会的决定，对业主具有约束力。业主大会或者业主委员会作出的决定侵害业主合法权益的，受侵害的业主可以请求人民法院予以撤销。"第 286 条第 2 款规定："业主大会或者业主委员会，对任意弃置垃圾、排放污染物或者噪声、违反规定饲养动物、违章搭建、侵占通道、拒付物业费等损害他人合法权益的行为，有权依照法律、法规以及管理规约，要求行为人停止侵害、排除妨害、消除危险、恢复原状、赔偿损失。"

（四）业主与物业服务机构的关系

物业服务，是指由业主自行或者委托物业服务机构以及其他管理人，对业主共有财产和共同事务进行管理和服务的行为。《民法典》和《物业管理条例》对物业服务的问题进行了比较全面的规定。

《民法典》第 284 条规定："业主可以自行管理建筑物及其附属设施，也可以委托物业服务企业或者其他管理人管理。对建设单位聘请的物业服务企业或者其他管理人，业主有权依法更换。"第 285 条规定："物业服务企业或者其他管理人根据业主的委托，依照本法第三编有关物业服务合同的规定管理建筑区划内的建筑物及其附属设施，接受业主的监督，并及时答复业主对物业服务情况提出的询问。物业服务企业或者其他管理人应当执行政府依法实施的应急处置措施和其他管理措施，积极配合开展相关工作。"据此，业主在物业服务中享有的权利有：（1）自行管理权；（2）自主聘任权；（3）解聘权。

五、建筑物区分所有权人的其他权利与义务

区分所有权人即业主不得违反法律、法规以及管理规约，将住宅改变为经营性用房。业主将住宅改变为经营性用房的，除遵守法律、法规以及管理规约外，应当经有利害关系的业主一致同意（《民法典》第 279 条）。

建设单位、物业服务企业或者其他管理人等利用业主的共有部分产生的收入，在扣除合理成本之后，属于业主共有（《民法典》第 282 条）。

建筑物及其附属设施的费用分摊、收益分配等事项，有约定的，按照约定；没有约定或者约定不明确的，按照业主专有部分面积所占比例确定（《民法典》第 283 条）。

业主应当遵守法律、法规以及管理规约，相关行为应当符合节约资源、保护生态环境的要求。对于物业服务企业或者其他管理人执行政府依法实施的应急处置措施和其他管理措施，业主应当依法予以配合。业主不得任意弃置垃圾、排放污染物或者噪声，不得做出违反规定饲养动物、违章搭建、侵占通道、拒付物业费等损害他人合法权益的行为。业主或者其他行为人拒不履行相关义务的，有关当事人可以向有关行政主管部门报告或者投诉，有关行政主管部门应当依法处理（《民法典》第 286 条）。

业主对建设单位、物业服务企业或者其他管理人以及其他业主侵害自己合法权益的行为，有权请求其承担民事责任（《民法典》第 287 条）。

第三节　相邻关系

一、相邻关系的概念和特征

相邻关系，是两个或两个以上相互毗邻的不动产的所有人或使用人，在行使不动产的所有权或使用权时，因相邻各方应当给予便利和接受限制而发生的权利义务关系。简单地讲，相邻关系就是不动产的相邻各方因行使所有权或使用权而发生的权利义务关系。例如，甲有一块承包地处于乙的地块中间，甲要行使自己的土地使用权，必须经过乙使用的土地，这样甲乙之间就产生了相邻关系。

相邻关系，从权利角度来看又称为相邻权，是指两个或两个以上相互毗邻的不动产所有人或使用人之间，一方行使所有权或使用权时，享有要求另一方提供便利或接受限制的权利。

相邻关系具有以下特点：

1. 相邻关系是依据法律规定而产生的（是法定的）

其本质上体现了法律对不动产权利的干预。当事人一般来说是不能通过约定来排除有关相邻关系法律规范的适用。

2. 相邻关系的主体是相邻不动产的所有人或使用人

相邻关系是因为主体所有或使用的不动产相邻而发生的，如因为房屋相邻产生了通风采光的相邻关系。在许多情况下，相邻关系的发生也与自然环境有关。例如，甲、乙两个村处于一条河流的上下两个相连的地段，就自然构成了甲、乙两村互相用水的相邻关系。

3. 在内容上，相邻关系因种类不同而具有不同的内容

但基本上包括两个方面：一是相邻一方有权要求他方提供必要的便利，他方应给予必要的方便。所谓必要的便利，是指非从相邻方得到便利，就不能正常行使其所有权或使用权。二是相邻各方行使权利，应尽量避免和减少给对方造成损失，不得滥用其权利。这种相邻权的内容实质上是消极的不作为。

4. 相邻关系的客体不同于一般物权的客体

在中国法学界，对相邻权的客体有三种看法。一种观点认为，相邻权的客体是不动产本身；另一种观点认为，相邻关系的客体是行使不动产权利所体现的利益。相邻各方在行使权利时，既要实现自己的合法利益，又要为邻人提供方便，尊重他人的合法权益。所以，相邻关系的客体是行使不动产的所有权或使用权所体现的财产利益和其他利益。还有一种观点认为，相邻权的客体是相邻各方面实施的行为(作为或不作为)。笔者认为，相邻权的种类十分复杂，不同的相邻权因其内容不同，权利义务所指向的对象及客体也不同。例如，在因土地使用权而发生的相邻关系中，其客体是不动产本身，但是大多数相邻权的客体是行使不动产的所有权或使用权所体现的财产权益和其他权益。所以，相邻权的客体只是行使不动产权所体现的利益。至于相邻各方行为，应视为相邻权的内容而不是客体。

二、相邻关系的种类

相邻关系产生的原因很多，种类复杂。根据中国《民法典》的规定，可以分为两大类型：一是提供积极便利的相邻关系，即用水、排水、通行等关系。二是消极不作为的相邻关系，即要求不动产相邻义务人不得从事一些特定的行为。主要的相邻关系有以下几方面：

(一)因用水、排水产生的相邻关系

《民法典》第290条规定："不动产权利人应当为相邻权利人用水、排水提供必要的便利。对自然流水的利用，应当在不动产的相邻权利人之间合理分配。对自然流水的排放，应当尊重自然流向。"

对自然流水的利用，应当在不动产的相邻权利人之间合理分配。多方共临一水源时，各方均可以自由使用水源，但不得因此损害邻地的用水。土地使用人不得滥钻井眼、挖掘地下水，使邻人的生活水源减少，甚至使近邻的井泉干涸。

对相邻各方都有权利用的自然流水，应当尊重自然形成的流向。任何土地使用人

都不得为自身利益而改变水路、截阻水流；在水流有余时，低地段的相邻人不得擅自筑坝堵截，使水倒流，影响高地的排水；水源不足时，高地段的相邻人不得独自控制水源，断绝低地段的用水。水源一般应按照"由近到远、由高至低"的原则依次灌溉、使用。一方擅自堵截或独占自然流水影响他方正常生产、生活的，他方有权请求排除妨碍；造成他方损失的，应负赔偿责任。相邻一方必须利用另一方的土地排水时，他方应当允许；但使用的一方应采取必要的保护措施，造成损失的，应由受益人合理补偿。

相邻一方可以采取其他合理措施排水而未采取，以致毁损或者可能毁损他方财产的，他方有权要求加害人停止侵害、消除危险、恢复原状、赔偿损失。对于共同使用和受益的渡口、桥梁、堤坝等，相邻各方应共同承担养护、维修的义务。

建造房屋应尽量避免房檐滴水造成对邻人的损害，在发生相邻房屋滴水纠纷时，对有过错的一方造成他方损害的，应当责令其排除妨碍、赔偿损失。

（二）因通行所产生的相邻关系

《民法典》第291条规定："不动产权利人对相邻权利人因通行等必须利用其土地的，应当提供必要的便利。"

（三）因建造、修缮建筑物以及铺设管线所形成的相邻关系

《民法典》第292条规定："不动产权利人因建造、修缮建筑物以及铺设电线、电缆、水管、暖气和燃气管线等必须利用相邻土地、建筑物的，该土地、建筑物的权利人应当提供必要的便利。"

（四）因通风、采光而产生的相邻关系

《民法典》第293条规定："建造建筑物，不得违反国家有关工程建设标准，不得妨碍相邻建筑物的通风、采光和日照。"

（五）保护环境所产生的相邻关系

《民法典》第294条规定："不动产权利人不得违反国家规定弃置固体废物，排放大气污染物、水污染物、土壤污染物、噪声、光辐射、电磁辐射等有害物质。"

（六）因挖掘土地、建造建筑物等发生的相邻关系

《民法典》第295条规定："不动产权利人挖掘土地、建造建筑物、铺设管线以及安装设备等，不得危及相邻不动产的安全。"

三、处理相邻关系的原则

相邻关系是实践中普遍存在的民事关系，如不能正确处理好此种关系，则必然会影

响人们的生产和生活，严重的甚至会造成人身伤亡和财产重大损害，影响社会生产和生活秩序的稳定。所以，正确处理好相邻关系，对于保护相邻人的合法权益，合理使用社会财富，稳定社会正常秩序，具有十分重大的意义。

《民法通则》(2009年修正)第83条规定，"不动产的相邻各方，应当按照有利生产、方便生活、团结互助、公平合理的精神，正确处理截水、排水、通行、通风、采光等方面的相邻关系"。《民法典》第288条规定："不动产的相邻权利人应当按照有利生产、方便生活、团结互助、公平合理的原则，正确处理相邻关系。"根据这一规定，在处理相邻关系时，应遵循如下原则：

(一)兼顾各方的利益，互谅互让、互助团结

相邻各方对土地、山林、草原等自然资源的使用权和所有权发生争议，或因环境污染发生争议以后，必须本着互谅互让、有利团结的精神协商解决；协商不成的，由有关国家机关和人民法院解决。在争议解决以前，争议各方不得荒废土地、山林等自然资源，不得破坏有关设施，更不得聚众闹事，强占或毁坏财产。对故意闹事造成财产损害和人身伤害的，除追究当事人的民事责任外，还应追究其行政责任，甚至刑事责任。

不动产权利人因用水、排水、通行、铺设管线等利用相邻不动产的，应当尽量避免对相邻的不动产权利人造成损害(《民法典》第296条)。

相邻各方在行使所有权或使用权时，要互相协作，兼顾相邻人的利益。以邻为壑，损人利己，妨害社会公共利益的行为，是与相邻关系所应遵循的原则相悖的。人民法院处理相邻关系纠纷，也要兼顾各方的利益，使纠纷得以妥善解决。

(二)有利生产、方便生活

处理因相邻关系发生的纠纷时，应从有利于有效合理地使用财产，有利于生产和生活出发。例如在处理地界纠纷时，如果原来未划定地界，就应当根据如何便于经营管理和有利于生产发展的原则，来确定新的地界线。

(三)公平合理

相邻关系的种类很多，法律很难对各种相邻关系都作出具体规定，这就需要人民法院在处理相邻关系纠纷时，应该从实际出发，进行深入的调查研究，兼顾各方面的利益，适当考虑历史情况和习惯，公平合理地处理纠纷。

(四)依法给予补偿

依据《民法典》第296条规定，不动产权利人利用相邻不动产的，应当尽量避免对相邻的不动产权利人造成损害；造成损害超过合理、容忍范围的，应当给予赔偿。其构成条件为：(1)主要限定于因用水、排水、通行、铺设管线等利用相邻不动产的情形；

(2)利用相邻不动产已造成了实际损失；(3)造成的损害超过合理、容忍范围。

第四节　所有权的取得

一、所有权取得概述

所有权的取得分为原始取得和继受取得。原始取得，是指所有权第一次产生或者不依靠原所有权而取得所有权或者根据法律规定取得新物。原始取得也称最初取得，依这种方式取得的所有权是独立的，或者是原来无所有权，或者与原所有人的所有权和意志无关。法律一般认为，前者包括劳动生产、收取孳息、没收财产、先占、拾得遗失物或发现埋藏物、添附以及善意取得等；后者包括征收等行为。原始取得的主要形式有：

(1)国有化和没收。这是剥夺原所有权的行为。例如，社会主义国有化是剥夺帝国主义、封建主义和官僚资本主义财产的一种方法。没收是对违法所得的财产或用来作为违法手段的财产的剥夺。依国有化取得的所有权是独立的，其所有权归国家；依没收取得的所有权，与原所有人的所有权和意志无关。

(2)生产。任何生产都是对自然界的占有、利用和改造。例如，对自然界的直接占有、捕鱼、采矿，对自然界的间接占有、使用原料制造产品。

(3)添附，包括：(1)附合，如用他人的建筑材料建造房屋；(2)混合，如不同所有人的财产混合不能分别；(3)加工，如在他人的布上画油画。

(4)收益，也称孳息，它分为：(1)天然孳息，如果树、木的结果；(2)法定孳息，如存款利息。

(5)无主财产的取得。无主财产包括抛弃物、拾得物、漂流物、走失动物、埋藏物、隐藏物和无人继承财产等，这是指所有人不明或没有所有人的财产。取得这类财产亦属原始取得。

《民法典》明确规定了善意取得、拾得遗失物、漂流物、埋藏物的权利归属和孳息等所有权取得方式。

继受取得，又称传来取得，指新的所有人通过某种民事法律行为或法律事件而从原所有人那里取得财产所有权，包括买卖、互易、赠与、继承与接受遗赠等其他合法原因。与原始取得不同，它是以原所有人的所有权和/或原所有人转让所有权的意志为根据的。

继受取得的主要依据：

(1)买卖合同：民事主体双方达成协议，出卖人一方将出卖财产交给买受人一方所有，买受人接受此项财产并支付价款。通过买卖，由买受人取得了原属出卖人的财产所有权。

(2)赠与、互易：赠与人自愿将其财产无偿转移给受赠人，或者一方以金钱之外的某种财产与他方的财产相互交换，也可导致所有权的移转。

（3）继承遗产：继承人按照法律的直接规定或者合法有效遗嘱的指定，取得被继承人死亡时遗留的个人合法财产。

（4）接受遗赠：自然人、集体组织或者国家作为受遗赠人，按照被继承人生前所立的合法有效遗赠的指定，取得遗赠的财产。

（5）其他合法原因：因其他合法原因，也可以取得或形成财产所有权，如参加合作经济组织的成员通过合股集资的方式组成合法经济组织，形成新的所有权形式。

二、善意取得

（一）概念和适用范围

善意取得，又称即时取得，是指无处分权人将其动产或不动产转让给受让人，若受让人取得该动产或不动产时出于善意，则受让人将依法取得该动产或不动产的所有权或其他物权。

善意取得是适应商品交换的需要而产生的一项法律制度。在广泛的商品交换中，从事交换的当事人往往并不知道对方是否有权处分财产，也很难对市场上出售的商品逐项调查。如果受让人善意取得财产以后，根据转让人的无权处分行为而使交易结果处于不稳定状态时，买到的商品随时都有可能退还。这样就会造成当事人在交易时的不安全感，也不利于商品交换秩序的稳定。可见，善意取得制度虽然限制了所有权之上的追及权的效力，从而在一定程度上牺牲了所有人的利益，但是它对于维护商品交换的安全和良好秩序具有重要的作用。因此，许多西方国家的民法都确认了善意取得制度。中国《民法典》第311～313条规定了善意取得制度。

根据《民法典》规定，善意取得适用范围是：（1）动产所有权；（2）不动产所有权；（3）其他物权。《民法典》第311条第3款规定："当事人善意取得其他物权的，参照适用前两款规定。"因此，在符合法定条件的情况下，不动产用益物权以及抵押权、质权等担保物权，也可以发生善意取得。

中国以往的法律制度上原则上否定善意取得对遗失物、盗赃物的适用。现在《民法典》第312条对遗失物的善意取得问题作了特别规定："所有权人或者其他权利人有权追回遗失物。该遗失物通过转让被他人占有的，权利人有权向无处分权人请求损害赔偿，或者自知道或者应当知道受让人之日起二年内向受让人请求返还原物；但是，受让人通过拍卖或者向具有经营资格的经营者购得该遗失物的，权利人请求返还原物时应当支付受让人所付的费用。权利人向受让人支付所付费用后，有权向无处分权人追偿。"

（二）善意取得适用的条件

依照《民法典》第311条规定，无处分权人将不动产或者动产转让给受让人的，所有权人有权追回；除法律另有规定外，符合下列情形的，受让人取得该不动产或者动产的所有权：

(1)让与人须为动产的占有人或者登记的不动产权利人。该条件实质上是说让与人（无处分人）对其所处分的他人之物，须具有权利的外观。这一条件是善意取得发生的前提。

(2)让与人须无处分权。包括根本无处分权，也包括欠缺完整的处分权。如一共有人未经其他共有人同意而处分共有物，包括夫妻一方将双方共有不动产登记在自己的名下后，未征得另一方同意私自将该不动产让与他人。

(3)受让人须基于交易行为而支付合理的对价。至于约定的"合理对价"是否已由受让人实际支付，一般并不影响善意取得的成立。

(4)受让人受让财产须为善意。

(5)转让的标的物须已经完成移转登记或者交付给受让人。

对遗失物适用善意取得还有特别条件(《民法典》第314~318条)。

(三)善意取得的效力

(1)发生物权的变动。

(2)动产上的原有利消灭。《物权法》第108条规定："善意受让人取得动产后，该动产上的原有权利消灭，但善意受让人在受让时知道或者应当知道该权利的除外。"

(3)无权处分人的法律责任。原权利人可以基于债权上的请求权要求转让人承担合同责任、侵权责任或不当得利的返还责任，但不能向受让人和其他权利人追及。

三、拾得遗失物

(一)遗失物的概念

遗失物是所有人遗忘于某处，不为任何人占有的物。遗失物只能是动产，不动产不存在遗失的问题。遗失物也不是无主财产，只不过是所有人丧失了对于物的占有，不为任何人占有的物。遗失物须具备以下几个条件：

(1)须是占有人不慎丧失占有的动产。

(2)须是无人占有的动产。

(3)须是拾得人拾得的动产。

(二)拾得人的义务

根据《民法典》第312条规定，遗失物原则上不适用善意取得。也就是说，某人在拾得他人的遗失物以后，将该物非法转让给第三人，受让人即使在受让该财产时是善意的、无过失的，也不能善意取得遗失物的所有权。失主可以继续主张所有权，并请求所有物的返还。《民法典》第314条规定："拾得遗失物，应当返还权利人。拾得人应当及时通知权利人领取，或者送交公安等有关部门。"第316条规定："拾得人在遗失物送交有关部门前，有关部门在遗失物被领取前，应当妥善保管遗失物。因故意或者重大过失致使遗失物毁损、灭失的,应当承担民事责任。"

（三）拾得人的权利

1. 请求支付保管费用。《民法典》第317条第1款规定:"权利人领取遗失物时,应当向拾得人或者有关部门支付保管遗失物等支出的必要费用。"

2. 请求失主按照承诺履行义务。第317条第2款规定:"权利人悬赏寻找遗失物的,领取遗失物时应当按照承诺履行义务。"第317条第3款规定:"拾得人侵占遗失物的,无权请求保管遗失物等支出的费用,也无权请求权利人按照承诺履行义务。"

（四）招领公告期过后遗失物的归属

《民法典》第318条规定:"遗失物自发布招领公告之日起一年内无人认领的,归国家所有。"

四、漂流物的拾得、埋藏物和隐藏物的发现

《民法典》第319条规定:"拾得漂流物、发现埋藏物或者隐藏物的,参照适用拾得遗失物的有关规定。法律另有规定的,依照其规定。"拾得遗失物的有关规定指《民法典》第314~318条。

五、孳息

《民法典》第321条规定:"天然孳息,由所有权人取得;既有所有权人又有用益物权人的,由用益物权人取得。当事人另有约定的,按照其约定。法定孳息,当事人有约定的,按照约定取得;没有约定或者约定不明确的,按照交易习惯取得。"

Chapter 3   Ownership

Section One   Survey of the Ownership

1. Ownership: Concept, Features and Nature

1.1   Concept

In civil law jurisprudence, ownership is usually considered as three kinds of meanings:

First, it may be referred to as the legal system of the ownership, namely, the body of laws and regulations concerning the ownership as a whole. It serves not only as a basic system for the real right law but also for the whole civil law system. Meanwhile, it encompasses other legislations regarding property ownership found in such legal departments as the constitutional, administrative and criminal law.

The second circumstance where ownership is used is when it refers to the legal relations under ownership, which is, the legally defined rights and obligations vested in particular right holders and non-specific duty holders, which arise from the attribution and domination of the property.

As a civil relationship, the ownership relation includes three essential elements: namely, its subject, object and contents (see Section One, Chapter 2 of this book). According the numerus clausus principle, objects of real rights or those of ownership include movable and immovable property, which are mainly tangible things. But the law also stipulates that rights can also be objects of real rights. Hence, where there are special rules regulating such issues, such rules shall prevail.

Third, ownership may allude to the lawful rights an owner enjoys over his property, i. e. , such contents concerning rights under an ownership relation.

The third approach is adopted almost unanimously by various civil law juristicions when defining ownership. Article 544 of the French Civil Code provides that "Ownership is the right of enjoying and disposing of things in the most absolute manner, provided they are not used in a way prohibited by the laws or statutes". This clause presents a rather abstract clarification on the function of ownership. According to Article 240 of the Civil Code stipulates that " An owner is entitled to possess, use, benefit from, and dispose of his own immovable or movable property in accordance with law". This provision only regulates the contents of right enjoyed by an owner.

1. 2 Features of Ownership

As one type of real right, the ownership distinguishes itself from other kinds of real rights with its special features, in addition to those common characteristics of real right.

1. 2. 1 Ownership is jus in re propria. Ownership is a real right enjoyed by the owner over his own property, while jus in re aliena is one right over others' properties.

1. 2. 2 Ownership is an absolute right and a "right against the whole world". To exercise the ownership right, the active assistance of another is not necessary, as the noninterference on the latter's part would suffice. As such, any individual other than the owner is a duty bearer in an ownership relation, assuming an obligation of inaction, which is, not interfering in the realization of ownership right. Unlike this, a creditor's right is exercised by means of the obligor's performance, or more specifically and in most cases, assuming an obligation for action.

1. 2. 3 Ownership is an exclusive right. The owner exclusively possesses the property and enjoys its value or the use value thereof. As he exercises his right, the owner doesn't have to pay any price to any party under private laws, though certain tax and fees may be paid to the State according to public laws. Any interests derived from the disposal of the property by another people goes to the owner as a carrier or manifestation of the general value vested in the ownership right, rather than to the person who has made such disposal. Alternatively, a counter-price should be paid to an owner when the owner's property has been used unless the law provides otherwise or the parties stipulate otherwise. In view of this, a line of demarcation may be drawn between ownership and jus in re aliena by judging whether the right holder has to transfer or safekeep for another the income he has acquired through or profited from the use of the property.

1. 2. 4 Ownership is an original real right. This means that it is not derived from other property rights but rather, comes from the direct attribution of property by law. Different from ownership, other real rights are derived from ownership as a result of power division of ownership.

1. 2. 5 Ownership is a complete real right. Ownership is an all-inclusive dominating right that encompasses the powers to possession, utilization, profit and disposition, all of which may be exercised freely within the legal framework and not subject to any unilateral restriction imposed by others. Unlike ownership, jus in re aliena is limited, incomplete and inadequate,

its right holder in general cases holds only part of the use or the exchange value of a property and may only exercise one, two, or three of the afore-mentioned four powers. Even if all the four powers could be enforced, the right is still subject to the restraints imposed by the owner. Thus, it is insufficient compared with the ownership right.

1.2.6   Ownership is with incompatibility. The ownership owner enjoys over his property excludes any illegal interference and allows for no impairment or infringement. This makes indispensable the principle of "one property one right", namely, one thing allows for only one ownership. In the context of jus in re aliena, however, the same principle is not to be so strictly implemented. Multiple real rights (e. g. , ownership and one or several jus in re aliena) may coexist in one property. The owner is entitled to claim for restitution of property, cessation of infringement, removal of the nuisance or compensation for loss when the property is unlawfully possessed by another people or the ownership is otherwise encroached upon.

1.2.7   Finally, ownership is with restoring power or elasticity. Undoubtedly, an owner may, in the pursuit of his own interests, create a jus in re aliena in his property. In such case, the ownership remains no longer complete due to the limitations brought up by the created right. However, the state of completeness will be restored once such jus in re aliena is eliminated and the restrictions removed. For jus in re aliena, on the other hand, there is no such effect as restoring power or elasticity, as the contents of the right themselves are fixed with limitations and will lead to the extinguishment of jus in re aliena in due course.

1.3   Differences between Ownership, Property and Property Right

Property is a concept commonly adopted in Anglo-American law system, and scholars in continental law jurisdictions also do use it. Property and ownership are interchangeable under most circumstances but still distinguish from each other in strict sense. First, property can be tangible or intangible, as a general term covering the two forms. However, ownership may only have tangible things as its object. Otherwise, if the ownership's object could be intangible the boundary between the ownership and other forms of rights may be obscured. Second, the connotation of property is much broader than ownership. It can be an absolute right or other rights or interests. In other words, ownership, other real rights, intellectual property rights and creditor's right may all fall into the category of property. In this sense, one may say that ownership is one subcategory of property.

Differences may also be observed between ownership and property right. The property right refers to the right whose contents are property-related and that embodies certain substance interests. As the counterpart of property right, non-property right has contents that are not related to property but rather, to those interests reflected in person. Basically, it encompasses such personal rights as personality right and right of status, which are all civil rights that are inseparable from the person. Since any right with economic value may be categorized as property right, the contents of the latter are rather wide-ranging, making property right a superordinate of ownership. As one category of property right, ownership, together with other real rights, contributes to form a relatively independent system in civil law, namely, the real right law (system). In comparison, property right indicate not any single type of right but a bunch of civil rights. It is a collection of excerpts from various civil law systems such as the real right law, the law of obligations the intellectual property law, etc. Admittedly, property rights, such as real rights, claims and right to inheritance all encompass contents related to economic interests, but their natures, features and means of protection are largely different from each other. Suffice it to say, their individuality prevails over their similarities.

2. Powers of Ownership

Powers of ownership are the various measures that are legally adoptable by an owner in the pursuit of his exclusive interests over the property he owns. The powers of ownership reflect its various functions and indicate the possibilities of the owner or a person authorized by the owner to conduct certain category or series of acts. For instance, the power to disposition enables the owner to use his property for consumption, payment, donation, transaction, lease or processing. Among these various acts of disposition, most may be entrusted to another person except living consumption. The powers of ownership are increasingly important due to the growing number of ways to utilize things as a result of social and economic development.

According to Article 240 of the Civil Code, possession, utilization, profit and disposition are the four kinds of powers vested in ownership.

2. 1 Power of Possession

Possession is the fact that a subject holds a property with an intention to possess or control it. It is a state of actual control that requires physical contact with the property, thus also known as a management over a thing. In any case, an intention to possess is still indispensable. De facto possession doesn't mean that it is without legal significance. On the contrary, it forms the basis of legal relations. A possessor acquires possessory right or even ownership over a thing by means of possession. In fact, the state of possession itself is legally protectable even if no right has been created. As such, possession is of great legal significance.

Possession can either be authorized or unauthorized, depending on whether it is founded on authorization. Authorized possession is such possessory right that is established by law or through agreement. The right on which possession is based is legally termed as title. Contractual claims (e. g. , deposit or lease) or real rights (e. g. , ownership or usufruct) may be possible titles. In cases of authorized possession, a title is also present. As to its relationship with possession, a title is safeguarded by means of protecting possession when there is usurpation. On the other hand, a title strengthens the state of possession in that the latter state will be maintained so long as the title is defended. In a word, possession in the presence of a title is authorized or with justified source, while that without title it is unauthorized, such as a thief's possession of stolen goods, or a lessee's overdue possession of a leased property.

Unauthorized possession may be further divided into possession in good faith and possession in bad faith. The former means that the unlawful possessor does not know and should not have known that his possession is unlawful when his possession started. For instance, a purchaser who acquires possession of a property without any knowledge that the person who sold it to him at a reasonable price was unauthorized is deemed as in good faith. In cases where a possessor is with actual knowledge or has already raised doubts about his title of possessing the property, he is deemed in bad faith.

The division between possession in good and bad faith is meaningful in light of the following aspects:

First, in cases where the possessor has illegally transferred a movable property to a third party, such transferee may acquire ownership if he possesses the property in good faith.

Second, a person who possesses a property peacefully, openly and continuously for a statutory period with an intention to own may acquire the ownership thereof under the doctrine of acquisitive prescription if he has acted in good faith.

Third, when it involves return of unjust enrichment, a possessor in good faith is only obliged to return that benefit, to the extent of which the benefit exists. He is not responsible for the damaged interests. However, a possessor in bad faith will still be obliged to compensate under such circumstance.

Fourth, in cases of restitution of property, an owner shall compensate the possessor, if the possessor is a bona fide one, for his expenses necessitated for safekeeping of the property. The owner may request the person to return the fruits that have been obtained. For a possessor in bad faith, however, the fruits may be required back and his expenses incurred will not be reimbursed by the owner.

2. 2 Power of Utilization

Utilization is the use of property in accordance with their nature and functions for the purpose of satisfying one's need in production and living. Power to utilization is one set of right contents of such nature.

Essentially, it is determined by the use value of a property, which value is realized to satisfy the owner's need, thereby reflects the owner's will and interests. Any individual other than the owner shall not impair such exercise of right on the part of the owner.

As to the owner, the power to utilization enables him to freely use the property and obtain the natural and legal fruits thereof subject to restrictions of the law.

Power to utilization is directly effected over a thing thus requires physical possession. When a property is separated from its owner, the power of utilization is then set apart from the ownership, which means, the power to utilization may be vested in a non-owner. As such power vested in a non-owner is derived from ownership, the non-owner shall exercise it in accordance with statutory or contractual provisions.

2. 3   Power of Profit

Power to profit means to obtain economic interests from a property, namely, to acquire the newly-increased economic value gendered by the property, including natural and legal fruits.

Ownership should be economically realized. The purpose of owning a property is to acquire its use value (utilize), exchange value (dispose) and other possible value derived therefrom (profit). This is the aim of commodity producers especially in market economy.

In the modern market economy, power of profit is not only a component but also a most fundamental content of ownership. In economic life, it is closely related to the use of a property and usually materializes as the fruits generated by the production and operation of means of existence. However, the process and fruits of operation belong to different categories, making it possible that powers of utilization and to profit go to different subjects in a legal context. For example, shareholders who make capital contribution may obtain profit therefrom on the basis of their equity while the target company possesses and utilizes the assets contributed by its shareholders. The case with enterprise leasing business is much similar to this. As the modern market economy is also a monetary one, a property owner may not attach much weight to the possession and utilization of his property because he is more interested in the economic value. As long as his property is appreciated in value, the powers of possession, utilization or even disposition may be transferred. The power of profit stands out starkly against such economic background, becoming the most fundamental content of ownership.

Power to profit may also be independent from ownership, thus vested in a non-owner. In the modern economy non-proprietary management, the separation of the power to profit and ownership often takes place as the following forms: (1) The owner makes a contract with a manager, in which the owner transfers the manager the power to possession, utilization and disposition over his asset. The owner partially retains the power to profit in proportion to what has been agreed upon. (2) The owner transfers another people his power of possession and utilization, retaining the power of disposition and part of the power of profit, as is the case with the right of land use in China. (3) An owner transfers the power of utilization and profit within a certain period, reserving only the power of disposition. For instance, the State allocates bare hills and tidal flats to collectives or individuals for development and does not obtain profit therefrom within a certain period to encourage the development of these natural resources. Of course, the permanent transfer of the full power of profit is impossible as ownership cannot be economically realized under such condition.

2.4　Power of Disposition (or Jus Disponendi)

It means to manage a property and decide its fate within the legal limits.

Disposal may be either de facto or de jure. De facto disposal refers to the consumption of a property either for production or living purposes. It physically disposes a property, transforming or extinguishing its physical existence. Production consumption sometimes may cause a property to be physically expanded, as products of labor accumulated in production can be converted into commodity. As for living consumption, it usually results in the simultaneous extinction of a property itself and its value, like in the case where the rice is boiled and consumed. Still, it is to be noticed that de facto disposal is not the same as the utilization of a property, which causes only depreciation rather than transformation or extinction, though it may finally lead to disposal (e. g. , abandonment) when the property can no longer be used.

De jure disposal means disposition of properties through juristic acts, i. e. , transfer. It shifts the exchange value of a property.

De facto and de jure disposal respectively cause ownership to vanish absolutely or relatively. Therefore, the power to disposition is the core of ownership right because it determines to whom the property goes. Nonetheless, such power may be vested in a non-owner as the result of statutory stipulation or the realization of will on the part of the owner, which is in the cases with lien, mortgage and pledge.

3. Categories of Ownership

The category of the ownership refers to the different types of the ownership, and reflects the form of ownership, which at this stage in China, mainly consists of three basic forms, namely, ownership of the State, the Collective and the individual person. Although all three forms reflect the characters of the system of socialist pubic ownership, they separately display their own natures, requirements as well as legal features. These features manifest not only in the differences of right holders, the scope of the objects (e. g. , the land only can be owned by State or collective organizations but not by individuals) but also in the ways of exercising the rights (e. g. , the State ownership is exercised through certain administrative acts). These distinctions constitute the standards in categorizing different ownership. In addition, the Civil Code also regulates the ownership of social-organization legal persons and donation-funded legal persons.

3. 1   Ownership of the State

3. 1. 1   Concept and Features of State Ownership

For China, the socialist country is not only the undertaker of state power, but also the proprietor of state-owned property. As one subcategory of ownership under a socialist regime, ownership of the State refers to such right that enables the State to possess, utilize, obtain profit from and dispose of state-owned property. Essentially, it is a manifestation of the socialist system of ownership by the whole people① in the law.

Ownership by the whole people is a system under which members of a society collectively possess the community's means of production. At the current stage, direct possession is impossible, and the chance of one individual exercising the right of disposal on behalf of all the community members is also slim. Therefore, the control over the nation's means of production has to be realized through a social center which, as long as states exist, has to be the State. The system of public ownership ensures the socialist nation to exercise unified leadership and administration over economic activities under such ownership system for the common interests of the whole people. For this reason, the socialist system of ownership by the whole people is inevitably reflected as the State ownership in law.

3. 1. 1. 1   Specific right holder. The ownership of the State is essentially a legal relationship. Its right holder is the State and its duty holders are any indeterminate entities or individuals other than the State. All duty holders are obliged not to encroach upon the state-owned property. As for the right holder, it is also the subject of the administrative power. The two different identities are separable when the accordant right is being exercised. Such separation between the State's status as an owner and that as the subject of administrative power is a prerequisite for the separation of government functions from enterprise management②, as well as the development of the socialist market economy. Under China's current state system, the State ownership is exercised by the State Council on the right holder's behalf. When exercising its ownership, the State may alienate certain power to other social organizations or individuals for their holding or exercise, but the latter cannot become the owner in any event. Likewise, state agencies, regardless of their administrative hierarchy, are not the owner even if

---

①   It means that the working people, as a community, collectively own the means of production. Such ownership is indivisible and shall be exercised collectively by the right holder. At present , it is one specific form of the ownership by the whole people and exercised by the State on the proprietor's behalf.

②   It means to establish healthy relationship between the State and state-owned enterprises, make clear the different status of the state and state-owned enterprises in social economic system, divide the ownership and operation right of state-owned properties in economic performance, and turn the enterprises to legal person and subjects of market competition that can make its own managerial decision, can assume sole responsibility for its own profits or losses, can realize self-development and can take self-discipline.

they do exercise certain ownership right on behalf of the State. Otherwise, the unified ownership system may be at the peril of falling apart into ownership of the State, the local government and the State department, thereby fundamentally reforming the nation's system of ownership by the whole people.

3.1.1.2   Wide scope of object. Article 242 of the Civil Code provides that "Where an immovable or movable property is provided by law to be exclusively owned by the State, no organization or individual may acquire ownership of it". According to the Constitution and other civil law provisions, "natural resources such as land in the cities, mineral resources, waters, forests, grassland, unreclaimed land, fishing ground, etc. are exclusively owned by the State and shall not be encroached upon or illegally transferred by sales or other means". Articles 247 to 254 of the Civil Code give detailed stipulation on the state-owned properties, which include wild animal and plant resources that are provided by law to be owned by the State, radio-frequency spectrum resources, and cultural relics that are provided by law to be owned by the State. Compared with the ownership of the collective and the individual persons, the ownership of the State has a wider scope of object which covers almost everything, while the former two kinds of ownership do not. Nonetheless, the wide sphere of state-owned property does not mean that property owned by the collective or individual persons may be arbitrarily "upgraded" into state-owned property or nationalized.

3.1.1.3   Special ways of acquisition. Because of its special status as both the sovereignty holder and undertaker of state power, the State may either compulsorily acquire private or collective properties through such ways as expropriation, nationalization or confiscation with its public power, or levy taxes using its administrative power thus appropriating state-owned property. In addition, it can also obtain ownership by other means including taking unclaimed lost property, drift-stuff or buried or hidden things whose right holders are unclear, or attaining things that are without inheritors or legatees[1].

3.1.1.4   Unique ways of exercising the right. Direct exercise of State ownership is difficult as the right holder is an abstract entity. Therefore, the right has to be realized through legally authorized state agencies, other business and institutions as well as enterprises invested by the State in accordance with laws.

3.1.2   Protection of Ownership of the State

One joint mission of all legal departments in China is to protect the ownership of the State. The Constitution provides with clarity that, "Socialist public property is sacred and inviolable". Article 258 of the Civil Code prescribes that, "The State-owned property is protected by law, and no organization or individual may misappropriate, loot, secretly distribute, intercept, or

---

[1]   Legatee means someone who receives a legacy money or property from a decedent.

destroy such property". Here, illegal possession refers to possession of state-owned property without authorization from the State or any consent of its agencies, for example, unauthorized use of state-owned land and other natural resource, seizure of the state-owned realities or other properties, defalcation, abuse of power for personal interest, embezzlement of state properties, etc. As for looting, it means deliberately and illegally taking state-owned property with force, for instance, plundering properties of the state-owned enterprises by taking advantage of its closure, merger or transfer. Private division is the distribution of state-owned property among individuals or organizations without approval, for example, payment of bonus or physicals under various invented pretexts. "Withholding" means none or incomplete transfer of such taxes or other interests which are due to the State. Destruction is directly destroying state-owned property by illegal means, for instance, to carry out mining without concession, denude forest or other woodlands, to kill precious animals, to excavate ancient tombs without permission, or to intentionally damage historic sites. The afore-mentioned unlawful acts all encroach upon the ownership of the State and shall entail civil liabilities on the part of the tortfeasor. The protection of state-owned property also requires safeguards for dynamic benefits. It is necessary to place importance on the Protection of state-owned assets for the ownership of the state being economically realized.

Special provisions to avoid the loss of state assets may be found in the Para. 1, Article 259 of the Civil Code provides that "Institutions and their staff with the duties of administration and supervision over the State-owned property shall strengthen the administration and supervision of the State-owned property in accordance with law, strive to preserve and increase the value of such property and prevent any loss thereof; they shall assume legal liabilities in accordance with law if losses are caused to the State-owned property as a result of their abuse of powers or dereliction of duties". The second paragraph of the same article further stipulates that "A person, who causes losses to the State-owned property by transferring it at low prices, secretly distributing it in conspiracy with other persons, creating a security interest on it without authorization, or by other means in the course of enterprise restructuring, merger or division, affiliated transactions, and the like, in violation of the provisions on the administration of the State-owned property, shall bear legal liability in accordance with law".

3. 2   Collective Ownership

3. 2. 1   Concept and Features of Collective Ownership

The Constitution stipulates that the basis of the socialist economic system of the People's Republic of China is socialist public ownership of the means of production, namely, ownership by the whole people and collective ownership by the working people. The sector of economy under the ownership of the collective constitutes an important component of the public sector of the nation's economy. In China, the ownership of the collective is the right of the collective organizations of the working masses or their members to possess, utilize, obtain profit from and dispose of the collective property. It is a reflection of the collective ownership of the working people in law. Its features may be observed from the following three aspects:

3.2.1.1 Subject of Collective Ownership

Nationwide, the subject of collective ownership is by no means uniform. It may be any independent but equal collective organization of the working masses. These organizations, mostly with the status of legal persons, are in mutual cooperation with or independent from each other. They are mainly rural collectives, but also include urban-town collectives and cooperative collectives. Their members may also be the subject the collective ownership when taken as a whole. Article 261 of the Civil Code regulates on this matter, stipulating that "The immovable and movable property of a farmer collective are collectively owned by the members of this collective". Property collectively owned by the working masses and that privately owned by the individual member of the collective organization are to be distinguished by law. An individual member or a part of the members of the collective organization cannot be the subjects of the collective ownership. Viewed in this, the concept "collective" does have its special meaning in civil law. It may either refer to an organization or the members of such organization. In any case, however, it does not include organizations without legal personality such as partnership or other unincorporated bodies.

3.2.1.2 Object of Collective Ownership

Land belonging to the collectives as is provided for by law is an important object of the collective ownership. In China, the land ownership may either be vested in the whole people or the collectives. According to Article 10 of the Constitution, "Land in the cities is owned by the State. Land in the rural and suburban areas is owned by collectives except for those portions which belong to the State as prescribed by law; house sites and privately farmed plots of cropland and hilly land are also owned by collectives". The Civil Code also has specific provision regarding the object of the collective ownership. Article 260 states that "The collectively-owned immovable and movable property include: (1) the land, forests, mountain ridges, grasslands, unreclaimed land and mudflats that are provided by law to be owned by collectives; (2) the buildings, production facilities, and farmland water conservancy facilities that are owned by collectives; (3) the educational, scientific, cultural, public health, sports, and other facilities that are owned by collectives; and (4) any other immovable and movable property that are owned by collectives". Although property exclusively owned by the State, for example, natural resources belonging to the State, are excluded, the object of the collective ownership still has a wide scope when compared with that of the private property.

3. 2. 1. 3   Contents of Collective Ownership

Contents of the ownership of the collective refer to the right of a collective to possess, utilize, obtain profit from and dispose of its properties. In general, all the powers under the ownership of the collective are exercised by the collective itself, but they may be partially transferred to an individual if it is necessary for production or operation.

3. 2. 2   Collective Ownership: Exercise and Protection

According to Article 17 of the Constitution, "Collective economic organizations have decision-making power in conducting independent economic activities, on condition that they obey the relevant laws". As production and operation organization are with full responsibility for profits and losses, the collective economic organization is entitled by law to conduct production and operate activities according to the local conditions, to decide on its production and operation pattern and to independently engage in civil transactions. As to the after-tax profit produced by these activities, the collective organization may dispose them at its sole discretion. The management bodies of the collective may exercise unified management over the rural collective organization's house sites and plots of cropland and hilly land allotted for their private use, and make adjustment accordingly. While enforcing ownership, the collective organization must abide by laws and state plans and implement democratic management. During production and distribution, such organization shall well compromise the interests of the State, the collectives and individuals. Specific provisions regarding the exercising of the collective ownership may be found in the Civil Code.

Property collectively owned by the working masses is an important component of China's socialist public property system, thus protected by Law. The Constitution stipulates that socialist public property is sacred and inviolable, which includes property collectively owned by the working masses. Based on such principle, Para. 3, Article 74 of the General Principles of the Civil Law (2009 Amendment) provides that "Collectively owned property shall be protected by Law, and no organization or individual may seize, encroach upon, privately divide, destroy or illegally seal up, distrain, freeze or confiscate it. " Article 265 of the Civil Code stipulates that "The property owned by a collective is protected by law, and no organization or individual may misappropriate, loot, secretly distribute, or destruct such property. Where a decision made by a rural collective economic organization, a villagers' committee, or the person in charge thereof infringes upon the lawful rights and interests of a member of the collective, the infringed member may request the people's court to revoke the decision". Any unit or individual should refrain from interfering with the internal affairs of a collective organization, or transferring, misappropriating, privately dividing for whatever reasons assets of a collective-owned enterprise including its funds, profit, workshops, facilities, equipment, raw materials and products, or using without consideration labor force of such enterprises. A collective-owned enterprise is entitled to resist any act that is in violation of its lawful interests, or to file a suit or claim for protection in accordance with the law. Such modes as confirmation of ownership, restitution of property, restoration of the original state, removal of the nuisance and compensation for loss are also the major measures for the protection of ownership of the collective. In addition to civil liabilities, administrative or criminal liability may also be entailed according to the circumstances and degree of the wrongdoer's encroachment upon the collective property.

3. 3　Private Ownership

3. 3. 1　Concept and Features of Private Ownership

The private ownership is the right of an individual to possess, utilize, obtain profit from and dispose of its movable property or immovable property. It is a reflection of the system of ownership of individual persons in law. It is the inevitable product of ownership under any social condition. This is because if private ownership were eliminated, namely, all properties became publicly-owned, then the existence of ownership itself would lose its meaning. In the stage of socialism, private ownership is inevitable. As is put by Karl Marx and Friedrich Engels, "Communism deprives no man of the power to appropriate the products of society; all that it does is to deprive him of the power to subjugate the labor of others by means of such appropriations. " To assert that private ownership and socialism stand in opposition to each other is incorrect. In the primary stage of socialism, private property cannot be eliminated in China, rather, it should make steady progress within the legal limit for the advancing of competition and market as well as the prospering of the nation's socialist commodity economy.

Features of private ownership may be summarized as follows:

First, its subject is a natural person.

Second, the scope of its object is wide. Under its concept as framed by the Civil Code, private ownership has a much broader object scope compared with individual ownership. Its object encompasses both means of subsistence and of production. Article 266 of the Civil Code provides that "A private individual has the right to own his lawful income, houses, articles for daily use, production tools, raw materials, as well as other immovable and movable property". This provision adopts an enumerative approach combined with abstraction when defining the object of private ownership.

Third, the ways to acquire private ownership are diverse, including lawful labor, investment, inheritance, donation, etc. , as long as not legally prohibited.

Fourth, it boasts rather rich contents.

3. 3. 2　Exercise and Protection of the Private Ownership

Article 13 of the Constitution states that "Citizens' lawful private property is inviolable. The State, in accordance with law, protects the rights of citizens to private property and to its inheritance. The State may, in the public interest and in accordance with law, expropriate or requisition private property for its use and shall make compensation for the private property expropriated or requisitioned. " Article 267 of the Civil Code regulates that "The property lawfully owned by a private individual is protected by law, and no organization or individual may misappropriate, loot, or destruct such property". An individual is legally entitled to possess, utilize, obtain profit from and dispose of his means of production and subsistence. Such lawful exercise of ownership regarding means of the production, undertaking of production and operating activities and utilization of means of subsistence for individual needs, are all legally protected. No units or individuals may transfer without compensation for another's property. Citizens have the rights to resist illegal apportions and charges, to claim for cessation of infringement, restitution of property, removal of the nuisance or compensation for loss and to file an action in a people's court in accordance with law.

When exercising his ownership right, an individual should comply with the laws, social ethics and the principle of good faith. Meanwhile, he should not abuse his right.

3. 4　Ownership of Social-organization Legal Persons and donation-funded legal persons

3. 4. 1　Concept and Features of Ownership of Social Organization Legal Persons and donation-funded legal persons

The ownership of social-organization legal persons and donation-funded legal persons is the right legally enjoyed by a social-organization legal person or a donation-funded legal person over its immovable property or movable property. Article 270 of the Civil Code provides that "The immovable and movable property that is lawfully owned by a social-organization legal person or a donation-funded legal person is protected by law". A social-organization legal person or a donation-funded legal person enjoys direct control over property lawfully owned by it free from illegal interference of other persons. No organization or individual may embezzle, misappropriate, loot, destruct or arbitrarily allocate such property. No expropriation or requisition may be carried out without statutory authority and procedure. The ownership of social-organization legal persons and donation-funded legal persons have the following legal features:

First, it cannot be categorized into any form of ownership under the ownership system standard. In fact, it is a type of ownership besides ownership of the State, the Collective and the individual person.

Second, it is a special kind of property owned by legal persons.

Third, its subjects are social organizations including social-organization legal persons and donation-funded legal persons.

3.4.2　Other provisions on social-organization legal persons and donation-funded legal persons, please refer to Articles 87 to 95 of the Civil Code.

Section Two　Ownership of a Building's Units

1. Concept and Features of Ownership of a Building's Units

According to Article 271 of the Civil Code, the ownership of a building's units means that a unit owner has the ownership over an exclusive unit of a building, such as a dwelling space or a space used for operating businesses, and has the right to co-own and jointly manage the common space other than the unit.

The ownership of a building's units finds its counterpart in the German law as "Wohnungseigentum", in French law as "la copropriete des immeuloles bates", in Swiss law as "Stockwerkeigentum", and in Anglo-American law as "condominium ownership". In Japan, it is termed "building unit ownership", and most scholars of Chinese mainland adopt the term "owners' partitioned ownership of building areas" or "divisional ownership of buildings". The Civil Code also adopts this view. The ownership of a building's units consists of exclusive ownership and joint co-ownership. Article 271 of the Civil Code provides that "A unit owner has the ownership over an exclusive unit of a building, such as a dwelling space or a space used for operating businesses, and has the right to co-own and jointly manage the common space other than the unit". The establishment of the condominium right system in law helps to define the attribution of property rights and interests, settle disputes arising therefrom, maintain the stable life of inhabitants and provide a boost to the economy through prospering real estate transactions. Its features may be listed as below:

First, the ownership of a building's units is a group of rights compounded of ownership of the exclusive or special parts, the right of sharing and jointly managing the common parts other than the special parts. This is different from such single real right as ownership or mortgage.

Second, the ownership of the exclusive units is dominant among the three components of the condominium right, as is indicated in the following few aspects. (1) An owner acquires joint co-ownership and membership right once he obtains the exclusive ownership of the special parts. (2) The scope of the exclusive right determines that of the joint co-ownership and membership right (e.g., the right to vote). (3) Upon establishment of the condominium right, only the exclusive ownership is required to be registered, while the joint co-ownership and membership right are spared. (4) If an owner transfers his ownership of the exclusive units, his joint co-ownership and membership right of the parts other than the exclusive units will be deemed as transferred along with what is transferred.

Third, the ownership of a building's units is a cohesive unit. Its three components are to be viewed in integrity. The right holder may not separate the three when exercising, transferring, mortgaging, inheriting or abandoning his ownership of a building's units.

Fourth, the subject of the ownership of a building's units has multiple identities, as may be observed from the following few aspects. (1) He may possess, utilize, obtain profit from and dispose of the exclusive units subject to the limits set by the exclusive ownership of other property owners. In other words, he is obliged not to prejudice the interests of others. (2) The proprietor may, as a joint owner of the common parts, utilize such common properties that are indispensable to daily life as the common stairs, corridors and or the gates, etc. Also, he may exclusively use such common properties that are subject to his sole use according to law or the mutual agreement of all owners, e. g. , underground parking spaces, yards conjoined to the first floor, etc. (3) The proprietor enjoys the management right as a member of the proprietors' committee or assembly.

Fifth, the ownership of a building's units has rather complicated object. Generally, its objects are buildings, but are not limited to buildings. In China, as the commodity houses are usually developed and constructed as a whole neighborhood, the divisional ownership accordingly extends from the buildings to the entire neighborhood including the greens, roads as well as other public places and facilities located therein.

2. Ownership of the Exclusive Units

2. 1   Concept and Features of Ownership of the Exclusive Units

Exclusive ownership, also known as exclusive right or special ownership, is the right enjoyed by an owner to possess, utilize, gain benefit from and dispose of the special parts of the building, whose features may be illustrated from the following aspects:

2. 1. 1   It is essentially a type of ownership, thus encompasses all the effects of the category of ownership.

2. 1. 2   Its object is very special because it may only be special parts severed from a building, which are independent and open for publication.

2. 1. 3   The exercise of the right is special and restrictive. It must be subject to certain restrictions set by the regulations agreed upon among the owners based on their co-inhabitance of the building. Article 272 of the Civil Code sets two limits regarding this matter: first, the owner shall not endanger the safety of the building; second, he shall not infringe the lawful rights and interests of other owners therein. Article 279 of the Civil Code provides that "No unit owner may turn a dwelling space into a space used for operating businesses in violation of laws, regulations, or the stipulations on management. A unit owner who intends to turn a dwelling

space into a space used for operating businesses shall, in addition to abiding by laws, regulations, and the stipulations on management, obtain unanimous consent from all interested unit owners".

2.1.4 It is a dominant component of the ownership of a building's units.

2. 2 Object of the Ownership of the Exclusive Units

The object of the ownership of the exclusive units is the special or exclusive units of a building. These parts are technically separated and exclusive units of a building with independent functions. They are the basis of ownership of a building's units because there may only be independent ownership or co-ownership over a building without them.

The following elements are indispensable for a special part:

First, structural or physical independence. This means that each part is structurally severable from each other in the building. Only in this way can the building be divided into different parts for the independent disposal of various owners. For instance, a house may be subdivided into several single households by partition walls. The legal necessity of structural independence lies in that, on the one hand, divisional ownership requires that a building must be subdivided into various parts for the sole ownership of various proprietors. Therefore, the object to which the disposal effect of each single ownership extends must be clearly defined, which makes walls, floors and doors important identifying symbols for partition. On the other hand, it is possible to fix the boundary of a right and in turn, to determine whether certain acts violate such exclusive right, only when the object of such right is clearly defined. Otherwise, the identification of damage will become an arduous work.

Second, independent functions. After being severed from a building, each single part should be of independent use or economic efficacy without any aid of other parts. For instance, the partitioned part may be used as a residential unit, stores, offices, warehouses, parking lots, etc. In cases where a partitioned room has no entrance or exit of its own and the access to it requires the servitude of an adjacent unit, such room may not become object of divisional ownership due to lack of independent functions.

Third, publication by way of registration manifesting its legal independence. Tectonic and functional independence are both economic characters. They may become legal parts only though registration. In other words, the partitioned parts become possible objects of the various partitioned ownerships after registration. At the same time, the building as a whole remains no longer an independent property. It is worth pointing out that legal independence manifests in registration and is grounded on tectonic and functional independence. Absent these two characters, the legal independence will also no longer exist. For example, when two separate parts come to be owned by one person and the partitions are removed, the two parts will lose their tectonic and functional independence and become one. Under such circumstance, it shall be deemed that there exists only one ownership.

2. 3   Determining the Exclusive Units

The Civil Code does not stipulate a clear scope or definition regarding the exclusive units. In theory, there are five opinions on this matter.

2. 3. 1   The first one is the "center theory", or "theory of the center of the wall", whereby the special parts extend to the center lines of such partitions as walls, pillars, floors, and the ceilings. Under this theory, the scope of right is clearly defined but the maintenance and management of the building have not been taken into full consideration.

2. 3. 2   The second one is the "space theory". According to this theory, the special parts reach only so far to the space encircled by walls, floors and ceilings. As to the partitions that separate such space, namely, the aforementioned walls, floors and ceilings, etc. , are jointly owned by all or at least some of the owners. Clearly, this theory provides a contrast to the "center theory" by excluding an owner's exclusive disposition over partition parts and accordingly expanding the scope of the common parts.

2. 3. 3   The third one is known as the "theory of last coated cladding", whereby the special parts also include the coated claddings of walls, pillars, etc. , In other words, walls as well as other partitions are categorized as common parts while the last coated claddings thereof special parts. The strength of this theory is that it gives full consideration to both the actual domination of property owners and the safety of the whole building. Nonetheless, it brings difficulty to the calculation of construction area in realty transactions. In trade practices, areas between the coated claddings and the center lines of partitions are calculated into the construction area, differing from this theory. In view of this, the theory of last coated claddings may not be easily accepted by the masses.

2. 3. 4   The fourth approach is provided by the "compromise theory", whereby the claddings are still categorized as special parts while the space between the claddings and center lines as common parts. The ingeniousness of the theory lies in its distinction of internal and external relations in dealing with the special parts. When it comes to the internal relations among property owners, the scope of special parts extends as far as to the coated claddings of walls, ceilings and other partitions. But when it comes to the external relations with a third party in cases of sales or insurance, etc. , then the special parts will extend further to the center lines. Clearly, this theory is a concession to the theory of last coated cladding while preserving the basic prevalence of trading practices and balancing the interest of parties concerned. This fourth theory seems to be the most appealing one.

2. 3. 5   The last one is the so-called "theory of dualism". Under this theory, walls have the dual characters of exclusively and jointly owned property.

The prevailing theory is the compromise theory. It is the most delicate one among the five because it well defines a solid but flexible boundary between the special parts and common parts of a portioned building. The flexible boundary is the center line while the solid one is the last coated cladding.

3. Co-ownership

3. 1   Concept and Features of Co-ownership over Co-owned Space

Co-ownership, or the so-called "the sharing right to the co-owned space", or "the shared part of the co-ownership", is the right of property owners to possess, utilize and obtain profit from the co-owned space of a partitioned building in accordance with the laws or management rules. In comparison with co-ownership, it has the following few features:

3. 1. 1   The co-owners are with multiple identities. They are co-owners, exclusive owners and a member of management community respectively, while co-owners of general co-ownership only have the first identity.

3. 1. 2   Its object has a wide scope. The co-owned space mainly include the following six sections. First, basic structures of a building such as the stanchions, roofs, external walls and basements; second, co-owned space of a building, appurtenant establishments thereof including staircases, firefighting equipment, corridors, water towers, water pipelines, as well as such co-owned space owned by a certain number of owners as the floor slabs between storeys; third, the right to the use of land which the building's foundations are located thereon; fourth, the green lands, roads and houses or rooms used for property management within the district; fifth, public spaces and facilities such co-owned surface or underground structures as gateway architectures and artistic ornaments, water, electricity, lighting, firefighting, safeguards and other appurtenant establishments, and things located within the district that belong to the owners other than what are legally owned by the State or legal persons concerned; last, the unused land located within the neighborhood.

3. 1. 3   Its contents are rather broad including four parts, namely, first, those rights and obligations shared by all owners to the whole building; second, shared rights over specific parts of the building; third, rights and obligations emanating from the exclusive right of use regarding certain co-owned space on the part of some property owners; fourth, the rights and obligations between property owners and the land owner arising from the use of the land on which the building's founded.

3. 1. 4   It may be further divided into various sub-categories according to different criterions, e. g. , co-ownership by law and co-ownership by agreement, collective co-ownership and partial co-ownership, co-ownership over the building and co-ownership over the appurtenant establishments, co-ownership with encumbrance and co-ownership without encumbrance, etc. In comparison, the general co-ownership may only be classified into co-ownership by shares and joint co-ownership. ①

3. 1. 5   In terms of the changes in the right, the acquisition, extinction, and alteration of partitioned co-ownership are largely determined by that of the exclusive ownership. The former is subordinate to and dominated by the latter. The acquisition, extinction and alteration of the general co-ownership, however, are separately initiated by each co-owner in the absence of such principal-subordinate relationship.

3. 1. 6   Persons who shares the partitioned ownership may not request to sever the object as persons who share general co-ownership do.

3. 2   Scope of Co-owned Space

3. 2. 1   Statutory Co-ownership

Statutory co-ownership is co-ownership that is legally stipulated to be shared by property owners. Parties concerned may not exclude it in their purchase contract for a house through mutual agreement. Article 274 of the Civil Code stipulates that "Roads within the construction zone are co-owned by all unit owners, except for those that are part of the urban public roads. Green spaces within the construction zone are co-owned by all unit owners, except for those that are part of the urban public green spaces and those expressly indicated to be owned by private individuals. Other public places, public facilities, and spaces used for property management service within the construction zone are co-owned by all unit owners". Para. 2, Article 275 of the Civil Code provides that "The parking spaces for parking vehicles that occupy the roads or other spaces co-owned by all unit owners are co-owned by all unit owners". Article 281 states that "The maintenance funds for buildings and their auxiliary facilities are co-owned by the unit owners". In view of these, statutory co-ownership mainly covers the following parts: (1) the roads within the building areas; (2) the greens within the building areas; (3) houses or rooms used for property management; (4) parking places which occupy the roads or other fields commonly owned by all the owners; (5) other public places or facilities within the building areas; and (6) the funds of maintenance of the building and its affiliated facilities.

---

① There are two kinds of co-ownership, namely, co-ownership by shares and joint co-ownership. Persons who share the ownership shall enjoy their rights and assume their obligations in proportion to the amount of their shares. Persons who jointly own a thing shall enjoy the ownership jointly.

3.2.2   Co-ownership by Agreement

Co-ownership by agreement is such co-ownership as agreed upon by parties concerned in accordance with the law.

First, garages and parking places. Para. 1, Article 275 of the Civil Code provides that "The ownership of the parking spaces and garages planned for parking vehicles within the construction zone shall be agreed upon by the parties by way of selling, giving away as gifts, leasing, and the like". Article 276 of the Civil Code stipulates that "The parking spaces and garages planned for parking vehicles within the construction zone shall first meet the needs of the unit owners".

Second, clubs. The Civil Code provide no rules regarding this point. Among practitioners there exists two opinions. One holds that to whom the clubs shall be attributed depends on the specific stipulation in the sales contract for the commodity house. Where the parties have not stipulated regarding this issue, the ownership goes to the developer. The other holds that, under such circumstances, the ownership shall vest in all the owners.

4. Management Rights

4.1   Concept and Features of Co-owners' Management Right

Co-owners' management rights are the rights and obligations vested in those owners to a partitioned building based on their status as members of building's management community. These rights and obligations arise from the close relationship among owners that is established on the basis of the structure, attribution and utilization of the building. Another definition of it may be, the management right of co-owners over their co-owned properties and mutual affairs on basis of their respective ownership over the special parts. The features of property owners' management right may be observed from the following few aspects:

4.1.1   It is exclusively owned by the owners based on their ownership of the special parts.

4.1.2   It is a right that is independent from the exclusive ownership and the co-ownership and encompasses the rights and obligations of all the owners regarding their co-owned properties and mutual affairs. The management right is not simply a property right in that it concerns managerial relationship to a great extent and involves much interpersonal elements (management mechanism). For exclusive ownership and co-ownership, in contrast, there involve mainly property elements.

4.1.3   It is grounded on the mutual relationship among co-owners.

4.1.4   It is a renewable right. As the mutual relationship among property owners is rooted in the close bond between the exclusive and co-owned space of the building and that between the exclusive ownership and co-ownership, the community formed by them remains as long as the building exists. In principle, such community will not be dissolved. The membership right arises from and shares the fate of the mutual relationship among property owners, thus is sustainable.

4.1.5   It is closely intertwined with the exclusive ownership and co-ownership. The three together constitute a complete partitioned ownership.

4.1.6   It is a right over co-owned properties and mutual affairs. Like the exclusive ownership and co-ownership, the management right is an indispensable and fundamental element of the modern partitioned ownership. Essentially, it may be divided into the personal right of the ownership of a building's units which mainly deals with the determination and the enforcement of intentions among property owners regarding mutual affairs. For this reason, it cannot serve as an independent object of a transaction.

4.2   Contents of the Management Right

According to Article 278 of the Civil Code, "The following matters shall be jointly decided by the unit owners: (1) to formulate and amend the procedural rules of the owners' assembly; (2) to formulate and amend the stipulations on management; (3) to elect or replace members of the owners' committee; (4) to employ and remove the property management service enterprise or other managers; (5) to use maintenance funds for buildings and auxiliary facilities thereof; (6) to raise maintenance funds for buildings and auxiliary facilities thereof; (7) to renovate and reconstruct buildings and auxiliary facilities thereof; (8) to change the intended use of the co-owned space or making use of the co-owned space to engage in business activities; and (9) to handle other major matters relating to co-ownership and the right to joint management. The quorum for matters subject to the unit owners' joint decision shall be two thirds or more of the exclusive units both by area and by number of unit owners. Decisions of matters provided in Subparagraphs (6) through (8) shall be subject to the consent of the unit owners representing three quarters or more of the participating exclusive units both by area and by number of unit owners. Decisions of other matters provided in the preceding Paragraph shall be subject to the consent of the unit owners representing more than half of the participating exclusive units both by area and by number of unit owners".

4.3   Owners' Assembly and Owners' Committee

Stipulations regarding the proprietors' assembly and proprietors' committee may be found in the Civil Code and Regulations on Property Management. The latter was promulgated on June 8, 2003 and revised respectively on August 26, 2007 and February 6, 2016.

4.3.1 Owner's Assembly

The proprietors' assembly is an autonomous organization constituted by all the owners within a property management area for the purpose of managing their co-owned properties and various affairs in their community life.

According to Article 10 of the Regulations on Realty Management, proprietors in the same realty management area shall, under the guidance of the competent real estate administrative department of the people's government of the district or county, or the neighborhood office, or the people's government of the town or township, where the realty is located, establish a proprietors' assembly and elect proprietors' committee. However, where there is only one owner, or there are only a small number of owners who unanimously agree not to establish an owners' assembly, the owner(s) shall perform, by himself or in common, the functions and duties of a owners' assembly and proprietors' committee.

The proprietors' assembly shall represent and safeguard the lawful rights and interests of all the owners within the realty management area in their realty management activities. Its authorities are determined by laws, regulations and management rules and agreements. The definition given by the Para. 1, Article 278 of the Civil Code regarding matters that shall be determined by all the owners may be categorized as one stipulation on the authorities of the proprietors' assembly. Other stipulations of the same nature may be settled by management rules and agreements aside from laws.

Meetings of an proprietors' assembly include regular sessions and interim sessions.

4.3.2 The Proprietors' Committee

The proprietors' committee is the executive organ of the proprietors' assembly, it is entrusted by the latter to manage the co-owned properties or community affairs of property owners. The owners may set up a proprietors' assembly and elect a proprietors' committee. The proprietors' committee shall, within 30 days from the date of establishment by election, make a report for the record to the competent real estate administrative department of the people's government of the district or county, the neighborhood office and the people's government of the town or township, where the realty is located. Membership of the proprietors' committee shall be held by proprietors ardent in promoting public good with a strong sense of responsibility and considerable capacity of organization. The chairperson and vice-chairpersons of the proprietors' committee shall be elected from among the members of the proprietors' committee.

The proprietors' committee executes the decisions of the proprietors' assembly, and shall perform its duties in accordance with the laws and regulations.

4.3.3 Effects of Decisions Made by the Proprietors' Assembly and the Proprietors' Committee and Daily Management

Article 280 of the Civil Code stipulates that "Decisions of the owners' assembly or the owners' committee are legally binding on unit owners. Where a decision made by the owners' assembly or the owners' committee infringes upon the lawful rights and interests of a unit owner, the infringed owner may request the people's court to revoke it". Para. 2, Article 286 of the Civil Code further regulates that "With respect to an act impairing the lawful rights and interests of others, such as arbitrarily discarding garbage, discharging pollutants or noises, feeding and keeping animals in violation of the stipulations, constructing structures against rules and regulations, encroaching on passages, and refusing to pay property management fees, the owners' assembly or the owners' committee has the right to request the actor to discontinue such infringements, remove the nuisance, eliminate the danger, restore to the original condition, and compensate for the losses entailed".

4. 4   Relations between the Proprietors and Realty Service Enterprises

Realty service means the activities in which the proprietors, either by themselves or by way of entrusting to a realty service enterprise or other managers, manage their co-owned properties and deal with their community affairs. With respect to this matter, the Civil Code and Regulations on Realty Management provide thorough regulations.

Pursuant to Article 284 of the Civil Code, "The unit owners may either manage the buildings and the auxiliary facilities on their own, or entrust a property management service enterprise or another manager for such a purpose. The unit owners have the right to replace, in accordance with law, the property management service enterprise or the other managers employed by the developer". Article 285 requires that, "The property management service enterprise or otherwise a manager shall, as entrusted by the unit owners, manage the buildings and their auxiliary facilities within the construction zone in accordance with the provisions of Book Three of this Code relating to contracts for property management service, subject itself to the supervision of the unit owners, and respond to the unit owners' inquiries about property management services in a timely manner. The property management service enterprise or other managers shall carry out emergency measures and other management measures implemented by the government in accordance with law and actively cooperate in the performance of the relevant work". In light of these provisions, a proprietor enjoys the following rights in realty management services: right of self-management, right of self-determination regarding appointing and dismissing the realty service enterprise.

5. Other Rights and Obligations of Holder of Ownership of a Building's Units

No holder of ownership of a building's units or unit owner may turn a dwelling space into a space used for operating businesses in violation of laws, regulations, or the stipulations on management. A unit owner who intends to turn a dwelling space into a space used for operating businesses shall, in addition to abiding by laws, regulations, and the stipulations on management, obtain unanimous consent from all interested unit owners (Article 279 of the Civil Code).

The income generated from the space co-owned by the unit owners that is received by the developer, the property management service enterprise, or other managers are co-owned by all unit owners after reasonable costs are deducted (Article 282 of the Civil Code).

Where there is an agreement on matters such as allocation of expenses on and distribution of income gained from a building and its auxiliary facilities, such matters shall be determined in accordance with the agreement; where there is no agreement or the agreement is unclear, such matters shall be determined in proportion to the area of each unit owner's exclusive unit to the total area (Article 283 of the Civil Code).

The unit owners shall abide by laws, regulations, and the stipulations on management, and their relevant acts shall meet the requirements of conserving resources and protecting the ecological environment. With respect to the emergency measures and other management measures implemented by the government in accordance with law that are carried out by the property management service enterprise or other managers, the unit owners shall, in accordance with law, be cooperative. No unit owner shall conduct any an act impairing the lawful rights and interests of others, such as arbitrarily discarding garbage, discharging pollutants or noises, feeding and keeping animals in violation of the stipulations, constructing structures against rules and regulations, encroaching on passages, and refusing to pay property management fees. Where a unit owner or an actor refuses to perform the relevant duties, the party concerned may make a report to, or lodge a complaint with the competent administrative department, which shall handle the case in accordance with law. (Article 286 of the Civil Code)

A unit owner has the right to request the developer, the property management service enterprise or other managers, and other unit owners to bear civil liability for any act done by them that infringes upon his lawful rights and interests. (Article 287 of the Civil Code)

Section Three Adjacent Relationships

1. Concept and Features of Adjacent Relationships

Adjacent relationship is a kind of relationship combining rights and obligations between or among owners or users of neighboring immovable properties that require the subjects to provide convenience or accept other restrictions when exercising his ownership or right to use. To put it simply, adjacent relationships relate to the rights and obligations that arise from the exercise of ownership or right to use by parties of neighboring immovable properties. For example, A possesses a piece of contracted land that located in the middle of B's land. When A exercises his right to use the land, he unavoidably has to pass the land of B. An adjacent relationship thus is established between the two parties.

When viewed as right, adjacent relationships may also be called the neighboring right, under which any one of the owners or users of neighboring immovable properties may require other neighboring property owner to provide convenience or accept other restrictions when exercising his ownership or right to use.

The features of adjacent relationships may be summarized as follows:

First, it is created by law or is statutory. In essence, it reflects the interference of law in the right of immovable property. The application of the relevant provisions cannot be excluded though mutual consent in most cases.

Second, the subjects of adjacent relationships are owners or users of neighboring immovable property. The adjacent relationship arises from the neighboring location of immovable property owned or used by various parties. For instance, it may arise from the ventilation and natural lighting of a neighboring building, or, in many cases, be generated because of issues concerning natural environments. For example, village A and B are located respectively on the upper and lower reaches of one same river. As a result, the two may draw water from the section occupied by each other, constituting thus such adjacent relationships regarding use of water.

Third, the contents of adjacent relationships may vary according to the categories, but basically include two parts. Firstly, a neighboring party may require the other party to provide necessary convenience and the latter is obliged to do as required. The necessary convenience refers to such assistance as is indispensable for the proper exercise of ownership or right of use. Secondly, each neighboring party must try his best to avoid or reduce the damages caused to other neighboring party and not abuse his rights. Quintessentially, this is an obligation of inaction.

Fourth, the objects of adjacent relationships are different from that of a general real right. In the Chinese legal academia, there are three theories regarding this matter. According to the first theory, the objects of adjacent relationships are the neighboring immovable properties. The second theory defines the objects of adjacent relationships as the interests manifested in exercising rights over immovable properties. To be specific, it is a kind of property interest or other interest that is manifested when an ownership of or a right to use an immovable property is realized, because a neighboring party, while exercising his rights, must provide convenience to his neighbor and respect the latter's lawful rights and interests while fulfilling his own rights. Under the last theory, the objects of the adjacent relationships are the acts (either action or inaction) conducted by parties concerned. In my opinion, the object should be the interests manifested in exercising rights over immovable properties. This is because adjacent relationships may be divided into various and complicated categories and the rights and obligations under each category may point to different objects or targets according to its contents. In terms of the acts conducted by the neighboring parities, they are the contents of the rights rather than its objects.

2. Categories of Adjacent Relationships

Causes of adjacent relationships are numerous and complex. According to the Civil Code, adjacent relationships may be divided into two categories: those that require actively providing convenience and arise from the use or discharge of water or passage, and those that require only passive inaction such as forbidding a neighboring obligor conducting certain acts. Major neighboring relations may be summarized as follows:

2. 1   Adjacent Relationships Arising from the Use or Discharge of Water

According to Article 290 of the Civil Code, "A person entitled to the real rights in immovable property shall provide a person entitled to an adjacent right the necessary convenience for the use of water or drainage. The right to utilization of natural flowing water shall be reasonably allocated among the persons entitled to the adjacent rights of the immovable property. When discharging the water, the direction of the natural water flow shall be respected".

The natural flowing waters shall be reasonably distributed among the neighboring right holders of immovable properties. Where parties use the same source of water, each party may freely use the water to the extent that the utilization of the neighbor is not prejudiced. The land user shall not drill wells or extract ground water in a manner, thus reducing the neighbor's source of living water or even drying the neighboring wells.

With respect to the natural flowing waters that all the neighboring parties are entitled to use, its direction shall be set store on. No land user shall, for the purpose of his own interests, change the route of or block the water flow. In cases there the water flow is adequate, the neighboring right holders upstream shall not illegally build dams so as to impede and reverse the direction of the water flow, thus exerting negatively impact on the discharge of water upstream. In cases where the water flow is insufficient, the users upstream shall not exclusively control the source of water and cut off the water supply downstream. The water flow shall be used for utilization or irrigation in such sequence as "from the near to the distant, from upstream to downstream".

In the event that the routine production activities or daily life of a neighboring right holder are negatively impacted as a result of the neighbor's illegal block or exclusive control of natural flowing waters, such influenced party have the right to require the latter to clear away the obstructions and compensate the losses caused thereby.

Where a neighboring right holder has to use for discharging water the land of another, the latter shall grant consent. The former, on the other hand, should provide proper safeguards and reasonably compensate for any loss caused thereby. In cases where a neighboring right holder could have taken appropriate measures while discharging the water but didn't, thus damaged or endangered the property of others, the latter may require such right holder to discontinue such infringement, eliminate the hazards, clear away the obstructions and compensate the losses entailed. Each neighboring right holder assumes the obligation for the preservation and maintenance of such ferries, bridges, dams, etc. as are commonly used. When building houses, an obligee shall do his best to avoid causing damage to the neighbor because of eavesdrop. In the event that dispute arises therefrom, the party at fault shall remove the obstacles and compensate the other party for damages caused thereby.

2. 2   Adjacent Relationships Arising from Passage

Pursuant to Article 291 of the Civil Code, "A person entitled to the real rights in immovable property shall provide necessary convenience to the persons entitled to an adjacent right who have to utilize his land for passage, and the like".

2. 3   Adjacent Relationships Arising from Construction or Maintenance of Buildings, or Laying of Wires and Pipelines

Article 292 of the Civil Code states that, "Where a person entitled to the real rights in immovable property has to utilize the adjacent land or building for constructing or maintaining a building, or for laying electrical wires, cables, or the pipelines for water, heating, gas, or the like, the person entitled to the real rights in the adjacent land or building shall provide the necessary convenience".

2. 4   Adjacent Relationships Arising from Ventilation or Lighting

Article 293 of the Civil Code stipulates that, "The construction of a building may not violate the relevant construction standards of the State or obstruct the ventilation, lighting, or sunlight of the adjacent buildings".

2. 5 Adjacent Relationships Arising from Environmental Protections

Article 294 of the Civil Code regulates that, "A person entitled to the real rights in immovable property may not, in violation of the regulations of the State, discard solid wastes or emit harmful substances such as atmospheric pollutants, water pollutants, soil pollutants, noises, light radiation, and electromagnetic radiation".

2. 6 Adjacent Relationships Arising from Excavation or Construction of Building(s)

Article 295 of the Civil Code provides that, "A person entitled to the real rights in immovable property may not endanger the safety of the adjacent immovable property when excavating land, constructing buildings, laying pipelines, installing facilities, or the like".

3. Principles in Handling Adjacent Relationships

As a type of common relations that commonly materializes in practices, neighboring relations should be properly handled. Otherwise, the routine production and livelihood of citizens may be negatively impacted, and in the worst-case scenario, even entail personal injuries or major property damages, threatening the social order of life and production. For these reasons, the proper maintenance of adjacent relationships is of great significance for both the protection of the lawful rights and interests of neighboring property owner and the appropriate utilization of social wealth.

Article 83 of General Principles of the Civil Law regulates that, "In the spirit of helping production, making things convenient for people's lives, enhancing unity and mutual assistance, and being fair and reasonable, neighboring users of real estate shall maintain proper adjacent relationships over such matters as water supply, drainage, passageway, ventilation and lighting". Article 288 of the Civil Code stipulates that, "The persons entitled to adjacent rights in immovable property shall properly deal with adjacent relationships in accordance with the principles of facilitation to production, convenience for daily lives, solidarity and mutual assistance, and fairness and reasonableness". According to these provisions, the following principles should be obeyed when handling the is dealt with.

3. 1 Principle of Balancing Interests, Mutual Understanding and Accommodation, and Unity and Mutual Help

Where disputes arise over the ownership or use of natural resources such as land, forests, mountains and grasslands, or from environmental pollution, owners of neighboring immovable properties shall negotiate on the settlement thereof in the spirit of mutual understanding and mutual accommodation and unity; if such negotiation collapses, the issue should be settled by competent government agencies or the people's court. Before a settlement is finally provided, the disputed parties shall not disuse such natural resources as land, forests and mountains, destroy the facilities, assemble a crowd to create disturbances, or take by force or damage the properties. Any person who willfully creates disturbances and causes personal injuries or property damages shall assume administrative and even criminal liabilities after taking his civil liabilities.

A person entitled to the real rights in immovable property who utilizes the adjacent immovable property for the purpose of using water, drainage, passage, laying pipelines, and the like, shall spare no effort to avoid causing damage to the person entitled to the real rights in the adjacent immovable property. (Article 296 of the Civil Code)

Owners of neighboring immovable property shall mutually cooperate and take account of each other's interests when exercising their ownership or right of use. The beggar-my-neighbor policy, self-aggrandizing at the expense of one's neighbors, or other acts that contradict the public and social interests are all opposed to the principles that one should adhere to while handling the adjacent relationships. The people's court shall also take into consideration the interests of each party in the trial of disputes over adjacent relationships, so that a reasonable settlement may be finally reached.

3. 2   Principle of Conduciveness to Production, Convenience for Daily Lives

When dealing with disputes over adjacent relationships, effective and reasonable utilization of properties, conduciveness to production and convenience for daily lives should be taken into account as prime considerations. For instance, when a dispute arises from unsettled land boundaries, new boundaries should be established in a way that is conducive to operation, management, production and development.

3. 3   Principle of Fairness and Rationality

As adjacent relationship is multifarious, it is impossible for the law to specifically regulate on each form. Therefore, the people's courts, in the trial of disputes over adjacent relationships, are expected to base themselves on realities, conduct in-depth investigation, balance the interests of all parties, and take into consideration of the historical conditions and customs to finally find a solution that is both fair and reasonable.

3. 4 Principle of Proper Compensation

According to Article 296 of the Civil Code, a person entitled to the real rights in immovable property who utilizes the adjacent immovable property, shall spare no effort to avoid causing damage to the person entitled to the real rights in the adjacent immovable property; where damage exceeding reasonable and tolerable scope is caused, compensation shall be made accordingly. The requirements include: First, it applies mostly in cases concerning use of the neighboring immovable properties for the drawing or draining off of water, for passage or for laying of pipelines, etc. Second, the utilization of the adjacent immovable property caused actual losses. Third, the damage caused exceeded reasonable and tolerable scope.

Section Four Acquisition of Ownership

1. Acquisition of Ownership: An Overview

The acquisition of ownership may be either original acquisition or derivative acquisition. Original acquisition means that an ownership is created for the first time or obtained independent of an existing ownership, or that a new property is acquired by law. Original acquisition is also known as initial acquisition. Ownership acquired in this way is independent. Either there is no previously existing ownership or the original right holder's ownership or will is not concerned. In law the former cases mainly include production, collection of fruits, confiscation of property, first possession, finding of lost things or discovery of buried things, accession, and good faith acquisition, etc. ; the latter cases include requisition, and the like. Original acquisition mainly takes the following forms:

First, nationalization and confiscation. These activities directly deprive one of his original ownership. For example, the socialist nationalization is a means by which the properties of imperialism, feudalism and bureaucrat-capitalism nature are deprived. As to confiscation, it is the deprivation of properties that have been illegally obtained or used. Ownership acquired through nationalization is independent and goes to the State, and properties confiscated are isolated from the ownership or will of the original owner.

Second, production. Any form of production involves the possession, utilization and transformation of the nature. Such activities as fishing, mining, etc. may involve direct possession, while activities like products manufacturing necessitate indirect possession.

Third, accession. This further includes: (1) attachment, for example, constructing houses with another's building materials; (2) mixture, for example, mixing properties of different owners to the extent that they are inseparable; (3) processing, for example, painting on the canvas of another.

Fourth, gains, or the so-called fruits. They can be divided into: (1) natural fruits, such as yields of fruiters; and (2) statutory fruits such as interests of savings.

Fifth, acquisition of ownerless properties. Ownerless thing refers to such property whose owner is absent or indefinite as abandoned thing, lost thing, drift-stuff, stray animals, buried or hidden property, property without inheritor, etc. These are property whose owner is unknown or does not exist. Acquisition of these property is original acquisition.

In the Civil Code, the rule of bona fide acquisition, the attribution of lost properties, drift-stuff, buried things, fruits, etc. are clearly defined.

As to derivative acquisition, it is also known as secondary acquisition, meaning the acquisition of ownership by a new owner from the former one by way of certain civil juristic acts or legal events, including sales, barter, donation, inheritance, legacy and other lawful causes. Unlike original acquisition, the derivative acquisition relies on the original owner's ownership and/or his intention to transfer such right.

The main causes for derivative acquisition include:

1. Sales contract. Where civil persons reach agreement that the seller hands over the sold property the buyer and the buyer in turn accepts such property and pay the purchase accordingly, the buyer obtains the property ownership that belonged to the seller through the transaction.

2. Gift and barter. Where a donor voluntarily gives his own property to a eve gratuitously, or where a party exchanges with another party with his own non-monetary property, the ownership may also be transferred in this way.

3. Inheritance. This is the case where a successor obtains the lawful personal property left a decedent upon death in accordant with stipulation of law or a legal and valid will.

4. Bequest. Where a donee-by-will is a natural person, collective organization or the State, the estate is obtained according to the legal and valid agreement established by the donor-by-will during his lifetime.

5. Other lawful causes. Property ownership could also be obtained or created through other legal ways. For instance, members of cooperative economic organization may establish lawful economic organization through share consolidation and fundraising, and thereby creating new forms of ownership.

2. Good Faith Acquisition

2. 1　Concept and Scope of Application

The rule of good faith acquisition, or the so-called immediate acquisition, bona fide acquisition, refers to such circumstances where a person transfers to a transferee immovable properties or movable properties while he has no right to dispose of and that the transferee is in good faith upon the acquisition of such property, then the ownership or other real rights over the properties shall go to the transferee.

The rule of good faith acquisition is instituted in response to the demands of commodity trade. As is often the case, a party in a goods transaction may lack the knowledge that whether the other side has the right to dispose of the property. It can also be difficult for him to conduct thorough investigation into each piece of the goods that is sold in the market. Under such circumstance, any goods purchased may have to be returned at any time if the transaction is made based on the unauthorized disposal of the transferor even if the transferee has taken over the goods in good faith. Undoubtedly, parties concerned may feel extremely unsecured about their transaction in such cases, and the order of trading will become unstable. Viewed in this, the good faith acquisition system does play a significant role in safeguarding a safe and desirable order for commodity transactions, though it unavoidably restricts the owner's right to pursuit, in turn sacrifices the proprietor's interests to a certain extent. For this reason, major western jurisdictions have all established such rule in their civil law systems. In China, this system of rules may be found in Articles 311 to 313 of the Civil Code.

According to the Civil Code, the rule of good faith acquisition is applicable to: (1) ownership over movable properties; (2) ownership over immovable properties; and (3) other real rights. Para 3. Article 311 of the Civil Code provides that "Where a party acquires, in good faith, a real right other than ownership, the provisions of the preceding two paragraphs shall be applied mutatis mutandis". Therefore, the rule may also apply to usufructs over immovable property and such security interests as right to mortgage and pledge, provided that other legal prerequisites have been satisfied.

In the past, the good faith acquisition of lost or stolen goods were in principle denied by Chinese laws. At present, Article 312 of the Civil Code has given specific stipulations regarding the good faith acquisition of lost goods. "An owner or any other right holder has the right to recover a lost thing. Where the lost thing is possessed by another person by way of transfer, the right holder has the right to claim damages against the person who disposes of the thing without the right to disposition, or to request the transferee to return the original thing within two years from the date on which the right holder knows or should have known of the transferee, provided that where the transferee has acquired the lost thing at auction or from a qualified business operator, the right holder shall, at the time of requesting the return of the original thing, reimburse the expenses that have been paid by the transferee. The right holder has, after having reimbursed the expenses paid by the transferee, the right to indemnification against the person who disposes of the thing without the right to disposition".

2. 2   Conditions for Applying the Rule of Good Faith Acquisition

Pursuant to Article 311 of the Civil Code, where a person with no right to dispose of an immovable or movable property transfers it to another person, the owner has the right to recover it; unless otherwise provided by law, the transferee acquires the ownership of the immovable or movable property under the following circumstances:

2. 2. 1   The transferor should be a possessor of a movable property or a registered right holder of an immovable property. This in fact requires the right appearance of the transfer (unauthorized disposer) over the thing he has disposed of. It is the precondition of the application of the rule.

2. 2. 2   The transferor is without the right to disposal. This includes two circumstances: his right to disposal is absent or incomplete. For instance, one of the co-owners disposes of a co-owned property without the consent of the other owners, like it does in the case where the wife or the husband transfers to a third party an immovable property that is registered under his or her name without the consent of his or her spouse.

2. 2. 3   The transferee should have offered reasonable consideration in the transaction. Of course, whether such consideration has been actually paid, doesn't matter for establishing a good faith acquisition.

2. 2. 4   The transferee must be in good faith when the property is transferred to him.

2. 2. 5   The transferred property must have been registered or delivered to the transferee.

It is to be noted that additional and special conditions may apply to lost things (Articles 314 to 318 of the Civil Code).

2. 3   Effects of Good Faith Acquisition

2. 3. 1   A change in real right occurs.

2. 3. 2   The existing rights over the movable properties extinguish. According to Article 108 of the Real Right Law, "After a bona fide transferee acquires a piece of movables, the rights previously attached to the said piece shall extinguish, unless where the bona fide transferee is or ought to be aware of the attached rights at the time of transfer of the piece".

2. 3. 3   Legal responsibilities that the unauthorized disposer assumes. He may be required by the original right holder to take liabilities under such claims as arising from a contract, tort or return of unjust enrichment. The original right holder, nonetheless, may not require the transferee or other parities for the restitution of the property.

3. Finding of Lost Things

3. 1   Concept of Lost Things

A lost thing refers to a thing that is left by its owner somewhere and under no one's possession. It must be a piece of movable property since immovable property cannot be lost. A lost thing is distinguished from an ownerless thing because it is only unpossessed either by its owner or anyone else. A lost thing requires the following few elements.

First, it is a piece of movable property over which the owner has inadvertently lost possession.

Second, it is unpossessed.

Third, it is found by the finder.

3. 2   Obligations of the Finder

According to Article 312 of the Civil Code, in principle, the doctrine of good faith acquisition doesn't apply to lost-and-found properties. That is to say, if a finder of a lost property has illegally transferred it to a third party, the transferee cannot acquire the ownership thereof even if he is in good faith when the property is transferred to him. The original right holder may claim his ownership and demand for return of the lost property. This is provided by Article 314 of the Civil Code, which states that, "Where a lost thing is found, it shall be returned to its right holder. The finder shall, in a timely manner, notify its right holder or hand it over to the relevant departments such as the department for public security". Article 316 further stipulates that "A finder shall well keep a lost thing before it is delivered to the relevant department, and the relevant department shall well keep it before it is collected. A person who, intentionally or by gross negligence, causes the lost thing in his custody to be destructed, damaged, or lost shall bear civil liability".

3. 3   Rights of the Finder

3. 3. 1   Claim for reimbursement of safekeeping expense. Para. 1, Article 317 of the Civil Code stipulates that, "The right holder of a lost thing shall, at the time of collecting it, pay to the finder or the relevant department the necessary expenses, such as the expense for safekeeping the lost thing".

3. 3. 2   Claim against the right holder for fulfillment of obligation as promised. Under Para. 2, Article 317 of the Civil Code, "Where a right holder has offered a reward for finding the lost thing, he shall, at the time of collecting the lost thing, perform his obligations as promised". Para. 3 of the same provision states that, "Where a finder misappropriates the lost

thing, he is neither entitled to request reimbursement of expenses such as the expense for safekeeping the lost thing, nor entitled to request the right holder to perform the obligations as promised".

3. 4   Attribution of Lost Properties after Expiration Date

Article 318 of the Civil Code regulates that, "Where a lost thing has not been claimed by anybody within one year from the date the lost-and-found notice is publicized, the lost thing is to be escheated to the State".

4. Finding of Drifting, Buried or Hidden Things

According to 319 of the Civil Code, "Where a drifting thing is found or a thing buried underground or hidden is discovered, the provisions relating to the finding of lost things shall be applied mutatis mutandis, unless otherwise provided by law". Provisions relating to the finding of lost things refer to Articles 314 to 318 of the Civil Code.

5. Fruits

Article 321 of the Civil Code provides that "Unless otherwise agreed by the parties, the natural fruits of a thing shall be acquired by the owner of the thing, or by a usufructuary if there are both an owner and a usufructuary of the thing. The legal proceeds of a thing shall be acquired as agreed by the parties if there is such an agreement, or, where there is no agreement or the agreement is unclear, in accordance with the course of dealing".

第四章 共　　有

第一节　共有的概述

一、共有的概念和特征

财产的所有形式可分为单独所有和共有两种形式。单独所有是指财产所有权的主体是单一的，即一个权利主体单独享有对某项财产的所有权。所谓共有，是指某项财产由两个以上的权利主体共同享有所有权。换言之，是指多个权利主体对一物共同享有所有权。《民法典》第297条规定："不动产或者动产可以由两个以上组织、个人共有。共有包括按份共有和共同共有。"例如，两个人共同所有一间房屋，三人共同所有一台机器。共有的主体称为共有人，客体称为共有财产或共有物。各共有人之间因财产共有形成的权利义务关系，称为共有关系。共有的法律特征包括：

(1)共有的主体不是一个而是两个或两个以上的公民、法人或非法人组织。但是，多数人共同所有一物，并不是说共有是多个所有权。在法律上，共有财产只有一个所有权，而由多人享有。

(2)共有的客体即共有物是特定的，既可以是独立物，也可以是集合物(如共同继承的遗产)。共有物在共有关系存续期间不能分割，不能由各个共有人分别对某一部分共有物享有所有权。每个共有人的权利及于整个共有财产，因此共有不是分别所有。

(3)共有的内容，是共有人对共有物按照各自的份额享有权利并承担义务，或者平等地享有权利、承担义务。每个共有人对共有物享有的占有、使用、收益和处分的权利，不受其他共有人的侵犯。在行使共有财产的权利，特别是处分共有财产时，必须由全体共有人协商，按全体共有人的意志行事。

共有是多个权利主体基于共同的生活、生产和经营目的，将其财产联合在一起而产生的财产形式。共有既可以是同一种类型的所有权的联合，如集体组织所有权的联合；也可以是不同类型的所有权的联合，如集体组织所有权与公民个人所有权之间的联合。在前一种情况下，共有反映特定的所有制关系的性质，而在后一种情况下，则具有所谓"混合所有制"关系的性质。

共有和公有不同。"公有"一词具有双重含义，一是指社会经济制度，即公有制；

二是指一种财产形式。共有既可以是公有制在法律上的表现形式，也可以是个人或私人所有制在法律上的反映。就公有财产权来说，其与共有在法律性质上也是不同的，表现在：第一，共有财产的主体是多个共有人，而公有财产的主体是单一的，在中国为国家或集体组织。全民公有的财产属于国家所有，集体公有的财产则属于某一个集体组织所有。第二，公有财产已经脱离个人而存在，既不能实际分割为个人所有，也不能由个人按照一定的份额享有财产权利。在法律上，任何个人都不能成为公有财产的权利主体。而在共有的情况下，特别是在公民个人的共有关系中，财产往往并没有脱离共有人而存在。共有财产在归属上为共有人所有，是共有人的财产。所以，单个公民退出或加入公有组织并不影响公有财产的完整性，但是公民退出或加入共有组织（如合伙），就会对共有财产发生影响。

财产共有是社会经济生活中大量存在的财产形式。对于共有的形式，各国民法的规定是不一样的。中国《民法典》确认了两种共有形式，即按份共有和共同共有，这是两种基本的共有形式。

二、准共有

准共有，是指两个以上组织、个人共同享有用益物权、担保物权等权利。《民法典》第 310 条规定："两个以上组织、个人共同享有用益物权、担保物权的，参照本章的有关规定。"

严格地说，共有本为一所有权分属于数人的状况。因此，所有权以外的权利，本不应称为"共有"。然而，所有权以外的用益物权、担保物权为数人的共有时，其法律关系与所有权共有并没有什么区别，因此民法对于此等财产共有，无论是按份共有，还是共同共有，都准用所有权共有的规定，除非法律另有相反规定。

准共有，究竟应当适用按份共有还是共同共有的规定，应当视具体情况而定。如果是数人基于某种共同关系而共有一财产权时，应准用共同共有的有关规定，其他则应准用按份共有的有关规定。

准共有的特征主要包括：
(1)它是所有权之外的共有。
(2)客体是用益物权、担保物权，人身权不可以作为准共有的标的。
(3)准用所有权共有的一般规则。

第二节　按份共有

一、按份共有的概念

按份共有，又称分别共有，是指两个以上的共有人按照各自的份额分别对共有财产享有权利和承担义务的一种共有关系。《民法典》第 298 条规定："按份共有人对共有的不动产或者动产按照其份额享有所有权。"例如，甲、乙分别出资合购一幢房屋，甲出资200万元，乙出资300万元，甲、乙各按出资的份额对房屋享有权利。

在按份共有中，各共有人对共有物享有不同的份额。各共有人的份额，又称应有份，其具体数额一般是由共有人的意志决定的。例如，按出资比例决定各自的份额时，法律要求共有人在共有关系产生时明确各自的份额，如果各共有人的份额不明确，则推定其份额均等。在按份共有中，每个共有人对共有财产享有的权利和承担的义务，是依据其不同的份额确定的。共有人的份额决定了其权利义务的范围。共有人对共有物持有多大的份额，就对共有物享有多大权利和承担多大义务，如份额不同，则对共有财产的权利义务也不同。

按份共有与分别所有是不同的。在按份共有中，各个共有人的权利不是局限在共有财产的某一部分上，或就某一具体部分单独享有所有权，而是各共有人的权利均及于共有财产的全部。当然，在许多情况下，按份共有人的份额可以产生和单个所有权一样的效力，如共有人有权要求转让其份额，但是各个份额并不是一个完整的所有权，如果各共有人分别单独享有所有权，则共有也就不复存在了。

二、按份共有人的权利和义务

（一）按份共有人按照预先确定的份额对共有财产享有占有、使用、收益和处分的权利

按份共有人依据其份额享有并行使权利，份额越大，则使用共有财产并获取经济利益的权利就越大，反之这种权利就越小。《民法典》第309条规定："按份共有人对共有的不动产或者动产享有的份额，没有约定或者约定不明的，按照出资额确定；不能确定出资额的，视为等额享有。"

（二）按份共有人对共有物的管理权利和义务

《民法典》第300条规定："共有人按照约定管理共有的不动产或者动产；没有约定或者约定不明确的，各共有人都有管理的权利和义务。"

（三）按份共有人有权处分其份额

《民法典》第305条规定："按份共有人可以转让其享有的共有的不动产或者动产份额。其他共有人在同等条件下享有优先购买的权利。"《民法通则》（2009年修正）第78条第3款规定，"按份共有财产的每个共有人有权要求将自己的份额分出或者转让"。所谓分出，是指按份共有人退出共有，将自己在共有财产中的份额分割出去。在分出份额时，通常要对共有财产进行分割。所谓转让，是指共有人依法将自己在共有财产中的份额转让给他人。共有人可以自由参加或退出共有。为了保护共有人的权益，应允许共有人自己转让其共有份额。但共有人转让其份额，不得损害其他共有人的利益。如果共有

是合伙形式的，则共有人退出共有和转让份额，都要受合伙合同的约束。《民法典》第306 条规定："按份共有人转让其享有的共有的不动产或者动产份额的，应当将转让条件及时通知其他共有人。其他共有人应当在合理期限内行使优先购买权。两个以上其他共有人主张行使优先购买权的，协商确定各自的购买比例；协商不成的，按照转让时各自的共有份额比例行使优先购买权。"

《民法典》第 303 条规定："共有人约定不得分割共有的不动产或者动产，以维持共有关系的，应当按照约定，但是共有人有重大理由需要分割的，可以请求分割；没有约定或者约定不明确的，按份共有人可以随时请求分割，共同共有人在共有的基础丧失或者有重大理由需要分割时可以请求分割。因分割造成其他共有人损害的，应当给予赔偿。"各按份共有人转让或分出其份额，一般是不受时间限制的，只要共有关系存在，共有人就享有该项权利。但是，如果各共有人事先约定在共有关系存续期间，不得转让和分出份额，则视为各共有人自愿放弃转让或分出其份额的权利，无论哪一个共有人转让或分出其份额，都将构成对其他共有人的违约行为。按份共有人的份额具有所有权的某些效力，如按份共有人死亡以后，其份额可以作为遗产由继承人继承。

（四）按份共有人出售其份额时，其他共有人在同等条件下享有优先购买的权利

为防止某一按份共有人转让其份额造成对其他共有人的损害，《民法典》第 305 条规定："按份共有人可以转让其享有的共有的不动产或者动产份额。其他共有人在同等条件下享有优先购买的权利。"也就是说，某一共有人在出售其份额时，应告知其他共有人。在出价大体相等的情况下，其他共有人可以优先于非共有人购买所出售的份额。例如，甲、乙、丙三人合建一房屋，各占 1/3 的份额，在丙欲出让其份额时，甲、乙二人有权优先于他人购买该份额。

（五）共有财产的处分和修缮

共有财产属于全体共有人所有。因此，对共有财产的处分和修缮，必须依法进行。《民法典》第 301 条规定："处分共有的不动产或者动产以及对共有的不动产或者动产作重大修缮、变更性质或者用途的，应当经占份额三分之二以上的按份共有人或者全体共同共有人同意，但是共有人之间另有约定的除外。"不过，多数人或份额多的共有人在处分共有财产时，不得损害少数人或份额少的共有人的利益。

共有人未依法对共有财产进行法律上的处分的，对其他共有人不产生法律效力。如果其他共有人事后追认该行为，则该处分行为有效。如果转让的共有财产为动产，受让人取得该动产时出于善意，则可以按善意取得的原则处理。某个或某几个共有人未依法对共有财产进行事实上的处分，如毁弃共有物等，应对其他共有人负侵权行为责任。

（六）按份共有人的义务

对共有物的管理费用以及他负担。《民法典》第 302 条规定："共有人对共有物的管

理费用以及其他负担，有约定的，按照其约定；没有约定或者约定不明确的，按份共有人按照其份额负担，共同共有人共同负担。"按份共有人按照各自的份额，对共有财产分享权利，同时也要按各自的份额分担义务。按份共有人享有的份额越大，其承担的因经营共有财产所产生的义务和责任也就越大，反之则越少。

各共有人的义务，正如各共有人的权利一样及于全部共有财产，每个共有人不能仅对共有财产的某一部分承担义务。例如，两人共同出资购买了两辆汽车搞运输，其中任何一辆被损坏或者肇事造成他人损失，各共有人都应承担损失或责任。共有人对整个共有财产承担义务，还包括共有人应按其份额承担的共有财产的管理费用、税款及保险费等。如果某个共有人支付上述费用时，超出其份额所应分担的部分，该共有人有权请求其他共有人偿还。

因共有产生的债权债务。《民法典》第307条规定："因共有的不动产或者动产产生的债权债务，在对外关系上，共有人享有连带债权、承担连带债务，但是法律另有规定或者第三人知道共有人不具有连带债权债务关系的除外；在共有人内部关系上，除共有人另有约定外，按份共有人按照份额享有债权、承担债务，共同共有人共同享有债权、承担债务。偿还债务超过自己应当承担份额的按份共有人，有权向其他共有人追偿。"

三、共有人对共有的事实没有约定或者约定不明视为按份共有

《民法典》第308条规定："共有人对共有的不动产或者动产没有约定为按份共有或者共同共有，或者约定不明确的，除共有人具有家庭关系等外，视为按份共有。"这一规定改变了在中国司法实践中长期实施的推定为共同所有的做法。《最高人民法院关于贯彻执行〈中华人民共和国民法通则〉若干问题的意见（试行）》（1988年）第88条规定："对于共有财产，部分共有人主张按份共有，部分共有人主张共同共有，如果不能证明财产是按份共有的，应当认定为共同共有。"《物权法》及之后《民法典》实施后，该规定不再适用。

按份共有因共有人之间的协议、共有财产归于一人所有、共有财产丧失和被转让等原因而发生消灭。

第三节 共同共有

一、共同共有的概念和特征

共同共有是共有的另一种形式。《民法典》第299条规定："共同共有人对共有的不动产或者动产共同享有所有权。"共同共有是指两个以上的公民或法人，根据某种共同关系而对某项财产不分份额地共同享有权利并承担义务。共同共有的特征是：

（1）共同共有根据共同关系而产生，以共同关系的存在为前提。例如，因夫妻关系、家庭共同劳动而形成的夫妻财产共有关系和家庭财产共有关系。

（2）在共同共有中，共有财产不分份额。只要共同共有存在，共有人对共有的财产就不划分各人的份额。只有在共同共有关系终止以后，才能确定各共有人的份额，以分割共有财产。这是共同共有与按份共有的主要区别。

（3）在共同共有中，各共有人平等地享受权利和承担义务。也就是说，各共有人对整个共有财产享有平等的占有、使用、收益和处分的权利，同时对整个共有财产平等地承担义务。由于共同共有人的权利和义务都是平等的，因此较之于按份共有，共同共有人之间具有更密切的利害关系。

二、共同共有人的权利和义务

1. 共同共有人对共有财产享有平等的占有、使用权

对共有财产的收益，不是按比例分配，而是共同享有。

2. 对共有物的管理

《民法典》第 300 条规定："共有人按照约定管理共有的不动产或者动产；没有约定或者约定不明确的，各共有人都有管理的权利和义务。"

3. 共有人对共有财产的处分和修缮

《民法典》第 301 条规定："处分共有的不动产或者动产以及对共有的不动产或者动产作重大修缮、变更性质或者用途的，应当经占份额三分之二以上的按份共有人或者全体共同共有人同意，但共有人之间另有约定的除外。"因此，在对共有财产的处分和修缮方面，共同共有与按份共有的权利义务是相同的。

4. 对共有物的管理费用以及其他负担

《民法典》第 302 条规定："共有人对共有物的管理费用以及其他负担，有约定的，按照其约定；没有约定或者约定不明确的，按份共有人按照其份额负担，共同共有人共同负担。"

5. 因共有产生的债权债务

《民法典》第 307 条规定："因共有的不动产或者动产产生的债权债务，在对外关系上，共有人享有连带债权、承担连带债务，但是法律另有规定或者第三人知道共有人不具有连带债权债务关系的除外；在共有人内部关系上，除共有人另有约定外，按份共有人按照份额享有债权、承担债务，共同共有人共同享有债权、承担债务。偿还债务超过自己应当承担份额的按份共有人，有权向其他共有人追偿。"

共同共有关系存续期间，各共有人无权请求分割共有财产，部分共有人擅自划分份额并分割共有财产的，应认定为无效。

共同共有也可以通过合同设立。在合同确定了共有人之间的权利义务后，共有人应按合同的规定行使权利并承担义务。共同共有因共同关系解除、共有物丧失等原因而消灭。

三、共同共有的形式

在中国，共同共有的基本形式有两种，即夫妻共有和家庭共有。

(一) 夫妻共有财产

根据《民法典》规定，婚姻关系存续期间夫妻一方所得和双方共同所得的收入和财产，均归夫妻双方共同共有，但特有财产和约定为夫妻一方所有的财产除外。夫妻对共同所有的财产，有平等的处理权。所谓婚姻关系存续期间，是指从男女双方登记结婚之日起，至双方离婚或一方死亡之日止的期间。

夫妻的婚前财产属于个人所有，不是夫妻共同财产。在婚姻关系存续期间，夫妻一方或双方的劳动所得、夫妻双方继承和受赠的财产、双方用合法收入共同购买的财产以及难以确定为个人所有还是共有的财产都是夫妻共有财产。婚前是个人财产，婚后双方用共有财产进行了重大修理和改造的，也属于夫妻共有财产。夫妻双方通过协商，以其他方式确定夫妻间的财产归属的，如不违背法律的规定，可依夫妻的约定。

夫妻在婚姻关系存续期间，对于共有财产享有平等的占有、使用、收益和处分的权利。夫妻双方出卖、赠与属于夫妻共有的财产，应取得一致的意见。夫妻一方明知另一方处分财产而未作否定表示的，视为同意。夫妻共同财产只有在夫妻离婚，或夫妻一方死亡、遗产继承开始时，才能进行分割。

(二) 家庭共有财产

配偶、父母、子女和其他共同生活的近亲属为家庭成员(《民法典》第 1045 条)，家庭共有财产是指家庭成员在家庭共同生活关系存续期间，共同创造、共同所得的财产。例如，家庭成员交给家庭的财产，家庭成员共同受赠的财产，以及在此基础上购置和积累起来的财产等。概言之，家庭共有财产是家庭成员的共同劳动收入和所得。

家庭共有财产以维持家庭成员共同的生活或生产为目的，每个家庭成员都对其享有平等的权利。除法律另有规定或家庭成员间另有约定外，对于家庭共有财产的使用、处分或分割，应取得全体家庭成员的同意。家庭共有财产只有在家庭共同生活关系终止以后，才能进行分割。

家庭共有财产和家庭财产的概念是不同的。家庭财产是指家庭成员共同所有和各自所有的财产的总和，包括家庭成员共同所有的财产、夫妻共有财产和夫妻个人财产、成年子女个人所有的财产、其他家庭成员各自所有的财产等。家庭共有财产则不包括家庭成员各自所有的财产。

区分家庭共有财产与家庭成员个人财产的主要意义在于：(1)家庭成员分家析产时，只能对家庭共有财产而不能对个人财产进行分割。家庭共有财产的某一共有人死亡，财产继承开始时，必须把死者在家庭共有财产中的应有部分分出，作为遗产继承，而不能把家庭共有财产都作为遗产继承。(2)因生产经营活动负债时，个人经营的，以个人财产承担清偿债务的责任；家庭经营的，以家庭共有财产承担清偿债务的责任。《民法典》第 56 条规定："个体工商户的债务，个人经营的，以个人财产承担；家庭经营的，以家庭财产承担；无法区分的，以家庭财产承担。农村承包经营户的债务，以从事农村土地承包经营的农户财产承担;事实上由农户部分成员经营的,以该部分成员的财产承担。"在这里,"家庭财产"就是指家庭共有财产。(3)在家庭共同生活期间,为家庭的共同生活和生产需要所付出的开支,由家庭共有财产负担。不是为家庭的共同生活和生产的需要,而是为满足个人需要作出的开支,应由个人财产负担。

第四节 共有财产的分割

一、分割的原则

按份共有人有权请求从共有财产中分割出属于他的份额,共同共有人在共有关系解体以后(如夫妻离婚、分家等),也要对共有财产进行分割。共有财产分割应遵循如下原则:

(一)应遵守共有人的约定

《民法典》第303条规定:"共有人约定不得分割共有的不动产或者动产,以维持共有关系的,应当按照约定,但是共有人有重大理由需要分割的,可以请求分割。"如果共有人之间事先订立合同,明确规定了共有财产的分割方式,则各共有人应依合同的规定分割共有财产。在按份共有中,合同禁止在共有存续期间分割共有财产,或规定共有人在一定期限内不得退出共有的,则在合同规定的期限内不得分割共有财产。某个共有人将其份额转让给共有人之外的其他人,该受让人加入共有的,也应遵守合同的规定。

(二)应遵循法律的规定

分割夫妻共有财产,必须遵循婚姻法的规定。《民法典》第303条规定:"共有人约定不得分割共有的不动产或者动产,以维持共有关系的,应当按照约定,但是共有人有重大理由需要分割的,可以请求分割;没有约定或者约定不明确的,按份共有人可以随时请求分割,共同共有人在共有的基础丧失或者有重大理由需要分割时可以请求分割。因分割对其他共有人造成损害的,应当给予赔偿。"

分割共有财产不得损害国家、集体和他人的利益,不能把属于国家、集体的财产,例如承包的土地、借用集体组织的工具、他人存放的财产等作为共有财产分割。如有隐匿的赃款、赃物等非法所得,必须依法追缴,也不能作为共有财产分割。此外,分割共有财产不得损害债权人和其他利害关系人的利益。分割房屋以后,要按法律规定的方式办理登记过户手续。

二、分割的方式

《民法典》第304条规定:"共有人可以协商确定分割方式。达不成协议,共有的不动产或者动产可以分割且不会因分割减损价值的,应当对实物予以分割;难以分割或者因分割会减损价值的，应当对折价或者拍卖、变卖取得的价款予以分割。共有人分割所得的不动产或者动产有瑕疵的，其他共有人应当分担损失。"对共有财产的分割可以采取三种方式：

（一）实物分割

共有的不动产或者动产可以分割并且不会因分割减损价值的，应当对实物予以分割。可以进行实物分割的共有物一般是可分物，如草料、粮食、布匹等。

（二）变价分割

如果共有财产难以分割或者因分割会减损价值的，应当对折价或者拍卖、变卖取得的价款予以分割。

（三）作价补偿

对于不可分割的共有物，若共有人中的一人愿意取得共有物的，可以由该共有人取得该共有物。对于共有物的价值超出其应得份额的部分，取得共有物的共有人应对其他共有人作价补偿。

三、分割的效力

共有财产分割以后，共有关系归于消灭。不管是就原物进行分割还是变价分割，各共有人就分得的份额取得单独的所有权。分割以后某个共有人的财产由于分割以前的原因而为第三人追索或发现有瑕疵的，原共有人应当分担损失。因为原共有人有义务担保各人分得的共有财产不受第三人的追索，对原共有财产负有瑕疵担保责任。例如，甲乙在分割共有财产以后，发现甲分得的"红旗 HS7"轿车是甲乙原来借用丙的车辆，因此甲应将该项财产返还给丙，而乙则应补偿甲一定的损失。

Chapter 4　Co-ownership

Section One　Survey of Co-ownership

1. Concept and Features of Co-ownership

Ownership consists of sole ownership and Co-ownership. The former has only one subject, namely, only one right holder exclusively enjoys the ownership over a particular property. As for the latter, it refers to such ownership as shared by two or more parties. In other words, multiple subjects share one ownership over a property. Article 297 of the Civil Code states that "Immovable or movable property may be co-owned by two or more organizations or individuals. Co-ownership consists of co-ownership by shares and joint co-ownership". For example, two persons collectively own a house or three individuals commonly own a machine. Subjects of co-ownership refer to the co-owners, and the objects are the properties in co-ownership or commonly owned object. The rights and obligations between or among co-owners on the basis of their shared property are thus termed "the relations of co-ownership". The legal characters of co-ownership may be summarized as follows:

First, its subject is not single but plural in number. They may be citizens, legal persons or unincorporated organizations. Nonetheless, that several parties share one property doesn't mean there exists multiple ownership in one object. In the legal sense, only one ownership exists in one property though such right is shared by several parties.

Second, its object may either be an independent or collective property (e. g. , co-inherited legacy), but must be specified. During the existence of co-ownership, the joint property shall not be partitioned, any of its part cannot be respectively owned by the co-owners. This means, the right enjoyed by each co-owner directs to joint property as a whole. As such, co-ownership doesn't amount to own something respectively.

Third, the contents of co-ownership includes the rights enjoyed and obligations undertaken by co-owners either in proportion to the amounts of their respective shares or jointly and equally. The rights of each co-owner to possess, utilize, benefit from and dispose of the common property is free from any encroachment of other co-owners. The exercise of co-ownership, especially disposal of the common property, shall be subject to the consultation of all the co-owners of their free will.

Co-ownership is a form of property whereby two or more right holders combine their properties together for the purpose of common life, production or operation. It may either be a combination of the same type of ownership as ownership by the collectives, or that of different kinds of ownership, e. g. collective ownership and individual ownership. In the former scenario, characters of certain type of ownership system will be reflected; in the latter scenario, characters of the so-called "mixed ownership system" may be observed.

It is to be noted that co-ownership is distinguished from public ownership. Under "public ownership", there are two meanings. First, it could refer to a social economy system, namely, the system of public ownership. According to another possible definition, it means a form of property. Co-ownership may either be a manifestation of the public ownership system in law, or that of private or individual ownership system. As regards public ownership as a property right, its legal characters are different from those of co-ownership, as can be seen from the following aspects. First, a common property is owned by two or more common owners, while a public property is solely owned by the State or a collective organization in China. Properties owned by the whole people go to the State, and those properties collectively owned go to a certain collective organization. Second, a publicly owned property has been alienated from individuals, thus it is subject to no actual partition among them. In any case, the individual person may not enjoy such right by a share of a certain amount. As the law stands, no individual person may be the right holder over public properties. In comparison, in a co-ownership relation, especially under co-ownership relation between or among individual persons, the property has not been detached from the co-owners. It still belongs to all the co-owners. Therefore, when an individual person leaves or joins a community for public ownership, the integrity of public property will not be impacted. In the case of a community for co-ownership (e. g. , partnership), however, it will be the other round.

In the social and economic life, co-ownership is a very common form of property, on which civil laws of various nations rule differently. In China, the Civil Code stipulates two basic categories of co-ownership, namely, several ownership and joint co-ownership.

2. Quasi Co-ownership

Quasi co-ownership refers to such usufructs or security interests as enjoyed by two or more organizations or individuals. According to Article 310 of the Civil Code, "Where two or more organizations or individuals are jointly entitled to a right to usufruct or a security interest, the relevant provisions of this Chapter shall be applied mutatis mutandis".

Strictly speaking, co-ownership in concept is adopted under such circumstances where one ownership is shared by several parties. As to other rights apart from ownership, they may not be termed "commonly owned" rights. On the other hand, no major difference in legal relations may be observed where such rights as rights to usufruct and security interests are shared by several persons. For this reason, the Chinese civil law allows for the mutatis mutandis application of rules on co-ownership to these real rights, they may be enjoyed by share or jointly, unless otherwise is provided.

It depends on the specific situations that whether the rules on joint co-ownership or that on several ownership should be applied to cases of quasi co-ownership. In the event that several persons share a property right based on certain common relations, the provisions on joint co-ownership shall apply; otherwise, those on several ownership shall be applied.

The features of quasi co-ownership may be summarized as follows:

First, what is shared thereunder is such rights as other than the ownership.

Second, its object may be usufructs or security interests but not personal rights.

Third, general principles of co-ownership are applicable to it.

Section Two   Co-ownership by Shares

1. Concept of Co-ownership by Shares

Co-ownership by shares, is such common relations whereby two or more co-owners enjoy rights and undertake obligations regarding the common property in proportion to their respective amount of share. According to Article 298 of the Civil Code, "Co-owners by shares have the ownership of the co-owned immovable or movable property according to their shares". For example, A and B collectively purchased a house, contributing respectively 2 million and 3 million yuan. The two enjoy their rights over the house in proportion to their contributions in the transaction.

Under co-ownership by shares, co-owners respectively enjoy different shares over the common property. The amount of the share to which each co-owner is entitled, or the so-called "due shares", is determined by mutual consent of co-owners in most cases. For example, the amount of share may be ascertained in accordance with the capital contributions made by each party. In any event, the share must be definite when a co-ownership relation is created; in case of ambiguity, it is assumed that each party enjoys an equal share. Because right holders of a co-ownership by shares enjoy their rights and assumes their responsibilities in proportion to the amount of their respective shares, it may be concluded that the scope of their rights and obligations is actually determined by their shares. The amount of share determines the scope of the rights and obligations; different shares indicate different rights and obligations over the common property.

Co-ownership by shares doesn't amount to respective ownership. Under co-ownership by shares, each co-owner's rights are not limited within certain part of a property. Neither is it the case that the co-owners respectively and solely own a particular portion of the property. Rather, the rights of every co-owner overspread the entire common property. Admittedly, in many aspects, the effects of a co-ownership by shares and those of a single ownership are seemingly identical, like in the case where a co-owner intends to transfer his due share. However, in the final analysis, such share is not complete as a single ownership. A co-ownership relationship will fall apart if each owner respectively enjoys the entirety of an ownership.

2. Rights and Obligations of Right Holders under Co-ownership by Shares

2.1 Right to Possess, Utilize, Obtain Profit from and Dispose of the Common Property in Proportion to the Predetermined Shares

Right holders who share the ownership hold and exercise their rights in proportion to their shares. The larger one's share is, the broader his right becomes in utilizing or obtaining economic interests from the property in co-ownership, and vice versa. Article 309 of the Civil Code provides that "The share of a co-owner by shares in the immovable or movable property shall be determined according to his capital contribution where there is no agreement or the agreement is unclear. Where it is impossible to determine the amount of capital contribution, each co-owner by shares shall be entitled to an equal share".

2.2 Rights and Obligations of Management over the Property in Co-ownership by Shares

Under Article 300 of the Civil Code, "The co-owners shall manage the co-owned immovable or movable property in accordance with their agreement. Where there is no agreement or the agreement is unclear, each co-owner is entitled and obligated to manage it".

2.3 Right to Dispose of Shares

According to Article 305 of the Civil Code, "A co-owner by shares may transfer the portion of shares he owned in the co-owned immovable or movable property. The other co-owners have the right of pre-emption to buy the shares under equivalent conditions". Para. 3, Article 78 of the General Principles of the Civil Law (2009 Amendment) echoes the above provision, stipulating that "Each co-owner by shares shall have the right to withdraw his own share of the common property or transfer its ownership". Here, the "right to withdraw" refers to the right of a co-owner to partition off his share in the commonly owned property. Upon the withdrawal of the share, it is usually necessary to partition the common property. As to the "right to transfer", it means that a co-owner is entitled to assign his share in the property of co-ownership to others according to the law. A co-owner may join or leave a co-ownership relation of his free will. To protect their rights and interests, they shall also be allowed to transfer his due share to the extent that such transaction doesn't prejudice the interests of other co-owners. In the case of a partnership, such withdrawal or transfer is further subject to the stipulation of the partnership agreement. Article 306 of the Civil Code provides that "Where a co-owner by shares transfers the portion of shares he owned in the co-owned immovable or movable property, he shall notify the other co-owners of the conditions of transfer in a timely manner. The other co-owners shall exercise their right of pre-emption within a reasonable period of time. Where two or more co-owners assert their rights of pre-emption, they shall determine through negotiation the proportion of shares each may purchase; where no agreement is reached, they shall exercise their right of pre-emption in proportion to the shares they each own at the time of transfer".

Article 303 of the Civil Code stipulates that "Where the co-owners have agreed not to partition the co-owned immovable or movable property in order to maintain the co-ownership, the agreement shall be followed, provided that a co-owner may request partition if there is a compelling reason for partition. Where there is no agreement or the agreement is unclear, a co-owner by shares may request partition at any time, whereas a joint co-owner may request partition in case the basis for the joint ownership ceases to exist or there is a compelling reason for partition. Compensation shall be made if partition causes damage to the other co-owners". In general cases, the right to withdraw or transfer the share is not subject to temporal limits, they are enjoyed by the co-owners as long as the co-ownership relation exists. However, if it has been previously agreed upon by all the co-owners that during the existence of the co-ownership relation, their shares shall not be transferred or partitioned, then any act that departs from such agreement is to be deemed as breach of contract in that all the co-owners have voluntarily given up their rights to transfer or partition the share. A co-ownership by shares also has certain effects of the ownership, such as the share may be inherited as a legacy upon the decease of the co-owner.

2.4　Priority to Purchase under Equal Conditions

To avoid damage to other right holders from the transfer of one co-owner's due share, Article 305 of the Civil Code stipulates that, "A co-owner by shares may transfer the portion of shares he owned in the co-owned immovable or movable property. The other co-owners have the right of pre-emption to buy the shares under equivalent conditions". This imposes upon the transferor an obligation to notice when he sells his share. In the event that price offered is nearly equal, the rest co-owners have the priority over other non-owners to purchase the share for sale. For instance, A, B and C collectively constructed and equally shared a house. When C intends to transfer his share, A and B has the priority over others to purchase it.

2.5　Disposal and Maintenance of Property in Co-ownership

The disposal and maintenance of property in co-ownership should be made in accordance with the law in view of the fact that the property is shared by all the co-owners. According to Article 301 of the Civil Code, "Unless otherwise agreed by the co-owners, any disposition of the co-owned immovable or movable property, or any major repair or change of the nature or intended use of the co-owned immovable or movable property shall be subject to the consent of the co-owners by shares whose shares account for two thirds or more of the total shares, or to the consent of all joint co-owners". Nonetheless, the interests of the minority owners or those who enjoy a small share in the property shall not be prejudiced when such common property is disposed of by the majority of owners or owners whose shares are dominant in the property.

Any legal disposal of the shared property that is in violation of the law will not exert any legal effect on other co-owners, unless subsequent ratification is acquired. Here, the rule of good faith acquisition may be applicable if the object transferred is a movable property and the transferee is with bona fide when he takes over the property. In case where one or some of the co-owners arrange factual disposal of the common property in violation of the law, for example, by destroying the shared thing, they should undertake tort liability towards other co-owners.

2.6　Obligations of Right holders under Co-ownership by Shares

Regarding the bearing of management costs and other expenses, Article 302 of the Civil Code regulates that, "The management expenses of and other burdens on a thing co-owned by the co-owners shall be borne according to the agreement among the co-owners where there is such an agreement; where there is no agreement or the agreement is unclear, these expenses shall be borne by the co-owners by shares proportionally, and by the joint co-owners jointly". While co-owners share their rights regarding the common property in proportion to the amount or their respective shares, they shall also assume their obligations in the same manner. A larger share indicates more obligations and liabilities arising from the management of the common property, and vice versa.

As is the case with the rights enjoyed by co-owners, the obligations they undertake also overspread the whole common property. None of owners may take obligations on part of the property. For instance, if two persons collectively make capital contribution to the purchase of two trucks for transportation business, they shall share the losses or liabilities when either of the truck get destroyed or have caused damages to another person. Other possible liabilities related to the common property that are to be shared by all the co-owners may also include the management fees, taxes and insurance premium, etc. Where a person who shares ownership pays the aforementioned costs in excess of his share, he shall have the right to recourse from other co-owners.

As regards claims and debts involved in a co-ownership relation, Article 307 of the Civil Code regulates that, "In terms of external relations, the co-owners are jointly and severally entitled to claims and are jointly and severally obligated to perform obligations arising from the co-owned immovable or movable property, unless it is otherwise provided by law or where the third person is aware that the co-owners are not in a relationship of joint and several claims and obligations. In terms of internal relations, unless otherwise agreed by the co-owners, the co-owners by shares are entitled to claims and obligated to perform obligations in proportion to the shares they each own, and the joint co-owners are jointly entitled to claims and obligated to perform obligations. A co-owner by shares who has performed the obligation in excess of his shares has the right of contribution against the other co-owners".

3. Presumption of Co-ownership by Shares in Absence of Agreement or Indefinite Stipulation Regarding the Type of Co-ownership

Article 308 of the Civil Code stipulates that, "Where there is no agreement among the co-owners or the agreement is unclear as to whether the co-owned immovable or movable property is under co-ownership by shares or under joint co-ownership, the immovable or movable property shall be deemed to be under co-ownership by shares, unless the co-owners are in a relationship such as familial relationship and the like". This provision has reversed the long-standing judicial tradition that favors a presumption of joint co-ownership while dealing with identical matters, which was provided for by Article 88 of Notice of the Supreme People's Court on Issuing the Opinions on Several Issues concerning the Implementation of the General Principles of the Civil Law of the People's Republic of China (For Trial Implementation) (1988), "For a common property, if some of the co-owners claim for several ownership, but other co-owners claim for joint co-ownership, if the property cannot be proved to be severally owned, it shall be regarded as jointly owned". Of course, this provision is no longer applicable after the implementation of the Real Right Law and the Civil Code.

A co-ownership by shares may extinguish upon co-owners' agreement, acquisition of the joint property by one of the co-owners, or the destruction or transfer of the property in co-ownership.

Section Three   Joint Co-ownership

1. Concept and Features of Joint Co-ownership

Joint co-ownership is another form of co-ownership. Article 299 of the Civil Code states that, "Joint co-owners jointly have the ownership of the co-owned immovable or movable property". Joint co-ownership means that two or more natural persons or legal persons commonly enjoy rights and undertake liabilities of a property without shares according to specific common relationship. The features of joint co-ownership may be summarized as follows:

First, joint co-ownership arises from and is premised on such common relations as marriage, ownership of marital assets formed on the basis of a family's joint labor and ownership of family assets.

Second, the joint property is not partitioned into shares in a joint co-ownership. As long as the joint co-ownership exists, the co-owners cannot request severance of their respective shares. They may do that only after the joint relationship is terminated. This constitutes the major difference between joint co-ownership and co-ownership by shares.

Third, each co-owner equally enjoys rights and assumes obligations in a joint co-ownership. In other words, all of them may equally possess, utilize, obtain profit from and dispose of the joint property as a whole, and undertake liabilities accordingly. Since the rights and obligations are equally shared by all the co-owners, the interests among the subject are much more closely related compared with those under a co-ownership by shares.

2. Rights and Obligations of Co-owners under Joint Co-ownership

2. 1   Equal Rights of Possession, Utilization Regarding the Property of Joint Co-ownership

Profits obtained from the property of joint co-ownership are not distributed in a certain proportion, but rather, equally shared among all the co-owners under joint co-ownership.

2. 2   Management over Joint Co-owned Property

Article 300 of the Civil Code states that "The co-owners shall manage the co-owned immovable or movable property in accordance with their agreement. Where there is no agreement or the agreement is unclear, each co-owner is entitled and obligated to manage it".

2. 3   Disposal and Maintenance of the Property of Joint Co-ownership

Article 301 of the Civil Code provides that "Unless otherwise agreed by the co-owners, any disposition of the co-owned immovable or movable property, or any major repair or change of the nature or intended use of the co-owned immovable or movable property shall be subject to the consent of the co-owners by shares whose shares account for two thirds or more of the total shares, or to the consent of all joint co-owners". Viewed from this, in terms of the disposal and repair of co-owned property the rights and obligations under joint co-ownership and co-ownership by share are the same.

2. 4　Bearing of Management Costs and Other Expenses

According to Article 302 of the Civil Code, "The management expenses of and other burdens on a thing co-owned by the co-owners shall be borne according to the agreement among the co-owners where there is such an agreement; where there is no agreement or the agreement is unclear, these expenses shall be borne by the co-owners by shares proportionally, and by the joint co-owners jointly".

2. 5　Claims and Debts Involved in the Co-ownership Relation

Pursuant to Article 307 of the Civil Code, "In terms of external relations, the co-owners are jointly and severally entitled to claims and are jointly and severally obligated to perform obligations arising from the co-owned immovable or movable property, unless it is otherwise provided by law or where the third person is aware that the co-owners are not in a relationship of joint and several claims and obligations. In terms of internal relations, unless otherwise agreed by the co-owners, the co-owners by shares are entitled to claims and obligated to perform obligations in proportion to the shares they each own, and the joint co-owners are jointly entitled to claims and obligated to perform obligations. A co-owner by shares who has performed the obligation in excess of his shares has the right of contribution against the other co-owners".

During the existence of a joint co-ownership relationship, co-owners may not claim division of their community property. Where some co-owners arbitrarily partition off their shares from the common property, such acts have no validity.

The joint co-ownership may also be established through contract. Where a contact has clearly defined the rights and obligations of the co-owners, the subjects shall act in accordance with the agreement. A joint co-ownership may expire upon termination of the common relationship or the destruction of the property of co-ownership.

3. Forms of Joint Co-ownership

In China, there are two forms of joint co-ownership, namely, joint co-ownership between husband and wife and joint co-ownership among family members.

3. 1 Properties Jointly Owned by Spouse

According to the Civil Code, properties incurred during the existence of marriage shall be jointly owned by both husband and wife, including earnings and assets acquired during this period by either or both of the spouses, but certain special properties and those agreed upon to be owned by one party should be excluded therefrom. Each husband or wife has equal rights in the disposal of jointly owned property. The existence of marriage refers to such period as starting from the registration of marriage and lasting until divorce or the decease of one party.

The pre-marital property that is owned by one party remains his or her personal assets and it will not become jointly owned. Properties incurred during the existence of marriage shall be jointly owned by both husband and wife, which include income from labor incurred by either of the parties, property inherited or bestowed by the parties, property jointly purchased by the parties with their lawful income, and properties whose status is not clear as to whether are jointly owned or not. As pre-marital property that is owned by one party before marriage but has undergone major repair or transformation t by using the property jointly owned by the parities, it also falls into the category of jointly owned properties. In cases where parties come to an agreement regarding the attribution of their properties, such agreement prevails provided that it doesn't violate any laws.

During the existence of marriage, the husband and wife enjoy equal rights of the possession, utilization, seeking from profits' and disposal of the property of their joint co-ownership. Agreement should be reached upon the sale or donation of such property. In the event that a party doesn't object upon the knowledge of the other party's disposal of a property, he or she is presumed to have acquiesced to such act. Division of joint property is granted only upon divorce or inheritance entailed by the decease of a party.

3. 2 Properties Jointly Owned by Family Members

Spouses, parents, children, and other close relatives living together are family members (Article 1045 of the Civil Code). Properties jointly owned by family members are those properties that are jointly created or incurred by family members during the existence of family life. It includes property contributed to the family by a family member, property bestowed on the family as well other assets that are purchased or accumulated on the basis thereof. In a word, properties jointly owned by family refer to income and earnings from the joint labor of family members.

As the joint property serves to maintain the life or production of the family, each member is equally entitled to enjoy it. Unless otherwise provided by law or agreed upon by the family members, the utilization, disposal or partition of the joint property is subject to the unanimous consent of all the family members. The severance of such property is possible only after the termination of family life.

Property jointly owned by family members is different from property of the family. The latter refers to such property as jointly or respectively owned by all family members, including common property owned by family members or husband and wife, personal property owned by the husband or wife, or adult children, etc. As to property jointly owned by family members, it doesn't encompass what is respectively owned by individual family members.

It is meaningful to differentiate a property jointly owned by family members from that individually owned, because first, members may only sever the properties that are jointly owned and not those individually owned when dividing up their family property and living apart. As succession begins upon the decease of a co-owner, only the decedent's due share should be partitioned off from the family's common property and pass to his heir, not the entirety of the family's community property. Second, the debts in production and operation should be secured with the individual's property if the business is operated by an individual, and with the family's property when the business is operated by a family. Article 56 of the Civil Code states that, "The debts of an individual-run industrial and commercial household shall be paid from the assets of the individual who operates the business in his own name or from the individual's family assets if the business is operated in the name of the household, or, if it is impossible to determine whether the business is operated in the name of the individual or in the name of the individual's household, from the individual's family assets. The debts of a rural-land contractual management household shall be paid from the assets of the household that is engaged in the operation on the contracted rural land, or from the portion of the assets of the family members who actually engage in such operation". The family's property denotes the property jointly owned by family members. Third, during the period of the family's common life, the expenses jointly incurred for the common life or production shall be paid with the family's jointly owned property. As to expenses incurred for the individual life of a member, they shall be borne by individual person with his own property.

Section Four　Partition of Co-owned Property

1. Principles of Partition

Co-owners under co-ownership by shares may claim for partition of his due share from the common property, and owners under joint co-ownership may do the same after the co-ownership relation terminates (e. g., divorce, division of family). The following principles shall be complied with when it comes to partition the common property:

1. 1 Compliance with Agreement Reached by Co-owners

According to Article 303 of the Civil Code, "Where the co-owners have agreed not to partition the co-owned immovable or movable property in order to maintain the co-ownership, the agreement shall be followed, provided that a co-owner may request partition if there is a compelling reason for partition". Where it is previously agreed upon by the co-owners as to how the common property should be partitioned, such agreement shall prevail. Under co-ownership, if the contract has forbidden any severance of the joint property during the existence of the co-ownership relation, or is prohibited the withdrawal of co-owners within a certain period of time, then the joint property may not be partitioned within the time stipulated by the contract. In cases where a co-owner transfers his share to a person other than the co-owners and let him join the co-ownership, the agreement should also be complied with.

1. 2 Compliance with Laws

The division of property jointly owned by husband and wife shall be conducted in compliance with the Marriage Law. Article 303 of the Civil Code stipulates that, "Where the co-owners have agreed not to partition the co-owned immovable or movable property in order to maintain the co-ownership, the agreement shall be followed, provided that a co-owner may request partition if there is a compelling reason for partition. Where there is no agreement or the agreement is unclear, a co-owner by shares may request partition at any time, whereas a joint co-owner may request partition in case the basis for the joint ownership ceases to exist or there is a compelling reason for partition. Compensation shall be made if partition causes damage to the other co-owners".

Partition of joint property shall not prejudice the interests of the State, collective organizations or other persons. Properties that are owned by the State or the collective organization, for example, contracted land, tools borrowed from the collective organization, articles left by another for safekeeping, etc. , shall not be taken as jointly owned and thereby partitioned. Illicit income such as concealed funds and articles that are illegally earned shall be recovered in accordance with the law, and are not to be partitioned as joint property. In addition, the partition may not infringe the interests of creditors or other concerned parties. In cases where a real estate is partitioned, certain formalities for transfer registration should be gone through as required by the law.

2. Methods for Partition

According to Article 304 of the Civil Code, "The co-owners may determine through negotiation the way of partition of the co-owned thing. Where they fail to reach an agreement, and where the co-owned immovable or movable property is divisible and its value is not diminished upon division, partition in kind shall be effected; where it is difficult to divide the co-owned thing or where its value would be impaired upon division, partition shall be carried out through dividing the proceeds based on appraisal or obtained from auction or a sale of it. Where the immovable or movable property acquired by a co-owner by means of partition is defective, the other co-owners shall share the losses". Pursuant to this provision, the partition of co-owned property may assume the following forms.

2. 1   Partition of Physical Objects

When the immovable properties or movable properties co-owned can be severed and its value will not be reduced because of such partition, the actual property shall be partitioned. Generally, such properties should be divisible objects such as fodder, cereals, cloths, etc.

2. 2   Partition after Conversion

If it is difficult to partition the property or its value will be reduced because of such partition, the partition shall be made after the property is converted into money, auctioned, or sold.

2. 3   Compensation after Conversion

In the event that a common property is indivisible, the co-owner who intends to acquire it may obtain the ownership provided that he compensates other co-owners for the value that exceeds his due share in the form of money.

3. Effects of Partition

Co-ownership terminates upon the partition of the common property. Each co-owner thereby exclusively owns his due share when the partition is conducted on the physical object or after conversion of such property. If the immovable properties or movable properties of a co-owner obtained from the partition are pursued by a third party or flawed due to facts that occurred before the partition, other co-owners shall share the losses. This is because all the co-owners are obliged to guarantee that each share partitioned from the common property shall be flawless and free from any third party's claim. For instance, when a former co-owner A, after partitioning his due share from the properties he shared with B, found out that one of the objects he got, e. g. , a "Hong Qi HS7" limousine was actually borrowed from C, he shall return the car to C and be properly compensated by B.

第五章 用益物权

第一节 用益物权概述

一、用益物权的概念和特征

《民法典》第 323 条规定："用益物权人对他人所有的不动产或者动产，依法享有占有、使用和收益的权利。"据此，所谓用益物权，是非所有人依法占有、使用和收益他人所有的不动产或动产的物权。

用益物权作为物权的一种，着眼于财产的使用效能、使用价值。在现代民法上，各国物权法贯彻效益原则，已经逐渐放弃了传统民法注重对物的实物支配、注重财产归属的做法，转而注重财产价值形态的支配和利用。两大法系有关财产的现代法律，都充分体现了"利用"为中心的物权观念。传统的以物的"所有"为中心的物权观念，已经被以物的"利用"为中心的现代物权观念所取代。用益物权正是这种以"利用"为中心的物权的主要表现。正是因为这一原因，许多学者认为，现代物权法的核心在于用益物权。[①]用益物权是以对标的物使用、收益为目的的权利。如何理解用益的含义，却存在分歧。有的学者认为应兼具使用和收益两个目的；有的学者认为不必同时兼具使用和收益两个目的。笔者赞成第二种观点。

与财产所有权、担保物权相比较，用益物权的特征有：

（1）是他物权、限制物权、有期限物权

（2）是以物的使用和收益为目的而设立的物权

用益性是用益物权的基本属性，是用益物权与担保物权相区别的基本标志。马克思主义哲学认为，物具有价值和使用价值的双重属性。用益物权和担保物权是就这两种不同的价值而设立的权利：用益物权侧重于物的使用价值，担保物权侧重于物的价值或曰交换价值。正因如此，用益物权又称为使用价值权，而担保物权又称为价值权。由于用益物权的目的在于对物的使用和收益，因而它不可能具有担保物权的变价受偿性和物上代位性等属性。也就是说，用益物权不涉及以用益物的价值清偿债务问题，也不涉及用

---

① 房绍坤等：《用益物权三论》，载《中国法学》1996 年第 2 期。

益物灭失后以其他物代替的问题。用益物权的用益性因用益物权的种类不同而存在着范围和程度上的差别。例如，传统民法上的地上权和永佃权都是以土地为用益物的权利，但两者的用益范围和程度却存在明显的不同：地上权以在土地上营造建筑物和种植树木为用益范围，而永佃权则以在土地上耕作或畜牧为用益范围。

3. 以对标的物的使用、收益为其主要内容，以占有为前提，不包括处分权

用益物权的内容是对标的物的占有、使用、收益，不包括法律上的处分权（在传统民法上，消费物也可以作为用益权标的物，消费物用益权包含了处分权）。具体而言，在用益物权设定以后，物的所有人并没有将其所有权的处分权能移转给用益物权人。用益物权人不具有对标的物的处分权，但可以对其享有的某些用益物权本身进行处分，如土地使用权、典权可以转让，也可以设定抵押。这有利于提高不动产的利用效率并扩大担保物权的客体范围。

用益物权须以实体上支配用益物为成立条件。物权是一种支配权，用益物权和担保物权都是如此，但用益物权和担保物权的支配形态不尽相同。用益物权的内容在于对物的实体进行使用收益，即对物的使用价值的使用收益，因而它必然以对物的实体上的支配，即实体占有为必要前提。用益物必须转移给用益物权人实际占有支配，否则用益物权人的用益目的就无法实现。例如，若不转移土地，地上权人或永佃权人就无法在土地上营造建筑物、种植树木或进行耕作；担保物权的内容在于取得物的交换价值，因而可不必对物进行实体上的有形支配，也可以无形支配为满足。在担保物权中，质权和留置权以标的物实体上的有形支配为必要，但这种支配并不是用益性的。在质权和留置权中，都有权利人非经物之所有人的同意，不得使用收益质物或留置物的规定，否则权利人应负民事责任。

4. 客体主要是不动产

从《民法典》第 323 条的规定和《民法典》中列举的各类用益物权形态来看，中国的用益物权的客体主要是不动产，例外情况下包括不动产权利。此外，为给将来的发展留有空间，还允许动产作为用益物权的客体。

（1）不动产。用益物权是在他人土地上或土地使用权上设立的。动产以占有为公示方法，很难表现较为复杂的用益物权关系，因此不能在动产之上设立用益物权。即使确需要利用他人的动产，也可以通过借用、租赁等方式在短期内满足。动产的价格一般来说并不太贵，如果确有必要长期利用，可以直接购买，而不必依赖用益物权制度。不动产则往往由于其数量有限、价值较大，因而价格十分昂贵。民事主体较难取得其所有权从而使其使用价值得到充分利用，尤其是不动产的买卖往往更难达成，因为在一般情况下，一方常常不愿意支付较高的费用，另一方又因各种原因不愿意轻易转让。因而只有设定用益物权，才能解决非所有人对他人之物使用价值的支配。所以，有必要在不动产之上设立用益物权。

（2）不动产权利。如以土地承包经营权、土地经营权、建设用地使用权为他人设定地役权的情况下，地役权的客体就为不动产权利，而非土地本身。

(3)动产。根据《民法典》第 323 条的规定，动产可以作为用益物权的客体，但根据物权法定原则，动产作为用益物权的客体，只能在法律作出特别规定的情况下才被允许。目前在中国还没有法律明确规定什么动产能够设立用益物权，也没有规定什么样的用益物权可以动产为客体。第 323 条的规定为以后的立法提供了依据。

5. 是独立物权

用益物权不以用益物权人对所有人享有其他财产权利为其存在的前提。用益物权的独立性表明用益物权不具有担保物权所具有的从属性和不可分性的属性。也就是说，用益物权不以他权利的成立为成立前提，不随他权利的让与而让与，亦不随他权利的消灭而消灭。同时，用益物的变化，如部分灭失或价值减少等都将引起用益物权的变化。在用益物权独立性问题上，地役权似有例外。通说认为，地役权具有从属性和不可分性。这似乎与担保物权相同，其实不然。地役权的从属性和不可分性与担保物权的从属性和不可分性存在明显的差别。地役权的从属性是指地役权不得与需役地所有权分离而存在，不得保留地役权而处分需役地所有权。这种从属性具体表现在：地役权必须与需役地所有权一同让与，地役权不得与需役地分离而成为其他权利的标的。地役权的不可分性是指地役权不得被分割为两个以上的权利，也不得使其部分消灭。可见，地役权的从属性和不可分性是为保证需役地人的用益目的而采取的措施，而非为保证某一债权的实现而设置的。

作为物权的一种，权利人不仅可以依用益物权限定的范围支配不动产，而且有权对抗包括所有人在内的任何人对其行使权利的干涉。用益物权的设定使物的利用关系物权化，巩固当事人间的法律关系，得对抗第三人，此为用益物权在法律结构上异于债权的特色。这就使在非所有人对他人之物的利用方面，用益物权制度具有债权制度无可比拟的优越性。在物权法中，用益物权以其对不动产进行特定支配的性质，成为与所有权、担保物权鼎足而立的一类物权。

《民法典》规定的用益物权有土地承包经营权、土地经营权、建设用地使用权、宅基地使用权、居住权、地役权和特许物权。

二、特许物权

（一）特许物权的概念和意义

特许物权，是指自然人、法人或者其他组织依法通过特别行政许可方式取得的对特定空间内的自然资源进行开发和利用的权利，包括海域使用权、探矿权、采矿权、取水权、养殖权、捕捞权等。由于这些权利的设定、流转、内容和效力等多通过《海域使用管理法》《矿产资源法》《渔业法》《水法》等特别法加以规定，因此也被称为特别法上的物权，也有学者称之为准物权。《民法典》第 328 条规定："依法取得的海域使用权受法律保护。"第 329 条规定："依法取得的探矿权、采矿权、取水权和使用水域、滩涂从事养殖、捕捞的权利受法律保护。"可见，物权法对特许物权的种类作出了规定，但其具体内容仍需要特别法加以规定。

特许物权与一般的用益物权的区别在于：

(1)权利客体上，特许物权的客体，是特定空间范围内的水资源、矿产资源、海域等，而非土地、房屋等不动产，因为这些资源都是国家所有。

(2)支配方式上，特许物权的权利人并不直接支配特定的不动产，而只是对某种不动产从事某种特定的开发、利用行为。

(3)在权利设定上，特许物权的设定往往受到更多的限制，权利的内容和期限大多是由行政机关界定的。

(4)在权利行使上，特许物权通常涉及自然资源的开发和利用，特许物权的行使往往具有较高的危险性，因此对权利人的资质以及权利的行使方式，法律往往加以强制性规定。

在《民法典》中规定特许物权具有重要意义：一是明确了特许物权是物权的一种，因此应当适用物权规则；二是明确了特许物权的私权性质，有利于对其保护。

(二)特许物权的主要种类及内容

1. 海域使用权

根据《中华人民共和国海域使用管理法》(以下简称《海域使用管理法》)的规定，所谓海域是指中华人民共和国内水、领海的水面、水体、海床和底土。随着科学技术的发展、人口的增加和自然资源的减少，"二战"以后，海域的经济价值越来越引起重视，各沿海国家纷纷制定法律对海域进行保护和规范。中国是一个海洋大国，海域管辖总面积超过300万平方公里，约为陆地面积的三分之一，该部法律的实施意义重大。该部法律规定：海域属于国家所有，国务院代表国家行使海域所有权。单位和个人使用海域，必须依法取得海域使用权。《民法典》第328条明确规定了依法取得的海域使用权受法律保护。尽管上述两部法律均确认了海域使用权的存在，却未明确规定海域使用权的性质和含义。

海域使用权是指单位或者个人依法取得对国家所有的特定海域的排他性使用权。单位或个人使用海域，必须依法取得海域使用权。海域使用权取得的方式主要有三种：一是单位或个人向海洋行政主管部门申请，申请被批准后取得；二是招标；三是拍卖。有关单位或个人使用海域的申请被批准或者通过招标、拍卖方式取得海域使用权后，海域使用权人应当办理登记手续。依照《不动产登记暂行条例》第7条第1款、第3款规定，海域使用权登记由海域所在地的县级及县级以上人民政府不动产登记机构办理；国务院批准项目用海、用岛等不动产登记，由国务院国土资源主管部门会同有关部门规定。根据使用海域不同的用途，海域使用权最高期限分别为：养殖用海十五年；拆船用海二十年；旅游、娱乐用海二十五年；盐业、矿业用海三十年；公益事业用海四十年；港口、修造船厂等建设工程用海五十年。海域作为国家重要的自然资源实行有偿使用制度。单位或个人使用海域，应当按照国务院的规定缴纳海域使用金。为了切实保护养殖用海渔民的利益，目前海域主管部门在实际工作中对有争议的海域、海洋自然保护区、渔业资源保护区、传统赶海区等涉及公共利益的海域不进行招标或拍卖。同时，对于专业渔民使用海域从事养殖生产的，可以在规定的面积内减缴或者免缴海域使用金。海域使用权作为一项重要的财产性权利，可以依法转让、继承。

2. 采矿权

采矿权是指具有相应资质条件的法人、公民或其他组织在法律允许的范围内，对国家所有的矿产资源享有的占有、开采和收益的一种特别法上的物权，采矿权在《民法典》概括性规定基础上由《中华人民共和国矿产资源法》予以明确细化。采矿权客体包括矿产资源和矿区，具有复合性，并且矿区及其所蕴含的矿藏种类规模不同对采矿权的取得及行使有重要影响。采矿权可有限制地转让，中国法律应明确并完善采矿权的抵押、出租和承包等流转形式。

2009 年 8 月 27 日修订的《中华人民共和国矿产资源法》第 3 条第 3 款规定："勘查、开采矿产资源，必须依法分别申请、经批准取得探矿权、采矿权，并办理登记；但是，已经依法申请取得采矿权的矿山企业在划定的矿区范围内为本企业的生产而进行的勘查除外。"此规定明确了采矿权的取得方法和程序。设立采矿权本身是国家行使矿产资源所有权的结果，也是合理利用自然资源，促进资源有效利用的重要方式。[①]

3. 探矿权

探矿权是指权利人在依法取得的勘查许可证规定的范围内勘查矿产资源的权利。依法取得探矿权的自然人、法人或其他经济组织称为探矿权人。享有法定主体资格的单位或个人依法向国家管理机关提出申请，经审查批准后取得勘查许可证，在规定的区块范围和期限内，按批准的内容进行矿产资源勘查的权利。国家将原本属于国家的矿产资源所有权以设置特许权的方式授予探矿权人使用，它是矿业权的组成部分，其主体为获得探矿权的单位或个人，其客体为批准的区块范围内特定的矿产资源。探矿权具有物权的性质或称为他物权，具有排他性，即在批准的区块范围和期限内不允许设立第二个探矿权，也不允许任何其他单位和个人在该区块内勘查矿产资源。

4. 取水权

取水权是指直接从地下、江河、湖泊等水资源中取水的权利。它是为必须改变自然状态下的水的空间位置，才可以对水进行利用而设立的重要权益，如农业灌溉、工业用水、生活用水和人工养殖渔业用水等。《中华人民共和国水法》第 48 条规定，直接从江河、湖泊或者地下取用水资源的单位和个人，应当按照国家取水许可制度和水资源有偿使用制度的规定，向水行政主管部门或者流域管理机构申请领取水许可证，并缴纳水资源费，取得取水权。但是，家庭生活和零星散养、圈养畜禽饮用等少量取水的除外。

5. 渔业权(捕捞权、养殖权)

(1)渔业权(捕捞权、养殖权)概念

根据《中华人民共和国渔业法》的规定，渔业权是指权利人根据渔业法的规定所取

---

① 王燕国、肖国兴：《浅议采矿权》，载《中国地质》1993 年第 11 期。

得的从事渔业的权利。主要包括水面、滩涂的使用权，养殖权，捕捞权等。渔业权不是一项独立的民事权利类型，渔业权制度的存废与海域的法律地位紧密相连。作为国内法上的渔业权制度，在英美法系国家并非一种财产权，而是一种公权，体现为国家对海洋渔业资源进行管理的许可证制度；在以日本为代表的大陆法系国家，渔业权是一种由本权和派生权利共同组成的双层权利结构。由于中国明确宣示海域为国家所有，传统法上的渔业权制度被现有的不动产物权体系所吸收，若创设渔业权，将破坏物权法上的一物一权原则。

渔业一般包括捕捞渔业和养殖渔业，因而，渔业权一般可划分为捕捞权和养殖权。捕捞权是指权利人依法对自然状态的特定水域(包括特定领海水域、内水水域、专属经济区水域、江河、湖泊水域)生物资源予以获取和收益的权利，属于自然资源使用权的一种。在一般情况下，行使捕捞权不需要也不能对特定水域进行排他性的使用，这种权利虽然没有排他性，但也属于对一定水域的持续利用。有人甚至一生都在固定的海域捕鱼，因而，在特定领海水域、内水水域、专属经济区水域这种捕捞权也是一种海域使用权。

养殖权是指权利人依法在国家或者集体所有的水域、滩涂从事养殖活动并排斥他人干涉的权利，目的是对养殖生物予以获取和收益，行使养殖权需要对特定水域进行排他性的使用。因此，海域使用权与渔业权属于交叉概念，海洋渔业权中的养殖权包括于海域使用权中，而海域使用权不限于养殖权。

《民法典》第 329 条规定："依法取得的探矿权、采矿权、取水权和使用水域、滩涂从事养殖、捕捞的权利受法律保护。"这就从法律上确认了养殖权、捕捞权为一种准用益物权，如此规定的主要意义在于：第一，其使渔业权成为一种长期稳定的权利。因为准用益物权的取得虽然需要经过行政许可，但是在取得之后就成为一种准用益物权，行政机关不得随意干涉，这就有利于维护渔业经营者的权利。中国有许多渔业经营者，完全靠水产养殖为生，且有的祖祖辈辈均从事水产养殖，水面就是其赖以生存的基本生产资料，如果其对养殖经营的水面不能享有物权，有关政府机关可以随意调整或收回权利，这就势必极大地损害养殖经营者的利益。第二，这有利于鼓励养殖经营者从事各种投资行为，有恒产者有恒心，由于渔业权成为一种长期稳定的财产权利，经营者基于对养殖的合理期待从而能够大胆地对养殖业进行投资，如果养殖权不能成为物权，则很难鼓励养殖业者作长远的投资。[①] 第三，其为渔业权在未来进行制度完善提供了一定的空间。由于渔业权是一种准用益物权，所以，在权利的设定、内容等方面，如果《渔业法》等特别法没有进行规定，则适用《民法典》的相关规定，尤其是确认其是一种准用益物权之后，对于此种权利的流转、保护等都可以适用《民法典》的相关规定，这就更加有利于保护渔业权人的利益，并为以后渔业权制度的完善提供了制度空间。

[①]　王利明：《试论〈物权法〉中海域使用权的性质和特点》，载《社会科学研究》2008 年第 4 期。

渔业权在法律效力上具有优先性，表现在以下几个方面：①渔业权在法律效力上优先于债权。某特定水域本来存在租赁权，当该水域成为渔业权的客体时，该租赁权终止。在严格的意义上，这是渔业权排他性的表现。②渔业权在法律效力上优先于水资源所有权。水资源所有权虽然是渔业权产生的母权，但在特定水域的利用方面，渔业权优先于水资源所有权，水资源所有权人不得妨碍渔业权的行使；在取得所捕捞的水生动物所有权方面，属于捕捞权的效力，水资源所有权不发挥作用，否则，渔业权就没有存在的价值。③渔业权在法律效力上优先于其他用益物权。有时渔业权与取水权虽然可以并存于同一水域，但渔业权优先受到保护。

（2）养殖权与海域使用权辨析

养殖权和海域使用权这两种权利可能同时涉及对海域的利用问题，在内容上具有一定程度的交叉，因而，在《民法典》的制定过程中，对海域使用权和养殖权的相互关系存在不同的看法：一是单一海域使用权说，该学说认为《民法典》只应当规定海域使用权，而不应当规定养殖权，因为，海域使用权可以涵盖养殖权的所有内容。而在其他水面上的养殖权，可以通过土地承包经营权的扩大解释来解决。养殖权从来不是，也不应当成为民法上的权利。[1] 二是单一养殖权说，此种观点认为，《民法典》只应当规定养殖权，而不应当规定海域使用权，因为，养殖权可以包括所有水面上的养殖，而海域使用权只能包括在海域上的养殖，且海域使用权缺乏调整目的和功能，如果海域用于养殖，就应当通过养殖权来代替；如果海域是用于捕捞，就应当通过捕捞权来代替。[2] 三是双重权利承认说，此种观点认为，尽管养殖权与海域使用权之间存在一定的交叉，但它们实际上是两种不同性质的权利，因此，《民法典》应当同时承认这两种准用益物权。多数国家的立法采纳了第三种观点。

《民法典》也采纳了第三种观点，分别在《民法典》第 328 条和第 329 条规定了海域使用权和养殖权。可以看出，海域使用权与养殖权这两种权利在内容上确实存在交叉，主要表现在：如果权利人要利用特定的海域从事养殖活动，将可能同时涉及海域使用权和养殖权的内容。如何解决两者之间在取得、行使时可能产生的冲突和矛盾，应当引起立法者的重视。

《海域使用管理法》第 25 条规定："海域使用申请人可以利用海域从事养殖。"《中华人民共和国渔业法》第 11 条规定："单位和个人使用国家规划确定用于养殖业的全民所有的水域、滩涂的，使用者应当向县级以上地方人民政府渔业行政主管部门提出申请，由本级人民政府核发养殖证，许可其使用该水域、滩涂从事养殖生产。"由于国有的水域包括了海域，据此申请人可以申请利用国有的海域从事养殖业，那么，海域使用权人经过申请和批准，获得海域使用权证书之后，是否还必须取得养殖权证书？反过来说，养

---

① 尹田：《中国海域物权制度研究》，中国法制出版社 2004 年版，第 159 页。
② 崔建远：《海域使用权制度及其反思》，载《政法论坛》2004 年第 6 期。

殖权人如果经过申请批准，获得养殖许可证书之后，是否还必须取得海域使用权证书？两种权利之间是重叠的还是相互冲突的？这些问题值得探讨。

尽管海域使用权与养殖权在内容上存在重叠和交叉，但两者毕竟是两种不同性质的准用益物权，在法律上也是可以作出区分的，其主要表现在：第一，二者的设定目的不同。养殖权的设立目的是利用水域从事水生动植物的养殖，但并不需要利用水域之上的空间；而海域使用权设立的目的非常广泛，除可以从事养殖活动外，还包括从事拆船，旅游娱乐、盐业矿业、公益事业、建设工程等诸多活动。当然，随着海洋经济以及科学技术的发展，海域的利用方式日益丰富发展，海域使用权的具体内容还将有新的发展。第二，两种权利的客体不同。海域使用权的客体是海域，而养殖权的客体是所有的水面和滩涂，包括江、河、湖、泊等的水面。根据《渔业法》第 2 条，在内水、滩涂、领海、专属经济区以及一切其他海域均可设立养殖；而海域使用权的范围仅限于海域本身。尤其是养殖权人可以在集体所有的水域进行养殖，从而使养殖权与承包经营权具有类似性；而海域使用权人只能利用专属于国家所有的海域。第三，两者适用的法律不同。《民法典》只是对养殖权和海域使用权作了原则性规定，两者的具体内容要根据特别法来具体确定，其中养殖权主要依据《渔业法》确定，而海域使用权要适用《海域使用管理法》的规定。

针对养殖权和海域使用权之间可能发生的冲突，法律上有必要作出一个整体的设计，不能够让权利人在取得一项权利之后，还要办理两次手续，增加取得此项用益物权利益的成本。如果能够通过颁发一个权证解决权利归属，则对保护权利人的权益是非常必要的。笔者认为，首先，应该根据当事人设立权利的目的来考虑，如果当事人仅仅只是从事养殖业，则可以考虑申请设立养殖权；而如果当事人要从事养殖以外的活动。例如开采、建造等活动，则应申请设立海域使用权。其次，也要考虑简化当事人的登记申请程序。例如，如果申请人要利用特定的海域从事养殖，而且已经获得一个权利的权属证书，就视为其同时获得了两种权利的资格，已经取得了另一个部门的审批，但是如果不是利用特定的海域从事养殖活动，而是从事其他的活动，或者主要是从事养殖活动但同时还要从事一些其他附属性活动，则必须要取得海域使用权证。如果申请人不仅仅利用海域，还要利用其他土地进行养殖，那就还需要取得养殖许可证。当然，负有审批两项权利的政府部门之间必须要有必要的协调和信息共享机制。另外，在同一海域范围内，如果不同的申请人都获得了许可证书。例如，某人从事养殖业，另一人从事建造、开采等活动，在此情况下，可以考虑根据两项规则来解决：一是根据物权法中的"先来后到"规则，如果两项权利之间发生直接冲突，譬如一人根据养殖权要求从事养殖，另一人根"海域使用权也要求进行养殖活动，则应根据两项权利设立的时间顺序来解决冲突。二是参照《民法典》第 346 条的规定，新设定的用益物权不得损害已设定的用益物权。例如，一人首先在特定的海域取得了养殖权从事养殖，另一人以后又取得海域使用权来从事开采、建造等活动，则开采，建造等行为不得影响他人的养殖活动。

第二节　土地承包经营权、土地经营权

一、土地承包经营权的概念和特征

中国《宪法》第 8 条规定："农村集体经济组织实行家庭承包经营为基础、统分结合的双层经营体制。……参加农村集体经济组织的劳动者，有权在法律规定的范围内经营自留地、自留山、家庭副业和饲养自留畜。"《民法典》第 330 条重申了这一基本体制，规定："农村集体经济组织实行家庭承包经营为基础、统分结合的双层经营体制。农民集体所有和国家所有由农民集体使用的耕地、林地、草地以及其他用于农业的土地，依法实行土地承包经营制度。"而土地承包经营权就是对家庭承包经营为基础、统分结合的双层经营体制在民事法律中的具体体现。

(一) 土地承包经营权的概念与特征

《民法典》第 331 条规定："土地承包经营权人依法对其承包经营的耕地、林地、草地等享有占有、使用和收益的权利，有权从事种植业、林业、畜牧业等农业生产。"据此，所谓土地承包经营权，是指自然人、法人或其他组织因从事种植业、林业、畜牧业、渔业生产或其他生产经营项目而对集体所有或国家所有的土地或森林、山岭、草原、荒地、滩涂、水面等享有的占有、使用和收益的权利。

从现行立法的规定和中国农村土地制度改革的方向来看，此种权利具有下列特征：

1. 土地承包经营权的主体具有限定性。

在此种权利产生之初，法律禁止其流转，故而其主体限于农村集体经济组织成员或者农村承包经营户。但随着中国农村土地制度改革的深入进行，法律逐渐放开了对土地承包经营权、土地经营权的流转限制。因此，土地承包经营权的主体不仅包括农村集体经济组织成员，还包括农村集体经济组织成员之外的自然人以及法人和其他组织。当然，对于农用地，其只能通过本集体经济组织家庭承包的方式设定土地承包经营权，故而其初始取得的权利人只能是集体经济组织成员。就"四荒"等其他土地而言，其初始取得的权利人也可以是集体经济组织成员之外的民事主体。

2. 土地承包经营权的客体具有广泛性。

《农村土地承包法》①第 2 条规定："本法所称农村土地，是指农民集体所有和国家所有依法由农民集体使用的耕地、林地、草地，以及其他依法用于农业的土地。"这就确立了土地承包经营权的客体范围。从这一规定来看，此种权利的客体具有广泛性，体现在如下两个方面：

---

①　该法 2018 年 12 月 29 日全国人民代表大会常务委员会第二次修正。

（1）其客体不仅可以是集体所有的土地，还包括国家所有依法由农民集体使用的土地。从中国法律的规定来看，国家所有的土地主要集中在城市，但是由于一些历史因素，在农村国家也拥有大量的农用地，例如，在"土改"时没有将土地所有权分配给农民的土地、实施1962年《农村人民公社工作条例修正草案》未划入农民集体范围内的土地、国有农场的土地等。这些土地，其中不少是国家交给集体使用的。对于这些土地，国家允许集体长期使用，而不能随意收回。这些土地，也属于《农村土地承包法》所言的农村土地的范围，可以成为土地承包经营权的客体。

（2）其客体不仅包括耕地、林地、草地，还包括其他依法用于农业的土地。所谓"依法用于农业的土地"，依据《土地管理法》第4条对土地用途的分类，应当包括各种农用地，即耕地、林地、草地、养殖水面等。荒山、荒沟、荒丘、荒滩等"四荒"土地也在土地承包经营权的客体之列，当然"四荒"土地就其土地用途而言，属于"未利用地"。换言之，土地承包经营权的客体实际上包括农村中建设用地之外的各种土地。

3. 土地承包经营权的内容是对土地通过农业生产的方式加以利用、收益。

土地承包经营权人对其土地应当通过农业生产的方式加以利用。所谓农业，依据《农业法》第2条的界定，"是指种植业①、林业、畜牧业和渔业等产业，包括与其直接相关的产前、产中、产后服务"。因此，权利人对土地的支配方式，体现为在土地上进行耕作、造林、畜牧、养殖等农业生产活动。这与建设用地使用权及宅基地使用权以在土地上下建造、保有建筑物、构筑物和附属设施，显然是不同的。因此，内容上或者说土地用途上的差别是土地承包经营权与建设用地使用权的根本区别。当然，在进行农业生产过程中，也不排除建造一定的建筑物、构筑物，如看果园的简易房屋、农田水利设施等。此种建造本质上是附属、辅助于农业生产的。土地承包经营权人进行此种建造行为，并未超出土地承包经营权的内容。需要指出的是，鉴于中国的粮食安全问题，中国法律对农村土地转为建设用地进行了严格的限制，严禁土地承包经营权人将其土地用作建设用途或者变相进行开发、建设。这主要是因为这个国家人口众多、土地资源匮乏，仅凭进口是无法满足整个国家的食品需求的。农用耕地制度、农业生产是中国国家安全、经济发展和社会稳定的基础，正所谓"无农不稳、无农不昌"。因此，《土地管理法》第30条规定："国家保护耕地，严格控制耕地转为非耕地。"此外，即便没有改变农用地的性质，也不得在其上进行农业之外的其他开发活动。《土地管理法》第37条第2、3款明确强调："禁止占用耕地建窑、建坟或者擅自在耕地上建房、挖砂、采石、采矿、取土等。"而且基于粮食安全的考虑，对于基本农田，只能进行种植业，禁止占用基本农田发展林果业和挖塘养鱼。

4. 土地承包经营权性质上属于物权且是有期限物权。

在《物权法》起草过程中，对于法律中土地承包经营权性质的判断，存在争议。长

---

①　指利用植物的生活机能，通过人工培育以取得粮食、副食品、饲料和工业原料的社会生产部门。在中国通常指粮、棉、油、糖、麻、丝、烟、茶、果、药、杂等作物的生产，亦指狭义的农业；种植业同林业、畜牧业、副业和渔业合在一起，为广义的农业。

期以来，法律和司法解释都将土地承包经营权作为债权来处理：土地承包经营权非经发包人同意不得转让、转包或者互换；对于土地承包经营权纠纷，一律是依据合同规则来处理。

《物权法》《民法典》则直接将土地承包经营权界定为一类物权形态，从而为农民享有长期稳定的土地权利打下了坚实的法律基础。土地承包经营权作为一种用益物权，性质上为他物权，即对他人(国家或集体)所有的土地而享有的物权。正是基于此种性质，中国实现了对于农村土地所有权和使用权的分离，创建了家庭承包经营为基础、统分结合的双层经营体制。土地承包经营权作为一种用益物权，性质上为限制物权，不仅在对土地的支配方面受到法律的限制，即只能以从事农业生产的方式来实现土地的使用价值，而且其支配有期限限制。作为限制物权，其有限制所有权的作用，其效力优先于所有权。所有权人亦须尊重其权利，不得侵害或妨害权利的行使。此外，土地承包经营权作为一种用益物权，并不依附于特定人格或者特定土地而存在，可以通过转让、互换等方式流转。因此，它是一种独立的财产权，具备了较大的权利处分权能。

(二)土地承包经营权的物权化及其意义

土地承包经营权的物权化，具有十分重要的意义：

1. 有利于保持权利的长期性和稳定性

如果将土地承包经营权界定为债权，基于债权的期限性，其期限只能按照承包合同的约定来确定。这就可能导致个别地方故意压缩承包期。这种做法将导致农户的短期行为：农户不愿做长期的投入以及合同期限将满时进行掠夺性经营，严重不利于农村经济的长期、稳定发展。而承包经营权物权化，就意味着以法律的形式确认承包经营权的期限。根据物权法定原则，《物权法》《民法典》对土地承包经营权的规定具有强制性，当事人不能进行另外的约定。例如，《民法典》规定耕地的承包期为30年，即便农村集体经济组织与农户之间约定为10年，该约定也没有法律效力，耕地承包期应当按照30年计算。这显然有利于稳定土地承包经营关系，使承包经营权确实成为长期稳定的权利。

2. 有利于土地所有者与承包权人双重利益的兼顾和平衡，赋予了土地承包经营权排他效力

如果将土地承包经营权界定为债权，由于债权在法律上的效力较物权低，不具有排他性，因此不能抗拒来自发包人(土地所有人)和乡村行政组织的各种干涉、侵害。

农村土地承包权的物权化有利于遏止发包方的非法干预，充分保护经营权人的合法权益。经营权人所面临的危险主要来自于发包方的越权干预，依法直接明确承包经营权人的权利范围并赋予其强有力的救济方式，将十分有助于承包权人地位的提升，充分实现其应得的承包经营收益。承包合同的发包人大多是集体组织，在合同的签订、执行过程中往往处于较优势的地位，以致经常发生发包方单方面修改承包合同，加重农户负担、损害农户利益的情形。而承包经营权的物权化就要求对承包经营权的内容由物权法

作出明确规定，不能由发包人随意确定，从而有利于保护承包经营权人的利益。而且作为物权，土地承包经营权具有对抗第三人的效力，并获得物权法的保护。如果他人对物权进行了侵害或者妨害，权利人有权行使物权请求权，无论加害人是否存在过错，都可以要求其返还财产、停止侵害、排除妨害、消除危险。土地承包经营权物权化，就意味着在发包人或者第三人对权利进行侵害的情况下，权利人可以直接主张物权请求权。在造成实际损失的情况下，权利人不仅可以依据合同要求发包人承担违约责任，还有权要求第三人承担侵权责任。

3. 为征收补偿提供法律基础

如果承包人的权利被界定为债权，在国家征收集体土地时，其只能就地上附着物（如修建的水渠等设施）、青苗等获得补偿，而不能对土地享有任何权利。因此，只有作为发包人和土地所有人的集体组织可以成为被征收的当事人和受补偿人，作为承包人的农户的利益得不到妥当的保障。换言之，农民不能就自己丧失土地承包经营权获得补偿。但是，在土地承包经营权物权化后，承包权人就有权单独就土地要求补偿。《民法典》第243条第2款规定：“征收集体所有的土地，应当依法足额支付土地补偿费、安置补助费以及农村村民住宅、其他地上附着物和青苗等的补偿费用，并安排被征地农民的社会保障费用，保障被征地农民的生活，维护被征地农民的合法权益。”其之所以对土地承包经营权人就土地加以补偿，法理基础就在于土地承包经营权的物权化。

4. 促进土地流转，有利于实现农村土地效益的最大化

作为一种相对权，债权及其移转直接关系到合同另一方当事人的利益，因此债权中权利义务的转让在法律上往往受到限制。也就是说，如果把农村土地承包经营权认定为债权，该权利的转让、转包需要经过发包人同意，就不利于农用地进行市场流转。而物权的绝对权属性，决定了其转让原则上无须经过他人同意或者通知。依法赋予农村土地承包经营权以物权的效力，不仅保证承包经营权人自身拥有使用土地获得收益的权利，还充分保障土地能够朝着最佳的使用方向合理流转，确保作为物的土地在流动中发挥其最佳的效益。

5. 土地承包经营权的物权化有利于对集体土地的管理，防止耕地的大量流失。目前，耕地流失的一个重要原因就是集体经济组织的负责人对于土地的转让享有事实上的决定权，而广大农民对土地的转让没有决定性的发言权。在耕地的流失之中，农民完全处于一种被动的无可奈何的状态，实际上被排斥在农地保护之外，这在很大程度上是由于农民没有对承包经营权享有一种稳定性的权利。在承包经营权真正成为农民的长期稳定的物权以后，农民就会切实地从维护自身的物权出发对抗非法的占地、转让等行为，使农民也能够积极参与对耕地的保护。如果乡镇、村或村民小组的负责人擅自非法转让土地，承包经营权人也能以其承包经营权受到侵害为由，基于物权法的规定请求法院宣告非法转让行为无效。

（三）为充分维护农民的合法权益，在土地承包经营权的实践中，应注意的问题

首先，就权利期限而言，基于物权法定原则，土地承包经营权的期限、消灭事由只能由法律规定，双方在合同中另行对此进行的约定，原则上都是无效的。否则，可能造成权利不稳定、集体经济组织过度干预生产等弊端。

其次，在发包方任意撕毁合同，随意调整承包的土地的情况下，权利人更应当通过违约责任而非侵权责任来获得救济。就来自发包人的侵害而言，土地承包经营权性质上为物权，可以得到侵权责任法（民法典第七编 侵权责任）的保护。同时，发包人侵害土地承包经营权显然违反了承包合同的约定，因此也构成违约。《农村土地承包法》在第57条规定了所谓发包人的侵权责任，在第59条又规定了发包人违反承包合同的违约责任。承包人完全可以基于合同主张继续履行，从而继续占有和使用土地，并就因此受到的损失要求损害赔偿。当然，承包经营权作为物权，发包人非法收回其承包的土地的，承包经营权人也可以行使物上请求权，请求返还承包的土地。

最后，在第三人对土地承包经营权进行侵害的情况下，权利人显然可以行使物上请求权。但在土地承包经营权本身存在争议的情况下，权利人也不妨直接基于《民法典》规定的占有保护请求权，请求返还原物、排除妨害或者消除危险。

二、土地承包经营权的设定

《民法典》第333条规定："土地承包经营权自土地承包经营权合同生效时设立。"可见，土地承包经营权应当通过土地承包合同来设定。按照《农村土地承包法》的规定，土地承包经营权的设定，可以通过家庭承包的方式和家庭承包以外的方式来进行。对于农村土地，原则上采取农村集体经济组织内部的家庭承包方式，不宜采取家庭承包方式的荒山、荒沟、荒丘、荒滩等农村土地，可以采取招标、拍卖、公开协商等方式承包。

（一）以家庭承包方式设定土地承包经营权

1. 签订承包合同

所谓以家庭承包方式设定土地承包经营权，是指本集体经济组织成员以家庭为单位，与集体经济组织之间通过合同设定土地承包经营权的行为。《民法典》对土地承包经营权的规定，主要适用于通过家庭承包方式设定的土地承包经营权。承包合同应当以书面形式为之，一般包括以下条款：发包方、承包方的名称，发包方负责人和承包方代表的姓名、住所；承包土地的名称、坐落、面积、质量等级；承包期限和起止日期；承包土地的用途；发包方和承包方的权利和义务；违约责任。家庭承包的承包方是本集体经济组织的农户。发包方则应当根据土地所有权的归属来确定：农民集体所有的土地依法属于村农民集体所有的，由村集体经济组织或者村民委员会发包；已经分别属于村内两个以上农村集体经济组织的农民集体所有的，由村内各该农村集体经济组织或者村民

小组发包。国家所有依法由农民集体使用的农村土地，由使用该土地的农村集体经济组织、村民委员会或者村民小组发包。

承包方案应当经本集体经济组织成员的村民会议 2/3 以上成员或者 2/3 以上村民代表同意方可通过。通过后，应当依法公开组织实施承包方案，并签订承包合同。

2. 集体经济组织的强制缔约义务

在家庭承包的情况下，承包人都是本集体经济组织成员，其土地在历史上是农民响应党的号召、自愿放弃其土地所有权而形成的，因此农村集体经济组织应当以无偿提供土地供其使用作为一种补偿。而作为社会主义公有制的实现形式，集体经济组织有义务为其成员提供基本的农业生产资料——土地。因此，基于历史因素以及集体作为社会主义公有制形式的本质，在原有的集体所有、集体经营的体制结束之后，作为发包人的集体经济组织负有强制缔约义务，应当满足其成员提出签订合同从而取得土地承包经营权的要求。《农村土地承包法》第 5 条规定："农村集体经济组织成员有权依法承包由本集体经济组织发包的农村土地。"实际上就科加了集体经济组织此种强制缔约义务①。而农村集体经济组织成员主张自己进行承包的权利，实际上是其作为集体经济组织成员的成员权的内容之一。但是，对于新增的集体成员，按照《农村土地承包法》第 29 条的规定，只能通过集体经济组织依法预留的机动地、通过依法开垦等方式增加的土地以及承包方依法、自愿交回的土地，来满足其承包要求。如果已经没有此种土地，则鉴于客观上不能履行，集体经济组织无法与其签订承包合同。

3. 承包方为本集体经济组织的农户

依据《农村土地承包法》第 16 条之规定，家庭承包的承包方是本集体经济组织的农户。农户内家庭成员依法平等享有承包土地的各项权益。这主要是因为在 20 世纪 80 年代普遍推行联产承包责任制时，采取了包产到户的做法。此后，国家力求稳定承包关系，并提倡"增人不增地、减人不减地"。这样，以户为单位的做法就一直保留下来，为现行法所沿用。当然，实践中如果出现家庭成员要求分家析产的，因为土地承包经营权是家庭共有财产，可以参照共同共有财产的分割规则来处理。

4. 土地承包经营权设定的方式

虽然《民法典》对不动产物权变动原则上采登记要件主义，但是土地承包经营权的设定则为法律规定的例外情形，其设定不以登记为要件。《民法典》第 333 条第 1 款实际上是重申了《农村土地承包法》第 23 条的规定："土地承包经营权自土地承包经营权合同生效时设立。"这就是说，此种合同一经成立就立即生效，而且该效力并非指承包人有权请求发包人交付土地并移转土地承包经营权的债权效力，而是直接发生物权创设的效力。

是否登记与土地承包经营权是否设定并无直接关系。这与建设用地使用权等不动产物权必须通过登记方可设定，形成了鲜明的对比。

---

① 广义上的缔约义务是指特定主体有法定义务与第三人缔结合同。

发放产权证也不是土地承包经营权的设定条件。《民法典》第 333 条第 2 款规定："登记机构应当向土地承包经营权人发放土地承包经营权证、林权证等证书，并登记造册，确认土地承包经营权。"该条实际上是重申了《农村土地承包法》第 24 条第 1 款的规定，即"国家对耕地、林地和草地等实行统一登记，登记机构应当向承包方颁发土地承包经营权证或者林权证等证书，并登记造册，确认土地承包经营权"。为了制止乱收费，《农村土地承包法》第 24 条同时强调："登记机构除按规定收取证书工本费外，不得收取其他费用。"农村土地承包经营权证是农村土地承包合同生效后，国家依法确认承包方享有土地承包经营权的法律凭证。

在广袤的中国农村、城市郊区，通过承包合同而无须登记来直接设定土地承包经营权，符合中国的实际情况。由此设定的权利，虽然未经登记，也应当具有对抗第三人的效力。这主要是因为，如前所述，土地承包合同的承包方只能是集体经济组织内部的成员。中国农村目前仍然属于熟人社会，在承包合同签订之后，即便没有登记，第三人也知悉或应该知悉该土地并非自己的，从而不得对其进行侵害。因此，公示的权利保护功能无从发挥。在农村集体土地没有初始登记的情况下，第三人也不可能受让该权利或者对之享有抵押权。因此，根本不可能存在标的物上有多个权利、从而哪项权利更为优先的问题，自然也不存在因权利瑕疵而影响交易安全的情况。中国农村尚处于熟人社会的特点，决定了土地承包经营权的设定，无须登记即可完成。而此种权利天然地具有对抗第三人的效力。此外，从中国农村的实际情况来看，农村土地幅员辽阔，各地情形千差万别，而农村土地承包合同的订立又往往赶在同一时间。因此，一概要求进行登记，在技术上存在难度。如果强行要求登记设立，反而可能引发一系列问题。当然，在土地承包经营权初始设立之后，如果权利人意欲对之处分，则为维护交易安全，应当先行办理登记。否则，不能发生对抗善意第三人的效力。

5. 土地承包经营权的期限

《民法典》第 332 条第对承包期进行了规定："耕地的承包期为三十年。草地的承包期为三十年至五十年。林地的承包期为三十年至七十年。前款规定的承包期限届满，由土地承包经营权人依照农村土地承包的法律规定继续承包。"《农村土地承包法》第 21 条规定："耕地的承包期为三十年。草地的承包期为三十年至五十年。林地的承包期为三十年至七十年。前款规定的耕地承包期届满后再延长三十年，草地、林地承包期届满后依照前款规定相应延长。"

这里的承包期，严格地讲，是指土地承包经营权的存续期限。

《物权法》《民法典》对承包期限的规定性质上为强制性规定，当事人应当在法律规定的范围内加以约定。对于《农村土地承包法》实施之后，尤其是《物权法》实施之后订立的家庭承包合同，则如果期限长于法定期限，则超出部分无效；如果期限短于法定期限，则应当按照法定最低期限来确定。

此外，考虑到在农村实行土地承包经营制度是中国将长期坚持的一项基本制度，为了赋予农民长期而有保障的土地使用权，促进农业、农村经济发展和农村社会稳定，

《民法典》第 332 条第 2 款规定："前款规定的承包期届满，由土地承包经营权人按照国家有关规定继续承包。"至于具体的条件，应当依据当时的规定来具体确定。按照现行《农村土地承包法》的规定，本轮承包期满后耕地承包期再延长三十年，草地、林地承包期届满后依照该法第 21 条第 1 款规定相应延长。

(二) 以家庭承包以外的方式设定土地承包经营权

对于不宜完全采取家庭承包方式的"四荒"等土地，现行法律允许其以其他方式进行承包。因此，以家庭承包以外的方式设定土地承包经营权时，其客体的范围受到了法律的严格限制。《民法典》第 342 条规定："通过招标、拍卖、公开协商等方式承包农村土地，经依法登记取得权属证书的，可以依法采取出租、入股、抵押或者其他方式流转土地经营权。"因此，在法律适用上，以家庭承包以外的方式设定的土地承包经营权，应当适用特别法的规定，而不应直接适用《民法典》的规定。依据相关法律、法规，此种承包经营权的设定，主要涉及如下内容：

1. 承包人与家庭承包不同

此种承包，承包人可以是集体经济组织之外的自然人、法人或其他组织。通过家庭承包方式在集体所有或者使用的农用地上设定土地承包经营权，主要是基于历史因素以及农村集体经济组织的社会主义性质，集体负有为其成员提供土地以供开展农业生产的义务，或者说是为了维护每一个集体经济组织成员的平等的承包资格。基于承包经营权，农村集体经济组织的成员可以要求集体将其所有或者使用的全部农用地通过承包的方式分配给农民使用。

但是，对于"四荒"土地这种未利用地，其并不当然具备农业生产条件，可能需要进行特别的投入方可用于耕作或种植，而农户本身未必具有相应的资金、技术、劳动力等开发能力。如果强行将之平均分配给农村集体经济组织成员进行开发，无异于给其增加了负担，而且不利于对"四荒"土地的利用。此外，还要考虑到，对于"四荒"土地的开发，通常要支付较大的开发成本，这就需要以一定的规模为基础，从而才能在合理的期限内收回投资。如果将"四荒"土地平均分配给农村集体经济组织成员进行开发，则可能无法实现规模效益，从而得不偿失。

因此，现行法律对"四荒"土地的承包设定了不同的规则，允许集体经济组织成员之外的自然人、法人或其他组织经过集体经济组织民主程序决定之后，承包"四荒"土地并取得承包经营权。但为了维护本集体经济组织及其成员的利益，法律规定，以其他方式承包农村土地，在同等条件下，本集体经济组织成员享有优先承包权；本集体经济组织以外的单位或者个人承包，应当事先经本集体经济组织成员的村民会议 2/3 以上成员或者 2/3 以上村民代表的同意，并报乡（镇）人民政府批准；而且，应当对承包方的资信情况和经营能力进行审查后，再签订承包合同。

2. 直接发包与折股后发包

《农村土地承包法》对于其他方式的承包，规定了两种发包程序：一是直接通过招标、拍卖、公开协商等方式对外发包。也就是说，通过民主决定程序确定承包方案之后，直接对外发出将"四荒"土地发包的要约邀请。二是将土地承包经营权折股分给本集体经济组织成员后，再实行承包经营或者股份合作经营。也就是说，先将集体所有的"四荒"土地先设定承包经营权，而所有的集体经济组织成员对之持有平等的份额。然后，或者通过股份合作制的方式由全体集体经济组织成员共同经营，而不再另行发包，各成员按照股份从经营收益中获得分红并共担风险；或者将该土地承包经营权以集体的名义再行对外发包，各集体经济组织成员按照份额来分享承包费。

实践中，直接发包的方式占了绝大多数。立法者之所以规定折股后发包，主要是为了保护集体经济组织成员尤其是没有经营能力成员的利益，从而维护各成员之间的公平、平等地位。而且此种做法，由于其公平性，也避免了个别成员对承包的结果不服从而可能导致的纠纷。笔者认为，折股分配的办法，在公平和效率之间实现了完美的平衡，有利于实现社会的和谐稳定，应当成为未来主要的发包方式。

3. 设定方式

现行法律规定了招标、拍卖、公开协商等承包合同的订立方式。关于招标、拍卖，应当遵循《拍卖法》和《招标投标法》的规定，并结合土地承包合同的特点进行进一步具体规定，确保招标、拍卖能够为有竞买意向者尤其是本集体经济组织成员所知悉。

而所谓的公开协商，从实践中的情况来看，主要是强调承包的方法、程序、过程和结果，应当进行公开，尤其是向本集体经济组织成员公开，从而避免少数人操纵之下的私自承包。但是大致看来，其本质仍然与建设用地使用权的协议出让一样，是通过一对一的谈判来完成的。

笔者认为，为了维护农民的利益，避免集体财产流失，应当考虑借鉴中国建设用地使用权出让的做法，一律采取公开竞价的方式来订立承包合同。也就是说，应当将现行法中的公开协商进一步具体化为挂牌出让的方式，从而通过公开竞价实现"四荒"土地的价值。

4. 承包合同及其性质

在通过招标、拍卖及公开协商方式确定承包人之后，应当签订承包合同。换言之，承包合同应当以书面形式为之。当事人的权利和义务、承包期限等，由双方协商确定。以招标、拍卖方式承包的，承包费通过公开竞标、竞价确定；以公开协商等方式承包的，承包费由双方议定。需要指出的是，此种权利存续期限或者说承包期限，虽然可以由当事人自由约定，但按照现行政策，耕地不得超过 30 年，草地不得超过 50 年，林地不超过 70 年。

值得注意的是，《农村土地承包法》第 53 条规定，通过招标、拍卖、公开协商等方式承包农村土地，经依法登记取得权属证书的，可以依法采取出租、入股、抵押或者其他方式流转土地经营权。按照该法律制定的本意，在没有登记的情况下，承包人取得的只是债权，而登记发生创设物权的效力。之所以如此，是因为"四荒"土地为非利用地，在中国土地分类管理、登记的情况下，土地用途没有确定，无法进行登记。因此，应当待"四荒"土地的初步治理完成后，根据其主导经营内容，依法分别由登记机构发放土地证、林权证、草原证或养殖使用证等其他相应的权属证明。

农村土地承包合同，是国家出于保障农村经济发展和社会安定，使得农民依法长期享有土地使用权的目的而订立。根据上文对承包合同的内容、特征分析，承包合同体现出了主体法定、契约内容法定、缔约强制和解约限制义务等特征，据此，有学者把农村土地承包合同的性质确定为行政合同。

签订农村土地承包合同的主要目的在于设立农村土地承包经营权。考察《农村土地承包法》《民法典》的相关规定，可以发现在发包方和承包方签订承包合同时设立的土地承包经营权是民事权利，但作为发包方的集体还是享有一定的行政性权力，同时承包方也应当承担一定的公法性义务，这些规定的确与民事合同的性质背道而驰，但其中发包方享有的这些行政性权力并不是所谓的行政合同中行政主体的特权，而是法律在定位作为发包方的集体的职能时所造成的错位。《最高人民法院关于审理涉及农村土地承包纠纷案件适用法律问题的解释》①第1条甚至明确将承包合同纠纷、承包经营权侵权纠纷、承包经营权互换、转让纠纷、承包经营权流转纠纷、承包地征收补偿费用分配纠纷、承包经营权继承纠纷、土地经营权继承纠纷界定为民事纠纷。因此，从农村土地承包合同的设立目的、合同主体定位、救济方式等综合分析，笔者认为其应当定位为民事合同，而不是行政合同。

三、土地承包经营权的内容

(一)土地承包经营权人的权利

土地承包经营权性质上为用益物权，故而权利人有权占有承包地，以农业生产的方法使用承包地，并获取土地上的出产物等天然孳息。至于如何进行生产，承包人享有经营自主权。《农村土地承包法》强调承包人有权自主组织生产经营和处置产品，发包方应当尊重承包方的生产经营自主权，不得干涉承包方依法进行正常的生产经营活动。此外，基于依法行政的理念以及物权对世效力的要求，地方政府也无权对承包人的经营自主权加以干涉。"承包经营人享有在承包的土地上自由耕种、自由经营的权利，只要不改变农业用地，不建造永久性建筑，不影响邻人的经营和邻人的种植，任何人都不得以所谓'规模经营''特色经营''一县一品''一乡一品'为由来干涉农民的经营。"②

(二)土地承包经营权、土地经营权及其流转

1. 概述

土地承包经营权为一种独立的用益物权，具有权利处分权能，权利人有权将其权利流转以获得相应的收益。《民法典》第334条对通过家庭承包取得的土地承包经营权的流

---

① 2005年3月29日最高人民法院制订，2020年12月23日修正。
② 王利明：《物权法论》(修订本)，中国政法大学出版社2003年版，第457页。

转进行了规定："土地承包经营权人依照法律规定，有权将土地承包经营权互换、转让。未经依法批准，不得将承包地用于非农建设。"《农村土地承包法》第 9 条规定："承包方承包土地后，享有土地承包经营权，可以自己经营，也可以保留土地承包权，流转其承包地的土地经营权，由他人经营。"这里要区分土地承包经营权、土地承包权、土地经营权三个概念。

2018 年 12 月 29 日《农村土地承包法》第二次修正后，土地所有权、承包权和经营权"三权分置"。"三权"的个性特征在于权利归属不同：土地所有权，归属集体；承包权，归属农户；经营权，归属经营者。"三权分置"下，所有权、承包权和经营权既存在整体效用，又有各自功能。实施"三权分置"的重点是放活经营权，核心要义就是明晰赋予经营权应有的法律地位和权能。

首先，关于土地的所有权是由我国国家性质所决定的。我国宪法明确规定"农村和城市郊区的土地，除由法律规定属于国家所有的以外，属于集体所有；宅基地和自留地、自留山，也属于集体所有"。因此，农村土地集体所有权的根本地位不变。

其次，土地承包经营权属用益物权。在权利内容上，多数观点认为，土地承包经营权系承包权与经营权的双重属性混合。其中，承包权属于成员权，只有集体成员才有资格拥有，具有身份依附性和不可对外转让性；经营权属于财产权，在权利属性上具有可交易性。

由此，在"两权分置"下，土地所有权和土地承包经营权其实并不具备自由流转的物权属性。但"三权分置"体制实现了集体、承包农户、新型经营主体对土地权利的共享，从法律制度的角度看，其本质就是确定在不改变土地公有制的基本经济制度前提下，在土地上分离出一个更加符合市场交易要求的私权——土地经营权。重点是承包方流转土地经营权后，其与发包方的承包关系不变。

依据《农村土地承包法》第 40 条，土地经营权流转合同应当采取书面形式，土地经营权流转合同一般包括以下条款：(1)双方当事人的姓名、住所；(2)流转土地的名称、坐落、面积、质量等级；(3)流转的期限和起止日期；(4)流转土地的用途；(5)双方当事人的权利和义务；(6)流转价款及支付方式；(7)土地被依法征收、征用、占用时有关补偿费的归属；(8)违约责任。承包方将土地交由他人代耕不超过 1 年的，可以不签订书面合同。在流转过程中，不得改变土地所有权的性质和土地的农业用途；流转的期限不得超过承包期的剩余期限；受让方须有农业经营能力；在同等条件下，本集体经济组织成员享有优先权。承包方依法采取出租(转包)、入股或者其他方式向他人流转土地经营权，应向发包方备案。

2. 转让

在通过家庭承包方式设定的土地承包经营权的转让问题上，《民法典》沿用了《农村土地承包法》的规定。《农村土地承包法》第 44 条规定："承包方流转土地经营权的，其与发包方的承包关系不变。"第 46 条规定："经承包方书面同意，并向本集体经济组织备案，受让方可以再流转土地经营权。"这就是说，对于通过家庭承包方式获得的土地承包经营权，土地经营权转让无需发包人的同意；承包方承包土地后，享有土地承包经营权，可以自己经营，也可以保留土地承包权，流转其承包地的土地经营权，由他人经营。但是受让人再流转土地经营权时，应经承包方书面同意，并向本集体经济组织备案。流转期限不得超过承包期的剩余期限。该法第41条规定："土地经营权流转期限为五年以上的，当事人可以向登记机构申请土地经营权登记。未经登记，不得对抗善意第三人。"

3. 互换

《农村土地承包法》第33条规定："承包方之间为方便耕种或者各自需要，可以对属于同一集体经济组织的土地承包经营权进行互换，并向发包方备案。承包方之间为方便耕种或者各自需要，可以对属于同一集体经济组织的土地承包经营权进行互换，并向发包方备案。"这就是说，其允许同一集体经济组织内部的权利人将各自的权利进行互易。但是，我们认为，就法理而言，互易与转让并无实质区别。如果允许本集体经济组织成员之外的人成为转让的受让人，则互换的当事人也应当不受同一集体经济组织之限制。需要探讨的是，《民法典》第335条规定："土地承包经营权互换、转让的，当事人可以向登记机构申请登记；未经登记，不得对抗善意第三人。"这一做法维持了《农村土地承包法》的做法，其理由在于：其一，目前土地承包经营权登记尚不健全，而且承包地数量巨大、地块分散，难以普遍进行登记；其二，流转的范围大部分是附近的农民，互相比较熟悉，从公示、公信的角度来看，登记的必要性不大；其三，如果必须登记，则必然发生登记费用，增加农民负担。

4. 土地经营权抵押

《农村土地承包法》第47条规定："承包方可以用承包地的土地经营权向金融机构融资担保，并向发包方备案。受让方通过流转取得的土地经营权，经承包方书面同意并向发包方备案，可以向金融机构融资担保。担保物权自融资担保合同生效时设立。当事人可以向登记机构申请登记；未经登记，不得对抗善意第三人。"

此时的抵押登记没有设权效力，只有对抗效力。

5. 出租与转包

中国法律中，出租与转包的根本区别在于：土地承包经营权出租中的承租人承租的标的仅为土地经营权，不含承包权（成员权），承租人可以是本集体经济组织之外的人员，也可以是本集体经济组织成员；土地承包经营权在转让、互换的情况下，转让、互换的对象限于本集体经济组织成员，互换时需向发包方备案，但转让时需经发包方同意。

2018年12月29日《农村土地承包法》第二次修正后，"三权分置"，该法第36条规定允许土地经营权自由流转，承包方可以自主决定依法采取出租（转包）、入股或者其他方式向他人流转土地经营权，并向发包方备案。

6. 入股

《民法典》第339条、《农村土地承包法》第36条允许承包人将土地经营权入股，承包人对承包权予以保留，并按照该股份获取一定的收益。

7. 土地承包经营权的继承

《民法典·物权编》并未涉及土地承包经营权的继承问题，《农村土地承包法》则规定了两种不同的情况：第一，对于家庭承包的，依据《农村土地承包法》第32条第2款，只有林地承包的承包人死亡，其继承人才可以在承包期内继续承包；而耕地或草地等农业用地上的土地承包经营权不能继承。之所以这样规定，其理由在于：家庭承包取得的土地承包经营权不发生继承的问题，因为即便家庭中某个或部分成员死亡，作为承包方的农户依然存在，如果家庭成员全部死亡，而最后一个死亡的家庭成员的继承人又不是本集体经济组织的成员，那么此时土地承包经营权应当归于消灭，否则将损害集体经济组织其他成员的权益；至于林地，则具有一定的特殊性，因为林地的投资周期长、收益慢，所以，对于以家庭承包方式取得的林地使用权，在该农户的最后一个家庭成员死亡时，无论其继承人是否为集体经济组织成员，都应当享有继承权。第二，对于其他方式的承包，依据《农村土地承包法》第54条的规定，在承包期内，承包人死亡的，其继承人可以继续承包，其理由在于，其他方式的承包通常是以承包人个人的名义而非农户进行，因此承包人死亡时，其继承人自然可以继承。

依据《农村土地承包法》第36条规定，承包方可以自主决定依法向他人流转土地经营权，并未禁止土地经营权的继承。

（三）承包人的义务

《农村土地承包法》规定了承包人的义务，包括：第一，维持土地的农业用途，不得用于非农建设；第二，依法保护和合理利用土地，不得给土地造成永久性损害；第三，法律、行政法规规定以及合同约定的其他义务。其中，前两项义务为法定义务，不得通过合同约定来排除。农业税在中国已经被废除，但是承包方应当依照承包合同缴纳"承包费"。在拖欠承包费的情况下，承包人应当承担违约责任。

在此需要讨论的是，拖欠承包费达到一定期限或数额，能否成为发包人解除承包合同、收回承包地的理由？《农村土地承包法》第57条明确强调，对于家庭承包，"不得将承包地收回抵顶欠款"。明确此种行为系侵害土地承包经营权的行为。这就明确禁止了因欠缴承包费而收回家庭承包方式设立的土地承包经营权。但是，对于其他方式设定的土地承包经营权以及继受取得的土地承包经营权、土地经营权，承包费是承包人或者土地经营权受让人使用土地的对价，是通过市场形成的土地使用价格。在欠缴达到一定标准的情况下，为了维护农村集体经济组织的利益，发包人、转让人应当有权解除合同，撤销土地承包经营权或者土地经营权。

（四）土地承包经营权、土地经营权的终止

《民法典》和《农村土地承包法》对土地承包经营权的消灭事由进行了严格的限制。发包方应当维护承包方的土地承包经营权，除法定消灭事由之外，发包人不可以通过约定合同解除条件和解除权来消灭该权利。例如，在承包期内，发包方不得单方面解除承包合同；不得假借少数服从多数强迫承包方放弃或者变更土地承包经营权；不得收回承包地搞招标承包；不得将承包地收回抵顶欠款。

现行法律中，土地承包经营权消灭的法定事由具体包括：

1. 期限届满

土地承包经营权有确定的期限。在期限届满时，如果当事人并未就续期另行约定，权利消灭。

需要注意的是，基于家庭承包时农村集体经济组织的强制缔约义务，实际上在期限届满之后，只要承包人提出续期的请求，发包人应当续期。而对于以其他方式取得的土地承包经营权期限届满后，则由于"四荒"地已经改造为农用地，故而应当通过家庭承包方式重新设定土地承包经营权，承包人不享有申请续期的权利。

2. 土地严重毁损或灭失时的依法调整

《民法典》第 336 条规定："承包期内发包人不得调整承包地。因自然灾害严重毁损承包地等特殊情形，需要适当调整承包的耕地和草地的，应当依照农村土地承包的法律规定办理。"《农村土地承包法》对承包地的调整进行了严格限制，该法第 28 条规定："承包期内，发包方不得调整承包地。承包期内，因自然灾害严重毁损承包地等特殊情形对个别农户之间承包的耕地和草地需要适当调整的，必须经本集体经济组织成员的村民会议 2/3 以上成员或者 2/3 以上村民代表的同意，并报乡(镇)人民政府和县级人民政府农业农村、林业和草原等主管部门批准。承包合同中约定不得调整的，按照其约定。"按照立法者的解释，这里的特殊情形，还包括承包地被依法征用、占用，人口增减导致人地矛盾突出的情况。

在依法调整的情况下，就意味着承包合同变更，从而导致被调整的土地上承包经营权消灭。

3. 承包人自愿交回土地

所谓自愿交回，实际上就是承包人对其权利的抛弃，从而导致权利的消灭。中国法律允许承包期内承包方可以自愿将承包地交回发包方。承包方自愿交回承包地的，可以获得合理补偿，应当提前半年以书面形式通知发包方。承包方在承包期内交回承包地的，在承包期内不得再要求承包土地。

关于没有提前通知的法律后果，法律并未规定。有学者认为如没有通知，应当于抛弃权利时，交付通知期间的租金。我们认为，权利人抛弃土地，集体经济组织无偿取得该权利而且无须再行对之分配承包地，这已经使集体经济组织获得了很大的利益，再要求权利人交付相应租金，并不合理。

4. 收回承包地

《民法典》第 337 条规定："承包期内发包人不得收回承包地。法律另有规定的，依照其规定。"可见，原则上不允许发包人收回承包地。从《农村土地承包法》第 27 条来看，可以收回承包地的情形主要是指因承包人全家迁居而收回土地的情形。承包期内，承包农户进城落户的，引导支持其按照自愿有偿原则依法在本集体经济组织内转让土地承包经营权或者将承包地交回发包方，也可以鼓励其流转土地经营权。承包期内，承包方交回承包地或者发包方依法收回承包地时，承包方对其在承包地上投入而提高土地生产能力的，有权获得相应的补偿。

值得探讨的是，集体能否因土地撂荒而收回土地。我们认为对于家庭承包的土地，一般不宜以撂荒为由收回，而应当由集体经济组织通过组织人员义务劳动、代为出资雇佣他人耕作等方式避免土地撂荒。他人也可以对之进行无因管理来避免土地闲置。对于其他方式承包的土地或者通过流转而继受取得的承包地，则可以通过收取相应的违约金等方式督促其开发，长期迟延经催告后仍然不予使用的，可以考虑收回，而不宜直接收回。

5. 因婚姻关系的设定与变更可否收回承包地

《农村土地承包法》第 31 条规定："承包期内，妇女结婚，在新居住地未取得承包地的，发包方不得收回其原承包地；妇女离婚或者丧偶，仍在原居住地生活或者不在原居住地生活但在新居住地未取得承包地的，发包方不得收回其原承包地。"换言之，在妇女婚姻关系发生或者消灭的情况下，除非另行取得承包地，否则发包方不得收回土地。但是如果其另行在新的居住地又取得了承包地，则其原先的承包经营权因承包地被收回而消灭。这里的"在新居住地未取得承包地"，应当是指通过家庭承包方式取得承包地，而非通过转让等继受取得承包地。此外，婚姻关系中男方入赘，也应当准用这一规定。

6. 其他消灭事由

土地承包经营权可以因国家的征收而消灭。在征收的情况下，不仅应当对土地上的青苗、附着物进行补偿，还应当对承包经营权本身进行合理补偿。《农村土地承包法》第 17 条规定，"承包地被依法征收、征用、占用的，有权依法获得相应的补偿"。

根据《土地管理法》第 61 条，乡（镇）村公共设施、公益事业建设，需要使用土地的，经相关单位审核批准，也可以占用农用地，从而导致土地承包经营权消灭。此种情况下，集体经济组织应当为权利人另行提供相同面积、质量的农用地，并为其设定土地承包经营权。此外，对土地上的青苗、附着物应当进行补偿。

承包人死亡后无人继承又无人受遗赠，土地承包经营权消灭。

但是对土地经营权的流转《农村土地承包法》第 42 条明确规定："承包方不得单方解除土地经营权流转合同，但受让方有下列情形之一的除外：（一）擅自改变土地的农业用途；（二）弃耕抛荒连续两年以上；（三）给土地造成严重损害或者严重破坏土地生态环境；（四）其他严重违约行为。"

7. 土地承包经营权、土地经营权的终止、消灭的法律效果

在权利消灭时，承包人有权取回其在土地上的青苗、竹木以及相关附属设施。如果发包人希望获得，其应当以市场价格购买，发包人提出购买要求时承包人不得拒绝。承包方对其在承包地上投入而提高土地生产能力的，有权获得相应的补偿。

第三节 建设用地使用权

一、建设用地使用权的概念

(一)建设用地使用权的概念

《民法典》第 344 条规定:"建设用地使用权人依法对国家所有的土地享有占有、使用和收益的权利,有权利用该土地建造建筑物、构筑物及其附属设施。"本条虽然将建设用地使用权的客体原则上限定为国有土地,但第 361 条仍然允许在集体土地上设定建设用地使用权。此外,第 345 条规定:"建设用地使用权可以在土地的地表、地上或者地下分别设立。"据此,所谓建设用地使用权,是指自然人、法人或其他组织依法享有的在国有或集体土地及其上下建造、保有建筑物、构筑物及其附属设施的用益物权。

这一概念的内涵,包括如下几个方面:

1. 建设用地使用权的客体原则上为国有土地,也可以为集体所有的土地

用益物权为支配他人之物使用价值的物权,用益物权之客体原则上为他人之物。就建设用地使用权而言,其支配的标的为土地。与其他国家通常土地归个人所有不同的是,中国《宪法》第 10 条第 1 款、第 2 款规定:"城市的土地属于国家所有。农村和城市郊区的土地,除由法律规定属于国家所有的以外,属于集体所有;宅基地和自留地、自留山,也属于集体所有。"《物权法》《民法典》《土地管理法》等法律也重申了这一规定。可见,中国采土地所有权公有制,土地的所有权只能为国家和集体所有,私人不能享有土地的所有权。因此,要对土地加以利用,在其上建造并保有建筑物和其他构筑物,只能在国家或集体所有的土地上为之。这与比较法上地上权以土地私有制为基础,多为对其他自然人、法人所有的土地而设定地上权,显然是不同的。

2. 国有土地和集体所有土地的界限与范围

从中国现行规定来看,建设用地使用权的客体可以为国有土地,也可以是集体所有的土地。依据《土地管理法》第 59 条、第 60 条等规定:任何单位和个人进行建设,需要使用土地的,可以依法申请使用国有土地;兴办乡镇企业和村民建设住宅经依法批准可以使用本集体经济组织农民集体所有的土地,乡(镇)村公共设施和公益事业建设经依法批准也可以使用农民集体所有的土地。这就是说,根据中国现行法律的规定,建设用地原则上为国家所有的土地;但为兴办乡镇企业或者乡(镇)村公共设施和公益事业而设定建设用地使用权时,或者村民建设住宅使用本集体经济组织土地作为宅基地的,其客体则可以为集体所有的土地。

关于国有土地和集体所有土地的范围,《民法典》第 249 条规定:"城市的土地,属于国家所有。法律规定属于国家所有的农村和城市郊区的土地,属于国家所有。"《土地

管理法》第 9 条确定了在中国土地所有权的归属："城市市区的土地属于国家所有。农村和城市郊区的土地，除由法律规定属于国家所有的以外，属于农民集体所有；宅基地和自留地、自留山，属于农民集体所有。"在国务院颁布的《土地管理法实施条例》中，对国有土地的范围进一步加以明确，依据该条例第 2 条的规定，属于全民所有即国家所有的土地为：

（1）城市市区的土地；（2）农村和城市郊区中已经依法没收、征收、征购为国有的土地；（3）国家依法征用的土地；（4）依法不属于集体所有的林地、草地、荒地、滩涂及其他土地；（5）农村集体经济组织全部成员转为城镇居民的，原属于其成员集体所有的土地；（6）因国家组织移民、自然灾害等原因，农民成建制地集体迁移后不再使用的原属于迁移农民集体所有的土地。如果某块土地的所有权归属发生争议，而无法证明该争议土地属于农民集体所有的，依据 1995 年 4 月 9 日原国家土地管理局发布的《确定土地所有权和使用权的若干规定》第 18 条的规定，该土地属于国家所有。目前，中国在土地供应机制上，国家垄断建设用地一级市场，集体建设用地原则上不能直接入市。因此，建设用地使用权的客体，原则上为国有土地，也可以是集体所有土地。正因为此，过去的法律将建设用地使用权称为国有土地使用权。法律并不禁止在集体土地上设定建设用地使用权，但是根据中国现行法律的规定，由于土地的所有权人不同，在其上设定的建设用地使用权在权利内容等方面也有不同之处，在集体土地上设定的建设用地使用权的权利处分权能受到一定的限制，但是随着土地二级市场的完善，国有建设用地与集体建设用地"同地同权"。

3. 土地的横向范围

传统民法学者观点认为："绵延无垠之土地，在形式上或物理上本非独立之物，但依社会经济观念，仍可依认为方式予以划分。"[1]因此，在技术上，对于土地主要是依据其横向范围的四至通过登记将陆地区变为地块。根据国务院颁布实施的《不动产登记暂行条例》[2]第 8 条的规定："不动产以不动产单元为基本单位进行登记。不动产单元具有唯一编码。"这就是说，可以通过土地登记，将土地分割为各个相互独立的地块，就各地块分别设定所有权及其他物权。

4. 与土地有关的物的排除

土地所有权人和使用权人的权利虽然及于土地上下的空间，但依据中国法律的规定，土地中的有些部分并非土地的重要成分，而是与土地相独立的物，土地权利人并不当然对其享有权利，具体包括林木、矿产资源、文物、水资源等。对于上述附着物或者埋藏于土地之下，但在法律上又独立于土地之外的物，即便取得了相关土地的所有权或使用权，也不能认为同时取得了这些物的所有权。土地使用权人对土地使用价值的支配权也不能及于这些物。

---

[1] 谢在全：《民法物权论》（上册），中国政法大学出版社 1999 年版，第 20 页。

[2] 该条例 2015 年 3 月 1 日生效，2019 年 3 月 24 日国务院令第 710 号《国务院关于修改部分行政法规的决定》第一次修订。

5. 建设用地使用权的客体，还包括土地上下的空间

传统民法中，土地的所有权被认为上至寰宇、下至地心。现代民法则基于社会本位，对土地所有权的空间范围通过法律以及禁止权利滥用、相邻关系等规则加以限制。其典型如《德国民法典》第905条对所有权的界限的规定，依据该条："土地所有人的权利，及于地表上的空间和地表下的地壳。但所有人不得禁止在高到或者深到如此程度，以至所有人对排除干涉没有利益的地方所进行的干涉。"中国法律未对土地所有权人对其土地上、下的空间范围进行明确的规定，但解释上应当认为土地所有权人对其土地上、下的空间享有永久、全面的支配权，其有权对该空间加以支配和利用。而此种上、下的界限，应当限于法律的规定及第三人的权利，在此范围之外，他人在其地上和地下的干涉，土地权利人不得排除之，例如，所有权人建筑房屋的高度应当符合城建规划；集体土地所有权人不得对其土地之下埋藏的矿藏行使权利。而且，对于过高或过低，以至于其不可能享有的空间，所有权人也不应再主张其权利。

随着科学技术的飞速发展，特别是随着现代化土木、建筑技术的进步，对土地上下空间的开发、利用或者说对土地的立体利用，成为可能。而且由于土地资源的日渐稀缺，其在现代社会中具有越来越重要的意义。空间成为一种具有重要经济价值的财产，从而有必要对其归属和利用在法律上加以规范。

《民法典》第345条规定："建设用地使用权可以在土地的地表、地上或者地下分别设立。"将空间利用权作为建设用地使用权的类型之一进行了规定，其理由在于：对于土地使用权人尤其是建设用地使用权人来说，其取得土地使用权的目的在于对土地的使用价值加以利用，如建造房屋、耕作。这自然以取得土地上、下的一定空间为必要。尤其是在城镇规划范围内，建设用地使用权的出让受到规划设计条件的限制，在规划设计条件中，对于建筑物或构筑物的高度、深度都有明确要求；在出让合同中，对此也有明确的约定。建设用地使用权人只能取得规划设计许可的高度和深度之内的空间加以使用，超出即为违法或者越权。因此，建设用地使用权的客体，应当及于土地表面以及规划范围内的土地上下空间。故而，我们在对建设用地使用权的定义中，强调其为在国有或集体土地"上下"建造、保有建筑物、构筑物及其附属设施的用益物权。

需要强调的是，从第345条来看，单纯对土地上下空间设定的建设用地使用权，其涉及的土地未必仅限于建设用地，还可能包括农用地。例如，当事人可以通过设定建设用地使用权的方式，在集体所有的农用地之下修建地铁、输油管道、车库；在集体所有的农用地上空修建架设管线、轻轨、空中走廊等。当然，在地表已经设立建设用地使用权、土地承包经营权等用益物权的情况下，新设立的建设用地使用权，原则上不得损害已设立的用益物权。一方面，建设用地使用权、土地承包经营权等用益物权系基于合同设定。虽然合同中对建设用地使用权的高度和深度已有约定，但是如果所有权人再在其上下设定建设用地使用权，且妨害了在先权利，显然所有权人的行为有悖诚信原则。

在判断同一土地上在先和在后设定的用益物权的关系时，应当考虑相邻关系规则。一方面，在后设定的权利如果对在先权利妨害不大，在先权利人也应当负有一定的容忍

义务。例如，为了架设电缆而必须通过他人建设用地使用权的上空时，如果对其权利并无太大妨害，对地表享有用益物权的权利人应当依据相邻关系的规则容忍他人的架设行为。如果确实造成了损失，例如，电缆的通过确实影响了土地承包经营权人的农作物，在后权利人应当予以赔偿。另一方面，如果超出了容忍的范围，则在先权利人有权主张排除妨害，甚至有权请求宣告在后设定的建设用地使用权合同无效。例如，某宗地四周业已设定建设用地使用权，但其高度仅为六层楼；而中间的宗地出让时，合同不仅约定建设用地使用权人可以对该宗土地上下加以利用，而且允许在地表以上八层楼高的空间向外延伸。最终，中间宗地的建设用地使用权人建造了一栋蘑菇形的大楼，在八层以下，该大楼是垂直的；但八层以上，该大楼则向外延伸，影响了四周各宗地的采光。这种做法显然侵害了其他建设用地使用权人的利益，宗地四周的业主则可依据相邻关系的规则主张权利。

6. 建设用地使用权的内容为建造和保有建筑物、构筑物及其附属设施

在建设用地使用权最初被所有权人设定之时，通常都是空地，该土地上尚不存在建筑物，而建设用地使用权人取得土地使用权后再根据自己的需求在土地上下进行建设、另行建造建筑物、构筑物及其附属设施。因此，建设用地使用权的内容包含建造。

需要指出的是，建造只是建设用地使用权的权利内容之一，并非所有的建设用地使用权都必须具备建造这一内容。在因建筑物等的所有权发生变动而导致其占用的建设用地使用权一并转移时，土地上现存的建筑物能够满足建设用地使用权人的需要，故而其无须另行建造，权利内容仅为保有。当然，对已经建设的土地，权利人也不妨根据自己的需要，在不违反土地使用目的的前提下拆除现有的房屋而另行建造。而且，此项权利在法律规定的特定情况下为建设用地使用权人的义务。例如，依据中国法律和行政法规的强制性规定，在国有建设用地使用权以出让方式设定后，建设用地使用权人必须在合同约定的期限内开始进行建造行为。但是，建造本质上为建设用地使用权人的权利，其自然可以在不违反法律规定的情况下，暂时不进行建造。

《城镇国有土地使用权出让和转让暂行条例》第 17 条第 2 款规定："未按合同规定的期限和条件开发、利用土地的，市、县人民政府土地管理部门应当予以纠正，并根据情节可以给予警告、罚款直至无偿收回土地使用权的处罚。"这里的"合同"指的是国有土地使用权出让合同，如果权利人没有依照合同规定进行开发、利用土地的，相关部门有权责令其改正。

此外，建设用地使用权在比较法上称地上权，产生于罗马法。基于当时"地上物添附于土地"的规则，在他人土地上建造的房屋等地上物，只能归土地所有权人所有。为解决由此带来的土地所有权和使用权合一之弊，罗马法上创设了地上权，以允许在他人所有的土地上拥有地上物。这一规则为后世所效仿。因此，建设用地使用权或者说地上权制度的产生，就是为了满足在他人土地上保有房屋的需求而设立的，中国也是如此。因此，有必要在建设用地使用权的概念中对此加以强调。

故而，笔者认为建设用地使用权的权利内容，应当界定为权利人在国有或集体土地

上下建造、保有建筑物、构筑物及其附属设施。

(1)建造的标的为建筑物、构筑物及其附属设施

建设用地使用权作为用益物权,自然以对土地的使用价值的支配为内容。但是,《土地管理法》①第4条明确规定:"国家实行土地用途管制制度。国家编制土地利用总体规划,规定土地用途,将土地分为农用地、建设用地和未利用地。……建设用地是指建造建筑物、构筑物的土地,包括城乡住宅和公共设施用地、工矿用地、交通水利设施用地、旅游用地、军事设施用地等。"因此,建设用地使用权的权利人对土地的支配,并非对土地使用价值的概括支配,而是在建设用地特定用途内的支配。此种用途,在比较法上通常以"在土地之上保有工作物"来表述,其外延相当于中国法律中的建筑物、构筑物和附属设施。由于"工作物"一词不为中国法律所采用,《民法典》第344条直接采用了中国法律中惯用的用语,从而以在土地上建造并保有建筑物、构筑物及其附属设施来表述建设用地使用权所支配的土地之用途。

(2)建筑物、构筑物及其附属设施的概念

建筑物与构筑物是中国法律中广泛采用的概念。例如,《土地管理法》第65条规定:"在土地利用总体规划制定前已建的不符合土地利用总体规划确定的用途的建筑物、构筑物,不得重建、扩建。"

对于建筑物和构筑物的概念,中国法律并未直接加以界定。从相关法律、法规的表述来看,建筑物与构筑物的区分在于建筑物可以供人在其中进行生产、生活,如居住用房、生产用房、办公用房等,仓库、地下室、空中走廊、立体停车场等均包括在内;而构筑物则是建筑物之外的其他人工建造的物体,提供的并非人们生产、生活的空间,主要包括道路、桥梁、隧道、堤坝、水渠等农田水利工程设施、人工养殖设施、地窖、地下管网等人工构筑物。

为充分发挥建筑物、构筑物的效能,建设用地使用权人通常会在土地上铺设一定的附属设施,如电线杆、电缆、变压器等电力、广播、通信设施,雕塑、纪念碑等。这些附属设施严格地讲并非不动产,自然也非建筑物或构筑物,但其系辅助建筑物、构筑物而修建,自然应当为法律所容许。因此,建设用地使用权人也有权在他人土地上建造、保有这些附属设施。

(3)关于种植竹木、花草

笔者认为,在中国法律中已经存在土地承包经营权、土地经营权,其中包含了对林地以造林为目的的使用。要使用他人土地进行植树造林完全可以通过土地承包经营权来解决,而且建设用地的土地使用费相对更为高昂,人们通常也不愿将重金取得的土地用来植树造林。因此,在建设用地使用权中自然没有必要将对林木的保有作为权利内容之一。但是,建设用地使用权人在保有建筑物、构筑物的同时,在其有权使用的土地上种植树木、设置绿地的行为也应当是允许的,因为良好的环境是正常生产、生活的重要保

---

① 该法于2019年8月26日第三次修订。

证。通过种植树木等行为对环境加以改良应当看做权利人建造、保有建筑物、构筑物的附属行为,"既不违背设定地上权之目的,自不得认为已超出地上权之范围"。①

(二)建设用地使用权的法律特征

用益物权是对他人之物的使用价值加以支配的物权,其着眼于对物使用价值的利用。建设用地使用权是自然人、法人和其他组织使用国有或集体所有土地的权利,其对土地的利用,主要是指占有、使用和收益。权利人有权实际对土地加以占有,既可以对土地实行一种消费性的使用(如居民在土地上建造住宅以自用),也可以从事一种经营性的使用(如开发商在土地上建造商品房以出售)。因此,建设用地使用权的设立目的在于使权利人获得土地的使用价值,从土地利用活动中获取经济利益和为其他活动提供空间场所,属于用益物权的范畴。建设用地使用权作为一种他物权、限制物权、用益物权,其法律特征体现在下列几个方面:

1. 标的上的他物性

建设用地使用权作为一种用益物权,性质上为他物权,即对他人(国家或集体)所有的土地而享有的物权。在国家或集体自行使用自己的土地之时,自然无设定建设用地使用权的必要,但在建设用地使用权与所有权发生混同时,为了维护第三人的利益,建设用地使用权不应立即消灭,从而出现了特殊情况下所有权人享有建设用地使用权的情况。例如,某块建设用地使用权出让之后,使用权人以该土地使用权设定了抵押权,现因未按照约定交纳土地使用权出让金该土地使用权被收回,则基于对抵押权人利益的保护,不应使建设用地使用权因混同而消灭。

2. 内容上的限制性

建设用地使用权作为一种用益物权,性质上为限制物权。一方面,其对作为权利客体的土地的支配并非全面、无期限的支配,受到法律和土地出让合同的限制。具体来说,建设用地使用权作为一种用益物权,其对标的土地的支配不仅在范围上限于对土地使用价值的支配,而且这种支配也是有期限的。《城市房地产管理法》第3条规定:"国家依法实行国有土地有偿、有期限使用制度。但是,国家在本法规定的范围内划拨国有土地使用权的除外。"国务院颁布的《城镇国有土地使用权出让和转让暂行条例》第12条规定:"土地使用权出让最高年限按下列用途确定:(一)居住用地七十年;(二)工业用地五十年;(三)教育、科技、文化、卫生、体育用地五十年;(四)商业、旅游、娱乐用地四十年;(五)综合或者其他用地五十年。"可见,建设用地使用权原则上是有期限的。对于国家划拨而设定的建设用地使用权,其主要是为了满足国家利益或者社会公共利益的需要而设定,故而不宜采用市场方式设定固定的期限并据此确定相应的土地使用权出让金。因此,《城市房地产管理法》将划拨国有土地使用权作为国有土地有偿、有期限使用制度的一种例外和补充方式作了规定,并对其使用期限除法律、行政法规另有

---

① 谢在全:《民法物权论》(上册),中国政法大学出版社1999年版,第347页。

规定外未作限制。但划拨土地使用权在设定条件上有着严格的限制，没有期限限制并不意味着此种权利就是永续存在的权利。一旦划拨的法定条件不复存在，划拨土地使用权则可能因国家收回而消灭，或者转化为普通的建设用地使用权而受到期限限制。另一方面，建设用地使用权系因土地所有权人的意思而设定，虽然其基于使用权而产生，以所有权的一定权能为内容，但有限制所有权的作用，其效力优先于所有权。所有权人亦须尊重其权利，不得侵害或妨害权利的行使。

3. 土地用途上的特定性

建设用地使用权的标的——土地的用途具有特定性。正如对该权利的定义所揭示的，其用途只能是在土地上建造、保有建筑物、构筑物和附属设施。

《城市房地产管理法》第 24 条规定："下列建设用地的土地使用权，确属必需的，可以由县级以上人民政府依法批准划拨：（1）国家机关用地和军事用地；（2）城市基础设施用地和公益事业用地；（3）国家重点扶持的能源、交通、水利等项目用地；（4）法律、行政法规规定的其他用地。"划拨土地的用途固定，权利人虽然可以在土地上种植竹木、花卉，但这种行为只能是建造、保有建筑物的附属行为，而不能在土地上以耕作为目的来进行此种种植，由此也使建设用地使用权区别于土地承包经营权。

还需要指出的是，建设用地使用权的标的土地的用途，并不包括农民利用集体土地修建住宅，此种用途应当为宅基地使用权的标的土地所拥有。

4. 权利本身的独立性

建设用地使用权虽然基于所有权而产生，但它是一种独立的权利，而不依附其他权利的存在而存在，具体来说：首先，建设用地使用权的设定与其说以所有权的存在为前提，不如说以作为权利客体的土地的存在为前提；其次，建设用地使用权一经设定，并不因土地所有权的转让而转让，而可以单独转让；最后，在所有权绝对消灭的情况下，建设用地使用权虽然同时消灭，但其是因自己的消灭原因而消灭的。例如，某块集体所有的土地因被国家征收而消灭，其上的建设用地使用权则是同时因征用而消灭，而非因所有权的消灭而消灭，因此建设用地使用权人有权就此请求国家单独提供补偿。至于所谓建设用地使用权上附有义务，亦不应作为证明其具有从属性的理由。在现代社会中，民事权利一旦确定，实际上就意味着权利人自由行为的边界已被确定。而且，即使在权利范围内，其行使也无不受到强行法、基本原则等规范的限制。在所有权都附有义务的情况下，建设用地使用权附有义务是很正常的。我们既然不能称所有权具有从属性，自然也不能据此认为建设用地使用权具有从属性。

5. 权能上的完备性

正是由于建设用地使用权是一种独立物权，其并不依附于其他不动产所有权、使用权或者特定的人身而可以独立存在。因此，建设用地使用权的权能上具有完备性。其不仅包括对土地本身的占有、使用和收益权能，而且权利人对权利本身可以自由处分，可以依法转让、赠与、出资、抵押、继承。这就使建设用地使用权可以独立进入交易机制，成为市场流转的客体。在中国现有的制度下土地所有权不能流转的情况下，通过土地使用权尤其是建设用地使用权制度的构建，在建设用地使用权的基础上建立了中国的土地市场。之所以如此，也正是基于建设用地使用权作为独立物权而可以进入市场交易机制的本质。

(三)关于建设用地使用权的名称

《民法典》出台前，关于建设用地使用权的名称，在法律、法规中有不同的名称。如前所述，在《民法通则》中采用的是"国有土地使用权"的提法，《土地管理法》则称之为"建设用地使用权"。在中国《物权法》立法过程中，对于建设用地使用权的权利名称如何称呼，也出现了基地使用权、地上权等观点。《民法典》采用了建设用地使用权的提法，我们赞同此种观点，其理由在于：

第一，中国现行法律中已经广泛使用这一概念，其在中国大陆已经深入人心，在保留这一概念的基础上对其不符合市场经济发展的内容加以适当调整，不会引起法律概念体系的巨大变动，节约了普法成本。

第二，这一概念，直接明确表明了土地的用途和权利内容，符合中国民众的日常用语习惯，容易为人们理解。而且，这一概念的产生是在保留土地使用权概念而对之加以细化的基础上完成的，它实现了改革开放之初包罗万象的土地使用权制度的进一步科学化。这种保持法律继承性的做法，基本保留了中国法律和司法实践的现行规定。此外，在德国法中地上权的德文本意就是"建筑权"，瑞士民法中也是如此。因此，采用建设用地使用权一词，实际上也实现了与其本源的接轨。

第三，这一概念在内容上具有较大空间，完全可以将其扩展到土地上下的空间。实际上，建造建筑物的目的就在于为人们提供一定的生产、生活的空间，只在地皮上是不可能建造房屋的。因此，建设一词本身就包含了对土地上下空间的利用。

第四，土地使用权的概念，没有突出土地使用的目的、功能，而且在法律上没有依据。中国《物权法》的起草、审议过程中，土地使用权的类型及其内容进一步的细化是物权法精确调整原则的必然要求，而这种细化的主要任务，是按照各种权利的性质建立更为细密的法律制度，以满足市场经济和人民群众生活的需要。而建设用地使用权这一概念，是依据土地用途和权利内容对中国目前略显大而无当的土地使用权加以细分、从而实现其类型化的结果，这显然符合中国物权法构建过程中立法技术上的客观需要。

第五，衡诸各国民法，对各种用益物权的区分，尤其是独立用益物权的区分，主要基于土地用途来进行，如地上权旨在在土地上下保有工作物，永佃权旨在对土地进行耕作。故而，采建设用地使用权一语，直接指明了土地用途和权利内容，与以农用为目的的土地承包经营权相得益彰。而且，这一概念又避免了依据土地所有制加以划分之弊，符合中国市场经济的发展需要。

(四)建设用地使用权的意义

中国的土地只能是国家所有或者集体所有。但是，国家和集体毕竟只是一种社会组织，其通常无法直接对土地加以利用从而获得收益，而只能委诸他人对之加以利用。在市场经济条件下，此种利用既可以以债权的方式如土地租赁为之，也可以通过设定用益物权的方式为之。从中国现行法律的规定以及《民法典》的规定来看，建设用地使用权在性质上为一种用益物权，即权利人对国家或集体所有的土地的使用价值加以利用的权利。权利人有权对该土地占有、使用、收益，有权对其权利加以处分，并排除他人干涉。土地使用权作为一种用益物权，亦不同于租赁权等以土地的使用为标的的债权，其具有对世性、排他性，而且是一种长期稳定的财产权利。

需要指出的是，由于中国土地所有权不能流转的法律限制，土地所有权不能进入市场流通。而在市场经济条件下，土地作为一种重要的生产要素，应当通过市场进行资源配置。在此情况下，建设用地使用权虽然是一种基于所有权而产生的用益物权，但是在中国的实践中，国有建设用地使用权实际上是一种类似于所有权的权利，权利人不仅可以对土地直接占有、使用，还对其权利享有充分的处分权能，有权将其权利转让、出租或者抵押，从而在建设用地使用权基础之上建立和发展起了中国的地产市场。这就有效克服了中国土地所有权不能流转与市场经济发展之间的矛盾。也就是说，中国的土地制度、土地权利，在很大程度上是建构在建设用地使用权等土地使用权的基础上的。实际上，在中国土地制度上，建设用地使用权也并非如中国台湾地区那样作为土地上的他项权利而登记，而是与所有权一样作为基础权利来登记。换言之，在土地之上设定的抵押权、地役权等他项权利，大多是基于建设用地使用权等土地使用权而非土地所有权而设定的。

建设用地使用权作为类所有权，在中国物权法具体制度构建上，还应当体现在如下几个方面：

第一，在传统民法中，当地上物与土地发生添附时，地上物添附于土地为一基本原则。也就是说，在地上物与土地紧密结合而不能分割或者强行分割成本过于高昂之时，应当由土地所有权人取得地上物的所有权。但是，鉴于中国"在土地公有制的条件下，一般公民与法人享有的是近似于所有权的土地使用权"。如果土地上存在建设用地使用权，则在发生添附时，该地上物应当归建设用地使用权人所有。

第二，建设用地使用权的存续具有稳定性。由于建设用地使用权具有类所有权的性质，是中国土地市场构建的重要基础，此种权利必须具有长期稳定性，否则难以维护交易安全。此种稳定性，主要表现为法律通过禁止所有权人对土地使用权的设定附解除条件、限制所有权人的合同解除权等方式限制所有权人的合同自由，避免其利用自己的强势地位对建设用地使用权加以过分限制，从而使之无法稳定存续。

第三，建设用地使用权的内容具有广泛性。在建造和保有建筑物、构筑物和附属设施的范围内，除非为社会公共利益的需要，法律不应对建设用地的用途施加更具体的限制。根据现行立法，法律对建设用地的用途又进一步区分为商业用地、住宅用地、旅游用地等各种具体类型。对各类型的限制必要性如何，有待商榷。尤其是目前实践中甚至对建设用地的容积率等十分具体的问题都要求经过审批，过分将公权力或者说所有权人的所有权渗透到建设用地使用权的行使方面。

二、建设用地使用权的类型

从《土地管理法》的规定来看，建设用地使用权依据其土地所有权的不同，分为国有建设用地使用权和集体所有土地的建设用地使用权。国有建设用地使用权依据其设定方式的不同，又可以分为三种，即通过出让设立的建设用地使用权、通过划拨设立的划拨土地使用权以及中外合资企业与外资企业中的、以合同加审批方式设定的场地使用权。集体所有土地的建设用地使用权根据其设立目的的不同，也可以分为三种，即乡（镇）村公共设施、公益事业建设用地使用权、乡镇企业建设用地使用权以及宅基地使用权。当然，《民法典》将宅基地使用权作为一种独立的用益物权类型，不应再属于建设用地使用权法律规范。

《民法典》规定了建设用地使用权和宅基地使用权，而且《民法典》在建设用地使用权一章主要规定的是关于通过出让设立建设用地使用权。故而以下对通过出让设立的建设用地使用权和宅基地使用权之外的其他建设用地使用权的内容、性质等问题，加以论述。

（一）划拨土地使用权

与出让一样，通过划拨设立建设用地使用权，也是建设用地使用权从国有土地所有权中分出而从无到有的初始设立。《民法典》第 347 条规定："设立建设用地使用权，可以采取出让或者划拨等方式。……严格限制以划拨方式设立建设用地使用权。"可见，其在允许通过划拨方式设定建设用地使用权的同时，对此种建设用地使用权的设定、内容进行了严格的限制。

《城市房地产管理法》第 23 条第 1 款规定："土地使用权划拨，是指县级以上人民政府依法批准，在土地使用者缴纳补偿、安置等费用后将该幅土地交付其使用，或者将土地使用权无偿交付给土地使用者使用的行为。"划拨与出让不同，本质上完全是通过行政命令来授予使用人一定的土地使用权，事实上涵盖了所有国有建设用地通过市场之外的方式设定的情形，因此《城镇国有土地使用权出让和转让暂行条例》第 43 条规定："划拨土地使用权是指土地使用者通过各种方式依法无偿取得的土地使用权。"原国家土地管理局 1992 年 3 月 8 日发布的《划拨土地使用权管理暂行办法》第 2 条更是明确规定："划拨土地使用权，是指土地使用者通过除出让土地使用权以外的其他各种方式依法取得的国有土地使用权。"这就将所有历史上非经市场方式设立的建设用地使用权都统称为划拨土地使用权，从而区别于以出让方式设立的建设用地使用权。

通过行政方式来授予或者拨付用地者一定的土地使用权是建国后中国的一贯做法，在国有土地用地制度改革之前，也几乎是唯一方式。其大致的程序是：（1）经过批准，建设单位方可申请用地。（2）提出用地申请，即建设单位必须持国务院主管部门或者县级以上地方人民政府按照国家基本建设程序批准的设计任务书或者其他批准文件（其中对用地数量、用地选址方案已经明确规定），向县级以上地方人民政府土地管理部门提出用地申请。（3）审批划拨，即经县级以上人民政府根据法定批地权限，对建设单位提出的用地申请进行审查，如法律手续齐备，即以行政命令的方式，确定具体使用的土地，由土地管理部门把土地划拨给建设单位。在接到县级以上人民政府批准用地文件之后，其可以持批准用地文件申请国有土地使用权设定登记。如果批准用地之后，土地尚为集体所有，则由建设单位自己依照批准用地文件办理征地手续，支付土地补偿费、安置补助费、剩余劳动力生活补助费，还应安排部分剩余劳动力就业等。而且所征用的集体所有的土地，所有权属于国家，用地单位只有使用权。但随着的发展、用地制度的改革，划拨制度的范围也在缩小。现在，只是就法律规定的一些关系国家利益和社会公共利益的用地，经建设单位申请和政府批准，才可以进行土地划拨。

通过划拨设立的国有建设用地使用权具有如下法律特征：

（1）以划拨方式设立建设用地使用权的客体限于国有土地。划拨作为一种行政方式，本质上是国家以其行政命令而授予用地者一定的土地使用权。而中国的土地资源分别由国家和集体所有，因此国家只能授予用地者国有土地。如果需要使用集体土地，也要先经过征地程序，将集体土地征收为国有土地之后再行划拨，而不能直接划拨。有学者认为，在划拨情形下，土地管理部门显然是以主权者和管理者的身份出现的。此种见解并不妥当。事实上，划拨虽然是通过行政命令来进行，但其依据仍然是国家的国有土地所有权人身份。

（2）划拨的条件受到法律的严格限制。在《城市房地产管理法》颁布以前，根据当时的土地管理法的规定，通过划拨的方式取得土地使用权的主要是全民所有制法人单位和城市集体经济性质法人单位。但随着经济体制改革尤其是国有土地用地制度改革的深入进行，划拨的条件从依据所有制判断转向根据土地用途来限制，不再区分所有制，而是依据国家利益和社会公共利益的需要来划拨土地。依据《城市房地产管理法》第23条以及国土资源部2001年10月22日发布的《划拨用地目录》的规定，下列建设用地的土地使用权，确属必需的，可以由县级以上人民政府依法批准划拨：

①国家机关用地和军事用地。包括党政机关和人民团体用地。

②城市基础设施用地。包括城市供水、供热、供气设施；环境卫生用地设施；公共交通设施以及道路、广场、绿地等的用地；公益事业用地，包括非营利性邮政设施、教育设施、体育设施、公共文化设施、医疗卫生设施以及公益性科研机构用地。

③国家重点扶持的能源、交通、水利等项目用地。包括石油天然气设施、煤炭设施、电力设施、水利设施，铁路、公路、水路交通设施以及民用机场设施用地。

但需要注意的是，对国家重点扶持的能源、交通、水利等基础设施用地项目，可以以划拨方式提供土地使用权。对以营利为目的的，非国家重点扶持的能源、交通、水利等基础设施用地项目，应当以有偿方式提供土地使用权。

④法律、行政法规规定的其他用地，主要包括监狱、劳教所以及戒毒所、看守所、治安拘留所、收容教育所的用地。这些用地都是基于国家利益和社会公共利益而使用的

土地。因此也有学者主张将划拨设立的土地使用权称为公益性用地使用权，即用于国家管理、教育、科研、消防、各种不营利的公用设施和公共福利设施等非营利目的，并且不允许用于任何营业目的的国有土地。这一见解是有道理的。

（3）划拨是行政机关的单方行为。从划拨的程序可以看出，对于符合法律要求的用地，先由建设单位提出申请，经有批准权的人民政府批准，方可以划拨方式提供土地使用权。因此，土地划拨在性质上应当是一种依申请的行政行为：土地划拨是国家为了维护国家利益和社会公共利益，应用地者的申请而许可其使用国有土地的行为。

（4）划拨行为具有一定的无偿性。通过划拨设立建设用地使用权旨在对具有国家利益或社会公共利益的项目加以扶持，其并非为市场化设立并移转建设用地使用权的手段。因此，从理论上讲划拨行为应当是无偿的，国家并未考虑取得划拨土地使用权的土地价值。但是，被划拨的土地上已经设立了建设用地使用权或者拟被划拨的土地本身就是集体所有的土地。在此情况下，就需要通过征收或者征用，消灭该土地上的建设用地使用权或者将之收归国有，再进行划拨。此时，就涉及征收、征用的费用问题。有些情况下，国家会直接动用财政力量完成征收、征用补偿并对土地进行"三通一平"①，然后再将可以直接用来开发建设的"熟地"进行划拨，从而完全无偿地将土地使用权交付给土地使用者使用。但实践中大多数情况下，都是由用地者来承担土地征用及拆迁补偿等费用。按照相关法律、法规，这些费用主要包括土地征用费、耕地占用税、劳动力安置费及有关地上、地下附着物拆迁补偿费、安置动迁用房支出等；以及规划、设计、项目可行性研究和水文、地质、勘察、测绘、"三通一平"等支出。换言之，此时虽然未就土地使用权本身支付对价，但是土地使用人使用土地也并非是无偿的，因为土地使用人实际上支付了国家获取集体土地所有权的对价。因此，我们在下文中主张对这些支付了一定费用的划拨土地使用权与完全无偿的划拨土地使用权应当区别对待。

当然，由于中国目前对征收和征用补偿数额的限制，这些费用并不等于所取得的土地所有权的市场价格，其数额与土地使用权的市场价格之间也并没有内在的联系，在本质上划拨仍然是一种非市场化的建设用地使用权设立方式。

（5）划拨土地使用权是一种没有确定期限的权利。基于划拨用地的公共目的，法律并未对划拨土地使用权的期限加以明确的限制，也未像通过出让方式设定的建设用地使用权那样规定明确的期限。根据相关法规的规定，无偿取得划拨土地使用权的土地使用者，因迁移、解散、撤销、破产或者其他原因而停止使用土地的，市、县人民政府应当无偿收回其划拨土地使用权。市、县人民政府根据城市建设发展需要和城市规划的要求，也可以无偿收回划拨土地使用权。因此，在法定事由发生时，国家可以收回土地，从而消灭该权利。

---

① "三通一平"是指基本建设项目开工的前提条件，具体指：水通、电通、路通和场地平整。水通（专指给水）；电通（指施工用电接到施工现场具备施工条件）；路通（指场外道路已铺到施工现场周围入口处，满足车辆出入条件）；场地平整（指拟建建筑物及条件现场基本平整，无需机械平整，人工简单平整即可进入施工的状态），简称"三通一平"。

（6）划拨土地使用权的内容受到法律的严格限制。根据中国现行法律的规定，划拨土地使用权，原则上不得转让、出租、抵押。其例外在于，如果具备下列条件，经过批准则允许进行流转：领有国有土地使用证（完成土地使用权初始登记）、具有地上建筑物、其他附着物合法的产权证明（需要连同土地上附着物一并流转而不能单独流转），以及签订土地使用权出让合同并补交土地使用权出让金或者以转让、出租、抵押所获收益抵交土地使用权出让金。例如，根据《城市房地产管理法》第51条的规定，在建筑物抵押时，其占用的划拨土地使用权一并抵押，但是抵押权应当通过拍卖实现，而且拍卖划拨的国有土地使用权所得的价款，在依法缴纳相当于应缴纳的土地使用权出让金的款额后，抵押权人才有优先受偿权。在此情况下，实际上进行流转的已经是经出让而设定的建设用地使用权而非划拨土地使用权。因此，中国法律并不承认划拨土地使用权具有权利处分权能。

（二）国有土地使用权的出让

国有土地使用权的出让，是指国家以国有土地所有人的身份将土地使用权在一定年限内让与土地使用者，并由土地使用者向国家支付土地使用权出让金的行为。通过出让方式取得的土地使用权，土地使用者有权以开发利用、生产经营为目的使用国有土地。

土地使用权出让可以采取下列方式：协议、招标、拍卖、挂牌等公开对价的方式。

根据《城镇国有土地使用权出让和转让暂行条例》第8条的规定，协议出让国有土地使用权，是指国家以协议方式将国有土地使用权在一定年限内出让给土地使用者，由土地使用者向国家支付土地使用权出让金的行为。《民法典》第347条第3款规定："严格限制以划拨方式设立建设用地使用权。"出让国有土地使用权，除依照法律、法规和规章的规定应当采用招标、拍卖或者挂牌方式外，还可采取协议方式。

《民法典》第347条第2款规定："工业、商业、旅游、娱乐和商品住宅等经营性用地以及同一土地有两个以上意向用地者的，应当采取招标、拍卖等公开竞价的方式出让。"根据国土资源部2002年4月发布的《招标拍卖挂牌出让国有土地使用权规定》（2007年9月28日修订），招标出让国有土地使用权，是指市、县人民政府土地行政主管部门（以下简称出让人）发布招标公告，邀请特定或者不特定的公民、法人和其他组织参加国有土地使用权投标，根据投标结果确定土地使用者的行为。拍卖出让国有土地使用权，是指出让人发布拍卖公告，由竞买人在指定时间、地点进行公开竞价，根据出价结果确定土地使用者的行为。挂牌出让国有土地使用权，是指出让人发布挂牌公告，按公告规定的期限将拟出让宗地的交易条件在指定的土地交易场所挂牌公布，接受竞买人的报价申请并更新挂牌价格，根据挂牌期限截止时的出价结果确定土地使用者的行为。商业、旅游、娱乐和商品住宅等各类经营性用地，必须以招标、拍卖或者挂牌方式出让。其他用途的土地的供地计划公布后，同一宗地有两个以上意向用地者的，也应当采用招标、拍卖或者挂牌方式出让。

《民法典》第348条规定："通过招标、拍卖、协议等出让方式设立建设用地使用权的，当事人应当采取书面形式订立建设用地使用权出让合同。"土地使用权出让合同由市、县人民政府土地管理部门与土地使用者签订。建设用地使用权出让合同一般包括下列条款：（1）当事人的名称和住所；（2）土地界址、面积等；（3）建筑物、构筑物及其附属设施占用的空间；（4）土地用途、规划条件；（5）建设用地使用权期限；（6）出让金等费用及其支付方式；（7）解决争议的方法。

土地使用者应当在签订土地使用权出让合同后 60 日内，支付全部土地使用权出让金。逾期未全部支付的，出让方有权解除合同，并可请求违约赔偿。出让方应当按照合同规定，提供出让的土地使用权。未按合同规定提供土地使用权的，土地使用者有权解除合同，并可请求违约赔偿。土地使用者在支付全部土地使用权出让金后，应当依照规定办理登记，领取土地使用证，取得土地使用权。土地使用者应当按照土地使用权出让合同的规定和城市规划的要求，开发、利用、经营土地。未按合同规定的期限和条件开发、利用土地的，市、县人民政府土地管理部门应当予以纠正，并根据情节可以给予警告、罚款直至无偿收回土地使用权的处罚。

对国有土地转让合同的性质，是行政合同还是民事合同理论上有争议，实务界认定为民事合同。

土地使用权的出让，从经济学角度来看，属于土地的一级市场，与土地使用权的转让即土地的二级市场是密不可分的。

（三）国有土地使用权的转让

土地使用权的转让，是指土地使用权人通过买卖、互易和赠与等方式将土地使用权以合同方式再转移的行为。依据《城市房地产管理法》第 37 条规定，房地产转让行为包括买卖、赠与或者其他合法方式将土地使用权转移给他人的行为。根据《城镇国有土地使用权出让和转让暂行条例》的规定，未按土地使用权出让合同规定的期限和条件投资开发、利用土地的，土地使用权不得转让。土地使用权转让应当签订转让合同。土地使用权转让时，土地使用权出让合同和登记文件中所载明的权利、义务随之转移。土地使用者通过转让方式取得的土地使用权，其使用年限为土地使用权出让合同规定的使用年限减去原土地使用者已使用年限后的剩余年限。土地使用权转让时，其地上建筑物、其他附着物所有权随之转让。土地上建筑物、其他附着物的所有人或者共有人，享有该建筑物、附着物使用范围内的土地使用权。土地使用者转让地上建筑物、其他附着物所有权时，其使用范围内的土地使用权随之转让，但地上建筑物、其他附着物作为动产转让的除外。土地使用权和地上建筑物、其他附着物所有权转让，应当依照规定办理过户登记。土地使用权和地上建筑物、其他附着物所有权分割转让的，应当经市、县人民政府土地管理部门和房产管理部门批准，并依照规定办理过户登记。

（四）国有土地使用权的租赁

土地使用权出租是指土地使用者作为出租人将土地使用权随同地上建筑物、其他附着物租赁给承租人使用，由承租人向出租人支付租金的行为。未按土地使用权出让合同规定的期限和条件投资开发、利用土地的，土地使用权不得出租。

土地使用权出租，出租人与承租人应当签订租赁合同。租赁合同不得违背国家法律、法规和土地使用权出让合同的规定。土地使用权出租后，出租人必须继续履行土地使用权出让合同。土地使用权和地上建筑物、其他附着物出租，出租人应当依照规定办理登记。

（五）农村集体所有土地建设用地使用权的取得、出让与转让

《民法典》第361条规定："集体所有的土地作为建设用地的，应当依照土地管理的法律规定办理。"按照《土地管理法》的规定，集体土地上的建设用地使用权包括乡（村）公共设施、公益事业建设用地使用权，乡镇企业建设用地使用权以及宅基地使用权三种形态。鉴于宅基地使用权是《民法典》规定的一种独立的用益物权，因此，第361条规定实际涉及的是前两种形态。兴办乡镇企业的，因乡村公共设施、公益事业建设需要使用土地的，应当依照法律的规定办理审批手续。

关于集体经营性建设用地的出让、出租，《土地管理法》第63条规定："土地利用总体规划、城乡规划确定为工业、商业等经营性用途，并经依法登记的集体经营性建设用地，土地所有权人可以通过出让、出租等方式交由单位或者个人使用，并应当签订书面合同，载明土地界址、面积、动工期限、使用期限、土地用途、规划条件和双方其他权利义务。

前款规定的集体经营性建设用地出让、出租等，应当经本集体经济组织成员的村民会议三分之二以上成员或者三分之二以上村民代表的同意。

通过出让等方式取得的集体经营性建设用地使用权可以转让、互换、出资、赠与或者抵押，但法律、行政法规另有规定或者土地所有权人、土地使用权人签订的书面合同另有约定的除外。

集体经营性建设用地的出租，集体建设用地使用权的出让及其最高年限、转让、互换、出资、赠与、抵押等，参照同类用途的国有建设用地执行。具体办法由国务院制定。"

中央全面深化改革委员会审议通过的《关于完善建设用地使用权转让、出租、抵押二级市场的指导意见》于2019年7月由国务院办公厅印发，对促进一二级土地市场协调发展、加快建立城乡统一的建设用地市场、推动经济高质量发展具有重要意义。措施主要包括完善转让规则促进要素流通、优化划拨土地转让流程、保障出让土地交易自由，促进存量土地进入二级市场转让盘活；放宽对抵押权人的限制、大力支持民营经济发展，自然人、企业均可作为抵押权人依法办理不动产抵押相关手续，并探索允许养老、教育等社会领域企业以有偿方式取得的建设用地使用权、设施等财产进行抵押融资等。

（六）建设用地使用权的设立公示

《民法典》第349条规定："设立建设用地使用权的，应当向登记机构申请建设用地使用权登记。建设用地使用权自登记时设立。登记机构应当向建设用地使用权人发放权属证书。"可见，建设用地使用权的设立，采取登记要件主义。

三、建设用地使用权人的权利和义务

（一）权利

建设用地使用权人有权对国家所有或者集体所有的土地占有、使用和收益，在该土地上建造并经营建筑物、构筑物以及其他附着物。

建设用地使用权人建造的建筑物、构筑物以及其他附着物，除有相反证据的以外，其所有权属于建设用地使用权人。

建设用地使用权人有权将建设用地使用权转让、互换、出资、赠与或者抵押，但法律另有规定的除外。

通过土地划拨取得的建设用地使用权，只有在下列几种情况下，才可以转让、抵押、出租：（1）土地使用者为公司、企业、其他经济组织和个人；（2）领有国有土地使用证；转让房地产时，应当按照国务院规定，报有批准权的人民政府审批；（3）具有地上建筑物、其他附着物合法的产权证明；（4）签订土地使用权出让合同，向当地市、县人民政府补交土地使用权出让金或者以转让、出租、抵押所获收益抵交土地使用权出让金。在其他情况下，通过划拨土地取得的建设用地使用权不得转让、出租、抵押。

建设用地使用权转让、互换、出资、赠与或者抵押的，当事人应当采取书面形式订立相应的合同。使用期限由当事人约定，但不得超过建设用地使用权的剩余期限。

建设用地使用权转让、互换、出资或者赠与的，应当向登记机构申请变更登记。

房随地走和地随房走。《民法典》第356条、第357条规定，建设用地使用权转让、互换、出资或者赠与的，附着于该土地上的建筑物、构筑物及其附属设施一并处分。建筑物、构筑物及其附属设施转让、互换、出资或者赠与的，该建筑物、构筑物及其附属设施占用范围内的建设用地使用权一并处分。

附属行为。建设用地使用权人可以在其地基范围内进行非保存建筑物或其他工作物的附属行为，如修筑围墙、种植花木、养殖等。

建设用地使用权期间届满前，因公共利益需要提前收回该土地的，有权依照法获得该土地上的房屋及其他不动产补偿，并有权获得退还相应的出让金。

（二）义务

建设用地使用权人应当合理利用土地，不得改变土地用途。需要改变土地用途的，应当依法经有关行政主管部门批准。

建设用地使用权人应当依照法律规定以及合同约定交付出让金等费用。

四、建设用地使用权的消灭

(一)消灭事由

1. 土地灭失

指因不可抗拒的自然灾害(如地震、火山爆发、洪水等)或人为原因导致土地实际使用价值消失的现象。土地灭失是权利的标的物的灭失,以灭失的土地为对象的所有权或其他各项权利,也随土地的灭失而消灭

2. 使用期限届满

《民法典》第 359 条规定:"住宅建设用地使用权期限届满的,自动续期。续期费用的缴纳或者减免,依照法律、行政法规的规定办理。非住宅建设用地使用权期间届满后的续期,依照法律规定办理。该土地上的房屋及其他不动产的归属,有约定的,按照约定;没有约定或者约定不明确的,依照法律、行政法规的规定办理。"

3. 征收

《民法典》第 243 条规定:为了公共利益的需要,依照法律规定的权限和程序可以征收集体所有的土地和组织、个人的房屋以及其他不动产。征收集体所有的土地,应当依法及时足额支付土地补偿费、安置补助费以及农村村民住宅、其他地上附着物和青苗等的补偿费用,并安排被征地农民的社会保障费用,保障被征地农民的生活,维护被征地农民的合法权益。征收组织、个人的房屋以及其他不动产,应当依法给予征收补偿,维护被征收人的合法权益;征收个人住宅的,还应当保障被征收人的居住条件。任何组织或者个人不得贪污、挪用、私分、截留、拖欠征收补偿费等费用。第 245 条规定:因抢险救灾、疫情防控等紧急需要,依照法律规定的权限和程序可以征用组织、个人的不动产或者动产。被征用的不动产或者动产使用后,应当返还被征用人。组织、个人的不动产或者动产被征用或者征用后毁损、灭失的,应当给予补偿。

4. 因行政处罚——而由政府无偿收回土地使用权

在以下两种情况下政府可以无偿收回土地:闲置土地和违反国有土地使用权出让合同的开发条件。

5. 其他事由

包括建设用地使用权被提前收回、建设用地使用权被撤销等事由。

(二)消灭的法律后果

地上物的补偿。《民法典》规定:征收应补偿建设用地使用权期间届满前,因公共利益需要提前收回该土地的,应当依照法律规定对该土地上的房屋及其他不动产给予补偿,并退还相应的土地出让金。对于其他原因而消灭的是否补偿目前法律无规定。

建设用地使用权消灭的，出让人应当及时办理注销登记。登记机构应当收回建设用地使用权证书。

第四节　宅基地使用权

一、宅基地使用权概述

（一）宅基地使用权的概念和特征

《民法典》第362条规定："宅基地使用权人依法对集体所有的土地享有占有和使用的权利，有权依法利用该土地建造住宅及其附属设施。"可见，宅基地使用权是指自然人（主要是农村村民）依法享有的，在集体所有的土地上下建造、保有房屋及附属设施的用益物权。按照《土地管理法》对土地用途的分类，宅基地属于建设用地，宅基地使用权也是为了对他人土地使用价值加以利用而设定的权利。关于建造、保有房屋及附属设施等内容，在建设用地使用权的概念中已做分析，在此不再赘述。从中国民法典物权制度以及相关法律规定来看，宅基地使用权具有下列特点：

1. 权利主体的限定性

宅基地使用权的主体，限于自然人，且从现行立法来看，原则上限于农村村民或者说农村集体经济组织成员。

宅基地使用权是对集体所有的土地享有的权利。因此，至少就其初始取得而言，其权利人只能是本集体经济组织成员。"外乡、外村的农村村民也不具备该项权利的主体资格，除非其依法将户口迁入本乡或本村。"①按照地方法规的规定，集体经济组织招聘的技术人员要求在当地落户的，回乡落户的离休、退休、退职的干部职工、复退军人和回乡定居的华侨和港、澳、台同胞，也可以申请取得宅基地使用。

2. 权利客体的特定性

宅基地使用权的客体，限于集体所有的土地。《土地管理法》保留了对土地所有权的宣示规定，其第9条强调："宅基地……属于农民集体所有。"

3. 土地用途的特定性与灵活性

经出让设定的建设用地使用权，其土地用途多种多样，包括居住用地，工业用地，教育、科技、文化、卫生、体育用地，商业、旅游、娱乐用地等。现行法律虽然对其用途加以限制，但权利人仍不可通过审批来改变其用途。但是，就宅基地使用权来说，现行法规定其只能用作农村村民住宅的建设。所谓住宅，是指农村村民所建住房；所谓附属设施，是指与住房的居住生活有关的其他建筑物和设施。例如，车库、厕所、沼气池、牛棚、猪圈等。正是由于宅基地的用途主要在于住宅及其附属设施的建设，故而在

---

① 王利明主编：《民法学》，复旦大学出版社2004年版，第335页。

土地之上建造的，应当是建筑物及其附属设施，而构筑物通常用于生产而非居住如水塔、烟囱等。因此宅基地使用权并不以建造、保有构筑物为其内容。2019 年 9 月 11 日下发的《中央农村工作领导小组办公室 农业农村部关于进一步加强农村宅基地管理的通知》中明确：鼓励村集体和农民盘活利用闲置宅基地和闲置住宅，通过自主经营、合作经营、委托经营等方式，依法依规发展农家乐、民宿、乡村旅游等。城镇居民、工商资本等租赁农房居住或开展经营的，要严格遵守合同法的规定，租赁合同的期限不得超过二十年。合同到期后，双方可以另行约定。在尊重农民意愿并符合规划的前提下，鼓励村集体积极稳妥开展闲置宅基地整治，整治出的土地优先用于满足农民新增宅基地需求、村庄建设和乡村产业发展。

4. 取得上的无偿性

中国现行法律强调宅基地使用权的初始取得，应当是无偿的。虽然中共中央、国务院包括有些地方政府曾提出对宅基地使用权进行有偿使用试点、征收有偿使用费，有些地方对宅基地超出法定面积的征收超占费等。也有学者基于有偿使用是集体土地所有权中收益权和处分权的体现，认为应当允许集体经济组织自由决定是否收取使用费。中办和国办在 2015 年 11 月联合下发的《深化农村改革综合性实施方案》提出了"宅基地制度改革的基本思路，确立：对农民住房财产权作出明确界定，探索宅基地有偿使用制度和自愿有偿退出机制"改革思路。但是，考虑到农民负担过重的问题，《中共中央办公厅、国务院办公厅关于对涉及农民负担项目审核处理意见的通知》（中发〔1993〕10 号）中明令取消在农村收取农村宅基地有偿使用费、农村宅基地超占费、土地登记费、村镇规划建设管理费、建设用地规划许可证费、房屋所有权登记费等收费。甚至对于因设定宅基地使用权而占用耕地，需要缴纳耕地开垦费的，根据相关规章，该费用也因农村集体经济组织为开垦义务人，而应当由农村集体经济组织交纳开垦费。该费用不得向申请宅基地使用权的农村居民收取，因为农民建房用地属农村集体经济组织所有，土地所有权没有发生转移，不应交纳土地补偿费、青苗补偿费、新菜地开发基金等费用。

这与建设用地使用权尤其是国有建设用地使用权有偿使用，原则上通过出让方式设立，形成了鲜明的对比。

5. 没有期限限制

中国现行法律没有对宅基地使用权的期限进行限制性规定，因此宅基地使用权不会因期限届满而消灭。因此，也有学者将宅基地使用权界定为，经过依法审批由农村集体经济组织分配给其成员用于建造住宅的没有使用期限限制的集体土地使用权，或者认为宅基地使用权是农民以户为单位在集体所有的土地上，在规定的地段享有建筑住房、添置生活设施，在庭院种植树木，永久居住的权利。其之所以具有无期限性，主要因为其以户为单位设立，虽然由户主代表家庭享有，但是户主或者某个家庭成员的死亡并不影响宅基地使用权的存续。

此外，中国现行法律禁止宅基地使用权的流转，即权利人不得单独就其宅基地使用权转让、出租或者设定抵押。《深化农村改革综合性实施方案》下发后，宅基地使用权的流转已经解禁。

(二)宅基地使用权与建设用地使用权的比较

从宅基地使用权的内容来看，其本质上也属于传统民法中地上权的范畴；其占用的土地也应当是建设用地。实际上中国《土地管理法》中也正是将之作为建设用地使用权的一种特殊类型加以规定的。如前所述，中国目前建设用地使用权包括国有建设用地使用权和集体所有土地的建设用地使用权，而宅基地使用权正是与乡(镇)村公共设施、公益事业建设用地使用权、乡镇企业建设用地使用权共同构成了集体所有土地上的建设用地使用权。

但是，正如前文所述的，相对于建设用地使用权，宅基地使用权具有自己特点。即便未来解除对其用途、流转的限制，但是其取得上的无偿性、初始设定时主体上的特定性，也决定了其与建设用地使用权之间仍然存在巨大的差别。故而，《民法典》未将之作为建设用地使用权的下位概念，而应当将其作为一种独立的用益物权形态。

宅基地使用权的初始取得，系基于集体经济组织成员的身份而为之，其初始取得的主体具有特定性，限于集体经济组织的成员；而建设用地使用权的设定，基于国家所有权的充分实现以及培育土地市场的考虑，应当尽可能公开其出让信息，吸引尽可能多的人参与公开竞价，从而实现其价值。在初始取得的主体上，宅基地使用权的封闭性和建设用地使用权的开放性，形成了鲜明的对比。

在二者的期限、地租支付等方面，也应当有不同的制度设计。例如，宅基地使用权主体为本集体经济组织成员时，不应当有期限限制；而建设用地使用权则应当有明确的期限。再如，如前所述，建设用地使用权出让时，笔者认为应当采用一次性交纳出让金的方式；而宅基地使用权主体为本集体经济组织成员时，应当是无偿的。

需要指出的是，正是由于二者存在上述差异，从而作为两种独立的用益物权规定在《民法典》中。但是从长远来看，笔者认为，随着农村改革的深入，宅基地使用权应当具备充分的权利处分权能，允许其直接入市；在制度建构上应当尽量限制宅基地使用权的消灭事由，从而使其成为一种稳定的、长期的、类似所有权的土地利用权，并能够与建设用地使用权一起成为中国土地市场的基础。

二、宅基地使用权的取得与消灭

《民法典》并未对宅基地使用权的具体内容进行直接规定。《民法典》第363条规定："宅基地使用权的取得、行使和转让，适用土地管理的法律和国家有关规定。"可见，关于宅基地使用权的具体制度，《民法典》将其委诸特别法来处理。以下详述之：

(一)宅基地使用权的初始取得

依据相关法律的规定，宅基地使用权的初始取得，主要包括以下几种方式：

1. 法律的直接规定

自 20 世纪 60 年代完成社会主义改造以来，中国农村建立起了农村土地集体所有制。通过集体化，农民对其通过土改获得的土地包括宅基地失去了所有权，但国家承认并保护其对宅基地的使用权，而且不准该使用权出租和买卖。

改革开放之后，随着法律的健全，对于既存的宅基地使用权，法律承认了其效力，并通过登记等方式将之确立为长期稳定的权利，逐渐赋予了其物权性质。根据当时的相关规定，"按土改时所确定的宅基地的所有权，改变为使用权的，该宅基地的使用权不变；凡是当地宅基地已经统一规划过的，按所规划后确定的社员宅基地的使用权处理；凡是经过合法手续已进行调整的，按调整的决定处理。社员在宅基地上种植的果树和竹木等，均应归社员所有"。

此后，尽管相关法律法规对于宅基地使用权的面积等问题进行了一定的限制，但仍然坚持了法律不溯及既往的原则，根据实际使用面积确定了其享有的宅基地使用权。例如，根据国家土地管理局 1995 年 4 月 9 日发布的《确定土地所有权和使用权的若干规定》，对于法律没有进行规范（1982 年 2 月国务院发布《村镇建房用地管理条例》）之前建房占用的宅基地，法律规范后未经拆迁、改建、翻建的，法律原则上承认其宅基地使用权。而在法律规范之后，则应当根据法律进行处理，按处理后实际使用面积确定宅基地使用权。非农业户口居民（含华侨）原在农村的宅基地，房屋产权没有变化的，也继续承认其宅基地使用权。可见，在中国建立宅基地使用权制度之后，对当时存在的农村居民建房占用宅基地的情形，除有擅自占地、乱占耕地等违法情形之外，法律直接赋予了其宅基地使用权。严格地讲，此种情形，也不妨视为法律对通过先占取得权利的一种承认。

2. 村民依法申请与集体经济组织依法无偿授予

作为集体经济组织成员，农村村民自愿将其土地等生产和生活资料转移给集体经济组织，从而建立起了中国大陆农村土地的集体所有制。而农民自愿联合起来组成的农村集体经济组织由此也负有为其成员提供基本生活保障的义务。故而，在农村村民存在实际的居住需求的情况下，集体经济组织负有设定宅基地使用权并移转给村民，供其建造并保有房屋及其附属设施的义务。

但是，为了避免农村集体经济组织滥批宅基地、造成土地浪费和占用耕地，法律对授予的条件进行了严格的限制：对宅基地的面积规定了上限，而且要求集体经济组织的授予决定需要经过相关政府的审核。

（1）申请人的条件

从《土地管理法》《中华人民共和国土地管理法实施条例》①等现行法律、行政法规以及地方性法规的规定来看，其对于申请人或者说宅基地使用权的初始取得人规定了三个方面的条件：

---

① 该条例 2021 年 7 月 2 日中华人民共和国国务院令第 743 号第三次修订，以下简称《土地管理法实施条例》。

第一，申请人必须具有特定身份。如前所述，宅基地使用权的初始取得，其权利人限于本集体经济组织成员。按照地方法规的要求，不仅包括既存的集体经济组织成员，也包括新加入的集体经济组织成员，如集体经济组织招聘的技术人员要求在当地落户的；回乡落户的离休、退休、退职的干部职工、复退军人和回乡定居的华侨和港、澳、台同胞，以及其他经县级以上人民政府批准回原籍落户的人员。

第二，申请人存在合理的住房需求。也就是说，申请人没有宅基地，或者因结婚等原因原有的宅基地不敷所需的。例如，农村村民从未取得过宅基地的；曾取得宅基地但因兴建乡（村）镇公共设施和公益事业建设等原因被收回宅基地的；或者原宅基地影响村镇建设规划，需要收回而又无宅基地的；成年子女因结婚等原因确需另立门户而已有的宅基地低于分户标准的；但基于扶老育幼的考虑，一般要求父母身边留一子女，而不能所有子女都另立门户。此种需求并非必需，只要根据当地的实际情况认为合理即可。例如，某户人家共有五口人，现有宅基地120平方米，现长子结婚需要另立门户。在此情况下，如果按照当地习俗确实需要另行授予宅基地，或者通常每人应当有30平方米的宅基地，即应当认为存在合理的居住需求，不能以其现有的宅基地尚能居住为由认定其不符合申请条件。

此外，依据《民法典》第364条的规定，在宅基地因自然灾害等原因灭失的情况下，宅基地使用权消灭。此种情况下，对失去宅基地的村民，显然存在合理的住房需求，因此《民法典》要求对其重新分配宅基地。

第三，不存在法律规定的禁止申请事由。例如，依据《土地管理法》第62条第5款的规定："农村村民出卖、出租、赠与住宅后，再申请宅基地的，不予批准。"据此，如果申请人曾经获得过宅基地，但其又通过出卖、出租、赠与而失去该宅基地使用权的，则不能再行申请。

（2）申请与授予程序

依据《土地管理法》第62条第4款的规定："农村村民住宅用地，由乡（镇）人民政府审核批准；其中，涉及占用农用地的，依照本法第44条的规定办理审批手续。"原则上，依照《土地管理法实施条例》第34条规定，农村村民申请宅基地的，应当以户为单位向农村集体经济组织提出申请；没有设立农村集体经济组织的，应当向所在的村民小组或者村民委员会提出申请。宅基地申请依法经农村村民集体讨论通过并在本集体范围内公示后，报乡（镇）人民政府审核批准。涉及占用农用地的，应当依法办理农用地转用审批手续。

需要指出的是，宅基地的授予是农村集体经济组织行使自己土地所有权的一种形式。而乡、县政府本身并非土地的所有权人，是作为土地使用和流转秩序的管理者而出现的，其进行的审核、批准内容应当限于该申请是否按照村庄和集镇规划；是否符合合理布局，综合开发，配套建设的要求；是否符合乡（镇）土地利用总体规划和土地利用年度计划相关规划以及土地利用计划；是否在有荒地的情况下占用农用地等。政府审核、批准的目的在于监督集体经济组织合理利用土地、避免随意将农用地转为建设用地。因此，此种审批严格地讲应当是一种核准，只要不违反相关规划和计划，就不应驳回其申请。审批机关不能越权干预集体经济组织对申请的审核，也不能对集体经济组织没有通过的宅基地进行审批。正是由于宅基地的授予是集体经济组织行使其土地所有权的方式，本书采用了民法中常用的"授予"的提法，而没有将之表述为"经审批设立"等常用的概念。

在授予宅基地时，应当尽量使用原有的宅基地和村内空闲地。如果该宅基地涉及占用农用地的，则应当依法办理农用地转用审批手续。但是，相关费用如耕地开垦费，仍然应当由农村集体经济组织承担，而不能向申请人收取。

(3)关于宅基地的面积上限

中国耕地紧缺，故而法律强调宅基地不能过大，而应当在法定上限之内。按照《土地管理法》第62条第1款的规定，农村村民一户只能拥有一处宅基地。考虑到中国各地实际情况差别较大，宅基地的面积上限则授权省、自治区、直辖市自行确定。

关于宅基地面积的上限，各省、自治区、直辖市根据本地土地稀缺程度进行了不同的规定，在标准确定上也有不同特点，以下选取较有代表性的几个地方加以介绍：

人口大省河南，将宅基地面积上限与人均耕地和地形地貌挂钩来确定宅基地上限。山区、丘陵区可耕作的土地较少，相对宅基地面积也比较宽松，《河南省实施〈土地管理法〉办法》(2009年11月27日修订)第53条第2款规定：(1)城镇郊区和人均耕地667平方米以下的平原地区，每户用地不得超过134平方米；(2)人均耕地667平方米以上的平原地区，每户用地不得超过167平方米；(3)山区、丘陵区每户用地不得超过200平方米，占用耕地的适用本款(1)、(2)项的规定。

而根据《河北省土地管理条例》第53条的规定，农村村民新建住宅，将宅基地面积上限与人均耕地挂钩，宅基地的用地标准是：(1)城市郊区，每处宅基地不得超过167平方米；(2)平原地区和山区，人均耕地不足1000平方米的县(市)，每处宅基地不得超过200平方米，人均耕地1000平方米以上的县(市)，每处宅基地不得超过233平方米；(3)坝上①地区，每处宅基地不得超过467平方米。在前款规定的限额内，市、县人民政府可以根据当地实际，具体规定本行政区域内的农村宅基地标准。

青海省则区分与城市的远近及耕地的具体情况来确定宅基地面积上限，依据《青海省实施〈中华人民共和国土地管理法〉办法》(2006年7月28日修订)第54条，其宅基地上限为：(1)城市郊区及县辖镇郊区不得超过200平方米；(2)其他地区：水地250平方米，旱地300平方米，非耕地350平方米。牧民的固定居民点可以适当放宽，但不得超过450平方米。如此高的面积上限，显然与其地广人稀有关。四川省则依据人口数量来确定宅基地面积上限，《四川省实施〈中华人民共和国土地管理法〉办法》第52条规定："宅基地面积标准为每人20～30平方米；3人以下的户按3人计算，4人的户按4人计算，5人以上的户按5人计算。其中，民族自治地方农村村民的宅基地面积标准可

---

① "坝上"是一地理名词，特指由草原陡然升高而形成的地带。坝上在华北平原和内蒙古高原交接的地方陡然升高，呈阶梯状，故名"坝上"。

以适当增加，具体标准由民族自治州或自治县人民政府制定；扩建住宅所占的土地面积应当连同原宅基地面积一并计算。"

新建住宅全部使用农用地以外的土地的，用地面积可以适当增加，增加部分每户最多不得超过 30 平方米。此种做法对于鼓励尽量不占用耕地，颇有意义。

浙江省则是区分占用土地用途来分别确定上限，《浙江省实施〈中华人民共和国土地管理法〉办法》第 35 条规定，"……鼓励自然村向中心村集聚；鼓励统建、联建和建造公寓式住宅；严格控制占用耕地建造住宅。……宅基地的面积标准（包括附属用房、庭院用地），使用耕地的，最高不得超过 125 平方米；使用其他土地的，最高不得超过 140 平方米，山区有条件利用荒地、荒坡的，最高不得超过 160 平方米。农村村民宅基地的具体标准，由市、县人民政府在前款规定的幅度内根据当地实际确定"。这种做法显然有利于减少占用耕地的行为，而且有利于对荒地的开发利用。可见，中国各地政府都根据自己的实际情况，因地制宜地对宅基地使用权的面积上限、确定标准等进行了规定。

（4）关于宅基地使用权的无偿性、长期性

我国现行宅基地制度起源于计划经济时期，其主要特征是"集体所有、成员使用，无偿分配、长期占有"。宅基地集体成员无偿取得和长期使用的制度设计初衷是保障农民的基本居住，承载的是社会保障功能，是集体作为社会主义公有制形式的本质所决定的，表达的是维护社会公平的国家意志，在保障农民住有所居、促进社会和谐稳定中发挥了基础作用。中国必须长期坚持宅基地初始取得的无偿性、长期性，其理由具体来说：

首先，是维护农民利益、减轻农民负担的政策考虑。一旦放开允许农村集体经济组织就宅基地使用权收取使用费，则加重了农民负担，可能助长腐败现象，危及社会稳定，不利于构建和谐社会。

其次，是基于历史补偿的考虑。此种历史补偿，是指农村集体经济组织的土地，在历史上是农民响应党的号召、自愿放弃其土地所有权而形成的，因此农村集体经济组织应当以无偿提供土地供其使用作为一种补偿。农民的私人土地通过集体化而转化为集体的土地所有权。集体不能在无偿取得农民土地所有权之后，再要求其（或者其子孙）有偿使用这些土地。在中国经济已经获得高速、平稳发展，基本实现工业化的情况下，工业反哺农业、城市反哺农村，应当通过财政、税收等措施尽力减轻农民负担，这已经成为社会的共识。在此情况下，要求有偿使用宅基地，理由不足，是说不通的。

虽然宅基地的初始取得是无偿的，本书采用了"授予"的提法来体现宅基地使用权的初始取得是集体土地所有权的实现方式而非基于政府的审批而设定。但是基于上述考虑，不能以宅基地使用权是集体经济组织无偿提供为由，允许其随意收回土地。《土地管理法实施条例》第 36 条规定："依法取得的宅基地和宅基地上的农村村民住宅及其附属设施受法律保护。禁止违背农村村民意愿强制流转宅基地，禁止违法收回农村村民依法取得的宅基地，禁止以退出宅基地作为农村村民进城落户的条件，禁止强迫农村村民搬迁退出宅基地。"这与民法中无偿行为的规则是完全不同的。

(5)宅基地使用权的确权及其设定、移转和消灭登记

建设用地使用权的设定,以登记为要件。宅基地使用权是否需要以登记为要件,值得探讨。《民法典》并未规定宅基地使用权登记设立或者登记发生对抗第三人的效力。

宅基地使用权的设定,应当以完成审批程序为条件,当事人可以申请而无须登记。中国农村幅员辽阔,要求对其进行全面的、实质性审查的土地登记并不现实。因此,只要完成批准程序,宅基地使用权就应当认定为依法设定了,登记不是宅基地使用权的设立的必要条件。依照《不动产登记暂行条例》第5条规定,宅基地使用权已经纳入不动产登记范围。

2010年以来,中央一号文件多次对宅基地、集体建设用地使用权确权登记工作作出部署和要求。为进一步做好宅基地和集体建设用地使用权确权登记工作,自然资源部组织编制了《宅基地和集体建设用地使用权确权登记工作问答》①,明确了确权登记的具体细节。

《国土资源部关于进一步加快宅基地和集体建设用地确权登记发证有关问题的通知》(国土资发〔2016〕191号)规定,宅基地使用权应按照"一户一宅"要求,原则上确权登记到"户"。符合当地分户建房条件未分户,但未经批准另行建房分开居住的,其新建房屋占用的宅基地符合相关规划,经本农民集体经济组织或村民委员会同意并公告无异议或异议不成立的,可按规定补办有关用地手续后,依法予以确权登记;未分开居住的,其实际使用的宅基地没有超过分户后建房用地合计面积标准的,依法按照实际使用面积予以确权登记。

对于因继承房屋占用宅基地,形成"一户多宅"的,可按规定确权登记,并在不动产登记簿和证书附记栏进行注记。

关于非本农民集体的农民可否获得宅基地使用权,国土资源部、中央农村工作领导小组办公室、财政部、农业部《关于农村集体土地确权登记发证的若干意见》(国土资发〔2011〕60号)要求严格规范确认宅基地使用权主体,宅基地使用权应该按照当地省级人民政府规定的面积标准,依法确认给本农民集体成员。非本农民集体的农民,因地质灾害防治、新农村建设、移民安置等集中迁建,在符合当地规划的前提下,经本农民集体大多数成员同意并经有权机关批准异地建房的,可按规定确权登记发证。已拥有一处宅基地的本农民集体成员、非本农民集体成员的农村或城镇居民,因继承房屋占用农村宅基地的,可按规定登记发证,在《集体土地使用证》记事栏应注记"该权利人为本农民集体原成员住宅的合法继承人"。非农业户口居民(含华侨)原在农村合法取得的宅基地及房屋,房屋产权没有变化的,经该农民集体出具证明并公告无异议的,可依法办理土地登记,在《集体土地使用证》记事栏应注记"该权利人为非本农民集体成员"。对于没有权属来源证明的宅基地,应当查明土地历史使用情况和现状,由村委会出具证明并公告

---

① 自然资源部办公厅于2020年7月22日以自然资办函〔2020〕1344号印发。

30 天无异议，经乡（镇）人民政府审核，报县级人民政府审定，属于合法使用的，确定宅基地使用权。

该意见规定要求，按照不同的历史阶段对超面积的宅基地进行确权登记发证，1982 年《村镇建房用地管理条例》实施前，农村村民建房占用的宅基地，在《村镇建房用地管理条例》实施后至今未扩大用地面积的，可以按现有实际使用面积进行确权登记；1982 年《村镇建房用地管理条例》实施起至 1987 年《土地管理法》实施时止，农村村民建房占用的宅基地，超过当地规定的面积标准的，超过部分按当时国家和地方有关规定处理后，可以按实际使用面积进行确权登记；1987 年《土地管理法》实施后，农村村民建房占用的宅基地，超过当地规定的面积标准的，按照实际批准面积进行确权登记。其面积超过各地规定标准的，可在土地登记簿和土地权利证书记事栏内注明超过标准的面积，待以后分户建房或现有房屋拆迁、改建、翻建、政府依法实施规划重新建设时，按有关规定作出处理，并按照各地规定的面积标准重新进行确权登记。

对农民进城落户后其宅基地能不能确权登记的问题，《中共中央 国务院关于实施乡村振兴战略的意见》（中发〔2018〕1 号）明确要求，依法维护进城落户农民的宅基地使用权、土地承包经营权、集体收益分配权，引导进城落户农民依法自愿有偿退出上述权益，不得以退出承包地和宅基地作为农民进城落户条件。《国土资源部关于进一步加快宅基地和集体建设用地确权登记发证有关问题的通知》（国土资发〔2016〕191 号）规定，农民进城落户后，其原合法取得的宅基地使用权应予以确权登记。

在宅基地和集体建设用地使用权确权登记工作中要坚持"不变不换"原则。《不动产登记暂行条例》第 33 条规定，"本条例施行前依法颁发的各类不动产权属证书和制作的不动产登记簿继续有效"。《不动产登记暂行条例实施细则》第 105 条规定，"本实施细则施行前，依法核发的各类不动产权属证书继续有效。不动产权利未发生变更、转移的，不动产登记机构不得强制要求不动产权利人更换不动产权属证书"。坚持"不变不换"是不动产登记法律制度的要求，是对原有登记成果的尊重和延续，也是保持工作稳定性和连续性的需要。因此，已分别颁发宅基地、集体建设用地使用权证书和房屋所有权证书的，遵循"不变不换"原则，原证书仍合法有效。

需要探讨的是：宅基地使用权没有经过登记，是否能够对抗第三人？所谓第三人，通常理解为标的物上的第三人。换言之，即对该物享有物权的人。但是，在没有初始登记的情况下，第三人也不可能受让该宅基地使用权或者对之享有抵押权。因此，根本不可能存在标的物上有多个权利，从而哪项权利更为优先的问题。这就是说，如果宅基地使用权没有进行初始登记，根本就不可能存在物上的第三人。如果将第三人理解为权利人之外的第三人，在中国目前的情况下，农村仍然是熟人社会。在此情况下，如果宅基地使用权没有发生流转，其设定登记是没有实际意义的。在取得宅基地使用权之后，即使没有登记，第三人也知悉该宅基地并非自己的，从而不会对其侵害。可见，无论登记与否，其都应当负有不得侵害的义务。因此，所谓不经登记不能对抗第三人之说，并无规定的必要。即便没有登记，宅基地使用权也是具有对抗效力的。当然，如果宅基地使用权人意欲对其权利进行处分，则为维护交易安全，应当先行办理登记。

《民法典》第 365 条规定："已经登记的宅基地使用权转让或者消灭的，应当及时办理变更登记或者注销登记。"对此，笔者解读为，宅基地使用权需登记方可处分，如果宅基地使用权已经办理了登记，则可以对之加以转让。转让时，应当办理宅基地使用权的转移登记。此种登记究竟是发生物权变动的效力，还是发生对抗善意第三人的效力，《民法典》并未规定。笔者认为此种登记产生登记对抗效力。

（二）宅基地使用权的继受取得

中国目前法律没有规定宅基地使用权是否可以单独流转，但政策层面已经解禁。目前农村村民的私有房屋的流转并不为法律所禁止。《关于农村集体土地确权登记发证的若干意见》（国土资发〔2011〕60 号）明确规定，因继承房屋占用农村宅基地的，可按规定登记发证，在《集体土地使用证》记事栏应注记"该权利人为本农民集体原成员住宅的合法继承人"。《国土资源部关于进一步加快宅基地和集体建设用地确权登记发证有关问题的通知》（国土资发〔2016〕191 号）规定，历史上接受转让、赠与房屋占用的宅基地超过当地规定面积标准的，按照转让、赠与行为发生时对宅基地超面积标准的政策规定，予以确权登记。因此，宅基地使用权也可以通过房屋转让时的一并转让而取得。此外，中国法律承认私有房屋为继承的标的，宅基地使用权也可因房屋的继承而取得。

三、宅基地使用权的内容、流转与限制

（一）宅基地使用权的内容

宅基地使用权人享有对其宅基地占有、使用、收益的权利。其有权占有、使用宅基地，在其上下建造房屋和附属设施；有权获得由于使用宅基地而产生的收益，包括在宅基地空闲处（如房前屋后）种植果树等经济作物而产生的收益。

（二）宅基地使用权的流转

关于宅基地使用权的内容，需要探讨的是其是否包括权利处分权能或者说宅基地使用权能否流转。应当看到，中国现行法律对宅基地使用权的处分进行了一定限制，主要包括如下几个方面：

1. 宅基地使用权单独处分与流转

《民法典》没有明确宅基地使用权的单独处分，但可以连同房屋一并处分。《民法典》第 363 条规定："宅基地使用权的取得、行使和转让，适用土地管理的法律和国家有关规定。"

中国《民法典》第 399 条第 2 款对于宅基地使用权的抵押给予了明确的禁止，从而禁止了宅基地使用权的单独处分。但是法律规定可以抵押的除外。

上述规定为宅基地使用权的流转提出方案。土地管理的法律和国家有关规定可以对

宅基地使用权的取得、行使和转让作出新的安排。从中国现行的政策规定来看，宅基地"三权分置"见诸 2018 年《中共中央、国务院关于实施乡村振兴战略的意见》，是其首次在中央文件中正式提到。文件认为三权是"所有权、资格权、使用权"，在权能上对宅基地集体所有权落实，宅基地农户资格权和农民房屋财产权要保障，宅基地和农民房屋使用权要适度放活。2021 年中央一号文件《中共中央、国务院关于全面推进乡村振兴加快农业农村现代化的意见》提出，稳慎推进农村宅基地制度改革试点，探索宅基地所有权、资格权、使用权分置的有效实现形式。推进宅基地"三权分置"改革。《中共中央 国务院关于做好 2022 年全面推进乡村振兴重点工作的意见》提出，稳慎推进农村宅基地制度改革试点，规范开展房地一体宅基地确权登记。稳妥有序推进农村集体经营性建设用地入市。推动开展集体经营性建设用地使用权抵押融资。适度放活使用权是宅基地"三权分置"改革的重点，放活后的使用权承载了优化资源配置和保障农民财产权利的功能，其价值需要通过流转交易才能实现；结合宅基地有偿使用、自愿有偿退出等改革事项，打通宅基地与集体建设用地转换通道，完善盘活闲置宅基地和农房的政策体系，赋予利用主体完整的权能。

在农村人口大规模进入城市定居的情况下，法律应当尽可能为农民进城创业提供条件，如果严格限制宅基地的流转，则由于受让人限于农村居民，则转让价格显然会比较低，不利于实现宅基地使用权的交换价值，也会使农村的不动产难以进入市场进行交易。这样一来，一方面，在许多农民已经进城定居并购置了房产，其在农村的房屋已经闲置的情况下，考虑到客观上又不可能强制收回其闲置的房屋和宅基地，如果不允许农民转让房屋，将会造成农村房屋的长期空闲，无疑将造成中国目前已经紧缺的土地资源的极大浪费。另一方面，农村人口融入城市，首先面临的就是经济地位方面的巨大差异。如果限制宅基地使用权的流转，农村人口很难通过对其土地、房屋的处分，如买卖、抵押等，获得其进城创业、定居所必需的资金。这一点在中国农村金融尚不发达的条件下尤为重要。此外，在中国农村目前社会保障尚不健全的情况下，过分限制宅基地的流转，将使农民在面临重大疾病、子女上学等大笔开销的情况下，无法筹措资金。

广东省等省份已经开始了宅基地使用权流转的试点，宅基地使用权依法流转，已经是中国法律中的一个必然趋势。综上所述，笔者认为，应当放开对宅基地使用权的限制，进一步强化其权利处分权能，允许宅基地使用权单独转让和抵押，使其能够作为一种类所有权，与建设用地使用权共同承担起构建中国土地市场的重任。

2. 宅基地处分后另行申请的限制

一经处分，宅基地使用权人就不能再申请宅基地使用权。《土地管理法》第 62 条第 5 款规定："农村村民出卖、出租、赠与住宅后，再申请宅基地的，不予批准。"此规定有利于维护宅基地使用权初始取得的公平。

3. 宅基地受让主体的限制与政策上的解禁

1999 年 5 月 6 日《国务院办公厅关于加强土地转让管理严禁炒卖土地的通知》明确强调："农民的住宅不得向城市居民出售，也不得批准城市居民占用农民集体土地建住宅，有关部门不得为违法建造和购买的住宅发放土地使用证和房产证。"这就基本上禁止了宅基地使用权以及农村房屋的流转。最终《民法典》采取了比较审慎的态度，规定宅基地使用权的流转"适用土地管理的法律和国家有关规定"。政策上的解禁见本节三之论述。

4. 一户只能拥有一处宅基地及宅基地面积的限制

对此，在前文中已做详述，于此不再赘述。

(三)宅基地的用途能否变动

宅基地使用权之设立，旨在解决村民合理的居住需要，故而应当以有合理居住需要作为授与宅基地使用权的条件。但是在已经设定宅基地使用权之后，如果村民通过其他手段能够解决自己的居住问题，而在其宅基地上建设厂房，从发展农村经济而言也无不妥。2019 年 9 月 11 日 下发的《中央农村工作领导小组办公室 农业农村部关于进一步加强农村宅基地管理的通知》中明确：鼓励村集体和农民盘活利用闲置宅基地和闲置住宅，通过自主经营、合作经营、委托经营等方式，依法依规发展农家乐、民宿、乡村旅游等。城镇居民、工商资本等租赁农房居住或开展经营的，要严格遵守合同法的规定。因此宅基地的用途可以根据需要适当变动。

四、"三权分置"中农村宅基地所有权、资格权、使用权概念与含义

(一)宅基地所有权

宅基地的所有权归农村集体经济组织，宅基地使用权人不享有宅基地所有权。宅基地使用权虽然是物权的一种，但在本质上属于农村集体土地使用权。在我国农村集体土地使用权具有特定的含义，法律规定，土地使用权的取得，除国有划拨土地外，必须通过出让、转让、租赁等方式，实质上是等价交换的交易方式。宅基地使用权主要发生在农村地区，当宅基地使用权作为用益物权的一种特定形式被《物权法》确定后，"宅基地使用权"与"土地使用权"在法理上被区分开来，不能继续以土地使用权代替宅基地使用权。因为《中华人民共和国宪法》第 10 条第 1 款规定："宅基地和自留地、自留山，也属于集体所有。"农民宅基地属于集体所有土地的一部分，而集体土地又分为农业用地和农村建设用地，所以宅基地属于农村建设用地的那一部分。

(二)宅基地资格权

2018 年中央一号文件《中共中央 国务院关于实施乡村振兴战略的意见》中，"探索宅基地所有权、资格权、使用权'三权分置'"，"三权分置"的构思被正式提出。对于"资格权"内涵，法律与规范性文件并没有做出明确的界定，实务界和学术界也没有对此也尚未达成统一认识。何为宅基地资格权？学界有财产权说、复合性权利说、宅基地使用权流转后的剩余权说等。不过，按照《深化农村宅基地制度改革试点方案》"保障资

格权、放活使用权"的思路，资格权是保障农户对宅基地的取得权，属于成员权的组成部分。

根据宅基地"三权分置"的政策目标，结合《民法典》《土地管理法》的规定，宅基地"资格权"既不是财产权也不是复合性权利，更不是宅基地使用权流转后的剩余权。它其实只是一种资格，是农户基于集体经济组织成员的特定身份而享有的可以申请在本集体土地上建造住宅及其附属设施的一种资格。它并非是一项新的权利，也不能权利化。

资格权并不具备权利应有的特定利益要素，其仅意味着利益实现之可能。宅基地资格权只是一种物权期待权，属于农户资格权的一种，专指农户基于集体成员地位而获得的对申请宅基地请求权的资格。

集体成员以其成员资格取得对本集体土地的宅基地使用权是集体土地所有权的占有、使用权能分离的结果，由集体土地所有权分离的占有、使用权能构成宅基地使用权的权能内容，这些权能内容决定了该权利的性质，其最核心的是在本集体土地上建造、保有住宅及其附属设施的权利。因此，资格权并不构成宅基地使用权的权能内容，它不体现权利的本质属性。

（三）宅基地"三权分置"中的使用权

宅基地"三权分置"的资格权、使用权应如何定性，学者之间存在不同的主张。第一种：用益物权+用益物权，学者席志国认为，"三权分置"中的"资格权、使用权"均为物权性质上的用益物权。第二种：用益物权+债权，学者宋志红的观点："三权分置"中的"资格权"为现行法律中的宅基地使用权，属于用益物权，而"三权分置"中的"使用权"为（法定）租赁权，属于债权。第三种：多权并存，"三权分置"的资格权与使用权，不一定只能均为用益物权、用益物权+债权或者成员权，相反，用益物权、债权、成员权可以兼容共存。[①]

笔者认为：《中共中央 国务院关于实施乡村振兴战略的意见》指出："完善农民闲置宅基地和闲置农房政策，探索宅基地所有权、资格权、使用权"三权分置"，落实宅基地集体所有权，保障宅基地农户资格权和农民房屋财产权，适度放活宅基地和农民房屋使用权……"此时的"三权分置"并不是"三权新置"，宅基地制度本身的应有之义即包括："所有权、资格权、使用权"三个权利束。因此"三权分置"中的宅基地使用权与《民法典》第362条至第365条、《土地管理法》第62条规定的"宅基地使用权"内涵与外延完全一样。但要强化其功能。

五、宅基地使用权的消灭

从《民法典》以及相关法律、法规的规定来看，宅基地使用权因下列原因而消灭：

---

① 江青梅：《宅基地"三权分置"法律研究综述》，载澎湃政务网，https://m.the_paper.cn/baijiahao_15347769，最后浏览时间：2022年11月6日。

（一）因为乡（镇）村公共设施和公益事业建设需要使用宅基地

因为乡（镇）村公共设施和公益事业建设，需要使用宅基地，而使宅基地使用权消灭。此种情况类似于建设用地使用权因国家的征用而消灭的情形。在因公共设施的建造而收回宅基地使用权的情况下，一方面，应当另行授与权利人宅基地使用权；另一方面，应当对附着物加以合理的补偿。而且，为了避免集体经济组织滥用这一事由损害村民利益，可以考虑提高对地上物的补偿标准，通过经济手段来减少此种事由的适用。

（二）不按照批准的用途使用土地

如前文所述，应当放开宅基地的用途限制，不应以违反用途限制为由收回宅基地。如果在初始设定时申请人并没有居住需求，而是通过欺诈手段隐瞒其无合理居住需求的事实，或者与相关人员串通而取得宅基地使用权，可以考虑撤销授与行为，从而收回宅基地使用权，而且此种撤销不应给予补偿，但是不能因在使用过程中违反居住用途而收回宅基地使用权。

当然，这里的居住需求应当是合理的居住需求。如果村民按照习俗另立门户而申请宅基地使用权，但是其自愿与父母、兄弟姐妹共同居住，从而以忍受狭窄的居住空间为代价而空出新获得的宅基地兴办企业，自然也应当为法律容许，而不能撤销其宅基地使用权。

（三）长期闲置宅基地

国家土地管理局 1995 年 3 月 11 日发布的《确定土地所有权和使用权的若干规定》第 52 条规定："空闲或房屋坍塌、拆除两年以上未恢复使用的宅基地，不确定土地使用权。已经确定使用权的，由集体报经县级人民政府批准，注销其土地登记，土地由集体收回。"从而将长期闲置土地作为宅基地使用权消灭的原因。地方法规也有类似规定，如《河南省农村宅基地用地管理办法》第 20 条规定："经批准的宅基地划定后，超过一年未建房的，由原批准机关注销批准文件，收回土地使用权。"

对于已经进城定居的农户，如果宅基地长期闲置又与权利人无法联系，则可以考虑收回宅基地使用权。但是如果其重新返乡落户，则应当另行授与宅基地使用权。

（四）宅基地面积超标

《土地管理法》第 62 条强调："农村村民一户只能拥有一处宅基地。"《确定土地所有权和使用权的若干规定》第 51 条则规定，对于相关法律出台之前面积超标的宅基地，通过继承、转让房屋而导致面积超标的宅基地，符合当地政府分户建房规定而尚未分户的农村居民，其现有的宅基地没有超过分户建房用地合计面积标准但超出单一宅基地面积上限的宅基地，可在土地登记卡和土地证书内注明超过标准面积的数量。以后分户建房或现有房屋拆迁、改建、翻建或政府依法实施规划重新建设时，按当地政府规定的面积标准重新确定使用权，其超过部分退还集体。可见，如果原有宅基地面积超标，则在房屋灭失之后应当收回超标部分的宅基地使用权。

（五）房屋灭失

《确定土地所有权和使用权的若干规定》第 48 条规定，非农业户口居民（含华侨）原在农村的宅基地，房屋拆除后没有批准重建的，土地使用权由集体收回。而是否批准重建并不取决于宅基地使用权人，这实际上是以房屋的灭失作为宅基地使用权消灭的原因。

（六）土地的灭失

宅基地使用权为用益物权，权利人系对宅基地的使用价值加以利用，不具有物上代位性。因此宅基地灭失的情况下，宅基地使用权自然也应当消灭。故而，《民法典》第 364 条规定："宅基地因自然灾害等原因灭失的，宅基地使用权消灭。对失去宅基地的村民，应当依法重新分配宅基地。"

除上述原因外，宅基地使用权也可能因国家的征收等事由而消灭。当然，国家的征收应当限于公益性用途。而且在国家征收时，应当结合国家社会经济发展状况以及各地实际情况，逐步提高补偿标准。因撤销、迁移等原因而停止使用土地的，所有人可以收回土地使用权，宅基地使用权消灭。

此外，依据《继承法》第 32 条之规定，"无人继承又无人受遗赠的遗产，归国家所有；死者生前是集体所有制组织成员的，归所在集体所有制组织所有"。依据《中华人民共和国土地管理法实施条例》第 35 条规定，国家允许进城落户的农村村民依法自愿有偿退出宅基地。退出的宅基地归所在集体所有制组织所有，原宅基地使用权消灭。

宅基地使用权乃权利，故而权利人当然有权抛弃。因此权利人自愿交回宅基地的，权利消灭。该抛弃的意思表示，应当向集体经济组织作出。

第五节 居 住 权

中国共产党在十九大报告中明确指出，要加快建立多主体供给、多渠道保障、租购并举的住房制度。为达到人人有居所的目标，中国立法机关认为有必要创设居住权制度。《民法典》设立居住权。按照《民法典》第 366 条之规定，"居住权人有权按照合同约定，对他人的住宅享有占有、使用的用益物权，以满足生活居住的需要"。同时，因居住权不得转让、继承（《民法典》第 369 条）而有别于地役权。实质上，居住权体现了对物的利用，从立法例上看，各国和地区的民法对居住权的规定都很简单，其原因在于，有关居住权的设立、效力与消灭等都准用用益权的相关规定。[1]《民法典》对居住权的规

---

① 参见《法国民法典》第 625 条、《德国民法典》第 1093 条第 1 款、《瑞士民法典》第 776 条第 3 款、《意大利民法典》第 1026 条、《葡萄牙民法典》第 1490 条、《西班牙民法典》第 528 条和第 529 条、《智利民法典》第 812 条。

定只有六个条文(第 366~第 371 条),仅规定居住权的含义、设立与消灭等内容。

一、居住权的含义与设立

居住权的含义,即居住权是对他人的住宅占有、使用,以满足生活居住需要的用益物权。此处的"占有、使用"权能既包括实际地居住房屋,即满足生活居住的需要,也包括居住权人为了实现居住目的而进行的其他行为,如堆放生活必需的用品、为了更好地居住而对房屋进行的修缮等。居住权本质上属于利用他人的住宅满足权利人居住需要的权利,归于中国物权体系中用益物权的范畴。实质上,居住权体现了对物的利用,应当属于财产权的范畴。肯定其财产权本质,既能为公民多元化利用其财产,满足各方需求提供制度保障,也能为"以房养老""分时度假"等新兴模式提供适用的依据。

中国法上的居住权应突破婚姻、继承等传统适用领域的限制,并扩展到房屋多元化利用的投资领域,甚至于利用居住权制度对经济适用房、共有产权房、公租房等保障性住房进行改造,以充分发挥居住权的制度功能和实现社会主体对住房的多元化需求。彰显了《民法典》对于公民权利给予全面保障的基本精神。但是在实务中必须反对利用居住权制度来逃避债务或者规避法院的强制执行。

从《民法典》的规定来看,居住权的设立方式有合同、遗嘱两种。

(一)通过合同设立

《民法典》第 367 条规定,设立居住权,当事人应当采取书面形式订立居住权合同,其条款主要包括当事人的姓名或者名称和住所、住宅的位置、居住的条件和要求、居住权期间、解决争议的方法等。

居住权合同主要有如下表现形态:

其一,所有权人与买受人签订居住权合同,这是居住权合同的常见形态。

其二,所有权人与买受人同时签订买卖合同与居住权合同。在这种合同形态中,所有权人将住宅出卖于买受人,同时保留居住权。

其三,所有权人将住宅的所有权转让给买受人,并为第三人设立居住权。

其四,所有权人将住宅出卖给买受人,同时要求买受人为第三人设立居住权。

其五,所有权人与第三人签订居住权合同,为第三人设立居住权。例如所有权人为其年老的保姆设立居住权。

居住权的登记。居住权是设立于不动产之上的物权,按照我国物权变动之法律规定,不动产物权变动采取登记生效主义。因此,当事人仅签订居住权合同并不能导致居住权的设立,必须办理登记。当然居住权合同自合同签字、盖章或者捺指印后即生效。根据《民法典》第 374 条,在此种情况下,居住权未经登记,同样不得对抗善意第三人,以保护交易秩序。对此,《民法典》第 368 条规定,设立居住权的,当事人应当向登记机构申请居住权登记,居住权自登记时设立。

(二) 通过遗嘱设立

通过遗嘱设立居住权,是各国和地区的普遍做法,《民法典》亦将遗嘱作为居住权的设立方式之一。

关于遗嘱设立居住权,居住权何时设立问题。《民法典》第 371 条规定:"以遗嘱方式设立居住权的,参照适用本章的有关规定。"从《民法典》关于居住权的规定来看,通过遗嘱设立的居住权可以参照适用有关居住权不得转让与继承、无偿设立、消灭原因的规定、同时应当采用书面形式。需要探讨的是,关于居住权登记的规定,可否参照适用? 也就是说,以遗嘱方式设立居住权的,是否适用当事人"应当向登记机构申请居住权登记。居住权自登记时设立"的规定? 对此,本书作者认为,无论是登记生效主义还是登记对抗主义,其适用的基础都是基于双方民事法律行为而产生的物权变动。遗嘱虽然是民事法律行为,但导致遗嘱生效的原因是遗嘱人的死亡,即遗嘱人死亡的事实是导致物权变动的原因。因此,通过遗嘱方式设立居住权的,可以参照《民法典》第 230 条规定,自遗嘱生效即继承开始时,居住权设立,而不以办理登记为设立条件。否则,若实行登记生效主义,则继承人拒绝办理登记的,遗嘱设立的居住权将落空,其也违背了遗嘱的意愿。

这类遗嘱的形式与效力问题,本书认为:遗嘱是一种单方民事法律行为,《民法典》对设立居住权的遗嘱的形式和效力并没有规定。这类遗嘱的形式和效力应当参照《民法典》继承编中遗嘱的形式和效力的规定加以认定。《民法典·继承编》第 1134 条至第 1139 条规定了遗嘱的形式包括自书遗嘱、代书遗嘱、打印遗嘱、录音录像遗嘱、口头遗嘱、公证遗嘱等。鉴于《民法典》第 367 条规定了居住权的设立必须订立书面合同,因此按照"参照适用"的理解,设立居住权的遗嘱也必须采用书面的形式,按照民事法律行为效力规定认定其效力。

二、居住权的主体

居住权的主体也即居住权人,其范围应包括哪些人,《民法典》并没有界定。本书作者认为,关于居住权的主体范围,仅限于自然人不包括法人与非法人组织。《民法典》第 367 条中的"当事人的名称"指向法人、非法人组织,但法人、非法人组织只能作为居住权的设立主体,而不能作为居住权人。

自然人作为居住权的主体,有无范围的限制,笔者认为,中国法律不应予以限制。尽管法律上明确了居住权的设立目的,但不能就此否定有房者也有这方面的需求。因此,没有否定为有房者设立居住权的合理理由。

以农村房屋设立居住权的,居住权人是否应限于本村的村民? 从目前相关的法律、政策规定来看,农村房屋的转让还受到一定的限制,通常只能在农村集体经济组织内部成员之间转让。但是,设立居住权并不涉及房屋转让问题,故为非农村集体经济组织内部成员设立居住权并无不许之理。但应当指出,农村住宅所有权人为他人设立居住权后,不得再申请宅基地。这是因为,按照《土地管理法》第 62 条第 5 款之规定,"农村村民出卖、出租、赠与住宅后，再申请宅基地的，不予批准"。而住宅所有权人以住宅设立居住权与出租住宅具有类似的性质，转移住宅的使用权，也应当受到"再申请宅基地，不予批准"的限制。

关于所有权人可否为两个以上的自然人共同设立居住权问题，对此，应作肯定回答。居住权可以为两个以上的人共同设立，由权利人共有居住权。这里的共有为一种准共有，而且是准共同共有。笔者认为同住之人可以与居住权人同住，但他们并不是居住权人；而且如果当事人有明确约定，房屋只能由居住权人自己居住的，其他人不得同住。

三、居住权的客体

关于居住权的客体，《民法典》第 367 条限定为"住宅"。但基于居住权的设立目的在于"生活居住"，而不得做办公或者商业使用。即使是建筑物、房屋，其也只能是供生活居住使用，故在居住权中，建筑物、房屋、住宅所代表的意义并无不同，可以通用之。当然，《民法典》直接使用"住宅"的概念，能够更直观地体现居住权的设立目的。就住宅的范围而言，无论是城镇住宅还是农村住宅，无论是建筑物区分所有权中的住宅还是其他住宅，均可以作为居住权的客体，但经营性用房应当排除在外。"住宅的位置"即居住权的客体范围，亦可表述为居住权人的权利范围。对于住宅的位置，应当由双方当事人协商一致后，在不动产登记簿上予以明确登记。如果所有权人以整体房屋为居住权人设立居住权，则对于"住宅的位置"一栏应当登记为整套房屋。但如果房屋的所有权人只是以房屋的一部分为他人设立居住权，即实践中可能出现房屋所有权人以整套房屋的某一个房间为居住权人设定居住权，亦应允许，不动产登记机构应当予以登记，设立居住权。

四、居住权的法律效力

居住权设立后，即在当事人之间产生相应的效力，这种效力主要体现为居住权人的权利、义务。在立法例上，各国和地区的民法大多规定用益权规范准用于居住权。因此，居住权的效力可以按照民法上关于用益权效力的规定加以确定。

(一)居住权人的权利

居住权人在取得居住权后，即可以对住宅行使相关的权利，具体体现在如下几个方面：

1. 合理使用住宅的权利

居住权是住宅所有权人为满足居住权人的生活居住需要而设立的用益物权，因此，居住权人对住宅享有占有、使用的权利。合理使用住宅，应明确以下几个细节：

(1)居住权人使用住宅只限于个人生活居住必需。

(2)居住权人有权使用住宅的附属设施。同时，住宅有从物的，若当事人没有禁止性约定，居住权人亦有权使用该从物。

(3)居住权人有权使用住宅内的生活设施。为生活居住需要使用住宅的非权利部分。居住权的制度功能在于保障居住权人的居住利益,如果居住权人在住宅中享有的有权部分不足以满足基本居住需要,必须利用住宅中的一些非权利部分,如住宅的出入口、通道、阳台、厨房、卫生间等,那么所有权人应当容忍居住权人的使用。

(4)居住权人对住宅的使用权不因住宅所有权人的变更而受影响。居住权虽然是对住宅所有权所施加的权利负担,但并不影响所有权人转让该住宅,如出卖、赠与等。

对于合理使用住宅所造成的合理损耗,居住权人不承担责任。

2. 允许他人同住的权利

如前所述,在当事人没有禁止性约定的情况下,居住权人有权允许其他人在住宅中居住。当然,这里的其他人并非没有限制,只限于特定范围内的人。笔者认为,同住之人可以包括三类:一是家庭成员,包括配偶、父母、子女和其他共同生活的近亲属(《民法典》第 1045 条第 3 款);二是为居住权人提供生活服务的人员,如保姆、护工等;三是居住权人供养的近亲属以外的人员。

3. 出租住宅的权利

根据《民法典》第 369 条规定,居住权人原则上不得出租住宅,除非当事人另有约定。也就是说,如果居住权合同或者居住权遗嘱中明确允许居住权人出租住宅的,则居住权人有权出租住宅。

4. 对房屋进行修缮、添附的权利

居住权对住宅中的有权使用部分享有排他性权利,因此只要不超出生活居住的用途限制,且不影响所有权人对住宅其他部分的使用,居住权人有权为保障居住条件对房屋进行修缮,或为提高生活质量对房屋进行装修等添附行为,不受房屋所有权人的制约。但基于权利义务的对等性,居住权消灭后,居住权人也不得基于修缮、添附的支出向所有权人要求补偿。

5. 取得补偿费、赔偿金的权利

住房被征收、征用、灭失。房屋被征收、征用,以及房屋灭失,都会使居住权消灭。住房所有权人因此取得补偿费、赔偿金的,居住权人有权请求分得适当的份额;如果居住权人没有独立生活能力,也可以放弃补偿请求权而要求适当安置。

(二)居住权人的义务

居住权人享有居住权权利的同时,也应当承担相应的义务,以维护所有权人的合法权益。一般而论,居住权人的主要义务如下:

1. 妥善管理、维护住宅的义务

居住权人有权对住宅进行占有、使用,相应地,居住权人就有妥善管理、维护的义务。居住权人应当按照合同的约定合理使用住宅,维持住宅的原有用途,不得改变房屋的结构。

2. 住宅的通常维修义务

本书认为,关于住宅的维修问题,首先应由当事人约定,在当事人没有约定或约定不明确的情况下，应按如下原则处理：

其一，应当区分居住权的设立有偿与否。在居住权系无偿设立的情况下，各国和地区的民法基本上区分通常维护与重大修缮两种情形分别确定义务人：通常维修即必要维修（如修复被毁坏的门窗、脱落的墙皮等）由居住权人承担，重大修缮即特殊维修（如屋顶、房梁的翻修、更换等）由所有权人承担。[①] 国外立法例的规则是合理的。但是，在居住权系有偿设立的情况下，是否还应当适用上述规则呢？对此，笔者认为应予否定回答。按照民法上权利与义务相一致的原则，住宅所有权人有权收取使用费，就应当承担与该项权利相适应的义务，这种义务就是维修义务，这也是保护合同约定的"居住的条件和要求"所必须的。因此，在居住权有偿设立的情况下，无论是通常维修还是重大修缮均应由所有权人承担。在所有权人承担修缮义务的情况下，居住权人有通知义务。

其二，在居住权人承担通常维修义务的情况下，若居住权人占有全部住宅，则居住权人应负担全部维修费用；若居住权人仅占有住宅的一部分，则居住权人应按比例承担通常维修费用。

3. 不得擅自出租住宅和转让居住权的义务

笔者认为，尽管《民法典》没有禁止居住权的抵押，但因在抵押权实现时会发生居住权的主体变更，这就相当于居住权的转让，而这已经违背了居住权的设立目的，因此，居住权不得抵押。

4. 支付使用费的义务

《民法典》采取了以无偿为原则、以有偿为例外的立法模式（第368条）。在当事人对居住权的设立是否有偿没有约定或约定不明确时，居住权的设立应视为无偿。如果当事人系有偿设立居住权，那么居住权人负有支付使用费的义务。

5. 容忍义务

居住权人的容忍义务主要包括几个方面：

其一，在设立居住权时住宅上已存在抵押权、地役权等权利负担的，则居住权人应承受该权利负担。

其二，居住权设立后，所有权人仍有权对住宅进行必要的检查。对此，居住权人应予容忍。

五、居住权的类型分析

（一）家庭保障性居住权

家庭保障性居住权主要以权利主体的特定身份为基础，承担家庭生活保障的基本功

[①]　参见《法国民法典》第605条和第606条、《瑞士民法典》第778条、《意大利民法典》第1025条和第1005条、《葡萄牙民法典》第1489条、《阿根廷民法典》第2968条。

能。家庭保障性居住权主要用来保障老人、离婚一方、保姆等弱势群体的利益，能够作为解决养老、丧偶、离婚时住房问题的工具。特别是在中国，普遍存在父母为子女出资买房、建房的现象；购买或建成的房屋登记在孩子名下的同时，父母保留一份居住权，可以有效地解决父母将来的基本住房问题。

（二）社会保障性居住权

中国的住房社会保障体系较为紊乱，譬如国家安居工程住房、经济适用房、廉租房、公租房、房改房、拆迁或棚户改造安置房、职工安置房、人才安置房（或人才公寓）等，当事人享有的权利形态有单独所有权、共有权、租赁权或居住权，有时产权界分根本不清晰，导致纠纷不断。

有鉴于此，本书认为应采取居住权的法律构造来解决上述保障性住房的权属纠纷问题，如将公租房的承租人的租赁权改造为居住权，从而对公租房承租人提供更加稳定的法律保障。

（三）投资性居住权

享有投资性居住权的当事人可能并无住房困难，可能还拥有其他住房，居住于该房之内并非其首要目的，而其真正目的在于投资。投资性居住权主要包括如下情形：（1）合作建房时设置的居住权；（2）合资购房时设置的居住权；（3）住房合作开发模式中的居住权。如由政府出地、房地产开发商出资合作开发房地产，房地产建成后为开发商设置 30~50 年长期居住权，并允许开发商转让或出租。此外，单位集资房也可采取该模式。

（四）消费性居住权

与投资性居住权中投资人（主要为自然人）自己直接享有居住权不同的是，消费性居住权中投资人（多为企业组织）为自然人提供居住服务，而该投资人为居住服务的经营管理者，该自然人作为居住服务的消费者而享有居住权。主要包括如下情形：（1）时权式酒店的居住权。又称分时度假酒店，消费者为了度假目的，通过有偿的方式获得度假酒店一段时间的居住权。（2）以房养老模式中的居住权。老年人以相对低的价格将房屋"空虚所有权"出售给金融机构，同时为自己保留居住权，金融机构为老年人提供养老资金，待老年人去世后，金融机构获得房屋的完整所有权。

六、居住权的消灭事由及消灭的后果

关于居住权的消灭事由，各国和地区的民法基本没有具体规定，而是适用用益权消灭的规定。从《民法典》的规定来看，居住权的消灭事由仅涉及期间届满和居住权人死亡。笔者认为，居住权的消灭绝不仅限于这两个事由，还应有其他情形。

(一)居住权人死亡

居住权具有人役权的部分属性，而具有人身属性，与居住权人的人身不可分离，因此，居住权人死亡，居住权应归于消灭。关于居住权人死亡的消灭原因，需要说明两点：一是若居住权为两个以上的自然人共同设立时，应当以多个自然人中，最后一个自然人死亡的时间为居住权消灭的时间；二是无论居住权合同中是否约定居住权期间，居住权人死亡都是居住权消灭的事由。也就是说，居住权合同约定有期间的，若在该期间内居住权人死亡的，即使期间尚未届满，居住权亦归于消灭。

(二)居住权的期间届满

居住权是一种有期限物权。当居住权合同约定有存续期间时，期间届满的，居住权消灭。那么，如果居住权合同中对居住权期间没有约定或约定不明确的，可以有两种解释：一是居住权不受期间的限制，所有权人可以随时解除居住权；二是以居住权人的终生为期限，即居住权人终生享有居住权。笔者持第二种解释，因为这更符合居住权的设立目的。

(三)住宅灭失

居住权是以住宅的利用为目的而设立的用益物权，住宅的存在与否对居住权的目的实现具有决定性作用。因此，一旦住宅灭失，居住权的目的将无法实现，此时居住权也就没有存在的必要和价值了。关于住宅灭失，以下两点需要阐明：

其一，住宅全部灭失的，居住权消灭当无疑问。但住宅部分灭失的，若剩余部分仍可满足生活居住需要，则居住权于剩余部分继续存在。这是因为，住宅的部分灭失仅是居住权的客体范围发生变化，并不影响居住权的目的实现。同时，住宅附属设施灭失的，也不影响居住权的继续存在。

其二，住宅灭失后有代替物的，居住权是否消灭？笔者认为，只要住宅灭失，即使有代替物的，居住权也应归于消灭。如果所有权人愿意，可以就新的住宅重新设立居住权。

(四)居住权被撤销

当出现法定事由时，物权设立人有权撤销物权，从而使物权归于消灭。为保护住宅所有权人的利益，在特定情形下，应当允许所有权人撤销居住权。这些特定情形主要有：(1)居住权人滥用居住权，如对住宅造成严重损害、随意转让居住权、擅自出租住宅、改变住宅的用途、不进行正常修缮而任其毁损、允许非基于居住权人生活之需的人员居住情节严重等；(2)居住权为有偿的，在约定的付款期限届满后在合理期限内经两次催告仍未支付费用。

（五）住宅被征收、征用而使居住权消灭

（六）其他消灭事由

其他事由主要包括：（1）附停止条件成就或附终止期限届至。如前所述，居住权可以附条件或附期限。若居住权附停止条件或附终止期限的，则当条件成就或期限届至时，居住权消灭。（2）抛弃。居住权人抛弃居住权当属其自由，居住权归于消灭。（3）权利混同。住房所有权和居住权发生混同，即两个权利归属于同一人的，发生居住权消灭的后果。如：当所有权人将住宅出卖或赠与给居住权人时，住宅的所有权与居住权发生混同，此时居住权消灭。

在居住权因上述事由消灭后，发生如下法律后果：（1）返还住宅。居住权人所返还的住宅，应当符合合同约定的使用后状态或者自然损耗后的状态。因居住权人死亡而导致居住权消灭的，其继承人承担返还住宅的义务。（2）赔偿责任。如果因居住权人的原因导致住宅灭失的，不仅居住权归于消灭，而且居住权人还应承担相应的赔偿责任。在居住权人抛弃居住权时，应妥善处理好抛弃后的事宜。若因居住权人抛弃居住权而造成住宅损害的，亦应承担赔偿责任。（3）办理注销登记。居住权实行登记生效主义，因此，在居住权消灭的情况下，应当办理注销登记。如果居住权人拒不配合办理注销登记，则所有权人可向法院起诉要求居住权人履行相应义务。对此，《民法典》第370条规定："居住权消灭的，应当及时办理注销登记。"居住权人去世的，所有权人可持相关证据单方申请居住权注销登记。应当指出的是，在住宅部分灭失的情况下，虽然居住权并没有消灭，但当事人亦应当办理相应的登记，这种登记属于变更登记。（4）设置的取回。居住权人在其权利存续期间，为正常居住使用房屋，可在房屋内设置必要设施或者对房屋进行装修。这些设置在居住权消灭时，居住权人可将上述设施取回，但应恢复房屋的原状。

第六节　地　役　权

一、地役权的概念、特征、性质

（一）地役权的概念和特征

《民法典》第372条规定："地役权人有权按照合同约定，利用他人的不动产，以提高自己的不动产的效益。前款所称他人的不动产为供役地，自己的不动产为需役地。"地役权，是地役权人按照合同约定，利用他人的不动产，以提高自己的不动产的效益的用益物权。"他人的不动产"为"供役地"，"自己的不动产"为"需役地"。例如，甲和乙的农田相邻，甲为浇灌自家农田必须从乙的农田里挖一条渠，此时甲可以和乙签订地役权合同，甲付给乙一定的报酬，从而取得从乙的农田挖渠、通水的权利。甲就叫作需役地人，亦称地役权人；乙就叫作供役地人，亦称供役地权利人。地役权人，可以是土地所有权人，也可以是土地承包经营权、建设用地使用权、宅基地使用权等权利人。

地役权源于罗马法，是罗马法最古老的他物权。大陆法国家民法典都有规定。地役权的特征主要有：

1. 客体是他人的不动产，包括他人的土地、房屋和其他附属物。《民法典》虽然在名称上使用的是地役权，但在第 372 条中明确规定为地役权的客体为不动产，而不是仅限于土地。

2. 须有两个土地相邻为条件，即需役地和供役地相邻为条件

地役权的本质是因为增加一定土地的利用价值而支配于他人的土地，所以必须有两个土地相邻为条件，即需役地和供役地相邻为条件。其中，他人的不动产（提供方便和利益的土地）为供役地；自己的不动产（享有方便和利益的土地）为需役地。这里的相邻，不仅是指两个不动产相互邻接或者毗连，也包括两个不动产相邻近的意义在内。在特殊情况下，可设立地役权的两个不动产甚至相隔很远。另外，根据空间权的理论，在设立了空间所有权或空间土地使用权的相邻空间之间也可以设立地役权。因此对"相邻"，不必限于平面上的理解，基于需役地的需要去寻找能实现其利用价值的供役地即可。

3. 是利用他人土地的物权

地役权原则上以不作为为内容。此即是罗马法上的"作为不能成立设权"的原则。依该原则，供役地人对需役地人对他的土地的利用，只负容忍的义务或者不作为的义务，而不负实施一定行为的义务。如果设定合同约定需要实施一定的行为的，在解释上应认为不是地役权的内容，在当事人间仅有债权债务关系的效力，而无物权的效力。因为地役权是物权，其标的物为供役地，而非供役地人；地役权人可以直接支配的，是供役地，而不是供役地人。

4. 目的是提高自己的不动产的效益

所谓效益，不仅指物质上或财产上的方便与利益，也包括精神上或感情上的方便与利益，如为需用地的视野广阔而在供役地上设立眺望权等。需役地的方便和利益的内容，由当事人以地役权设定合同确定。

5. 内容具有较大的任意性，但其内容不得违反强行性规定或公序良俗

地役权是由需役地权利人和供役地权利人相互之间通过地役权合同约定设立的，其内容具有较大的任意性，如设立地役权可以有偿也可以无偿。但是，其内容不得违反强行性规定或公序良俗。例如，不得以其他用益物权的内容为内容；不得设立禁止邻地使用或袋地（包围地）通行为内容的地役权；或者设定容忍权利滥用的地役权等。

（二）地役权的性质：从属性和不可分性

1. 地役权具有从属性

这是指地役权虽然是一种独立的用益物权，但必须从属于需役地存在。具体包括：

（1）地役权不可与需役地分离而转让。《民法典》第 380 条规定："地役权不得单独转让。土地承包经营权、建设用地使用权等转让的，地役权一并转让，但是合同另有约定的除外。"第 382 条规定："需役地以及需役地上的土地承包经营权、建设用地使用权等部分转让时，转让部分涉及地役权的，受让人同时享有地役权。"第 383 条规定："供役地以及供役地上的土地承包经营权、建设用地使用权等部分转让时，转让部分涉及地役权的，地役权对受让人具有约束力。"

（2）地役权不可与需役地分离而为其他权利的标的。《民法典》第 381 条规定："地役权不得单独抵押。土地经营权、建设用地使用权等抵押的，在实现抵押权时，地役权一并转让。"

2. 地役权的不可分性

地役权的不可分性，包括地役权的取得上的不可分性、消灭上的不可分性和地役权的享有或负担上的不可分性。具体表现为：（1）需役地为共有的，各共有人的应有部分，不能取得地役权，要整体取得地役权。（2）需役地为共有的，各共有人不能就其应有部分，使已经存在的地役权一部分消灭或全部消灭。（3）地役权设定后，需役地或供役地变成共有时，地役权并不是分割而由需役地各共有人分别享有，也不是由供役地共有人分别负担。（4）需役地经分割的，地役权为各部分的利益，继续存在；供役地经分割的，地役权就其各部分，继续存在。

（三）地役权与相邻权的区别

相邻制度起源于罗马法，在近代各国民法中多有规定。虽然地役权和相邻权都是以邻人的不动产供自己不动产便宜之用的权利，但二者有明显区别：

（1）相邻权是法定的，当然的；地役权是由契约而生，是意定的。

（2）相邻关系是法律对邻近不动产的利用进行最小限度调节的结果；地役权则作为当事人双方超越相邻关系之限约定权利义务。

（3）相邻权非独立的物权，是所有权本身之限制或扩张；地役权是一种用益物权种，为独立之权利。

（4）相邻权与所有权俱存，不可能单独取得或丧失；地役权则可以不与所有权俱存。

（5）相邻关系一般是无偿；而地役权是可有偿可无偿。

（6）地役权可以登记以对抗第三人（在大陆法系国家一般采取登记成立要件主义），未经登记，不得对抗第三人；而相邻关系则不用登记。

（7）地役权调整的是广义相邻关系，不限于相互毗邻或近邻，而是基于需役地的需要去寻找能实现其利用价值的供役地即可，发生在建筑物或空间权中的地役权更是比相邻权要宽泛得多，对不动产权益的扩张或限制比相邻权程度要大得多。某种程度上，地役权还可以修正或补充相邻权的内容。地役权种类的发展使其传统法上的构成要件也在发生变化。在美国地役权制度中，存在有通行地役权和取益地役权之分，所谓取益地役权，是指进入他人土地，获取他人土地之土壤及土地产物的权利，如采矿权、采伐权均属此类。这种地役权完全脱离有需役地的要件，而仅存供役地即可，比相邻权有了更为宽广的调整区域。

二、地役权的取得

(一)基于民事法律行为而取得地役权

1. 以合同设定取得地役权

一是以合同设定地役权。根据《民法典》第 373 条的规定，设立地役权，当事人应当采取书面形式订立地役权合同。

地役权合同一般包括：

(1)当事人的姓名或者名称和住所；

(2)供役地和需役地的位置；

(3)利用目的或者方法；

(4)地役权期限；

(5)费用及其支付方式；

(6)解决争议的办法。

地役权自地役权合同生效时取得。当事人要求登记的，可以向登记机构申请地役权登记。未经登记，不得对抗善意第三人(《民法典》第 374 条)。地役权期限由当事人约定；但是，不得超过土地承包经营权、建设用地使用权等用益物权的剩余期限(《民法典》第 377 条)。

二是单独民事法律行为如遗嘱设定地役权，需要有设定地役权的遗嘱并经登记，才发生设定地役权。

2. 因连同需役地一并转让而取得相应地役权

地役权不得单独转让。土地承包经营权、建设用地使用权等转让的，地役权一并转让，但是合同另有约定的除外(《民法典》第 380 条)。

(二)基于民事法律行为以外的原因而取得利用权

继承。由于地役权的从属性，地役权的继承，应是因继承土地所有权、使用权、抵押权时同时继承。在中国，公民个人无土地所有权，但享有宅基地使用权、农村土地承包经营权等。继承人可因继承宅基地上建筑物而继续享有使用权。依《农村土地承包法》第 32 条第 2 款的规定："林地承包的承包人死亡，继承人可以在承包期内继续承包。"第 54 条规定："依照本章规定通过招标、拍卖、公开协商等方式取得土地经营权的，该承包人死亡，其应得的承包收益，依照继承法的规定继承；在承包期内，其继承人可以继续承包。"可见，农村土地承包经营权及其地役权符合法定条件的，可因继承而取得。

三、地役权的内容

(一)地役权人的权利义务

1. 权利

(1)利用供役地。根据《民法典》第372条规定，地役权人应当按照合同约定的利用目的和方法利用供役地。地役权人因通行取水、排水、通风、采光、铺设管线等需要，有权按照与供役地权利人签订的合同利用他人土地，以提高自己不动产的效益。

(2)因行使地役权的需要，有权在被利用的土地上修建必要的附属设施。

(3)物权请求权。地役权受到侵害时，可以向供役地权利人或者其他侵害人主张包括返还原物、排除妨碍、消除危险、恢复原状等物权请求权。

2. 义务

(1)地役权人应当按照合同约定的利用目的和方法利用供役地，尽可能减少对供役地的权利人物权的限制。

(2)维护附属设施的义务。

(3)支付费用的义务。有偿利用供役地的，地役权人应当按照约定支付费用。

(二)供役地权利人的权利义务

1. 权利

(1)收取费用的权利。

(2)使用附属设施的权利。供役地权利人可以使用地役权人修建的附属设施，但不得妨害地役权人之利用权。除当事人另有约定的以外，应当适当分担附属设施的维护费用。

(3)可以请求变更利用其土地的方式。因此增加的费用，由当事人协议负担；达不成协议的，由被利用土地的权利人负担。

2. 义务

应当按照合同约定，容许地役权人利用其土地，不得妨害地役权人行使权利。《民法典》第375条规定："供役地权利人应当按照合同约定，允许地役权人利用其不动产，不得妨害地役权人行使权利。"

四、地役权的消灭

(一)地役权人有下列情形之一的，供役地权利人有权解除地役权合同，该地役权消灭：

1. 违反法律规定或者合同约定滥用地役权；

2. 有偿利用供役地，约定的付款期间届满后在合理期限内经两次催告未支付费用。

(二)有以下情形之一的，地役权消灭：

1. 地役权期间届满；

2. 供役地因自然变化不能实现地役权目的；

3. 抛弃地役权；

4. 供役地或者需役地灭失。

已经登记的地役权变更、转让或者消灭的，应当及时申请变更或者注销登记。

Chapter 5   Right to Usufruct

Section One   Survey of Right to Usufruct

1. Concept and Features of Right to Usufruct

According to Article 323 of the Civil Code, "A usufructuary has the right to possess, use, and benefit from the immovable or movable property owned by another person in accordance with law". In view of this, the right to usufruct refers to the right of a non-owner to possess, use and benefit from others' movable properties or immovable properties.

As a type of real right, the right to usufruct focuses on the efficacy and use value of a property. In the modern civil laws, the principle of efficiency has dominated the real right legislations of various nations. The focus of civil laws has been gradually shifted from the physical disposal and attribution of properties onto the domination and utilization of their values. Modern legislations on properties, which are in the civil claw system or in the common law system, have unanimously exhibited a notion that focuses on utilization, replacing the traditional one that focuses on ownership. Such conception is greatly reflected by the system of right to usufruct. For this reason, it is held by many scholars that the core of modern real right lies in the right to usufruct[1], a set of rights that aim to utilize or obtain profit from a property. Besides, views are divided regarding what is right to usufruct. According to some scholars, it denotes dual purposes of utilization and benefit, while others doubt that it's not necessary. I personally agree with such opinion.

In comparison with ownership and security interests, the right to usufruct has the following features:

First, it is categorized as jus in re aliena, limited real right, and real right with a definite period of time.

Second, it is established to possess and obtain profit from a property.

---

[1]   Fang Shaokun, eds., "Three Essays on the usufructuary Right", *China Legal Science*, Vol. 2, 1996.

One of the most observable characters of the right to usufruct is its usufructuary nature, which also fundamentally distinguishes it from security interests. According to Marxist theory, commodity is with a two-fold character of value and use value. These two factors respectively give rise to the right to usufruct and security interests. In other words, On the one hand, the right to usufruct springs from and underlines the use value of a property, which is termed "right of use value"; the security interests, on the other hand, stems from the value or exchange value of a property, which is also-called "right of value". Therefore, the right to usufruct is not as subrogative in nature as the security interest. Nor can it be enforced by way of taking the variants of a property as replacement. Simply speaking, the right to usufruct does not touch on such issues as paying a debt with the property's value or seeking replacement when the object is lost. The extent of right to usufruct with different usufructuary nature may vary from each other according to the specific categories. One example is superficies and jus emphyteusis under traditional civil law. Both of them are rights to usufruct that involve use of land, but the scopes and intensity of their use of properties are noticeably dissimilar. The former's contents range over construction of buildings and plantation of trees, while those of the latter over cultivation and animal husbandry on land.

Third, its major contents encompass the use and seeking profit by making use of properties, both of which require possession. Nonetheless, disposal is not part of its contents.

As the right to usufruct is the right to possess, utilize and enjoy the fruit of its object, its contents don't encompass the right of legal disposal (under the conception of traditional civil law, the right to usufruct may also have a consumable property as its object, thus embodies a right of disposal). This is to be specifically accounted for by the fact that the owner has not transferred the usufruct right holder the power of disposal upon the creation of the usufruct. In spite of this, the right to usufruct holder is still with the right to dispose of the right to usufruct. For example, right to the use of land and pawning right may be transferred or mortgaged, thus promoting the utility efficiency and enlarging the scope of the objects under security interests.

The actual control over the object is a precondition for the creation of a right to usufruct. As real rights, both rights to usufruct and security interests are dominating rights, but their domination takes on different forms. For the right to usufruct, it underlines the utilization and seeking profit by making use of the physical object, or the use value thereupon, which makes the physical domination or actual possession indispensable. For example, if the possession of a tract of land were not transferred, then a right holder of superficies or jus emphyteusis could not construct buildings, plant trees or cultivate on the land. As to security interests, they focus on the exchange value of a property, thus the tangible control may be dispensed, and pure intangible domination may suffice. It is true that certain types of security interest such as pledge and lien do necessitate physical domination, but it is equally true that such domination is not usufructuary in nature, as can be seen from the fact that the right holders of such security interests are not allowed to use or obtain profit from the objects without the owner's consent. Otherwise, the right holder has to undertake civil liabilities.

Fourth, its objects are mostly immovable properties.

As may be observed from Article 323 of the Civil Code and other forms of rights to usufruct numerated therein, in China, the objects of Rights to usufruct are mostly immovable properties, and in exceptional cases, rights contain immovable properties. Apart from this, movable properties can also be objects of rights to usufruct that indicates room for interpretation with the development in the future.

(1) Immovable property. Rights to usufruct may be established on a tract of land or a right to use land. Usually, a right to usufruct may not be created over a movable property. The reason behind this is that movable properties are publicized by means of possession, thus it cannot easily reflect the complicated usufruct relations thereupon. When it is necessary to use another's property, a gratuitous loan or lease may satisfy such need in a short term. If it's necessary to keep in a long term, a direct purchase may also be a solution as a movable property is generally not very expensive. Therefore, in the latter case the system of right to usufruct is not unnecessary to be applied. In contrast, the immovable properties tend to be costly due to their scarcity and huge value. A civil subject doesn't have easy access to their ownership to give full play of their use value. This is impressive when taking into consideration of such circumstances where a sale of immovable property fails easily due to the buyer's unwillingness to pay a high consideration and the seller's reluctance to transfer out of various reasons. Therefore, a non-owner has no other ways than to establish a right to usufruct over an immovable property, if he wants to achieve domination over its use value. This is why it is necessary to establish right to usufruct on immovable property.

(2) Rights in immovable property. Where an easement is created over a right to contractual management of land, right to management of land or right to use land for construction purposes, its object is the right in immovable property rather than the land itself.

(3) Movable property. According to Article 323 of the Civil Code, the objects of right to usufruct also include movable property. However, under the doctrine of numerus clausus, this will be the case only if the law has specifically stipulated. In the nation's current legislations, it is still not clear as to what sort of movable property may be the objects of a right to usufruct or as to what kind of right to usufruct may take a movable property as its object. Still, Article 323 has left room for further legislation.

Fifth, the right to usufruct is an Independent Real Right.

The independence of right to usufruct may be observed from the fact that its existence doesn't rely on other rights enjoyed by the right to usufruct holder against the owner, which means, unlike security interests, right to usufruct are not appurtenant or inseverable. The creation, transfer or extinguishment of a right to usufruct doesn't necessarily follow those of other rights. On the other hand, any change in the object, for example, partial loss or depreciation, may possibly cause change to the right to usufruct. Notable exception to the independence of right to usufruct may be found in easements. According to the prevailing opinion, an easement is incidental and inseverable, thus seems to be much similar to security interests. In fact, such characters of the two are not in line with each other. The appurtenance of an easement denotes that an easement may not be separated from the ownership over the dominant estate. The easement cannot be solely reserved when one disposes of the ownership of the dominant estate. The two sets of rights have to be transferred concurrently. In other words, an easement cannot become the object of any right if it is stripped of the dominant land. These are the concrete manifestations of an easement's incidental character. As to its inseverability, it means that an easement cannot be partitioned into two or more rights; neither may it partially extinguish. As can be seen therefrom, the appurtenance and inseparability nature of an easement serves to satisfy the usufructuary need of the easement holder. It doesn't aim to safeguard a creditor's right.

As a real right, the right to usufruct enables a right holder not only to achieve domination over the immovable property within the limits of law, but also to assert such right against any other person who interferes with the enforcement of the right. The establishment of the right to usufruct makes relation arising from the utilization of properties evolve into a real right one, enhancing the legal relations between parties concerned by making it possible to challenge a third party. These features differentiate the right to usufruct from a claim and bestows upon it overwhelming superiority over the latter in terms of the utilization of another's property. The dominative character further enables the right to usufruct to stand up to the ownership and security interest as an equal in the realm of real right law.

Rights to usufruct regulated by the Civil Code include the right to contractual management of land, right to management of land or right to use land for construction purposes, right to the use house sites, rights of habitation, easements and charted real rights.

2. Chartered Real Rights

2. 1　Concept and Significance of Chartered Real Rights

Chartered real rights denotes the right of natural persons, legal persons or other organizations to develop and utilize natural resources that are located within certain space with special administrative licenses. These include rights of using sea areas, prospecting for mineral deposits, mining, water taking, using water for aquaculture or fishing, etc. Since the establishment, transfer, contents and effects of these rights are mostly stipulated in such special laws as the Law of the People's Republic of China on the Administration of Sea Areas, Mineral Resources Law of the Peoples' Republic of China, Fisheries Law of the People's Republic of China and Water Law of People's Republic of China, these rights are called "real rights in special laws", or as is termed by some scholars, "quasi real rights". As is provided for by Article 328 of the Civil Code, "The right to use the sea areas that is acquired in accordance with law is protected by law". Article 329 provides that, "The right to explore and mine minerals, to draw water, and to use waters and mudflats to engage in aquaculture or fishing that are acquired in accordance with law is protected by law". In view of these provisions, it may be said that the real right has only defined the categories of chartered rights. As to the concrete contents, they shall be clarified by special laws.

The differences between chartered real rights and general right to usufruct may be summarized as follows:

First, in terms of their objects, the chartered real rights' objects are such state-owned resources as water, minerals and sea areas, rather than immovable properties like land or houses.

Second, in terms of means of disposal, the right holder of a chartered real right doesn't directly own a specific piece of immovable property; he only develops and utilizes it.

Third, in terms of the creation of the right, a chartered right is subject to multiple limitations, with its contents and term mostly determined by administrative organs.

Fourth, in terms of the exercise of the right, a chartered right is exercised by such right holder and in such ways that are legally defined in mandatory provisions. This is because chartered real rights usually involve the development and utilization of natural resource and such process contains considerable danger.

Provisions on chartered real rights as provided by the Civil Code are of great significance. Because first, they confirm the real right status of these rights. Therefore, rules on real rights should be applied thereto. Second, the clear definition that chartered real rights are private in nature contributes to its protection.

2.2 Major Categories and Contents of Chartered Real Rights

2.2.1 Right to Use Sea Areas

According to Law of the People's Republic of China on the Administration of Sea Areas ("Law on the Administration of Sea Areas"), the term "sea area" refers to the interior waters, the surface, body, seabed and bottom soil of the territorial seas. With the development of science and technology, increase of population and decrease of natural resources, more and more importance has been attached to the economic value of sea areas since World War II. One after another, coastal countries promulgate laws to protect and regulate sea areas. As a maritime power, China takes up a sea area of over 3 million square kilometers, about one third of the land area. The implementation of this statute takes on profound significance. It stipulates that the sea areas shall belong to the State, and the State Council shall exercise ownership over the sea areas on behalf of the state; the right to use sea areas shall be lawfully obtained for the use of sea areas by any entity or individual. Article 328 of the Civil Code clearly states that the right to use the sea areas that is acquired in accordance with law is protected by law. Although these two statutes both acknowledge the right to use the sea areas, neither has clarified the nature or definition of the right.

The right to use sea areas refers to the exclusive right of an individual or entity to use particular sea areas. To utilize the sea area, the individual or entity must have acquired the right to use sea areas through one of the following three ways, namely, by applying to competent maritime administrative authority for approval, by bid invitation or by auction, all of which are to be followed by registration. According to Para. 1 and Para. 3 of Article 7 of the Interim Regulations on Real Estate Registration, the right to use sea areas shall be registered by the real estate registration authority of the county people's government at the place where the sea area is located; the registration of real estates such as the sea areas and islands used for projects approved by the State Council shall be provided for by the competent department of land and resources of the State Council together with other relevant departments. The maximum term for using sea areas varies according to the following purposes: 15 years for aquatic breeding; 20 years for shipbreaking; 25 years for tourism and entertainment; 30 years for salt production and mineral exploitation; 40 years for public interests; and 50 years for construction projects including ports, shipbuilding factories, etc. As one of the nation's important natural resources, the sea areas are used on paid basis. Any entity or individual user shall pay royalties for the use according to the rates as provided by the State Council. At present, administrative departments for sea areas don't adopt bidding or auction for assigning the right to use such sea areas as disputed ones, marine natural reserves, fishery resource conservation areas, the traditional areas for collecting shells and fishes, and those involving public interests, etc. The royalties for the use of the sea areas by fishermen to breed aquatics may be paid at reduced rates or be exempted within certain regulated areas. As an important property rights, the right to use sea areas may be legally transferred or inherited.

2. 2. 2   Right to Mining

The right to mining is a real right in special laws of qualified legal persons, individuals or other entities to possess, extract and derive benefits from state-owned mineral resources within the legal limit. In addition to the general rules found in the Civil Code on the right to mining, specific regulations are prescribed by the Mineral Resources Law of the People's Republic of

China. The object of the right to mining is compounded of mineral resources and mining areas, whose types and scopes exert great impact on the acquisition and exercise of the right. Under the Chinese law, the right to mining may be transferred subject to conditions, though ways of circulation such as mortgaging, lease and contractual management still need to be defined and further developed.

Para. 3, Article 3 of the Mineral Resources Law of the People's Republic of China, which was revised on August 27, 2009 gives specific regulation on the ways and procedures for obtaining the right to mining, "Anyone who wishes to explore or mine mineral resources shall separately make an application according to law and shall register after obtaining the right of exploration or mining upon approval, with the exception of the mining enterprises that have, in accordance with law, applied for and obtained the right of mining and are conducting exploration within the designated mining area for the purpose of their own production". The statute regulates clearly on the ways and procedures to obtain the right to mining. The establishment of the right to mining is the result of the realization of the ownership of mineral resources by the state. It is also an important way to make rational use of natural resources and to promote the effective utilization of resources. ①

2.2.3　Right to Explore Minerals

The right to explore minerals is the right of an obligee to explore mining resources within the areas designated in a legally acquired exploration license. Natural persons, legal persons or other economic organizations that have legally obtained the right to prospecting mineral deposits are termed as exploration licensees. Entities or individuals with statutory personalities may apply to the relevant state administrative authorities and get entitled to explore the mining resources within the designated areas in accordance with the terms and contents as stipulated after obtaining the exploration license upon examination and approval. Through concession, the State authorizes the exploration licensees to utilize the mineral resources that is under its ownership. The entity or individual that has been licensed the right to prospecting mineral deposits is its subject and the mining resources within the designated regions are its object. As a constituent of the mining rights, the right to prospecting mineral deposits is a real right, or to be more specific, a right over the property of another (jus in re aliena). It is exclusive, i. e., within the designated area and term, a second right to prospecting mineral deposits cannot be established, neither can the exploration of entities or individuals other than the licensee within the region be allowed.

2.2.4　Right to Draw Water

The right to draw water refers to the right to directly draw water from such water resources

---

① Wang Yangguo, Xiao Guoxing, "On the Right to Mining", China's Geology, Vol. 11, 1993.

as groundwater, rivers, lakes, etc. It is an important interest established for utilizing water in areas where the natural spatial distribution of water has to be changed, such as agricultural irrigation, industrial and domestic need for water, water need for industry breeding aquatics, etc. Article 48 of the Water Law of the People's Republic of China stipulates that, the entities and individuals that collect water resources directly from rivers, lakes, or underground shall, in accordance with the provisions of the water collection license system and the system of paid use of state water resources, apply to the water administration departments or watershed administration authorities for a water collection license, pay the water resource fees and obtain the right to draw water. However, small amount of water drawing for domestic need, drinking water for captive or free-range livestock and poultry is excluded.

2.2.5　Fishing Rights (Right to Use Water for Fishing and for Aquaculture)

2.2.5.1　Concept of Fishing Rights (Right to Use Water for Fishing and for Aquaculture)

According to the Fisheries Law of the People's Republic of China, the fishing right is the right acquired by a right holder in accordance with the fisheries laws to conduct activities of fisheries. It mainly includes the right to use waters or tidal flats, the right to use water for aquaculture, the right to use water for fishing, etc. The fishing right is not an independent civil right, as its establishment or extinguishment is closely related to the legal status of the particular sea areas. In sense of domestic law, the fishing right is taken by common law jurisdictions as a public right that reflects the state's administration of oceanic fishing resources through concession, rather than a property right as viewed in civil law jurisdictions represented by Japan, where the fishing right is with a dual structure consisting of the title and the right derived therefrom. As China has declared explicitly the state ownership of sea areas, the traditional fishing right system is embodied in the system of real rights in immovable properties. A separate system of fishing right will undermine the principle of one property one right.

As the fisheries is generally consisted of fishing and aquaculture, the fishing right accordingly includes the right to use water for fishing and that for aquaculture. The former is the right of a right holder to lawfully obtain and derive benefits from the biological resources within particular waters under natural state, including waters of territorial waters, internal waters, waters in exclusive economic zone, rivers, and lakes. It is one type of the rights to use natural resources. In general, the exercise of the right to use waters for fishing does and should not require the exclusive use of the related waters. Though it is not an exclusive right, this right still involves continuous utilization of waters. One may conduct fishing activities within one determinate sea area all his life. Therefore, in territorial waters, internal waters, and waters in exclusive economic zone, the right to use water for fishing is also a right to use sea areas.

As to the right to use water for aquaculture, it refers to the right of a right holder to legally conduct activities of aquaculture within state-owned or collectively owned waters or tidal flats free from others' interference. It aims at obtaining and deriving benefits from the reared aquatics and requires the exclusive utilization of the particular sea areas. In such sense, the right to use sea areas and the fishing rights overlap to the extent that the former incorporates but is not limited to the right to use water for aquaculture encompassed in the latter.

Article 329 of the Civil Code gives statutory confirmation to the quasi-usufruct status of the right to use water for aquaculture and for fishing by stipulating that "The right to explore and mine minerals, to draw water, and to use waters and mudflats to engage in aquaculture or fishing that are acquired in accordance with law is protected by law". The significance thereof lies in three aspects. First, it makes the fishing right a long-term and stable right. Though the right still necessitates administrative license for its acquisition, it is subject to no administrative interference once obtained as a quasi-usufruct. This protects the operators in fishing industry, many of whom in China make a living solely by rearing aquatics, and may have been doing so for generations. For them, the waters are the basic means of production. If the right granted is subject to the willful adjustment or revocation of the governmental entities, the interests of those conducting activities of aquaculture will be greatly jeopardized. Second, this encourages the operators to make more investments. Possessions make perseverance. As the fishing right becomes a long-term and stable property right, the operators can increase their investments in the aquaculture based on their reasonable expectation. On the other side, if the right to use water for aquaculture is not a real right, the long-term investment may less likely be made. ①
Third, it reserves certain room for the future development of the fishing right. As a quasi-usufruct, the fishing right is to be established and defined in accordance with the rules in the Civil Code, absent any stipulations in special laws such as the Fisheries Law. The recognition of the fishing right as quasi-usufruct renders the rules in the Civil Code on assigning and protecting such right applicable, and it is conducive to safeguarding the right holder's interests and leaves an institutional blank for improving the system of the fishing right.

The fishing right is with preferential effect, which mainly manifests in the following aspects. First, it has priority over creditor's right. A pre-existed leasehold ceases when the waters become an object of a fishing right. In a strict sense, this projects the exclusivity of the fishing right. Second, it has priority over the ownership of the water resources. Though the latter is the title from which the former emerges, it is inferior in terms of the utilization of certain waters. The owner of the water resources shall not hinder the exercise of the fishing right. With regard to the ownership of the aquatics caught, the right to use water for fishing takes effect, while the ownership of the waters does not. Otherwise, the existence of the fishing

① Wang Liming, "On the Nature and characters of the Right to Use Sea Areas of the Real Right Law", Research on Social Science, Vol. 4, 2008.

right will lose its meaning. Third, it takes priority over other usufructs. In some cases, though a fishing right coexists with a right to draw water, it is protected in a privileged position.

2. 2. 5. 2   Distinction between Right to Use Water for Aquaculture and Right to Use Sea Areas

Both right to use water for aquaculture and the right to use sea areas involve the utilization of sea areas, they may in contents overlap to certain extent. As a result, different views regarding the relationship of the two were raised in drafting the Civil Code. The first is the theory of the right to use sea areas. According to this theory, the Civil Code should only stipulate on the right to use sea areas, as it can cover all the contents of the right to use water for aquaculture. As to the right to use water for aquaculture in other waters, it may be established through the expanded interpretation of the right to contractual management of land. The right to use water for aquaculture has never been a right in the civil law, nor should it be. ①The second one is theory of right to use water for aquaculture. Under this view, the Civil Code should only regulate on the right to use water for aquaculture, as it may encompass aquaculture within any waters, while the right to use sea areas only encompass waters within sea areas. Moreover, there lacks purpose and need for regulation over the latter. Where a sea area is utilized for aquaculture, the right to use water for aquaculture can take its place; where the sea area is used for fishing, the right to use water for fishing may be its replacement. ② The third one is the dualism theory. According to this theory, the right to use water for aquaculture and the right to use sea areas are in fact two rights with different nature, though they partially overlap. Consequently, the Civil Code should stipulate the two usufructs concurrently. This view is also adopted by most foreign legislation in comparative law.

The Civil Code also takes the third view. The right to use sea areas and the right to use water for aquaculture are respectively stipulated in Articles 328 and 329 of the code. We have found it out that the two rights do have overlap in their contents, as is manifested in cases where an right holder intends to use particular sea area for aquaculture, thus involving both rights, The legislators should pay attention to how the potential conflict or contradiction to arise from the acquisition or exercise of the two rights.

Pursuant to Article 25 of the Law on the Administration of Sea Areas, the applicant for the use of sea area may use it for breeding aquatics. Article 11 of the Fisheries Law of the People's Republic of China provides that, where an entity or an individual uses a water area or tidal flat with ownership by the whole people which is determined by the State programming to be used

---

① Yin Tan, Research on Sea Area Real Right System of China, Beijing: China Legal Publishing House, 2004, P159.

② Cui Jianyuan, "The System of the Right to Use Sea Areas and Thoughts to It", Tribune of Political Science and Law, Vol. 6, 2004.

for aquatic breeding industry, the user shall apply to the department in charge of fishery administration of the local people's government at the county level or above for the aquatic breeding certificate which shall be checked and issued by the people's government at the same level. With this certificate, the user is permitted to be engaged in aquatic breeding production in the said water area or beach. Water areas owned by the state also include sea areas. As such, one may apply for utilizing a particular state-owned sea area for aquatic breeding industry based on the above article. Then such an issue may be raised: is it still necessary for a right holder to use sea areas to apply for a certificate for aquaculture, after he has been issued one for using the sea areas upon application and approval? Or to put it the other way round, can a holder of the right to use water for aquaculture be spared from the requirement of a certificate for the use of sea area, after he has obtained one for aquaculture upon application and approval? Do the two rights overlap or conflict with each other? This is a point worth digging into.

In spite of their overlapping contents, the two rights are legally distinguishable due to their different features as usufructs. First, their purposes of establishment are not identical. A right to use water for aquaculture is created mostly for using the waters for breeding aquatic plants or animals. The utilization of the space above is not a necessity. In contrast, a right to use sea areas may be established for various purposes other than aquatic breeding, including shipbreaking, tourism and entertainment, salt production and mineral exploitation, public interests and construction projects including ports, shipbuilding factories, etc. With the further development of oceanic economy and scientific technology, the ways of using sea areas will doubtlessly be increased and contents of the right be enriched. Second, the objects of the two rights differ. The object of the right to use sea areas is the sea areas, while that of the right to use water for aquaculture is waters or tidal flat, including rivers and lakes. According to Article 2 of the Fisheries Law, the right to use water for aquaculture may be created upon the inland waters, tidal flats, territorial waters, waters in the exclusive economic zone or any other sea areas, while the right to use sea areas only upon particular sea area. Particularly, in cases where a holder of the right to use water for aquaculture conduct activities of aquatic breeding in collectively-owned waters, similarities between this right and that of contractual land management may be well noticed. In contrast, the right to use sea areas is limited to the use of state-owned sea areas. Third, the two are subject to the regulation of different laws. The Civil Code regulates on the two rights only in a general sense, leaving their detailed contents to special laws. The right to use water for aquaculture is stipulated by the Fisheries Law, while the right to use sea areas by the Law on the Administration of Sea Areas.

In any case, an overall arrangement in law is still desirable to solve the possible conflicts between the two rights. An obligee should not be urged to go through the procedures for a second time after obtaining a right, thus incurring higher costs for acquiring the usufruct. The protection of the obligee necessitates that the issuance of one certificate shall suffice to determine to whom the right goes. In my view, the purposes for which the parties establish their rights should be first considered. If aquatic breeding is the sole purpose, then the creation of a right to use water for aquaculture might as well be applied for. Whereas activities other than aquaculture such as exploration, construction, etc. are also desired, then a right to use sea areas should be established upon application. Second, the procedures for registration and application should be simplified as possible. For instance, where an applicant intends to conduct activities of aquatic breeding within certain sea areas, the acquisition of one certificate for either right shall be the equivalent of qualifications for the two; where the approval from one authority has been obtained but activities other than or instead of aquatic breeding are planned to be conducted within the sea areas, then a certificate for the right to use sea areas is still necessary. In cases where an applicant not only uses the sea areas, but also utilizes other land for aquatic breeding, a license for aquaculture cannot be waived. In any case, the competent authorities for examination and approval should coordinate and share information with each other. Moreover, when several applicants are licensed to utilize the same sea areas, for instance, one to conduct aquatic breeding activities, the other to construct and explore, two rules may be adopted as a solution. One is the rule of "first in time, first in right" prescribed by the real right law. For the direct conflict between the two rights, for example, one party claims for conducting aquaculture based on the right to use water for aquaculture and the other claims for the same based on his right to use sea areas, the dispute can be settled after the temporal sequence in which the two rights are created. The other rule refers to Article 346 of the Civil Code, which stipulates that the newly created usufruct shall not infringe on the one that has already been created. For instance, when one party first conducted activities of aquatic breeding within particular sea areas after obtaining his right to use water for aquaculture, the other party, who later acquired the right to use sea areas for exploration or construction, must conduct his activities in such a manner that the aquatic breeding of the former party is not influenced.

Section Two   Right to Land Contractual Management and Right to Management of Land

1. Concept and Features of Right to Contractual Management of Land

Pursuant to Article 8 of the Constitution, "The rural collective economic organizations apply the dual operation system characterized by the combination of centralized operation with decentralized operation on the basis of operation by households under a contract. Working people who are members of rural economic collectives have the right, within the limits prescribed by law, to farm plots of cropland and hilly land allotted for their private use, and to engage in household sideline production and raise privately owned livestock". Article 330 of the Civil Code echoes the above provision, stating that "Rural collective economic organizations shall adopt a two-tier management system, with household contractual management as the basis and integrated with the collective management. A system of contractual management of land is adopted in accordance with law for cultivated land, forestland, grassland, and other land used for agricultural purposes which are owned by farmers collectively, or owned by the State and used by farmers collectively". In view of this, it may be concluded that the right to contractual management of land is a concrete manifestation of the aforesaid dual management system that is characterized by the combination of centralized management with decentralized management on the basis of management by households under a contract.

1.1 Concept and Features of Right to Contractual Management of Land

Article 331 of the Civil Code provides that "A person who has the right to contractual management of land is, in accordance with law, entitled to possess, use, and benefit from the cultivated land, forestland, and grassland contracted and managed by him, and to engage in agricultural production such as crop cultivation, forestry, and animal husbandry". According to this provision, the right to land contractual management may be defined as a right enjoyed by a natural person, legal person or other organizations to possess, use and benefit from collectively-owned or State owned land or forests, mountain ridges, grasslands, unreclaimed land, mudflats and waters when engaging in crop cultivation, forestry, animal husbandry, fishery, or other production activities.

Existing legislations and the trend of rural land reform in China have displayed the following features of this right:

1.1.1 Subjects of right to contractual management of land are restricted.

Upon the advent of the right, its circulation was legally forbidden and the subjects were largely restricted to the members of the collective economic organization or rural contracting households. With the development of rural land reform, the legal restrictions on circulation of right to contractual management of land and the right to management of land were gradually lifted. As a result, the subjects of the right to contractual management of land not only include members of the collective economic organization, but also natural persons, legal persons as well as other organizations outside this range. Admittedly, right to contractual management of land on farmland may only be established by such means as household contractual management within the collective economic organization, which means the right holder of original acquisition may only be members thereof. As to other land such as barren mountains, gullies, hills and beaches, their right holder of original acquisition may be civil persons outside the collective economic organization.

1.1.2　Objects of right to land contractual management are extensive.

Article 2 of the Law on Land Contract in Rural Areas① stipulates that, "For purposes of this law, land in rural areas includes the arable land, forestlands and grasslands that are owned collectively by the farmers and by the State but are used collectively by the farmers according to law, as well as other lands used for agriculture according to law". The provision defines the scope of the objects of the right to land contractual management. Viewed from this provision, the object of the right is very extensive, which is reflected in the following aspects:

First, the object may either be land owned by collective organizations or that owned by the State but collectively utilized by farmers according to law. Under Chinese law, the state-owned land is mostly located in the cities, but that in the rural areas for agriculture use also occupies vast area due to historical reasons. For example, the land whose ownership was not distributed to farmers during the Land Reform or land that was not attributed to the collective under the implementation of the Draft Amendment of the Regulation on the Work of Rural People's Commune in 1962, as well as land where state-owned farms are built, etc. Most of such lands were granted by the State to collective organizations for their long-term use and are not subject to arbitrary recovery. According to the Law on Land Contract in Rural Areas, the above-mentioned lands can be objects of the right to land contractual management.

Second, the objects include cultivated land, forest land and grassland. Besides, other land for agriculture is encompassed according to law, whose definition is given by the classification of land usages in Para. 3, Article 4 of the Land Administration Law, which stipulates that it shall contain various types of land including cultivated land, forestlands, grasslands, water surface for agriculture, etc. As for the four categories of barren lands, namely, barren mountains, gullies, hills and waste tidal flats, they may also be the objects though they are also categorized as unused land according to usages. In other words, objects of the right to contractual management of land, may be any type of land in the rural areas except for the land for construction.

1.1.3　Contents of the right to contractual management of land mainly lie in land utilization and profiting by means of agricultural production.

A right holder of the right to contractual management of land should utilize his land for agricultural production. Here, "agriculture" is defined by Article 2 of the Agriculture Law as

---

①　The law is Amended by the National People's Congress Standing Committee for the second time on December 29, 2018.

"consists of the industries of crop cultivation①, forestry, animal husbandry and fishery, including the services before, during and after the production process directly related with the above". Thus, disposition of the right holder over the land may conduct such forms of agricultural production activities on the land including cultivation, forestation, animal husbandry, fishery, etc. This is obviously different from the right to use land for construction purposes and the right to use a house site, both of whose contents consist of the utilization of lands for erecting and maintaining buildings, structures and affiliated facilities thereof. In view of this, it may be concluded that the fundamental difference between the right to contractual management of land and the right to use land for construction purposes lie in their contents or use. Of course, agricultural production may also involve constructing buildings or structures such as small houses built for guarding orchards, or water conservancy facilities in the farmland etc. Essentially, however, such act of construction is appurtenant to and still falls into the range of agricultural production. It is worth pointing out that, out of concerns for food security issues, the Chinese legislations have imposed strict restrictions on the transformation of the farmland into land for construction, and the use of it for development or construction in disguised forms. Such policy shall be accounted for by the large population of the nation, and its scarce land resources. A full reliance on import cannot meet the food demand of the entire country, which in turn makes the system of farmland and the industry of agricultural production a cornerstone of the national security, economic development and social stability of China. A popular saying goes, "There is no political stability and economic prosperity without agriculture development". For these reasons, Article 30 of the Land Administration Law stipulates that, "The State protects the cultivated land and strictly controls the conversion of cultivated land into non-cultivated land". Apart from this, no development activities other than agricultural production may be conducted on a farmland even if the purpose of the use of the land has not been altered. Para. 2 to 3, Article 37 of the Land Administration Law also explicitly emphasizes that "It is forbidden to use cultivated land for building kilns and graves and to build houses, dig sand, quarry, mine or collect earth on or from cultivated land without authorization". Meanwhile, out of concern for food security, it is also forbidden to use capital farmland for planting forest or fruit trees or to turn such land into ponds for raising fish. Capital land may only be used for plant production.

1.1.4　Right to contractual management of land is a real right with definite term.

While the Real Right Law was being drafted, the legal nature of the right to contractual

---

① It is a social production department that makes use of plants' life functions to artificially cultivate grains, non-staple food, feeding stuffs and industrial raw materials. In China, it usually refers to production of products such as grain, cotton, oil, sugar, hemp, silk, tobacco, Tea, fruit, medicine and miscellaneous. It also refers to agriculture in narrow sense. Agriculture in broad sense includes crop cultivation, forestry, animal husbandry, sideline, and fishery.

management of land provoked stark controversy. Over a long period of time, both legal and judicial interpretations treated the right to contractual management of land as a claim, which means transfer, subcontract or exchange are forbidden if the party offering the contract refuses to consent. Disputes over the right to contractual management of land are dealt with in accordance with rules on contract.

Nonetheless, the Real Right Law and Civil Code directly define the right to contractual management of land as real right, laying a solid legal foundation for the farmers to enjoy a stable right over lands for a long period of time. As a right to usufruct, the right to contractual management of land is jus in re aliena, meaning that it is a real right over lands owned by others (the State or collective organizations). Also, because of such nature, the nation has established the rule of separating this right from land ownership, and has applied the dual management system characterized by the combination of centralized management with decentralized management on the basis of management by households under a contract. The right to contractual management of land is also a limited real right, its disposition over a property is subject to legal restrictions, and it may only adopt such forms to use as agricultural production to realize the use value of land within a certain period. Meanwhile, it restricts and prevails over the ownership. The owner is obliged to respect the right to contractual management of land and may not infringe upon or hinder the exercise of the right. In addition, as a right to usufruct, the right to contractual management of land shall not be appurtenant to a specific personality or land, but it can be circulated through alienation, exchange, etc. Therefore, it is an independent property right with extensive power of disposal.

1. 2   Evolution of the Right to Contractual Management of Land into Real Right and Its Significance

The evolution of the right to contractual management of land into a real right bears great importance when viewed from the following few perspectives:

1. 2. 1   It contributes to stabilizing and extending the duration of the right. If the right to contractual management of land is a claim, whose duration is decided by the contract for the right to contractual management of land due to the time limit of a claim, then the term of such contract may likely be shortened in certain areas. A direct result of this would be the short sightedness in farmer households' acts and their reluctance to make long term investment, or even predatory operation upon the expiration of the contract, which will exert undesirable impact on the sustainable development of rural economy. Viewed from this, the evolution of the right to contractual management of land into a real right denotes a legal confirmation of its term. Under the doctrine of numerus clausus, parties concerned cannot agree otherwise since the relevant rules of the Real Right and the Civil Code are all mandatory. For example, the Civil

Code Law provides that the contractual term of cultivated land is thirty years, which may not be otherwise agreed upon by the farmer household and the collective economic organization as ten years. Term of this kind agreed between the parties is not legally effective and the contractual term of cultivated land shall be calculated as thirty years. This is obviously conducive to the stability of a contractual land management relation as the duration of the right is extended and stabilized.

1.2.2 It is conducive to balancing the interests of the land owner and contractor, and grants the right to contractual management of land an effect of exclusivity. If the right is defined as a claim, then infringements and interferences from the party offering the contract (the land owner) as well as rural administrative organs may not be easily avoided because a claim is not exclusive, thus inferior to a real right in terms of legal effects.

Evolution of the right to contractual management of land into a real right helps prevent the unlawful interference of the party offering the contract and sufficiently protect the lawful rights and interests of the contractor. The risk faced by the contractor mainly comes from the unauthorized interference of the party offering the contract. Hence, to directly clarify the scope of right enjoyed by the holder of right to contractual management of land in law and grant powerful remedies accordingly will contribute to improving the status of the contractor and amply fulfill his due contractual management interests. The amendment of a contract for the right to contractual management of land is easily dominated by the party offering the contract, which, in most cases is the collective organization, it means that the farmer household cannot be on an equal footing during the conclusion and enforcement of the contract. As a result, the farmer may have to bear heavier burden or lose certain interests under the amended contract. Conversely, the evolution of the right to contractual management of land into a real right requires that the contents of the right be clearly defined in the Real Right Law and subject to no whimsical domination of the party offering the contract. In this way, the interests of the right holder are safeguarded. Meanwhile, as a real right, the right to contractual management of land may be asserted against a third party and is protected by the real right law. Where a real right was infringed upon or obstructed by others, the right holder is entitled to contend for claims of real rights such as claim for restitution of property, removal of the nuisance, elimination of danger and restoration of original status, regardless of whether the tortfeasor is with fault or not. The evolution of the right to contractual management of land into a real right denotes that a right holder may directly cite his claims on real rights against any violation by the party offering the contract or a third party. In cases where any actual loss has been caused, the right holder may require that the party offering the contract take liability for breach of contract and the third party that of tort.

1. 2. 3   It lays a legal foundation for compensation in expropriation. A contractor is entitled to contend for compensations for the attachments and the young crops on land but not for the land itself in case of expropriation if a right to contractual management of land is deemed a claim. Under such circumstance, only the collective organization, as the party offering the contract and the land owner, acquires the status of a party which is expropriated and compensated, the farmer households have no access to safeguarding their interests as contractors. In other words, the farmers are not entitled to ask for compensations for their lost right to contractual management of land. As the right to contractual management of land is confirmed as a real right, the contractor may be compensated for the land itself. Para. 2, Article 243 of the Civil Code stipulates that "In the case of expropriation of collectively-owned land, land compensation fees, resettlement subsidies, and compensation fees for rural villagers' dwellings and other ground attachments as well as young crops shall be paid in full in a timely manner in accordance with law, and social security premiums of the farmers whose land has been expropriated shall be arranged, their lives secured, and their lawful rights and interests safeguarded". The jurisprudential basis of such compensation for right to contractual management of land itself lie in its real right status.

1. 2. 4   It promotes land circulation and contributes to maximizing the efficiency of rural land. The claim, as a relative right, cannot be transferred without any direct influence upon the other party's interests. Therefore, the transfer of the rights and obligations under a claim is generally restricted by law. That is to say, if the right to land contractual management is treated as a claim, then its alienation or subcontracting will have to be approved by the party offering the contract. This unfavorably impacts the circulation of farmland in the market. In contrast, the absolute nature of the real right determines that the right may in principle be alienated without the consent of or notice to others. To grant the right to contractual management of land the effects of a real right not only ensures that the holder of such right enjoys the right to benefit from the land, but also sufficiently safeguards the reasonable circulation of land in a direction that realizes the best utilization of the land and achieves the highest efficiency of land in the process of circulation.

1. 2. 5   It optimizes the management of land owned by collective organization, preventing large-scale wastage of cultivated land. At present, one of the major reasons for the wastage of cultivated lands lies in the fact that the leading person of collective economic organization factually determines the transfer of the land while the majority farmers have no final say regarding the matter. When faced with the loss of cultivated lands, the farmers are passively situated and feel completely powerless. They are actually excluded from protection largely due to the lack of stability in their rights to contractual land management. As such right evolves into a real right, the farmers acquire means to fight against illegal occupation or transfer of land to

protect their real rights. The farmers can thus actively participate in the protection of cultivated land. In cases where the leading person of a township, village or villagers' team has illegally alienated a tract of land, a right holder of the right to contractual management of land may apply to a people's court to invalidate such transaction on the basis that his right has been violated.

1.3　In practice, the following issues deserve special attention for safeguarding the farmers' legal rights and interests

First, the term of the right. The term and causes for extinguishment of the right to contractual management of land shall only be prescribed by law under the principle of numerus clausus. Any deviation from this in the agreement of the parties shall be invalid in principle. Otherwise, the right may become unstable and excessive interference in production by the collective economic organization is likely to be entailed.

Second, in cases where the party offering the contract disregards the contract and arbitrarily alters the contracted land, the right holder will be better remedied under liability for breach of contract than that of tort. As regards the damage caused by the party offering the contract, it may be recovered under the law of tort liability (Book Seven Tort Liability of the Civil Code) as the right to contractual management of land is a real right. On the other hand, it may also be repaired under the claim of breach of contract since the party offering the contract has blatantly violated the contract. Article 57 of the Law on Land Contract in Rural Areas has regulated on the tort liability of the party offering the contract, and Article 59 liability for breach of contract. The contractor may claim for specific performance so as to continue its possession and use of the land and get compensated for the loss incurred. Alternatively, he may enforce his claims on real rights and recover the contracted land when the party offering the contract has illegally taken it back, as the right to contractual management of land is a real right.

Finally, in cases where a third party has infringed the right to contractual management of land, the right holder may undoubtedly exercise his claims on real right. Nonetheless, if the right to contractual management of land itself is at dispute, then the right holder might as well directly rely on the claim for recovery of possession under the Civil Code and require the return of original property, removal of the nuisance or elimination of dangers.

2. Establishment of Right to Land Contractual Management

According to Article 333 of the Civil Code, "A right to contractual management of land is created at the time when the contract on the right to contractual management of land enters into effect". Clearly, the right to land contractual management shall be established by contract. According to the Law on Land Contract in Rural Areas, the right to contractual management of land may be either established through household contract or in other ways. In principle, rural land is to be contracted by household within the rural collective economic organization. As to other types of rural land that are not suited for household contract such as barren mountains, gullies, hills and beaches, they may be contracted through bid invitation, auction, public consultation etc.

2. 1　Establishment through Household Contract

2. 1. 1　Conclusion of Contract for the Right to Contractual Management of Land

The establishment of the right to contractual management of land by household contract refers to such act whereby the members of a collective economic organization conclude contract with the organization in households to create the right to land contractual management. The relevant provisions in the Civil Code mainly apply to those rights to land contractual management that are established in this way. The contract must be in written form and generally includes the following clauses : the names of party giving out the contract and the contractor, and the names and domiciles of the representative of the party giving out the contract and the representative of the contractor; the name, location, area and quality grade of the contracted land; the term of contract and the dates of beginning and end; the purpose of using the contracted land; the rights and obligations of the party giving out the contract and the contractor; liability for breach of the contract. The contractor in a household contract shall be the farmer household of the collective economic organization. As to the party offering the contract, it should be determined in accordance with attribution of the contracted land. Where the land owned collectively by the farmers belongs, in accordance with law, to collective ownership by the farmers in a village, contracts should be given out by the collective economic organization of the village or the villagers' committee; where the land is already owned collectively by the farmers of more than two rural collective economic organizations in a village, contracts should be given out respectively by the said organizations or villagers' groups in the village. Where the rural land is owned by the State but used collectively by farmers according to law, contract should be issued by the rural collective economic organizations, villagers' committees or villagers' groups that use such land.

The contracting plan shall be subject to consent by no less than two-thirds of the members of the villagers' assembly of the collective economic organization concerned or by no less than two-thirds of the representatives of the villagers. After the contracting plan is passed, arrangements for the implementation of the contracting plan should be conducted in public and the contract should be concluded.

2. 1. 2　Obligation to Contract of the Collective Economic Organization

Under household contract, the contractors are members of collective economic organizations who historically abandoned their ownership voluntarily to heed the call of the Communist Party.

For this reason, the collective economic organization in rural areas should allow the land to be used for free by the farmers as compensation. Also, they are obliged to provide their members with basic means of agricultural production, which is, the land. This is one scheme to realize the socialist public ownership system. Therefore, both history factors and the collective organization's nature as a form of the public ownership system require that the collective economic organization, as the party offering the contract, is obliged to contract after the former system of collective ownership and operation ended. It should grant the request of its members to conclude a contract for the right to land contractual management. Article 5 of the Law on Land Contract in Rural Areas stipulated that, "Members of the collective economic organizations in rural areas shall, according to law, have the right to undertake rural land contracts with their own collective economic organizations that give out the contracts". The provision in fact imposes a duty of compulsory contracting[1] on the collective economic organizations. As such, the right of members of a collective economic organization to contract is actually part of the contents of the membership right. Nonetheless, according to Article 29 of the Law on Land Contract in Rural Areas, new inhabitants are only entitled to such land as reserved by collective economic organizations according to law, or increased through reclamation according to law, or turned back by contractors according to law or on a voluntary basis, to meet their needs for contract. In cases where there is no such land, the collective economic organization can't conclude the contract with the new inhabitants Because performance of its contracting obligation is impossible.

2.1.3　Farm Households within Collective Economic Organization as the Contractor

According to Article 16 of the Law on Land Contract in Rural Areas, the contracting party for household contracts is to be farm households within the collective economic organization. Family members of a farmer household shall equally share all rights and interests in the contracted land in accordance with the law. This is to be accounted for by the practice "fixing farm output quotas on each household"[2] that was adopted in the 1980s along with the household contract responsibility system. The State has been striving to stabilize the contracting relationships and advocating the policy of "variation in members influences not the land area of the household". The practice of treating a household as a unit continues up to now. Of course,

---

[1]　The duty of compulsory contracting, interpreted in broad sense, means that a specific subject has the duty to issue promise to others.

[2]　It is originally called the system of household contracted responsibility linking remuneration to output, which is a production responsibility system of rural collective economic organizations of China and is firstly exerted by 18 peasants households of Xiaogang village, Fengyang county of Anhui province. Under conditions of adhering to the public ownership of production materials and adhering to unified planning, unified operation, unified accounting and unified distribution, the rural collective economic organization contracted cultivation land and some production tasks i. g. animal husbandry, aquaculture and other sidelines to peasant households and carry on a system of extra payment for overfufillment of work quotas and compensations for reduction of output.

if in practice such circumstance arises where family members require for dividing up family property and living apart, rules on partitioning property by joint co-ownership may apply mutatis mutandis because the right to contractual management of land is treated as a family common property.

2.1.4   Ways of Establishing Right to Contractual Management of Land

Although the Civil Code adopts the principle that change in real right regarding immovable properties requires registration as a requirement of validity, the establishment of the right to contractual management of land constitutes an exception to the rule by waiving the registration requirement. Para. 1, Article 333 of the Civil Code actually echoes Article 23 of the Law on Land Contract in Rural Areas, which stipulates that "A right to contractual management of land is created at the time when the contract on the right to contractual management of land enters into effect". In other words, such contract goes into effect upon conclusion. Moreover, the right exerts its effect not as a claim but a real right.

There is no direct link between registration and the establishment of the right to contractual management of land, which provides a clear contrast to the creation of right to use land for construction purposes, whereby registration is a requirement of validity.

Neither is the issuance of certificate of property rights a prerequisite for the establishment of the right to contractual management of land. Para. 2, Article 333 of the Civil Code provides that, "The registration authority shall issue a certificate, such as a certificate of the right to contractual management of land, a certificate of the right to forestry, and the like, to the person entitled to the respective right to contractual management of land, and establish a register for this purpose to record and confirm such rights". This provision is a repetition of Para 1, Article 24 of the Law on Land Contract in Rural Areas, which regulates that, "The state implements the unified registration of arable land, forest land, and grassland, among others, and a registration body shall issue a certificate of a conventional usufruct on rural land for agricultural operations or a certificate of a forest right, among others, to a grantee, and maintain a register thereof, to confirm the conventional usufructs on rural land for agricultural operations". Meanwhile, to avoid unreasonable charges, Article 24 of the Law on Land Contract in Rural Areas emphasizes that, "The registration body shall not charge any fees other than the certificate production costs collected as required". The certificates of the right to contractual management of land is a legal certificate used by the State to affirm the contractors' right to contractual management of land under the law after the contract goes into effect.

In the vast rural areas and urban suburbs of China, establishing the right to contractual management of land through contract without registration matches the practice of China; right thereby established may be asserted to a third party although it has not been registered. This is because, as earlier mentioned, contractors are all members from collective economic organizations, whose rights, in the current acquaintance society of the rural areas, are or should have been known to third parties who are subject to no infringement after the contract has been concluded though not registered. Viewed in this way, the function of publication in right protection cannot be brought into full play. On the other hand, a third party cannot take over the ownership or acquire a mortgage in the absence of original registration of collectively owned rural land. Hence, where multiple rights coexist in one property and priority needs to be determined will not occur. Neither will there be any negative impact on transaction security due to defects in right. For these reasons, the fact that the Chinese rural area is an acquaintance society determines that the establishment of the right to contractual management of land does not need to be registered, and that the right can inherently be asserted against a third party. Besides, the reality in the rural area is to be taken into consideration. Registration is not technically workable due to the vast area, various scenarios and the simultaneity in the conclusion of the contract. A series of problems may be caused if registration is made compulsory. Of course, registration is required for protecting transaction security if a right holder intends to dispose of his right to contractual management of land after it has been initially created. Otherwise, the disposal effect may not be asserted against a third party in good faith.

2.1.5　Term of the Right to Contractual Management of Land

According to Article 332 of the Civil Code, "The term of a contract for cultivated land is 30 years. The term of a contract for grassland ranges from 30 to 50 years. The term of a contract for forestland ranges from 30 to 70 years. Upon expiration of the term of contract as provided in the preceding paragraph, the person with the right to contractual management of land is entitled to renew the contract in accordance with the provisions of laws on rural land contracting". Article 21 of the Law on Land Contract in Rural Areas stipulates that, "The term of a usufruct on arable land shall be 30 years. The term of a usufruct on grassland shall range from 30 years to 50 years. The term of a usufruct on forest land shall range from 30 years and 70 years. The term of a usufruct on arable land in the preceding paragraph shall be extended by 30 years upon expiration, and the term of a usufruct on grassland or forest land shall be extended correspondingly upon expiration according to the provision of the preceding paragraph".

Here, strictly speaking, the term of contract means the duration throughout which the right to contractual management of land exists.

The rules in the Real Right Law and the Civil Code regarding the term of the contract are mandatory, and the parties should make agreement within the statutory scope. Where contracts are concluded after the Law on Land Contract in Rural Areas and especially after the Real Right Law is implemented with a term that is longer than the statutory limit, then the excessive part shall be invalid; if it's the other way around, then the term shall be the lowest legal limit.

In addition, considering that the system of contractual land management in rural areas is a basic system that will be held by the nation for a long period and for the purpose of granting the farmers a right to land use with long-term stability as well as promoting the economic development and social stability in the rural areas, Para. 2, Article 332 of the Civil Code stipulates that "Upon expiration of the term of contract as provided in the preceding paragraph, the person with the right to contractual management of land is entitled to renew the contract in accordance with the provisions of laws on rural land contracting". As to the specific requirements, they are to be determined in accordance with the governing law. According to the current Law on Land Contract in Rural Areas, the term of a usufruct on arable land shall be extended by 30 years upon expiration, and the term of a usufruct on grassland or forest land shall be extended correspondingly upon expiration according to Para. 1, Article 21 of the statute.

2. 2　Ways of Establishment other than Household Contract

The current legislations allow the four categories of barren land, which are not entirely suitable for household contract, to be established in other ways where there are strict statutory restrictions on the object. Under Article 342 of the Civil Code, "Where rural land is contracted by means including bidding, auction, or open negotiation, for which a title certificate is obtained through registration in accordance with law, the right to manage such land may, in accordance with law, be transferred by means of leasing, contributing it as shares, mortgaging, or by other means". In view of this, when it comes to the application of the law, special laws shall prevail over the Civil Code when a right to contractual management of land is established in ways other than household contract. According to relevant laws and regulations, such means of establishment mainly involves the following contents:

2. 2. 1　The Contractor is Different with that under Household Contract

Under such form of contract, the contractor may be natural persons, legal persons or other entities outside the collective economic organization. The household contract is adopted to establish the right to contractual management of land on such farmland as owned or used by the collective organization due to historical factors and the socialist character of rural collective economic organizations. The collective organization is obliged to provide its members with land for agricultural production, or in other words, to ensure its members' equal chances for contracting. Based on their rights to contractual land management, members of the collective economic organization may require that the collective organization distribute all the collectively-owned farmland to the members by contract.

In contrast, unused land such as the four categories of barren land doesn't naturally suit for agricultural production. Special investments are needed for such land to be cultivated or farmed. Nonetheless, the farmer households themselves may not have the necessary fund, technology or labor forces for development. Under such circumstances, if land is compulsorily distributed to its members of the collective economic organization in equal share for development, it is tantamount to imposing on them extra burdens, which in fact hinders the utilization of the barren land. In addition, it should also be noted that development of unused land entails huge cost, which cannot be covered within a reasonable period if the scale of the land is not large enough. When the barren land is equally distributed among the farmers for their development, economies of scale cannot be achieved and the cost may not be covered.

Therefore, the law sets various rules regarding the contracting of barren land, allowing such land to be contracted by natural persons, legal persons or entities that are not members of the collective economic organization concerned, after democratic procedure has been gone through within the organization. On the other hand, in order to safeguard the interests of the organization and its members, the law also provides that members of the collective economic organization concerned shall enjoy priority under equal conditions when land is contracted in other ways. Where the party gives out the contracts for rural land to units or individuals other than the ones of the collective economic organization concerned, the matter shall first be subject to consent by no less than two-thirds of the members of the villagers assembly, or of the villagers' representatives, of the collective economic organization concerned and it shall be submitted to the township (town) people's government for approval; Moreover, the contracts shall be concluded only after examination of the credit position and management capability of the contractors.

2.2.2 Giving out Contracts Directly or after Converting the Right into Shares

Apart from household contract, the Law on Land Contract in Rural Areas provides two sets of procedure for giving out contract. The first one is to give out contract directly by such means as bid invitation, auction and public consultation. This means to send out an invitation for offer which shows the intent to give out contract of barren land after the plan for contracting has been confirmed through a democratic process. The other one is to undertake the operation of lands for contractual management or joint-stock cooperative management① after the rights to contractual land management are converted into shares and distributed to the members of the collective economic organization concerned. Under this approach, the first step is to establish the right to contractual management of land on the four categories of barren land that is owned by the collective organization and held in equal shares by members of the organization. Second, the operation of land will be undertaken for contractual management or joint-stock cooperative

---

① The joint-stock cooperative system is a kind of cooperative economy which adopts some practices of joint-stock system. The cooperation of labour is the foundation, the labourers share works, jointly possess and utilize production materials, share benefits and risks; the cooperation of capital is realized in form of shares. The labourers are either workers or investors of the enterprise.

management by the whole members. It will not be otherwise contracted. Each member may acquire dividends from the operation profits and undertake risks according to their respective shares. Alternatively, the right to contractual management of land may be further contracted in the name of the collective organization, and all the members may share the contracting incomes according to their shares.

In practice, most contracts are given out directly. The reason why the legislator also regulates on giving out contract after the right to contractual management of land is converted into shares is that it aims to protect the interests of the members in the collective economic organization, especially those without management capacity, so as to ensure fairness and equal status among members, which in turn also avoids possible disputes among members arising from discontent with the result. In my view, the latter approach strikes a perfect balance between fairness and efficiency, thus contributing to the harmony and stability in society. It should be the dominant way of giving out contract in the future.

2. 2. 3　Ways of Establishment

The law has regulated on such ways as bid invitation, auction and public consultation for the conclusion of contract on the right to contractual management of land. Bid invitation and auction should be conducted in accordance with the Auction Law and Law on Tenders and Bids. Further and more specific rules should be stipulated in accordance with the characters of the contract itself so as to ensure that the bid invitation or auction is made known to all the potential bidders, especially members of the collective economic organization.

As to public consultation, practices show that it mainly focuses on the openness in the method, procedure, process and result of the contract. Particularly, it should be made known to members of the collective economic organization so that such secret contract manipulate by minority may be prevented. However, in general, it is essentially the same as the transfer of the right to use land for construction purposes since it is also concluded through individual negotiation.

In my opinion, as is the case with the transfer of the right to use land for construction purposes, all the contracts for the right to contractual management of land should also be concluded by way of public bidding so as to protect the interests of the farmers and avoid loss of collective properties. That is to say, the current practice of public consultation should be specified into listing, realizing the value of barren land by way of public bidding.

2. 2. 4　The Contract for the Right to contractual management of land and Its Nature

After the contractor is settled in such ways as bid invitation, auction or public consultation, a contract should be signed, which means that the contract should be in written form. For example, the rights and obligations of the parties, the term of the contract, etc., should be agreed upon by the parties. Where the land is contracted by way of bid invitation or auction, the contracting fees should be fixed through public bidding. Where the land is contracted through public consultation, the contracting fess should be decided by the parties through negotiation. It is worth pointing out that, the term of the right or contract concerned the cropland may not exceed 30 years and that concerned the grassland may not exceed 50 years, forest land not over 70 years according to the current policy, though it may be agreed upon by the parties of their free will.

It also should be noticed that, Article 53 of the Law on Land Contract in Rural Areas regulates that where a person enters into a contract for rural land through bid invitation, auction or public consultation and, after registration according to law, obtains the certificate of the right to land contractual management or the certificate of the right to forestland contractual management, his right to land contractual management may, according to law, be circulated though transfer, lease, pooling of rights as shares, mortgage or other means. The initial intention of this law is to grant the contractor a claim before registration. Registration is a requirement of validity. The reason behind this is that, as unused land, the four categories of barren land have not let their purpose of use determined, thus cannot be registered under the country's classified system of land management and registration. Therefore, certificate of the right to contractual management of land, or the certificate of forestry ownership, etc., are to be issued to the contractor by the competent registration organs according to major purpose of use of the barren land after it is primarily cultivated.

The contract on the right to contractual management of rural land contract is concluded by the State for the purpose of granting to the peasants lawful and long-term land-use right, thereby safeguarding the development of rural economy and social stability. As can be seen from the above analysis on its contents, features of the contract on contracted management of rural land include the legal prescription of its subjects and contents, obligation of compulsory contracting, restricted right of rescinding the contract, etc. In view of this, some scholars categorize this type of contract as administrative contract.

The main purpose of concluding a contract on the right to contractual management of rural land is to create a right to contractual management of land. If one reviews the relevant provisions in the Law on Land Contract in Rural Areas and the Chinese Civil Code, he may notice that the party offering the contract, namely the collective, enjoys certain degree of administrative powers whilst the contractor undertakes certain public law obligations, although the right to contractual management of land created by them through contract conclusion is a civil right. Admittedly, these provisions contravene the nature of civil-law contract. Nevertheless, the administrative powers enjoyed by the party offering the contract are different from the priorities enjoyed by an administrative subject in an administrative contract. They are merely a result of misplacement of the law in defining responsibilities of the collective that offer the contract. Art. 1 of the Interpretations of the Supreme People's Court about the Issues concerning the Laws Applicable to the Trial of Cases of Disputes over Rural Land Contracting[1] even explicitly defines disputes over contracting contract, disputes over the infringement upon the right to contractual management, disputes over the exchange and transfer of rights to contractual management of land, disputes over the circulation of the right to contractual management, disputes over the distribution of compensation for the requisition of contracted land, disputes over the inheritance of the right to contractual management, and disputes over the inheritance of land management right all as civil disputes. In light of the above, the author opines that based on the comprehensive analysis on its purpose of conclusion, positions of its contracting parties and the available remedies, the contract on contracted management of rural land shall be defined as a civil contract instead of administrative agreement.

3. Contents of the Right to Contractual Management of Land

3. 1　Rights of Holder of the Right to Contractual Management of Land

The right to contractual management of land is a right to usufruct, meaning that the right holder is entitled to possess and use the contracted land for agricultural production and obtain the natural fruits thereof. The contractor is entitled to make his own decision regarding the arrangement of production. It is stressed by the Law on Land Contract in Rural Areas that the contractor has the right to make its own decision regarding the arrangements for production and operation as well as the disposition of the products. The party offering the contract shall respect the contractor's right to make its own decision on production and operation, and refrain from interfering with the normal production and operation conducted by the contractor according to law. Furthermore, the conception of administration according to law and the absoluteness of the real right also require that, the local government shall not intervene with the right of self-determination of the contractor. "The contractor enjoys the right to freely cultivate and operate the contracted land as long as he does not change the land's purpose of use construct permanent structures, or adversely impact the management and cultivation of the neighbor. No one may interfere the farmers' operation with such excuses as 'operation of scale', 'characteristic operation', 'one village, one product', 'one county, one industry', etc."[2]

3. 2　Circulation of the Right to Contractual Land Management and Right to Management of Land

3. 2. 1　Overview

As a right to usufruct, the right to contractual management of land has the power of

---

[1]　The Interpretation was Issued by the Supreme People's Court on March 29, 2005, amended on Dec. 23, 2020.

[2]　Wang Liming, On Real Right Law, China University of Political Science and Law Press, 2003, p. 457.

disposal, meaning that the right holder is entitled to circulate his right in exchange for interests. Article 334 of the Civil Code regulates that, "The persons with the rights to contractual management of land are entitled to exchange or transfer such rights in accordance with law. The contracted land may not be used for non-agricultural construction purposes without being approved in accordance with law". Article 9 the Law on Land Contract in Rural Areas provides that "After land is contracted, the grantee shall have a conventional usufruct on rural land for agricultural operations, and may conduct such operations itself or retain its contracting right but circulate its land operating rights for others to conduct such operations". Here, the three concepts, namely, the right to contractual management of land, right to land contracting, and right to management of land shall be distinguished.

Since the second amendment of the Law on Land Contract in Rural Areas on December 29, 2018, the parallel separation of the ownership, management right, and contracting right has been implemented. The individual features of the three rights lie in their attribution to different entities: the land ownership belongs to the collectives, the contracting right is attributed to farm households, and the management right vests in operators. Under separation of the three rights, the ownership, management right, and contracting right not only achieve their efficiency as a whole but also have their own functions. The key of implementing the separation of the three rights is to loosen the control over land management right, and the core lies in granting the land management right its due legal status and powers.

First, attribution of the land ownership is decided by the nature of the state. The Constitution clearly states that "Land in rural and suburban areas is owned by collectives except for that which belongs to the state as prescribed by law; housing sites and cropland and hillsides allotted for private use are also owned by collectives". Hence, the status of the collective ownership of land in rural areas shall remain unchanged.

Second, the right to contractual management of land is a right to usufruct. Regarding contents of this right, the majority view is that the right to contractual management of land combines the dual natures of the contracting right and the right of management. Here, the contracting right is a membership right that can only be enjoyed by members within the collectives. It is attached to the collective's member identity and not alienable. The right of management in contrast is a proprietary right and marketable in terms of the nature of this right.

As such, under "separation of two rights", the land ownership and the right to contractual management of land are in fact not freely circulatable real rights. But the system of "separation of three rights" demonstrates the share of real rights in land by the collective, contracting farmer household and new operators. From a legal perspective, in essence this system severs a private right that is more suitable for marketing transaction, i. e., the right to management of land, from the land, without changing the basic economic system that upholds public ownership of land. The key is that the contractor's relationship with the party offering the contract remains the same after the right to management of land is circulated.

According to Article 40 of the Law on Land Contract in Rural Areas, a contract for circulation of the right to land management shall be concluded in written form. In general, the contract for the circulation of the right to land management shall include the following clauses: (1) the names and domiciles of the two parties; (2) the name, location, area and quality grade of land concerned; (3) the term of circulation and the dates of beginning and end; (4) the purpose of use of the land concerned; (5) the rights and obligations of the two parties; (6) the price for the right circulated and the method of payment; (7) attribution of compensation fees in case where the land is expropriated, requisitioned or occupied according to law, and (8) liabilities for breach of the contract. Where the period in which the contractor lets another person do farm work on his behalf does not exceed one year, a written contract may be dispensed with. When the right to land management is circulated, no change shall be made in the nature of the land ownership or the purpose of use of the land designed for agriculture, the term of the circulation may not exceed the remaining period of the term of contract; the transferee shall have the capability for agricultural operation, and under equal conditions, members of the collective economic organization concerned shall enjoy priority. Where lease (subcontract), contribution as shares, or other means is adopted for circulation, the matter shall be reported to the party giving out the contract for the record.

3.2.2   Transfer

Regarding the transfer of the right to contractual management of land established through household contract, the Civil Code follows the Law on Land Contract in Rural Areas. Article 44 of the Law on Land Contract in Rural Areas stipulates that, "When a right to land contractual management is circulated by the contractor, the contractual relationship between the contractor and the party giving out the contract shall remain unchanged". Article 46 of the same statute provides that "The transferee may further circulate the right to land management, and the matter shall be subject to consent by the party giving out the contract and reported to the party giving out the contract for the record". That is to say, the transfer of the right to contractual management of land established through household contracting is not subject to the consent of the party giving out contract. After contracting the land, the contractor enjoys the right to contractual management of land. He may either conduct such operations itself or retain its contracting right but circulate its land operating rights for others to conduct such operations. But if the transferee further circulates the right to lang management, he shall obtain the consent of the party offering the contract and report to the collective economic organization concerned for record. The term of the circulation may not exceed the remaining period of the term of contract. Article 41 provides that "Where the term of the circulation exceeds five years, the parties may apply to the registration authority for registration of the right to land management. Circulation that has not been registered is not effective against a bona fide third person".

3.2.3 Exchange

Article 33 of the Civil Code stipulates that "Where the rights to contractual management of land are exchanged or transferred, the parties may apply to the registration authority for registration; without registration, such exchange or transfer may not be asserted against a bona fide third person". That is to say, it allows the right holders within the same collective economic organization to exchange their rights. However, one may notice that jurisprudentially there is no essential distinction between exchange and transfer. If persons who is not from the collective economic organization concerned is allowed to be the transferee of the right to contractual management of land, then he may as well become one of the parties in the exchange. It is worth discussing what is regulated by Article 335 of the Civil Code. "Where the rights to contractual management of land are exchanged or transferred, the parties may apply to the registration authority for registration; without registration, such exchange or transfer may not be asserted against a bona fide third person". This provision follows the approach adopted by the Law on Land Contract in Rural Areas on grounds that first, the current registration system of the right to contractual management of land is still imperfect when in view of the huge number of scattered land tracts that are contracted. Second, registration is not so necessary in terms of its function in publication and presumption of validity if taking into consideration the fact that circulation is mainly conducted among farmers in the same neighborhood who are familiar with each other. Third, compulsory registration entails fees, thus increasing the burden of the farmers.

3.2.4 Mortgage of Right to Management of Land

Article 47 of the Law on Land Contract in Rural Areas stipulates that "The contractor may use the right to management of land for financing guarantee at financial institutions and shall report to the party offering the contract for records. Subject to the written consent of the party offering the contract and after reporting to the party offering the contract for record, the transferee who obtains the right to management of land through circulation may use his right for financing guarantee at financial institutions. The security interest takes effect at the time when the contract for financing guarantee becomes effective. The parties may apply for registration at competent registration authority. Without registration, the guarantee is not effective against a bona fide third person".

In such cases, mortgage registration has no effect for right establishment. Instead, it has mere perfection effect.

3.2.5 Lease and Subcontract

In Chinese law, the fundamental difference between lease and subcontract lies in the fact that the lessee of the right to contractual management of land only leases the right to management, not the contracting right (membership right), hence the lease could be a person outside the collective economic organization, whilst in cases of assignment or exchange of the right to contractual management of land, the transacting partner is limited to members within the collective economic organization concerned, the exchange shall be reported to the party offering the contract for record, and the assignment is subject to the consent of the party offering the contract.

Since the second amendment of the Law on Land Contract in Rural Areas on December 29, 2018, the parallel separation of the ownership, management right, and contracting right has been implemented. Article 36 of the statute allows the free circulation of the right to contractual management of land, and the contractor may, of its own free will, adopts lease (subcontract), contribution as shares, or other means for circulation, and the matter shall be reported to the party giving out the contract for the record.

3.2.6   Equity Contribution

Article 339 of the Civil Code and Article 36 of the Law on Land Contract in Rural Areas allow the contractor to contribute the right to land management as shares. The contractor retains the contracting right and obtains dividends based on such equity share.

3.2.7   Succession

The book on real rights of the Civil Code does not regulate on the succession of the right to contractual management of land. The Law on Land Contract in Rural Areas distinguishes two different situations. First, for household contract, according to Para. 2, Article 32 of the Law on Land Contract in Rural Areas, only in case where a contractor for forestland is dead, may his/her successor continue undertaking the performance of the contract within the term of contract. As to other types of farmlands such as cultivated land or grassland, they may not be inherited. This is because a farmer household continues existing as the contractor even if one or some of the family members were dead. Therefore, the right to contractual management of land that is obtained through household contract may not be succeeded. Where all the members of a household are dead, and the successor of the last survivor is not a member of the collective economic organization, then the right to contractual management of land terminates. Or else, the rights and interests of other members in the collective economic organization will be negatively affected. As regards forestland, it is special in that the investment cycle is long, and it takes time to get profit. Therefore, where the right to use forestland is acquired by way of household contract, the successor of the last survivor of the household shall have the right to inherit the right regardless of whether such successor is a member of the collective economic organization or not. The second situation concerns the contract that is given out in other ways. According to Article 54 of the Law on Land Contract in Rural Areas, when the contractor is dead, his successor may continue executing the contract within the term of contract. This is because contract given out in other ways is usually acquired in the name of individuals rather households. Thereby, the successor may inherit the right upon the death of the contractor.

Pursuant to Article 36 of the Law on Land Contract in Rural Areas, the contractor may decide of its own free will to circulate the right to management of land to other persons. This provision does not forbid the succession of the right to management of land.

3. 3   Obligations of the Contractor

The Law on Land Contract in Rural Areas regulates that, the contractor undertakes the following obligation: first, keeping or using the land for agricultural purposes, and refraining from using it for non-agricultural development; second, protecting and rationally using the land in accordance with law, and refraining from causing permanent damage to the land; and third, other obligations provided for in laws, administrative rules and regulations. The first and second one are statutory obligations that may not be excluded through agreement. While the agricultural tax has been abolished in China, contracting fees shall still be paid by the contractor in accordance with the contract. A contractor shall undertake liability for breach of the contract if the payment of contracting fees is delayed.

Another question that needs to be discussed here is that in cases where the unpaid contracting fees reach a certain amount or the default of debt has lasted for a certain period of time, is the party giving out contract entitled to dissolve the contract and take back the contracted land? Article 57 of the Law on Land Contract in Rural Areas clearly emphasizes that, regarding household contract, "the contracted land may not be taken back to pay off debts". The provision explicitly categorizes such act as a violation of the right contractual management of land. It obviously prohibits the taking back of right to contractual management of land that has been established through household contracting when contracting fees are defaulted. As for right to contractual management of land acquired in other ways and right to contractual management of land and right to management of land derivatively acquired, however, the contracting fees are the consideration paid by the contractor or assignee of the right to management of land for using the contracted land, and it is a price decided by the market. Thus, the party giving out contract or the assignor may dissolve the contract and revoke the right to the contractual land management or right to management of land when the unpaid fees exceed a certain amount, so that the interests of the collective economic organization may be thereby safeguarded.

3. 4   Extinguishment of Right to Contractual Management of Land and Right to Management of Land

Strict restrictions have been imposed on the extinguishment of the right to contractual management of land by the Civil Code and the Law on Land Contract in Rural Areas. The party offering the contract shall safeguard the contractor's right to contractual management of land and may not terminate the right by agreeing on the conditions for terminate the contract or exercising the right to termination absent the occurrence of statutory causes. For example, during the term of the contract, the party giving out the contract may not unilaterally revoke the contract, nor, under pretext that the minority is subordinate to the majority, compel the contractor to give up or modify his right to contractual management of land, nor recover the contracted land for bid invitation or paying off debts.

The current legislations have provided for the following statutory causes for the extinguishment of the right to contractual management of land:

3.4.1   Expiration of the Term

The right to contractual management of land exists for a definite term. Upon expiration of the term, the right terminates if the parties have not otherwise stipulated on renewal.

It should be noted that as rural collective economic organizations undertake the obligation of contract under household contract, it shall agree to renew the contract if the contractor requires so upon the expiration of the term. As for other right to contractual management of land that is acquired by other means, because the barren land has been transformed into arable land, the contractor doesn't have the right of renewal upon expiration of the term. The right to contractual management of land should be reestablished through household contract.

3.4.2   Statutory Readjustment Due to Serious Damage of the Contractual Land

Article 336 of the Civil Code provides that "Within the term of contract, the party offering the contract may not adjust the contracted land. Under special circumstances such as severe deterioration on the contracted land caused by natural disasters, appropriate adjustments shall be made in accordance with the provisions of laws on rural land contracting where necessary". Regarding readjustment, the Law on Land Contract in Rural Areas has stipulated strict restrictions. Article 28 of the statute states that, "Within the term of contract, the party offering the contract may not adjust the contracted land. Where during the term of the contract, if proper readjustment of the arable land or grasslands contracted by individual farmer households is necessary due to such special circumstances as natural calamities that greatly damage the contracted land, the matter shall be subject to the consent of at least two-thirds of the members of the villagers' assembly or of the representatives of villagers of the collective economic organization concerned and shall be reported for approval to the people's government of the township (town) and the competent departments of agriculture and rural affairs, forestry, and grassland, among others at the people's government at the county level. Where an agreement upon no adjustments is concluded in the contract, such an agreement shall prevail". According to interpretation made by the legislator, the special circumstances aforementioned further include the legal requisition or occupation of the contracted land, increase or decline of inhabitants that leads to serious conflict, etc.

Where statutory readjustment is made, the contract for the right to contractual management of land is amended and former right terminated.

3.4.3 Voluntary Returning of the Land

Voluntarily returning of the land means that the right holder has abandoned his right, thus terminating it. Chinese law allows the contractual land to be voluntarily turned back by the contractor to the party offering the contract during the term of the contract. Where a contractor wishes to do so, he shall, in six months in advance, inform the party giving out the contract of the matter in written form and may obtain reasonable compensation fees. After the land has been turned back, the former contractor may no longer request to undertake a new contract for land within the term.

The law doesn't provide for the legal consequences of failing to announce in advance. Some scholars deem that the contractor should pay the rent when the right is abandoned. As I see, the abandonment of the right itself has already greatly benefited the collective economic organization because has acquired the right without consideration; nor is it obliged to enter into a new contract. In view of this, it is not reasonable to demand that the former right holder pay his rent.

3.4.4 Recovery of the Contracted Land

Article 337 of the Civil Code provides that, "Within the term of contract, the party offering the contract may not take back the contracted land, unless otherwise provided by law". As can be seen, in principle, the party offering the contract shall not take back the contracted land. According to Article 27 of the Law on Land Contract in Rural Areas, circumstances under which the contracted land may be taken back mainly include cases where the whole family of the contractor move away and the contracted land is taken back. Where, during the term of contract, the farmer household as the usufructuary permanently settles down in an urban area, the farmer household shall be guided and supported in legally transferring the conventional usufruct on rural land for agricultural operations within the collective economic organization of which it is a member under the principles of voluntariness and non-gratuitousness or surrendering the contracted land to the grantor, and the farmer household may also be encouraged to circulate their land operating rights. During the term of contract, if the contracted land is returned by the contractor or legally taken back by the party offering the contract, the contractor is entitled to corresponding compensations for investment vested into the contracted land that improves the land productivity.

What may be worthy of discussion is whether the land contracted can be taken back if it has been lying waste. We opine that in general land contracted by household should not be taken back because it is wasted. A more desirable approach would be that the collective economic organization takes measures to avoid the land being wasted, for example, by arranging its staff to work voluntarily or hiring others to cultivate it. Meanwhile, other parties may also cultivate the land on the basis of negotiorum gestio. As for land that is contracted by other means or successively acquired via circulation, it may be taken back after such measures as penalty has been taken to urge the contractor to develop the land but the latter still don't utilize the land after being urged. The taking back may not be conducted directly.

3.4.5   Recoverability of Contracted Land in Cases of Conclusion and Alteration of Marriage

Article 31 of the Law on Land Contract in Rural Areas provides that, "During the term of the contract, if a woman gets married but no land is contracted to her in her new domicile, the party giving the land shall not withdraw the land originally contracted to her; if a women gets divorced or becomes a widow, but she still resides in the original place or although she resides in a new place but it fails to contract land to her, the party giving the land shall not withdraw the land originally contracted to her, either". In other words, the party offering the contract shall not take back the contractual land from a woman who has got married or divorced, unless she has been otherwise contracted a land. If she has obtained such right in her new residency, the original right based on the former contract will terminate and the party offering the contract can thereby take back the contracted land. Here, the land contracted to the woman by her new domicile should be acquired by way of household contract and not successively acquired via transfer. This rule applies mutatis mutandis in cases where a man gets married and lives with his bride's family.

3.4.6   Other Causes for Extinguishment

The right to contractual management of land may terminate due to expropriation by the State. In such cases, compensations for the attachments and the young crops on land shall be paid in full. Not only that, the right to contractual management of land itself should also be compensated. Article 17 of the Law on Land Contract in Rural Areas stipulates that, "Contractors are entitled to compensation in accordance with the law, where the contracted land is legally expropriated, requisitioned, or occupied".

According to Article 61 of the Land Administration Law, where land is needed for the construction of township (town) or village public utilities or public welfare undertakings, land for agriculture may be used for such purpose subject to approval of competent authorities. Under such circumstances, the right to contractual management of land thereupon may have to be terminated. As such, the collective economic organization concerned should offer to the right holder another piece of land for agriculture which is with the same area and similar quality, and then establish for him a right to contractual management of land thereupon. Meanwhile, compensations for the attachments and the young crops on land shall also be fully paid.

The right to contractual management may also terminate upon the decease of the contractor absent any successor and legatee.

Regarding the circulation of the right to management of land, Article 42 of Law on Land Contract in Rural Areas explicitly stipulates that "The contractor may not unilaterally terminate the contract for circulation of the right to land management, unless under any of the following circumstances where the transferee: (1) arbitrarily changes the agricultural purposes of the land; (2) abandons the arable land for more than two years; (3) causes serious damages to the land or severely destroys the land ecological environment; or (4) otherwise seriously breaches the contract".

3.4.7   Legal Effects of Termination and Extinguishment of Right to Contractual Management of Land and Right to Management of Land

When his right terminates, the contractor may recover the young crops, woods and attachments on land. In the event that the party offering the contract intends to obtain these objects, he should purchase them at the market price and the contractor shall not reject. The contractor, however, is entitled to get compensation for any input he has invested in the land that has improved the productivity.

Section Three   Right to Use Land for Construction Purposes

1. Concept of the Right to Use Land for Construction Purposes

1.1   Concept of the Right to Use Land for Construction Purposes

Article 344 of the Civil Code stipulates that "With respect to the State-owned land zoned for construction purposes, a person with the right to use a lot of such land is entitled to possess, use, and benefit from the lot, and to use it to construct buildings, structures, and auxiliary facilities". Although this provision restricts the object of the right to use land for construction purposes as State-owned land in principle, Article 361 still allows for the establishment of the right to use land for construction purposes on land that is owned by collective organizations. In addition, Article 345 stipulates that "The right to use a lot of land for construction purposes may be created separately on the surface of, above, or below the lot of land". In light of this, the right to use land for construction purposes may be defined as a right to usufruct legally enjoyed by natural person, legal person or other entities to erect and keep buildings, structures and the facilities attached to them above or under the land owned by the State or the collective organization.

This concept may be decoded in the following ways:

1.1.1   The Objects of the Right to use land for construction purposes is State-owned Land in Principle, but Exceptionally May also be Land Owned by Collective Organizations

The right to usufruct is a real right that concerns the disposal of the use value of a property owned by others. In principle, the object of a right to usufruct is a property owned by others. In the context of the right to use land for construction purposes, the object is the land. Unlike laws of other jurisdictions which attribute the land usually to individual persons, Para. 1 and Para. 2 of Article 10 of the Constitution adopts a different approach, regulating that, "Land in the cities is owned by the state. Land in the rural and suburban areas is owned by collective organizations except for those portions which belong to the state in accordance with the law; house sites and privately farmed plots of cropland and hilly land are also owned by collective organizations". This provision is further echoed by the Real Right Law, the Civil Code, and the Land Administration Law, etc. Clearly, China adopts a public ownership system regarding land resources. The land may only be owned by the state and the collective organizations, not by individual persons. Therefore, the utilization of the land, i. e. , the construction and maintenance of and to build buildings and other structures thereupon may only be carried out on the land that is owned by the state or the collectives. This obviously differs from the superficium system in comparative law, which is based on private land ownership and mostly established on the land owned by other natural persons or legal persons.

1. 1. 2   Boundary and Scope of State-owned Land and Collectively-owned Land

Under the current Chinese legislations, the object of the right to use land for construction purposes can be the land either owned by the state or by the collective organization. According to Articles 59 and 60 of the Land Administration Law, any unit or individual that needs land for construction purposes may apply for the use of state-owned land according to law, land collectively owned by farmers of a collective economic organization may be used for building township or town enterprises or houses for villagers or building public utilities or public welfare undertakings of a township (town) or village subject to lawful approval". That means, according to the current laws in China, land for construction is in principle owned by the state. However, it may also be owned by collective organization when such right to use land for construction purposes is established for building public utilities or public welfare undertakings of townships (town), or the land is used by villagers for construction of house sites.

Regarding the demarcation line of the land owned by the state and that owned by the collective organizations, Article 249 of the Civil Code regulates that, "Urban land is owned by the State. Land in rural and urban suburbs that is provided by law to be owned by the State is owned by the State". Article 9 of the Land Administration Law also defines the attribution of land ownership in the nation, stating that "Land in urban areas is owned by the State. Land in rural and urban suburbs is owned by farmer collectives, unless provided by law to be owned by the State. House sites, land and hills retained for household use are owned by farmer collectives by the state". In the Regulations for the Implementation of the Land Administration Law promulgated by the State Council, the scope of the state-owned land is further clarified. Article 2 of this regulation regulates that the following land belongs to the entire people, i. e., the State.

(1) land in urban areas of cities; (2) land in rural and suburban areas that is confiscated, expropriated or requisitioned through purchase as state-owned land; (3) land requisitioned by the state according to law; (4) forestland, grassland, wasteland, beaches and other land that is not under collective ownership according to law; (5) land collectively owned by all members of a rural collective economic organization where all such members have become urban dwellers; and (6) land previously collectively owned by farmers which is not used any longer after they have collectively moved in a lot as a result of organized migration by the state or of natural disasters and other reasons. In cases where dispute arises over the attribution of a tract of land whose status as collectively owned cannot be proved, Article 18 of Several Provisions on the Determination of Land Ownership and Use Right, a document promulgated by the former State Land Administrative Bureau on April 9, 1995, regulates that such land belongs to the state. Under the current land supply mechanism of the nation, the primary market of land for construction is monopolized by the state, and land collectively owned cannot directly be put into the market. Therefore, the object of the right to use land for construction purposes is in principle state-owned land, but may also be collectively owned land. For these reasons, the law used to term the right to use land for construction purposes as the right to state-owned construction land. The law does not prohibit the establishment of construction land on collectively owned land, but the current Chinese legislations stipulate different contents of the rights to use land for construction purposes created on land owned by different entities. The disposal power of the right to use land for construction purposes established on collectively owned land is to some extent restricted, but with the improvement of the secondary land market, the right to use land for construction purposes over state-owned and that over collectively owned land are treated equally.

1. 1. 3 Horizontal Scope of Land

In traditional civil law, scholars hold that the vast land is a non-independent thing in terms of its shape or physical characters; but under the economic conception of the society, it may still be artificially partitioned. ① As such, the land is technically divided into parcels by way of registration in accordance with its horizontal boundary. According to Article 8 of the Interim

---

① Xie Zaiquan, On the Law of Civil Real Estate (Volume One), China University of Political Science and Law Press, 1999, p. 20.

Regulations on Real Estate Registration① promulgated and implemented by the State Council, "Real estate shall be registered based on the real estate unit. The real estate unit has the exclusive code". That is to say, the land may be partitioned into independent land parcels by means of registration, after which ownership or other real right may be established on each parcels respectively.

1. 1. 4   Exclusion of Property Related to the Land

Though the right of the right holders of ownership or right to land use extends to the space above and underneath the land, such right doesn't necessarily extend to such non-essential parts of the land as taken by the Chinese law as independent thing including forests, mineral resources, cultural relics, water resources, etc. Regarding the above-mentioned things that are attached to or buried underneath the land but legally categorized as things independent from the land, their ownership doesn't simultaneously go to the right holder who obtains the land ownership or right to land use, the disposal of the right holder of the land's use value does not cover these property.

1. 1. 5   Object of the Right to Use Land for Construction Purposes also Includes the Space above and under the Land

Under the conception of traditional civil law, the ownership of the land extends upwards as far as to the outer space and downwards so far as to the core of the earth. The modern civil law system, however, has restricted the spatial radiation of the land ownership by such rules as prohibition of abuse of right, neighboring relations, etc. , on the basis of society standard. One typical example is Article 905 of the German Civil Code, which defines the ownership in its text. "The right of the owners of a plot of land extends to the space above the surface and to the subsoil under the surface. However, the owner may not prohibit influence that is exercised at such a height or depth that he has no interest in excluding them. " The Chinese law doesn't give clear definition as to what constitutes the vertical scope of the land, but such interpretation may be drawn that the land owner is entitled to the complete and eternal control over the space above and underneath the land. He may dominate or utilize such space subject to statutory restrictions and the right of a third party. Outside this scope, the right hold of the land may not exclude the interference of other persons above or underneath the land. For example, the height of the building erected by the right holder should comply with the urban policy; right holders of collectively-owned land may not exercise right regarding the underground mineral resources. Meanwhile, an owner is not entitled to enjoy such space whose height or depth doesn't allow control thereover.

The rapid advance of scientific technology, especially the progress of Modernized civil

---

① This statute Comes into effect on March 1, 2015, and first amended by the Decision of the State Council to Amend Certain Administrative Regulations (Order No. 710 of the State Council) on March 24, 2019.

engineering architectonic technology has made it possible to practice the exploitation and utilization of spaces above and underneath the surface of the land, or the so-called three-dimensional utilization of land, whose importance is growing in the modern society due to increasing scarcity in land resources. As the space has become a type of property with significant economic value, it is necessary to regulate its attribution and utilization by way of law.

Article 345 of the Civil Code regulates that "The right to use a lot of land for construction purposes may be created separately on the surface of, above, or below the lot of land". This provision stipulates the right to space utilization as a sub-category of the right to use land for construction purposes for the reason that, an right holder of the right to land use or particularly one of the right to use land for construction purposes acquires such right for the purpose of utilizing the use value of the land, e. g. , construction, cultivation, etc. , which naturally necessitates the acquisition of certain space above and under the ground. This is typical where the transfer of the right to use land for construction purposes is subject to multiple restrictions imposed by the urban planning which together with the transfer contract, clearly defines the height or depth of buildings and structures. The right holder of the right to use land for construction purposes may only use the space within the range that is specified in the planning. Otherwise, he may have violated or overridden his right. As such, the object of the right to use land for construction purposes shall include the surface of the land and space above and under the ground within the planned district. This is why we previously emphasized in the definition of the right to use land for construction purposes that the right is a right to usufruct which allows for construction and maintenance of buildings, structures and their attached facilities "above or under" the ground of the land owned by the state or the collective organization.

It should be emphasized that, under Article 345 of the Civil Code, the right to use land for construction purposes simply established regarding the space above or under the ground may involve not only land for construction but also that for agriculture. For example, the parties may construct subway, oil pipelines, and garages under farmland owned by collective organization or install pipelines, light rails, air corridors, etc. , above farmland owned by collective organization by way of establishing right to use land for construction purposes. Undoubtedly, the newly established right to use land for construction purposes in principle may not obstruct such right to usufruct as the right to use land for construction purposes or right to contractual management of land that has been created on the land surface. Such rights to usufruct as the right to use land for construction purposes and the right to contractual management of land are established by contract. In spite of the fact that parties usually have stipulated the height and depth in the contracts, the owner may still have violated the principle of good faith if a new right to use land for construction purposes is created and has obstructed the existing rights.

When determining the relations of a previous or a later established right to usufruct on the same land, the rules on adjacent relationship should be taken into consideration. On the one hand, if the later created right does not cause great impediment to the prior right, the right holder of the prior undertakes the obligation to tolerate. For example, where for running electric cables, a tract of land has to be crossed the right to usufruct who enjoys right over such land surface shall tolerate in accordance with rules on adjacent relationships if his right is not too greatly impacted. Where actual loss is caused, e. g. , during the running of the cables, the crops owned by the right holder of the right to land contractual management is damaged, then the posterior right holder shall compensate for it. On the other hand, if the impact goes beyond the scope of the due tolerance, the right holder of the prior right may request removal of impairment, or even demand that later concluded contract for the right to use land for construction purposes be invalidated. For example, where a tract of land is encircled by several tracts of land over which various rights to use construction land have already been established and the legal limit on the height of the buildings thereupon is six stories, it may be the case that upon the transfer of such land tract, parties stipulate that the right holder of the right to use land for construction purposes is entitled to utilize the space above and under the surface of land, and that the space above the land may extend to a height of eight stories. However, if the right holder of such parcel of land eventually constructs a mushroom-shaped building, namely, below the height of eight stories, the building is vertical, but above that height it expands horizontally, thus affecting the lighting of neighboring land parcels, then this clearly has violated the interests of other construction land users. The neighbors may enforce their rights in accordance with the rules on adjacent relationships.

1. 1. 6   Contents of Right to Use Land for Construction Purposes include Constructing and Maintaining Buildings, Structures, and the Auxiliary facilities

Upon the establishment of the right to use land for construction purposes, the land tract concerned is usually an opening without buildings thereupon. After acquiring his right, the right holder then starts to erect buildings, structures or attached facilities above or under the ground based on his needs. Therefore, one of the contents of the right to use land for construction purposes is construction.

It should be noted that construction is only one dispensable content of the right to use land for construction purposes. Because the right to use land for construction purposes is transferred as result of the change in the ownership of building thereupon, construction is not necessary as the existed building suffices to satisfy the need of the right holder. Of course, the right holder may as well demolish the existing building and reconstruct according to his own needs provided that the land's purpose of use is not changed. In fact, under certain conditions provided by law, such right to use land for construction purposes is a right as well as an obligation. For example, certain compulsory laws and regulations provide that right holder of the right to construction land must within the stipulated period start construction after his such right has been established according to assignment. Still, as construction is essentially a right of the right holder, it may be suspended absent the mentioned statutory stipulation.

Para. 2, Article 17 of the Interim Regulations of the People's Republic of China Concerning the Assignment and Transfer of the Right to the Use of the State-owned Land in the Urban Areas promulgated by the state council prescribes, "Should any land user fail to develop and utilize the land in accordance with the period of time specified in the contract and the conditions therein, the land administration departments under the people's governments at the municipal and county levels shall make corrections and, in light of the seriousness of the case, give such penalties as a warning, a fine or, in an extreme case, withdrawing the right to the use of the land without compensation". Here, "contract" refers to the contract for the transfer the right to use of state-owned land. Where the right holder fails to develop or utilize the land according to the stipulations of the contract, the competent agencies may order it to rectify.

Moreover, the right to use land for construction purposes is called superficies under comparative laws, a concept that originates from the Roman law. According to the doctrine that "buildings are attached to the land", the ownership of such buildings that are erected upon the land of another shall go to the land owner. To address the confusion of the land ownership and the right of use, the Roman law thereby created superficies to enable the ownership of buildings attached upon the land of another. This approach has been followed by the successors. Therefore, it may be concluded that superficies or the right to use land for construction purposes is created to meet the need of retaining buildings on the land of another. This is also the case with China. It is necessary to emphasize this point when defining the right to use land for construction purposes.

For the above reasons, I think the contents of the right to use land for construction purposes should include the construction and maintenance of buildings, structures and attached facilities above or under the land owned by the state or the collective organization.

1.1.6.1 Objects of Construction are Buildings, Structures and Attached Facilities

As a right to usufruct, naturally, the right to use land for construction purposes has contained its contents the control over the use value of the land. However, Article 4 of the Land Administration Law① clearly stipulates that "The State applies a system of control over the purposes of use of land. The State formulates overall plans for land utilization in which to define the purposes of use of land and classify land into land for agriculture, land for construction and

_____

① The law was Amended for the third time on August 26, 2019.

unused land…land for construction means land for constructing buildings and other structures, including land for housing in urban and rural areas, for public utilities, for factories and mines, for communications and water conservancy, for tourism and for military installations". As can be seen, the control of construction land user over the land is not concrete domination over the use value of the land, but such control as within the established special purpose, which is termed "ownership of structures on the land" in the comparative law. The counterpart of structures in the Chinese law are buildings, structures and their attached facilities. Since the Chinese law has adopted the word "structures" in its text, Article 344 of the Civil Code directly uses such words as commonly adopted in the Chinese legislations. Thus, it defines the purpose of use of the land over which the right to use land for construction purposes dominates by using the terms "construction and ownership of buildings, structures and their attached facilities on the land".

1. 1. 6. 2　Concept of Buildings, Structures and Attached Facilities

The terms "buildings and structures" are widely adopted in the Chinese law. For example, Article 65 of the Land Administration Law stipulates that, "No buildings or structures built before the overall plan for land utilization is drawn up and at variance with the purposes defined in such a plan may be rebuilt or expanded."

Clear definition of "buildings and structures" is nowhere to be found in the current law in China. It may be drawn from the texts of the relevant laws and regulations that the major distinction between the buildings and structures is that buildings such as residential units, units for production or business that can serve as accommodation for living or production. They further include warehouse, basement, air corridors, parking tower etc. As for structures, they are artificial fixtures other than buildings including roads, bridges, tunnels, dams, channel, water conservancy works for farmland, facilities for animal husbandry, cellars, underground pipe networks, etc.

To give full play to the utility of buildings and structures, the right holders of the right to use land for construction purposes may further establish such attached facilities on the land as facilities for electric power, broadcasting, and communication including poles, cables and transformers, sculptures, monuments, etc. In a strict sense, these facilities are not immovable properties, thus may not be categorized as buildings or structures. Nonetheless, because they are erected to assist the functioning of buildings and structures, they are accepted by law. As such, the right holder of the right to use land for construction purposes may construct and own these auxiliary facilities on the land owned by another.

1. 1. 6. 3　Plantation of Bamboo, Wood, Flowers, etc.

In my opinion, contents of the right to use land for construction purposes don't need to include the ownership of the trees on the land. This is because the right to contractual management of land and right to management of land have already included into its contents the utilization of the land for purpose of plantation. As such, any need for forestation on another's land may be well satisfied in this way. On the other hand, forestation on land for construction entails huge cost for land use, making it undesirable for one to plant trees thereupon. Still, the right holder should be allowed to plant trees and reserve areas as green belts while owning the buildings and structures. The reason is that a pleasant environment benefits the routine residence and production, thus such improvements made to the environment as planting may be deemed appurtenant acts to the construction and owning of buildings and structures. "This is not a violation against the purpose of establishing the superficies, and has by no means exceeded the scope of such right. "①

1. 2 Legal Characteristics of the Right to Use Land for Construction Purposes

The right to usufruct is a real right that dominates and focuses on the use value of a property owned by another people. As for the right to use land for construction purposes, it is the right of natural persons, legal persons, or other entities to possess, utilize and obtain profit from the use of the land owned by the state or collective organization. The right holder may take actual possession over the land for purposes of consumption (e. g. , construction of buildings for residence) or operation (e. g. , construction of commodity houses by the land developers). In light of this, the right to use land for construction purposes is established for the right holder to obtain the use value of the land, namely, to acquire the economic interests from its utilization or space for other activities. It falls into the category of right to usufruct. As jus in re aliena, a limited real right as well as a right to usufruct, the right to use land for construction purposes has the following legal characteristics:

1. 2. 1 The Object is Owned by Others

The right to use land for construction purposes is a right to usufruct and jus in re aliena, namely, is a real right over the land owned by the others (either the State or collective organization). Where the state or a collective organization intends to use its own land, the establishment of the right to use land for construction purposes is undoubtedly unnecessary; however, where such ownership confuses with the right to use land for construction purposes, the latter right shall not go extinct directly when taking into consideration of a third party's interests. As a result, it may be possible that an owner enjoys the right to use land for construction purposes over such land. For example, a right holder of a right to use land for construction purposes has its right mortgaged after the assignment. Where the land is to be taken back due to his failure in paying assigning fees, the right to use land for construction

---

① Xie Ziquan, On Real Right of Civil Law (Volume One), China University of Political Science and Law Press, 1999, p. 347.

purposes shall not terminate as a result of confusion if the interests of the mortgagee is not safeguarded adequately.

1. 2. 2　The Content is with Various Restrictions

The right to use land for construction purposes is a right to usufruct as well as a limited real right. This is reflected in the following aspects. On the one hand, its control over the object, i. e. , the land, is not complete and without time limit, but rather, subject to stipulations of the law and the contract for assignment. Specifically speaking, the right to use land for construction purposes, as a right to usufruct, exerts its control over the object not only within the scope of the land's use value but also within a certain period of time. Article 3 of the Law on the Administration of the Urban Real Estate, "The State practices compensatory and terminable system for the use of state-owned land in accordance with the law, however, allocation of the land-use right by the state under this Law shall be excepted". Article 12 of the Interim Regulations Concerning the Assignment and Transfer of the Right to the Use of the State-owned Land in the Urban Areas promulgated by the State Council stipulates that, "The maximum term with respect to the assigned right to the use of the land shall be determined respectively in the light of the purposes listed below: (1) 70 years for residential purposes; (2) 50 years for industrial purposes; (3) 50 years for the purposes of education, science, culture, public health and physical education; (4) 40 years for commercial, tourist and recreational purposes; and (5) 50 years for comprehensive utilization or other purposes". Clearly, the right to use land for construction purposes is in principle terminable. As regards such right to use land for construction purposes as established via state allocation, its term should not be simply determined by the market, neither shall its assigning fees be accordingly decided, because such right created for the state's interests or the common social benefits. In light of this, the Law on the Administration of the Urban Real Estate has made allocated right to use land for construction purposes an exception and supplement to the compensatory and terminable principle, subject to no time limit unless otherwise provided by the laws or regulations. On the other hand, the establishment of allocated right to use land for construction purposes is subject to strict restrictions. Such right without time limit doesn't mean that it stands eternal. Once the foundation for allocation ceased, the right might still terminate due to recovery by the State, or it might transform into a general right to use land for construction purposes by assignment, and become subject to time limit. Meanwhile, the right to use land for construction purposes restricts and prevails over the ownership because it is created by the owner out of his free will though the content of the right originates from and is based on certain powers of the ownership. The owner is obliged to respect such right, and not to infringe or obstruct its exercise.

1. 2. 3　The Land is for Special Purposes of Use

For the right to use land for construction purposes, the purpose of use of its object, namely, the land, is specialized. As has been indicated by the definition of the right, the purpose of use is limited to the construction and ownership of buildings, structures and attached facilities.

According to Article 24 of the Law on the Administration of the Urban Real Estate provides that, "The right of land use for the following construction land may, if really necessary, be allocated upon approval by the people's governments at or above the county level in accordance with the law: (1) land used for State organs of military purposes; (2) land used for urban infrastructures and public utilities; (3) land used for projects of energy, communications or water conservancy, etc. which are selectively supported by the State ; and (4) land used for other purposes as stipulated by laws and administrative rules and regulations". An allocated tract of land is for fixed purposes. A right holder may plant bamboo, wood, flowers, etc. but only as appurtenant use to the construction and maintenance of buildings. Use of such nature may not be made for the purpose of cultivation on the land. This is also what distincts a right to use land for construction purposes from the right to land contractual management.

It should be also pointed out that the purpose of use of the land, namely, the object of the right to use land for construction purposes doesn't include the construction of houses for residence by farmers on the land owned by collective organization. Such purpose of use is home to the object of the right to use a house site.

1.2.4　The Right is Independent

The right to use land for construction purposes is an independent real right though it originates from ownership. Its existence doesn't rely on any other rights. To be specific, first, the right to use land for construction purposes is more founded on the existence of its object, namely, the land, than on the ownership thereupon. Second, once established, the right to use land for construction purposes doesn't have to be transferred along with the ownership of the land. It may be transferred alone. Third, where the ownership on the land terminates, the right to use construction is simultaneously extinguished, but due to its own causes for extinguishment. For example, where the ownership on a tract of land owned by a collective organization terminates due to expropriation by the state, the right to use land for construction purposes thereupon is also extinguished for the same reason as the ownership being expropriated, rather than because the ownership terminates. As a result, the right holder of the right to use land for construction purposes is also entitled to state compensation. Finally, it should be noted that the encumbrance on right to use land for construction purposes cannot deny its independence. In the modern society, the boundary of a right holder's freedom is determined the moment when a particular civil right is confirmed, thus the exercise of the right is subject to restrictions imposed by mandatory laws and regulations. When the ownership is accompanied by certain obligations, it is normal for the right to use land for construction purposes to burden obligations. Neither can we take the ownership as appurtenant right. Nor can we deem the right to use land for construction purposes as subordinate for the same reason.

1. 2. 5　The Right Contains Complete Powers

As the right to use land for construction purposes is independent, it may solely exist, and be independent from the existence of other real rights regarding immovable properties or particular personalities. As such, the content of the right to use land for construction purposes is complete, which includes powers to possess, utilize and obtain profits from the land and dispose of the right itself by such way as transfer, donation, equity contribution, mortgage, succession, etc. All of the above enables the right to use land for construction purposes to enter into the market system and be circulated in the market. Under Chinese present system that the land ownership is not subject to circulation, the land market is built upon the system of the right to use land for construction purposes by structuring such right itself as well as other land-use rights. Such mechanism is made possible by the independent nature of the right to use land for construction purposes, which allows for its circulation in the market.

1. 3　Term of Right to use land for construction purposes

Before the Civil Code was enacted, laws and regulations termed differently regarding the right to use land for construction purposes. As has been mentioned earlier, the General Principles of the Civil Law adopts the term "the right to use state-owned land", while the Land Administration Law uses "right to use land for construction purposes". While the Real Right Law was being drafted, opinions as to what term should be adopted for the right to use land for construction purposes are diverse. Some scholars proposed such terms as "right to the use of sites", "superficies", etc. the Civil Code adopts the term "right to use land for construction purposes". This term is taken as a proper choice for the following reasons:

First, such choice saves the cost for popularizing the law. The existing laws in China has widely adopted this term, making it universally accepted in the Chinese mainland. Meanwhile, the existing system of legal concept system will not be greatly transformed provided that appropriate adjustment is made to harmonize the term with the development of the market economy.

Second, the term clearly indicates the purpose and contents of the right in a direct manner, adapting to the daily language habits to which the people are accustomed. It can be easily understood. Furthermore, the term is formed on the basis whereby the concept "right to land use" was reserved and further specified. It realized one step further the all-inclusive system of right to land use that was established at the early stage of reform and opening up. Under such approach which maintains the continuity of the legal system, the existing legislations and judicial practices are basically retained. In addition, it may be noted that the original meaning of "superficies" in German is "construction right", so is it with the Swiss civil law. In light of this, the term "the right to use land for construction purposes" also maintains its links with the right's origins.

Third, this term encompasses broad contents, which may be expanded to the underground and overhead space of the land. In fact, man constructs buildings as a shelter for production and living. It is impossible to keep the buildings only on the land surface. The word "construction" itself includes the utilization of the space above and under the land.

Fourth, the term "right to land use" does not emphasize the purpose and function of land use and fails to find any legal basis. During the draft and review of the Real Right Law, the principle of accurate adjustment necessitates further specification of the categories and contents of the right to land use, of which the major task lies in satisfying the needs of the market economy and the mass by establishing a more delicate legal system according to the characters of various rights. The term "right to use land for construction purposes" constitutes exactly a specification of the relatively overgeneralized concept "right to land use" in accordance with the land use and right contents. It contributes to the subcategorization of the right, thus adapting to objective needs of the legislative techniques in structuring of the Chinese real right law.

Fifth, civil laws in various nations tend to distinct different Rights to usufruct especially the independent ones based on the purpose of using land. For example, superficies aims to retain the structures above or under the land, while the jus emphyteusis aims to cultivate on the land. Thus, by its clear indication of the purpose of using land and the right's contents, the word "right to use land for construction purposes" provides a glaring contrast to the right to contractual management of land, whose purpose is majorly agricultural production. Furthermore, this concept avoids those disadvantages contained in the classifying the right according to the ownership system, thus more adapting to the development of the nation's market economy.

1. 4   Significance of the Right to Use Land for Construction Purposes

In China, the land is exclusively owned by either the state or the collective organization. However, as the state and collective organization are social organizations that can't directly utilize the land and acquire interests therefrom, they have to entrust their right to others for the purpose of such utilization, which, in market economy, may take the form of claims such as land lease or right to usufruct. According to current legislations including the Civil Code, the right to use land for construction purposes is a right to usufruct whereby the right holder acquires the use value in the land owned by state or collective organization. The right holder may possess, utilize and obtain profits from the land, dispose of his right, and exclude the infringement from others. Unlike such claims whose objects are land use as lease, the right to land use is absolute and exclusive as a right to usufruct. It is a property right with long-term stability.

It should be noted that the land cannot be circulated in the market due to legal restrictions on the circulation of land ownership in China. In a market economy, the land, as an important means of production, should be allocated by the market. In light of this, the right to use land for construction purposes is in practice much similar as the ownership although it is a right to usufruct based on the latter. Its right holder may not only directly possess, utilize the land, but also fully dispose of his right in such ways as transfer, lease or mortgage. The Chinese real estate market is established and developed on the basis of this right to use land for construction purposes, which efficiently addresses the conflict between non-transferability of land ownership and the development of the market economy. That is to say, the land system and such rights in China are founded, to a great extent, on the right to land use as the right to use land for construction purposes. In fact, under the land system of China, the right to use land for construction purposes is not registered as a derivative right, as it is the case with Chinese Taiwan, but as a basic right like ownership. In other words, other rights such as mortgages and easements, are established upon the right to use land for construction purposes which is classified into the right to land use, not on the land's ownership.

The similarity between ownership and the right to use land for construction purposes in terms of their role in structuring real right system may be further observed in these aspects:

First, in the traditional civil law, where accession between superficies and the land occurs, the basic principle is that the superficies becomes accession to the land, namely, if the superficies and the land with different owners are so close to each other that they cannot be partitioned, or that excessive expense would be consumed to separate them, ownership of the composite property on the surface shall vest in the land owner. However, in the Chinese context, since the land is publicly owned, and the right to land use that is enjoyed by citizens and legal persons bears much similarity with the ownership, the superficies shall vest in the right holder of the right to use land for construction purposes in cases of accession, if there exists such right on the land.

Second, the right to use land for construction purposes exists with continuity. As the right to use land for construction purposes shares certain characters of the ownership and serves as an important foundation for the Chinese land market, it must be a right of long-term stability. Otherwise, it will be too difficult to protect the transaction security. This aforementioned stability mainly manifests in the restrictions imposed by the law on the owner's freedom to contract by such ways as prohibiting the owner from setting collateral conditions on the dissolution of a right to land use, limiting the right holder's right to dissolve, etc. By such means, it may avoid that the land owner, by using its favorable position, unreasonably restricts the right to use land for construction purposes to such extent as it can influence the stability of land use right.

Third, the contents of the right to use land for construction purposes are extensive. Within the range of constructing and owning buildings, structures and attached facilities, the law should not impose more specific restrictions on purpose of use regarding the land for construction, unless the public interests of the society require so. The existing legislations further divide the land for construction into various sub-categories including that for commercial, tourist, residential purposes. The necessity of such restrictions is questionable. Especially, taking into consideration the current practices where every concrete matters such as the plot ratio of the land for construction requires approval, the public power or the ownership seems to have gone too far in terms of the exercise of the right to use land for construction purposes.

2. Categories of the Right to Use Land for Construction Purposes

According to the Land Administration Law, the right to use land for construction purposes, based on the different land ownership, may be further divided into state-owned construction land use right and construction land use right owned by collective organizations. The former category may further be divided into three sub-categories according to ways in which it is established, namely construction land use right established by assignment, allocation, and the right to the use of a site established by Sino-foreign joint equity ventures or foreign-invested enterprises or by a contract that is subject to administrative approval. And construction land use right owned by collective organization can also be classified into three types according to the purposes of establishment, which includes right to use land for construction purposes for public utilities or public welfare undertakings of a township (town) or village, that for township and town enterprises and the right to use a house site. However, as the right to use a house site has been taken as a separate category of right to usufruct in the Civil Code, thus it should be excluded from the right to use land for construction purposes.

The Civil Code has regulated on the right to use land for construction purposes and the right to use a house site. In the chapter on the right to use land for construction purposes, it mainly focuses on such right as acquired through assignment. In light of this, the rest of this section will mainly discuss the contents, characteristics, etc. of those rights to use construction land that are not expounded previously.

2.1 The Allocated Right to Use Land for Construction Purposes

As the case with assigned right to use land for construction purposes, the allocated right to use land for construction purposes also refers to the original establishment of the right to use land for construction purposes by way of separating it from the ownership of state-owned land. Article 347 of the Civil Code stipulates that "The right to use a lot of land for construction purposes may be created by way of transfer or gratuitous grant...The creation of a right to use a lot of land for construction purposes by way of gratuitous grant is strictly restricted". As can be seen, the law allows for establishing the right to use land for construction purposes by allocation, but such approach is accompanied by strict restrictions on the establishment and contents of the right.

According to Article 23 of the Law on the Administration of the Urban Real Estate, "allocation of the right to land use refers to acts that the people's government at or above the county level approves, in accordance with the law to allocate the land to a land user after the latter has paid compensation and expenses for resettlement, etc. , or gratuitously allocates the right to land use to the land user". Unlike assignment, allocation essentially refers to granting a land user the right to land use through administrative orders. It in fact encompasses all the means outside the market by which the right to land use is established. For this reason, Article43 of the Interim Regulations Concerning the Assignment and Transfer of the Right to the Use of the State-owned Land in the Urban Areas states that, "The allocated right to land use refers to the right to the use of the land which the land user acquires in accordance with the law, by various means, and without compensation". According to Article 2 of the Interim Measures for the Administration of Allocated Land Use Right, which was promulgated on March 8, 1992 by the former State Bureau of Land Administration, "Allocated land use right' denotes the right to use state-owned land as has been legally obtained by the land users through means other than the grant of land use right". This provision has encompassed all types of right to use land for construction purposes that are historically established by non-market means under the concept of allocated right to land use, thus distinguishing from those established by assignment.

After the founding of the People's Republic of China, the universal practice for conferring or allocating a right to land use is by means of administrative approval. This is also the only way before the reform of the state-owned land system. The procedure generally goes like this: (1) Construction units may apply for land use after acquiring governmental approval. (2) Application thereof must be submitted by the construction units to the land administration department of a local people's government at or above the county level by presenting a project plan description or other documents of approval (whereby the amount of land and the intended site has been clearly defined) issued by the competent authority under the State Council or a local people's government at or above the county level in accordance with procedures specified for state capital construction. (3) Examination, approval and allocation. After the local people's government at or above the county level has examined the application for land use of the construction units in accordance with its legal authority, the competent land administration department will confirm the land concerned and then allocate it to the construction units by means of administrative order provided that all the legal formalities are complete. After receiving the documents of approval issued by the local people's government at or above the county level, the construction units may apply for establishment registration for the right to use state-owned land. Where after approval, the land is still owned by collective organization, the construction units should go through the formalities for expropriation with the document of approval for land use and pay the land compensation, resettlement subsidy, living subsidies for the surplus labor force, and provide jobs for some of them. The ownership of the requisitioned land vest in the state and the land use entity only has the right to use. With the development and the reform of the system of land use, the scope of the application for the allocation system is shrinking. At present, only such use of land that is related to the interests of the state and the social welfare as provided for by law may be allocated after the application of the construction units and the approval of the competent governmental authorities.

The allocated right to use land for construction purposes have following legal characteristics:

(1) The object of the allocated right to use land for construction purposes is the state-owned land. As an administrative act, allocation is essentially the grant by the state to the land users certain right to land use by means of administrative orders. Since the land resource in China are respectively owned by the state and the collective organizations, the state can only assign or allocate such land as owned by the State. Should the land owned by collective organization be needed for use, the procedures for land expropriation shall first be gone through, and then the land may be allocated. The land owned by collective organizations can't be allocated directly. According to some scholars, in cases where the land is allocated, the competent land administrative department obviously assumes the identity of the administrator and the governor. This opinion is inappropriate because the foundation of allocation is that the state is the owner of the land concerned though the allocation which is conducted by way of administrative orders.

(2) The conditions for allocation are restricted strictly by the law. Before the Law on Administration of the Urban Real Estate was promulgated, according to the Land Administration Law effective at that time, the right holders of the allocated right to use land for construction purposes are mainly such legal persons owned by the whole people or with nature of urban collective economy. As the reform of the economic system, especially the system of state-owned land deepens, the conditions for allocation transform from those based on the ownership to those on the land's purpose of use, namely, based on the State's interests and public interests. According to Article 23 of the Law on Administration of the Urban Real Estate and Directory of the Allocated Land that was promulgated by the Ministry of Land and Resources on October 22,

2001, the land-use right for the following land used for construction may, if really necessary, be allocated upon approval by the people's government at or above the county level in accordance with the law:

First, land used for the State organs or military purposes. Land used for the State organs mainly includes land used by the Chinese Communist Party and government organizations and people's organizations.

Second, land used for urban infrastructure or public utilities, including facilities for water supply, heat supply, gas supply, environmental sanitation, public traffic, road and square plaza, greenbelt, etc.; land used for public utilities includes land used for non-profit post facilities, education facilities, physical exercise facilities, public cultural facilities, medical facilities, and commonweal scientific research institutes.

Third, land used for projects of energy, communications or water conservancy, etc. which are selectively supported by the state. Specifically, they include land used for petroleum and natural gas, coal facilities, electric utilities, water conservancy facilities, railway, highway, waterway communications and civil airport facilities.

It should be noted that, regarding land used for projects of energy, communications or water conservancy, etc., that are selectively supported by the state, the right to land use may be allocated. However, for such land used for projects of energy, communications or water conservancy, etc., that are conferred for profit and not selectively supported by the state, the right to land use should be allocated with compensation.

Fourth, land used for other purposes as provided by laws or administrative rules and regulations, including land for prisons, reform-through-labour farms; drug addict education center, detention houses, lockup, collecting post, etc. Land for these purposes are all for interest of the state or public interests. For this reason, some scholars proposed that the allocated right to use land for construction purposes should be called right to use land for public utilities, i. e., land for non-profit purposes such as administration, education, scientific research, firefighting as well as various facilities for public service and social welfare etc., that is state-owned and subject to no business purposes. This opinion is well grounded.

(3) Allocation is a unilateral administrative act. As can be seen from the procedures of allocation, the construction units should first apply for the land in accordance with the law, and then acquire the allocated right to use land after getting the competent local people's government's approval. In light of this, the allocation of the land may be deemed administrative acts on basis of application. Such act is conducted by the state upon the application of the land users to permit the latter's use of state-owned land for purpose of the state's interests or public interests.

(4) Allocation is without recompense. The state allocates the right to use land for construction purposes to support those projects concerning the state's interests or public interests. Such approach doesn't aim to establish or transfer the right to land use for purpose of marketization. Thus theoretically, allocation should be without compensation, and the state has not taken into consideration the value of allocated land for construction. However, cases could be that the allocated land tract is one on which there already exists a right to use land for construction purposes or that is owned by the collective organizations. Under such circumstances, expropriation or requisition becomes necessary for extinguishing the right to land use or for nationalizing it, which then will be followed by allocation. In such cases, fees for expropriation or requisition may be involved. On certain occasions, the state directly uses its budget to compensate for the expropriation or requisition of the land and pay fees for preparation work of a construction that is incurred for building electricity, running water and gas supply projects for the construction site and ensuring smooth road transport, before it allocates the "mature land" for development and construction. In such cases, the right to use land for construction purposes is delivered to the land users completely without any cost. However, in most cases, the land users shall reimburse the fees for requisition compensation. According to relevant laws and regulations, these fees mainly include fees for requisition, farmland occupation tax, the resettlement of labor force, the net expenses incurred as compensation for dismantling and removing the attached items aboveground or underground, fees for arranging houses for evacuation and resettlement, expenses for planning and design, feasibility studies, hydrological and geological research, surveys and mapping, fees for building electricity, running water and gas supply projects, and fees for the construction site and ensuring smooth road transport. Put simply, in such cases, although the land user does not pay any consideration for the right to use land for construction purposes, its acquisition of right, however, is by no means costless. In fact, it has to pay on behalf of the state for the consideration for the land owned by the collective organization. For this reason, we will argue that the aforementioned two types of allocated right to use land for construction purposes should be taken differently.

Of course, due to the restrictions set by the state on compensation fees for expropriation and requisition, the above listed fees are not equal to the market price for the acquired right, neither is there any internal link between them. Therefore, allocation is fundamentally still not a way to establish the right to use construction right for marketization.

(5) The allocated right to use land for construction purposes by allocation is a right with indefinite duration. Considering that the allocated land is for public interests, the law does not set a definite time limit on the allocated right to use land for construction purposes as it does in

the case with assigned ones. According to the relevant law and regulations, if the land user who has acquired the allocated right to use land for construction purposes without compensation ceases using the land because of moving to another site, dissolution, disbandment, or bankruptcy or other reasons, the municipal or county people's government shall withdraw the allocated right to use land for construction purposes without compensation. The municipal or county people's government may also, based on the needs of urban construction or development or the requirements of urban planning, withdraw the allocated right to use land for construction purposes without compensation. As can be seen, the state may recover the land and terminate the right upon occurrence of statutory causes.

(6) The contents of the allocated right to use land for construction purposes is subject to strict statutory restrictions. Under the current legislations, in principle, the allocated right to use land for construction purposes shall not be transferred, leased or mortgaged. Nonetheless, exceptions are made in the following circumstances. The land may be transferred after approval where a certificate for the use of state-owned land is obtained (i. e. , primary registration of the right should have been completed); where there are valid certificates of title to over-ground buildings and appurtenances thereto (i. e. , appurtenances should be concurrently rather than separately transferred), or where a contract for the grant of land use right is executed and the land grant premium is paid to the local people's government of the city or county, or is paid with the proceeds from transfer, lease or mortgage. For example, according to Article 51 of Law on the Administration of the Urban Real Estate, where a building is mortgaged, the allocated right to use land for construction purposes within the area occupied by the building shall be mortgaged along with the building. As a mortgage is to be realized only by auction, the mortgagee is entitled to priority in having his claim paid only when he has paid such amount that is equal to the land grant premium. In such cases, what is to be circulated has already become the assigned right to use land for construction purposes instead of the allocated one. Therefore, it may be concluded that the Chinese law does not grant to the right to use land for construction purposes the power of disposal.

2. 2   Assignment of the Right to use land for construction purposes Owned by the State

The assignment of the right to use state-owned land refers to the act of the state as the owner of the land who, within the term of a certain number of years, assigns the right to use land for construction purposes to land users who shall in turn pay fees for the assignment thereof to the State. The right holder of the assigned right to use land for construction purposes may have access to develop, utilize, operate and manage the land that is owned by the state.

Assignment of the right to use land for construction purposes may take such forms of open bidding via consultation, bid invitation, auction, listing, etc.

According to Article 8 of the Interim Regulations Concerning the Assignment and Transfer of the Right to the Use of the State-owned Land in the Urban Area, the agreed assignment of the right to use state-owned land means that the state assigns the right to use state-owned land to the land user by agreement for a fixed period on payment of fees for assignment to the state by the users concerned. Para. 3, Article 347 of the Civil Code provides that, "The creation of a right to use a lot of land for construction purposes by way of gratuitous grant is strictly restricted". The assignment of the right to use state-owned land may be conducted by agreement only when the law doesn't require other means such as bid invitation, auction or listing, etc.

Para. 2, Article 347 of the Civil Code states that, "The bidding, auction, or other means of public bidding shall be adopted in transferring a lot of land used for business purposes, such as for industrial, commercial, tourism, recreational, and commercial residential purposes, or where there are two or more intended users competing for the right to use the same lot of land". In accordance with the Provisions on Assignment of the Right to Use State-owned Land Through Bidding, Auction and Listing promulgated by the Ministry of Land Resources in April, 2002 (revised on September 28, 2007), assignment of the right to use state-owned land through bid invitation refers to the act of the competent land administrative department under the people's government at the city or county level publishing the announcement of tender to invite definite or indefinite natural persons, legal persons, and other entities to participate in bidding on the right to use state-owned land and determining the owner of the right to use the same object according to the result of bidding. Assignment of the right to use state-owned land through auction refers to the acts of the transferor publishing the announcement of auction for the bidder to bid in public at the specified time and location and determining the owner of the right to use state-owned land subject to the result of bidding. Assignment of the right to use state-owned land through listing refers to the acts of the transferor publishing the announcement of listing, publicizing the trading conditions of the land parcel to be transferred at the designated land trading location within the time prescribed in the announcement, accepting the applications of the bidders, updating the listing price and determining the owner of the right to use state-owned construction land subject to the result of bidding upon the expiration of the listing period or the result of on-site bidding. The transfer of business land for commerce, tourism, entertainment and commercial residential building purposes must be effected by means of tendering, auction and listing. After the supply plan on land for other purpose has been publicized, the transfer of a land parcel that has more than two potential land users shall also be effected through biding, auction and listing.

Article 348 of the Civil Code stipulates that, "Where a right to use a lot of land for construction purposes is created through bidding, auction, agreement, or other means of transfer, the parties shall enter into a contract in writing for the transfer of the right to use the lot of land for construction purposes". The contract be concluded by the land administration departments under the people's governments at city or county level and the land user. A contract for the transfer of the right to use a lot of land for construction purposes generally contains the following clauses: (1) the name and address of each party; (2) the metes and bounds and area of the lot of land; (3) the space occupied by the buildings, structures, and the auxiliary facilities thereof; (4) the planned use and zoning conditions of the lot; (5) the term of the right to use the lot of land for construction purposes; (6) the transfer fee and other fees, and the mode of payment thereof; and (7) the means of dispute resolution.

The land user shall, within 60 days after signing of the contract for the assignment of the right to use land, pay the total amount of the assignment fee. If it defaults, the assigning party is authorized to terminate the contract and may claim compensation for breach of contract. The assigning party shall, in compliance with the stipulations of the contract, provide the right to use land thus assigned. If it fails to do so, the land user is entitled to terminate the contract and may claim compensation for breach of contract. After paying the total amount of the fee for the assignment of the right to use land, the land user shall, in accordance with the relevant provisions, finish the registration thereof, obtain the certificate of land use and enjoy the right to use land. The land user also shall, in conformity with the stipulations of the contract for the assignment of the right to use land and the requirements of city planning, develop, utilize and manage the land. Where the land user fails to develop or utilize the land in accordance with the period of time specified in the contract and the conditions therein, the land administrative departments of the people's governments at the municipal and county levels shall require immediate utilization of the land user and, based on the seriousness of the case, give such penalties as a warning, a fine or, in an extreme case, withdrawing the right to land use without compensation.

Regarding the issue whether the contract for assigning the state-owned land is one of administrative or civil nature, it is disputed. The practitioners favor the view that such contract is of civil nature.

From an economic point of view, the assignment of the right to land use deals with the primary land market of land, which is closely related to the secondary land market, namely, the transfer of the right to land use.

2.3   Transfer of the Right to Use State-owned Land

The transfer of the right to use land refers to such act whereby the right holder of the right to land use transfers his right in such ways as sale, exchange, or giving as a gift, etc. According to Article 37 of the Law on the Administration of the Urban Real Estate, transfer of real estate refers to acts that a right holder of real estate transfers his real estate to another person through sale, donation or other legal means. According to the Interim Regulations Concerning the Assignment and Transfer of the Right to the Use of the state-owned Land in the Urban Areas if the land has not been developed and utilized in accordance with the period of time specified in the contract and the conditions therein, the right to use and thereof may not be transferred. A transfer contract shall be signed for the transfer of the right to use land. With the transfer of the right to land use, the rights and obligations specified in the contract for assigning the right to use land and in the registration, documents shall be transferred accordingly. The land user who has acquired the right to use land by means of the transfer thereof shall have a term of use which is the remainder of the term specified in the original contract for assigning the right to use land minus the number of years in which the original land user has used the land. With the transfer of the right to use land, the ownership of the above-ground buildings and other attached objects shall be transferred accordingly. The owners or joint owners of the above-ground buildings and other attached objects shall have the right to use land within the limits of the use of the buildings and objects. With the transfer of the ownership of the above-ground buildings and other attached objects by the land users, the right to use land within the limits of use of the buildings and objects shall be transferred accordingly, with the exception of the movable properties. With respect to the transfer of the right to use land and of the ownership of the above-ground buildings and other attached objects, registration for the transfer shall be undertaken in accordance with the relevant provisions. Transfer of divided parts of the right to use land and of the ownership of the above-ground buildings and other attached objects shall be subject to the approval of the land administration department and the housing administration departments under the people's governments at the municipal and county levels, and registration for the transfer of the divided parts shall be undertaken in accordance with the relevant provisions.

2. 4 Lease of the Right to Use State-owned Land

The lease of the right to use state-owned land use refers to the act of the land user as the lessor to lease the right to use land along with the above-ground buildings and other attached objects to the lessee for use, who shall in turn pay lease rentals to the lessor. If the land has not been developed and utilized in accordance with the period of time specified in the contract and the conditions therein, the right to use land thereof may not be leased.

A lease contract shall be signed for leasing the right to use land between the lessor and the lessee. The lease contract shall not be against to the laws and regulations of the state or the stipulations of the contract for assigning the right to use land. After leasing the right to use land, the lessor must continue performing the contract for assigning the right to use land. With respect to the lease of the right to use land together with the above-ground buildings and other attached objects, the lessor shall undertake registration in accordance with the relevant provisions.

2.5　Acquisition, Transfer and Assignment of the Right to use land for construction purposes Owned by Rural Collective Organization

Article 361 of the Civil Code stipulates that " The using of a lot of collectively-owned land for construction purposes shall be dealt with in accordance with the provisions of the laws on land administration ". According to the Land Administration Law, the right to use land for construction purposes owned by collective organization takes three forms, namely, that for public utilities or public welfare undertakings of a township (town) or village, for township and town enterprises, and the right to use a house site. Since the right to use a house site is taken as an independent right to usufruct by the Civil Code, only the former two kinds are involved in Article 361. Where township or town enterprises are established, or that land is to be used for public utilities or public welfare undertakings of a township (town) or village, the relevant procedures for examination and approval shall be gone through in accordance with the law.

Regarding the assignment and lease of the collective construction land, Article 63 of the Land Administration Law provides that " Concerning collective construction land that is for industrial, commercial, etc. operation purposes according to the general land utilization planning and urban planning and legal registered, a land owner may by means of transfer or lease consign it to a unit or an individual for their utilization, and shall enter into a contract thereon in writing clearly stating the metes and bounds, area, term of the construction, term of the use, purpose of use, planning conditions of the lot of land and the parties' other rights and obligations.

Where the aforementioned collective construction land is transferred or leased, etc. , as stated in the preceding paragraphs, the consent from over two-thirds majority vote of the villagers' assembly or over two-thirds of villagers' representatives shall be obtained.

Where a right to use a collectively owned lot of land for construction purposes is created through transfer, the right holder is entitled to transfer, exchange, offer as capital contribution, give away as a gift, or mortgage such right, unless otherwise provided by laws or administrative regulations or otherwise agreed in writing by the land owner and the holder of the right to land use.

With regard to lease of the right to use a collectively owned lot of land for construction purposes, transfer of collective construction land use right and I maximum term, assignment, exchange, offering as capital contribution, giving away as a gift, or mortgage, rules governing state-owned construction land use right for same purposes of use shall be referred to. The specific measures shall be formulated by the State Council. "

In July 2019 the Guiding Opinions on Improving the Secondary Market for Assigning, Leasing, and Mortgaging Rights to Use Land for Construction Purposes as adopted by the central committee for deepening overall reform was issued by the General Office of State Council. It is of immense significance for promoting the coordinated development of the primary and secondary land market, accelerating the establishment of a unified construction land market for urban and rural areas, and fostering high-quality economic development. The measures taken mainly include perfecting assignment rules and promoting the circulation of factors, optimizing the process for assignment of allocated land, ensuring the transaction freedom for land assignment, promoting the revitalization and utilization of existing land, loosening restrictions on mortgage holders, strongly supporting the development of private economy, allowing both natural persons and enterprises to go through relevant procedures for realty mortgage as mortgage holders in accordance with the law, exploring permitting the mortgage financing by enterprises in the social fields such as elderly care, education, etc. , with onerously acquired property such as right to use land for construction purposes, equipment, etc.

2.6 Publication for the Establishment of the Right to Use Land for Construction Purposes

Article 349 of the Civil Code provides that "To create a right to use a lot of land for construction purposes, application shall be filed with the registration authority for the registration of the right. The right to use a lot of land for construction purposes is created upon registration. The registration authority shall issue a title certificate to the person entitled to the right". In light of this, establishing the right to use land for construction purposes requires registration as a requirement of validity.

3. Rights and Obligations of the Right Holder of the Right to use land for construction purposes

3.1 Rights

3.1.1 The right holder of the right to use land for construction purposes has the right to possess, use and obtain profits from the land owned by the state or collective organizations, and has got access to construct buildings, structures and attached facilities thereupon.

3.1.2 Unless evidence indicates otherwise, the ownership of the buildings, structures and their attached facilities erected by the right holder of the right to use land for construction purposes shall vest in him.

3.1.3 The right holder of the right to use land for construction purposes may use his right for transfer, exchange, equity contribution, donation or mortgage, unless otherwise provided by the law.

The allocated right to use land for construction purposes may be transferred, mortgaged, leased only on condition that the following requirements are satisfied: (1) the land users are companies, enterprises, or other economic organizations, or individuals; (2) a certificate for the right to use state-owned land has been obtained; where a real estate is transferred, the approval from competent people's government shall have been obtained in accordance with measures formulated by the State Council; (3) possess legitimate certificates of property rights to the above-ground buildings and other attached objects; and (4) a contract for assigning the right to use land is signed and the land user makes up for the payment of the assignment fee to the local municipal or county people's government or uses the profits resulting from the transfer, lease or mortgage to pay the assignment fee. Otherwise, the allocated right to use land for construction purposes shall not be transferred, mortgaged or leased.

For the transfer, exchange, use for equity contribution, donation or mortgage of the right to use land for construction, the parties shall accordingly conclude a contract in written form. The period of time is to be stipulated by the parties concerned but not exceeds the remainder of the term of the right to use land for construction purposes.

Where the right to use land for construction purposes is transferred, exchanged, used for equity contribution or given as a gift, application should be made to registration organ for modification registration.

The buildings are transferred along with the land and vice versa. According to Articles 356 and 357 of the Civil Code, Where a right to use a lot of land for construction purposes is transferred, exchanged, offered as capital contribution, or given away as a gift, the buildings, structures, and auxiliary facilities thereof attached to the land shall be disposed of concomitantly; where a building or structure, and auxiliary facilities thereof are transferred, exchanged, offered as capital contribution, or given away as a gift, the right to use the lot of land for construction purposes in the lot of land occupied by the building, structure, and auxiliary facilities thereof shall be disposed of concomitantly.

3.1.4 Appurtenant acts. The right holder of the right to use land for construction purposes may, within the range of the foundation, carry out such appurtenant acts which are not related to the maintenance of the buildings or other structures as building walls, planting flowers and trees, practicing animal husbandry, etc.

3. 1. 5　Where for public interests, the land has to be recovered before the expiration of the right to use land for construction purposes, the right holder is entitled to get compensations for the buildings and other immovable properties on the land according Article 42 of the Real Right Law, together with the refund of the assigning fees.

3. 2　Obligations

3. 2. 1　The right holder of the right to use land for construction purposes shall utilize the land in a reasonable manner and not change the land's purpose of use. In cases where such change is necessary, the approval of the relevant administrative departments should be acquired in accordance with the law.

3. 2. 2　The holder of the right to use land for construction purposes shall pay the assigning fees according to the laws and the contract.

4.　Extinguishment of the Right to Use Land for Construction Purposes

4. 1　Causes of Extinguishment

4. 1. 1　Loss of the Land. This refers to circumstances where insurmountable natural disasters (such as earthquake, volcano eruption, flood, etc.) or human acts lead to the loss of use value in the land. Loss of the land means the loss of a right's object. Hence, the ownership or other rights in the lost land also extinguishes together with the loss of the land.

4. 1. 2　Expiration of the term for use. Article 359 of the Civil Code stipulates that "The right to use a lot of land for construction of residential buildings is automatically renewed upon expiration of the term. The payment, reduction, or exemption of the renewal fees shall be dealt with in accordance with the provisions of laws and administrative regulations. The renewal of the right to use a lot of land for construction of buildings other than residences, upon expiration of the term, shall be dealt with in accordance with the provisions of the laws. The ownership of the buildings and other immovable property on such lot of land shall be determined in accordance with the agreement, or, where there is no agreement or the agreement is unclear, in accordance with the provisions of laws and administrative regulations".

4. 1. 3　Expropriation. Article 243 of the Civil Code provides that "For the need of the public interest, the collectively-owned land and the houses and other immovable property of an organization or individual may be expropriated within the scope of authority and pursuant to the procedures provided by law. In the case of expropriation of collectively-owned land, land

compensation fees, resettlement subsidies, and compensation fees for rural villagers' dwellings and other ground attachments as well as young crops shall be paid in full in a timely manner in accordance with law, and social security premiums of the farmers whose land has been expropriated shall be arranged, their lives secured, and their lawful rights and interests safeguarded. In the case of expropriation of houses or other immovable property of organizations or individuals, compensation for the expropriation shall be made in accordance with law in order to safeguard the lawful rights and interests of the person whose immovable property has been expropriated. In the case of expropriation of individuals' dwelling houses, the housing conditions of such individuals shall also be guaranteed. No organization or individual may embezzle, misappropriate, secretly distribute, intercept, default on the payment of the expropriation compensation fees, or the like". Article 245 of the code stipulates that "An immovable or movable property of an organization or individual may, in response to an emergency such as providing disaster relief and preventing and controlling pandemics, be requisitioned within the scope of authority and pursuant to the procedures provided by law. The requisitioned immovable or movable property shall be returned to the aforementioned organization or individual after use. Where the immovable or movable property of an organization or individual is requisitioned, or where it is destructed, damaged, or lost after being requisitioned, compensation shall be made. ".

4.1.4   Administrative penalty. The right to use land may be withdrawn without compensation in the following two situations: letting the land lie waste, or violation of the stipulations for development regulated in the assignment contract for the right to use state-owned land.

4.1.5   Other Causes. These includes cases where a right to use a lot of land for construction purposes is taken back prior to expiration of its term or revoked, and the like.

4.2   Legal Effects of Extinguishment

Compensation for the superficies will be made. The state shall compensate for expropriation. The Real Right Law stipulates that, where, before the expiration of the period of time for the right to use land for construction purposes, the land needs to be taken back for public interests, compensations for the houses and other immovable properties on the land shall be paid in accordance with the law, and the fees paid for assignment shall appropriately be returned.

Upon the extinguishment of the right to use land for construction purposes, the transferor shall go through reregistration procedures in a timely manner, and the registration organ shall take back the certificate for the right to use land for construction purposes.

Section Four　The Right to Use a House Site

1. Survey of the Right to Use a House Site

1. 1　Concept and Features of the Right to Use a House Site

Article 362 of the Civil Code provides that, "A person who has the right to use a house site is entitled to possess and use the lot of land owned by the collective, and to utilize such lot of land to build a dwelling and auxiliary facilities in accordance with law". Thus, the right to use a house site is such a right to usufruct as enjoyed by natural persons (mainly the rural farmers) to construct and own houses and affiliated facilities above or under the land owned by the collective organization. According to the classification of the land's purpose of use in the Land Administration Law, the house sites fall into the category of land for construction, and the right to use them are also established for the utilization of the use value of the land owned by others. As for the contents of constructing and owning houses and their affiliated facilities, they have been covered by the last chapter in the concept of the right to use land for construction purposes, thus will not be repeated here. According to the real right system in the Civil Code and the relevant laws and regulations in China, the right to use house site has following features:

1. 1. 1　Its Subject is Restricted

The right holder of the right to use a house site is restricted into natural persons. If viewed from the current laws and regulations, it should be villagers or members of a collective economic organization in the rural areas.

The right to use a house site is a right over land owned by collective organizations. For this reason, its right holder must be members of the collective economic organizations concerned, at least so when the right is originally acquired. "Villagers outside the township or village do not obtain the subject qualifications of this right, unless they are registered as permanent residents in this township or village."[1] According to certain local regulations, technicians who are recruited by the collective economic organizations requiring to be registered as local residents, retired cadres, ex-servicemen, overseas Chinese, and compatriots of Hong Kong, Macao or Taiwan who are to resettle in their ancestral place may apply for the right to use a house site.

1. 1. 2　Its Object is Specialized

The object of the right to use a house site is restricted into the land owned by collective

---

[1]　WangLiming, Science of Civil Law, Fudan University Press, 2004, p. 335.

organization. The current Land Administration Law keeps the declaratory provision on land ownership. Article 9 of this statute states that, "...house sites... are owned by farmer collective organizations".

1.1.3   Specificality and Flexibility of Land's Purposes of Use

As regards the assigned right to use land for construction purposes, its object may be utilized for various purposes such as residence, industry, education, science, culture, public health and physical exercise, or for commercial, tourist, entertainment purposes, etc. Admittedly, the law does impose restrictions on the purpose of use, but the right holder may change it through procedures for examination and approval. In comparison, for the right to use a house site, its object may only be used for the construction of residences for villagers. Residence means houses constructed by villagers and the attached facilities refer to other buildings and utilities that are connected with the living in the houses, including garages, washrooms, methane pools, cowsheds, pigsties, etc. As the house sites are mainly used for purposes of residence and erecting attached facilities, what is constructed thereupon incudes only buildings and attached facilities. Structures are not included in that they are mostly used for production purposes (e. g. water towers, chimneys, etc.) rather than for residence. Therefore, the contents of the right to use a house site don't encompass the construction and maintenance of structures. The Notice by the Office of the Central Rural Work Leading Group and the Ministry of Agriculture and Rural Affairs of Further Enhancing the Administration of Rural House Sites issued on September 11, 2019 explicitly states that village economic collectives and farmers are encouraged to revitalize and utilize idle house sites and dwelling houses, develop agritainment, rural homestay, rural tourism, etc. in accordance with laws and regulations by means of self-management, cooperative management and entrusted management. Urban citizens, industrial and commercial capital that lease rural housing for residence or business operation must strictly comply with the Contract Law, and term of the lease contract shall not exceed twenty years. After the lease contract expires, the parties may make new agreement; on the premise that farmers' wills are respected and planning are complied with, village economic collectives are encouraged to actively and steadily conduct idle house sites consolidation, and land made available through consolidation shall be first used to satisfy farmer's need for adding new house sites, village construction and development rural industries.

1.1.4   Gratuitousness in Acquisition

The law in China emphasizes that the original acquisition of the right to use a house site should be free. The Central Committee of CPC, the State Council and some local government once proposed that fees be collected for the use of house sites in some pilot counties, and in some regions fees are collected for house site areas that exceed the statutory limits. Also, some scholars argues that the collective organization should be left for its own discretion as to whether fees should be collected for the use of house sites, because onerous use indicates the powers of the collective ownership to profit and dispose. The Comprehensive Implementation Plan for Deepening China's Rural Reform jointly issued by General Office of the CPC Central Committee and the General Office of the State Council in November 2015 proposes the fundamental thinking for the reform of house site system, establishing the reform approach of "clarifying farmers' housing property rights and exploring onerous utilization system of house sites and voluntary exit mechanism". But it is equally true that the burden's on the farmers should be taken into account. In Notice of General Office of the CPC Central Committee and General Office of the State Council on Opinions on Handling the Examination of Projects Concerning Burdens of the Farmers (Zhong Fa [1993] No. 10), it is clearly ordered that fees for the use of house sites, occupation of excessive areas in the house sites, land registration, planning, construction and management of the village or township, construction land use permit, registration for ownership of the house, etc. shall be cancelled. In cases where land reclamation fees are incurred due to occupation of cultivated land for establishment of right to use a house site, the relevant documents require that the rural economic organization should pay for them as it is the obligor for land reclamation. Such fees shall not be collected from the villagers who apply for the right to use a house site. Moreover, the land on which the houses are built belongs to the collective economic organization, and compensation for the land, young crops and fund for cultivating new vegetable fields should not be paid before the ownership of the land is transferred.

The right to use a house site makes a sharp contrast to the right to use land for construction purposes, especially to the land to use state-owned land, which is acquired with recompense and in principle established through assignment.

1.1.5 It is Subject to No Time Limit

As the current legislations have not set time limit on it, the right to use a house site doesn't terminate upon expiration of the term of the contract. For this reason, some scholars define the right as an interminable right granted by the rural collective economic organization to its members after legal examination and approval to use the land owned by collective organization for constructing residential houses. Alternatively, it may also be defined as the right enjoyed by farmer households to build houses, install living facilities, plant trees in the yard and live there permanently. The reason for its interminability lies in that the right is established for household units, which are represented by the head of the households but will not extinguish upon the death of such person or any other family member in the household.

Apart from the above mentioned, it is to be noted that under the current law in China, the circulation of the right to use a house site is legally prohibited, meaning that the right holder may not solely transfer, lease or mortgage his right to use a house site. Since the issuance

Comprehensive Implementation Plan for Deepening China's Rural Reform, circulation of the right to use a house site is no longer forbidden.

1. 2   Comparison of Right to Use a House Site and Right to Use Land for Construction Purposes

If taking into consideration the contents of the right to use a house site, then essentially, the right might as well be categorized as superficies under the conception of the traditional civil law; the land that may become its object should also be land for construction. In fact, the Land Administration Law regulates on it as a special subcategory of the right to use land for construction purposes. As has been mentioned earlier, currently, the right to use land for construction purposes includes the right to use land for construction purposes owned by the state and the right to use land for construction purposes owned by collective organizations, while the right to use a house site, the right to use land for construction purposes for public facilities or public welfare undertakings of a township (town) or village, and the right to use land for construction purposes for township and town enterprises jointly constitute the right to use land for construction purposes owned by collective organizations.

However, as has been also stated, compared with the right to use land for construction purposes, the right to use a house site does have its own characters. Even if the restrictions on its purpose and circulations are to be removed in the foreseeable further, that the acquisition of the right doesn't require compensation and that its subject is specified may still well distinguish from the right to use land for construction purposes. Therefore, the Civil Code does not treat it as a subcategory of the right to use land for construction purposes, but rather, takes it as an independent category of right to usufruct.

The original acquisition of the right to use a house site is based on the subject's status as a member of the collective economic organization. As a result, the subject is specified and limited to members of the collective economic organization. As for the right to use land for construction purposes, its establishment and transfer should be made as public as possible when taking into the account of the need for giving full play to the ownership of the state and fostering the land market. The more bidders take part into the public bidding, the more thorough the land value will be realized. Therefore, in terms of the subjects' original acquisition, that of the right to use a house site is self-enclose while that of the right to use land for construction purposes is open and publicized. The two approaches form a glaring contrast.

Different arrangement should be made for the two rights in terms of their term and payment of the lease. For example, when the subjects of the right to use a house site are members of the collective economic organization, the term restriction should be removed, while the right to use land for construction purposes should have a definite term. Another example would be that, as aforementioned, when the right to use land for construction purposes is assigned, the assigning fees shall be paid off all at once, while in the case of the right to use a house site, there shall be no compensation if the right holder is a member of the collective economic organization.

It should be pointed out that though the two are separately stipulated in the Civil Code as two different types of Rights to usufruct due to their differences, in the long run, the author opines that as the reform in rural areas deepens, the right to use a house site should obtain the power of disposal and be allowed to directly enter into the market. In terms of the system structuring, the causes for extinguishment of the right should be restricted as much as possible, so that it will become a right to land use with long-term stability and more like the ownership, forming the basis of the Chinese land market together with the right to use land for construction purposes.

2. Acquisition and Extinguishment of the Right to Use a House Site

The Civil Code does not directly regulate on the specific contents of the right to use a house site. According to Article 363 of the Civil Code, "The acquisition, exercise, and transfer of the right to use a house site are governed by the laws on land administration and the relevant regulations of the State". Obviously, the Civil Code has entrusted to the special laws such specific institutions on the right to use a house site. The contents are as follows.

2.1 Original Acquisition of the Right to Use a House Site

According to the relevant laws, original acquisition of the right to use a house site may be effected mainly by the following means:

2.1.1 Statutory Regulations

Since the socialist transformation was completed in 1960s, the system of collective ownership regarding the land in the rural areas has been established. Due to collectivization, the farmers lost their ownership in the land acquired during the land reform, which included their house sites. Nonetheless, the State acknowledged and protected their rights to use house sites, which are subject to no lease or transfer.

After the adoption of the reform and opening up policy, the law recognizes the legal status of the existing system of right to use a house site with the improvement of the legal system. The right has been established with long-term stability and gradually granted with the nature of a real right through registration. According to the relevant provisions effective at that time, "where the ownership of house sites established during the land reform were changed into the right to use land, such right to use a house site shall remain; where the local house sites have been under unified planning, the right should be dealt with as such commune members' right to use a house site as has been established after the planning; where readjustment has been made in accordance with the legal formalities, the decision in the readjustment shall prevail. The fruit trees, bamboo, wood, etc. planted on the commune members' house sites shall belong to the members".

Although relative laws and regulations have set certain restrictions regarding the areas involved in the right to use a house site, the scope of the right is still determined in accordance with the land area that is actually used under the principle of non-retroactivity. For example, according to Several Provisions on the Determination of Land Ownership and the Right to Use, which was promulgated by the State Bureau of Land Administration on April 9, 1995, regarding those house sites upon which buildings were erected and the law did not regulate thereupon (namely, before the promulgation of the Regulations on the Administration of Land Used by Villages and Towns for House Building by the State Council in February 1982) the law in principle recognized their status as the right to use a house site provided that the houses are not removed, rebuilt or renovated. After the law has provided regulation on the matter, the above issue shall be dealt with in accordance with the law, and the right to use a house site should be determined according to the actually used area. Where ownership of original house sites and houses legally obtained by non-agricultural residents (including overseas Chinese) in the countryside are not changed, the right to use a house site of such persons should be acknowledged. As can be seen, after the system of the right to use a house site was established, the law directly granted the rural residents the right to use a house site over such land as taken by them for house building provided that such occupation was not legal, or unauthorized, or made over cultivated land according to the law at that time. In a strict sense, it may be concluded that the law has recognized that right may be acquired by occupation in such circumstances.

2. 1. 2   Villager's Lawful Application and Gratuitous Transfer Legally Conducted by the Collective Economic Organizations

As members of the collective economic organizations, the farmers voluntarily transferred such means of production and existence as the land to the collective economic organizations, thus built up the system of collective ownership in rural areas of the Chinese mainland. For this reason, the rural collective economic organization which is united by the farmers of their free wills is obliged to secure its members the basic living conditions. As such, the collective economic organization undertakes the obligation to establish for and transfer to the farmers such right to use a house site and allow them to construct and maintain houses and attached structures thereupon when the latter have actual demand for dwelling.

However, to avoid the abuse of right by the rural collective economic organization in approving house sites and the consequent land waste or occupation of the cultivate land, the law sets strict restrictions on the conditions for granting the right to use a house site. It also puts an upper limit on the land area of the house sites, and requires that the decision on approval is subject to the examination of the competent government departments.

2.1.2.1 Qualifications of the Applicant

According to the current laws, administrative regulations and local regulations such as the Land Administration Law and Regulations for the Implementation of the Land Administration Law of the People's Republic of China①, etc. , the applicant or the original acquirer of the right to use a house site shall meet at least three requirements:

First, the applicant must be with certain identities. As has been mentioned above, the right holder in the original acquisition of the right to use a house site must be members of the collective economic organization concerned. According to some local regulations, this contains both existed members and new inhabitants, including technicians who are recruited by the collective economic organizations requiring to be registered as local residents, retired cadres, ex-servicemen, returned overseas Chinese, compatriots from Hong Kong, Macao or Taiwan who resettles in their native country, and other persons who are approved by the local people's government at or above the county level to be re-registered as local residents.

Second, the applicant shall have reasonable demand for dwelling. That is to say, the applicant has not ever used house sites, or his original house sites haven't met the need for reasons of marriage, etc. Examples for this may include: where rural residents have never obtained house sites, or the house sites have been taken back for building public utilities or public welfare undertakings of townships (town), or the original house sites have been taken back due to construction planning of townships; or where the adult children need to be divided from the family after marriage, but the available house sites areas are smaller than the standard, though it's not likely that all the children of a family will do so because at least one of them will be required to stay with the parents for nursing the old and the young. Such requirement is not compulsory; and the need is taken as reasonable as long as the actual conditions of the local towns or villages admit so. For example, a household with five members has a house site that takes an area of 120 square meters, and the eldest son is to be separated from the family after marriage. In such case, the need for residence will be deemed reasonable if local practices have so decided or required that every person is entitled to a house site area of 30 square meters. One should not conclude that the application qualifications are not met because the house site still suffices for residence.

In addition, Article 364 of the Civil Code regulates that, where a house site is destroyed due to natural disasters or for other reasons, the right to use the house site is extinguished. Under such circumstances, the villager who has lost his house site has reasonable demand for

---

① This statute was amended for the third time on July 2, 2021 by Order No. 743 of the State Council, hereafter referred to as "Regulations for the Implementation of the Land Administration Law".

residence, thus is allocated by the Civil Code with new house sites.

Third, there are no such statutory causes that prohibit the application. For example, Para. 5, Article 62 of the Land Administration Law stipulates that, "Application for other house sites by villagers who have sold, leased or given away their house sites as a gift shall not be approved". According to this provision, if the applicant has once obtained house sites but lost such right because of sale, lease or giving the house site away as a gift, he will no long be entitled to apply for it.

2. 1. 2. 2　Procedures for Applying for and Granting of Right to Use a House Site

According to Para. 4, Article 62 of the Land Administration Law, "The use of land for building houses should be examined and approved by the township (town) people's governments. Whereas occupation of agricultural land is involved the examination and approval procedure provided for in Article 44 of this law is required". In principle, pursuant to Article 34 of Regulations for the Implementation of the Land Administration Law, when applying for house sites, farmers in rural areas shall submit their applications in household to the rural collective economic organization concerned, and in cases where no rural collective economic organization is established, to the villagers' group or villagers' committee in which they have memberships. After applications for house sites are collectively discussed and adopted by villagers and posted within the collective in a public notice, the relevant formalities shall be performed for the examination and approval of the people's government of a town or township. Where agricultural land is concerned, the relevant formalities for examination and approval of converted use of agricultural land shall be performed in accordance with law.

It should be pointed out that the conferring of house sites is one of the ways in which a rural collective economic organization exercises its land ownership. As for the government of the town or township, it is not the land owner and functions only as the administrator who monitors the utilization and circulation procedures of the land. Matters subject to examination and approval therefore shall be restricted to matters such as whether the applications are filed in a manner of rational distribution, comprehensive development and construction with supporting facilities, whether it does keep with the overall plan and annual plan for land utilization of the townships (towns), whether any land for agriculture is used when there is waste land, etc. The purpose of the government's examination and approval is to supervise the collective economic organization and make sure that it reasonably utilizes the land, avoiding the random conversion of land for agriculture changing into that for construction. Thus, in a strict sense, such examination and approval is in fact an act of confirmation. As long as the relevant plans are not violated, the application shall not be rejected. The authority may not abuse its power and interfere with the examination and application of the collective economic organization; neither shall it examine or approve the house sites application that has been rejected by the collective economic organization. Since the allocation of house sites is one of the ways by which the rural collective economic organization exercises its land ownership, this book adopts the term "grant" that is commonly used in civil law instead of such commonly used expression as "establishment subject to examination and approval".

When granting house sites, it is encouraged to use previous house sites or idle lots in the village as much as possible. If land for agriculture is to be used for the purpose, the matter shall be subject to examination and approval in accordance with the law. Meanwhile, the rural collective economic organization shall pay expenses such as fees for land reclamation and shall not collect them from the applicant.

2.1.2.3   The Upper Limit of the Area of House Sites

Due to shortage of cultivated land in China, the law sets an upper limit on the area of house sites to make it not oversized. Under Para. 1, Article 62 of the Land Administration Law, for villagers, one household shall only have one house site. Considering that conditions vary in different regions, the limits of the area of such house sites are to be fixed by provinces, autonomous regions and municipalities directly under the Central Government.

Various provinces, autonomous regions and municipalities directly under the Central Government have fixed different upper limits on the areas of the house sites according to the local land situation, and the standards adopted are determined under the influence of different factors. In the rest of this section, we have chosen several representatives for further introduction.

In Henan, which is a very populous province, the upper limit of the house sites' area is determined according to the per capita cultivated land area and the topographic features of the province. In mountainous and hilly regions where cultivated land is scarce, the house sites are relatively thinly scattered. Para. 2, Article 53 of the Measures of Henan Province on the Implementation of the Land Administration Law (revised on Nov. 27, 2009) prescribes: (1) in suburban areas and in flat lands where per capita cultivated land area is under 667 square meters, the area occupied by the house site of each household shall not exceed 134 square meters; (2) in flatlands where per capita cultivated land area is above 667 square meters, the area occupied by the house site of each household shall not exceed 167 square meters; and (3) on mountainous and hilly areas, the area occupied by the house site of each household shall not exceed 200 square meters, and paragraphs (1) and (2) apply in cases where cultivated land is used.

According to Article 53 of the Measures of Hebei Province on Land Administration, regarding newly constructed whole houses of farmers in rural areas, the upper limit of house site area is linked to the per capita cultivated land. The utilization standard for house sites is as follows: (1) in suburban areas, the area occupied by each house site shall not exceed 167 square meters; (2) in flat areas and mountain areas, the area occupied by each house site for county or county-level city whose per capita cultivated land is below 1000 square meters shall not exceed 200 square meters, for county or county-level city whose per capita cultivated land is above 1000 square meters shall not exceed 233 square meters; (3) in Bashang area, the area occupied by each house site shall not exceed 467 square meters. Within the limit stipulated by the preceding paragraph, the people's governments of at city or county level may, based on the local conditions, specify the standard for rural house sites in their administrative regions.

In Qinghai Province, the distance from the cities and the specific conditions of the cultivated land are taken into consideration when setting the upper limit of house site area. According to Article 34 of the Measures of Qinghai Province on the Implementation of the Law of Land Administration (revised on July 28, 2006), the upper limit of house site area is determined as follows: (1) in suburban areas and towns governed by county, the area occupied by the house site of each household shall not exceed 200 square meters; (2) other areas: 250 square meters for irrigable land, 300 square meters for non-irrigable land, and 350 square meters for non-cultivated land. The limit may be adjusted reasonably higher in the fixed dwelling places of herdsmen but shall not exceed 450 square meters. Obviously, such higher upper limit undoubtedly resorts to the province's vast area and sparse population. As for Sichuan Province, it determines its upper limit of house site area according to the numbers of the residents. Article 52 of the Measures of Sichuan Province on the Implementation of the Land Administration Law prescribes that, "the standard area of a house site is 20 to 30 square meters per capita; where a household has less than 3 persons, it should be accounted as 3 persons; where a household is with 4 persons, it should be accounted as 4 persons; where a household has more than 5 persons, it should be accounted as 5 persons. Among other things, the standard area of a house site may be moderately increased for rural villagers in national autonomous areas, and the specific limit should be set respectively by the people's government of national autonomous prefectures or national autonomous counties. Where houses are expanded, the area of extension should be calculated together with the original area of the house site".

Where the whole house is newly built on land for non-agricultural purposes, the area of the house sites may be moderately increased, but the added part should not exceed 30 square meters for each household. Such practice is significant because it encourages the households not to occupy farmland.

Zhejiang Province sets its upper limit on house site area in accordance with purpose of using the land. Article 35 of the Measures of Zhejiang Province on the Implementation of Land Administration Law provides that, "···to encourage natural villages to gather around the central villages; to encourage unified housing and construction of apartments; to strictly control the use of farmland for house construction. As for the area of house sites (including houses attached to it and the yard), it shall not exceed 125 square meters where cultivated land is used, 140 square meters where other land is used, and 160 square meters where waste land or bare hillside is used in mountainous areas. The specific standard for house sites of rural villagers should be established by the local people's government at city or county level within the range stipulated in the preceding paragraph". Clearly, such approach contributes to discouraging the possession of cultivated land while boosting the development and utilization of waste land. As can be observed local governments in China have set the upper limit and standard for determination regarding the area of house sites according to the practical and local conditions.

2. 1. 2. 4   Gratuitousness and Long-term Feature of the Right to Use a House Site

China's current house site system originates in the planned economy period. Its main characteristic is "ownership by collectives and utilization by members, gratuitous allocation and long-term possession". The system whereby members within collectives are entitled to gratuitous acquisition and long-term use of house sites was originally designed to ensure the basic living conditions of farmers and assumes a social security function. This is decided by the collective nature of the socialist public ownership system. It demonstrates the State's will of maintaining social equity, and plays a fundamental role in meeting the housing needs of farmers and promoting the harmony and stability of the society. The State should stick to the long-term policy that the original acquisition of house sites is gratuitous and long-term. The reason are as follows:

First, there should be such policy consideration as safeguarding the farmers' benefits and easing their burdens. Once the rural collective economic organizations are allowed to collect fees from the farmers for use of house sites, the burden of the farmers will increase. Such measure may encourage corruption, make the society unstable, thus hindering the process of building a harmonious society.

Second, this policy contains the notion of making historical compensation. The historical compensation refers to that the system of the collective land ownership is thus formed because the farmers historically abandoned their ownership voluntarily to heed the call of the Communist Party. For this reason, the collective economic organization in rural areas should provide the land to be used for the farmers freely as a kind of compensation. The farmers private land has been collectivized into collective one, and the rural collective economic organization shall not require the farmers or their descendants to use the land with recompense while itself has acquired the land without paying any consideration. At present, with industrialization being already basically realized and the Chinese economy under rapid and stable growth, it has already become a common understanding that industry should nurture agriculture, cities shall support countryside, and the burdens on the farmers should be eased as much as possible through financial or tax measures. Under such circumstances, it makes no sense and lacks solid ground to require the farmers to pay for the use of house sites.

The original acquisition of house sites is gratuitous and may be deemed one of the ways in which the land ownership of the collective organization is realized, rather than taken as the result of governmental approval. Thus, it is referred to in this book as the "grant" of the right to use a house site. In spite of this, the collective economic organization shall still not arbitrarily take back the land on the basis that the land has been offered gratuitously. Article 36 of Regulations for the Implementation of the Land Administration Law stipulates that "Rural villagers' dwellings and auxiliary facilities thereof that are lawfully obtained are protected by law. Compulsory circulation of houses sites against the will of rural villagers, illegal taking back of house sites lawfully obtained by rural villagers, imposition of surrendering a house site as condition for rural villagers' settling down in an urban area, and forcing rural villagers to relocate and surrender their house sites are all forbidden". This is completely different from the doctrines on gratuitous acts in the civil law.

2.1.2.5　Confirmation and Registration for Establishment, Transfer, and Extinguishment of the Right to Use a House Site

The establishment of the right to use land for construction purposes requires registration. Whether this is also true with the right to use a house site is worth discussion. The Civil Code does not regulate that the establishment of the right to use a house site requires registration; neither has it stipulated that the right may be asserted against a third party after registration.

The establishment of the right to use a house site shall be conditioned upon the completion of relevant formalities for examination and approval. The parties may apply for registration. So long as the relevant formalities for examination and approval have been gone through, the right to use a house site may be deemed as established. Registration is not a necessary requirement for creating a right to use a house site. According to Article 5 of Interim Regulation on Real Estate Registration, the right to use a house site has been encompassed into to the scope of real rights in immovables that shall be registered.

Since 2010, the central government has for multiple times in the No. 1 Document of the Central Committee of the CPC made arrangement and requirements for the confirmation and registration of the right to use a house site and construction land in collective ownership. To better implement the confirmation and registration of rights to use a house site and construction land in collective ownership, the Ministry of Natural Resources edited the Q&A on Confirmation and Registration of the Right to Use a House Site and the Construction Land in Collective Ownership[1], which regulates the details for confirmation and registration.

_____

[1]　The Q&A was Issued by the General Office of the Ministry of Natural Resources on July 22, 2020 (Zi Ran Zi Ban No. 1344 [2020]).

The Notice by the Ministry of Land and Resources Concerning Issues of Accelerating the Registration and Certification to Verify the Rights to Use House Sites and Construction Land in Collective Ownership (Guo Tu Zi Fa No. 191 [2016]) stipulates that the right to use a house site shall, according to the requirement of "one household one house site", in principle be confirmed and registered under relevant households. Where conditions for separating household and building new houses have been satisfied, new houses haven been built and family members live separately but relevant approval has not been obtained, a right to use house site may be confirmed and registered after relevant formalities for land use are completed, provided that the house site occupied by the newly built house complies with the relevant planning, and the matter is approved by the rural collective economic organization or villagers' committee and posted in a public notice without being objected or validly objected. Where family members are not living separately and area of the house site in actual use does not exceed the area of land for house building calculated after household separation, the actually used area shall be confirmed and registered.

When a house site is possessed due to inheritance of houses attached thereupon, thus causing a circumstance of "multiple house sites for one household", confirmation and registration may be conducted in accordance with relevant rules and marked in the real right certificate and register of immovable property in the column of "Remarks".

Regarding the issue whether farmers outside a rural collective may obtain the right to use a house site, Several Opinions of the Ministry of Land and Resources, Central Leading Group Office for Rural Work, the Ministry of Finance, and the Ministry of Agriculture on Registration and Certification to Verify Collectively-Owned Land in Rural Areas (Guo Tu Zi Fa No. 60 [2011]) requires that confirmation on holders of the right to use a house site be strictly regulated. The right to use a house site shall be granted to member of the rural collective in accordance with the area standard set up by the provincial government. In cases of centralized relocation caused by prevention and control of geologic disasters, construction of a new countryside, resettlement, and the like, a farmer outside a rural collective may have his right confirmed and registered and be granted with the right certificate, provided that his acquisition of the house site complies with the relevant planning, and the matter is approved by the majority members of the rural collective economic organization concerned and approval for building houses in a different place is obtained from competent authority. Where a rural house site is possessed due to inheritance of houses by a local member of the rural collective who already owns another house site or a rural or urban resident outside the rural collective, registration and issuance of certificate may be conducted accordingly. On the corresponding Collective Land Use Certificate it should be marked in the "Notes" column that "The right holder is a lawful heir of the dwelling owned by a deceased member of this rural collective". House sites and houses lawfully obtained in rural areas by residents engaged in non-agriculture (including Overseas Chinese) may be registered in accordance with law, if ownership of the house remains unchanged and the matter is certified by the rural collective concerned and posed in a public notice without being objected. On the corresponding Collective Land Use Certificate it should be marked in the "Notes" column that "This right holder is not a member of this rural collective". Regarding house sites without certification on the source of right, the right to use a house site may be confirmed after the utilization history and current status of the land is identified, a corresponding certification is issued by the villagers' committee and posted in a public notice without objection for 30 days, the matter is examined by the people's government of town (township) and submitted to the people's government at county level for scrutinization and confirmation on the legality of utilization.

The above Opinions stipulate that house sites of which the areas exceed the permissible limits shall be confirmed, registered and issued with certificates according to their different historical stages. Where a house site was occupied by the house built by a rural villager before the Regulation on the Administration of Land Use for Buildings in Villages and Townships 1982 was implemented and the area of the house site has not been expanded after the implementation of this Regulation, the area in current actual use may be confirmed and registered. Where a house site was occupied by the house built by a rural villager during time when the Regulation on the Administration of Land Use for Buildings in Villages and Townships 1982 was first implemented and the time when the Land Administration Law 1987 was first implemented and the area occupied exceeds the local standard, the exceeding area that is in actual use may be confirmed and registered in accordance with the relevant State and local regulations. Where a house site was occupied by the house built by a rural villager after the Land Administration Law 1987 was implemented and the area occupied exceeds the local standard, the exceeding area that has been actually approved may be confirmed and registered in accordance with the relevant State and local regulations. If the house site area occupied exceeds the local standard, the exceeding area may be marked in the "Notes" columns of the corresponding register of immovable property and land right certificate. In the event that the household is separated and new houses built on the house site or the existing house is demolished, converted, renovated, or rebuilt in accordance with the government planning, the relevant regulations shall be complied with, and a new confirmation and registration shall be conducted according to the local area standard.

Concerning the issue whether house sites of farmers who have settled down in urban areas may be confirmed and registered, the Opinions of the CPC Central Committee and the State Council on Implementing the Rural Revitalization Strategy (Zhong Fa No. 1 〔2018〕) explicitly states that, the right to use a house site, right to contractual management of land, and right to collective income distribution of farmers who settle down in an urban area shall be safeguarded in accordance with law, farmers who settle down in an urban area shall be guided and supported in surrendering such rights under the principles of voluntariness and non-gratuitousness. Farmers' settlement in urban areas shall not be conditioned upon the surrender of their rights to contractual management of land and rights to use house sites. The Notice by the Ministry of Land and Resources Concerning Issues of Accelerating the Registration and Certification to Verify the Rights to Use House Sites and Construction Land in Collective Ownership (Guo Tu Zi Fa No. 191 [2016]) regulates that, after farmers settle down in an urban area, their lawfully obtained right to use house sites shall be confirmed and registered.

The principle of requiring no change and replacement of original certificates shall be adhered to in carrying out the confirmation and registration of the right to use a house site and right to contractual management of land. Article 33 of the Interim Regulation on Real Estate Registration provides that "All kinds of real estate ownership certificates issued and real estate registers produced in accordance with law before this Regulation comes into force shall remain valid". Article 105 of the Detailed Rules of Implementation of the Interim Regulations on Real Estate Registration provides that "All kinds of real estate ownership certificates issued in accordance with law before the Rules comes into force shall remain valid. Where real rights are not altered or transferred, the real estate registration authority shall not oblige the right holder to replace their real estate ownership certificates". Adhering to the principle of requiring no change and replacement of original certificates is a requirement from the legal system of real estate registration. It is a sign of respect for and the continuation of the previous registration results. It is also a necessity for maintaining the work stability and continuity. As such, following the principle of requiring no change and replacement of original certificates, certificates for the use of house site, collective construction land and certificate of house property right that have been respectively issued shall remain valid.

One issue to be considered is whether a right to use a house site may be asserted against a third party before it is registered. A third party is usually interpreted as a third party regarding the subject matter, i. e., the person who enjoys real right over the property. However, it should be noted that a it is impossible for a third party to obtain the right to use a house site or mortgage over the right absent the initial registration of the right. Thus, the priority among several rights that coexist on one property will not become the issue under such circumstances. In other words, if the right to use a house site is not initially registered in the first place, a third party in the sense of real right can't exist at all. If the third party is interpreted as a third person other than the right holder, then since the rural area is still an acquaintance society in China currently, the establishment registration will be of no material significance if the right to use a house site doesn't go into circulation. When such right is acquired, even if the right is not yet registered, a third party still has the knowledge that he doesn't hold it, thus is not likely to encroach upon it. As can be seen, he is obliged not to infringe upon the right, whether the right is registered or not. In light of this, it is unnecessary to stipulate that the right to use a house site may not be asserted against a third party before it is registered. The perfection effect stays with the right even if there is no registration. Of course, when the right holder of the right to use a house site intends to dispose of his right, then registration is required to safeguard the transaction security.

Article 365 of the Civil Code stipulates that "Where a registered right to use a house site is transferred or extinguished, registration of the change or deregistration of the right shall be made in a timely manner". The author's interpretation of this provision is that, registration is required for the disposal of the right to use a house site. Once the right is registered it, can be transferred and transfer registration should be handled accordingly. Nonetheless, the Civil Code doesn't provide whether such registration will case a change in the real right, or it only perfects a third party in good faith. In my opinion, this registration shall be a requirement of perfection.

2. 2   Successive Acquisition of the Right to Use a House Site

Current Chinese legislations have not stipulated the issue whether a right to use a house site may be separately circulated, but the ban at policy level has already been lifted. At present, circulation of houses privately owned by villagers in rural areas are not forbidden by law. The Several Opinions on Registration and Certification to Verify Collectively-Owned Land in Rural Areas (Guo Tu Zi Fa No. 60 [2011]) explicitly stipulates that where a rural house site is possessed due to inheritance of houses thereto, registration and issuance of certificate may be conducted accordingly. On the corresponding Collective Land Use Certificate it should be marked in the "Notes" column that "The right holder is a lawful heir of the dwelling owned by a deceased member of this rural collective". The Notice by the Ministry of Land and Resources Concerning Issues of Accelerating the Registration and Certification to Verify the Rights to Use House Sites and Construction Land in Collective Ownership (Guo Tu Zi Fa No. 191 [2016]) regulates that, where a rural house site is possessed due to historical acceptance of assignment or gift concerning the house thereupon and the area occupied exceeds the local standard, confirmation and registration of the right shall be conducted in accordance with the policies and rules effective at the time when the assignment or gift was accepted which regulated house sites area exceeding standard. In light of this, a right to use a house site may also be acquired through the concomitant transfer of the house built thereupon. Moreover, as the Chinese law recognizes private houses as inheritable property, a right to use a house site may also be acquired through inheritance of the house built upon the house site.

3. Contents, Circulation and Restrictions of the Right to Use a House Site

3.1 Contents of the Right to Use a House Site

The right holder of the right to use a house site enjoys the right to possess, utilize and obtain profit from the house sites. He may use the land for constructing residences and the facilities attached to them and obtain such gains derived from the land including yields of economic crops such as fruit trees that are planted in the openings of the house sites (e. g. , around the house).

3.2 Circulation of the Right to Use a House Site

As regards whether the right to use a house site contains the power of disposal, or in other words, whether this right is transferrable, further discussion is required. It should be noted that the current law in China has set some restrictions on the disposal of this right, which include the following a few aspects:

3.2.1 Separate Disposal and Circulation

The Civil Code does not explicitly regulate on the issue where the right to use a house site may be disposed of separately. What is regulated is that this right may be disposed of together with the houses on the house sites. Article 363 of the Civil Code stipulates that "The acquisition, exercise, and transfer of the right to use a house site are governed by the laws on land administration and the relevant regulations of the State".

Para. 2, Article 399 of the Civil Code explicitly forbids the mortgage of the right to use a house site. This indicates that the right to use a house site may not be separately disposed of, unless otherwise provided by law.

The above rules proposed an approach for circulation of the right to use a house site. The laws on land administration and the relevant regulations of the State may make new arrangement for the acquisition, exercise, and transfer of the right to use a house site. Viewed from China's current policy on this right, "separation of three rights" was stated in the Opinions of the CPC Central Committee and the State Council on Implementing the Rural Revitalization Strategy (2018). This is the first time it is officially mentioned in a document of the CPC Central Committee The Opinions stated that the three rights are the ownership, membership right and utilization right. Collective ownership on the house sites shall be implemented, the farmer households' membership right over the house sites shall be stabilized, and the control over the right to use a house site and farmer's houses shall be loosened appropriately. The No. 1 Central Document of the year 2021, the Opinions of the CPC Central Committee and the State Council on Comprehensively Promoting Rural Revitalization and Accelerating the Modernization of Agriculture and Rural Areas, proposed to steadily and properly advance the pilot reform on house site system in rural areas, explore the effective way of realizing the separation of ownership, membership right and utilization right concerning house sites, and push through the reform of the three-right separation system on house sites. The Opinions of the CPC Central Committee and the State Council on Effectively Completing the Key Work for Comprehensively Promoting Rural Revitalization in 2022 proposed to steadily and properly advance pilot reform on house site system in rural areas, carry out the house site confirmation and registration featuring integration of buildings and land in accordance with the requirements and norms, steadily and orderly push through the marketization of collective construction land in rural areas, and foster the mortgage financing of collective construction land. Moderately loosening the control over right utilization right is a key to the reform of the three-right separation system on house sites. After the control on it is loosened, the utilization right can function to optimize the resource allocation and protect the farmers' property right. Such value needs circulation and transactions to be realized. Together with reforms on the non-gratuitous utilization and voluntary surrender of house sites, the transfer channel between house site and collective construction land shall be opened up to revitalize the policy system for idle house sites and farm houses and grant complete rights and abilities to the right holders.

Against the background where people in rural areas emigrate from rural regions to settle down in urban areas in a large scale, the law should, where possible, create the conditions for the farmers to start their business in the cities. If the circulation of house sites is strictly restricted, the transfer price can obviously get lower because eligible transferees are limited to rural residents. This is not conducive to fully realize the exchange value of the right to use a house site. It can also make it more difficult for real estates in rural areas to enter into the market. As a result, houses in rural areas could be left idle for a long time because many farmers who settle down in urban areas may have purchased realties there thus leaving their houses in rural areas idle, and at same time, compulsory taking back of such idle houses and house sites is not allowed by policy. Hence, if farmers are not allowed to assign their houses, a huge waste could be caused to the land resources, which is already in scarcity in China. Moreover, the first great gap faced by the rural population when adapting to the cities is the great disparity in economic status. Restricting the circulation of house sites would set obstacles for the rural population to acquiring the funds needed to start business or settle down in urban areas through disposing of their land and houses by means such as sale or mortgage, etc. This fact is especially important if one takes into consideration the under developed financing industry in China's rural areas. In addition, against the background that the social security system in rural areas is still incomplete, overstrict restrictions on the circulation of house sites may lead to farmer's inability of raising funds needed in cases of severe diseases or children's education.

Pilot sites have also been established in provinces such as Guangdong for the circulation of the right to use house sites, which is already an irreversible trend for the Chinese law. To sum up, the author would suggest that the restrictions on the right to use house sites be removed so that this right's power of disposal may be further strengthened. Allowing the assignment and mortgage of the right to use house sites can also serve to building up the Chinese land market as an ownership-like right together with the right to use construction land.

3.2.2 Restrictions on New Applications after the Disposal

Once a right holder has disposed of his right to use a house site, he may not apply for a new right. Para. 5, Article 62 of the Land Administration Law prescribes that, "Applications for other house sites made by villagers who have sold, leased or given away their house sites as gift shall not be approved". This provision contributes to achieving fairness in the original acquisition of the right to use a house site.

3.2.3 Restrictions on the Transferee of a House Site and Loosened Control in Policy

In the Notice of the General Office of the State Council on Strengthening Administration in Land Assignment and Strictly Prohibiting Land Speculation, which was promulgated on May 6, 1999, clearly emphasizes that, "Houses of the farmers shall not be sold to urban residents, nor shall the land owned by the rural collective organizations be used by city residents for building houses. The competent department shall not issue any land-use certificate or certificate of title to houses that are illegally built or purchased". This provision has basically prohibited the circulation of the right to use a house site and the transfer of houses in the rural areas. Regarding this issue, the Civil Code has taken a relatively conservative attitude by stipulating that circulation of the right to the use of house sites "are governed by the laws on land administration and the relevant regulations of the State". For loosened control in policy please refer to Part 3 of this Section.

3.2.4 One household may possess one house site, of which the area is restricted

As this issue has already been covered by the previous discussion, here we will not go over it again.

3.3 Alterability of a House Site's Purpose of Use

The right to use a house site is established to meet the reasonable need of villagers for residence. Thus, such need shall constitute a precondition for the allocation of the right. However, if, after the right to use a house site has been established, the villager manages to secure himself accommodation in some other way so as to build a workshop on his house site, such practice shall also be allowed in light of developing the rural economy. The Notice by the

Office of the Central Rural Work Leading Group and the Ministry of Agriculture and Rural
Affairs of Further Enhancing the Administration of Rural House Sites issued on September 11,
2019 explicitly states that village economic collectives and farmers are encouraged to revitalize
and utilize idle house sites and dwellings, develop agritainment, rural homestay, rural
tourism, etc. in accordance with laws and regulations by means of self-management,
cooperative management and entrusted management. Urban citizens, industrial and
commercial capital that lease rural housing for residence or business operation must strictly
comply with the Contract Law. Hence the purpose of use of a house site could be altered
based on practical need.

4. Concept and Definition of Ownership, Membership right and Utilization Right of House Sites under the System of "Separation of Three Rights"

4.1　Ownership of a House Sites

The ownership of a house site belongs to the relevant rural collective economic organization
instead of the holder of the right to use the house site. Although the utilization right of a house
site is a type of real right, it is in essence categorized as a right to use collectively owned rural
land, which has a specific definition in China. It is stipulated by relevant statute that except for
allocated right to use state-owned land, the right to land use must be acquired through
assignment, transfer or lease, which essentially are all transaction methods for exchanges at
equal values. The right to the use of house sites is mainly practiced in rural areas. After the
right to use a house site is stipulated by the Real Right Law as a particular form of usufructuary
right, the "right to use a house site" and the "right to land use" is jurisprudentially
distinguished, so that the right to land use can no longer replace the right to use a house site.
Because according to Article 10 of the Constitution of the People's Republic of China, "…house
sites and privately farmed plots of cropland and hilly land are also owned by collectives", the
farmers' house sites constitute a part of the collectively owned land, which could be further
divided into farmland and land for rural construction purpose. The house sites shall then fall
into the latter category.

4.2　Membership Right of House Sites

In the No. 1 Central Document of the year 2018, i. e., the Opinions of the CPC Central
Committee and the State Council on Implementing the Rural Revitalization Strategy, it is
proposed to "explore the separation of 'three rights', i. e., ownership, membership right and
utilization right of house sites". The idea of "separation of three rights" is thereby officially

proposed. Regarding the connotation of the "membership right", the laws and normative documents have not provided any clear definition. Neither have the practitioners and scholars reached any consensus in this regard. In respect of what is a membership right of house sites, the scholars have presented the proprietary right theory, compound right theory, and the theory of residual right after circulation of the right to use house sites. However, according to the thinking of Pilot Program Plan for Deepening the Reform of Rural House Sites System to "protect the membership right and loosen the control over the utilization right", the membership right guarantees the households' right to acquire house sites, and constitutes a component of the membership right in collective economic organizations.

According to the policy goal of the "separation of three rights" concerning house sites and in view of the relevant provisions of the Civil Code and Land Administration Law, the membership right of house sites is neither a proprietary right nor a compound right, and much less the residual right after circulation of the right to use house sites. It is in fact a qualification enjoyed by a household to apply for the construction of residential buildings and attached facilities over the collectively owned land because of its particular identity as a member of the collective economic organization. It is not a new right, and shall not obtain the status of a right.

The membership right does not embody the element of specific interest, which is an integrant part of a right. It only means the possibility of realizing an interest. As an expectant real right, the membership right of house sites is a type of households' membership right that specially refers to a household's qualification for apply a house site that is obtained because of its status as a member of the collective.

That a member of a collective obtains the right to use of a house site over collectively owned land because of its membership is a result of the separation of powers of possession and utilization from the power of collective land ownership. Such powers constitute the contents of the right to use a house site and these contents further decide the nature of this right, of which at the core is the right to construct and retain the residential buildings and attached facilities over the collectively owned land. For the said reasons, the membership right does not compose the contents of the right to use a house site or show the nature of the right.

4. 3　Utilization Right of House Sites

It is disputed among scholars as to how the nature of membership right and utilization right of house sites under the system of "separation of three rights" should be determined. The first opinion is that both rights are usufructuary right. According to scholar Zhiguo Xi, both membership right and utilization right of house sites under the system of "separation of three rights" are usufructuary rights. The second view combines the usufructuary right and creditor's right. It is argued by Zhihong Song that the membership right of house sites under the system of "separation of three rights" equals the right to use house sites stipulated under the current laws, which is a type of usufructuary right, whilst utilization right of house sites under the system of "separation of three rights" is a (statutory) right to lease, which is a type of creditor's right. According to the third opinion, multiple types of rights may coexist. The membership right and utilization right of house sites under the system of "separation of three rights" shall not necessarily be categorized as either both are usufructuary rights or one is a usufructuary right and the other a creditor's right or membership. On the contrary, a usufructuary right, a creditor's right or membership may coexist. [1]

The author notices that it is pointed out by the Opinions of the CPC Central Committee and the State Council on Implementing the Rural Revitalization Strategy to "improve the policies on idle house sites and farm houses in rural areas, explore the separation of 'three rights', i. e. , ownership, membership right and utilization right of house sites, solidify the collective ownership of house sites, safeguard the households' qualifications concerning house sites and the farmer's proprietary rights on houses, moderately loosen the control over house sites and the farmer's utilization rights on house…" Here, the "separation of three rights" does not mean the "creation of three rights", and the house site system per se shall include three bundles of rights: ownership, membership right and utilization right. As such, connotation and denotation of the right to use a house site shall be the same under the system of "separation of three rights" as in Articles 362 to 365 of the Civil Code and Article 62 of the Land Administration Law, but the function of this right under the system of "separation of three rights" must be strengthened.

5. Extinguishment of a Right to Use a House Site

According to the Civil Code and the relevant laws and regulations, the right to use a house site may terminate for the following reasons:

5. 1   House Sites Used for Building Public Utilities or Public Welfare Undertakings of a Township(town) or Village

Where the house site is used for build public utilities or public welfare undertakings of a township(town) or village, right to use house site terminates accordingly. This is very similar to the situation whereby the right to use land for construction purposes terminates because of state requisition. Where the right to use a house site is taken back for building public facilities, the right holder should be allocated a new site, and the all the attachment above the ground should be compensated accordingly. Moreover, to prevent the collective economic organizations from abusing its right and taking advantage of this provision, thus harming the villager'' interests

---

[1]   Qingmei Jiang, Legal Research on the System of "Separation of Three Rights" of House Sites, Pengpai Governmental Affairs, https://m. thepaper. cn/baijiahao_15347769, last accessed on November 6, 2022.

the standard of compensation for the superficies might as well be raised, so that the application of such provision may be reduced by way of economic measures.

5.2 Not Using the Land in Accordance with the Approved Purposes

As mentioned earlier, restrictions on the house sites' purposes of use should be removed, and house sites should not be taken back for the reason that their purposes of use have been changed. Where the applicant has no need for residence and conceal such facts by fraud or collude with persons concerned, thus has acquired the right to use a house site, the collective organization may consider withdrawing the grant and recovering the house site without making compensation. However, the right to use a house site should not be taken back because the residence purpose is changed during the exercising of the right.

Of course, the need for residence here referred to must be reasonable. Where a villager applies for the right to use a house site after dividing from the family and establishing a new household in accordance with the local customs but voluntarily continues living with his parents and siblings in narrow space while using the newly acquired land for the establishment of enterprise, such practice should also be legally allowed and the right to use a house site shall not be taken back.

5.3 The House Site is Vacant for a Long Time

Article 52 of Several Provisions on the Determination of Land Ownership and Use Right promulgated by the State Land Administrative Bureau on March 11, 1995 prescribes that "Where the house site is vacant, or that the house thereupon has been collapsed or dismantled for two years without being reutilized, the right to land use is not established. Where the establishment of such right has been confirmed, the collective organization should report to the people's government at the county level for approval of the deregistration thereof and the recovery of the land". Similar rules may also be found in local regulations. For example, Article 20 of Measures of Henan Province on the Administration of Rural House Sites stipulates that, "where houses have not been built for more than one year after the approved house site has been demarcated, the document of approval should be deregistered by the registration organ who issued it, and the right to land use should be taken back".

As regards farmer households who have settled in cities, their right to use a house site may be taken back if the house site has been vacant for a long time and the right holder cannot be reached. Nonetheless, if the household returns and resettles in the local, a new house site shall be allocated to it.

5.4 Excessive Area of the House Site

Article 62 of the Land Administration Law emphasizes that: "For villagers, one household shall only have one house site". Article 51 of Several Provisions on the Determination of Land Ownership and Use Right prescribes that, as regards house sites whose areas are beyond prescribed standard before the promulgation of the relevant laws or as a result of succession or assignment of houses, and for house sites owned by villagers who have not divided from the family though qualified under local administrative regulations and whose areas exceed the upper limit of single house site area but is smaller than the aggregate limit of the areas if the family have been divided, the amount of the area that exceeds the prescribed standard may be registered in the land registration card and the land certificate. When the right to land use is later reconfirmed according to the area standard set by the local government under such circumstances as building of houses upon family division, demolition, reconstruction, renovation, or reconstruction due to the government re-planning of existing houses, the exceeding area should be returned to the collective organization. Thus, it may be concluded that where the area of the original house site exceeds the prescribed standard, the right to use a house site regarding the exceeding part should be taken back after the house thereupon is lost.

5. 5   Loss of the House

Under Article 48 of Several Provisions on the Determination of Land Ownership and Use Right, where house site of a non-agricultural resident (including overseas Chinese) is not allowed for reconstruction after the house thereupon is demolished, the right to land use should be taken back by the collective organization. In fact, the right holder of the right to use a house site is not in the place to decide whether the reconstruction is to be approved. As such, the loss of the house has become a cause for the extinguishment of the right.

5. 6   Loss of the Land

The right to use a house site is a right to usufruct. As its right holder acquires the use value of the house site, the right is not subrogative. Where the house site disappears, the right to use it naturally comes to an end. As such, Article 364 of the Civil Code prescribes that "Where a house site is destroyed due to natural disasters or for other reasons, the right to use the house site is extinguished. A new house site shall be allocated in accordance with law to the villagers who have lost their house site".

Apart from the cases mentioned above, the right to use a house site may also extinguish because of the expropriation of the State. Of course, the expropriation of the State should be restricted within the purpose of the public interests. Meanwhile, the standard for compensation in such case should gradually be raised according to the nation's social and economic progress and the specific local conditions. Where a land is no longer used due to revocation or migration, the land owner may take back the right to land use, thereby causing the extinguishment of the right to use a house site.

In addition, Article 32 of the Succession Law prescribes that "An estate which is left with neither a successor nor a legatee shall belong to the state or, where the decedent was a member of an organization under collective ownership before his or her death, to such organization". According to Article 35 of the Regulations for the Implementation of the Land Administration Law, the State allows farmers in rural areas who settle down in an urban area to voluntarily and non-gratuitously surrender their house sites in accordance with law. The house sites surrender belong to the collective organization concerned and the original right to use a house site shall extinguish.

The right to use a house site is a right, thus, may be abandoned. When a right holder voluntarily gives back the house site, the right terminates. The intention of the abandonment should be manifested to the collective economic organization.

Section Five   Right of Habitation

The Report at the 19th National Congress of the CPC pointed out that we will move faster to put in place a housing system that ensures supply through multiple sources, provides housing support through multiple channels, and encourages both housing purchase and renting. To achieve the goal of meeting the housing needs of all the people, the Chinese legislator finds it necessary to establish the system of the right of habitation. The Civil Code established the right of habitation. According to Article 366 of the code, "A person with a right of habitation is entitled to the right to usufruct of possessing and using another person's dwelling as agreed in the contract, so as to meet his needs of habitation". In addition, the right of habitation distinguishes itself from the easement by its lack of transferability and inheritability (Article 369 of the Civil Code). The right of habitation essentially reflects the utilization of property. Legislative practices of various jurisdictions around the world on the right of habitation seem to demonstrate a tendency for simplicity. This reason therefor is that the relevant provisions concerning the right to usufruct usually apply to the creation, effects and extinguishment of the right of habitation mutatis mutandis. ① The Civil Code only has six provisions (Articles 366 to 371) on the right of habitation, stipulating the definition, establishment and extinguishment of this right.

1. Definition and Establishment of the Right of Habitation

Right of Habitation is defined as a right to usufruct of possessing and using another person's

---

① See Article 625 of the French Civil Code, Para. 1, Article 1093 of the German Civil Code, Para. 3, Article 776 of the Swiss Civil Code, Article 1026 of the Italian Civil Code, Article 1490 of the Portuguese Civil Code, Articles 528 and 529 of the Spanish Civil Code, and Article 812 of the Chilean Civil Code.

dwelling so as to meet his needs of habitation. Here, the power of "possessing and using" not only encompasses acts of actual dwelling, namely, meeting the needs of habitation, but also other acts conducted by the right holder to achieve the aim of habitation, such as storing necessary articles of daily use, maintenance of the dwelling for better habitation, etc. In essence, the right of habitation is a right of using another person's dwelling for the purpose of meeting one's own needs of habitation. It is categorized as a right to usufruct in the Chinese real right system. Essentially, the right of habitation reflects the utilization of property, thus falls into the scope of proprietary rights. Confirming the proprietary nature of this right not only provides institutional safeguard for the citizens' diversified uses of their property and the satisfaction of various parties' needs, but also forms a basis for applying various modes that have newly emerged such as the house-for-pension scheme, timeshare, etc.

The application right of habitation in Chinese law should not be constrained in traditional areas such as marriage and succession, but should expand to investment areas where uses of houses are diversified, and even to reform government-supported residential housing such as economically affordable housing, housing with co-ownership, public rental housing, etc. , so as to give full play to the institutional function of the right of habitation and achieve the diversified housing need of social subjects. This system demonstrates the fundamental spirit underlying the Civil Code of comprehensively safeguarding citizens' right. That said, in practice, practices of such using the right of habitation to avoid debts or circumvent the court's enforcement must be combatted.

Viewed from the provisions in the Civil Code, the right of habitation may be created in two ways: by contract or by will.

1. 1   Establishment by Contract

Article 367 of the Civil Code provided that, to create a right of habitation, the parties shall enter into a contract on such a right in writing. A contract on a right of habitation generally contains clauses such as the name and address of each party, the location of the dwelling, the conditions and requirements for the habitation, the duration of the right of habitation, and the means of dispute resolution.

A contract on a right of habitation may take the following forms:

First, the owner of the dwelling and the buyer may enter into a contract on a right of habitation. This is a common form.

Second, the owner of the dwelling and the buyer may enter into a sales contract and a contract on a right of habitation at the same time. Under this form, the owner retains a right of habitation when selling the dwelling to the buyer.

Third, the owner of the dwelling may assign his ownership to the buyer and establish a right of habitation for a third party.

Fourth, the owner of the dwelling may assign his ownership to the buyer and require the buyer to establish a right of habitation for a third party.

Fifth, the owner of the dwelling and a third party may enter into a contract on a right of habitation whereby a right of habitation is established for such third party. For instance, an ownership creates a right of habitation for his old housekeeper.

With respect to the registration of the right of habitation, one may note that this right is a real right established in immovable property, which, according to the Chinese law on changes to real rights, takes effect upon registration. Hence, the conclusion of a contract on a right of habitation between the parties cannot give rise to the creation of the right; registration is required. Of course, the contract takes effect upon the time when the parties all sign, stamp, or put their fingerprints on the written agreement. According to Article 374 of the Civil Code, without registration, a right of habitation cannot be asserted against a bona fide third person, so as to protect the transaction order. Article 368 of the Civil Code stipulates that to create a right of habitation, an application for the registration of the right shall be filed with the registration authority. The right of habitation is created upon registration.

1.2 Establishment by Will

Establishing a right of habitation by will is a common practice among countries and regions around the world. The Civil Code also adopts will as a way of creating a right of habitation.

As to when a right of habitation is created in cases of establishment by will, Article 368 of the Civil Code stipulates that "Where a right of habitation is created by will, the relevant provisions of this Chapter shall be applied mutatis mutandis". Viewed from this provision, the provisions regulating the non-transferability and non-inheritability, succession, gratuitous establishment, causes for extinguishment, and requirement for written form of the right of habitation may be applied mutatis mutandis in cases where the right is created by will. One issue worth discussing is whether the provisions on registration may also be applied mutatis mutandis. In other words, where a right of habitation is created by will, should an application for the registration of the right be filed with the registration authority? The author holds the view that the answer should be negative. Be it the mode of registration as a validity requirement or the mode of registration as a perfection requirement, the common application basis is the change of real rights caused by bilateral civil juristic acts. Although a will is a civil juristic act, the cause for the will's coming into effect is the death of the testator. In other words, the cause for the change in real right is the death of the testator. As such, where a right of habitation is created by will, Article 230 of the Civil Code may be applied mutatis mutandis. When the will takes effect, namely, when the succession opens, the right of habitation is thus created and the registration is not a requirement for establishment. Otherwise, if taking the approach of registration as a validity requirement the right of habitation established by the will would fall through if the successor refuses to complete the registration, which is against the testator's will.

Concerning the forms and effects of such type of will, the author notes that a unilateral civil juristic act, and the Civil Code did not stipulate the forms and effects of wills establishing a right of habitation. The relevant provisions of the book on succession in the Civil Code regulating the forms and effects of wills should be applied mutatis mutandis here. Articles 1134 to 1139 in Book Six Succession of the Civil Code stipulate that wills may take forms of holographic wills, wills written on behalf of the testator, will in printed form, wills made in the form of an audio or video recording, nuncupative wills, notarized wills, etc. Considering that Article 367 of the Civil Code requires the parties to enter into a contract in writing for the creation of a right of habitation and according to the understanding of "mutatis mutandis", wills establishing the right of habitation shall also be in writing. Their effects shall be determined pursuant to that of civil juristic acts.

2. Subjects of the Right of Habitation

Subject of the right of habitation refers to the person entitled to the right. The Civil Code does not define the scope. The author opines that the subjects of the right of habitation shall be confined to natural persons and not include legal persons or unincorporated organizations. Article 367 of the Civil Code uses the term "the parties", which could encompass both legal persons and unincorporated organizations. However, these two types of civil persons may only be subjects establishing a right of habitation, not subjects of the right of habitation.

2. 1   Scope of Natural Persons Eligible for being Subjects of Right of Habitation

Regarding the issue whether the scope of natural persons that are eligible for being subjects of the right of habitation shall be restricted, the author opines that the answer should be no. Although the law explicitly states that the purpose of establishing the right of habitation is to meet the needs of habitation, it is undeniable that persons with houses may also have needs in this regard. There seems no convincing reason for denying the establishment of the right of habitation by persons with houses.

Where a right of habitation is established on a dwelling in rural areas, it could be questionable whether the person entitled to the right shall be limited to villagers of the same village. Based on the current laws and policies, assignment of houses in rural areas is still subject to certain restrictions. They may only be assigned among members within the same rural collective economic organization. However, the establishment right of habitation does not involve assignment of the houses. Hence, there seems no reason for forbidding the establishment of such right for a person who is not member of the same rural collective economic organization. It should be noted that an owner of a rural dwelling shall not apply for a new house site after establishing a right of habitation for another person on the current house site. This is because Para. 5, Article 62 of the Land Administration Law prescribes that, "Applications for other house sites made by villagers who have sold, leased or given away their house sites as gift shall not be approved". Since the establishment of a right of habitation by the owner of the dwelling is similar to leasing in that both transfers the utilization right on the dwelling, it shall also subject to the restriction that "applications for other house sites shall not be approved".

Concerning the issue whether an owner may establish a right of habitation for more than two natural persons for their joint enjoyment, the author opines that the answer should be positive. A right habitation may be established for more than two persons for their joint enjoyment. Here the joint enjoyment is a quasi co-ownership, or more specifically, a quasi joint co-ownership. The author holds the view that the person with the right of habitation may cohabit with other persons, but such cohabitants are not holders of the right of habitation. Where the parties explicitly agree that the dwelling may only be dwelled by the person with the right of habitation, other persons may not cohabit.

3. Objects of the Right of Habitation

Regarding the object of the right of habitation, Article 367 of the Civil Code limits it as "dwelling". Nonetheless, since the purpose of establishing the right of habitation is to "meet the needs of habitation", instead of for office or business, even buildings or houses may only be used for habitation. As such, in the setting of the right of habitation, there is no substantial difference in building, houses or dwellings. These terms are interchangeable. Of course, the direct use by the Civil Code of the term "dwelling" can more vividly demonstrate the purpose of establishing the right of habitation. In terms of the scope of dwellings, be it dwellings in urban areas or in rural areas, regardless of whether subject to the ownership of a building's units or not, they may all be objects of the right, except those houses for business purposes which shall be excluded therefrom. The location of the dwelling refers to the scope of the right's object. It may also be termed as the scope of the rights enjoyed by the person with right of habitation. The location of the dwelling shall be negotiated by the parties and registered in the register of immovable property. Where an owner creates a right of habitation on the entire real estate, in the column for "location of the dwelling" it should be recorded as the entire real estate. Where the owner only creates a right of habitation for another person on part of the estate, as in the case where an owner only establishes a right of habitation on one room of the estate, such practice shall also be allowed. The real estate registration authority shall register accordingly to create a right of habitation.

4. Legal Effects of the Right of Habitation

A right of habitation exerts effects between the parties after being established. Such effects mainly manifest in the rights and obligations of the person entitled to the right. As the legislative practices of jurisdictions around the world tend to apply rules on the right to usufruct to the right of habitation, the effects of the right of habitation may be ascertained in accordance with the civil law rules on the effects of the right to usufruct.

4. 1   Rights of the Person with a Right of Habitation

After obtaining the right of habitation, the person entitled to the right may exercises the following rights over the dwelling:

4. 1. 1   Right to appropriately use the dwelling

Right of Habitation is a right to usufruct of possessing and using another person's dwelling so as to meet his needs of habitation. Hence, the person with a right of habitation may possess and utilize the dwelling. Regarding the appropriate use of the dwelling, the following details should be clarified.

(1) The purpose of utilizing the dwelling is only for meeting the right holder's needs of habitation.

(2) The person with the right of habitation is entitled to use the auxiliary facilities of the dwelling. Where the dwelling has accessary, the person entitled to the right may also use such accessary, unless otherwise agreed by the parties.

(3) The person with the right of habitation is entitled to use the living facilities within the dwelling as well as other part of dwelling that is not covered by the right, when it is necessary to meet his needs of habitation. The function of the right of habitation is to ensure its right holder's habitation interests. Where the part of the dwelling covered by the right doesn't to suffice to meet the basic needs of habitation, and the utilization of the part not covered by the right is necessary, for instance, the use of the entrance and exit, passageway, balcony, kitchen or toilette, then the owner shall tolerate such use.

(4) The use of the person with the right of habitation is not influenced by the change of the dwelling owner. Although the right of habitation is an encumbrance to the ownership of the dwelling, it does not influence the assignment of the dwelling by ways of sales, giving away as a gift, etc.

The person with the right of habitation is not liable for the reasonable wear and tear on the dwelling.

4. 1. 2　Right to have cohabitants

As has been mentioned above, the person with the right of habitation is entitled to have cohabitants in the dwelling, unless otherwise agreed upon by the parties. Of course, such cohabitants are not free from restriction. They are confined to persons within certain scope. The author opines that eligible cohabitants may be divided into three categories. The first category are family members, which include spouses, parents, children, and other close relatives living together (Article 1045 of the Civil Code). The second category are persons providing life services to the person with the right of habitation, such as housekeepers, nursing workers, etc. The third category are persons supported by the person with the right of habitation who are not his close relatives.

4. 1. 3　Right to let the dwelling on lease

Article 369 of Civil Code provides that, in principle the dwelling in which a right of habitation is created may not be let on lease, unless otherwise agreed by the parties. Following that, if it is explicitly stipulated in the contract on a right of habitation or a will establishing such right that the dwelling may be let on lease, then the person with right of habitation may do so.

4. 1. 4　Right to repair or make improvement to the dwelling

The person with right of habitation enjoys exclusive right over the part of the dwelling covered by the right, and may, free from the owner's restraint, repair such part to meet his needs of habitation, or make improvement to the dwelling through remodeling, etc. to improve his living quality, provided that such change does not exceed the need for his habitation or influence the owner's utilization of the other part of the dwelling. On account of the reciprocity of rights and obligations, the person with right of habitation would not be entitled to require compensation from the owner for the repair or improvement upon extinguishment of the right.

4. 1. 5　Right to obtain compensation fees

If the dwelling is expropriated, requisitioned, or lost, the right of habitation extinguishes accordingly. Where the owner obtains compensation fees, the person with the right of habitation is entitled to claim proper shares thereof. Where the person with the right of habitation is incapable of supporting himself, he may also surrender his claim for compensation fees and require property resettlement instead.

4. 2　Obligations of the Person with a Right of Habitation

While enjoying the relevant rights, the person with the right of habitation shall assume the corresponding obligations to protect the owner's lawful rights and interests. Generally speaking, obligations of the person with the right of habitation include the followings:

4. 2. 1　Obligation of appropriately managing and maintaining the dwelling

The person with the right of habitation is entitled to possess and utilize the dwelling. Accordingly, he is also obliged to appropriately manage and maintain it. He shall make reasonable use of the dwelling as agreed in the contract, maintain the originally intended use of the dwelling and refrain from changing the dwelling's structure.

4.2.2   Obligation of normal repairing of the dwelling

The author holds view that regarding the repair of the dwelling, the parties' agreement shall prevail. Where there is not agreement or the agreement is unclear, the matter should be handled as follows.

First, it should be considered whether the right of habitation is established free of charge. Where the right is created free of charge, according to civil laws of foreign jurisdictions, two cases, namely that of daily maintenance and that of major repair, are usually distinguished in ascertaining the obligor. For daily maintenance, i.e., necessary repair (e.g., repair of damaged doors and windows or peeling paint from walls), the person with the right of habitation is liable for the costs. For major repair, i.e., special repair (e.g. repair of the roof, fixing or replacement of beams, etc.), the owner shall bear the fees. [1] The legislations are well-reasoned. The problem is whether the above rules are applicable when a right of habitation is created not free of charge. The author opines that the answer should be negative. According to the principle of consistency in rights and obligations, if the owner of the dwelling Charges utilization fees, he shall also assume the corresponding obligations of making repair. This is necessary for ensuring the living conditions as agreed in the contract. Hence, if a right of habitation is created not free of charge, the owner shall be liable for both daily repair and major repair, and the person with the right of habitation undertakes obligation of notification.

Second, where the person with the right of habitation assumes the obligation of daily repair, if he takes possession of the whole dwelling, he shall bear all the repair costs; if he only occupies part of the dwelling, he shall bear the costs for daily repair according to the relevant proportion.

4.2.3   Obligation of refraining from arbitrarily leasing out or assigning the dwelling

The author notes that the Civil Code does not forbid the mortgage of the right of habitation. However, since enforcement of mortgage would lead to change in the subject of the right of habitation, which equals to an assignment, thereby going against the aim of establishing this right, the right of habitation shall be not mortgageable.

4.2.4   Obligation of paying utilization fees

The Civil Code adopts the approach that the right of habitation shall in principle be created free of charge, and in exception case established onerously. (Article 368) Where the parties

---

[1]   See Articles 605 and 606 of the French Civil Code, Article 778 of the Swiss Civil Code, Articles 1025 and 1005 of the Italian Civil Code, Article 1489 of the Portuguese Civil Code, and Article 2968 of the Argentine Civil Code.

have no agreement or the agreement is unclear as to whether the right of habitation is created free of charge, the establishment shall be treated as gratuitous. Where the parties agree that the right of habitation is created with charge, then the person with the right of habitation is obliged to pay utilization fees.

4. 2. 5   Obligation of tolerance

The obligation of tolerance of the person with the right of habitation include the following aspects:

First, where right encumbrances such as mortgages or easements existed before the right of habitation is created, the person entitled to the right shall be subject to such encumbrances.

Second, after the right of habitation is created, the owner has the right to conduct necessary check of the dwelling, and the person entitled to the right of habitation shall tolerate such act.

5. Analysis on Categories of the Right of Habitation

5. 1   Right of Habitation for Family Support of Housing

Right of habitation for family support of housing is based on the special identity of the right holders, and performs the function of securing the family housing. It is mainly established to protect the interests of disadvantaged groups such as old people, the divorced, housekeeper, etc. , and serves as a solution to the housing issues faced by these groups in cases of elderly care, divorce or becoming widowed. In the Chinese society, it is a common practice the parents provide funds to their children for purchasing houses. While the houses purchased or built are registered under the name of their children, establishing a right of habitation for the parents can effectively solve the parents' future housing problem.

5. 2   Right of Habitation for Social Security

The Chinese system of social security housing is somehow rather disorderly. For instance, there are national comfortable housing, economically affordable housing, low-rent housing, public rental housing, housing-reform house, resettlement houses for demolition and relocation or squatter settlement, employee settlement housing, settlement housing for talents (talent apartment), and the like, whereby parties enjoy rights of various forms such as separate ownership, co-ownership, right of lease or right of habitation. The boundaries of these property rights can sometimes be rather vague, thereby causing endless disputes.

In light of this, the author opines that the above disputes caused by the attribution of rights in government-supported residential housing should be solved through the legal institution of the right of habitation. For instance, a lessee's right to rent public rental housing may be converted to a right of habitation, so that legal protection with more stability can be provided to such lessee of public rental housing.

5. 3   Right of Habitation for Investment

A party enjoying a right of habitation for investment may face no housing problem, and even possess other dwellings. For such person, the top priority is not to live in the dwelling, but lies in making investment. A right of habitation for investment may be established in the following cases: (1) The right could be established in cooperative house-building; (2) The right could be established in house-purchasing using joint funds; or (3) The right could be established when the parties cooperated to in realty development. For instance, a government provided the land and the realty developer brings capital to cooperate in real estate development. After the houses were built, a right of habitation with duration of 30 to 50 years was created for the developer, who was also permitted to assign such right or let the dwelling on lease. Such mode can also be adopted in cases of cooperative house-building with funds raised by the enterprise.

5. 4   Right of Habitation for Consumption

Unlike the investors (mostly natural persons) in a right of habitation for investment who directly enjoy the right of habitation by themselves, the investors (mostly enterprises) in a right of habitation for consumption usually provides residential services to natural persons. These investors are the operating manager for the residential services, and the natural persons are consumers for the residential services who enjoy the right of habitation. A right of habitation for consumption may be established in the following cases: (1) Right of habitation created in a time share hotel, which is also known as timeshare. The consumers usually obtain the right of habitation in a resort with charge for the purpose of spending holidays there; (2) Right of habitation created in the house-for-pension scheme, whereby the elderly sell the "empty ownership" of their houses to financial institutions at relatively prices while keeping the right of habitation for themselves. The financial institutions provide the elderly with old-age annuity and obtain the complete ownership after the elderly deceases.

6. Causes for and Effects of Extinguishment of the Right of Habitation

The causes for the extinguishment of the right of habitation are not specifically stipulated by the civil laws in jurisdictions around the world, but the relevant provisions concerning the right to usufruct apply to the right of habitation mutatis mutandis. In the Civil Code, causes for the extinguishment of the right of habitation only include expiration of the term of the right and or the death of the person entitled to the right. The author opines that the causes for the extinguishment of the right of habitation should also include other circumstances.

6. 1　Death of the Person with the Right of Habitation

The right of habitation embodies certain nature of a personal servitude right and thus is personal. It is inseparable from the person with the right of habitation. As such, the right extinguishes upon the death of the right holder. Regarding the death of the person entitled to the right of habitation as a cause for the extinguishment of the right, two points need to be explained here further. First, where a right of habitation is jointly established for more than two natural persons, the time when the right of habitation extinguishes shall be determined by the death of the last natural person who is entitled to the right. Second, regardless of whether the term of the right is stipulated in a contract on a right of habitation, the death of the person entitled to the right is always a cause for the extinguishment of the right. In other words, where a contract on a right of habitation contains clauses on the term of the right, and the person entitled to the right deceases during such term, the right of habitation shall extinguish even though the term has not expired.

6. 2　Expiration of Term of the Right of Habitation

The right of habitation is a real right with definite term. Where a contract on a right of habitation contains clauses on the term of the right, the right of habitation extinguishes upon expiration of the term. Where there is no such clause or the clause is unclear, there exists two possible interpretations. One interpretation is that the right of habitation is not subject to the term restriction, and the parties may terminate the right at any time. The other interpretation is that the term shall be the life time of the person entitled to the right of habitation. In other words, the right holder enjoys life-long right of habitation. The author supports the second approach in that it fits the establishment purpose of the right of habitation better.

6. 3　Loss of the Dwelling

The right of habitation is a right to usufruct that designed for the utilization of dwellings. The existence of the dwelling is decisive for achieving the goals set by the right of habitation. Hence, once the dwelling is lost, such goals would be unattainable, and the right of habitation would be no longer necessary and meaningful. Concerning the loss of the dwelling, two points shall be elaborated here.

First, if the entire dwelling is lost, the right of habitation shall undoubtedly also extinguish. However, if the dwelling is lost only in part, and the residue can still meet the need of living and dwelling, then the right of habitation shall continue to exist on the residual part. The reason for this is that partial loss of the dwelling only alters the object scope of the right of habitation, and has no impact on realizing the aim of the right. Similarly, loss of the auxiliary facilities of a dwelling shall also make no impact on the continual existence of the right of habitation.

Second, if a dwelling is lost but leaves a substitute, does the right of habitation extinguish? The author opines that the right should extinguish so long as the dwelling is lost, even if there exists a substitute. If the owner agrees, he may nevertheless create a new right of habitation upon the new dwelling.

6. 4　Revocation of the Right of Habitation

When certain statutory causes occur, the person establishing a real right may revoke the right, thereby causing the extinguishment of such real right. To protect the interests of the dwelling owner, the right of habitation shall be allowed to be revoked by the owner under the special circumstances, which mainly include: (1) where the person with the right of habitation abuses his right, for instance, causing severe damage to the dwelling, arbitrarily assigning the right of habitation, leasing out the dwelling without permission, altering the dwelling's purpose of use, failing to conduct normal repair and maintenance and leaving the dwelling destructed or damaged, accommodating persons who are not necessary for meeting his needs of habitation, and the circumstances are serious, etc. ; and (2) in case of non-gratuitous right of habitation, failing to pay the relevant fees despite of receipt of two warning notices within a reasonable period of time after the payment is due according to the agreement.

6. 5　Expropriation or Requisition of the Dwelling

Expropriation or requisition of the dwelling may cause the extinguishment of the right of habitation.

6. 6　Other Causes for Extinguishment

These mainly include: (1) Where the right of habitation is attached to a condition subsequent, and the condition is fulfilled, or where the right of habitation is subject to a term of termination and the term expires. As has been mentioned, a right of habitation may be subject to a condition or a term. If a right of habitation is attached to a condition subsequent or subject to a term of termination, and the condition is fulfilled or a term of termination expires, the right of habitation shall extinguish; (2) Where the right is abandoned. The person with the right of habitation has the freedom to abandon his right, thereby causing the extinguishment of the right of habitation; and (3) Where rights are merged to be held by the same person. When the ownership of the dwelling and the right of habitation thereupon are merged, namely, they are to be held by the same person, the right of habitation also extinguishes. For instance, when the owner of the dwelling sells the dwelling or gives it away as a gift to the person with the right of habitation, the ownership of dwelling and the right of habitation thereupon are merged, and the right of habitation would extinguish under such circumstance.

Extinguishment of the right of habitation has the following legal effects: (1) Return of the dwelling. The dwelling returned shall be in a status in line with the stipulations in the agreement or the natural wear and tear. Where the extinguishment of the right of habitation is caused by the death of the person entitled to the right, the heir of the deceased is obliged to return the dwelling. (2) Liabilities for compensation. Where the dwelling is lost due to reasons attributable to the person with the right of habitation, not only shall the right extinguish in such case, but also the person entitled to the right must assume the liability for compensation. Where a right of habitation is abandoned by the holder, the ensuing matters shall be properly handled. If the abandonment of the right of habitation causes damages to the dwelling, the person entitled to the right shall also assume compensation liability. (3) Deregistration. The right of habitation takes effect upon registration. Hence, when the right extinguishes, deregistration of the right shall be made accordingly. Where the person with the right of habitation refuses to render cooperation in deregistering the right, the owner of the dwelling may file an action at the court, requiring the person entitled to the right of habitation to fulfill his obligation. Article 370 of the Civil Code provides that "Where a right of habitation is extinguished, deregistration of the right shall be made in a timely manner". If the person with the right of habitation deceases, the owner of the dwelling may unilaterally apply for deregistration by submitting the relevant evidence. It is to be noticed here that if a dwelling is lost in part, the parties shall still go through the correspondent registration formalities, though the right of habitation on the dwelling does not extinguish. Under such circumstance, what is to be dealt with is the registration of the change to the right. (4) Taking back of facilities. During the term of the right of habitation, the person entitled to the right may, for the purpose of normal habitation and utilization, set up necessary facilities in the dwelling or remodels the dwelling. Upon the extinguishment of the right of habitation, the person entitled to the right may rake back such facilities but shall restore the dwelling to its original status.

Section Six   Easements

1. Concept, Features and the Nature of the Easements

1. 1   Concept and Features of the Easements

Article 371 of the Civil Code prescribes that "A person who has a right to easement is entitled to utilize the immovable property of another person as agreed in a contract so as to enhance the efficiency of his own immovable property. The immovable property of another person referred to in the preceding paragraph is the servient land, and the immovable property of the person entitled to the easement is the dominant land". The easement is a right to usufruct whereby the right holder of easement utilizes another person's immovable property in compliance with the stipulations in the contract to get better results from his own immovable property. Another person's immovable property is "the servient estate", and one's own immovable property is "the dominant estate". For example, the farmland tracts of A and B are adjacent, and A has to dig a ditch in B's land tract to irrigate his own. In such case, A may sign a contract of easement and pay B a certain amount of remuneration in exchange for the right to dig a ditch on B's land to have the access to water. Here, A is the holder of the dominant estate or holder of the right to easement, while B is the holder of the servient estate, or obligee of the servient estate. The right holder of may easement be a land owner, the right holder of the right to contractual management of land, the right holder of the right to use land for construction purposes or the right holder of the right to use a house site.

The easement originates from the Roman law, and is one of the oldest jus in re aliena therein. Almost all the civil codes in the civil law system include this institution. The features of the easement may be concluded as follows:

1.1.1   The object is other's immovable properties, including land, premise, and other attached facilities. Although the Civil Code uses the term "easement", it has clearly stipulated in Article 372 that the object of the easement is the immovable property, not limited to land.

1.1.2   That two land tracts, namely, the servient estate and the dominant estate, should be adjacent to each other is a precondition. The essential purpose of an easement is to increase the use value of a particular land tract through dominating someone else's land. thus, Consequently, it is a precondition that two land tracts, i. e. , the servient estate and the dominant estate are adjacently located. Another person's immovable property (the land providing convenience and interests) is the servient estate, and one's own immovable properties (the land enjoying convenience and interests) are the dominant estate. Here, "adjacently located" doesn't necessarily mean that two land tracts are next to each other or adjoined, it could also be that the two are merely close to each other. In particular cases, they may even be geographically remote from each other. Moreover, according to the "space theory", an easement may be established between two adjacent spaces where space ownership or right to use space over land is legally recognized. Therefore, "adjacent" is not limited to the two dimensions. The most simple and accurate approach to understand it is that to seek for the dominant estate a servient estate that can the dominant estate best realized its use value.

1.1.3   It is a real right that requires the use of other's immovable property. In principle, the content of an easement is inaction, which is echoed by the doctrine "action establishes no easement" in the Roman law. According to this principle, the holder of the servient estate is only obliged to tolerate the utilization of his estate on the part of the holder of the dominant estate. He is not obliged to take any action. If the contract stipulates that he should take certain action, then such provision shall not be interpreted as a content of the easement, but may only be taken as valid in the sense of claim instead of real right. This is because the easement is a real right whose object is the servient estate, and consequently, the holder of servient estate may only exert direct control over the servient estate rather than over the holder of the servient estate.

1. 1. 4　An easement is established to get better results from one's own immovable property. Here, the result may refer to convenience and interests regarding material possessions or property, but it can also include such convenience or interests of in the spiritual or emotional sense as establishing the right of view on a servient estate for tenement for a grandstand view from the dominant estate. The specific convenience or interests need by the dominant estate shall be stipulated by the contract for easement.

1. 1. 5　The contents of the easement are optional but shall not violate the mandatory rules or public policies.

The easement is established between the holder of the dominant estate and that of the servient estate by agreement. Its contents are optional. For instance, the right may either be gratuitous or onerous at the parties' choice. However, such contents shall still not violate mandatory rules or the public policies. For example, the contents shall not be the same as those of another type of right to usufruct, and an easement my not prohibit the utilization of the neighboring land or the right to pass of a locked land; neither may it make its content obligation of tolerating right abuse.

1. 2　Nature of the Easement: Appurtenance and Indivisibility

1. 2. 1　The easement is a right with appurtenance nature, meaning that its existence is subordinate to that of the dominant estate in spite of its independent status as a right to usufruct. Such nature may be observed from the following aspects:

First, it may not be assigned apart from the dominant estate. Article 380 of the Civil Code provides that "An easement may not be transferred separately. Where a right to contractual management of land, a right to use a lot of land for construction purposes and the like rights are transferred, the easement shall be transferred concomitantly, unless otherwise agreed in the contract". Article 382 prescribes that, "Where a right to easement is involved when the dominant land and a right to contractual management of land, a right to use a lot of land for construction purposes, and the like rights thereon are partially transferred, the transferee is simultaneously entitled to the easement". Article 383 further states that "Where a right to easement is involved when the servient land and a right to contractual management of land, a right to use a lot of land for construction purposes, and the like rights thereon are partially transferred, the easement is legally binding on the transferee".

Second, it may not be made the object of the other rights apart from the dominant estate. Article 381 of the Civil Code provides that, "An easement may not be mortgaged separately. Where a right to contractual management of land, a right to use a lot of land for construction purposes, and the like rights are mortgaged, the easement shall be transferred concomitantly upon enforcement of the mortgage".

1.2.2   The easement is with indivisibility nature, which further includes indivisibility in terms of its acquisition, its extinguishment and its exercise or encumbrance. (1) where the dominant estate is commonly owned, one of the co-owners may not acquire, with respect to his own share, the easement over the estate. The right may only be acquired by the co-owners as a whole. (2) where the dominant estate is commonly owned, one of the co-owners may not extinguish or partially extinguish, with respect to his own share, the existed easement over the estate. (3) where the servient or dominant estate becomes commonly owned after the easement has been established, the easement is not partitioned for the separate exercise of each co-owner of the dominant estate, or for the separate encumbrance of each co-owner of the servient estate. (4) where the dominant or servient estate is partitioned, the easement shall exist on behalf of or in relation to the respective portions of the estate.

1.3   Differences between the Easement and Adjacent Relationships

The rule of adjacent relationship originates from the Roman law, and has been encompassed by the civil law in most modern jurisdictions. Both easement and adjacent relationships involve the use of another person's immovable properties for the convenience of one's own, but the two are noticeably different in terms of the following aspects:

1.3.1   The adjacent relationship is a statutory right whose establishment is automatic; while the easement is created by contract as a result of the meeting of minds.

1.3.2   The adjacent relationship is brought by the minimum adjustment made by the law regarding the utilization of neighboring immovable; while the easement goes beyond such limit as the rights and obligations agreed upon by the parties.

1.3.3   The adjacent relationship is not an independent real right. It is only a restriction on or expansion of the ownership; As for the easement, it is one subcategory of the right to usufruct and is an independent right.

1.3.4   The adjacent relationship coexists with the ownership and may not be separately obtained or terminated; while for the easement, the ownership may be dispensed with.

1.3.5   The adjacent relationship is usually without recompense; but the easement may be either onerous or gratuitous.

1.3.6   An easement may be asserted against a third party after it is registered (In civil law jurisdictions, registration is usually a requirement for establishment), without registration the right is not effective against a third party; but the adjacent relationships need no registration.

1.3.7   The easement adjusts the adjacent relationships in a broad sense. Its application is not restricted into such cases where two land tracts are next to each other or neighboring. It may arise where there is need to seek for the dominant estate a servient estate that can realize its use value. Especially in cases where the buildings or space are involved, it is much more widely applied than the adjacent relationships, and the extent to which it the expands or restricts to the immovable property is also much greater than the adjacent relationships. To certain extent, the easement can correct or make up for the contents of the adjacent relationships. The enrichment of categories of the easement brings up changes to its constitutive elements under the traditional law. Under the easement system of the United States, the easement is divided into easement of access and the easement for profit. The latter refers to "the right to enter into the land of another and obtain the soil or yields therefrom". Typical examples are right of mining, right of logging, etc. This type of easement completely waives existence of the dominant estate as one of its constitutive elements, and necessitates only the existence of the servient estate. This means it has a wider scope of application compared with the neighboring right.

2. Acquisition of the Easement

2.1   Acquisition by Civil Juristic Acts

2.1.1   Easement Established by Contract

The first approach for establishing easement is the conclusion of contract. According to Article 373 of the Civil Code, to create an easement, the parties shall enter into an easement contract in writing.

An easement contract generally contains the following clauses:

(1) the name and address of each party;

(2) the location of the servient land and the dominant land;

(3) the purposes and methods of utilizing the servient land;

(4) the duration of the easement;

(5) the fees and the mode of payment; and

(6) the means of dispute resolution.

An easement is established at the time when the easement contract comes into effect.

When the parties request registration, they may apply to the registration organ for registration of easement. When lacking the registration, such right may not be used against a third party in good faith (Article 374 of the Civil Code). The duration of an easement shall be agreed upon by the parties, provided that it may not exceed the remaining term of the right to usufruct, such as the right to contractual management of land or the right to use a lot of land for construction purposes (Article 377 of the Civil Code).

The second approach of establishing easement is by means of such unilateral civil juristic act as making a will. An easement is established when a valid will is made and registered.

2. 1. 2   Establishment by Way of Concurrent Transfer with the Dominant Estate

An easement may not be transferred separately. Where a right to contractual management of land, a right to use a lot of land for construction purposes and the like rights are transferred, the easement shall be transferred concomitantly, unless otherwise agreed in the contract (Article 380 of the Civil Code).

2. 2   Acquisition not Caused by Civil Juristic Acts

Succession. Due to the appurtenance nature of the easement, the succession of this right occurs upon the succession of the ownership, right to land use or mortgage in the land. In China, individual citizens don't enjoy land ownership, but may have the right to use a house site or the right to contractual management of land, etc. A successor may enjoy the right to use a house site as a result of succeeding the buildings thereupon. Para. 2, Article 31 of the Law on Land Contract in Rural Areas stipulates that: "In the case a contractor of forestland is dead, his successor may continue undertaking the contract within the term of the contract". Article 54 prescribes that "In the event that rural land is contracted through such means as bid invitation, auction, and open consultation in accordance with this Chapter and the contractor is dead, the benefits derived from the contract which are due to him shall be inherited in accordance with the provisions of the Succession Law; and within the term of the contract, his successors may continue executing the contract". The right to contractual management of land under a contract in rural areas and the relevant easements can be obtained through succession when it meets the legal condition.

3. Contents of Easements

3. 1   Rights and Obligations of Right Holder of Easement

3. 1. 1   Rights

3. 1. 1. 1   Right to utilize the servient estate. According to Article 376 of the Civil Code, A person entitled to an easement shall utilize the servient land in accordance with the purposes

and methods of utilization as agreed in the contract, and minimize restrictions on the real rights of the right holder in the servient land. Where a right holder of easement need to utilize the adjacent immovable property for the purpose of using water, drainage, passage, ventilation, light laying pipelines, and the like, he is entitled to utilize the immovable property of another person as agreed in his contract with the holder of the servient land so as to enhance the efficiency of his own immovable property.

3.1.1.2 A right holder of easement is entitled to build such attached facilities on the servient land as is necessary for exercising his easement.

3.1.1.3 Claims on real rights. Where an easement is encroached upon, claims on real rights for restitution of property, removal of the nuisance, elimination of danger, and restoration of the original state, etc. may be brought up against the right holder of the servient land or other tortfeasor.

3.1.2 Obligations

3.1.2.1 A right holder of easement shall utilize the servient estate according to the purpose and means of use as stipulated in the contract, and lighten as much as possible the restrictions on the real right of the holder of the servient estate.

3.1.2.2 The obligation to maintain the affiliated facilities.

3.1.2.3 The obligation to pay the fees for utilization. The right holder of easement should pay the fees as agreed upon if the utilization is onerous.

3.2 Rights and Obligations of the Holder of the Servient Estate

3.2.1 Rights

3.2.1.1 The right to collect fees for utilization.

3.2.1.2 The right to utilize the attached facilities. The holder of the servient estate may utilize the attached facilities constructed by the easement holder to the extent that he doesn't obstruct the latter from exercising his right. Unless otherwise stipulated, the holder of the servient estate should take a reasonable share of the fees for maintaining the attached facilities.

3.2.1.3 Right to require the right holder of easement to change his manner of utilizing the servient land. The extra fees incurred should be borne by the parties through agreement; if the parties are unable to reach an agreement, the fees shall be paid by the holder of the servient estate.

3.2.2 Obligations

According to Article 375 of the Civil Code, "A right holder of the immovable property served as the servient land shall allow the person entitled to an easement to utilize the immovable property as agreed in the contract and may not interfere with the exercise of the right to easement by such person".

4. Extinguishment of the Easements

First, if an easement holder is under any of the following circumstances, the holder of the servient estate has the right to terminate the easement contract, and the easement extinguishes:

(1) Abusing the easement in violation of the provisions of law or the contract;

(2) In the case of compensated use of servient estate, upon expiration of the duration for payment, failing to pay the fees after two exigent demands are given within a reasonable period.

Second, an easement extinguishes in any of the following circumstances:

(1) Expiration of the easement;

(2) The servient estate can no longer serve for the purpose of the easement due to natural forces;

(3) Abandonment of the easement;

(4) Loss of the servient estate or the dominant estate.

If a registered easement is altered, transferred or lost, the alteration registration or deregistration shall be made in a timely manner.

第六章　担 保 物 权

第一节　担保物权概述

一、担保物权的概念

担保物权，是为了担保债务的履行，在债务人或第三人的特定物或权利上所设定的物权。

《民法典》第 386 条规定："担保物权人在债务人不履行到期债务或者发生当事人约定的实现担保物权的情形，依法享有就担保财产优先受偿的权利，但是法律另有规定的除外。"担保物权的主要功能是担保债权的实现。由于担保人要以一定的物或权利作为担保，这就为债权的实现提供了切实的保障。担保物权制度对于鼓励交易、促进交易的迅速达成起到十分重要的作用。在现代市场经济下，担保物权本身作为社会融资的基本手段，对经济的繁荣有积极的作用。企业和个人在向金融机构融资时，最有效的手段即提供物的担保。因此，担保物权已经成为成功获得社会融资的重要保障。

担保物权是在私有制条件下形成的古老的民事法律制度。在传统民法中，担保物权包括抵押权、质权、留置权。中国《民法通则》只规定了抵押权、留置权，未区分出质权。1995 年 6 月全国人大常委会通过，1995 年 10 月 1 日起实施的《担保法》则对抵押权和质权进行了区分，并对抵押权、质权、留置权作了具体的规定。最高人民法院于2000 年 12 月 13 日起发布了《最高人民法院关于适用〈中华人民共和国担保法〉若干问题的解释》(共 134 条，以下称《担保法司法解释》)。《物权法》将《担保法》中的担保物权的内容纳入自己的体系。

《民法典》整合了《物权法》与《担保法》规定的内容。由于《民法典》采取了债权与物权二分的立法方式，故分别在第二编物权编的第四分编规定了"担保物权"，《民法典·物权编》共 5 个分编、《物权编》第 4 分编 担保物权 共 4 章、71 条。担保制度是《民法典》的重要内容，对于巩固和完善社会主义基本经济制度、推动经济高质量发展，具有极其重要的作用。考虑到民法典对担保制度作出了重大完善和发展，最高人民法院在清理以往与担保有关的司法解释的基础上，根据民法典关于担保制度的新规定，制定了《最高人民法院关于适用〈中华人民共和国民法典〉有关担保制度的解释》(以下称：《民法典担保制度司法解释》），共有71个条款。

二、担保物权的特征

1. 担保物权是为担保主债权的实现而设定的从权利

设定担保物权的目的是以一定的物或权利作为担保来保证债务的履行和债权的实现，而债权人的债权因一定的担保物的存在而得到充分的保障。

2. 担保物权是债务人或第三人提供一定的物或财产权利进行担保的限制物权

或者说，是在债务人或第三人的特定财产上设定的权利。

3. 担保物权是以支配担保物的价值为内容的权利

交换价值是一物与他物相交换而表现出来的价值，为什么说担保物权支配一定的交换价值呢？因为，一方面，担保物权是以获取担保物的交换价值为目的而设定的，担保物权注重支配的是物和权利在拍卖、变卖时的价值。正因为如此，同一物之上可以基于对交换价值的分割而设立多个物权，并且担保物权可以实行物上代位。所谓物上代位权一般是指物权担保中（如抵押、质押）担保物因意外损害或其他原因，使担保物消失而换来赔偿金（或受让款等其他财产时），担保权人仍享有的对担保物换来的该赔偿金（或受让款等其他财产）的担保物权。另一方面，担保物权中重要的内容是换价权，所谓换价权是指在债务人不履行债务时，债权人有权将担保物进行拍卖、变卖，并就所得价款优先受偿。德国学者哈里·韦斯特曼主张，担保物权就是"物权的换价权"。交换价值是一个抽象的概念，而普遍存在于各种物之上。担保物权人对于物的支配表现在对其交换价值的支配，而一般不是对其使用价值的支配。正是从这个意义上说，担保物权被称为价值权。担保物权的价值权和换价权是担保物权的本质特征。

4. 担保物权是从物权

设定担保物权是为了确保债务人履行债务。担保物权的存在，是以债权的存在为前提的，并且随着债权的转移而转移，随着债权的消灭而消灭。因此，它是从属于债权的从物权。

5. 担保物权是他物权

担保物权是在他人的所有物设定的，担保物的所有人是债务人或其他第三人。对于担保物权人来说，担保物是他人的所有物。因此，这就是为什么我们称担保物权为他物权。担保物权人享有排除他人干涉权和追及权。担保物落入他人之手，担保物权人可以追及主张其权利。同时，在债务人不履行债务时，可以行使对担保物的处分权，并取得受偿的权利。

6. 担保物权实现方式有其特点

对其他物权而言，权利人不仅可以直接支配其物，而且可以直接依法享有对物的占有、使用等权能，并可以排除他人的非法干涉。但对担保物权来说，权利人一般不能直接地实现担保物权，必须通过法定的方式，如依据拍卖、变卖程序来实现其担保物权。例如，抵押权的实现，必须由抵押权人在债务人不履行债务时，将抵押物依法交付给有关机构，依据一定的程序，进行拍卖或变卖，而抵押人不能直接没收抵押物，或擅自拍卖抵押物而从中优先受偿。这就是说，担保物的换价权必须要通过一定的程序才能实现。强调担保物权实现的特殊性对保护债务人及一般债权人的合法权益是十分必要的。

7. 担保物权具有从属性、不可分性和代位性

担保物权的属性，和一般物权相比较，除具有一般物权所共同具有的支配性、优先性、排他性等特性之外，还具有：

(1)从属性。所谓从属性，是指在一般情况下担保物权是从属于主债权的从权利，其在效力上必须依附于被担保的主债权。不过，担保物权的从权利性质并不影响其可以作为一种物权独立存在。担保物权的从属性主要表现在三个方面：

①成立上的从属性。在一般情况下，担保物权的成立应当以已经成立并生效的债权的存在为前提。如果债权根本不成立或未生效，则担保物权即使成立也并不生效。如果债权在成立以后被宣告无效或撤销，则担保物权也相应无效。需要注意的是，因担保物权的价值权化，担保物权与其所担保的债权之间的主从关系有转化的倾向。可以预期，在未来的债权的担保中，担保物权可能先于债权成立，而担保物权设立的目的可能在于诱导债权成立。

②移转上的从属性。如果债权发生转让，则担保物权也应当相应地转让，因为担保物权不得与债权相分离。担保物权人不得单独将担保物权转让给他人，而自己保留债权，否则转让无效；也不得将债权转让给他人，而自己保留担保物权，更不得将债权和担保物权区别开而分别转让给不同的受让人。

③消灭上的从属性。是指担保物权随着债权的消灭而消灭。

(2)不可分性。所谓不可分性，是指担保物权的各个部分应担保债权的全部，享有担保物权的债权人有权就担保物的全部行使担保物权。担保物是否被分割或产生部分的毁损灭失，或担保物权所担保的债权是否已经部分履行，都对担保物权的存在不产生影响。具体而言：

①担保物的各个部分担保债权的全部，享有担保物权的债权人可以就担保物的全部行使担保物权。

②债权是否被分割对担保物权的存在不产生影响。例如，甲对丙享有 10 万元的债权，丙以其房产作为抵押，后来，甲将债权分割并分别转让给两人，两人分别享有一部分债权。分割后的债权人就各自的债权对丙的全部房产享有抵押权。

③担保物权所担保债权是否已被部分履行，对担保物权的存在不产生影响。例如，甲以其自行车 5 辆作为质物向乙借款 2000 元，此后甲清偿了 1000 元的债务。此时，甲是否可以要求乙返还两部自行车呢？从担保物权的不可分性而言，即使债务已履行了一部分，但债权人在债务未完全清偿以前，可以就担保物的全部行使权利。

(4)如果担保物发生部分灭失，则未灭失的部分仍应担保全部债权，而不能相应地缩小担保的债务范围。当然，如果担保物因为可归责于担保人的原因发生部分灭失，担保人有义务以其他财产补充担保物所灭失的部分价值。

(3)物上代位。所谓物上代位，是指担保期间，担保财产毁损、灭失或者被征收等，担保物权人可以就获得的保险金、赔偿金或者补偿金等优先受偿。例如，甲为了向乙借款，将其汽车1辆出质给乙，后因为发生火灾，该汽车被烧毁，甲从保险公司获得赔偿，该赔偿金应当成为质押的标的，债权人可以对此赔偿金优先受偿。关于物上代位，《民法典》已经对此做出了明确规定。担保物毁损灭失之后，担保人获得的赔偿金或者保险金极易被担保人挪作他用，为了保障担保物权人的权利的实现，《民法典》第390条规定："担保期间，担保财产毁损、灭失或者被征收等，担保物权人可以就获得的保险金、赔偿金或者补偿金等优先受偿。被担保债权的履行期限未届满的，也可以提存该保险金、赔偿金或者补偿金等。"

担保物权形成以后，权利人有权采取必需措施以保全担保物的价值。如果担保物因担保人的原因而发生价值的减少时，担保物权人有权就担保物减少的价值而要求担保人提供相应的担保。《民法典》第408条规定："抵押人的行为足以使抵押财产价值减少的，抵押权人有权请求抵押人停止其行为；抵押财产价值减少的，抵押权人有权请求恢复抵押财产的价值，或者提供与减少的价值相应的担保。抵押人不恢复抵押财产的价值，也不提供担保的，抵押权人有权请求债务人提前清偿债务。"

三、担保物权的取得和担保的债权的范围

(一)担保物权的取得

取得担保物权的法律事实可以分为两类。

1. 基于民事法律行为而取得担保物权

这包括担保物权的设定和担保物权的让与。

(1)担保物权的设定。《民法典》第388条第1款第1句规定："设立担保物权，应当依照本法和其他法律的规定订立担保合同。"理解这一规定应明确：第一，留置权是法定担保，留置权的成立无须订立担保合同，这种情况是特例；第二，担保合同必须采取书面形式。

(2)担保物权的让与。基于担保物权的从属性，除非当事人另有相反的约定，当作为主权利的债权转让时，作为从权利的担保物权将一并转让。

2. 非基于民事法律行为而取得担保物权

包括：(1)因法律规定而直接取得担保物权。如留置权、建筑工程的承包人的建设工程价款优先受偿权(《民法典》第807条)、民用航空器优先权(《民用航空法》第18条及以下第19~25条)、船舶优先权(《海商法》第21条及以下第22~30条)。

(2)因继承而取得担保物权。

(3)因取得时效而取得担保物权(《民法典》未规定)。

(二)担保物权担保的债权范围

《民法典》第389条规定："担保物权的担保范围包括主债权及其利息、违约金、

损害赔偿金、保管担保财产和实现担保物权的费用。当事人另有约定的，按照其约定。"

四、反担保

《民法典》第 689 条及《民法典》第 387 条第 2 款对反担保做了明确规定。《民法典》第 387 条第 2 款规定："第三人为债务人向债权人提供担保的，可以要求债务人提供反担保。反担保适用本法和其他法律的规定。"

反担保，是指债务人或第三人向担保人作出保证或设定物的担保，在担保人因清偿债务人的债务而遭受损失时，向担保人作出清偿。在反担保中，与反担保相对应并作为设定反担保前提的担保称为本担保。反担保只是与本担保相对应的概念。本担保中的担保人称为本担保人，而反担保中的担保人称为反担保人。

反担保的主要功能在于，使担保人的追偿权得以实现，其宗旨在于保障担保人的追偿权。担保人为债务人承担责任之后，其对债务人享有追偿权，为了保障这种追偿权的实现，就有必要设立反担保。反担保可以适用于各种担保形式，不管是物的担保还是人的担保，担保人都可以要求债务人提供反担保。

反担保的成立需具备下列条件：

(一)反担保是以本担保的存在为前提

一般认为，反担保是从属于本担保的，反担保依附于本担保而存在，本担保是反担保存在的前提和基础。本担保不成立，反担保也就不成立。但是反担保的责任又具有一定的独立性，不完全依附于本担保。《民法典》第 388 条规定："设立担保物权，应当依照本法和其他法律的规定订立担保合同。担保合同包括抵押合同、质押合同和其他具有担保功能的合同。担保合同是主债权债务合同的从合同。主债权债务合同无效的，担保合同无效，但是法律另有规定的除外。担保合同被确认无效后，债务人、担保人、债权人有过错的，应当根据其过错各自承担相应的民事责任。"担保人因无效担保合同向债权人承担赔偿责任后，可以向债务人追偿，或者在承担赔偿责任的范围内，要求有过错的反担保人承担赔偿责任。担保人可以根据承担赔偿责任的事实对债务人或者反担保人另行提起诉讼。另外，当事人可以在反担保合同中约定，反担保合同的效力可以独立于本担保合同的效力，此种约定也是有效的。

(二)提供反担保的主体不限于债务人，还包括债务人以外的其他人

反担保方式可以是债务人提供的抵押或者质押，也可以是其他人提供的保证、抵押或者质押。债务人充任反担保人时，只能提供物的担保，不能将保证作为反担保的形式。因为债务人本身不能作为保证人，以保证作为反担保，则债务人成为反担保人毫无实际意义。如果反担保人是债务人以外的其他人，则不仅可以提供物的担保也可以提供人的担保。

（三）关于反担保适用的范围，原则上限定为保证、抵押或者质押

这就是说，在留置等法定担保物权中，不可能产生反担保，而只能在约定担保中才能产生。因为法定担保是基于特定事实出现而产生的，当事人无法预见其担保责任的承担，所以也不可能以约定反担保的方式对其追偿权的实现作出事先的安排。另外，在法定担保中，担保责任的承担人往往就是债务人，一般不会产生追偿权，也没有必须采取反担保的形式。

（四）反担保也应当有一定的形式要求

《民法典》第387条第2款规定："第三人为债务人向债权人提供担保的，可以要求债务人提供反担保。反担保适用本法和其他法律的规定。"反担保合同及担保权的设立适用《民法典》担保的规则，一般要求书面形式，同时必要时履行登记手续等。

反担保成立以后，必须在担保人实际承担了担保责任，并据此对债务人、反担保人产生了追偿权，追偿权成立并生效。

五、物的担保、人的担保、混合共同担保

担保物权通常称为物的担保。严格地说，物的担保与担保物权仍然有一定的区别。担保物权中所说的物并不限制有体物。在担保物权中，还存在权利质权、优先权等以无体物（权利）为标的物的情况。但由于担保物的典型形式是动产和不动产，所以一般认为，它是与人的担保相对应的一种形式。

所谓人的担保，是指自然人或法人以自身的资产或信用担保债务的履行的一种担保制度。人的担保最早起源于古代的"人质"，即债务人以人身作为保证。但近现代意义上的人的担保，主要是指以第三人的信用以及全部财产作为债权实现的担保。人的担保的典型方式是保证。人的担保属于债权请求权担保。在这种担保中，担保权人不能直接支配担保人的特定财产，而只能在债务人不履行债务时，请求担保人承担担保责任。

人的担保和物的担保的区别主要有：

（一）用于担保的财产或者信用不同

人的担保通常以第三人的一般责任财产及信用财产做担保，或者说是以债务人不履行债务时的第三人的全部财产做担保。而物的担保则是以特定的财产作担保，其中包括动产、不动产和权利等。人的担保是增加可供清偿的一般责任财产，如果保证人在债务人不清偿债务时，具有足够的代债务人清偿的财产能力，人的担保将对债权的实现起到可靠的保障。但是，由于一般责任财产具有浮动性、不稳定性，在债务人不履行债务时，保证人可能没有足够的财产承担债务。因此，债务不能得到完全履行的危险仍然存在。而物的担保不受个人财产变动的影响，所以，比人的担保更加可靠。

（二）主体不同

人的担保的主体只能是债务人以外的第三人，而物的担保的主体则包括债务人和第三人。

（三）法律效力不同

人的担保本质上仍然是一种合同关系，其产生的是一种债权，不具有优先受偿性。债权人所享有的对保证人的请求权只能与其他债权人按比例分配保证人的财产。而物的担保产生的是一种物权，具有优先受偿性。正因为如此，一般认为，当两种担保同时存在时（混合共同担保），物的担保在法律效力上一般优先于人的担保。

《民法典》第 392 条对混合共同担保作出了规定，"被担保的债权既有物的担保又有人的担保的，债务人不履行到期债务或者发生当事人约定的实现担保物权的情形，债权人应当按照约定实现债权；没有约定或者约定不明确，债务人自己提供物的担保的，债权人应当先就该物的担保实现债权；第三人提供物的担保的，债权人可以就物的担保实现债权，也可以要求保证人承担保证责任。提供担保的第三人承担担保责任后，有权向债务人追偿"。这一条规定分为两类情形三种情况：（1）当事人之间就如何实现债权有约定的，债权人应当按照约定实现债权，按照约定实现担保物权。（2）当事人之间就如何实现债权没有约定的或者约定不明的，分两种情况：①债务人自己提供物的担保的，债权人应当先就该物的担保实现债权；②第三人提供物的担保的，债权人可以就物的担保实现债权，也可以要求保证人承担保证责任。（3）提供担保的第三人承担担保责任后，有权向债务人追偿。

六、流质契约的认定与法律后果

（一）流质契约的概念和特征

所谓流质契约，又称绝押契约，是指当事人双方在设立抵押或质押时，在担保合同中规定，债务履行期限届满而担保物权人尚未受清偿时，担保物的所有权移转为债权人所有。流质契约的特点主要有：

第一，主要在约定担保物权中采用。当事人通过订立抵押或者质押合同设立担保物权时才可能在担保合同中约定流质契约条款。直接根据法律规定产生的物权，一般不会出现流质条款。

第二，流质契约不仅能在担保合同中事先约定，也可以在担保合同之外另行约定。在担保物权实现时，当事人约定担保物折价协议并不属于流质条款。

第三，流质契约通常规定担保物的所有权完全归债权人所有。

（二）流质契约的效力及法律后果

大陆法系历来有禁止流质契约的传统。《民法典》持放任态度，该法典第 401 条规定："抵押权人在债务履行期限届满前，与抵押人约定债务人不履行到期债务时抵押财产归债权人所有的，只能依法就抵押财产优先受偿。"第 428 条规定："质权人在债务履行期限届满前，与出质人约定债务人不履行到期债务时质押财产归债权人所有的，只能依法就质押财产优先受偿。"流质契约的表面意思无效，按照法律规定只能就担保财产优先受偿，实现担保物权。流质契约的法律规范在中国的立法目的主要表现在：

1. 保护债务人。

2. 有利于保护担保物权人以外的其他债权人的利益。

3. 防止国有资产流失。

当事人违反了担保法关于禁止流质契约的规定，并非指设定担保物权的行为无效，设定行为因符合法律而有效，其无效仅以预先约定担保物所有权移转的部分为限。流质契约无效并不影响整个担保合同的效力。

七、担保物权的消灭

《民法典》第 393 条规定："有下列情形之一的，担保物权消灭：（一）主债权消灭；（二）担保物权实现；（三）债权人放弃担保物权；（四）法律规定担保物权消灭的其他情形。"

第二节 抵 押 权

一、抵押权的概念和特征

抵押权，是债权人对于债务人或者第三人提供的担保债的履行的不动产及其他财产不转移占有，在债务人不履行债务时，可以用该财产的价值（折价或者以拍卖、变卖该财产的价款）优先受偿的权利。本书所言的"折价"是指由具有债权债务关系的双方按照市场价格或共同委托的估价机构对标的物的实际价值进行评估，以双方均认可的价格将标的物的所有权由一方当事人转让给另一方当事人，从而全部或部分地了结双方间的债权债务关系。在抵押权关系中，享有抵押权的债权人称为抵押权人；提供担保财产的债务人或第三人，称为抵押人；抵押人提供的担保财产，称为抵押物或抵押财产。

从古代罗马市民法到现代欧洲大陆民法，抵押权都是与质权相区别的一类担保物权：抵押权是以不移转占有的不动产作为履行债务保证的担保物权；而以移转占有的动产或权利作为履行债务保证的，则称为质权。但是，在俄罗斯则创造了另一种立法例。从苏联 1922 年民法典到现在的俄罗斯联邦民法典，都没有再区分抵押权与质权，而是把二者合并起来，统称为抵押权。按照这种立法例，抵押权的标的物可以是包括不动产、动产和财产权利在内的任何财产。设立抵押权，除法律规定不移转财产占有者外，其他财产抵押可以由当事人约定移转占有或不移转占有；约定不移转占有的动产抵押，抵押权人可以在抵押物上打上抵押标记或者在抵押人处将抵押物封存。

在抵押权的立法体例上，《民法通则》采取的是苏联的立法例。《民法通则》没有规定质权，仅规定了抵押权。1995 年制定的《担保法》则改采了传统民法的立法例，对抵押权与质权分别作了规定，从而也形成了较为科学的抵押概念和制度。《民法典》仍然对抵押权与质权分别作了规定。抵押权的特征如下：

（一）抵押权是一种物权

抵押权虽然具有债权的属性，但仍然属于物权的范围。一方面，抵押权人对抵押人提供抵押的特定财产享有支配权，抵押物虽不移转占有，但抵押权人可以支配抵押物的价值，即使抵押人转让抵押物的所有权，抵押权也不因此而受到影响。如果在抵押期间，抵押物发生毁损灭失，抵押物将发生物上代位，抵押权的效力及于抵押物变价后的价值。另一方面，抵押权人享有优先受偿的权利。也就是说，当抵押权与普通债权并存时，抵押权人要优先于普通债权人而受偿。如果同一物上设定了数个抵押权，则先设定的抵押权要优先于后设定的抵押权。此外，在抵押财产受到他人不法侵害时，抵押权人可以基于抵押请求权除去妨害。这些特点都表明抵押权是一种物权。

（二）抵押权是一种担保物权

抵押权是以担保债权为目的，即是以确保债务的履行为目的的物权。抵押权的产生与存在必须以一定的债权关系的发生与存在为前提和基础，没有所担保的债权，就不能成立抵押权。抵押权既不能与其所担保的债权相分离而单独转让，也不能与其所担保的债权相分离而作为另一个债的担保。押权设定的目的就是确保主债务的履行。

（三）抵押权是在债务人或第三人的财产上所设定的物权

（四）抵押权是不移转标的物占有的担保物权

所谓不移转占有，是指抵押权设定后，抵押物仍留在抵押人手中，由抵押人继续占有抵押物。不移转占有是抵押权与质权的重要区别。由于抵押的设定不移转占有，抵押人能够继续占有和使用抵押财产，从而使物的使用价值得到充分发挥。由于抵押权的设定不需要移转占有，因此抵押权不能采用占有移转的公示方法，而必须采用登记或其他方法进行公示。这也决定了在实践中抵押的标的主要为不动产而非动产。

（五）抵押权是以抵押财产的变价而优先受偿的权利

所谓优先受偿是指债务人不履行债务时，债权人有权依照法律规定以抵押财产折价或者以拍卖、变卖该财产的价款优先受偿。抵押权的优先受偿性是抵押权作为担保物权的重要特征，但这种优先受偿并不是指在债务人不履行债务时直接移转抵押物的所有权，而是指在债务人不履行债务时将抵押物变价，使抵押权人就抵押物变价后的价值而优先于其他债权人受偿。正是从这个意义上说，抵押权是一种价值权或变价受偿权。

二、抵押权的设定

(一)抵押权设定方式

1. 基于民事法律行为而取得抵押权

这可以分为抵押权的设定与抵押权的转让两种。基于民事法律行为而取得的抵押权,学说上称为约定抵押或意定抵押权。

实践中,通过抵押合同而设定抵押权的情形最为常见。所以,《民法典》第 388 条第 1 款第 1 句规定:"设立担保物权,应当依照本法和其他法律的规定订立担保合同。"

抵押合同的形式。《民法典》第 400 条规定:"设立抵押权,当事人应当采取书面形式订立抵押合同。"

抵押合同的内容。《民法典》第 400 条第 2 款规定:"抵押合同一般包括下列条款:(一)被担保债权的种类和数额;(二)债务人履行债务的期限;(三)抵押财产的名称、数量等情况;(四)担保的范围。"

通过转让取得抵押权。《民法典》第 407 条规定:"抵押权不得与债权分离而单独转让或者作为其他债权的担保。债权转让的,担保该债权的抵押权一并转让,但法律另有规定或者当事人另有约定的除外。"因此,当一债权人向他人转让债权时,抵押权随同该债权一并转让,受让人因此而取得抵押权。此种取得抵押权的方式即为抵押权的转让。

2. 非基于民事法律行为而取得抵押权

这包括基于法律规定而取得抵押权即法定抵押权、基于公信原则而取得抵押权,以及通过继承而取得抵押权。

(二)抵押当事人

抵押当事人包括抵押人和抵押权人。抵押权人就是指债权人,因为抵押权是担保主债权而存在的,所以只有被担保的主债权中的债权人才能成为抵押权人。抵押人即抵押财产的所有人,是以自己的财产为自己或他人的债务设定抵押的人,既可能是债务人,也可能是第三人。由于抵押在性质上是一种处分财产的行为,因此抵押人必须对设定抵押的财产享有所有权或处分权。

(三)抵押物

抵押物又称为抵押财产,是抵押权的标的或客体,然而并不是所有的财产都可以用来作为抵押标的物。一方面,抵押财产必须是某项特定的财产,或者该财产具有特定的范围。如果不能特定,抵押权人就无法支配抵押财产,从而不可能顺利地实现抵押权。另一方面,由于抵押权的实现要将抵押物拍卖、变卖,因此抵押物必须是可以转让的物。凡是法律禁止流通或已被强制执行的财产是不得作为抵押物的。还要看到,由于抵押权的设定不是以标的物的占有移转为公示要件,而是以登记或其他的方法进行公示,因此抵押权必须能以登记或其他的方式予以公示。

《民法典》第395条规定了可以用来抵押的财产的范围："债务人或者第三人有权处分的下列财产可以抵押：（一）建筑物和其他土地附着物；（二）建设用地使用权；（三）海域使用权；（四）生产设备、原材料、半成品、产品；（五）正在建造的建筑物、船舶、航空器；（六）交通运输工具；（七）法律、行政法规未禁止抵押的其他财产。抵押人可以将上列财产一并抵押。"第396条还规定，"企业、个体工商户、农业生产经营者可以将现有的以及将有的生产设备、原材料、半成品、产品抵押，债务人不履行到期债务或者发生当事人约定的实现抵押权的情形，债权人有权就抵押财产确定时的动产优先受偿。"第397条规定："以建筑物抵押的，该建筑物占用范围内的建设用地使用权一并抵押。以建设用地使用权抵押的，该土地上的建筑物一并抵押。抵押人未依照规定一并抵押的，未抵押的财产视为一并抵押。"这种被视为已经做成的抵押，本书称为法定抵押或者法定抵押权。第398条规定："乡镇、村企业的建设用地使用权不得单独抵押。以乡镇、村企业的厂房等建筑物抵押的，其占用范围内的建设用地使用权一并抵押。"

《民法典》在从正面规定可以抵押的财产的同时，第399条又从反面规定了不得用于抵押的财产范围，包括："（一）土地所有权；（二）耕地、宅基地、自留地、自留山等集体所有的土地使用权，但法律规定可以抵押的除外；（三）学校、幼儿园、医疗机构等为公益为目的成立的非营利法人的教育设施、医疗卫生设施和其他社会公益设施；（四）所有权、使用权不明或者有争议的财产；（五）依法被查封、扣押、监管的财产；（六）法律、行政法规规定不得抵押的其他财产。"

（四）抵押权的登记

由于抵押权的设立的法律效果不仅直接涉及抵押人和抵押权人，而且还涉及抵押人的一般债权人和其他与抵押物有利害关系的人。因此，法律要求抵押权的设立必须具备严格的形式要件。

1. 必须办理登记

根据《民法典》第402条规定，以本法第395条第1款第1项至第3项规定的财产或者第5项规定的正在建造的建筑物抵押的，应当办理抵押登记。抵押权自登记时设立。包括(1)建筑物和其他土地附着物；(2)建设用地使用权；(3)海域使用权；(4)正在建造的建筑物。

2. 自愿办理登记

根据《民法典》第403条之规定，"以动产抵押的，抵押权自抵押合同生效时设立；未经登记，不得对抗善意第三人"。这里的动产主要包括(1)生产设备、原材料、半成品、产品；(2)正在建造的船舶、航空器；(3)交通运输工具。企业、个体工商户、农业生产经营者以现有的以及将有的生产设备、原材料、半成品、产品抵押的，可以向登记机构办理登记。

三、抵押关系当事人的权利

(一)抵押权人的权利

1. 对抵押权的处分，是指抵押权人对抵押权的支配力的维持、消灭或减少所为的具有法律效力的行为，包括：(1)抵押权的让与(抵押权必须随同其所担保的主债权一并转让)；《民法典》第 407 条规定，"抵押权不得与债权分离而单独转让或者作为其他债权的担保。债权转让的，担保该债权的抵押权一并转让，但是法律另有规定或者当事人另有约定的除外。"可见，《民法典》没有承认抵押权可以另行设立担保。(2)将抵押权作为其他债权的担保。(3)抵押权的抛弃。抵押权虽然不能与主债权分离而为其他债权提供担保，但可以连同债权一起为其他债权提供担保，设定附随抵押权的债权担保。抵押权抛弃的要办理注销登记；抵押权转让的要办理变更登记；抵押权为其他债权提供担保的要办理设定登记。

《民法典担保制度司法解释》第 39 条规定："主债权被分割或者部分转让，各债权人主张就其享有的债权份额行使担保物权的，人民法院应予支持，但是法律另有规定或者当事人另有约定的除外。主债务被分割或者部分转移，债务人自己提供物的担保，债权人请求以该担保财产担保全部债务履行的，人民法院应予支持；第三人提供物的担保，主张对未经其书面同意转移的债务不再承担担保责任的，人民法院应予支持。"当主债权被分割或者部分转让时，受让的抵押权可以不作变更登记。

《民法典担保制度司法解释》第 38 条第 2 款规定："担保财产被分割或者部分转让，担保物权人主张就分割或者转让后的担保财产行使担保物权的，人民法院应予支持，但是法律或者司法解释另有规定的除外。"

同时根据《民法典》第 392 条规定，被担保的债权既有物的担保又有人的担保的，债务人不履行到期债务或者发生当事人约定的实现担保物权的情形，债权人应当按照约定实现债权；没有约定或者约定不明确，债务人自己提供物的担保的，债权人应当先就该物的担保实现债权；第三人提供物的担保的，债权人可以就物的担保实现债权，也可以请求保证人承担保证责任。提供担保的第三人承担担保责任后，有权向债务人追偿。债权人对第三人提供的抵押财产所担保的债权份额或者顺序没有约定或者约定不明的，抵押权人可以就其中任一或者各个财产行使抵押权。抵押人承担担保责任后，可以向债务人追偿，也可以要求其他抵押人清偿其应当承担的份额。《民法典》第 409 条规定："债务人以自己的财产设定抵押，抵押权人放弃该抵押权、抵押权顺位或者变更抵押权的，其他担保人在抵押权人丧失优先受偿权益的范围内免除担保责任，但是其他担保人承诺仍然提供担保的除外。"

2. 抵押财产价值的保全与恢复权

根据《民法典》第 408 条的规定，"抵押人的行为足以使抵押财产价值减少的，抵押权人有权请求抵押人停止其行为；抵押财产价值减少的，抵押权人有权请求恢复抵押财产的价值，或者提供与减少的价值相应的担保。抵押人不恢复抵押财产的价值，也不提供担保的，抵押权人有权请求债务人提前清偿债务"。该条实际上确认了三种权利，即请求停止实施减少抵押物价值行为的权利、抵押权人对抵押物的价值保全权和请求提前清偿债务的权利。

3. 侵权损害赔偿请求权与物权请求权

支配抵押物并排除他人侵害的权利。在抵押期间，尽管抵押权人并未实际占有抵押物，但抵押权人对抵押物仍享有相应支配权与控制权。如果抵押物受到第三人的侵害，抵押权人有权要求侵害人停止侵害、恢复原状、赔偿损失。当抵押物被第三人侵夺时，抵押权人依法可对抵押物行使物权请求权，以保障其权利实现。

4. 变价优先受偿权

所谓变价优先受偿权，主要是指在债务人不履行债务或出现当事人约定实现抵押权的情形时，抵押权人可以与抵押人协议以该抵押财产折价，或者以拍卖、变卖该抵押财产所得的价款优先受偿的权利。除此之外，还包括如下几个方面：第一，对内的优先权，即在抵押权与抵押权发生冲突的情况下，应当按照《民法典》第414条的规定确定抵押权实现的先后顺序。第二，对外的优先权，如果在抵押物被查封、被执行时，抵押权优先于执行的债权。对于抵押财产被扣押或强制执行的，抵押权人应当从抵押物的变价中优先受偿。如果债务人被宣告破产，抵押权应当优先于一切债权破产清偿财产。

（二）抵押人的权利

1. 同一抵押物上设定多个抵押权

多重抵押设定权，是指抵押人可以在同一抵押物上设立多个不相矛盾的抵押权，具体包括重复抵押设定权和再抵押设定权。

2. 在抵押财产上设定用益物权

在中国大陆，由于土地等自然资源只能归属于国家或集体所有且禁止抵押，而用益物权均为从土地等自然资源的所有权中派生出来的，如建设用地使用权、宅基地使用权、海域使用权等。因此，中国的不动产抵押人很少有可能在抵押物上设定用益物权。但是，建设用地使用权人可以在该使用权抵押之后，再设定地役权。

3. 出租抵押财产

《民法典》基本承接《物权法》的主旨，该法第405条"抵押权设立前，抵押财产已经出租并转移占有的，原租赁关系不受该抵押权的影响。"订立抵押合同前抵押财产已出租的，原租赁关系不受该抵押权的影响。抵押权设立后抵押财产出租的，该租赁关系不得对抗已登记的抵押权。

4. 转让抵押财产的权利

根据《民法典》第406条的规定，抵押期间，抵押人可以转让抵押财产。当事人另有约定的，按照其约定。抵押财产转让的，抵押权不受影响。抵押人转让抵押财产的，应当及时通知抵押权人。抵押权人能够证明抵押财产转让可能损害抵押权的，可以请求抵押人将转让所得的价款向抵押权人提前清偿债务或者提存。转让的价款超过债权数额的部分归抵押人所有，不足部分由债务人清偿。

四、抵押权的实现

(一)抵押权实现的条件

抵押权的实现，是指抵押物所担保的债权已到清偿期而债务人未履行债务时，抵押权人可以通过行使抵押权，以抵押物的价值优先受偿。故抵押权的实现必须具备如下条件：

(1)必须债务人的债务已到清偿期。

(2)债务人未履行债务。债务人未履行债务包括债务人拒绝履行、迟延履行和不适当履行。如果债务人到期已履行了债务，或者虽未履行，但依照法律和合同的规定应免除责任的，则主债权人不得行使抵押权，否则抵押人有权提出抗辩。

(3)必须存在合法有效的抵押。抵押权的实现是以抵押权合法有效地存在为前提的。如果抵押所担保的主合同被宣告无效或撤销，则抵押合同也应相应被宣告无效，抵押权自然不能有效成立，抵押权人也不得行使抵押权。

(二)抵押权实现的方法与期限

根据《民法典》第410条规定："债务人不履行到期债务或者发生当事人约定的实现抵押权的情形，抵押权人可以与抵押人协议以抵押财产折价或者以拍卖、变卖该抵押财产所得的价款优先受偿。协议损害其他债权人利益的，其他债权人可以请求人民法院撤销该协议。抵押权人与抵押人未就抵押权实现方式达成协议的，抵押权人可以请求人民法院拍卖、变卖抵押财产。抵押权的实现方式主要有三种：

1. 以抵押物折价

所谓以抵押物折价，是指抵押权人与抵押人达成协议，将抵押物折价用于清偿债务，并使抵押权人取得抵押物的所有权。可见，以抵押物折价必须由双方订立折价合同，而不能由抵押权人单方面决定抵押物的价格。如果抵押权人单方面决定了某种价格，抵押人表示同意或未表示异议，可以认定双方已达成了折价协议。在决定抵押物价格时，应当参照市场价格，合理地确定。折价合同必须是在实现抵押权时才能订立，且抵押物的所有权必须在折价合同订立以后才能移转。

2. 抵押物的拍卖

拍卖，是指公开地以竞争方式出卖。通常是指在特定的时间、特定的场合，依据《拍卖法》规定的程序，在拍卖人的主持下，由多个竞买人竞相报价，确定报价最高的数额为抵押物的出售价金，抵押物出售给报最高价额的人。

3. 抵押物的变卖

变卖，是指由抵押权人或者法院出卖抵押物。从广义上讲，拍卖也属于变卖的方式，但此处所说的变卖主要是指由抵押物通过一般的买卖或者以招标转让等方式实现的变卖。

对通过上述三种方式处分抵押物所获得的价款，抵押权人享有优先受偿的权利。

优先受偿权主要针对债权而言，即如果在同一项抵押物上设定了抵押权同时又存在其他需要清偿的普通债权，抵押权人应以该抵押物在处分后所获得的价值优先受偿，而普通债权人只能就抵押权人优先受偿后以剩余的部分受偿。

建设用地使用权抵押后，该土地上新增的建筑物不属于抵押财产。该建设用地使用权实现抵押权时，应当将该土地上新增的建筑物与建设用地使用权一并处分，但新增建筑物所得的价款，抵押权人无权优先受偿。依照《土地承包法》第47条，承包方可以用承包地的土地经营权向金融机构融资担保，并向发包方备案。受让方通过流转取得的土地经营权，经承包方书面同意并向发包方备案，可以向金融机构融资担保。土地经营权抵押或者依照《民法典》第418条规定以集体所有土地的使用权依法抵押的，实现抵押权后，未经法定程序，不得改变土地所有权的性质和土地用途。

抵押权人应当在主债权诉讼时效期间行使抵押权；逾期行使的，人民法院不予保护。[①]

抵押权的实现应严格依照《民法典》的规定内容及《民事诉讼法》中关于"实现担保物权案件"相关程序规定执行。《民法典》第410条第3款规定："抵押财产折价或者变卖的，应当参照市场价格。"

实现担保物权案件的管辖、审理程序、法院不予受理后的救济渠道《民事诉讼法》均有详细安排，该法第203条规定："申请实现担保物权，由担保物权人以及其他有权请求实现担保物权的人依照民法典等法律，向担保财产所在地或者担保物权登记地基层人民法院提出。"第204条规定："人民法院受理申请后，经审查，符合法律规定的，裁定拍卖、变卖担保财产，当事人依据该裁定可以向人民法院申请执行；不符合法律规定的，裁定驳回申请，当事人可以向人民法院提起诉讼。"

(三)抵押权的顺位

1. 抵押权顺位的概念与确定

抵押权的顺位(或次序、顺序)，是指抵押人因担保两个或两个以上债权，就同一财产设定两个或两个以上的抵押权时，各抵押权人之间优先受偿的先后次序。

根据《民法典》第414条之规定，"同一财产向两个以上债权人抵押的，拍卖、变卖抵押财产所得的价款依照下列规定清偿：(1)抵押权已经登记的，按照登记的时间先后确定清偿顺序；(2)抵押权已经登记的先于未登记的受偿；(3)抵押权未登记的，按照债权比例清偿。其他可以登记的担保物权，清偿顺序参照适用前款规定"。

---

① 《民法典》第419条。

2. 抵押权顺位固定主义与顺位升进主义

顺位在先的抵押权因实行抵押权以外的原因而消灭时，顺位在后的抵押权是否依次升进，对此有两种不同的立法例，即抵押权的顺位固定主义与抵押权顺位升进主义。

抵押权的顺位固定主义，即前一顺位的抵押权所担保的债权即便因清偿等非抵押权实现之外的原因而消灭时，该抵押权并没有消灭而依然存在，因此后一顺位的抵押权无法相应地晋升。抵押权顺位升进主义，即前一顺位的抵押权所担保的债权如果因清偿等非抵押权实现之外的原因而消灭时，该抵押权也消灭，后一顺位的抵押权的顺位相应的晋升。

3. 中国《民法典》采取的是抵押权顺位升进主义

对《民法典》第409条、第414条进行文义解释，《民法典》采取的是抵押权顺位升进主义。关于在抵押权与其他物权并存的情况下抵押权人是否可以优先于其他物权受偿，一般认为应采取先来后到的原则，即先设定的物权应优先于后设定的物权。《民法典》第415条规定："同一财产既设立抵押权又设立质权的，拍卖、变卖该财产所得的价款按照登记、交付的时间先后确定清偿顺序。"

五、动产浮动抵押权

(一)动产浮动抵押权的概念和特征

《民法典》第396条规定："企业、个体工商户、农业生产经营者可以将现有的以及将有的生产设备、原材料、半成品、产品抵押，债务人不履行到期债务或者发生当事人约定的实现抵押权的情形，债权人有权就抵押财产确定时的动产优先受偿。"这是中国《民法典》确立的一类新型抵押权——动产浮动抵押权。其特征主要包括：

(1)抵押人的特殊性：只能是企业、个体工商户、农业生产经营者。

(2)抵押客体的特殊性：只能是动产，包括现有的以及将有的生产设备、原材料、半成品、产品。

(3)抵押权的效力特殊性：浮动抵押权中，抵押期间抵押人用于抵押的动产是变动不定的，抵押人可以出售、出租甚至抵押这些动产，只有发生法律规定的情形，该抵押财产才被特定化，抵押人未经抵押权人同意不得随意处置。

(二)动产浮动抵押权的登记——登记对抗主义

《民法典》第403条的规定："以动产抵押的，抵押权自抵押合同生效时设立；未经登记，不得对抗善意第三人。"第404条规定："以动产抵押的，不得对抗正常经营活动中已经支付合理价款并取得抵押财产的买受人。"

(三)浮动抵押财产的确定

根据《民法典》第411条的规定，"依据本法第396条规定设定抵押的，抵押财产自下列情形之一发生时确定：（1）债务履行期届满，债权未实现；（2）抵押人被宣告破产或者解散；（3）当事人约定的实现抵押权的情形；（4）严重影响债权实现的其他情形"。

六、共同抵押权

（一）共同抵押权的概念和特征

共同抵押权又称为"总括抵押权"或"聚合抵押权"，是指为担保同一个债权而在数项不动产、动产或权利上设定的抵押权。这数个不动产、动产或权利，可以分别属于同一个人，也可以分别属于不同的人。从中国《民法典》第 395 条第 2 款的规定来看，中国法律是承认共同抵押权的。共同抵押权的特征有：

（1）担保的是同一债权。同一债权就是指基于同一债的发生原因而产生的债权，而非债权的数额同一。因此共同抵押权担保的债权中债权人、债务人以及给付的内容都必须完全相同的。至于各个抵押物所担保的债权范围是否同一，在所不问。

（2）存在多个抵押财产。共同抵押权的标的物是数项财产而非一项财产，而且这数项财产并非是集合物而是各自独立的财产。

（3）共同抵押权是由数个抵押权担保同一债权。

（4）如果当事人没有对各抵押人提供的抵押财产所担保的债权份额作出约定或者约定不明，则抵押权人有权就各个抵押物所卖得的价金，满足其全部或者一部分的债权（共同抵押权的数个抵押物对于其所担保的债权各负全部的担保责任）。

（二）共同抵押权的成立

可以分为两种类型：一是初始的共同抵押权设立，即债务人或者第三人同时以数个抵押物担保同一债权而设立共同抵押权；二是追加的共同抵押权设立，即在某一抵押权设立之后，另行增加一个或数个抵押物设立抵押权担保同一债权。就共同抵押权成立的要件而言，与普通的抵押权没有多大的差别。

（三）共同抵押的效力

1. 约定了抵押物所担保的债权份额的共同抵押的效力

如果同一抵押人与抵押权人就其提供的抵押物上担保的债权份额作出了约定，或者数个抵押人分别与抵押权人就其提供的抵押物担保的债权份额作出了约定，则当债务人届期不履行债务时，抵押权人虽然仍可以将抵押物全部予以拍卖或变卖，但是应算清各个抵押物变价价款，并依照约定的范围就各个抵押物变价价款优先受偿。

2. 未约定各个抵押物所担保的债权份额的共同抵押权的效力

如果同一抵押人对其提供的各个抵押物上担保的债权份额，或者不同的抵押人对其各自提供的抵押物上担保的债权份额没有与抵押人作出约定或者约定不明，则当债务人届期不履行债务时，抵押权人是否能够或者是否必须将各个抵押物一并拍卖？根据《民法典担保制度司法解释》第 20 条规定，人民法院在审理第三人提供的物的担保纠纷案件时，可以适用民法典第 695 条第 1 款、第 696 条第 1 款、第 697 条第 2 款、第 699 条、第 700 条、第 701 条、第 702 条等关于保证合同的规定。《民法典》第 699 条规定："同一债务有两个以上保证人的，保证人应当按照保证合同约定的保证份额，承担保证责任；没有约定保证份额的，债权人可以请求任何一个保证人在其保证范围内承担保证责任。"如果担保合同没有约定抵押担保的债权份额的，抵押权人既可以将抵押物全部加以拍卖并就卖得的价款优先受偿，也可以拍卖其中的一个或多个抵押物并就价款优先受偿，对多余价款可以按约定比例或者法律规定退还给抵押人。

七、最高额抵押权

（一）最高额抵押权的概念、特征

《民法典》第 420 条第 1 款规定："为担保债务的履行，债务人或者第三人对一定期间内将要连续发生的债权提供担保财产的，债务人不履行到期债务或者发生当事人约定的实现抵押权的情形，抵押权人有权在最高债权额限度内就该担保财产优先受偿。"所谓最高额抵押，是指债务人或第三人与抵押权人达成协议，在最高债权额限度内，以抵押物对一定期间内将要连续发生的债权作担保。当债务人不履行债务或发生当事人约定的实现抵押权的情形时，抵押权人有权在最高债权额限度内就该担保财产优先受偿。如甲乙双方于 2004 年 2 月 5 日约定 2004 年 3 月 1 日至 2004 年 12 月底，在此期间所发生的债务均以某栋楼房作抵押。由于该楼房当时估价为 2000 万元，因此双方约定担保借款最高限额为 2000 万元，若借款超过 2000 万元，甲将以其他财产担保。最高额抵押的特征有：

1. 为将来发生的债权提供的担保

在一般抵押中，必须是先有债权，然后才能设定抵押权，亦即抵押权的设定是以债权的存在为前提的，抵押权是为担保已存在的债权而存在的，债权不存在，抵押权也不存在。这就是所谓抵押权在发生上的从属性。然而，最高额抵押权的设定，则不以债权的已经存在为前提，而是对将来发生的债作担保。因此最高额抵押已不具有抵押权在发生上的从属性。

2. 被担保债权具有不特定性

一般抵押所担保的债权都是特定的，这不仅表现在债权类型是特定的，而且表现在债权的数额也是特定的。但最高额抵押所担保的未来债权则是不特定的，即将来的债权是否发生、债权类型是什么、债权额多少，均不确定。在最高额抵押的情况下，必须到决算时，才能确定抵押权担保的实际债权数额。

3. 抵押的债权具有最高限额

对于一般抵押而言，由于设定抵押时担保的债权已经确定，因此不存在最高或最低数额的限定，而最高额抵押则不同。由于在抵押设定时担保债权不确定，而抵押物是特定的，其价值是确定的，不能以价值有限的抵押物担保将来发生的无数的债务，否则将会给债权人造成极大的损害。正是由于这一原因，需要对抵押所担保的未来债权设定最高限额。

4. 对一定期限内连续发生的债作担保

一般抵押仅对已经存在的债权作担保，通常这些债权是独立的。而最高额抵押是对一定期限内连续发生的债权作担保，适用于连续发生的债权法律关系，而不适用于仅发生一个独立债权的情况。因此，一般抵押权应随着主债权的移转而发生移转，但最高额抵押权在决算期未到来而主债权未确定时则不能移转的。因此，最高额抵押权也无转让上的从属性。《民法典》第 421 条规定，最高额抵押担保的债权确定前，部分债权转让的，最高额抵押权不得转让，但是当事人另有约定的除外。最高额抵押担保的债权确定前，部分债权转让的，最高额抵押权不得转让，但当事人另有约定的除外。

（二）最高额抵押权的设立

《民法典》第 424 条规定："最高额抵押权除适用本节规定外，适用本章（第 17 章抵押权）第一节（一般抵押权）的有关规定。"最高额抵押权的设立规则与一般抵押权相同，其特殊性在于：

（1）用于担保一定期间内将要连续发生的债权。

（2）合同条款的特殊性。①在设定最高额抵押权的合同中应当包括最高债权额限度，未约定最高额抵押权，抵押合同无法成立；②通常要约定决算期即"债权确定期间"。它是使得最高额抵押权所担保的不特定债权得以特定的日期确定。如果没有约定债权确定期间或者约定不明确的，抵押权人或者抵押人自最高额抵押权设立之日起满二年后请求确定债权（《民法典》第 423 条第 2 项）。

最高额抵押权的登记，适用《民法典》关于一般抵押权登记的规定，且只需要办理一次登记即可。

（三）最高额抵押权的效力

1. 最高额抵押权担保的债权范围

（1）以现在及将来的债权为限，不能回溯至过去的债权。但是最高额抵押权设立前已经存在的债权，经当事人同意，可以转入最高额抵押担保的债权范围（《民法典》第 420 条第 2 款）。（2）如果实际债权额超过最高额的，应以最高额为抵押权所担保的债权额；超出部分的债权额为普通债权，不受最高额抵押权担保。

2. 最高额抵押权内容的变更

《民法典》第 422 条规定："最高额抵押担保的债权确定前，抵押权人与抵押人可以通过协议变更债权确定的期间、债权范围以及最高债权额，但是，变更的内容不得对其他抵押权人产生不利影响。"

3. 最高额抵押权的转让

《民法典》第 421 条规定："最高额抵押担保的债权确定前，部分债权转让的，最高额抵押权不得转让，但当事人另有约定的除外。"

（四）最高额抵押权担保的债权的确定及实现抵押权

最高额抵押权担保的债权的确定，也称"最高额抵押权担保的债权的特定"，是指最高额抵押权所担保的一定范围内的不特定债权，因一定事由的发生而归于具体特定。《民法典》第 423 条规定，最高额抵押权所担保的债权的特定化事由有：（1）约定的债权确定期间届满；（2）没有约定债权确定期间或者约定不明确，抵押权人或者抵押人自最高额抵押权设立之日起满二年后请求确定债权；（3）新的债权不可能发生；（4）抵押权人知道或者应当知道抵押财产被查封、扣押；（5）债务人、抵押人被宣告破产或者解散；（6）法律规定债权确定的其他情形。

最高额抵押要实现抵押权，必须具备两个条件：一是抵押权担保的债权数额已确定；二是债权已到履行期。所以，当事人在抵押合同中除应规定决算期以外，还应当规定债的履行期限。只有在决算期到来后，通过决算确定出债的实际数额，同时债务也已经到清偿期时，抵押权人才能实现其抵押权。

第三节 质 权

一、质权的概念和特征

质权，是指债务人或者第三人将其特定的财产移交债权人占有，作为债权的担保，债务人不履行债务时，债权人有就其占有的该财产折价或以拍卖、变卖所得价款优先受偿的权利。

由于质权是为担保债的履行而在担保物之上设定的，质权人对标的物的价值可予以支配并可以排除他人的干涉，因此质权是担保物权。但与抵押权相比，有如下特征：

（一）质权的标的——动产和某些权利

依据《民法典》，作为抵押标的的财产既包括动产也包括不动产，然而质权的标的则不包括不动产。《民法典》将质押分为动产质权和权利质押，因此可以用于质押的标的物乃是动产和某些权利。

（二）从是否要求移转占有来看——设定质权须移转对标的的占有

抵押权的设定并不要求移转抵押物的占有，而质权的设定则必须移转占有。质权以占有标的物为成立要件。以一些特殊的财产如以股票或知识产权中的财产权作质物时，还必须办理登记手续。

（三）从公示方式来看——设定质权须移转对标的占有或者登记

尽管抵押权和质权的产生都需要公示，但其方法不完全相同。抵押权的设立主要应采用登记方法。而对于质权的设立来说，根据《民法典》有关规定，权利质权的设立中，以汇票、支票、本票、债券、存款单、仓单、提单出质的，只有没有权利凭证的，质权才自有关部门办理出质登记时设立；以基金份额、证券登记结算机构登记的股权或以其他股权出质的，以及以注册商标专用权、专利权、著作权等知识产权中的财产权出质的，质权自有关主管部门办理出质登记时设立。一般动产和其他权利出质并不需要登记，因为质权的设定要移转占有，而占有移转本身就是一种公示方法。根据《民法典》第429条规定，动产质权自出质人交付质押财产时设立。

（四）从担保权人享有的权利来看质权人直接对质物行使占有权亦有权收取孳息

由于抵押权设定以后不移转占有，所以抵押物仍然置于抵押人占有，抵押人可以继续对抵押物占有、使用、收益。而抵押权人虽能享有对标的物的一定的支配权，但并不能对物直接行使占有、使用、收益权利。在质押的情况下，质权人因质物移转占有，可直接对质物行使占有权，亦有权收取质物所生的孳息（但合同另有约定的除外）。

二、动产质押

（一）动产质权的概念和标的物

动产质权，是债务人或第三人将其动产移交债权人占有以作为债权的担保，在债务人不履行债务时，债权人享有的依法以该动产折价或者以拍卖、变卖该动产的价款优先受偿的权利。简单地说，是指动产为其标的的质权。动产质权是质权的典型形式。

动产质权的标的物，是出质人须移交质权人占有的动产，但并非所有的财产均可以成为动产质权的标的物。作为质权的标的物应具备如下条件：

1. 必须具有可让与性

所谓可让与性，是指该财产依据法律、法规的规定能够移转其所有权。法律、行政法规禁止转让的动产不得出质，因此不具有可让与性的财产不能质押。

2. 须为特定物

如果物尚未特定，则质权缺乏特定的对象，同时物不特定也不能移转占有。债务人或第三人向债权人交付押金或保证金，实际上是通过移转该笔金钱的占有而设定担保，以担保主债务的履行。而在债务人不履行债务时，债权人有权以该笔金钱优先受偿。如果债务人履行债务，债务人则负有返还押金或保证金的义务。因押金或保证金为动产且要移转占有，所以交付押金或保证金而设定担保，符合质权的特征。从中国的实践来看，通常也是将押金交付作为质押的一种方式对待。

由于设定质权的占有仅限于直接占有，而直接占有无多重性或多次占有的可能，因此一物不能设立多项质权。

(二)动产质权的设定

根据《民法典》第 427 条之规定，设定动产质权，出质人和质权人应当以书面形式订立质权合同。如果当事人采用口头方式订立质押合同，该质押的设定是无效的。

质权合同一般包括下列条款：(1)被担保债权的种类和数额；(2)债务人履行债务的期限；(3)质押财产的名称、数量等情况；(4)担保的范围；(5)质押财产交付的时间、方式。

质押合同若不完全具备前款规定内容的，可以补正，但不能简单宣告合同无效。《民法典》第 428 条规定：质权人在债务履行期届满前，与出质人约定债务人不履行到期债务时质押财产归债权人所有的，该约定无效，只能依法就质押财产优先受偿。也就是说在中国法律认为流质契约按质押担保合同的规则执行，质权人只能依法就质押财产优先受偿。

动产质权的设定不仅要订立书面的质押合同，还必须要移转动产的占有。质权自出质人交付质押财产时设立。

(三)出质人的权利和义务

1. 出质人的权利

(1)质物的收益权。根据《民法典》第 430 条的规定，出质人可以与质权人约定仍然保留对质物的收益权。

(2)质物的处分权。动产出质以后，出质人虽然将质物的占有权移转给质权人，但是在法律上并没有丧失对质物的所有权。因此他仍然有权处分其已经出质的财产，但仅限于"法律上的处分"，而非"事实上的处分"。但出质人行使对质物的处分权，不应当影响原有的质权。质权人仍然对该质物享有质权。

(3)物上保证人的追偿权。当出质人是主债务人之外的第三人时，即为"物上保证人"。在代债务人清偿债务之后或因质权的实现而丧失质物的所有权时，物上保证人享有追偿权。

(4)保全质物的权利。《民法典》第 432 条第 2 款规定："质权人的行为可能使质押财产毁损、灭失的，出质人可以请求质权人将质押财产提存，或者请求提前清偿债务并返还质押财产。"

2. 出质人的义务

主要是，不得妨害质权人享有并行使对质物的权利。

(四)质权人的权利义务

1. 质权人的权利

(1)对质物的占有和留置权。

(2)收取质物的孳息权。如果在质押合同中当事人没有特别约定质物的孳息由出质人或第三人收取，则质权人有权收取质物所生的孳息。

(3)转质权。质权人在债权存续中，为了对自己的债务提供担保而将物移转占有给第三人，从而在该质物上设定了新的质权，此种情况称为转质。转质包括承诺转质和责任转质两种情况。《民法典》第434条规定："质权人在质权存续期间，未经出质人同意转质，造成质押财产毁损、灭失的，应当承担赔偿责任。"因此，《民法典》承认了承诺转质和责任转质。

所谓承诺转质，是指质权人取得出质人的同意，为担保自己的债务的履行，而将质物移转占有给第三人，并在质物上设立新质权的行为。质权人在转质时取得了出质人的同意，意味着出质人已将质物的处分权利授予了原质权人。

所谓责任转质，是指在质权存续期间，质权人未经出质人同意，而以自己的责任将物转质给第三人，从而设立新的质权。如前所述，转质涉及债务尚未到履行期时，质权人能否提前处分物的问题。对此学术界存在不同观点，各国立法也存在不同的规定。我们认为在法律上承认责任转质有利于充分发挥质物的效用，有利于促进交易并保障交易安全。因为允许责任转质，《民法典》实际上是允许质权人以质物为自己的债务作担保，从而可以起到鼓励担保作用。

(4)预先拍卖和变卖质物权(质物的保全)。《民法典》第433条规定："因不能归责于质权人的事由可能使质押财产毁损或者价值明显减少，足以危害质权人权利的，质权人有权请求出质人提供相应的担保；出质人不提供的，质权人可以拍卖、变卖质押财产，并与出质人协议将拍卖、变卖所得的价款提前清偿债务或者提存。"

(5)优先受偿权。是指质权人优先于其他债权人甚至优先于其他物权人受偿的权利。

2. 质权人的义务

(1)质权人的主要义务是妥善保管质物。《民法典》第432条规定："质权人负有妥善保管质押财产的义务；因保管不善致使质押财产毁损、灭失的，应当承担赔偿责任。质权人的行为可能使质押财产毁损、灭失的，出质人可以请求质权人将质押财产提存，或者请求提前清偿债务并返还质押财产。"

(2)不得擅自使用、处分质押财产的义务。《民法典》第431条规定："质权人在质权存续期间，未经出质人同意，擅自使用、处分质押财产，造成出质人损害的，应当承担赔偿责任。"

(3)返还质物的义务。《民法典》第436条第1款规定："债务人履行债务或者出质人提前清偿所担保的债权的，质权人应当返还质押财产。"

(五)动产质权的实现

所谓动产质权的实现，是指质权人在债务人到期不履行债务时，有权对通过折价拍卖和变卖方式所获得的价款优先受偿。《民法典》第436条第2款规定："债务人不履行到期债务或者发生当事人约定的实现质权的情形，质权人可以与出质人协议以质押财产折价，也可以就拍卖、变卖质押财产所得的价款优先受偿。"

1. 质物的折价

质物的折价是指质权人和出质人订立合同，由质权人依质物的价格取得质物所有权。质物在折价以后，如果质物折价后的价格高于担保的债权数额，质权人必须向出质人返还差额；如果低于担保的债权数额，质权人仍有权请求债务人清偿差额部分。不过，由于质权人已接受折价，因此该差额部分将成为无担保的债权。

2. 质物的拍卖与变卖

质押的标的一般是普通动产，价值不会太大，并且要转移占有，在质物上不大可能设定多个担保，因此所涉及的其他债权人较少，法律关系较为简单。《民法典》允许质权人自行对质物进行拍卖、变卖而无须和出质人达成协议。《民法典担保制度司法解释》第 45 条规定："当事人约定当债务人不履行到期债务或者发生当事人约定的实现担保物权的情形，担保物权人有权将担保财产自行拍卖、变卖并就所得的价款优先受偿的，该约定有效。因担保人的原因导致担保物权人无法自行对担保财产进行拍卖、变卖，担保物权人请求担保人承担因此增加的费用的，人民法院应予支持。"《民法典》第436 条第 3 款规定："质押财产折价或者变卖的，应当参照市场价格。"

（六）最高额质权

《民法典》第 439 条规定："出质人与质权人可以协议设立最高额质权。最高额质权除适用本节有关规定外，参照适用本编（物权编）第十七章第二节的有关规定。"最高额质权可以在动产质权上设立，也可以在权利质权上设立，适用《民法典·物权编》第十八章规定外，参照适用民法典"最高额抵押权"的有关规定。最高额质权的其他内容参见本书本章第六节 七 "最高额抵押权"的论述。

三、权利质权

（一）权利质权的概念

权利质权，是指为了担保债权清偿，就债务人或第三人所享有的可转让的权利为标的的质权。

动产所有权以外的可以让与的财产权，因其具有交换价值，所以也可以作为担保物权的标的。然而权利毕竟不同于一般的物，以权利作为担保物权的客体，表明权利本身也可以作为交易的对象。尤其是以权利作为物权客体，从而使传统物权的客体仅限于有体物的规则得以逐渐改变，物权的客体范围也得以拓宽。不过，权利作为质押客体与动产作为质押客体有许多相同之处，如关于移转占有、质押合同的主要内容、流质契约的认定与处理等都是大体相同的。基于这一原因，《民法典》和《物权法》仅就权利质押作了一些特殊规定，而并未对权利质押的一般问题作出规定。因此，凡是在权利质押中未作特殊规定的，应适用动产质押的规定。

（二）权利质权的标的

1. 权利质权标的的特点

权利质权的标的是权利，但并不是说任何权利都可以作为权利质权的标的。能够作为权利质权的标的的权利，在性质上必须具有以下特点：

（1）必须是财产权利，包括物权、债权及无体财产权等可以用金钱价格评估的权利。不具有财产价值的权利，如人格权、身份权等不能成为权利质权的标的。此外，不作为债权以及某些债权的书面证明本身因无财产价值，故此也不得设定权利质权。

（2）必须是依法可转让的财产权利。不可转让的财产权利主要包括：第一，依其性质不可转让的财产权利。包括基于特定的人身关系而专属于特定人的债权，即基于扶养关系、抚养关系、赡养关系、继承关系产生的给付请求权和劳动报酬、退休金、养老金、抚恤金、安置费、人寿保险、人身伤害赔偿请求权等权利（《合同法解释（一）》第12条）；基于特殊信任关系而产生的债权，如委托合同中委托人对受托人的处理委托事务的请求权、雇佣合同中雇主对雇员的劳务请求权等；具有个人收入性的财产权，例如抵押权、质权。第二，依据当事人约定不得转让的权利。但当事人的约定不能对抗善意第三人。第三，法律、行政法规规定不得转让的权利（《民法典》第446条、第426条）。

（3）必须是出质权利的债务人或者第三人有权处分的权利。

（4）以该权利设定质权不违背法律的规定以及权利质权的性质。依中国法律，此类权利主要包括：第一，《公司法》第142条第5款规定："公司不得接受本公司的股票作为质押权的标的。"第二，不动产上的物权。第三，动产所有权。第四，动产质权与动产抵押权。

2. 权利质权标的的范围

（1）汇票、支票、本票、债券、存款单、仓单、提单。以汇票、支票、本票、债券、存款单、仓单、提单出质的，当事人应当订立书面合同。质权自权利凭证交付质权人时设立；没有权利凭证的，质权自有关部门办理出质登记时设立。汇票、支票、本票、债券、存款单、仓单、提单的兑现日期或者提货日期先于主债权到期的，质权人可以兑现或者提货，并与出质人协议将兑现的价款或者提取的货物提前清偿债务或者提存。

（2）可以转让的基金份额、股权。以基金份额、股权出质的，当事人应当订立书面合同。以基金份额、证券登记结算机构登记的股权出质的，质权自证券登记结算机构办理出质登记时设立；以其他股权出质的，质权自工商行政管理部门办理出质登记时设立。基金份额、股权出质后，不得转让，但经出质人与质权人协商同意的除外。出质人转让基金份额、股权所得的价款，应当向质权人提前清偿债务或者提存。

（3）可以转让的注册商标专用权、专利权、著作权等知识产权中的财产权。以注册商标专用权、专利权、著作权等知识产权中的财产权出质的，当事人应当订立书面合同。质权自有关主管部门办理出质登记时设立。知识产权中的财产权出质后，出质人不得转让或者许可他人使用，但经出质人与质权人协商同意的除外。出质人转让或者许可他人使用出质的知识产权中的财产权所得的价款，应当向质权人提前清偿债务或者提存（《民法典》第 444 条）。

（4）应收账款。应收账款是会计学上的概念，是销售商品或提供劳务而应向购货单位或顾客收取的款项。在会计制度中，应收账款属于企业的非货币性资产。在民法理论中，应收账款其实就是一种债权，即卖方或劳务提供方依法享有的请求买方或接受劳务的一方支付价金或劳务费的请求权。《民法典》中规定的"应收账款"，是指"未被证券化的、以金钱给付标的的现有以及将来的合同债权"。以应收账款出质的，当事人应当订立书面合同。质权自信贷征信机构办理出质登记时设立。应收账款出质后，不得转让，但经出质人与质权人协商同意的除外。出质人转让应收账款所得的价款，应当向质权人提前清偿债务或者提存。

（5）法律、行政法规规定可以出质的其他财产权利。中国法律对质押的财产持开放的态度，给立法者、律师、法官、法律研究人员更大的创设、思维与适用空间。

第四节 留 置 权

一、留置权的概念和特征

留置权，是指当债务人不履行到期债务时，债权人可以留置已经合法占有的债务人的动产，并有权就该动产折价或者以拍卖、变卖的价款优先受偿的权利。其特征主要有：

（一）留置权是一种担保物权

留置权人对于其留置的物享有支配的权利并可以排斥他人干涉。留置权不仅可以对债权人主张，而且可以对抗留置标的物的受让人。留置权不仅是物权，而且是一种担保物权，因为它的主要作用是为了担保债权的实现。

（二）留置权是以动产为标的物的担保物权

留置权为基于动产占有而发生的法定担保物权，债权人因合法理由占有债务人的动产，始得发生留置权。不动产不能移动，不能作为留置权的客体。

（三）留置权是法定担保物权

在符合一定的条件时，依法律的规定产生，而不是依当事人之间的协议设定的。但是，依据《民法典》第 449 条规定，当事人可以通过约定不得留置的动产而排除留置权的适用。

（四）留置权可以两次发生效力

第一次发生效力是指在留置产生的时候，债权人在其债权没有得到清偿时，有权留置债务人的财产，留置本身是第一次发生效力。第二次发生效力是指债务人超过规定的期限仍不履行其债务，留置权人可以依法以留置物折价或拍卖、变卖的价款优先受偿。

（五）留置权不具有追及效力

留置权首先是一种物权，但是其并不具有作为物权属性的追及效力。《民法典》第457条规定："留置权人对留置财产丧失占有或者留置权人接受债务人另行提供担保的，留置权消灭。"留置权是以占有为基础的担保物权，在丧失占有后就消灭了权利本身。从这一点上说，留置权的物权性弱于其他担保物权。

关于商事留置权与民事留置权，《民法典》第448条规定："债权人留置的动产，应当与债权属于同一法律关系，但企业之间留置的除外。"据此，《民法典》已明确规定了商事留置权。商事留置权与民事留置权相比，一是主体不同，前者适用于商人之间因双方的商行为而产生的债权，其主体都必须是商人；二是成立要件不同，前者不要求债权的发生与债权人占有的债务人的该动产具有牵连关系。

二、留置权的成立条件

留置权的成立必须具备如下条件：

（一）债权人必须合法占有债务人的动产

债权人占有债务人的动产是留置权发生的前提。这里的占有不仅是指直接占有，而且是指合法占有。这里的债务人的动产，是指该财产为债务人所有的依法可以进行交易的财产。

《担保法》规定留置权只能发生在特定的合同关系中。《担保法》第84条规定："因保管合同、运输合同、加工承揽合同发生的债权，债务人不履行债务的，债权人有留置权。法律规定可以留置的其他合同，适用前款规定。当事人可以在合同中约定不得留置的物。"《物权法》《民法典》未对留置权适用作出这样的限定规定。根据《民法典》第447条第1款规定，只有债权人"合法占有的债务人的动产"，债权人才可能享有留置权。因此，不仅债权人依据合同关系而合法占有债务人的动产可以被留置，而且债权人基于其他法律关系而合法占有债务人的动产也可以被留置，如基于无因管理之债而占有的他人的动产，当受益人不偿付管理人由此而支付的必要费用时，管理人也有权留置该动产。

《民法典》第449条规定："法律规定或者当事人约定不得留置的动产，不得留置。"

（二）债权人占有的债务人的动产与债权属于同一法律关系

《民法典》第448条规定："债权人留置的动产，应当与债权属于同一法律关系，但企业之间留置的除外。""属于同一法律关系"也称为"有牵连关系"。如果没有牵连关系则将形成不同的债权,债权人应当向债务人分别提出请求。债权的发生与标的物的占有取得是因同一法律关系而发生,并且债务人不履行债务时,债权人有留置权。

(3)债权须已届满清偿期而债务人未按规定的期限履行义务

在具备上述三个条件时,留置权一般即可成立。因而上述三个条件被称为留置权成立的积极条件。但如果存在妨碍留置权成立的情形,即使具备了上述三个条件,留置权仍不能成立。因而该条件被称为留置权成立的消极条件。妨碍留置权成立的情形有以下几项:其一,当事人约定排除留置权的适用。留置权是一种财产权,应当允许当事人约定排除其适用;其二,留置财产违反社会公共利益或社会公德;其三,留置财产与债权人所承担的义务相抵触。

三、留置权人的权利和义务

(一)留置权人的权利

1. 对留置物的占有权

留置权人在其债权未受到清偿时有留置标的物的权利。这意味着留置权人有权占有债务人交付的财产,以督促债务人履行债务,即留置权人对留置标的物的占有权受民法占有制度的保护。在留置权人行使留置权以后,如果债务人请求债权人返还该物,债权人有权予以拒绝。留置权人所享有的占有权是一种持续的权利,这就使留置权人得以保持对留置物的持续占有,直至留置权消灭或者留置权实现。

但是,《民法典》第450条规定:"留置财产为可分物的,留置财产的价值应当相当于债务的金额。"这是对留置权不可分性的限制。如果严格地强调留置权的不可分性可能会对债务人不公平,也不利于对留置物的充分利用。

2. 留置资产孳息收取权

《民法典》第452条规定:"留置权人有权收取留置财产的孳息。前款规定的孳息应当先充抵收取孳息的费用。"留置权人在占有留置物期间内,有权就留置物的孳息享有收取的权利。如果孳息是金钱,则可直接以其冲抵债务;如果孳息是其他财产,留置权人可以以其折价或变价,优先受偿。当然留置权人对留置物的孳息应以善良管理人的注意进行妥善的管理,如果没有尽到这种注意义务,给债务人造成损失的应当承担赔偿责任。

3. 必要使用权

从原则上说留置权人对留置的物不享有使用权,但是在特殊情况下,出于保管留置物的需要,留置权人可适当地使用留置物。例如,为了防止留置的汽车生锈进行适度的使用。留置权人只能在具有保管上的必要时才能使用,而不能以获得收益为目的而使用留置物,否则将构成侵权行为。此外经债务人的同意,留置权人也有权使用留置物。

4. 实现留置权的权利

留置权人在留置债务人的财产后，债务人逾期仍不履行的，债权人可以与债务人商议以留置物折价，也可以依法拍卖、变卖留置物。留置权人有权就留置物的价值优先受偿，是保障留置权人债权实现的根本手段。

(二) 留置权人的义务

1. 妥善保管留置物

留置权人负有妥善保管留置财产的义务。因保管不善致使留置财产毁损、灭失的，应当承担赔偿责任。

2. 返还留置物的义务

当留置权所担保的债权消灭时，留置权人有义务将留置物返还于债务人。在债权虽未消灭，但债务人另行提供担保而使留置权消灭时，留置权人也有返还留置物的义务。留置权人违反返还留置物的义务的，构成非法占有，应向债务人或所有人承担民事责任。

四、债务人的权利义务

(一) 债务人的权利

(1) 损害赔偿请求权。留置权人负有妥善保管留置财产的义务。因保管不善致使留置财产毁损、灭失的，债务人有权请求留置权人承担赔偿责任。

(2) 返还留置物请求权。债务人履行债务，债务人有权请求返还留置的动产。

(3) 行使留置权请求权。《民法典》第454条规定："债务人可以请求留置权人在债务履行期届满后行使留置权；留置权人不行使的，债务人可以请求人民法院拍卖、变卖留置财产。"

(4) 消灭留置权的请求权。

(二) 债务人的义务

在留置权发生后，不得干扰、阻碍留置权人行使留置权，并应偿付因保管留置物而支出的必要费用。

五、留置权与质权、抵押权的冲突

《民法典》第456条规定："同一动产上已设立抵押权或者质权，该动产又被留置的，留置权人优先受偿。"

六、留置权的实现

根据《民法典》第453条第1款规定："留置权人与债务人应当约定留置财产后的债

务履行期限；没有约定或者约定不明确的，留置权人应当给债务人六十日以上履行债务的期间，但是鲜活易腐等不易保管的动产除外。债务人逾期未履行的，留置权人可以与债务人协议以留置财产折价，也可以就拍卖、变卖留置财产所得的价款优先受偿。"由此可见，留置权的实现应当遵循如下程序：

第一，确定留置财产后履行债务的期限；

第二，债务人在履行期限内仍然不履行债务；

第三，留置权人有权行使和实现留置权。债权人行使留置权的方式是首先可以与债务人协议将留置物实行折价。如果债务人不同意折价，则留置权人有权依法对留置物实行拍卖、变卖。拍卖可以参照《拍卖法》规定的程序进行，也可以不予参照。对于留置物的变价款和留置物的折价款额，留置权人应当优先受偿。在偿付债权之后，如有剩余额的，应返还给债务人；如无法返还的，应予提存，提存费用从该剩余额中支付。留置物折价或者拍卖、变卖后，其价款超过债权数额的部分归债务人所有，不足部分由债务人清偿。

Chapter 6   Security Interest

Section One   Survey of Security Interest

1. Concept of Security Interest

Security interest is a real right that is created upon a specific property or right owned by the debtor or a third party for guaranteeing the payment of debts.

Article 386 of the Civil Code provides that "Where a debtor fails to perform his obligations due, or any event upon which a security interest is to be enforced as agreed upon by the parties occurs, the person entitled to the security interest has priority to be paid from the collateral in accordance with law, unless otherwise provided by law". The major function of security interest is to guarantee the realization of a claim. As the guarantor has to secure the creditor's right with a specific object or right, a solid safeguard for the realization of the right is thus provided. For this reason, the system of security interest plays an important role in encouraging and promoting transactions. In the modern market economy, security interest exerts active impact on the property of the economy as a basic means of private financing. It is also a most effective way of guaranty where an enterprise or an individual raises financing from a financial institution. In light of this, it may be concluded that security interest has already become an important means of securing social financing.

The security interest is a civil law system of respectable antiquity that came into being against the background of private ownership. Under conception of traditional civil law, security interest includes right to mortgage, pledge and lien. The General Principles of the Civil Law stipulates only on right to mortgage and lien, leaving aside the definition of pledge. This job was later done by the Guaranty Law, which was adopted by the Standing Committee of the Eighth National People's Congress in June, 1995 and went into effect on October 1, 1995. This statute distinguishes the right to mortgage and pledge interest and gives further concrete stipulation on the right to mortgage, pledge and lien. On December 13, 2000, the Supreme People's Court announced the Interpretation of the Supreme People's Court on Certain Issues

Regarding the Application of the Guaranty Law of the People's Republic of China (with 134 articles, hereafter "Judicial Interpretation of the Guaranty Law"). The Real Right Law has incorporated the content on security interests in the Guaranty Law into its own system.

The Civil Code further incorporated the contents of the Real Right Law and the Guaranty Law. It adopted a legislation mode where the law of obligations and real rights are separated in two books, with security interests being regulated in the fourth part of Book Two Real Rights. Book Two Real Rights consist of 5 subdivisions. Its fourth subdivision "Part Four Security Interests" is further divided into 4 chapters in 71 provisions. As an important component of the Civil Code, the security system plays a significant role in strengthening and perfecting the basic socialist economic system and fostering the high-quality economic growth. Taking into consideration the major improvements and developments made by the Civil Code concerning the security system, the SPC, after reviewing the relevant judicial interpretations on security and in accordance with new rules on the security system stipulated by the Civil Code, formulated the Interpretation of the Supreme People's Court on the Application of the "Civil Code of the People's Republic of China" in Respect of Guarantee System (hereafter "Judicial Interpretation on Guarantee System in Civil Code"), which consists of 71 provisions.

2. Features of Security Interest

Frist, the security interest is the accessory right set to secure the realization of the principal claim. The security interest is created to secure the performance of the debt and the realization of the creditor's right by providing specific objects or rights as security. As a result, a claim may be sufficiently secured by the security properties.

Second, the security interest is a qualified right whereby the debtor or a third party provides specific objects or proprietary rights for security. In other words, it is a right set on the property owned by the debtor or the third party.

Third, the security interest is an interest whose contents include the domination of the value in the security property. Exchange value refers to the value of a property that manifests in its exchange with other properties. One may wonder, why it may be concluded that the security interest dominates particular exchange value? This is because, on the one hand, the security interest is created to acquire the exchange value of the security property. If focuses on dominating the value of a property or right in the process of auction or sale. That's why several security interests may be concurrently set on one object by dividing the exchange value of such property, and at the same time the security interest is subrogative, which generally means that where the security property in the occasion of a mortgage or pledge is lost or damaged due to accidents or for other reason, the right holder's security interest may extend to the proceed of the collateral and he may receive such payment out of compensation and damages. On the other hand, one important content of the security interest is the right of the exchange value, meaning that the right holder of the security interest is entitled to auction or sell the security property and has the priority in having his claim paid by the money when the debtor defaults. According to the German scholar Harry Westermann, the security interest is "the right to exchange value of the property right". Exchange value is an abstract concept that may be universally observed in properties. The domination over an object by the security interest manifests reflected in the control of the exchange value instead of the use value. It is in this sense that the security interest is also termed the "right of value", which essentially characterizes the security interest together with the right to exchange value.

Fourth, the security interest is an accessory real right. The security interest is created to ensure the performance of the debt. Its existence is founded upon the principal claim. When the claim is transferred or extinguishes, the security interest shall be transferred or extinguishes along with it. Therefore, the security interest is an accessory right to the claim.

Fifth, the security interest is jus in re aliena. The security interest is established on the property that belongs to another person. The owner the security property may either be the debtor or a third party. For the right holder of the security interest, the security property is owned by others. That's why we classify the security interest as jus in re aliena. The right holder of the security interest enjoys the right to exclude interference as well as the right of pursuit. If the security property is obtained by another person, the right holder of the security interest may pursue and claim his right. Meanwhile, he may dispose of the security property and enjoy the priority in having his claim paid when the debtor defaults.

Sixth, enforcement of the security interest is with its own features. Under other real rights, the right holder may not only directly dominate the object, but also directly possess and use the object as well as exclude illegal intervention from others. Nonetheless, for right holder of security interest, he may not directly do so but has to enforce his right through such legal procedures as auction or sale. For instance, the enforcement of a right to mortgage interest requires that the security property be delivered to competent institutions and auctioned or be sold in accordance with legal procedures when the debtor defaults. The mortgagee shall not directly confiscate the mortgaged property or auction it to get paid in priority. In other words, the right to the exchange value of the security property may be exercised only through particular procedures. It is of great importance to highlight the features in enforcement that characterize the security interest so as to better safeguard the lawful right and interests of the debtor and the general creditors.

Seventh, the security interest is with appurtenance, indivisibility and subrogation natures. The security interest shares such common characters as dominant nature, preferential nature and exclusive nature with general real rights. In addition, it also has the following characters that are unique:

2.7.1   Appurtenance nature. The appurtenance nature denotes that in general, the security interest is an accessory right to the principal claim and its validity largely depends on that of the latter. Still, that the security interest is an accessory right does not change the fact that it can independently exist as a real right. The appurtenance nature if the security interest mainly manifests in the following three aspects:

2.7.1.1   Appurtenance in establishment. In general, the establishment of a security interest is premised on the existence of valid claim. If the principal claim has never been established or is void, the security interest will never take effect even if it is created. Where the principal claim is invalidated or rescinded after being established, the security interest shall also be void as a result. It should be noted that as the security interest evolves into a right of value, the appurtenant and dominant relation between it and the principal claim may be reversed. It may be expected that in the near future, the security interest may be created prior to the principal claim, making it one of the purposes of the security interest to induce the establishment of a creditor's right.

2.7.1.2   Appurtenance in transfer. If the claim is transferred, the security interest shall be transferred along with it because such interest may not be separated from the principal claim. The right holder of the security interest may not separately transfer such right to another person while reserving the principal claim to himself. Deviation from this leads to void transfer. Neither may such right holder transfer his principal claim to another person without concurrently assigning the security interest thereof. It is also forbidden to transfer the claim and the security interest respectively to different transferees.

2.7.1.3   Appurtenance in extinguishment. It means that the security interest extinguishes together with the creditor's right.

2.7.2   Indivisible nature. It denotes that every part of the security property serves to secure the entire claim. A creditor who holds the security interest may exercise his security interest with respect to the entire security property. His right will not be influenced by, may the property be divided or partly destroyed, or that the secured claim has been has been partially performed. Specifically, it vied from the following perspectives:

2.7.2.1   Every part of the security property secures the entire claim, and the creditor who holds the security interest may exercise his right on the entire security property.

2.7.2.2   Division of the claim doesn't affect the existence of the security interest. For example, A had a claim of 100, 000 yuan against C, who mortgaged his house to secure the claim. A partitioned his claim into two and respectively transferred them to two persons. Both of the two transferees may realize their mortgage interest on the entire mortgaged house that was owned by C with respect to their claims.

2. 7. 2. 3   The partial fulfillment of the claim does not affect the existence of the security interest. For example, A borrowed 2,000 yuan from B and pledged his five bicycles. If later A pays back 1,000 yuan, will he be entitled to recover two of the bicycles? The answer is no, because the indivisibility of the security interest enables the creditor to exercise his security interest on the entire security property even if the claim is partially fulfilled as long as the debt has not been completely paid off.

2. 7. 2. 4   If the security property is partially lost, the remainder part left still shall secure the entire claim, meaning that the secured debt shall not be reduced accordingly. Of course, if such loss is attributable to the guarantor, the guarantor is obliged to provide other properties corresponding to the amount of the lost value.

2. 7. 3   Subrogative nature. Subrogative nature denotes the extension of security interest to the proceed of the collateral. The right holder of the security interest has the right of priority while receiving payment out of insurance money, compensation and damages if the security property is lost, damaged or requisitioned. For example, A pledged a car to B for the purpose of borrowing some money. If the car got destroyed in fire and A obtained an amount of insurance money from the insurance company, then such money should become the object of the pledge interest, and the creditor B may have his claim paid in priority with this compensation. Regarding such subrogative nature of the security interest, the Civil Code has made clear stipulations. After the security property is damaged or destructed, the compensation or the insurance money is easily embezzled by the guarantor for other use. To safeguard the realization security interest, Article 390 of the Civil Code stipulates that "Where a collateral is destructed, damaged, or lost, or is expropriated during the secured period, the person entitled to a security interest has priority to be paid ①from the insurance payment, compensation, or indemnity received on the collateral. Where the collateral is destructed, damaged, or lost, or is expropriated prior to the due date of performance of the secured claim, the insurance payment, compensation, or indemnity may also be placed in escrow".

After the security interest is established, the right holder is entitled to take necessary measures to preserve the value of the security property. In the event the value of the security property has declined due to reasons that can be attributed to the guarantor, the right holder of security interest may require the guarantor to provide security corresponding to the amount of the lost value. Article 408 of the Civil Code stipulates that "Where an act of a mortgagor suffices to reduce the value of the mortgaged property, the mortgagee is entitled to request the mortgagor to refrain from performing such an act. Where the value of the mortgaged property is reduced, the mortgagee is entitled to request the mortgagor to restore its value or provide additional security to

---

① It means the priority right of a particular creditor to receive compensations in comparison with other creditors, or even other real right holders.

the extent of the reduced value. Where the mortgagor neither restores the original value of the mortgaged property, nor provides additional security therefor, the mortgagee is entitled to request the debtor to pay off the debt before it is due".

3. Acquisition and Scope of Security Interest

3. 1   Acquisition of Security Interest

Legal facts that may cause the acquisition of a security interest can be divided into two categories.

3. 1. 1   Acquisition of the security interest through civil juristic act, including the establishment and assignment of the security interest.

3. 1. 1. 1   Establishment of the Security Interest. The first sentence of Para. 1, Article 388 of the Civil Code prescribes that "To create a security interest, a security contract shall be entered into in accordance with the provisions of this Code and other laws". It may be drawn from this provision that firstly, the lien is a statutory security interest, thus its establishment doesn't require the conclusion of a contract, which constitutes an exceptional case; secondly, the guarantee contract shall be in written form.

3. 1. 1. 2   Transfer of the Security Interest. In light of the appurtenance nature of the security interest, when the principal claim is transferred, the security interest shall be transferred concurrently as an accessory right, unless otherwise agreed upon by the parties.

3. 1. 2   Acquisition of the security interest not through civil juristic acts, which include the following circumstances:

3. 1. 2. 1   Acquisition of the security interest directly based on statutory stipulations including the lien, right of priority for repayment of construction project price of the contractor of a construction project (Article 807 of the Civil Code) , the preemptive right over civil aircraft (Article 18 of the Civil Aviation Law and Article 19 to 25) , maritime liens (Article 21 of the Maritime Law and Article 22 to 30).

3. 1. 2. 2   Acquisition of security interest by succession.

3. 1. 2. 3   Acquisition of security interest by prescription (not stipulated in the Civil Code).

3. 2   Scope of the Secured Claim

Article 389 of the Civil Code prescribes that, "Unless otherwise agreed by the parties, the scope covered by a security interest includes the principal claim and its interests based on the principal contract, liquidated damages, compensatory damages, and the expenses arising from safekeeping the collateral and enforcing the security interests".

4. Counter-security

Concerning counter-security Article 689 and Para. 2, Article 387 of the Civil Code provide clear rules. Para. 2, Article 387 of the Civil Code stipulates that "Where a third person provides security to the creditor for the debtor, the debtor may be requested to provide a counter-security. Counter-security shall be governed by the provisions of this Code and other laws".

Counter-security means that the debtor or a third party makes suretyship or sets security interest on property to assure the guarantor that it will liquidate the debt owed to the guarantor if any damage has incurred by the latter in liquidating the debt of the debtor. In a counter-security, the security based on which counter-security is set and which serves as the premise of the counter-security is called the original security. Counter-security is a concept relative to the original guarantee. The guarantor of the original guarantee is called original guarantor and that of the counter-security is called counter guarantor.

The major function of counter-security is to realize the guarantor's right of recourse. It aims to secure such right. The guarantor enjoys a right of recourse against the debtor after he undertakes the responsibility for the debtor. It thus becomes necessary to create the counter-security for the purpose of securing such right. Counter-security may apply to various forms of guarantee. Be it is in a personal guarantee or in a security on property, the security provider may require the debtor to provide counter-security.

The creation of the counter-security requires the following elements:

4.1 Counter-security is Premised on the Original Security

Generally speaking, the counter-security is appurtenant to and dependent on the original Security. The original Security is the premise and foundation of the counter-security. If it is not effective, so will be the counter-security. However, the responsibility involved in the counter-security is somehow independent from the original security. Article 388 of the Civil Code stipulates that "To create a security interest, a security contract shall be entered into in accordance with the provisions of this Code and other laws. Security contracts include mortgage contracts, pledge contracts, and other contracts with a function of security. A security contract is a contract secondary to the principal contract with the principal claims and obligations. Where the principal contract is void, the security contract is also void, unless otherwise provided by law. Where a security contract is determined to be void, if the debtor, the security provider, and the creditor are at fault, they shall each bear civil liability in proportion to their fault". In addition, the parties may stipulate in the Counter-security contract that the validity of the Counter-security is independent from that of the Original Security. Such stipulation is also legally valid.

4. 2   Security Provider of the Counter-security is Not Limited to the Debtor, but May Also be a Third Party

The counter-security may either be mortgages or pledges offered by the debtor, or guarantees, mortgages or pledges offered by a third party. When the debtor is the counter security provider, the Counter-security may only be security on property; it may not be personal guarantee. That is because the debtor himself may not be the security provider, thus it makes no real significance when he becomes the counter-security provider. When the counter-security provider is a third party, then the security interest may either be personal guarantee or security on property.

4. 3   Application Scope of Counter-security is in Principle Limited within Guarantee, Mortgage or Pledge

That is to say, the counter-security may not arise in such statutory security interest as lien. It only exists in security interest that is stipulated in a contract. Since statutory security is created upon the occurrence of certain facts, thus the parties cannot foresee their security responsibility; neither can they make prearrangement to secure their right of recourse by means of Counter-security. In addition, under statutory security, the right of recourse may not arise as it is usually the debtor who undertakes the security responsibility. In light of this, the Counter-security is unnecessary for the statutory security.

4. 4   Counter-security Shall Have Certain Formality Requirements

Para. 2, Article 387 of the Civil Code stipulates that "Where a third person provides security to the creditor for the debtor, the debtor may be requested to provide a counter-security. Counter-security shall be governed by the provisions of this Code and other laws". Provision on security in the Civil Code apply to the conclusion of contract for counter-security and establishment of the counter-security. In general cases the written form and registration shall be required.

After the counter-guaranty is created, the right of recourse takes effect only after the security provider has actually undertaken the security liability and thus acquired the right of recourse against the debtor and the counter security provider.

5. Security on Property, Personal Guarantee, and Mixed Joint Security

The security interest is generally termed security on property. Strictly speaking, the two still differ from each other. The property under the security interest is not limited to tangible property. Such rights whose objects are intangible properties as the pledge of rights, right of priority etc. may also be the object of the security interest. As a security property typically takes the form of movable property or immovable property, the security on property is generally regarded as the opposite counterpart of the personal guarantee.

The personal guarantee refers to such security system whereby a natural person or legal person secures the performance of the debt with their own assets or credit. It initially originated from the "hostage" in ancient times, meaning that the person himself is made as guarantee. In the modern sense, however, the personal guarantee mainly denotes that a security provider secures a claim with the credit or entire property of a third party. A typical form of personal security is guarantee. Personal security may be categorized as security of obligatory right in nature, meaning that the right holder of the security may not directly control the security property of the security provider but may only request performance when the debtor fails to fulfill such obligation.

Primary distinction between security on property and personal guarantee lies in:

5. 1 Differences in Properties or Credits Provided for Security

Under personal guarantee, the general liability property or credit property of a third party is usually provided for security, which means that the entire property of the third party is provided to secure the debt. In security interest on property, however, what is provided for security is such particular property as movable property, immovable property, rights, etc. On the one hand, personal guarantee may increase the amount of the general liability property that is available for liquidation. If the security provider is with sufficient capacity to pay off the debt when the debtor defaults, the personal guarantee may serve as a reliable safeguard for the realization of the creditor's right. On the other hand, due to the fluctuation and instability of the general liability property, it may be the case that a security provider also doesn't have enough property to pay off the debt when the debtor defaults. As a result, the debt is still at the risk of non-performance. In comparison, security on property is not affected by the fluctuation in personal property. Thus, it is more reliable than personal guarantee.

5. 2 Differences in Subjects

The subject of personal guarantee is limited to a third party other than the debtor, while that of the security on property may either be the debtor or a third party.

5. 3 Differences in Legal Effects

In essence, the personal guarantee is still a contractual relationship that may only give rise to claims, which cannot get paid in priority. The claim enjoyed by the creditor against the security provider may only enable him to share the distribution of the guarantor's property with other general creditors in certain proportion. However, the security on property gives rise to property right, which may be paid in priority. For this reason, it is generally held that the legal effect of security on property prevails over that of personal guarantee when the two coexist (mixed joint security).

Regarding mixed joint security Article 392 of the Civil Code stipulates that "Where a claim is secured by both a collateral and a surety, and the debtor fails to perform his obligations due or any event upon which a security interest is to be enforced as agreed upon by the parties occurs, the creditor shall enforce the claim in accordance with the agreement. Where there is no agreement or the agreement is unclear, if the collateral is provided by the debtor, the creditor shall first enforce the claim against the collateral, and if the collateral is provided by a third person, the creditor may elect to enforce the claim against the collateral or request the surety to assume liability. After the third person who provides security has assumed such liability, he has the right of indemnification against the debtor". This provision has differentiated the following two cases, including three situations: First, where there is agreement between parities regarding the payment of the claim, the creditor shall have his claim paid or enforce his security interest as agreed upon. Second, where there is no such agreement or the agreement is indefinite in this respect, the case should be further differentiated into two situations: if the debtor himself provides property as security, the creditor shall have his claim paid with such property first; where a third party provides property as security, the creditor may either have his claim paid with such property or request the security provider to undertake the suretyship. Third, after the third party has borne the suretyship, he shall have the right of recourse against the debtor.

6. Identification and Legal Effects of Forfeiture Agreement

6. 1   Concept and Features of Forfeiture Agreement

Forfeiture agreement, or the so-called utter guaranty contract, denotes such cases where the parties, upon establishing a mortgage or pledge interest, stipulate in the security contract that the ownership of the security property goes to the creditor if the debt is not liquidated after maturity. The main characteristics of the contract may be concluded as follows:

First, it is mainly adopted in cases where the security interest is created by agreement. It exists only when the parties create the security interest through concluding a contract for mortgage or pledge interest. It generally doesn't appear in statutory security interest.

Second, such contract may not only be stipulated in the security contract in advance, but also otherwise agreed upon independent of the security contract. The agreement between the parties on the conversion of the security property after the maturity of the debt is not taken as forfeiture articles.

Third, such contract usually states that the ownership of the security property completely goes to the creditor.

6. 2　Effects and Legal Results of Forfeiture Agreement

The civil law system traditionally prohibits the contract. The Civil Code leases the issue open. Article 401 of the code prescribes that "Where, prior to the due date of performance of an obligation, the mortgagor reaches an agreement with the mortgagor under which the mortgaged property belongs to the creditor in the event that the debtor fails to perform the obligation due, the mortgagee, regardless, may only have priority to be paid from the mortgaged property in accordance with law". Article 428 prescribes that, "Where, prior to the due date of performance of an obligation, the pledgee reaches an agreement with the pledgor under which the pledged property belongs to the creditor in the event that the debtor fails to perform the obligation due, the pledgee, regardless, may only have priority to be paid from the pledged property in accordance with law". The ostensible meaning of the forfeiture agreement is invalid, according to the law, the pledgee may only have priority to be paid from the pledged property, to realize the security interest. The legislative goals of the legal provisions of the forfeiture agreement may be mainly concluded as follows:

1. Protecting the obligor.

2. Protecting the interests of other creditors other than the right holder of the security interest.

3. Preventing the loss of state-owned assets.

Where parties violate the provision of the Guaranty Law on the prohibitive contract, it does not mean the act of establishing the relative security interest is also void. Such act for establishment is still effective if it is in compliance with the law. The invalidity is only with respect to the provision that stipulates the transfer before the maturity of the debt. The invalidity of the prohibitive contract does not affect the validity of the security contract.

7. Extinguishment of Security Interests

Article 393 of the Civil Code prescribes that "A security interest is extinguished under any of the following circumstances: (1) the claim under the principal contract is extinguished; (2) the security interest is enforced; (3) the creditor waives his security interest; or (4) there exists any other circumstance in which security interest is extinguished as provided by law".

Section Two　Right to Mortgage

1. Concept and Features of Right to Mortgage

The right to mortgage denotes such right whereby the creditor enjoys priority in having his claim paid with the converted property value (by means of converting the property into money, auction or selling off the property), the property includes movable property and immovable property that are mortgaged by the debtor or a third party for guaranteeing the payment of debts without transferring of the possession of such property when the debtor defaults to pay off his debt. "Converting the property into money" in the context of this book refers to the transfer of the ownership of the subject matter from one party to another, at the price of which both parties with debtor-creditor relationship recognize in accordance with the actual market price or evaluated value estimated by a valuation institution entrusted by both parties, which partially or completely pays off the debts of the debtor or a third party. The debtor or the third party is the mortgagor, the creditor is the mortgagee, and the property used as security is mortgaged property.

From the ancient Roman law to the modern civil law in Europe, the right to mortgage has always been a security interest separate from the pledge. It is a security interest that secures the performance of the debt without transferring possession of the property; while the pledge secures a claim by way of transferring the possession of movable property or rights. Nonetheless, Russia has come up with a new legislation pattern. From the 1922 Civil Code of the Soviet Russia to the current Civil Code of the Russian Federation, the two rights have never been differentiated in the law, but rather, they are combined into one and termed "mortgage right". According to such legislation pattern, the object of the mortgage interest can be any property including immovable property, movable property and proprietary rights right. As to the establishment of the mortgage interest, unless it is stipulated by law that transfer of possession is not needed, the parties may stipulate whether they would like to transfer the possession of the mortgaged property or not. Where it is agreed upon by the parties that the possession is not be transferred, the mortgagee may make a mark on the guaranty or have it sealed at its place.

The General Principles of the Civil Law follows the approach adopted by Russia while regulating on the mortgage interest. It only stipulates on the mortgage interest, thus sparing the pledge interest. The Guaranty Law of 1995 turns to the traditional civil law approach by making separate stipulations regarding the two rights, which leads to a relatively more scientific system of mortgage interest rules and concepts. The Civil Code sticks to the same by separately prescribing the two security interests. Features of a mortgage interest may be concluded as follows:

1. 1　Mortgage Interest is a Real Right

The right to mortgage is property right though it is with some characters of a claim. On the one hand, the mortgagee enjoys the right to control the specified mortgaged property provided by the mortgagor. Although the possession is not transferred, the mortgagee may still control the value of the mortgaged property, without being affected if such mortgaged property is assigned. Where the guaranty is damaged or lost during the mortgage period, it may be subrogated, meaning that the effects of mortgage interest will extend to the proceeds obtained after the mortgaged property is converted. On the other hand, the mortgagee enjoys priority in getting his claim paid. That is to say, when a claim that is secure by the mortgage interest coexists with a general claim on one property, the mortgagee shall have the priority in getting the claim repaid. Where several mortgage interests coexist concurrently on one property, the earlier mortgaged claim shall prevail over the later mortgaged claim. In addition, where the mortgaged property is damaged by others, the mortgagee may require removal of such impairment from his mortgaged interest. All of these indicates that the right to mortgage is a real right.

1. 2　The Right to Mortgage is a Security Interest

The right to mortgage is created to secure the obligatory right, namely the performance of the debt. Its establishment and existence are premised and based on the existence of certain claim. Where the mortgaged right extinguishes, so will the right to mortgage do. The right to mortgage may not be transferred apart from the mortgaged claim. Neither may it be the security of another claim apart from the claim it secures. The purpose of establishing the right to mortgage lie in the need to ensure the fulfillment of the principal claim.

1. 3　The Right to Mortgage is a Real Right Set on the Property Owned by the Debtor or a Third Party

1. 4　The Right to Mortgage is a Security Interest that Waives the Transfer of the Possession over the Object

Waiving transfer of possession means that the guaranty remains being possessed by the mortgagor after the right to mortgage is established. This constitutes the major distinction between the right to mortgage and the pledge. Also because of it, the mortgagor may continue possessing and using the mortgaged property so as to give full play to its usefulness. For the same reason, the right to mortgage may not be publicized by way of delivery, but only in the form of registration. This also determines that in practice the objects of the right to mortgage are mostly immovable property instead of movable property.

1.5　The Right to Mortgage is a Right to the Priority in Getting One's Claim Paid with the Converted Proceeds Obtained from the Mortgaged Property

The priority in compensation denotes that when the debtor fails to perform the matured debt, the creditor has the right of priority in getting liquidated with the proceeds obtained after the mortgaged property is lawfully disposed by such means as converting it into money (reference to page 583), auction or sale. The priority in compensation is a significant character for the right to mortgage as a security interest. However, it does enable the mortgagee to directly take over the guaranty when the debtor fails to perform his debt. Rather, it only allows the mortgagee to first let the mortgaged property converted into money and then have priority in having his claim paid with the proceeds. In this sense, the right to mortgage is a right of value or a right of priority in getting compensated with proceeds obtained from the conversion of the mortgaged property.

2. Ways of Establishing a Mortgage

2.1　Acquisition of a Mortgage Interest through Civil Juristic Acts

2.1.1　It further falls into two categories, namely, establishment of the right to mortgaged and assignment of the right to mortgage. The right to mortgage acquired through civil juristic acts is theoretically termed as stipulated or intended mortgage.

In practice, conclusion of a mortgage contract is most common way to establish the right. As a result, the first sentence of Para. 1, Article 388 of the Civil Code prescribes that, "To create a security interest, a security contract shall be entered into in accordance with the provisions of this Code and other laws".

Regarding formality of the mortgage contract, Para. 1, Article 400 of the Civil Code provides that, "To create a mortgage, the parties shall enter into a mortgage contract in writing".

Concerning contents of the mortgage contract, Para. 2, Article 400 of the Civil Code stipulates that, "A mortgage contract generally contains the following terms: (1) the type and amount of the secured claim; (2) the term during which the debtor shall perform obligations; (3) such particulars as the name and quantity of the mortgaged property; and (4) the scope of the security interest covered".

For cases where a mortgage interest is obtained through transfer, Article 407 of the Civil Code regulates that, "A mortgage may not be transferred separately from the underlying claim or be used as security for another claim. Where a claim is transferred, the mortgage securing the claim shall be transferred concomitantly with it, unless otherwise provided by law or agreed by the parties". Thus, if a creditor transfers his obligatory right to others, the right to mortgage shall be transferred accordingly, thus the transferee obtains the right to mortgage. This method to acquire the right to mortgage is just the transfer of the right to mortgage.

2.1.2 Mortgage interest not acquired through civil juristic acts. This includes acquisition of the right to mortgage based on statutory stipulation, i. e. , statutory mortgage interest, on the principle of presumption of accuracy, or through succession.

2.2 Parties in Mortgage Relationship

The parties in mortgage include the mortgagor and the mortgagee. The mortgagee refers to the creditor. As the mortgage interest is established to secure the principal claim, only the creditor in such secured principal claim may be the mortgagee. The mortgagor, or the owner of the mortgaged property, is the person who establishes the right to mortgage with his own property for himself or others. He may either be the debtor or a third party. As the right to mortgage is an act of disposal of the property in nature, the mortgagor must own or is with the right to dispose of the mortgaged property.

2.3 The Mortgaged Property

The collateral, or the mortgaged property, is the object of the right to mortgage. However, not any property may be the object of a right to mortgage. On the one hand, the mortgaged property shall be a specified property, or it covers a definite sphere of influence. If the mortgaged property is unspecified, the mortgagee cannot exert control over it the mortgaged property, thus unable to enforce it. On the other hand, as the enforcement of the right to mortgage requires auctioning or selling off the guaranty, the mortgaged property must also be transferable. As such, properties that are legally forbidden to be circulated or that are subject to compulsory enforcement may not be the guaranty. It should also be noted that as the establishment of the right to mortgage is not publicized by way of delivery, but rather by such means as registration or other means, the mortgaged property must be able to be registered or publicized.

Article 395 of the Civil Code prescribes the scope of mortgageable property, stating that "The following property, which the debtor or a third person is entitled to dispose of, may be mortgaged: (1) buildings and other things attached to the land; (2) the right to use a lot of land for construction purposes; (3) the right to use the sea areas; (4) production equipment, raw materials, work in process, and finished products; (5) buildings, vessels, and aircraft under construction; (6) vehicles for transport; and (7) other property not prohibited by laws or administrative regulations from being mortgaged. A mortgagor may mortgage the property listed in the preceding paragraph concurrently". Article 396 of the code stipulates that "An enterprise, an individual-run industrial and commercial household, or an agricultural production operator may mortgage their production equipment, raw materials, work in process, and finished products that they currently own or thereafter acquired, and if the debtor fails to perform his obligations due or any event upon which a security interest in the mortgaged property is to be enforced as agreed by the parties occurs, the creditor has priority to be paid from the movable property determined at the time when the mortgaged property is ascertained". Article 397 further prescribes that, "Where a building is mortgaged, the right to use the lot of land in the area occupied by the building for construction purposes shall be mortgaged concomitantly. Where a mortgagor fails to concomitantly mortgage the property as provided in the preceding paragraph, the unmortgaged property in question shall be deemed to be concomitantly mortgaged". Such assumed mortgage is termed as statutory mortgage or statutory mortgage interest in this book. Article 398 of Civil Code provides that "A right to use a lot of land for construction purposes of a township or village enterprise may not be mortgaged separately. Where a factory premise or any other building of a township or village enterprise is mortgaged, the right to use the lot of land in the area occupied by the building for construction purposes shall be concomitantly mortgaged".

Apart from the above provisions on mortgageable properties, the Civil Code also prescribes the scope of the property that are not mortgageable. Article 399 of the code provides that "The following property may not be mortgaged: (1) land ownership; (2) the right to use the land owned by a collective, such as house sites, land and hills retained for household use, unless it may be mortgaged as provided by law; (3) educational facilities, medical and health facilities, and other public welfare facilities of non-profit legal persons established for public welfare purposes, such as schools, kindergartens, and medical institutions; (4) property of which the ownership or right to the use is unclear or disputed; (5) property that has been seized, detained, or placed under custody in accordance with law; and (6) other property that may not be mortgaged as provided by laws or administrative regulations".

2. 4   Registration of Mortgage

Strict requirements on formalities are necessary for the establishment of the right to mortgage, as the effects of the right may directly affect not only the mortgagor and the mortgagee, but also the general creditors of the mortgagor and other persons concerned in relations to the mortgaged property.

2. 4. 1   Circumstances Where Registration is Compulsory

According to Article 402 of the Civil Code, "To create a mortgage on the property as specified in Subparagraphs (1) through (3) of the first paragraph of Article 395, or on the building under construction as specified in Subparagraph (5) of the first paragraph of this Code, registration shall be made for the mortgage. The mortgage shall be created upon registration". The mortgage on the following property shall be registered: (1) buildings and other things attached to the land; (2) the right to use a lot of land for construction purposes; (3) the right to use the sea areas; and (4) the buildings under construction.

2.4.2   Circumstances Where Registration is Voluntary

According to Article 403 of the Civil Code, "A mortgage on movable property shall be created at the time when the mortgage contract enters into effect; without registration, such a mortgage may not be asserted against a bona fide third person". The movable property here referred to include (1) production equipment, raw materials, work in process, and finished products; (2) vessels and aircraft under construction; and (3) vehicles for transport. Where an enterprise, a self-employed industrial or commercial household, or an agricultural producer or distributor mortgages their existing and anticipated production equipment, raw materials, work in process, and finished products, they may complete the registration with the competent registration authority.

3. Rights of the Parties in Mortgage Relationship

3.1   Rights of the Mortgagee

3.1.1   The right to the disposition of the mortgage. This refers to such acts that are with legal effect in sustaining, eliminating or reducing the sphere of influence on the right to mortgage, which include (1) transfer of a mortgage (a mortgage shall be transferred along with the principal claim it secures); Article 407 of the Civil Code provides that "A mortgage may not be transferred separately from the underlying claim or be used as security for another claim. Where a claim is transferred, the mortgage securing the claim shall be transferred concomitantly with it, unless otherwise provided by law or agreed by the parties". Viewed from this provision, the Civil Code does not recognize the creation of a security interest in mortgage. (2) using a mortgage to secure other claims; and (3) abandonment of a mortgage. A mortgage may not be used for securing other claim apart from the principal claim, but may be provided as security for other claims together with the principal claim or create a security on claim that co-exists with a collateral mortgage. Abandonment of the right to mortgage should be followed by deregistration, and transfer thereof the alteration registration. Where the right to mortgage is provided as a security for another claim, the establishment registration shall be gone through.

Article 39 of the Judicial Interpretation on Guarantee System in Civil Code stipulates that "Where a principal claim is divided or partially assigned, and each creditor claims exercise of a security interest for the share of the claim it has, the people's court shall uphold the claim, unless otherwise provided by law or agreed by the parties. If a main debt is divided or partially delegated, the debtor gives real guarantee, and the creditor requests that the property given as a guarantee should guarantee the performance of the debt in whole, the people's court shall uphold the claim; or if a third party gives a real guarantee and claims that it ceases to assume the guarantor's liability for the debt is delegated without its written consent, the people's court shall uphold the claim". When the principal obligation is divided or partially transferred, the registration thereof is not a must and may be waived.

Para. 2, Article 38 of Judicial Interpretation on Guarantee System in Civil Code provides that "If a collateral is divided or partially transferred, and the security interest holder claims the exercise of its security interest in the collateral as divided or transferred, the people's court shall uphold the claim, unless otherwise provided by law or judicial interpretation".

In addition, according to Article 392 of the Civil Code, "Where a claim is secured by both a collateral and a surety, and the debtor fails to perform his obligations due or any event upon which a security interest is to be enforced as agreed upon by the parties occurs, the creditor shall enforce the claim in accordance with the agreement. Where there is no agreement or the agreement is unclear, if the collateral is provided by the debtor, the creditor shall first enforce the claim against the collateral, and if the collateral is provided by a third person, the creditor may elect to enforce the claim against the collateral or request the surety to assume liability. After the third person who provides security has assumed such liability, he has the right of indemnification against the debtor". Where the mortgaged property is provided by a third person and there is no agreement or the agreement is unclear regarding the share or order of the claim secured by such property, the mortgagee may exercise his right on any or every of such property. After assuming security liability, the mortgagor may have recourse against the debtor or require other mortgagors to pay for their own shares. Article 409 of the Civil Code stipulates that "Where a debtor creates a mortgage on his own property, and the mortgagee waives his right to the mortgage and his priority order in the line of mortgagees, or changes the mortgage, the other security providers shall be exempted from the security liability to the extent of the rights and interests of the mortgagee that are forfeited owing to the waiver of his priority to be paid from the mortgaged property, unless the other security providers are committed to still provide security".

3. 1. 2   The right to preserve and restore the value of the mortgaged property.

Pursuant to Article 408 of the Civil Code, "Where an act of a mortgagor suffices to reduce the value of the mortgaged property, the mortgagee is entitled to request the mortgagor to refrain from performing such an act. Where the value of the mortgaged property is reduced, the mortgagee is entitled to request the mortgagor to restore its value or provide additional security to the extent of the reduced value. Where the mortgagor neither restores the original value of the mortgaged property, nor provides additional security therefor, the mortgagee is entitled to request the debtor to pay off the debt before it is due". This provision in fact confirmed three rights, namely, the right to request cessation of acts reducing the value of the mortgaged property, right to request restoring value of the mortgaged property and the right to request to pay off the debt before it is due.

3. 1. 3   Tort Claims for Compensation of Damages and Claims on Real Rights

These rights concern the control over the mortgaged property and exclude the infringement of other persons. During the term of the mortgage, the mortgagee still enjoys the corresponding dominance and control over the mortgaged property, though he does not actually possess it. Where the mortgaged property is encroached upon by a third party, the mortgagee is entitled to claim against the tortfeasor for cessation of the infringement, restoration or compensation of damages. When the mortgaged property is taken by a third party by force, the mortgagee may exercise his claims on real rights to ensure the enforcement of his rights.

3. 1. 4   Priority Right in Getting Claim Repaid

Priority right in getting claim repaid is the right enjoyed by the mortgagee in cases where a debtor fails to perform his obligation due or an event upon which a mortgage is to be enforced as agreed upon by the parties occurs, upon agreement with the mortgagor, to have the priority right to appraise and accept the mortgaged property, or apply the proceeds obtained from auction or sale of the mortgaged property to satisfy his claim against the mortgagor. In addition, this right also has the following contents. First, in terms of the internal priority, namely, in cases where different mortgages conflict with each other, the mortgages shall be enforced in accordance with the order stipulated by Article 414 of the Civil Code. Second, in terms of the external priority, a mortgage shall prevail over a creditor's right in cases where the mortgaged property is seized or enforced. Where the mortgaged property is detained or enforced, the mortgagee has the priority right to apply the proceeds obtained from auction or sale of the mortgaged property to satisfy his claim against the mortgagor. If the debtor is declared bankrupt, the mortgage shall prevail over any creditor's right, and the mortgaged property shall not be listed into the bankruptcy property.

3. 2   Rights of the Mortgagor

3. 2. 1   The right to establish several mortgages on one collateral. This means that the mortgagor may establish multiple non-conflicting mortgages on a same mortgaged property. More specifically, it includes repeated establishment of mortgage and remortgage.

3. 2. 2   The right to establish rights to usufruct on the mortgaged property. In China, where natural resources such as land only belongs to the state or collective organization and are forbidden to be mortgaged, the rights to usufruct are all derived from the ownership such natural

resources as is illustrated by the right to use land for construction purposes, the right to use a house site and the right to use sea areas, etc. As a result, mortgagors of immovable properties in China are less likely to be accesible to establish rights to usufruct on the guaranty. However, the right holder of the right to use land for construction purposes may establish easement on a mortgaged property.

3.2.3 The right to lease the mortgaged property. The Civil Code follows the approach adopted by the Real Right Law. Article 405 of the code prescribes that "Where a mortgaged property has been let to and possessed by another person prior to creation of the mortgage, the lease relationship shall not be affected by the mortgage". If a mortgagor leases the mortgaged property before the mortgage contract is concluded, the previously established leasing relation shall not be affected. If a mortgagor leases the mortgaged property after the creation of the mortgage interest, the leasing relation may not be asserted against the registered mortgage interest.

3.2.4 The right to transfer the mortgaged property. Pursuant to Article 406 of the Civil Code, "A mortgagor may transfer the mortgaged property to another person during the term of the mortgage unless otherwise agreed by the parties. The transfer of the mortgaged property shall not affect the mortgage. A mortgagor who transfers the mortgaged property to another person shall notify the mortgagee in a timely manner. The mortgagee may request the mortgagor to apply the proceeds of the transfer to pay off the obligation before it is due, or place such proceeds in escrow where he may establish that the transfer of the mortgaged property may impair his right to the mortgage. The portion of the proceeds obtained from the transfer in excess of the amount of the obligation owed shall belong to the mortgagor, while any deficiency shall be satisfied by the debtor".

4. Enforcement of a Mortgage

4.1 Requirements for Enforcing a Mortgage

The enforcement of a mortgage denotes that the mortgagee may exercise the right to mortgage and have priority in having his claim paid with the property if the debtor defaults. Enforcement of the right to mortgage is conditioned on the following elements:

4.1.1 The debt of the obligor shall have matured.

4.1.2 The debtor defaults. The default of the debtor includes non-performance, delay in performance and inadequate performance. Where the debt has been liquidated by the debtor, or though the debt is not paid off statutory or contractual basis exist for exempting the debtor from his liability, the principal creditor shall not exercise his right to mortgage. Otherwise, the mortgagor may address plea.

4.1.3 The mortgage is lawful and valid. The existence of a lawful and valid mortgage interest is a premise for the enforcement of the right to mortgage. If the principal claim contract secured by mortgage is declared invalid or rescinded, so shall the mortgage contract. Consequently, the mortgagee shall not exercise the right to mortgage when such right has not been created in the first place.

4.2 Means of Enforcing a Mortgage and its Term

According to Article 410 of the Civil Code, "Where a debtor fails to perform his obligation due or an event upon which a mortgage is to be enforced as agreed upon by the parties occurs, the mortgagee may, upon agreement with the mortgagor, have the priority right to appraise and accept the mortgaged property, or apply the proceeds obtained from auction or sale of the mortgaged property to satisfy his claim against the mortgagor. Where the agreement is detrimental to the interests of other creditors, the other creditors may request the people's court to rescind the agreement. Where a mortgagee and a mortgagor fail to reach an agreement on the methods of enforcing the mortgage, the mortgagee may request the people's court to have the mortgaged property sold at auction or in a sale". There are mainly three ways of enforcing a mortgage:

4.2.1 Repayment by obtaining the ownership of the collateral through converting the mortgaged property into money. It means that the mortgagee may conclude an agreement with the pledgor that the mortgaged property be converted into money for the liquidation of the debt, and that the mortgagee obtains the ownership of the mortgaged property. As can be seen, Repayment by obtaining the ownership of the collateral through converting the mortgaged property into money, the parties shall enter into a contract for it, that the price of the mortgaged property is not unilaterally determined by mortgagee. When the mortgagee has unilaterally determined the price and the mortgagor consents or acquiesces to it, it may be presumed that the conversion agreement has been concluded. The price of the mortgaged property shall be reasonably determined by the parties in accordance with the market price. The conversion contract may be concluded only upon the enforcement of the right to mortgage, and the ownership of the mortgaged property may be transferred t.

4.2.2 Auction of the mortgaged property. Auction refers to sell property through open competition. It usually refers to such case whereby bidders make offer in the specified time and location under the host of the presided person in accordance with the procedures provided by the Auction Law. The determination of the price for sale is subject to the highest offered price, and the mortgaged property goes to the person who has made such offer.

4.2.3 Sale of the mortgaged property. It refers to the mortgagee's or a court's selling of the mortgaged property. In a broad sense, auction is also a form of sale, but the sale here mainly means that the mortgaged property is sold through common mode of transaction, bid invitation, etc.

As regards the proceeds from the disposal of the mortgaged property made in the above three ways, the mortgagee has the priority right in getting his claim paid in comparison with other creditor's debt.

The priority right in getting claim repaid is a concept that mainly applies to the obligatory right, meaning that if a mortgaged claim and other general obligatory right coexist on a mortgaged property, the mortgagee has the right of priority in having his claim paid with the proceeds from the disposal of the mortgaged property, while other general creditors may only be paid with the remainder.

When a right to use land for construction purposes is mortgaged, the buildings erected are not mortgaged property. Where the right concerned is disposed of to enforce the right to mortgage, the newly-erected buildings on the land shall be disposed of concurrently; however, the mortgagee shall have no priority in having his claim paid with the proceeds obtained from the buildings concerned. Article 47 of the Law on Land Contract in Rural Areas stipulates that "The contractor may use the right to management of land for financing guarantee at financial institutions and shall report to the party offering the contract for records. Subject to the written consent of the party offering the contract and after reporting to the party offering the contract for record, the transferee who obtains the right to management of land through circulation may use his right for financing guarantee at financial institutions. Where a right to management of land is mortgaged, or where a right to use a lot of land owned by a collective is mortgaged in accordance with Article 418 of the Civil Code, the nature of the ownership and the purpose of use of the land may not be altered without going through statutory procedures after the mortgage is enforced.

A mortgagee shall exercise his right to mortgage within the limitation period for claiming against the principal obligation; otherwise no protection may be provided by the people's court. ①

The realization of a mortgage shall be conducted in compliance with the relevant provisions set forth by the Civil Code and the relevant procedural rules stated in the part concerning "Cases of Security Interest Enforcement" of the Civil Procedure Law. Para. 3 of Article 410 of the Civil Code states that "The appraisal or sale of the mortgaged property shall be based on the market price thereof".

The Civil Procedure Law stipulates detailed instructions on jurisdiction, the trial procedure, the relief approaches after the relative lawsuit of the realization of the right to

---

① Article 419 of the Civil Code

mortgage is rejected by the court, Article 203 of the law stipulates that, "If the right holder of a security interest applies to realize his security interest, he shall according to such laws as the Civil Code, etc. , apply to the basic people's court in the place where the property for security is located". Article 204 next states that, "After the application is entertained and examined by the people's court, if it conforms to the provisions of the law, the people's court shall issue a ruling to auction or sell the property posted as security, and the parties may, based on the ruling, apply for enforcement to the people's court; or if the application does not comply with legal provisions, the people's court shall issue a ruling to dismiss the application, and the right holder may file a lawsuit to the people's court".

4.3 Priority Order of the Right to Mortgage

4.3.1 Concept and Determination of Priority Order of Mortgages

The order (or sequence, arrangement) of the right to mortgage refers to the priority order among the mortgagees when the mortgagor has established two or more mortgage interests on one mortgaged property to secure two or more credits.

According to Article 414 of the Civil Code, "Where a property is mortgaged to two or more creditors, the proceeds obtained from auction or sale of the mortgaged property shall be applied in accordance with the following provisions: (1) where the mortgages have all been registered, the order of payment is based on the priority in time of registration; (2) a registered mortgage has priority over an unregistered mortgage to be paid; and (3) where none of the mortgages are registered, payment shall be made on a pro rata basis against the claims. The preceding paragraph shall be applied mutatis mutandis with regard to the priority order of payment for other security interests that are registrable".

4.3.2 The Theory of Fixed Priority Order and of Ascending Priority Order

Where a mortgage in preferential order extinguishes due to reasons other than the enforcement of the mortgage, whether a mortgage that are inferior to it may ascend accordingly? Regarding this issue, there are two legislative patterns: the doctrine of fixed priority order and that of ascending priority order.

The former mode denotes that mortgage in inferior order to will not ascend because the mortgage in preferential order does not extinguish even when the claim secured by the latter extinguishes due to reasons other than enforcement of mortgage such as repayment of the debt. According to the latter pattern, however, the mortgage in inferior order shall ascend in a priority order because the mortgage in preferential order has extinguished under such circumstance.

4.3.3 The Civil Code Adopts the Latter Approach

Adopting the literal interpretation to Articles 409 and 414 of the Civil Code, one may conclude that the Civil Code takes the approach of ascending priority order. Regarding whether the mortgagee enjoys priority over other real right holders when his mortgage coexists with other real rights, it is generally recognized that the doctrine of "first come, first served" shall apply here, meaning that real right that is earlier established prevails over a later established one. Article 415 of the Civil Code provides that "Where both a mortgage and a pledge are created on the same property, the priority order of payment with the proceeds obtained from auction or sale of the property shall be based on the priority in time of registration and delivery of the property".

5. Floating Charge of Movable Properties

5. 1   Concept and Features of Floating Charge of Movable Properties

Article 396 of the Civil Code prescribes that "An enterprise, an individual-run industrial and commercial household, or an agricultural production operator may mortgage their production equipment, raw materials, work in process, and finished products that they currently own or thereafter acquired, and if the debtor fails to perform his obligations due or any event upon which a security interest in the mortgaged property is to be enforced as agreed by the parties occurs, the creditor has priority to be paid from the movable property determined at the time when the mortgaged property is ascertained". This is a new type of right to mortgage that is established by the Civil Code, namely, the floating charge of movable property. Its features mainly include:

5. 1. 1   Particularity in the mortgagor: only enterprises, self-employed industrial and commercial households and agricultural producers and distributors and operators may establish floating charge of movable properties.

5. 1. 2   Particularity in the mortgaged objects: only movable properties such as the existing and anticipated production equipment, materials, semi-finished products and finished products may be mortgaged.

5. 1. 3   Particularity in the effects of the right to mortgage: under floating charge, the mortgaged movable properties owned by the mortgagor change and are uncertain during the mortgage term. They may be sold, leased or even mortgaged by the mortgagor until specified upon the occurrence of certain statutory circumstances. In such cases, the mortgagor may no longer entitled to freely dispose of them without the permission of the mortgagee.

5. 2   Registration under Floating Charge of Movable Properties—Registration as a Requirement for Perfection

Article 403 of the Civil Code stipulate that " A mortgage on movable property shall be created at the time when the mortgage contract enters into effect; without registration, such a mortgage may not be asserted against a bona fide third person". Article 404 provides that "A mortgage on movable property may not be asserted against a buyer who has paid a reasonable purchase price and acquired the mortgaged property in the ordinary course of business".

5. 3   Establishment of the Mortgaged Property in a Floating Charge

According to Article 411 of the Civil Code, "Where a mortgage is created in accordance with the provisions of Article 396 of this Code, the mortgaged property shall be ascertained at the time when one of the following circumstances occurs: (1) the claim is not satisfied upon expiration of the term of performance of the obligation; (2) the mortgagor is declared bankrupt or dissolved; (3) an event upon which the mortgage is to be enforced as agreed upon by the parties occurs; or (4) any other circumstance that seriously affects the enforcement of the claim".

6. Common Mortgage

6. 1   Concept and Features of Common Mortgage

Common mortgage, or the so-called "lump mortgage right" or "aggregated mortgage right", refers to the right to mortgage that are established on several immovable properties, movable properties or rights to secure one same right. The "several immovable properties, movable properties or rights" may belong to one or more different persons. Viewed from Para. 2, Article 395 of the Civil Code, the common mortgage is legally recognized in China. Its features include:

6. 1. 1   One same claim is secured. One same claim refers to the claim that occurs on the basis of one same reason, but not necessarily means that the number of the claim in single. Therefore, under common mortgage, the creditor, the debtor and the content of the performance in the claim secured shall be totally the same. It is not an important issue as to whether the scope of the claims that each security property secures are the same.

6. 1. 2   Multiple mortgaged properties co-exist. The objects of common mortgage are several properties rather than one. In addition, these properties are not one aggregative thing but several properties that are independent from each other.

6. 1. 3   Under common mortgage, several rights to mortgage are established to secure one same claim.

6. 1. 4   Where no agreement or an indefinite agreement is formulated on the proportion shared by each mortgaged property with respect to the secured claim, the mortgagee may satisfy all or part of his claim with the proceeds generated from the sale of any mortgaged property (each mortgaged property under joint mortgage undertake mortgage responsibility with respect to

the entire secured claim).

6. 2   Establishment of Common Mortgage

It can be divided into two kinds. The first one is initial establishment of common mortgage, which is such a common mortgage as established by the debtor or a third party using two or more mortgaged properties to concurrently secure one same obligatory right. The second is subsequent establishment of common mortgage, meaning that after one right to mortgage is established, one or several others are subsequently established on several mortgaged properties to secure the same claim. As for the requirements for the establishment, there are little difference between the common mortgage and general mortgage interest.

6. 3   Effects of Common Mortgage

6. 3. 1   The effects of the common mortgage where an agreement has been reached on the share of the claim secured by each mortgaged property. If the mortgagor and the mortgagee have agreed on the shares of the obligatory rights secured by the guaranty provided by the mortgagor, or several mortgagors separately make agreements with the mortgagee on the shares of the obligatory rights secured by their guaranties, when the debtor default to pay the debt, although the mortgagee may still be entitled to auction or sell off the whole security property, the proceeds shall be calculated separately, and the mortgagee shall have priority in getting paid with the money each guaranty is converted into within the limit of the agreed amount of share.

6. 3. 2   The effects of the common mortgage where an agreement has not been concluded on the share of the claim secured by each mortgaged property. Where no agreement whether clear or not has been reached between the mortgagor and the mortgagee regarding the shares in secured claim by each mortgaged property when the debtor defaults, can the mortgagee auction all the mortgaged properties concurrently? Must he do so? According to Article 20 of the Judicial Interpretation on Guarantee System in Civil Code, when trying a dispute over a collateral provided by a third party, the people's court may apply the provisions on suretyship contract of Para. 1, Article 695, Para. 1, Article 696, Para. 2, Article 697, Article 699, Article 700, Article 701, and Article 702, among others, of the Civil Code. Article 699 of the Civil Code states that "Where there are two or more sureties guaranteeing one obligation, the sureties shall undertake the suretyship liability in proportion to their share of suretyship in accordance with the suretyship contract. In the absence of such an agreement, the creditor may request any of the sureties to undertake the suretyship liability within the scope of his liability". Where there is no contract or the contract is unclear about the shares of claime secured by the mortgage, the mortgagee may auction any or every mortgaged property and enjoys the right of priority in getting his debt paid with the proceeds obtained therefrom. The residue amount may

be returned to the mortgagor in accordance with the proportion previously agreed upon or provided by law.

7. Maximum Mortgage for Floating Claims

7. 1　Concept and Features of Maximum Mortgage for Floating Claims

Para. 1, Article 420 of the Civil Code provides that "Where a debtor or a third person provides a collateral for future claims that will arise consecutively within a certain period of time to secure performance of the obligations, if the debtor fails to perform an obligation due or an event upon which such a mortgage is to be enforced as agreed upon by the parties occurs, the mortgagee has the priority to be paid from the mortgaged property up to the maximum amount of his claim. " The maximum mortgage for floating claims is a case where the debtor or a third party reaches a contract with the mortgagee that, within the extent of the maximum amount of the claims, the mortgaged property is used to secure the debts to be incurred consecutively within a given period of time. If the debtor defaults or the conditions for implementing the mortgage, as agreed upon by the parties, arise, the mortgagee shall have the priority in having his claims paid with the security to the extent of the maximum amount of the claims. For example, A and B entered into an agreement on February 5, 2004, which stipulated that the debts from March 1, 2004 to December 31, 2004 shall be mortgaged by a specified building. As the building was evaluated as worth 20 million yuan then, the parties agreed that the maximum amount of the mortgaged debts is 20 million yuan. If the debts exceed this amount, A shall provide other property as security property. The features of a maximum mortgage for floating claims include the followings:

7. 1. 1　It provides security for claims to be incurred in the future. Under general mortgage, the right to mortgage is established after the obligatory right has been established, namely, it is premised on the latter and serves to secure the latter. If there is no credit, neither will there be the right to mortgage. This is the appurtenance nature of the right to mortgage in establishment. However, the creation of a maximum mortgage for floating claims does not require a pre-existed obligatory right. It provides security for claims that will arise in the future. Therefore, a maximum mortgage for floating claims is no longer with appurtenance nature upon its establishment.

7. 1. 2　The secured claims are not specified. Under general mortgage, the claim secured is specified. This manifests not only in the certainty of the type of the obligatory right, but also in that of its amount. However, a maximum mortgage for floating claims provides security for such future obligatory rights whose occurrence, type and amount are all uncertain. These matters may be settled only at the time of final calculation.

7. 1. 3   The secured credits have a maximum amount. For general mortgage, there is no restriction on the maximum or minimum amount as the secured credits have been established. However, for the maximum mortgage for floating claims, the case is different because the secured credits are not established when the maximum mortgage for floating claims is created. The mortgaged property and its value are determined, which means that the security provider may not provide security for unlimited number of claims with a mortgaged property whose value is limited. Otherwise, the creditor may suffer great damage. This is why a maximum amount must be set with respect to the future claims.

7. 1. 4   It provides security for the debts to be incurred consecutively within a given period. General mortgage right only provides security for existed obligatory rights which are usually independent. However, the maximum mortgage for floating claims provides security for the obligatory rights to be incurred consecutively within a given period. It applies to the consecutive obligatory rights instead of a single claim. Thus, while general mortgage interest shall be transferred along with the principal claim, the maximum mortgage for floating claims is not until the final calculation when the principal claims are established. Therefore, a maximum mortgage for floating claims is with no appurtenance nature in terms of transfer, either. Article 421 of the Civil Code stipulates that "Before the claims secured by the maximum mortgage for floating claims are ascertained, where part of the claims is transferred, the mortgage may not be transferred unless otherwise agreed by the parties".

7. 2   Establishment of a Maximum Mortgage for Floating Claims

Article 424 of the Civil Code prescribes that "In addition to the provisions of this Section, the relevant provisions of Section 1 of this Chapter shall be applied to the maximum mortgage for floating claims". Rules regulating establishment of general mortgages also apply to the creation of a maximum mortgage for floating claims. The specialty of the a maximum mortgage for floating claims lies in the following aspects:

7. 2. 1   It provides security to credits to be incurred consecutively within a given period.

7. 2. 2   Particularity in the clauses of the contract: (1) The maximum amount of the credits shall be stipulated in the contract, otherwise the mortgage contract shall not take effect. (2) Normally the period of the final calculation, or the so-called "determination period of the obligatory right" shall be stipulated in the contract, which is the date on which the indefinite credits secured by a maximum mortgage for floating claims are determined. In absence of a definitely agreed term for establishing the claim or the term agreed upon is indefinite, the mortgagee or the mortgagor may request to ascertain the claim after the lapse of two years calculated from the date of creation of the maximum mortgage for floating claims (Item. 2, Article 423 of the Civil Code).

The registration of the maximum mortgage for floating claims shall be governed by the relevant provisions in the Civil Code on the registration of the general mortgage, and registration only needs to be conducted only once.

7.3   Effects of Maximum Mortgage for Floating Claims

7.3.1   Scope of the claims secured by maximum mortgage for floating claims. (1) Maximum mortgage right only provides security for the debts existing or to be incurred in the future, not those established in the past. However, a credit that exists before the creation of the maximum mortgage may, as agreed upon by the parties, be included in the credits secured by the maximum amount of mortgage (Para. 2, Article 420 of the Civil Code). (2) When exercising such hypothec, if the actual amount of the creditor's rights exceeds the maximum amount, the mortgagee can have priority right to get paid within the maximum amount excluding the exceeding portion. The excessive portion turns into general credit not secured by the maximum mortgage for floating claims.

7.3.2   Alteration in the contents of maximum mortgage for floating claims. Article 422 of the Civil Code prescribes that, "Before the claims secured by a maximum mortgage for floating claims are ascertained, the mortgagee and the mortgagor may change by agreement the period of time for the ascertainment of the claims, the scope of the claims, and the maximum amount of the claims, provided that such changes may not adversely affect other mortgagees".

7.3.3   Transfer of maximum mortgage for floating claims. Article 421 of the Civil Code stipulates that, "Before the claims secured by the maximum mortgage for floating claims are ascertained, where part of the claims is transferred, the mortgage may not be transferred unless otherwise agreed by the parties".

7.4   Determination of Claims Secured by a Maximum Mortgage for Floating Claims and Realization of the Mortgage

Determination of the credits secured by maximum mortgage, or the so-called "the specialization of claims secured by a maximum mortgage for floating claims", means that the uncertain credits that the maximum mortgage secure may be specified for certain reasons. Article 423 of the Civil Code prescribes the following circumstances where claims secured by a maximum mortgage are specified: (1) where the agreed period of time for the claims to be ascertained expires; (2) where there is no agreement on the period of time for the claims to be ascertained or the agreement is unclear , and the mortgagee or the mortgagor requests for ascertainment of the claims after the lapse of two years from the date of the creation of the mortgage; (3) where it is impossible for a new claim to arise; (4) where the mortgagee knows or should have known that the mortgaged property has been seized or detained; (5) where the debtor or the mortgagor is declared bankrupt or dissolved; or (6) any other circumstance under which the claims are to be ascertained as provided by law.

Enforcement of a maximum mortgage for floating claims requires two conditions: first, the amount of the claims has been ascertained; second, the time limit for the performance of the claims has expired. Therefore, the parties shall stipulate time limit for performance of the claims at the same time when they determine the date of final calculation. Only when such comes may the actual amount of the debts be fixed. Meanwhile, the mortgagee may enforce his right to mortgage only after the time limit for the performance of the debt expires.

Section Three   Pledge

1. Concept and Features of Pledge

The pledge refers to the right of a creditor to convert into money such pledged property whose possession is transferred to him by a debtor or a third party to guarantee the repayment of debts, or to enjoy priority in having his claim paid with the proceeds from auction or sale of the said property, if the debtor defaults.

Because the pledge is created on a security property to secure the performance of a debt, and the pledgee may dominate the value of the object and eliminate interference of others, the pledge is a security interest. However, it has following features compared with the mortgage right:

1.1   Object of Pledge—Movable Properties and Certain Rights

According to the Civil Code, the object of mortgage may be movable properties or immovable properties, while that of pledge excludes the immovable properties. As the Civil Code has divided the pledge into pledge of movable properties and pledge of rights, it may be concluded that object of pledge can be movable properties or certain rights.

1.2   Whether the Possession of the Property Must be Transferred— Establishing the Pledge Requires Transfer of the Possession

The establishment of the right to mortgage does not require the transfer of possession regarding the security property, while the establishment of the pledge requires so. The transfer of possession is a requirement of establishment for the pledge. In cases where special properties such as stocks, proprietary rights in the intellectual property are pledged, registration procedures shall be gone through before the interest is created.

1. 3 Means of Publication—Establishing the Pledge Requires Transfer of Possession or Registration

While the establishment of both the right to mortgage and the pledge requires publications, the means thereof are different. The establishment of the right to mortgage mostly requires registration. Nonetheless, for the establishment of the pledge, according to the Civil Code, when a bill of exchange, cheque, promissory note, bond, certificate of deposit, warehouse receipt or bill of lading is pledged, the right is created at the time when the pledge is registered with the relevant authority. When the certificate of right is lacking; when portions of funds or the shares that are registered with the securities registration and settlement authority are pledged, the right of the pledge is established at the time when the pledge is registered with the securities registration and settlement authority; when portions of funds or the shares that are registered with the securities registration and settlement authority are pledged, or when the proprietary rights consisted in the intellectual property rights, such as the right to exclusive use of registered trademarks, the patents and copyrights, are pledged, the right of the pledge is perfected at the time when the pledge is registered with the relative registration organ. Ordinary movable properties and other rights do not need to be registered when they are pledged, because transfer of the possession itself is a way of publication. According to Article 429 of the Civil Code, a pledge is created upon delivery of the pledged property by the pledgor.

1. 4 In view of the Rights of the Security Interest Holder—the Pledgee may Directly Possess the Pledged Property as well as Obtain its Fruits

As possession is not transferred upon the establishment of the mortgage, the security property is still possessed by the mortgagor, who shall still be entitled to possess, utilize and benefit from the mortgaged property. As for the mortgagee, he enjoys certain control of the object, but he may not possess, utilize or benefit from it. In the case of the pledge, since the possession of the pledged property is transferred, the pledgee may directly possess it as well as obtain its fruits (unless otherwise stipulated in the contract).

2. Pledge of Movable Properties

2. 1 Concept and Object of the Pledge of Movable Properties

The pledge of movable property refers to the right of a creditor to convert into money such pledged movable whose possession is transferred to him by a debtor or a third party to guarantee the repayment of debts, or to enjoy priority in having his claim paid with the proceeds from auction or sale of the movable property concerned, if the debtor defaults. In brief, pledge of movable property is a such right whose object is movable properties. Pledge of movables is a typical form of pledge interest.

The objects of the pledge of movable property are the movable properties whose possession of which shall be transferred from the pledgor to the pledgee. However, not all properties may become the object of the pledge of movable properties. To be qualified as the object of the pledge, they must satisfy the following requirements:

2.1.1 They must be transferable. "Transferability" means that the ownership of a property may be transferred according to laws and regulations. Properties that are not transferrable may not be pledged. Therefore, movable properties that are prohibited from being transferred by laws or regulations may not be pledged.

2.1.2 They must be specified. If a property is not specified, then the pledge will lack a specified object and it is also impossible to transfer the possession over the property when a debtor or a third party provides the creditor with funds of pledge or guarantee, they intend to secure the performance of the principal debt by establishing a security through the transfer of possession over the fund. If the debtor fails to perform his debt, the creditor has priority in getting the debt paid with the fund. If the debtor performs his debt, the creditor shall return the funds of pledge or guarantee. Since such funds are movable properties and shall be transferred in possession, the establishment of security through delivering funds of pledge or guarantee accords with the characteristics of pledge. In the nation's practice, delivery of funds of pledge is generally regarded as a form of rights of pledge.

As the establishment of the pledge requires direct possession which doesn't allow for the possibility of multiple possession or possession for multiple time, several rights of pledge may not be concurrently established on one property.

2.2 Establishment of the Pledge of Movable Properties

According to Article 427 of the Civil Code, To create a pledge, the parties shall enter into a pledge contract in writing. If the parties orally conclude a pledge contract, the pledge is not created.

A pledge contract generally contains the following clauses: (1) the type and amount of the secured claim; (2) the term for the debtor to perform the obligation; (3) such particulars as the name and quantity of the pledged property; (4) the scope of the security covered; and (5) the time for and the mode of the delivery of the pledged property.

If the pledge contract does not contain all the contents prescribed above, it may be modified but shall not be simply invalidated. Pursuant to Article 428 of the Civil Code, where, prior to the due date of performance of an obligation, the pledgee reaches an agreement with the pledgor under which the pledged property belongs to the creditor in the event that the debtor fails to perform the obligation due, the pledgee, regardless, may only have priority to be paid from the pledged property in accordance with law. In other words, under Chinese law the forfeiture agreement is enforced in accordance with what is stipulated in the pledge contract, and the pledgee is only entitled to have priority to be paid from the pledged property.

To create the pledge over a movable property, the parties shall not only conclude a pledge contract in written form, but also transfer the possession of the movable property concerned. The pledge is established upon the delivery of the pledged property.

2.3   Rights and Obligations of the Pledgor

2.3.1   Rights of the Pledgor

2.3.1.1   Right to collect the fruits from the pledged property. According to Article 430 of the Civil Code, through agreement with the pledgee the pledgor may reserve the right to collect the fruits from the pledged property.

2.3.1.2   Right to dispose of the pledged property. After the movable property is pledged, the pledgor has not lost his ownership over the pledged property in law, though he has transferred the possession of it to the pledgee. As such, he may still dispose of the pledged property but only in the legally sense, not in fact. The pledgor shall not affect the existed the pledge when exercising his right of disposal over the pledged property, meaning that the pledgee continue enjoying the pledge.

2.3.1.3   Right of recourse of the security provider on property. The third party who secures the obligation of the debtor is a "security provider on property". He shall have the right of recourse against the debtor after he clears the debt for the debtor or loses the ownership of the pledged property due to the pledgee's enforcement of the pledge.

2.3.1.4   The right to preserve the pledged property. Para. 2, Article 432 of the Civil Code prescribes that, "Where the pledgee's act is likely to cause the pledged property to be destructed, damaged, or lost, the pledgor may request the pledgee to place the pledged property in escrow, or request the pledgee to discharge the obligation before it is due and return the pledged property".

2.3.2   Obligations of the Pledgor

The main obligation of the pledgor is not to hinder the pledgee while the latter enjoys and exercises his right over the pledged property.

2.4   Rights and Obligations of the Pledgee

2.4.1   Rights of the Pledgee

2.4.1.1   Right to possess and set lien over the pledged property.

2. 4. 1. 2　Right to collect the fruits of the pledged property. If there is no special stipulation that the fruits of the pledged property shall be collected by the pledgor or a third party, the pledgee has the right to collect the fruits of the pledged property.

2. 4. 1. 3　Right to repledge. Repledge means, during the existence of the creditor's right, the pledgee transfers the possession of the pledged property to a third party and establishes a new pledge interest on the pledged property for the purpose of securing his own debt. Repledge may be further divided into commitment repledge and liability repledge. Article 432 of the Civil Code prescribes that " A pledgee shall be liable for compensation where he, during the effective period of the pledge, repledges the pledged property without the consent of the pledgor to a third person and thus causes destruction, damage, or loss to the pledged property". In light of this provision, the Civil Code recognizes both commitment repledge and the liability repledge.

The commitment repledge means that the pledgee, transfers the possession of the pledged property to a third party with the consent of the pledgor and establishes a new pledge right on the pledged property to secure his debt. The consent of the pledgor upon repledging means that the pledgor has conferred the right to dispose of the pledged property to the original pledgee.

The liability repledge means that without the permission of the pledgor, the pledgee transfers the possession of the pledged property to a third party at his liability and establishes a new pledge right on the pledged property. As has been stated above, repledge involves such issue as to whether the pledgee may dispose of the object before the time limit for performance. Opinions are divided within the academia and legislations of various jurisdictions taking different approaches. We opine that the legal recognition of liability repledge contributes to giving full play to the usefulness of the pledged property, encouraging transactions and promoting transaction security in that by allowing for the liability repledge, the Civil Code also allows the pledgee to use the pledged property to secure his own debt which encourages the setting of security.

2. 4. 1. 4　Right to auction or sell off the pledged property in advance (preservation of the pledged property). According to Article 433 of the Civil Code, "Where, due to a cause the pledgee is not responsible for, the pledged property is likely to be damaged or significantly diminished in value which suffices to jeopardize the pledgee's rights, the pledgee has the right to request the pledgor to provide additional security; where the pledgor fails to do so, the pledgee may have the pledged property sold at auction or in a sale and may, by agreement with the pledgor, apply the proceeds obtained from the auction or sale to discharge the obligation before it is due or place such proceeds in escrow".

2. 4. 1. 5　Priority right in getting claim repaid. This refers to the priority enjoyed by the pledgee over other creditors or even other real right holders in getting his claim repaid.

2. 4. 2　Obligations of the Pledgee

2. 4. 2. 1   The major obligation of the pledgee is to safekeep the pledged property. Article 432 of the Civil Code prescribes that "A pledgee is obligated to well keep the pledged property, and shall be liable for compensation where the pledged property is destructed, damaged, or lost due to his improper custody. Where the pledgee's act is likely to cause the pledged property to be destructed, damaged, or lost, the pledgor may request the pledgee to place the pledged property in escrow, or request the pledgee to discharge the obligation before it is due and return the pledged property".

2. 4. 2. 2   The pledgee shall not illegally use or dispose of the pledged property. Article 431 of the Civil Code prescribes that " A pledgee who, during the effective period of the pledge, uses or disposes of the pledged property without the consent of the pledgor and thus causes damage to the latter shall be liable for compensation".

2. 4. 2. 3   Obligation to return the pledged property. Para. 1, Article 436 of the Civil Code stipulates that "A pledgee shall return the pledged property after the debtor has performed his obligation or the pledgor has paid the secured claim before it is due".

2. 5   Enforcement of the Pledge Interest of Movable Properties

The enforcement of the pledge of movable properties means that the pledgee has priority in getting his credit paid with the money accrued from the conversion, auction or sale of the pledged property when the debtor defaults. Para. 2, Article 436 of the Civil Code provides that "Where a debtor fails to perform an obligation due or an event upon the occurrence of which the pledge is to be enforced as agreed upon by the parties occurs, the pledgee may, by agreement with the pledgor, appraise and accept the pledged property as satisfaction of his claim, or have priority to be paid from the proceeds obtained from auction or sale of the pledged property".

2. 5. 1   Conversion of the pledged property into money. Conversion of the pledged property into money means that the pledgee and the pledgor enter into a contract whereby the pledgee obtains the ownership of the pledged property to the extent of the actual price of the pledged property. If, after the pledged property is converted into money, the proceeds therefrom exceed the amount of the claim, the balance shall go to the pledgor, and if they are insufficient to cover the debt, the difference shall be paid by the debtor. However, as the pledgee has accepted the conversion, such difference is no longer secured as a credit.

2. 5. 2   Auction and sale of the pledged property. The object of the pledge is usually general movable properties whose value may not be huge and possession shall be transferred. Thus, it is unlikely that two or more rights of pledge are concurrently created over the same pledged property. Since in such cases, only a few creditors may be involved and the legal relation is simple, the Civil Code allows the pledgee to auction or sell the pledge property without entering into agreement with the pledgor. Article 45 of the Judicial Interpretation on

Guarantee System in Civil Code provides that "Where the parties agree that if the debtor does not perform the debts as they become due, or there occurs a circumstance for realization of security interest as agreed upon by the parties, the security interest holder has the right to auction or liquidate the collateral and has priority of payment form the proceeds, the agreement shall be valid. If the security provider renders the security interest holder unable to auction or liquidate the collateral, and the security interest holder requests that the security provider bear the resultant increase in costs, the people's court shall uphold the request". Para. 2, Article 436 of the Civil Code provides that "The appraisal or sale of the pledged property shall be based on the market price".

2. 6　Maximum Pledge for Floating Claims

Article 439 of the Civil Code prescribes that "A pledgor and a pledgee may create a maximum pledge for floating claims upon agreement. In addition to the relevant provisions of this Section, the relevant provisions of Section 2 of Chapter 17 of this Book shall be applied mutatis mutandis to the maximum pledge for floating claims". The maximum pledge for floating claims may be established on the pledge of chattels or the pledge of rights. In addition to the provisions of Chapter 18 of the Civil Code, the relevant provisions of "Maximum Mortgage for Floating Claims" of the Civil Code shall be applied mutatis mutandis to the maximum pledge for floating claims . On other contents of the maximum pledge for floating claims, see section 6 of this chapter, " Maximum Mortgage for Floating Claims. "

3. Pledge of Rights

3. 1　Concept of Pledge of Rights

Pledge of rights refers to such pledge whose object is transferable rights enjoyed by the debtor or a third party and whose aim is to secure the realization of the creditor's right.

Because of their exchange value, transferable property rights other than the ownership of movable properties may also be the object of security interests. Still, right is much different from general properties. To include them into the object of security interests indicates that the right itself may be the subject matter of a transaction. Particularly, as rights qualify for becoming the object of real rights, the traditional rule that only tangible properties may be the object of real right is gradually altered and the scope of object of the real right is thereby broadened. It is to be noted that many similarities between rights and movable properties may be observed when they serve as the object of a pledge in terms of such matters as transfer of possession, contents of the pledge contract, identification and treatment of forfeiture agreement, etc. For this reason, the Civil Code and the Real Right Law have only stipulated on certain special provisions for the pledge of rights, without providing any general provision for it. In light of this, provisions on the pledge of movable property also apply to the pledge of rights unless otherwise stipulated by law.

3. 2　Object of the Pledge of Rights

3.2.1　Characteristics of the Object of the Pledge of Rights

The object of the pledge of rights is a right. However, this does not mean that any right can become the object of pledge of rights. A right may become a competent object thereof only if it has the following characteristics:

3.2.1.1　It shall be a proprietary right that can be evaluated by price, which may be real right, creditor's right, intangible property right, etc. Rights like personality right, right of status, etc. , that is with no property value shall not be the object of the pledge of rights. In addition, a claim for inaction or a written certificate of a claim cannot serve as the object of the pledge of rights due to their lack of property value.

3.2.1.2　It must be a property right that is legally transferable. Property rights that are untransferable mainly include the following few categories: (1) property rights untransferable due to their nature, namely, claims exclusive to the debtor due to existence of specific personal relationship, including right to claim payment arising from maintenance of dependents, child support, maintenance of parents, or succession, or a right to claim for wage, retirement pension, annuity, pensions for the disabled or the family of a deceased, relocation allowance, life insurance, or compensation for personal injury, etc. (Article 12 of the Interpretation I on Certain Issues Concerning the Application of Contract Law); creditor's right based on special trust such as the claim of the principal against the agent for handling affairs under an entrustment contract, the claim of an employer against the employee for services under an employment contract; property right like mortgage or pledge interest that concerns personal income, etc. (2) untransferable right agreed upon by parties concerned. However, this stipulation by the parties may not be held against a third party in good faith. (3) rights the transfer of which is prohibited by laws or administrative regulations (Articles 446 and 426 of the Civil Code).

3.2.1.3　It shall be a right that the debtor or the third party is entitled to dispose of.

3.2.1.4　The laws and the nature of the pledge of rights are not violated when the right is pledged. In China, such right mainly includes: (1) right as is stipulated by Para. 5, Article 142 of the Company Law, "A company shall not accept any pledge with its own stocks as the subject matter". (2) property rights regarding immovable properties. (3) ownership of movable properties. (4) the pledge and the right to mortgage over movable properties.

3.2.2　Scope of the Object of the Pledge of Rights

3. 2. 2. 1　Bill of exchange, cheque, promissory note, bond, certificate of deposit, warehouse receipt and bill of lading. When a bill of exchange, cheque, promissory note, bond, certificate of deposit, warehouse receipt or bill of lading is pledged, the parties concerned shall conclude a contract in written form. The pledge is created at the time when the certificate of right is delivered to the pledgee; if there is no such certificate, the pledge is created at the time when the pledge is registered with the relevant authority. Where the date of payment or of delivery of goods in respect of a pledged bill of exchange, cheque, promissory note, bond, certificate of deposit, warehouse receipt or bill of lading is matured prior to the date of maturity of the principal claim, the pledgee may accept the payment or take delivery of the goods and may conclude an agreement with the pledgor that the payment or the goods accepted be used to pay the debts in advance or be deposited with a third party.

3. 2. 2. 2　Transferable portions of funds or certificates of stocks. Where portions of funds or shares are pledged, the parties concerned shall conclude a contract in written form. Where portions of funds or the shares that are registered with the securities registration and settlement authority are pledged, the pledge is established at the time when the pledge is registered with the securities registration and settlement authority. Where other kinds of shares are pledged, the pledge is established at the time when the pledge is registered with the administration department for industry and commerce. The portions of funds or the shares that are pledged may not be transferred, unless otherwise agreed upon by the pledgor and the pledgee. The proceeds the pledgor obtained from the transfer of the portions of funds or shares shall be used in advance to pay the debts owed to the pledgee or be deposited with a third party.

3. 2. 2. 3　Transferable proprietary rights consisted in the intellectual property, such as the right to exclusive use of registered trademarks, the patents and copyrights, etc. When the proprietary rights consisted in the intellectual property rights, such as the right to exclusive use of registered trademarks, the patents and copyrights, are pledged, the parties concerned shall conclude a contract in written form. The pledge is perfected at the time when the pledge is registered with the relevant authority. If the proprietary rights consisted in the intellectual property rights are pledged, the pledgor may not transfer or permit another person to use such rights, unless otherwise agreed upon by the pledgor and the pledgee through consultation. The proceeds obtained by the pledgor through transfer of such rights or through permitting another person to use such rights shall be used in advance to pay the debts owed to the pledgee or be deposited with a third party. (Article 444 of the Civil Code)

3. 2. 2. 4　Accounts Receivables. The account receivable is a concept in accounting. It refers to the money that shall be collected from a buyer or customer for the sale of goods or providing services. In the accounting system, the accounts receivable is included in the nonmonetary asset of a company. Under the theory of the civil law, the receivable is essentially

a claim whereby a seller or service provider is entitled to request for the price or service fees against the purchaser or the party receiving services. The account receivable as prescribed in the Civil Code refers to the existed and future credits under contractual relations that have not been securitized and can be cleared off by monetary payment. When the receivable is pledged, the parties concerned shall conclude a contract in written form. The pledge is created at the time when the pledge is registered with the credit information service. The pledged receivable may not be transferred, unless otherwise agreed upon by the pledgor and the pledgee through consultation. The proceeds obtained by the pledgor from the transfer of the receivable shall be used in advance to pay the debts owed to the pledgee or be deposited with a third party.

    3.2.2.5　Other property rights which may be pledged as provided for by laws and administrative regulations. The Chinese law leaves an opening for the pledgeable property, thereby giving the legislator, lawyers, judges and scholars more room for creation, thinking and application thereof.

Section Four　Lien

1. Concept and Features of Lien

The lien is the right of a creditor to retain a debtor's movable properties which have been legally possessed by the creditor and convert the retained property into money (reference to page 583), or enjoy the priority in having the debts paid with the proceeds from auction or sale of the property concerned, if a debtor defaults. The features of the lien include:

1. 1　It is a Security Interest

The right holder of lien has the right to control the property under lien and exclude the interference from others. The lien may be asserted not only against the debtor but also against the transferee of the retained property. The lien is a real right, and a security interest that mainly functions to secure a credit.

1. 2　Its Object is Movable Property

The lien is a statutory security Interest based on the possession of movable property. The lien is established from when the creditor occupies the movable property of the debtor upon a legal reason. Immovable property cannot be moved, and cannot be the object of a lien.

1. 3　It is a Statutory Security Interest

A lien is established in accordance with the law when certain conditions has been satisfied.

It is not to be created through agreement. However, according to Article 449 of the Civil Code, the parties may excluding the application of liens by concluding agreement on the movable property that may not be retained under a lien.

1. 4   It May Take Effect Twice

The lien takes effect for the first time upon its establishment. A creditor may retain the debtor's movable properties when the debtor fails to pay off its due debts. This is when the lien takes effect for the first time. It takes effect for a second time when the debtor defaults, under which circumstance the lien holder may convert the retained property into money, or enjoy priority in having the debts paid with the proceeds from auction or sale of the property.

1. 5   It Does Not Have Retroactive Effect

Although the lien is a real right, it does not have retroactive effect, which is one of the characteristics of the real right. Article 457 of the Civil Code prescribes that "A lien is extinguished where the lienholder loses possession of the retained property or accepts another form of security provided by the debtor". The lien is a security interest based on possession, thus may extinguish once the right holder losses possession of the retained property. Therefore, its real right nature is weaker than other security interests.

Concerning the commercial and general liens, Article 448 of the Civil Code stipulates that "The movable property retained under a lien by the creditor shall be in the same legal relationship as the underlying claim, unless the lienholder and the debtor are both enterprises". From this provision one may conclude that the Civil Code has stipulated on the general lien. Compared with commercial lien, the general lien is different in two aspects. First, the subjects of the two are different. Commercial lien applies to creditor's rights arising from commercial acts between merchants, thus its subject shall be merchants. Second, the elements for their establishment are different. Commercial lien waives the requirement that the claim of the creditor and the retained movable property owned by the debtor shall be linked.

2. Requirements for Establishing Liens

Establishment of a lien requires the satisfaction of the following elements:

2. 1   The Creditor Shall Legally Possess the Movable Property Owned by the Obligor

That the creditor possesses the movable property owned by the debtor is a premise for the establishment of a lien. The possession here shall be both direct and legal. The movable property owned by the debtor means that the property shall be owned by the debtor and legally transferrable.

The Guaranty Law prescribes that the lien may only be established in certain types of contractual relationships. Article 84 of the Guaranty Law stipulates that, "In the event of any credits arising from a storage, transportation or processing contract, if the debtor defaults, the creditor shall have the right to retain the property. The provisions of the preceding paragraph shall be applicable to other contracts whereby the creditor has the right of retention as provided by law. The parties may specify in the contract that the property may not be retained". The Real Right Law and the Civil Code do not set such limitations on the application of lien. According to Para. 1, Article 447 of the Civil Code, only those "debtor's movable properties which have been legally possessed by the creditor" may be retained by the latter. Therefore, the creditor may retain the debtor's movable properties which have been legally possessed by him through both contractual or other legal relationships. For example, where a creditor possesses a movable property owned by the debtor through negotiorum gestio, the manager may retain the movable property if the beneficiary fails to pay the expenses necessary for such assistance.

Article 449 of the Civil Code prescribes that, "The movable property that may not be retained under a lien as provided by law or agreed by the parties may not be so retained".

2.2 The Movable Property Retained by the Creditor Shall in the Same Nexus of Legal Relationships with the Creditor's Credits

Article 448 of the Civil Code stipulates that "The movable property retained under a lien by the creditor shall be in the same legal relationship as the underlying claim, unless the lienholder and the debtor are both enterprises". "In the same legal relationships" is also-called "in implicated relationship". Absence of implicated relationship indicates that the credits are different and should be claimed by the creditor separately. When the establishment of the credits and the acquisition of the possession over the retained object are in the same nexus of legal relationships and the debtor defaults, the creditor acquires the lien.

2.3 Period of Fulfillment Has Expired but the Debtor Fails to Timely Perform the Obligations

In general cases, a lien is established where the three above-mentioned requirements are satisfied. Hence, these three requirements are also called the active requirements for the establishment of liens. Nevertheless, if circumstances hindering the creation of liens occur, a lien still cannot be established even the above three requirements are all satisfied. Such requirements are termed negative requirements for the establishment of liens. Circumstances that may hinder the creation of liens include the followings. First, the parties may agree to exclude the application of lines. The lien is a property right and the parties shall be allowed to exclude its application through their agreement. Second, retaining of the property harms the public interests or social morality. Third, retaining of the property may set off the obligations assumed by the creditor.

3. Rights and Obligations of the Right Holder of Lien

3. 1   Rights of the Lienholder

3. 1. 1   The right to possess the retained property. The lienholder has the right to retain the property when the debtor fails to pay off his debt, which means that, in the first place, the lienholder has the right to possess the property delivered to him by the debtor so as to urge the latter to pay off his debt. Such possessory right regarding the retained property is protected by the rule system on possession under the civil law. After the lienholder has acquired the lien, he may refuse to return the property when the debtor requires him to do so. Such right of possession on the part of the lienholder is a continuous right, which enables him to maintain the possession of the property until the lien extinguishes or is enforced.

However, according to Article 448 of the Civil Code, where the property retained under a lien is a divisible thing, the value of the retained property shall be equivalent to the amount of the obligation. This is a restriction on the indivisibility character of the lien. Overemphasizing the indivisibility character of the lien may not only cause unfairness to the debtor but also set obstacles for making full use of the retained property.

3. 1. 2   Right to collect fruits and proceeds from the retained property. Article 452 of the Civil Code states that, "A lienholder has the right to collect the fruits and proceeds accrued from the property retained under a lien. The fruits and proceeds as specified in the preceding paragraph shall first be applied to offset the expenses for collecting them". As can be seen, the lienholder has the right to collect the fruits of the retained property during the term of possession. Such fruits may directly compensate the debt if they are money. Otherwise, they shall be converted or appraised into money, before the lienholder exercise priority in being paid with the proceeds from auction or sale of the property under lien. Undoubtedly, the lienholder shall safekeep such fruits with the due care of a manager in good faith. Failing that, he shall be liable for compensating the damage caused to the debtor.

3. 1. 3   Right of necessary use. In principle, the right holder may not use the property under lien. However, in particular cases and for the purpose of safekeeping the retained property, he may do that in a proper manner. For example, a lienholder may use the car he retained in a reasonable manner so that it doesn't rust. The lienholder may use the retained property only in such cases when the safekeeping of the property requires. He cannot do so to

obtain profit therefrom. Otherwise, his act may constitute a tort. Nonetheless, he may behave so if the debtor agrees.

3.1.4 Right to enforce the lien. After the property of the debtor is retained by the lienholder, if the debtor defaults, the lienholder may upon agreement with the debtor have the retained property converted into money, or may enjoy the priority in having the debts paid with the proceeds from auction or sale of the property. The priority of the lienholder in having his debt paid with the proceeds is a fundamental measure to ensure the realization of his credit.

3.2 Obligations of the Lienholder

3.2.1 Obligation to properly safekeep the property under lien. The lienholder shall have the duty to safekeep the retained property. If the retained property is damaged, destroyed or lost due to improper keeping, the lienholder shall be liable for compensation.

3.2.2 Obligation to return the property under lien.

Where the claim secured by the lien extinguishes, the lienholder is obliged to return the retained property to the debtor. Where the claim secured has not extinguished but the debtor has provided other security, thereby causing the extinguishment of the lien, the lienholder is also obliged to return the retained property. Violation of the obligation to return the returned property constitutes illegal possession, and lienholder shall assume civil liabilities towards the debtor or the property owner.

4. Rights and Obligations of the Debtor

4.1 Rights of the Debtor

4.1.1 Right to claim for damages. The lienholder shall have the duty to safekeep the retained property. If the retained property is damaged, destroyed or lost due to improper keeping, the debtor may request the lienholder to compensate for it.

4.1.2 The right to claim for returning the property under lien. After fulfilling the debts, the debtor may claim for returning the retained movable property.

4.1.3 The right to request the lienholder to enforce the lien. Article 454 of the Civil Code provides that, "A debtor may request the lienholder to enforce the lien after expiration of the term of performance of the obligation; where the lienholder fails to do so, the debtor may request the people's court to have the retained property sold at auction or in a sale".

4.1.4 The right to claim for eliminating the lien.

4.2 Obligations of the Debtor

After the lien is created, the obligor shall not obstruct or hinder the lienholder from exercising his right of lien, and shall pay the necessary expenses for retaining the property.

5. Conflicts between the Lien, the Pledge and the Right to Mortgage

Article 456 of the Civil Code prescribes that "Where a lien is created on a movable property on which a mortgage or pledge has already been created, the lienholder has priority to be paid".

6. Enforcement of the Lien

According to Para. 1, Article 453 of the Civil Code, "A lienholder and the debtor shall reach an agreement on the term of performance of the obligation after the property is retained under the lien; where there is no agreement or the agreement is unclear, the lienholder shall give the debtor a period of 60 or more days as the term of performance, unless the retained movable property is fresh, living, or perishable so that it is hard to keep it for long. Where a debtor defaults upon expiration of the term of performance, the lienholder may, upon agreement with the debtor, appraise and accept the retained property to fully or partially satisfy the obligation, or be paid with priority from the proceeds obtained from auction or sale of the retained property". In light of this provision, the enforcement of the lien shall made in compliance with following procedures:

First, a time limit for the debtor to pay the debts after the property is retained shall be determined;

Second, the debtor defaults at the expiration of the specified time limit;

Third, the lien holder has the right to exercise and enforce the lien. As the first step, the lienholder shall seek agreement from the debtor to have the retained property converted into money. If the debtor disagrees, the lienholder may have the property under lien auctioned or sold. The auction may be conducted according to the procedures set by the Auction Law. The right holder enjoys the priority in having the debts paid with the proceeds from auction or sale of the property. After the payment of the debt, the excessive proceeds shall be returned to the debtor, or deposited if the return fails, and the expenses for depositing shall be deducted from the remainder of the proceeds. If after the retained property is converted into money, auctioned or sold, the proceeds therefrom exceed the amount of the credit, the balance shall move to the debtor, and if they are insufficient to cover the debts, the difference shall be paid by the debtor.

第七章 占 有

第一节 占 有 概 述

一、占有的概念和性质

(一)占有的概念

占有，是指主体对于物基于占有的意思进行的控制的事实状态。占有是对物的一种事实上的控制。对物的控制也称为对物的管领，需要借助于身体与物发生一定的外部接触。不管占有人对物的控制是否具备据为己有的意思，只要存在客观上的控制状态就可以构成占有。

在实践中，占有可以采用多种方式来体现，但构成占有，至少必须要有两个要件：

1. 在主观上，必须具有占有的意思

占有并不要求占有人具备据为己有的意图，但占有人应当具有一种占有的意图。也就是说，所谓占有意思，指意识到自己正在占有某物。如果对自己占有某物毫无意识，或者意识到或应当意识到是在为别人占有某物，则不具有占有意思。因此无意识地占有财物、占有辅助人的占有都不构成占有。占有人应当具有占有的意图，但并不意味着占有人必须具有为自己的利益而占有的意图。在某些情况下，占有人并不一定是为自己利益而占有，如拾得遗失物、漂流物后占有该物，拾得人希望尽快返还失主，因此很难说拾得人具有为自己利益占有该物的意图。但拾得人完全意识到自己在占有该物，拾得人仍然具有占有意图，因而仍然构成占有。

2. 从客观上，占有要求占有人事实上控制或管领了某物

占有人事实上控制、管领是占有的外在形式，是占有的客观构成要件。判断占有人是否对物有事实上的控制或领管，应当依据占有人对物在空间、时间的支配来具体确认。在空间上，物应当处于人的力量作用范围内始得谓之占有，如对房屋、土地因使用而占有，放置在家中的衣物、家具等财产属于主人占有。在时间上，人对物的某种支配应当持续一定的时间方为占有。如别人的鸡进入自己的鸡舍后又迅即离去，虽然该鸡曾进入自己的支配范围，但这种偶然的转瞬即逝的支配不能构成占有。

(二) 占有的性质

关于占有的性质问题，是指占有是事实还是权利问题。自罗马法以来，对占有的性质一直存在争论。

在罗马法中，不同时代的法学家对占有的本质有不同的认识。罗马古代的法学家一致认为，占有是事实，但具有一定的法律效果。帝政后期，有的学者开始主张占有是一种权利，也如物权一样，可以援用救济程序加以保障。主张占有为事实的法学家认为，占有取得完全是事实行为，故违法行为(如盗窃等)也可以取得占有，法律行为的无效(如要式买卖的证人不适格)并不影响占有的转移。如果占有是权利，则违法行为人应无占有他人物件的权利，无效的法律行为也不能发生转移占有的效力。其实，占有在罗马法中受令状的保护，其真正的目的在于制止暴力，维持秩序，占有具有特殊地位不过是其间接地沾了光。如果真的以保护占有为目的，则占有令状早该成为对物诉讼了，就可以对持有任何物件的人提起了。主张占有为权利的法学家认为，权利的要素一为利益，二为法律的保障：占有使占有者得利用其物并受令状的保护，便已具备了权利的要件。至于令状也保护非法的占有人，作为占有非权利的佐证，论据似欠充分，因非法而取得权利之事并不少见，如恶意的加工人可成为加工物的所有人，猎人经土地所有人反对而仍在该地打猎的，对猎获物依法享有所有权等。在日耳曼法中，占有为物权法的核心概念，占有不是一种单纯的事实，而是一种物权。占有具有公示性，权利被包裹于占有之内，并借占有而体现。因此，日耳曼法上的占有又被称为"权利的外衣"。

在近现代民法中，学者们对于占有本质的认识也存在分歧：

有人主张占有为一种事实而非仅利，但此项事实在民法上却有一定的效力，受法律保护，具有法律意义。这种保护系对物的事实支配状态的保护，是否具有法律上的正当权利在所不问。

有人主张占有是一种权利。他们认为，从理论上讲，一切权利都是由法律保护的一定事实关系而发生。占有本身虽是一个事实，但法律既予以保护而赋予一定的效力，使占有人得享有由占有所发生的利益，即不得不谓之为权利。而且这种权利直接行使于物上，与所有权及其他物权均属相同。还有人认为，占有很难说是单纯的事实或权利，而是一种法律关系。美国学者哈瑞斯就曾指出，占有是某人和物之间针对另一个人所形成的关系。由于它是一种法律关系，所以要根据法律规则来解释一系列的事实。通说认为，占有是一种事实。占有本质的学说之争，在近现代民事立法中也有所体现。德国、瑞士民法认为，占有是一种事实，称为"占有"，即物的占有因对物有实际的控制而取得(《德国民法典》第 854 条第 1 项)；日本、意大利民法认为，占有是一种权利，称为"占有权"，即占有是一种以行使所有权或其他物权的形式表现出的对物的权利(《意大利民法典》第 1140 条)。

在中国大陆，尽管占有的问题一直没有得到应有的重视，但关于占有的本质，也存在不同的看法。早期的民法学著作基本上是将占有视为所有权的一项权利，即占有权能。该占有权能可以由所有人行使,也可以由非所有人行使。近年来,学者们普遍认为,不应将占有限于所有权的权能,而应将占有视为独立的法律制度。但对占有本质的认识,也存在事实说和权利说的分歧。多数学者认为,占有为事实,是占有人对物具有的事实上的管领力;但也有人认为,占有不仅为状态,更是重要的民事权利之一,即占有权,是行为人依法享有对他人财产或财产权利所行使的管领、控制、支配、收益之权。我认为,占有是一种事实,而不是一种权利,更不是单纯的所有权的权能。马克思指出:"私有财产的真正基础,即占有,是一个事实,是不可解释的事实,而不是权利。只是由于社会赋予实际占有以法律的规定,实际占有才具有合法占有的性质,才具有私有财产的性质。"①占有仅体现为人对物的支配管领关系,而并不反映某权利关系。无论是合法行为,还是违法行为,均可基于管领物的事实而成立占有。将占有定性为事实,旨在表示法律对物的事实支配状态的保护,而不问占有人是否具有法律上的正当权利。

中国《民法典》是将占有作为一种事实专编规定的。

二、占有的种类

(一)有权占有和无权占有

这是根据进行的占有是否依据本权所做的分类。所谓本权,是指基于法律上的原因,可对物进行占有的权利,如所有权、地上权、典权、质权、留置权。有权占有即指有本权的占有,如地上权人依地上权对土地的占有;无权占有是指无本权的占有,如拾得人对于遗失物的占有。

有权占有与无权占有区别的意义在于:无权占有人在本权人请求返还原物时,有返还的义务;另外,作为留置权要件的占有,限于有权占有。

(二)自主占有和他主占有

这是依占有人的意思为标准进行的分类。自主占有是指以物属于自己所有(所有的意思)的占有;无所有的意思,仅基于某种特定关系支配物的意思的占有是他主占有。

自主占有中的"所有的意思",是指具备所有人占有的意思,而不必是真正的所有人或要求其自信为所有人。因此,所有人对其物的占有为自主占有,盗贼对于盗赃的占有亦为自主占有。至于他主占有,包括如典权人对于典物的占有,承租人对于租赁物的占有,质权人对于质物的占有。

(三)直接占有和间接占有

直接占有和间接占有。直接占有是指直接对物的控制,而不问权源如何。所有人常常直接占有所有物。而在不少情况下,所有人并不直接占有,而为地上权人、典权人、

---

① 《马克思恩格斯全集》(第一卷),人民出版社1956年版,第382页。

质权人、承租人、借用人、保管人、受托人、承运人等直接占有，但所有人的所有权未变，依法或依约仍可请求返还。这种占有称为间接占有。直接占有也被称为实际占有。间接占有由于是从所有权推定的，因此又称为推定占有。

(四)合法占有和非法占有

民法上的"非法占有"是指没有法律规定和合同约定，没有占有权利来源的占有；反之即为合法占有。

(五)善意占有和恶意占有

善意占有，是无权占有的再分类。善意占有是指占有人不知道或者不应当知道自己无占有的权利而为的占有。

在善意占有中，根据占有人有无过失为标准，还可以再分为过失占有与无过失占有。但严格来说，只有不知自己无占有的权利且无重大过失者，方构成善意占有。

恶意占有是对无权占有的再分类，指占有人知道或者怀疑自己没有占有权而为的占有。

第二节　占有的效力和保护

一、占有的效力

占有的效力是指占有所具有的法律上的证明力和强制力。关于占有的效力，各国立法规定并不一致，学者们的认识也存在分歧。占有的效力通常有权利推定的效力、事实推定、动产物权的善意取得、占有物的使用收益、占有人与占有回复请求权人之间的权利义务等五项内容。关于动产物权善意取得，前面已有讲述，下文将对占有效力的其余四项内容进行论述。

(一)占有的权利推定效力

占有的权利推定效力又称占有权利的推定力，是指占有人于占有物上行使的权利，推定其为合法并有此权利。这是占有的最主要效力，为各国民法所明定。在现代民法中，占有是物权变动的要件，是权利存在的外观。占有存在时，通常均认为有实质或真实的权利为其基础。基于这种权利存在的盖然性，各国法律大多规定了占有的权利推定效力。例如，《德国民法典》第1006条规定，为了动产的占有人的利益，推定占有人即为物的所有人；《日本民法典》第188条规定，占有人在其占有物上行使的权利可推定为适法。关于占有的权利推定效力，应说明以下几点：

(1)在占有物上行使的权利为依占有所表现的一切权利，不限于物权，也包括债权。例如，占有人于占有物上行使所有权时，推定其具有所有权；于占有物上行使质权时，推定其有质权；于占有物行使租赁权或借用权时，推定其有租赁权或借用权。但是，不以占有为内容的权利不在推定之列，如抵押权等。

(2)受权利推定的占有人不负有权占有的举证责任。即如果他人对占有人的占有物提出权利主张时，占有人无须证明自己有占有的权利。但当该他人提出反证证明其有权利时，占有人应负有推翻反证的举证责任。

(3)权利的推定效力，不仅占有人可以主张，第三人也可以主张。例如，债权人对于债务人占有的动产得援用"推定为债务人所有"的效力，主张该动产为债务人所有。

(4)占有的权利推定效力适用于一切占有人，无论占有人的占有是否存在瑕疵。但德国民法规定，权利的推定不适用于占有物系被盗窃、遗失或以其他方式丢失的占有人，但占有物为金钱或无记名证券者，不在此限。同时，除现有占有人外，过去占有人，于其占有期间亦推定其有合法权利。

(5)权利的推定仅具有消极的效力，占有人不得利用此项推定作为行使权利的证明。例如，占有人不得援引权利的推定效力申请权利登记。

(6)权利的推定适用于动产当无疑问，但是否适用于不动产则意见不一。法国、德国、瑞士等国民法规定，权利的推定仅限于动产，不动产不发生权利推定问题。日本民法则认为，不动产也适用权利推定。本人认为，不动产以登记为公示方法。所以，不动产如已登记，则不发生权利推定问题；但如不动产没有登记，则可以适用权利推定。

(二)事实推定

(1)占有究竟是自主占有还是他主占有不易判断时，推定为自主占有。

(2)占有究竟是善意占有还是恶意占有，或者是公然占有还是隐秘占有不易判断时，推定为善意占有与公然占有。

(3)占有人先前曾经占有，现在也依然占有，则推定其在中间的时段也进行了占有(连续占有的推定)。

(三)占有物的使用收益

(1)有权占有人对占有物的使用收益依据合同和法律规定处理。《民法典》第458条规定："基于合同关系等产生的占有，有关不动产或者动产的使用、收益、违约责任等，按照合同约定；合同没有约定或者约定不明确的，依照有关法律规定。"

(2)无权占有人对占有物的使用收益取决于其是善意占有还是恶意占有。对占有的使用，《民法典》第459条规定："占有人因使用占有的不动产或者动产，致使该不动产或者动产受到损害的，恶意占有人应当承担赔偿责任。"对占有物的收益，《民法典》第460条规定："不动产或者动产被占有人占有的，权利人可以请求返还原物及其孳息，但是，应当支付善意占有人因维护该不动产或者动产支出的必要费用。"

(四)占有人的赔偿责任

《民法典》第461条规定："占有的不动产或者动产毁损、灭失，该不动产或者动产的权利人请求赔偿的，占有人应当将因毁损、灭失取得的保险金、赔偿金或者补偿金等返还给权利人；权利人的损害未得到足够弥补的，恶意占有人还应当赔偿损失。"

二、占有的保护

占有的保护是法律对占有人提供的以防占有遭受损害的保护手段。民法中对占有的保护可分为物权法上的保护与债法上的保护。物权法上的保护包括占有人的自力救济权，占有保护请求权。债法上的保护包括不当得利与侵权损害赔偿请求权。《物权法》规定了占有的保护请求权，但是不承认占有人可以自力救济。

对占有的侵夺或妨害。对占有的侵夺，是指占有人对于占有物的事实上的管领力，因被侵害而被持续的剥夺。对占有的妨害，是指虽未剥夺占有人对占有物的全部或任何一部分的管领力，但是妨害了占有人对其物的管领，以致占有人的利益遭受损害。侵夺占有或妨害占有须存在侵夺占有或者妨害占有的行为；非基于占有人的意思；具有违法性。

根据《民法典》第462条规定，对占有的保护有两种方法：

(一) 占有保护请求权

占有保护的请求权，是指占有人有权请求国家有权机关通过运用国家强制力来保护其占有，包括占有物返还请求权、排除妨害请求权和消除危险请求权。《民法典》第462条第1款规定："占有的不动产或者动产被侵占的，占有人有权请求返还原物；对妨害占有的行为，占有人有权请求排除妨害或者消除危险……"

占有人返还原物的请求权，自侵占发生之日起一年内未行使的，该请求权消灭（《民法典》第462条第2款）。

(二) 占有的损害赔偿请求权

《民法典》第462条第1款规定："因侵占或者妨害造成损害的，占有人有权请求损害赔偿。"

Chapter 7　Possession

Section One　Survey of Possession

1. Conception and Nature of Possession

1. 1　Concept of Possession

Possession is a factual state where a subject holds a property with an intention to possess. It is the factual control over a property, or management of a property, which requires certain external physical contact with the property through one's body. The possessory right may be acquired as long as the control over the property objectively exist, regardless of the fact as to whether the possessor has the intention to own it.

In practice, possession may take various forms but two elements must be satisfied:

First, subjectively, the possessor must be with an intention to possess. Though the possessor doesn't necessarily need to hold the property with an intention to own it, but an intention to possess is indispensable. That is to say, the possessor should be aware of the fact that he is holding the property. If such intention is lacking or he realizes or should have realized that he is holding the property for another person, then it may not be concluded that he is with an intention to possess. Thus, holding a property unconsciously or exercising control as an agent don't constitute possession. It is to be noted that holding a property with an intention to possess is not equal to holding it for his own interests. In some cases, the possession may be made not for one's own interests, as is in cases when one finds a lost property or drift-stuff and takes control over it. The finder may hope to return the property to its owner as soon as possible, thus can hardly be deemed holding it for his own interests. However, as he is fully aware that he is holding the property, his control still constitutes possession.

Second, objectively, the possessor should be actually controlling or managing the property. Such factual control or management is the external manifestation and an object constitutive element of possession. While deciding whether one actually controls or manages a property, the spatial and temporal domination of such person over the property should be taken into account. Spatially, the property should be within the scope where the person is able to exert influence. For example, a house and a tract of land is possessed by the person who uses them; the properties in the house such as clothes and furniture are also possessed by such owner. Temporally, the control over the property should last for a certain period of time. For example, where a hen owned by another person entered into one's henhouse but immediately left, the momentary control of the henhouse owner doesn't constitute possession though the hen did once enter into his sphere of influence.

1. 2   Nature of Possession

Whether possession is a fact or a right, is a long-disputed issue ever since the Roman Law came into existence.

Under the Roman law, jurists of different times have different interpretation regarding the nature of possession. In the ancient times, jurists shared the common understanding that possession is a fact but exerts certain legal effects. During the later period of the Roman Empire, some scholars started to argue that possession is a right that can be protected through relief procedures like the real right. Jurists who were for the view that possession is a fact held that the acquisition of possession is completely a matter of act. As a result, illegal acts (e. g. , theft, etc.) give rise to possession, and the invalidity of a juristic act (e. g. , incompetent witness in mancipatio) does not affect the transfer of possession. Conversely, if possession is not a right, then a tortfeasor may not acquire the right of possession over the property of another person, and invalid juristic act will not cause a transfer of possession. In fact, the Roman law rendered protection to possession through a writ for the purpose of containing violence and maintaining the order. That possession obtains a special status is merely an indirect bonus thereof. If the purpose lies in protecting the possession itself, then the writ should have evolved into an action in rem whereby a suit may be brought against any person who holds the property. As for those jurists who argued that possession is a right, they insisted that interest and legal protection are the two elements of a right. As possession enables the possessor to utilize the property and be protected by the writ, it has already been qualified as a right. To argue that possession is not right by citing the fact that a writ also protects a tortfeasor, the evidence is insufficient in that illegal acquisition of right is not a rare property, like in the case where a processor in bad faith may become the owner of the processed property, or a hunter who hunted on an estate in disregard of the objection of a land owner may still legally acquire the ownership regarding the prey. Under Germanic law, possession is the core concept of the real right law, which is taken as a real right rather than a mere fact. Possession is with publicity nature, meaning that it is a manifestation of the right that encloses such possession. Therefore, possession is also called "the clothes of the right" in the Germanic law.

In the modern civil law, dispute among the scholars regarding the nature of possession remains:

According to some scholars, possession is a fact rather than a right. However, such fact is with certain effects in the civil law, thus protected by law. Such protection is exerted on the factual state of possession over the property regardless of whether the possessor has the legitimate right to do so.

Others argue that possession is a right. They believed that, theoretically, all rights emerge from particular set factual relationship that is protected by law. Admittedly, possession itself is a fact, but if taking into consideration the effects granted to it by the law, thus the possessor is entitled to the profits brought up by the possession, then it may be concluded that possession is a right. Moreover, like the ownership and other real rights, such right may also be directly exercised upon the property. Another theory proposes that possession cannot be simply categorized as a fact or a right but has to be taken as a type of legal relationship. One supporter of such opinion is the American scholar Harsis, who once pointed out that possession is such relationship between a person and a property that might be asserted against another person. Since it is a legal relationship, the series of facts have to be interpreted in accordance with legal rules. According to the prevailing theory, possession is a fact. The theoretical debate over the nature of possession also rages during the legislative process of modern civil law. The civil codes of Germany and Switzerland take possession as a fact and adopt the term "Possession", meaning that possession of a property is acquired by obtaining actual control of the property (Para. 1, Article 854 of the German Civil Code). Civil laws of Japan and Italy adopt the other view that possession as a right, and term it "possessory right", meaning that possession is a right over a property that is manifested in the exercise of the ownership or other real rights (Article 1140 of the Italian Civil Code).

In Chinese mainland, opinions also split regarding the nature of possession, though the issue itself has not drawn its due attention. Early writings on civil law mainly view possession as a power of the ownership, namely, the power to possess. Such power may be exercised either by an owner or a non-owner. In recent years, scholars gradually come to the common understanding that possession does not only serve as a power of the ownership, but might as well be deemed an independent legal system. Still, the battle between the "fact theory" and the "right theory" continues. Majority opinion holds that possession is a fact. It is the factual management of a possessor over a property. Nonetheless, opposite opinion goes that possession is not only a state, but also an important civil right, namely, the possessory right, which is legally enjoyed by a possessor to manage, control, hold and benefit from the property or property right of another. In my opinion, possession is a fact rather than a right. It is not simply efficacy power of the ownership. As is put by Karl Marx, "the quite essential foundation of private property is possession, which is a fact that is unexplainable rather than a right. An actual possession is lawful, namely, with the nature of private property, merely because the society has provided laws on it". Possession merely reflects the control or management relationship of a person over a property. It doesn't indicate any right. Possession may arise as long as such fact of management exist, no matter it is legal or not. That possession is defined as a fact indicates that the law protects the factual control over a property, regardless of whether the possessor is with a legal right to do so.

The Civil Code defines possession as a fact and regulates it in a separate chapter.

2. Categories of Possession

2.1 Authorized Possession and Unauthorized Possession

Such classification is made based on the existence of a title. A title refers to such right that serves as a legal basis on which the possession is justified. It may be ownership, superficies, pawning right, pledge, lien, etc. Authorized possession means that the possession is based on a title, as in the case where a superficiarius possesses the land based on its superficies, while unauthorized possession means that the possession is not founded on a title, as in the case where a finder possesses a lost thing.

The significance in distinguishing authorized possession from unauthorized one lies in that an unauthorized possessor is obliged to return the property upon the request of a right holder. Moreover, only authorized possession may serve as a constitutive element of the lien.

2.2 Proprietary Possession and Non-proprietary Possession

Such division is made based on the intention of the possessor. Proprietary possession means that possessor is with an intention to own the property, while non-proprietary possession denotes that the possessor has no intention to own the property for himself, but do so only based on certain other relationship.

The "intention to own" under proprietary possession refers to an intention to own the property, but the possessor doesn't have to be the actual owner or have mistakenly believed that he is the actual owner. Therefore, the possession of a property by its owner constitutes proprietary possession, and the possession by a thief of a stolen thing may also constitutes proprietary possession. As for non-proprietary possession, it may be such possession by a pawnee regarding the pawn, by a lessee regarding the leased object, or that by a pledgee regarding a pledged property, etc.

2. 3　Direct Possession and Indirect Possession

Direct possession refers to the direct control over a property without tracing the title thereof. An owner usually possesses his property directly, yet in not rare circumstances, he doesn't take direct possession but have the property directly held by a superficiarius, pawnee, pledgee, lessee, borrowers, depository, agent or carrier, etc. , while retaining the right to request return based on his ownership. Such possession is termed indirect possession. While direct possession is also known as actual possession, indirect possession is also-called presumptive possession as it is presumed from the ownership.

2. 4　Legal Possession and Illegal Possession

In civil law, illegal possession denotes such possession that is not based on stipulation of the law or a contract and without a title. Conversely, it will be legal possession.

2. 5　Possession in Good Faith and Possession in Bad Faith

Possession in good faith is a result of the further division of the unauthorized possession. It denotes the possessor do not know and should not have known that the possession is without a title.

Possession may be further divided into negligent possession and non-negligent possession, based on the existence of negligence on the part of the possessor. In a strict sense, possession requires that the possessor is without the knowledge that he lacks the title to possess and he has no gross negligence in doing so.

Possession in bad faith is also a sub-category of the unauthorized possession. It means that the possessor knows or should have known that his possession is without a title.

Section Two　　Effects and Protection of Possession

1. Effects of Possession

The effects of possession denote the probative force and compelling force of possession in law. Legislations of various jurisdictions rule on the effects of possession differently, and opinions in the academia also split regarding the matter. In general, effects of possession include the following five points: presumptive effect for right, presumptive effect for fact, acquisition in good faith regarding movable properties, utilization of and benefits from the possessed properties as well as the rights and obligations between a possessor and the right holder for recovery of possession. As the effect on acquisition in good faith regarding movable properties has already been covered previously, the rest of this section will mainly discuss the other four effects.

1. 1   Presumptive Effect of Right of Possession

The presumptive effect of right is also-called the presumptive effect of the possessory right. It means that it is presumed that a possessor lawfully has the rights that a possessor exercises with respect to the property in his/her possession. This is the principal effect of possession and may be found in civil laws of every nation. Under the modern civil law, possession is a requirement for change in real right and serves as an external symbol of a right. Where it exists, it is generally presumed that such possession is based on a substantial or actual right. In light of such probability, the laws of various nations have concurrently prescribed the presumptive effect for right of possession. For example, Article 1006 of the German Civil Code prescribes that, it is presumed in favor of the possessor of a movable property that he is the owner of the property. Article 188 of the Japanese Civil Code prescribes that it shall be presumed that a possessor lawfully has the rights that a possessor exercises with respect to property in his possession. Regarding the presumptive effect the following few points should be clarified:

1. 1. 1   The right exercised by the possessor may be any right that is indicated by the state of possession, including but not limited to the real right. It may also be credits. For example, where a possessor exercises ownership, pledge, leasehold, right to borrow, etc. , it is presumed that he lawfully has such right with respect to the property. Nonetheless, if the contents of a right don't include possession, then such right may not be presumed to vest in the possessor. One example of this is the right to mortgage.

1. 1. 2   The burden of proof is not assumed by the possessor whose right is presumed. That is, in case where others raise a claim with respect to the possessed property, the possessor is not obliged to prove his title for the possession. However, if such other person has presented evidence of his title, the possessor shall assume the burden to disprove such title.

1. 1. 3   The presumptive effect for right may be asserted by the possessor or a third party. For example, a creditor may assert that the debtor owns a movable property the latter possessed by citing the presumptive effect for right.

1. 1. 4   The presumptive effect may apply to all possessors even those whose possession is with defect. Nonetheless, according to the German civil law, the presumptive effect of right does not apply in relation to a former possessor from whom the property was stolen or who lost it or whose possession of it ended in another way, unless the property is money or bearer instruments. Meanwhile, it is presumed in favor of a former possessor that during the period of his possession he was the owner.

1. 1. 5   The presumptive effect also functions in a negative way. The possessor shall not

use such effect as a proof in exercising his right. For example, a possessor may not apply for registering a right by citing the presumptive effect of possession.

1. 1. 6   It is without doubt that the presumptive effect applies to movable properties, but opinions are divided in the case of immovable properties. The civil laws of France, Germany and Switzerland prescribe that the presumptive effect of right applies only to movable properties, not to the immovable properties. However, their counterparts in Japan and Chinese Taiwan hold that such effect also applies to immovable properties. In my opinion, since the real right regarding immovable properties is usually publicized by way of registration, the presumptive effect is not an issue if a right on the immovable property has been registered. Where such registration is lacking, then the presumptive effect of right might apply as well.

1. 2   Presumption of Facts

1. 2. 1   When it is difficult to judge whether possession is proprietary or not, it is presumed to be proprietary.

1. 2. 2   If it is difficult to judge whether the possession is made in good faith or not, or whether the possession is in public or not, then it is presumed to be in good faith and in public.

1. 2. 3   If there is evidence of possession at two different points in time, it shall be presumed that possession continues during the interval (presumption of continuous possession).

1. 3   Utilization of and Benefits from the Possessed Property

1. 3. 1   The utilization of and benefits obtained from the possessed property of an authorized possessor shall be dealt with in accordance with the stipulation of the contract and the law. Article 458 of the Civil Code prescribes that "In the case of possession of immovable or movable property based on a contractual relationship, matters such as the use of the immovable or movable property, the benefits therefrom, and the default liability shall be subject to the agreement in the contract; where there is no agreement thereon in the contract or the agreement is unclear, the relevant provisions of laws shall be applied".

1. 3. 2   The utilization or and benefits obtained from the possessed thing by an unauthorized possessor are dealt with depending on whether the possessor is in good faith or not. Concerning utilization of the possessed property, Article 459 of the Civil Code prescribes that "Where damage is caused to the immovable or movable property by its possessor as a result of use of the property, a mala fide possessor shall be liable for compensation". As regards the fruits from the possessed property, Article 460 of the Civil Code provides that "Where an immovable or movable property is in the possession of another person, a person holding a right in the property may request the possessor to return the original property and its fruits and proceeds, provided that the necessary expenses incurred by a bona fide possessor for the

maintenance of the immovable or movable property shall be paid".

1. 4　Compensation Liability of the Possessor

Article 461 of the Civil Code stipulates that "Where the immovable or movable property in another person's possession is destructed, damaged, or lost, and a person holding a right in the property requests for compensation, the possessor shall return to the right holder the amount of insurance payment, compensation or indemnity he has received for the property destructed, damaged, or lost; where the right holder has not been fully compensated, a possessor mala fide shall also compensate for the loss".

2. Protection of Possession

The protection of possession denotes the legal measures for protecting a possessor against damages. In civil law, the protection may be either be based on real right law or credit law. Under the real right law, the legal protection takes such forms as the possessor's right of self-help, claims for protection of possession, etc. Under credit law, the legal protection takes such forms as claims on restitution of unjust enrichment, claim for compensation of damages on account of tort liability. The Real Right Law has regulated on the claim for protection of possession, but hasn't recognized the possessor's right of self-help.

Forcible dispossession or disturbance in possession. The forcible dispossession denotes that the possessor is continuously deprived of his actual control over the possessed property due to the act of infringement. The disturbance in possession means that a possessor is disturbed in his possession of the property possessed and his interests thus damaged, though he has not been deprived of all or any part of his actual control over the property. Forcible dispossession or disturbance in possession is established when the following elements are satisfied: there is an act that has forcibly dispossessed the possessor or disturbed his possession of the property; the possessor's intention regarding such act is absent; the act is unlawful.

Article 462 of the Civil Code prescribes two means for protecting possession:

2. 1　Claim for Protection of Possession

The Claim for protection of possession means that the possessor has the right to require the competent authority to render protection over his possession of a property by using the State's coercive force. It includes the right to claim for the return of the original property, for the removal of the nuisance and for elimination of danger. Para. 1, Article 462 of the Civil Code prescribes that, "Where an immovable or movable property is trespassed or converted, its possessor is entitled to request restitution. Where there is a nuisance against the possession, the possessor has the right to request the removal of the nuisance or the elimination of the danger. ..."

The possessor's right to request for restitution is extinguished if such a right has not been exercised within one year from the date the trespass or conversion occurs (Para. 2, Article 462 of the Civil Code).

2. 2 Claim for Compensation for Damage based on Possession

Para. 1, Article 462 of the Civil Code provides that "Where damage is caused as a result of the trespass, conversion, or nuisance, the possessor has the right to request compensatory damages in accordance with law".

附　录
Appendix

actual delivery 现实交付

registration of a priority notice 预告登记

alienation guarantee 让与担保

allocated right to use land for construction purposes 划拨土地使用权

bearer instrument 无记名证券

bid invitation, auction, public consultation 招标、拍卖、公开协商

bona fide acquisition / acquisition in good faith 善意取得

bona fide possession / possession in good faith 善意占有

buildings, structures and attached facilities 建筑物、构筑物及其附属设施

burden of proof 举证责任

chartered real right 特许物权

China / PR of China / PRC 中华人民共和国

China's rural land system reform 中国农村土地制度改革

claim for confirmation of real right 确认物权请求权

claim for restoration of the original state 恢复原状请求权

claim on real rights / claim on property rights 物上请求权

co-ownership 共有

compelling force 强制力

conceptual delivery 观念交付

ownership of a building's units 业主的建筑物区分所有权

confiscation 没收，征用

consensualism 意思主义

consortium 联合体

contractor 承包人

constructive transfer 占有改定

counter-security 反担保

creditor's right / credit / claim 债权

defalcation 挪用公款

de facto disposal 事实上的处分

de jure disposal 法律上的处分

drifting things 漂流物

dual operation system characterized by the combination of centralized operation with decentralized operation on the basis of operation by households under a contract 家庭承包经营为基础、统分结合的双层经营体制

duty of compulsory contracting 强制缔约义务

embezzle state properties 侵吞国家财产

enforcement of a mortgage 抵押权的实现

equity contribution 入股

forfeiture agreement 流押契约

formalism of creditor's right 债权形式主义

formalism of real right（物权）形式主义

giving out contract after it is converted into shares 折股后发包

illicit acquisition 非法所得

immovables / immovable properties 不动产

lost-and-found things 拾得物

joint-stock cooperative management 股份合作经营

joint co-ownership 共同共有

jus emphyteusis 永佃权

jus in re propria 自物权

mala fide possession / possession in bad faith 恶意占有

movables / movable properties 动产

nature of subordination / appurtenance nature 从属性

negotiorum gestio 无因管理

odic force / force of nature 自然力

original acquisition and derivative acquisition 原始取得和继受取得

ownership retention 所有权保留

pawning right 典权

power of possession, power of utilization, power to profit and power of disposition 占有权，使用权，收益权，处分权

principle of equal protection 平等保护原则

principle of numerus clausus 物权法定原则

principle of publication and presumption of accuracy 公示、公信原则

priority order of the mortgage interest 抵押权的顺位

probative force 证明力

real right for a definite period of time 有期限物权

real right for an indefinite period of time 无期限物权

real right in movables and real right in immovables 动产物权和不动产物权

account receivable 应收账款

registration as a requirement of perfection / antagonism 登记对抗要件

registration as a requirement of validity 登记生效要件

adjacent relationship / neighboring relationship 相邻关系

requisition 征收

right over property of another / jus in re aliena 他物权

right of first refusal 优先购买权

right of mining / mining right 采矿权

pledge 质权

right of explore minerals 探矿权

right of water taking 取水权

right to exclusive use of registered trademarks 商标专用权

right to contractual management of land 土地承包经营权

right to use land for construction purposes 建设用地使用权

mortgage 抵押权

right to land use 土地使用权

right to use a house site 宅基地使用权

right to use sea areas 海域使用权

right to use water for fishing and for aquaculture 捕捞权与养殖权

security interest 担保物权

self-help 自力救济

co-ownership by shares 按份共有

socialist ownership by the whole people 社会主义全民所有制

socialist public ownership 社会主义公有制

space utilization 空间利用权

superficies 地上权

theory of fixed priority order of mortgage and of ascending priority order of mortgage 抵押权顺位固定主义与抵押权顺位升进主义

thing 物

treasure trove / buried things 埋藏物

unjust enrichment 不当得利

right to usufruct 用益物权

参 考 文 献

1. 江平、米健：《罗马法基础》，中国政法大学出版社 1991 年版。

2. 杨振山：《民商法实务研究》（物权卷），山西经济出版社 1994 年版。

3. 邓曾甲：《日本民法概论》，法律出版社 1995 年版。

4. 王利明：《中国物权法草案建议稿及说明》，中国法制出版社 2001 年版。

5. 王利明：《物权法论》，中国政法大学出版社 1998 年版。

6. 王利明：《中国民法案例与学理研究》（物权篇），法律出版社 1998 年版。

7. 梁慧星等：《中国物权法草案建议稿》，社会科学文献出版社 2000 年版。

8. 梁慧星、陈华彬：《物权法》，法律出版社 1997 年版。

9. 梁慧星：《中国物权法研究》（上、下），法律出版社 1998 年版。

10. 孙宪忠：《论物权法》，法律出版社 2001 年版。

11. 孙宪忠：《德国当代物权法》，法律出版社 1997 年版。

12. 陈华彬：《物权法原理》，国家行政学院出版社 1998 年版。

13. 陈华彬：《现代建筑物区分所有权制度研究》，法律出版社 1995 年版。

14. 钱明星：《物权法原理》，北京大学出版社 1994 年版。

15. 王卫国：《中国土地权利研究》，中国政法大学出版社 1997 年版。

16. 苏力：《法治及其本土资源》，中国政法大学出版社 1996 年版。

17. 程啸、高圣平、谢鸿飞：《最高人民法院新担保司法解释理解与适用》，法律出版社 2021 年版。

18. 尹田：《法国物权法》，法律出版社 1998 年版。

19. 董学立：《中国动产担保物权法》，法律出版社 2020 年版。

20. 孟勤国：《物权二元结构论》，人民法院出版社 2002 年版。

21. 关涛：《我国不动产法律问题专论》，人民法院出版社 1999 年版。

22. 史尚宽：《物权法论》，中国政法大学出版社 2000 年版。

23. 谢在全：《民法物权论》（上、下），中国政法大学出版社 1999 年版。

24. 郑玉波：《民法物权》，台湾三民书局 1998 年版。

25. 王泽鉴：《民法物权》（第一册·通则·所有权），中国政法大学出版社 2001 年版。

26. 王泽鉴：《民法学说与判例研究》（第 1～8 卷），中国政法大学出版社 1998

年版。

27. 谢哲胜：《财产法专题研究》(三)，台湾元照出版有限公司 2002 年版。

28. 苏永钦：《民法物权争议问题研究》，台湾五南图书出版股份有限公司 1999 年版。

29. 前南京国民政府司法行政部编：《民事习惯调查报告录》，中国政法大学出版社 2000 年版。

30. [法]蒲鲁东：《什么是所有权》，孙署冰译，商务印书馆 1982 年版。

31. [日]我妻荣：《日本物权法》，有泉亨修订、李宜芬校订，台湾五南图书出版股份有限公司 1989 年版。

32. [意]桑德罗·斯奇巴尼：《物与物权》(中译本)，范怀俊译，中国政法大学出版社 1993 年版。

33. [美]博登海默：《法理学、法律哲学与法律方法》，邓正来译，中国政法大学出版社 1999 年版。

34. [美]亨利·汉斯曼：《企业所有权论》，于静译，中国政法大学出版社 2001 年版。

35.《德国民法典》，上海社会科学院法学研究所译，法律出版社 1984 年版。

36.《拿破仑法典》，李浩培等译，商务印书馆 1983 年版。

37.《美国统一商法典》，潘琪译，中国对外经济贸易出版社 1990 年版。

38.《日本民法典》，陈国柱译，吉林出版社 1993 年版。

39. 申惠文：《民法典担保制度司法解释适用指南》，法律出版社 2021 年版。

References

1. Jiang Ping, Mi Jian, Roman Law Basis, China University of Political Science and Law Press, 1991.

2. Yang Zhenshan, Study on Civil and Commercial Law Practice (Property Law Volume), Shanxi Economic Press, 1994.

3. Deng Zengjia, Introduction to the Civil Law of Japan, Law Press China, 1995.

4. Wang Liming, Proposal of China's Real Right Law Draft and Prescriptions, China Legal Publishing House, 2001.

5. Wang Liming, The Theory of Real Right Law, China University of Political Science and Law Press, 1998.

6. Wang Liming, Study on China's Civil Law Cases and Theory (Property Law Volume), Law Press China, 1998.

7. Liang Huixing, Proposal of China's Real Right Law Draft, Social Science Academic Press (China), 2000.

8. Liang Huixing, Chen Huabin, The Real Right Law, Law Press China, 1997.

9. Liang Huixing, Study on the Real Right Law of China (I , II), Law Press China, 1998.

10. Sun Xianzhong, The Theory of Real Right Law, Law Press China, 2001.

11. Sun Xianzhong, The Contemporary Real Right Law of German, Law Press China, 1997.

12. Chen Huabin, Real Right Law Principle, National School of Administration Press, 1998.

13. Chen Huabin, Study on the Modern Partitioned Ownership of Building Areas System, Law Press China, 1995.

14. Qian Mingxing, Real Right Law Principle, Peking University Press, 1994.

15. Wang Weiguo, Study on Land Rights of China, China University of Political Science and Law Press, 1997.

16. Su Li, The Rule of Law and Its Local Resources, China University of Political Science and Law Press, 1996.

17. Cheng Xiao, Gao Shengping, Xie Hongfei, Understanding and Applying New Judicial Interpretation on Security of the SPC, Law Press China, 2021.

18. Yin Tian, The Real Right Law of France, Law Press China, 1998.

19. Dong Xueli, Law of Security Interest of Moverble Properties of China, Law Press China, 2020.

20. Meng Qinguo, The Theory of Dualistic Structure of Real Right, People's Court Press, 2002.

21. Guan Tao, Monograph on China's Real Estate Issues, People's Court Press, 1999.

22. Shi Shangkuan, The Theory of Real Right Law, China University of Political Science and Law Press, 2000.

23. Xie Zaiquan, The Theory of Real Rights of Civil Law (I, II), China University of Political Science and Law Press, 1999.

24. Zheng Yubo, Real Rights of Civil Law, San Min Book Co., Ltd., 1998.

25. Wang Zejian, Real Rights of Civil Law (I-General Rules-Ownership), China University of Political Science and Law Press, 2001.

26. Wang Zejian, Study on Civil Law Theory and Cases (Volume1~8), China University of Political Science and Law Press, 1998.

27. Xie Zhesheng, Special Research on Property Law (Volume3), Angel Publishing Co., Ltd., 2002.

28. Su Yongqin, Study on Real Rights Disputes of Civil Law, Wunan Book Co., Ltd., 1999.

29. Ministry of Justice of Former Nanjing National Government, Survey Report of Civil Customary, China University of Political Science and Law Press, 2000.

30. Proudhon P. J, What Is Property?, translated by Sun Shubing, Commercial Press, 1982.

31. Wagatsuma Sakae, The Real Right Law of Japan, revised by You Quanhen, edited by Li Yifeng, Wunan Book Co., Ltd., 1989.

32. Schipani, S., Property and Property Right (Chinese Translation), China University of Political Science and Law Press, 1993.

33. Bodenheimer, E. Jurisprudence, The Philosophy and Method of the Law, translated by Den Zhenglai, China University of Political Science and Law Press, 1999.

34. Hansmann, H., The Theory of Enterprises' Ownership, translated by Yu Jing, China University of Political Science and Law Press, 2001.

35. Translated by Law Institute of Shanghai Academy of Social Science, German Civil Code (Chinese Translation), Law Press China, 1984.

36. Translated by Li Haopei, Napoleonic Code (Chinese Translation), Commercial

Press, 1983.

37. Translated by Pan Qi, Uniform Commercial Code, USA (Chinese Translation), China International Business and Economics Press, 1990.

38. Translated by Chen Guozhu, Japan Civil Code (Chinese Translation), Jilin Press, 1993.

39. Shen Huiwen, Guide to Judicial Interpretation of Guarantee System in Civil Code, Law Press China, 2021.